WITHDRAWN
HARVARD LIBRARY
WITHDRAWN

THE CHURCHES OF EASTERN CHRISTENDOM

Although the history of Western Christendom has been studied extensively, relatively little has been written about the Christian Churches of the East. Beginning with the ultimately divisive Council of Chalcedon in AD 451, Kidd traces the complex events and doctrinal differences, the schism between Rome and the Sees of Constantinople, Antioch, Alexandria and Jerusalem, and its far-reaching consequences. For those familiar only with the annals of the Western Church, this work presents a fascinating and enlightening parallel account of Christianity and the of rivalries between Church, State and Sects in the East. A particular feature of this work is the detailed account of the development of the Church in Byzantium and its relation to the Byzantine Empire and the dynasties that shaped and defended it, even against the Crusades that lay powers diverted to their own ends. After the fall of Constantinople, Kidd turns to the creed, rites and external histories of the two divisions of the Eastern Church – the Orthodox Church that flourished in Russia, Greece, Rumania, and the Balkan Peninsula, and the less well-known branch that includes the Nestorian and Monophysite Christians. This highly important work is essential reading for all those interested in the history and beliefs of the Christian Church as a whole, as well as for those interested in the Christian Church of the East as one of the influential faiths of the region.

The Author
Beresford James Kidd (1864-1948) was educated at Christ's Hospital and Keble College, Oxford. He was ordained in 1887, and was appointed examining chaplain to the Bishop of Oxford and to the Bishop of London. He was the Warden of Keble College, Oxford from 1920 to 1939.

www.keganpaul.com

THE KEGAN PAUL LIBRARY OF RELIGION AND MYSTICISM

The Bible of Tibet • *Fanton Von Schiefner and W.R.S. Ralston (trans)*

The Book of Governors • *E. A. Wallis Budge*

The Flora of the Sacred Nativity • *Alfred E. P. Raymund Dowling*

Guide for the Perplexed • *Moses Maimonides*

Hindu, Manners, Customs and Ceremonies • *Abbe J. A. Dubois*

The Lankavatara Sutra • *D. T. Suzuki*

Plants of the Bible • *Harold N. Moldenke and Alma L. Moldenke*

The Religions of Tibet • *Giuseppe Tucci*

The Religions of Mongolia • *Walther Heissig*

The Religion of the Ancient Celts • *J. A. MacCulloch*

The Sayings and Stories of the Christian Fathers of Egypt • *E. A. Wallis Budge*

Studies in the Lankavatara Sutra • *D. T. Suzuki*

Tibetan Yoga and Its Secret Doctrines • *W. Y. Evans-Wentz*

Western Mysticism • *Dom Cuthbert Butler*

The Liturgy of the Ethiopian Church • *Translated by Marcos Daoud*

Secret Sects of Syria and Lebanon • *Bernard H. Springett*

The Churches of Eastern Christendom • *B. J. Kidd*

KEGAN PAUL BOOKS OF RELATED INTEREST

The Alexiad of the Princess Anna Comnena • *Elizabeth A.S. Dawes*

The Latin Kingdom of Jerusalem • *Claude Reignier Condor*

THE CHURCHES OF EASTERN CHRISTENDOM

From A.D. 451 to the Present Time

B. J. KIDD

KEGAN PAUL
London • New York • Bahrain

First published in 2006 by
Kegan Paul Limited
UK: P.O. Box 256, London WC1B 3SW, England
Tel: 020 7580 5511 Fax: 020 7436 0899
E-Mail: books@keganpaul.com
Internet: http://www.keganpaul.com
USA: 61 West 62nd Street, New York, NY 10023
Tel: (212) 459 0600 Fax: (212) 459 3678
Internet: http://www.columbia.edu/cu/cup
BAHRAIN: bahrain@keganpaul.com

Distributed by:
Marston Book Services Ltd
160 Milton Park
Abingdon
Oxfordshire OX14 4SD
United Kingdom
Tel: (01235) 465500 Fax: (01235) 465555
Email: direct.orders@marston.co.uk

Columbia University Press
61 West 62nd Street, New York, NY 10023
Tel: (212) 459 0600 Fax: (212) 459 3678
Internet: http://www.columbia.edu/cu/cup

© Kegan Paul, 2006

Printed in the United States

All rights reserved. No part of this book may be reprinted or
reproduced or utilised in any form or by any electric, mechanical
or other means, now known or hereafter invented, including
photocopying or recording, or in any information storage or retrieval
system, without permission in writing from the publishers.

ISBN: 0-7103-1081-1

British Library Cataloguing in Publication Data
Kidd, B. J.
The churches of Eastern Christendom : from A.D. 451 to the present time
1. Eastern churches – History
I. Title
281.5
ISBN 0710310811

St. Sophia.

Frontispiece.

CONTENTS

Chap.		Page.
I.	THE EAST AFTER CHALCEDON ...	3
II.	JUSTINIAN, 527—†65 : VICTOR AND LAWGIVER ...	24
III.	JUSTINIAN, 527—†65 : THE THEOLOGIAN ...	35
IV.	CHURCH AND STATE UNDER JUSTINIAN ...	55
V.	THE SUCCESSORS OF JUSTINIAN, 565—610 ...	79
VI.	THE DYNASTY OF HERACLIUS, 610—95, AND THE FIRST ANARCHY, 695—717 : MOHAMMEDANISM AND MONOTHELETISM ...	103
VII.	THE ISAURIAN DYNASTY, 717—867, INCLUDING THE SECOND ANARCHY, 802—20 : ICONOCLASM. SCHISM ...	138
VIII.	THE MACEDONIAN DYNASTY, 867—1056, ENDING WITH THE THIRD ANARCHY, 1025—81. CONVERSION OF RUSSIA. SCHISM OF EAST AND WEST ...	181
IX.	THE COMNENI AND THE ANGELI, 1081—1204. THE CRUSADES ...	221
X.	THE RIVAL EMPIRES : 1204—61. LATIN AT CONSTANTINOPLE : GREEK AT NICÆA ...	247
XI.	THE RESTORATION OF THE EMPIRE AND ITS DOWNFALL : 1261—1453. THE PALAEOLOGI : RE-UNION AND ITS REPUDIATION ...	263
XII.	THE ANCIENT PATRIARCHATES WITH CYPRUS AND SINAI	297
XIII.	THE CHURCHES OF THE BALKAN PENINSULA : (I.) BULGARIA. (II.) JUGOSLAVIA ...	319
XIV.	THE CHURCHES OF THE BALKAN PENINSULA : (III.) RUMANIA. (IV.) GREECE ...	345
XV.	THE CHURCH OF RUSSIA OR THE PATRIARCHATE OF MOSCOW	367
XVI.	THE "NESTORIANS"; OTHERWISE THE CHURCH OF THE EAST	418
XVII.	THE MONOPHYSITES : (I.) ARMENIANS. (II.) JACOBITES. (III.) CHRISTIANS OF MALABAR. (IV.) COPTS. (V.) ABYSSINIANS ...	428
XVIII.	THE UNIATES ...	457
XIX.	CONCLUSION : (1) FAITH, (2) GOVERNMENT, (3) WORSHIP, (4) RE-UNION ...	467
	NOTES ...	475
	INDEX ...	525

LIST OF ILLUSTRATIONS

	Facing Page.
ST. SOPHIA	... Frontispiece.
HIS ALL HOLINESS, THE ŒCUMENICAL PATRIARCH, BASIL III. ...	48
HIS HOLINESS DAMIANUS, PATRIARCH OF JERUSALEM	97
CHRYSOSTOM, METROPOLITAN OF ATHENS AND ARCHBISHOP OF GREECE	144
THE MONASTERY OF H. BARLAAM, MT. METEORA	192
THE CATHEDRAL OF THE ASSUMPTION, MOSCOW	241
CHURCH OF ST. BASIL THE BEATIFIED, MOSCOW	288
THE LATE PATRIARCH TIKHON	337
THE ASSYRIAN PATRIARCH, ISSAI MAR SHIMUN	384
HIS BEATITUDE MAR IGNATIUS, ELIAS, PATRIARCH OF ANTIOCH AND OF THE SYRIANS	416
HIS BEATITUDE THE LORD PHOTIUS, PATRIARCH AND POPE OF ALEXANDRIA, AND ŒCUMENICAL JUDGE	449
AT WESTMINSTER ABBEY, JUNE 29, 1925	473

PREFATORY NOTE.

AFTER I had published my *History of the Church to A.D. 461* (Oxford, 1922), I thought at first of continuing it. But to have attempted it on the same scale would have been impossible, with official and other claims on my time. Nor was it necessary: there are plenty of books in English on the history of Western Christendom. But for the Churches of the East there are next to none. The older are out of date: and the more modern, though scholarly, are apt to be tendencious. I thought it possible, then, while avoiding this temptation, to try to fill the gap: and hence this present volume.

For lack of acquaintance with oriental languages, I have often been obliged to rely on secondary authorities: and I would express my obligations to the school of Byzantine history represented by Bury, Diehl, Gelzer, Krumbacher, Pargoire; to Dr. Frere for Russia; to M. Labourt and Dr. Wigram for the East; to the *Cambridge Mediæval History;* as well as to the great Dictionaries of Vacant and Mangenot, of Baudrillart, and of Hastings, and to the *Catholic Encyclopædia*. My references in the notes to these authorities are, by themselves, quite insufficient to express my debt.

Acknowledging, then, both my indebtedness and my limitations, I venture to offer this survey of *The Churches of Eastern Christendom* to the public : primarily to tell the story, but also, as I hope, to further the growing understanding between East and West. I have to thank Canon J. A. Douglas, Rev. R. A. French and Rev. A. Ward for allowing me the use of plates for many of the illustrations.

B.J.K.

Keble College, Oxford,
September, 1927.

CHAPTER I.

THE EAST AFTER CHALCEDON.

MARCIAN 450—†7; LEO I. 457—†74; ZENO 474—†91; ANASTASIUS 491—†518.

BISHOPS OF THE CHIEF SEES, 451—527.

ROME.		CONSTANTINOPLE.		ANTIOCH.	
Leo I.	440—61	Anatolius	449—58	Maximus I.	449—55
Hilary	461—8	Gennadius I.	458—71	Basil I.	456—8
Simplicius	468—83	Acacius	471—89	Acacius	458—9
Felix III.	483—92	Fravitta	489—90	Martyrius	
Gelasius I.	492—6	Euphemius	490—6		459—68/70
Anastasius II.		Macedonius II.		Peter II. (the Fuller)	
	496—8		496—511		468/70—1
Symmachus	498—514	Timothy I.	511—18	Julian	471—5/6
Hormisdas	514—23			Peter II.[2]	
John I.	523—6				475/6—477/8
Felix IV.	526—30			John II. (Codonatus)	
					477—8
				Stephen II.	478—81
				Calandion	481—5
				Peter II.[1]	485—8
	ALEXANDRIA.			Palladius	488(?)—98
Orthodox		*Monophysite*		Flavian II.	498—512
Proterius	452—7	Timothy II. (the Cat)		Severus	512—8
Timothy II. (Salo-			457—77	Paul II.	519—21
faciolus)	460—82	Peter III. (Mongus)		Euphrasius	521—6
John I. (Talaia)	482		477—90	Ephraim	526—45
		Athanasius II.			
			490—7	JERUSALEM.	
		John I.	497—506	Juvenal	421—58
		John II.	506—17	Anastasius	458—78
		Dioscorus II.	517—9	Martyrius	478—86
		Timothy III.	519—36	Sallustius	486—94
				Elias I.	494—516
				John III.	516—24
				Peter	524—52

CHAPTER I.

THE EAST AFTER CHALCEDON.

MARCIAN 450—†7; LEO I. 457—†74; ZENO 474—†91; ANASTASIUS, 491—†518.

AT its sixth session, 25th October, 451, the Council of Chalcedon promulgated its *Definition of Faith*. The *Definition* affirms that our Lord Jesus Christ is one Person in two Natures.[1] The Emperors Marcian 450—†7, and Pulcheria 450—†3, were present in state at the promulgation. They probably thought that they had given peace to the Church: and Marcian immediately accorded civil sanction to the decision of the Council by *Si quis igitur*[2] forbidding disputations against it. But a reaction set in which extended over the reigns of four Emperors, and lasted for seventy years, before a settlement was reached under the House of Justin.

§ 1. The progress of the reaction varied with changes in the political scene.[3]

The reign of Marcian 450—†7 was " a period of calm. . . . In later times it was looked back to as a golden age." He could not foresee the troubles to which the Council was to lead. He died early in A.D. 457 : and " with him the Theodosian Dynasty, to which, through his marriage, he belonged, ceased to reign at New Rome."[4] He had been chief of the staff to the Patrician Aspar; and was succeeded by Aspar's steward, Leo I.

Leo I.,[5] 457—†74, was the nominee of Aspar, an Alan by descent, and by religion an Arian. Aspar and his son Ardaburius were strong enough to give away the throne, but not to seize it; for it was impossible, as yet, for any but a Roman and a Catholic to succeed to the inheritance of Theodosius the Great. Leo, however, soon became aware that the German ascendancy, which in his day brought the Empire to a close in the West, might as easily dominate the East. In 468, in order to escape from the tutelage of Aspar and his Germans, he formed the plan of recruiting his regiments from " native subjects no less valiant and robust."[6] He placed himself under the protection of Zeno and a bodyguard of Isaurians, and gave him his daughter Ariadne in marriage. The Emperor then bestowed the succession on their little son Leo II., and died shortly afterwards. The first and only act of the child was to place the crown on the head of his father; and thus Zeno became Emperor, largely by the aid of the Dowager-Empress Verina.

" In his ecclesiastical policy Leo followed Marcian, and faithfully maintained orthodoxy as established by the Council of Chalcedon."[7] But during the reign of Zeno, 474—†91, a new policy took its place, of making terms with the Monophysites.[8] Verina was not minded to part with the authority which she had bestowed upon her son-in-law; and, finding him disinclined to share it with her, she took advantage of the unpopularity of the Emperor and his Isaurians to stir up against him her brother Basiliscus. The usurper had proved his incompetence when, as commander of the expedition which Leo I. sent against the Vandals, he had suffered signal defeat at the hands of Gaiseric; but he now maintained himself for a time—in the fateful year, 476, of the fall of the Western Empire—by relying upon the support of the Monophysite party; while Zeno and Ariadne took refuge in Isauria. Basiliscus was induced not only to abrogate the theological decisions of the Council of Chalcedon but also to abolish the Patriarchate which it created for Constantinople. But this was a blunder. The Patriarch Acacius, 471—†89, at once took up the challenge; and held out for his lawful sovereign till Zeno re-entered the city, July 477. The turn of events thus placed Chalcedonian orthodoxy once more in power. But Acacius became alarmed at the growing discords of the Empire; and persuaded himself that it would be wise to make terms, if possible, with the defeated party. Taking advantage, therefore, of the improvement manifest in Monophysite statements of doctrine by contrast with the original Eutychianism, the Patriarch advised the Emperor that, at last, reconciliation of Catholic and Monophysite was not impossible. In the " statesmanlike "[9] document called the *Henoticon*,[10] 482, or " Instrument of Union," Zeno made the attempt. Its effect also was " statesmanlike," to purchase the civil unity of the State at the expense of schism in the Church; for the churches of the Empire, during the Acacian Schism, 481—519, were out of communion with Rome and the West. They became, in effect, Monophysite under Zeno †491, and remained so under his successor Anastasius 491—†518. The re-union came with the accession of Justin, 519.

§ 2. We now proceed to trace these events in detail: especially as they developed in the Patriarchal Sees since the Council of Chalcedon.

(i.) In Palestine, Juvenal returned from the Council as Patriarch of Jerusalem, 451—†8, to find the monks of the three Palestines in an uproar at the instigation of an ex-Religious named Theodosius. This worthy had played his part at the Council; but, returning to Palestine before Juvenal, had set to work to vilify it for having, in effect, rehabilitated Nestorius and condemned Cyril by deposing his successor Dioscorus. Monks abounded in Palestine. There were the solitaries of the Jordan and the Dead Sea; undisciplined save for the few who had come under the hand of St. Euthymius, 377—†473. There were communities also, such as that of the archimandrite Passarion in Jerusalem; or the double convent for men and for women on the Mount of Olives. It had been founded by Melania the Younger; but, since her death, 439, it had been ruled by her almoner and confidant, Gerontius, †484. Pilgrims, as well as ascetics, flourished in Palestine; and, most illustrious of these, there now resided in Jerusalem a greater lady than Melania—Eudocia, the widow of Theodosius II. To her the Council of Chalcedon, which the monk Theodosius was so busy in denouncing, was the council of her sister-in-law, Pulcheria. Her Council, and that of her departed husband, was the second synod of Ephesus, 449, where Dioscorus, now in exile at Gangra, had had his triumph. The Empress, therefore, easily lent herself to the party of the insurgent Religious. It enjoyed also the favour of Gerontius, and of personages among the solitaries as well. Now Juvenal had once seconded Cyril and Dioscorus; but he had gone over to the "enemy" at Chalcedon. He was coming back, with the reward of a Patriarchate for his "treachery." Theodosius and the monks determined that he should be resisted; while, both into his own see and into the sees of his suffragans, bishops of one mind with the opposition were to be intruded. The programme was carried out to the letter; and Juvenal arrived, under imperial escort, only to find the gates of Jerusalem closed against him and Theodosius installed in the see. He took flight to Constantinople; and, while Theodosius proceeded to set up bishops of his party in the sees of Palestine, Juvenal managed to enlist the intervention of the Eastern Sovereigns. At his request, Marcian wrote, c. 453, to the monks of Palestine; bade them take no offence at the expression *In two Natures* as if it were a novelty; and vindicated the Council of Chalcedon against the accusation of having rehabilitated Nestorianism.[11] Pulcheria also wrote to the monks,[12] and to Bassa,[13] the abbess of a convent at Jerusalem, to justify her proceedings and to clear the Council against the calumnies of the intruder Theodosius. From letters, the Emperor at length went on to action; and issued orders for the arrest of Theodosius, who escaped to Mount Sinai, and the reinstatement of Juvenal, July 453. Juvenal got things back into good order by a Council, which wrote a synodal letter[14] to remove mistrust and was itself the recipient of a reassuring communication from Marcian.[15]

At the same time, Pope Leo, 440—†61, intervened. On 11th March, 453, he had already begun to ask for further information about the monks of Palestine in a letter[16] to his agent Julian, bishop of Cos; and, 21st March, he wrote to Julian to say that he had not only complied with a request from Marcian that he should remonstrate with the Empress Eudocia but had induced her son-in-law, Valentinian III., 425—†55, to do the same.[17] He wrote also, 15th June, to the monks[18] in explanation of his *Tome*;[19] and, in a letter of the same date to Eudocia,[20] he exhorted her to reclaim those of them to whom she had lent her patronage and to assure them that the Catholic Faith is equally opposed to Nestorianism and to Eutychianism; she will let him know, of course, how far she succeeds. We do not know how the Empress took this admonition at first; but the troubles that came upon her by the assassination of her son-in-law and by the captivity of her daughter Eudoxia and her granddaughters Eudocia and Placidia, who were carried off to Carthage, shook her resolution, and caused her to think about returning to the communion of the Catholic Church. She turned for advice to the oracles of the desert; and, while St. Simeon Stylites warned her that "that scoundrel Theodosius was the instrument of the devil," Euthymius informed her that the calamities which had befallen her family in Italy were a punishment for yielding to his villainy. Let her renounce the communion of Dioscorus, and return to the allegiance of Juvenal. She took the advice : and the effect of her reconciliation with the Patriarch did much to allay the disorders of Palestine. They disappeared with the capture of Theodosius by the Imperial police, and his death in a monastery at Constantinople, 30th December, 457. Marcian himself died on 26th January of that year; and next year died Juvenal, five years after restoration to his see. He had held it for nearly forty years, 421—†58.

(ii.) In Egypt the resistance of the Monophysites was much more serious. Dioscorus had been exiled to Gangra in Paphlagonia, where he died 4th September, 454. So long as he lived, the populace of Alexandria, with Egypt as a whole, refused to regard him as other than their lawful bishop. Four of his suffragans, however, had voted with the majority at Chalcedon; and they presently appeared with letters from the Emperor to the Prefect of Egypt bidding him proceed to the election of a bishop of Alexandria. The choice fell upon Proterius, 452—†7, to whom, as archpriest, Dioscorus had committed the care of the Church in his absence; and he was consecrated by the four. But the election was the work of the Court and the city nobles; and, in spite of the connection of Proterius with his late chief Dioscorus, the mob broke out into riots against him. With them it was a question not so much of preference for *Of two Natures* as against *In two Natures*, as for Egyptian nationalism against Byzantine Imperialism. The rioters, of course, were suppressed, at last, by a strong force of soldiery sent from Constantinople; but Proterius could never dispense with a military escort, so insecure was his hold, till the death of Marcian. That event gave his opponents the chance they were awaiting.

On the accession of Leo I., 457—†74, a monk named Timothy, nicknamed the Cat, took advantage of the absence in Upper Egypt of the General in command to raise a tumult. The result of it was that, 16th March, he was consecrated in the church of the Cæsareum to be Patriarch of Alexandria, 457—60 and 475—7, in true succession, as his adherents would say, to their late Patriarch Dioscorus, 444—51. Timothy had but two consecrators, both of whom had previously been deposed by Proterius and the Egyptian synod; and, after playing the anti-Patriarch for a few days, he was expelled by the General Dionysius. Whereupon his partisans took their revenge by hunting Proterius into the baptistery of the church of Quirinus, where they murdered him on Maundy Thursday, 28th March, 457. They then dragged his remains round the city and, after feasting upon them like cannibals, burnt them and scattered his ashes to the winds. The friends of Proterius lost no time in putting their case before the Emperor Leo I. and his Patriarch Anatolius, 449—58, at Constantinople. Meanwhile, " rumours of the misdeeds of the Alexandrian populace " reached Pope Leo by 1st June, 457; but it was only by " the report of his brother and fellow-bishop Anatolius "[21] that he was enabled to take precise note of the situation. The Monophysites, Anatolius informed him, had demanded another Council to revise the conclusions of Chalcedon, and the Emperor had refused their request. This, of course, was to the good: but Pope Leo still thought it desirable to keep the Government loyal to its refusal. He therefore wrote three letters,[22] on 11th July, to the Emperor, to Anatolius and to his agent Julian, bishop of Cos, pointing out the supreme importance of holding fast to the Synod of Chalcedon, and begging the Emperor to provide a Catholic bishop for Alexandria. These representations he followed up, on 1st September, by a second series:[23] to the Emperor, expressing his gratification that his Majesty had guaranteed the inviolability of Chalcedon—for, till the death of Aspar, †471, it must be remembered, Leo was surrounded by Arian influences; and to the bishops of leading sees, such as Basil, Patriarch of Antioch, 456—†8, and Euxitheus, bishop of Thessalonica, assuring them of his confidence that on this point the Government was sound. During the autumn, however, the partisans of Timothy sent petitions to put it to the proof; and, though these emanated only from four bishops,[24] the four had the hardihood to declare that their creed was that of Nicæa only, neither more nor less; that while they accepted the two Councils of Ephesus—the assemblies, that is, of Cyril and Dioscorus —they repudiated the Councils of Constantinople and Chalcedon, Court Councils both; and, in conclusion, that they would be obliged by an answer being forwarded to their archbishop, Timothy. The Emperor referred this communication to Anatolius, and asked for the opinion of the Home Synod as well on the validity of the consecration of Timothy as on the point of upholding the Council of Chalcedon. The Synod replied that Timothy's consecration was null, and that to reopen the decisions of Chalcedon would be to open the flood-gates of confusion in every church. A circular letter, in terms very much the same as those of the letter to Anatolius, was next sent to the chief bishops of Christendom and to three famous solitaries—Simeon Stylites, James and Baradai—who, in popular esteem, took rank with them. The replies were unanimous—against reopening questions closed at Chalcedon. The Government thus succeeded in circumventing the demand for a Council, and yet in securing the authoritative decision of the Church; for the consent of the episcopate, with the Pope at its head, is final by whatever method, of votes collected by letter or of votes given in Synod, it be attained. To this consent, Leo added the weight of his "second *Tome*,"[25] 17th August, 458, as the exposition which he promised to the Emperor in a letter of 1st December, 457, has been called.[26] It was intended for the benefit of Timothy. But, though the Emperor pressed it upon him, Timothy refused it absolutely. "Its statements," he said, "are Nestorian." Timothy therefore was banished: and in exile he remained till after the death of the Emperor Leo, fervently occupied in defending his own theological position and combating the tenets alike of Eutyches and of the Council of Chalcedon.

No sooner was he got rid of than the Government proceeded to fill his place. The Proterians elected another Timothy, 460—75 and 477—†82, nicknamed Salofaciolus, a name of uncertain meaning;[27] and by his opponents, the Royalist or Melkite. He was thus the first to bear the name by which the nationalist and Monophysite majority in Syria and Egypt afterwards marked their contempt for the Orthodox remnant as slaves to the religion of the Court. Personally, however, they liked Timothy Salofaciolus. He had a good heart, and a kind word for everybody, even for the fanatics who regarded his communion with horror. "We love you well," they used to say to him in the street, "though we do not want you for our bishop." The last three extant letters[28] of Pope Leo were written, 18th August, 460, to congratulate the new Patriarch, and his clergy, and certain Egyptian bishops, on his election. "Let him be on his guard against heresy, and keep us constantly informed at Rome." Leo, perhaps, had reason to think him too accommodating; and so it turned out. For the Catholic Patriarch of Alexandria consented to restore the name of Dioscorus to the diptychs; till 478, when he received a reprimand[29] from Pope Simplicius, 468—†83.

The accession of Zeno, 474—†91, made but slight difference at first to the ecclesiastical situation in Egypt; for though, when in command at Antioch, he had compromised himself with the Monophysites, as Emperor he suffered himself, like his predecessor, to be kept loyal to the *Tome* and the Council by the Patriarch of Constantinople. But Acacius carried less weight with the usurper Basiliscus, 475—7, who had in his train friends of the exiled Timothy of Alexandria. Yielding to their suggestions and, it is said, to the entreaties of his wife Zenonis, the intruder made a bid for the support of the Monophysites throughout the Empire. He recalled their leader Timothy, and handed him the *Encyclical*,[30] 476. It was a document entirely in harmony with Timothy's ideas; for by it the Government gave its sanction to the two Councils of Ephesus and denounced at once the errors of Eutyches and the novelties of Chalcedon. All the bishops were required to confirm it by their signatures; and, while for clerics refusal was to involve deposition, on the part of the laity any demonstration in favour of Chalcedon was to be visited with exile and confiscation. Timothy, after eighteen years of exile, 458—76, would now feel that his hour of triumph was come; and he lost no time in making the most of it. Hastening from the Crimea to Constantinople, he landed amid the cheers of Alexandrian sailors; and was escorted by the people to lodgings reserved for him in the Palace. Thence he intended, by making a solemn entry into St.Sophia, to force the hand of Acacius. But Acacius was well aware that, if the anti-Chalcedonian reaction were to succeed, then with the doctrine of that Council the newly-won powers of the see of Constantinople would also go by the board. So at his nod, no doubt, the Chalcedonian monks of the capital barred the way of Timothy to the cathedral. Acacius clothed its pulpit and altar in black for his reception, and closed all the other churches against him. The Eutychians also, who, equally with the Catholics, had come in for Timothy's displeasure, joined in to repel him. " Let him go back into exile, to where he came from!" Foiled in the capital, Timothy thought it prudent to withdraw; but, on his way home, he endeavoured to retaliate upon Acacius by stopping at Ephesus to reinstate in that see a bishop named Paul whom the Ephesians had put in without reference to the see of Constantinople, or to the canon of Chalcedon which gave it authority over them. Acacius had, therefore, deposed him; and Timothy halted to summon a Council at Ephesus. The Council re-affirmed the autonomy of Ephesus, deposed Acacius, and wrote to the Emperor to beg his support. Timothy then continued his journey to Alexandria, where he re-established himself without difficulty. The mild Salofaciolus retired to his Pachomian monastery at Canopus, content to live on an allowance from his rival of a penny a day. The remains of Dioscorus Timothy also brought back with him to Alexandria in a silver casket, and laid to rest by the side of his predecessors in the see. And thus Timothy awaited the next move of Acacius.

(iii.) Meanwhile, in Syria, the Monophysite reaction had enjoyed, up to the usurpation of Basiliscus, a like measure of success. From early times Antioch had produced a succession of teachers whose tendency was to look upon our Lord as a man who became God. The Ebionites, Paul of Samosata, Diodore, Theodore, Nestorius, were all inclined to minimise His Godhead for the sake of affirming His manhood. But there had also been in existence, from the first, a rival tradition at Antioch which tended to evacuate His humanity because it had so firm a conviction of His Deity. In the second century, the Docetics had denied the *reality* of our Lord's human nature, as early as the days of Ignatius. His condemnation of them may have been prompted by the Docetism of Saturnilus, his contemporary at Antioch and one of the Syrian school of Gnostics. In the fourth century, Apollinaris, bishop of the neighbouring Laodicea in Syria, had denied the *completeness* of our Lord's human nature. In the fifth century the tendency showed itself in Monophysitism, some forms of which were incompatible with the *permanence* of our Lord's human nature; and at Antioch the monk Maximus, though a deacon of John, the friend of Nestorius, and Patriarch of Antioch, 429—†42, adhered so ardently to the Christology of Cyril that the latter had to write and check his zeal.[31] There was thus a rift beginning to appear between the people and the hierarchy of Syria; and the theology of the Greek-speaking epis-

The East after Chalcedon

copate ran counter to the sympathies of the monks and the Syriac-speaking populace. The monks of Syria rallied to the Cyrilline party; while, to devout folk throughout Syria, Monophysitism alone appeared to guarantee the Deity of the Saviour. It was thus the religion of piety: whereas the belief of the Government, the Council and the Roman church was held to be indistinguishable from Nestorianism. If Monophysitism was persecuted, so much the stronger case for its being the truth!

Martyrius, Patriarch of Antioch, 459—70, was the first to encounter the forces of Monophysitism led by Peter the Fuller. Peter had belonged to the community of the Accœmetæ. But he quarrelled with them; and became a priest at Chalcedon where he presided over the monastery of St. Bassa. The Accœmetæ were ardent Chalcedonians; to the Monophysite chronicler, Zacharias of Mitylene †553, Nestorians.[32] Peter, therefore, transferred himself to the opposite party; and having attached himself to the retinue of Zeno who, upon his marriage, 468, with Ariadne, the daughter of Leo I., proceeded to Antioch as commander-in-chief of " The East," Peter not only took the lead of the Monophysite party there and drove out Martyrius but, with the aid of Zeno, established himself as Patriarch in his place. Martyrius carried complaint to Constantinople, where the Patriarch Gennadius, 458—†71, came to his rescue and procured the exile of Peter to the Oasis under an order now recalled by *Qui in monasteriis*[33] of 1st June, 471. But the exile was commuted to internment with the Accœmetæ. They kept him safe till the end of the reign of Leo I.; nor did Zeno, at his accession, 474, release him. But on the usurpation of Basiliscus and the arrival of Timothy the Cat in Constantinople, Peter was sent for and put into possession, for the second time, of the throne of Antioch, 476—7. The triumph of the Monophysites, however, proved short-lived; and, on the return of Zeno, 477, a second order was issued for the banishment of Peter, this time to Pityus in the Caucasus. Fortune again saved him from being sent so far afield; and again he was interned, this time with the Massalians at the sanctuary of St. Theodore in the province of Helenopontus. His friends endeavoured to enthrone in his place a *protégé* of his, John Codonatus, 477—8, but without success, for the Government put in Stephen, 478—†81. He fell a victim to the Monophysites, who murdered him in church by running him through with pointed reeds. An Orthodox election at Antioch was quite impossible : so Acacius " provided " Calandion. He was Patriarch 481—5; but then had to give way to Peter the Fuller who thus occupied the throne for the third time, 485—†8. The mere record of these events is enough to show the daring of the Monophysites, and to what impotence they had reduced both the see of Antioch and the school of Diodore and Theodore, of Nestorius and Theodoret, so long and so intimately associated with it. Nor was the situation different in Jerusalem, where the successor of Juvenal, Anastasius, was Patriarch, 458— †78, and signed the *Encyclical* of Basiliscus.

Thus twenty-five years after the Council of Chalcedon the Monophysite reaction had everywhere risen to the crest of the wave. At Alexandria, Antioch and Jerusalem, three out of the four Eastern Patriarchs had signed the *Encyclical.* But for the opposition of Acacius, everything was going well from the point of view of Timothy the Cat. It follows next to consider the check and the ultimate advantage that his cause sustained by the course of events in the capital.

(iv.) At Constantinople, Acacius refused to sign the *Encyclical,* and threw himself for support upon the monks of the city, mostly Chalcedonian; and, in particular, upon St. Daniel the Stylite. The saint descended from his column and, rousing the populace, so overawed Basiliscus by foretelling the speedy return of Zeno that the usurper at once endeavoured to forestall it by revoking his former pronouncement in the *Anti-encyclical.*[34] By this document he re-affirmed the decisions of Chalcedon in regard both to the Faith and to the privileges accorded to the see of Constantinople. But it was too late to save himself by any such expedient; and Zeno re-entered the city, July, 477. Having got rid of Basiliscus, whom the Patriarch

The East after Chalcedon

delivered up even from the sanctuary, Zeno put out an edict reversing his measures affecting religion and restoring the *status quo ante*. In a letter[35] of 9th October, 477, he received the congratulations of Pope Simplicius, 468—†83, on his recovery of the throne. " Let your Majesty," urged Simplicius, " now deliver the churches and, in particular, the church of Alexandria, from intruders; and suffer no indignity to be offered to the Council of Chalcedon or to the *Tome* of St. Leo." To Acacius also Simplicius wrote in similar terms on the same date.[36] " Let him put pressure on the Emperor to send Timothy the Cat into perpetual exile; and let him remind his Majesty that Paul of Ephesus, Peter the Fuller, and his *protégé*, John of Apamea, deserve the same sentence." These three last were quickly ousted; but Timothy the Cat, as the Prefect of Egypt represented to the Emperor, was too old to be disturbed; and, indeed, he died within a few months of the restoration. But his death did not end the schism in Egypt; for his archdeacon, Peter, surnamed Mongus, or the Stammerer, was elected by the Monophysite party to the see which he held, 477—90, the election taking place in spite of the fact that the Catholic Patriarch, Timothy Salofaciolus, was yet alive. Justly indignant at this irregularity, the Emperor sent orders to the prefect of Egypt to put Mongus to death, to punish his supporters, and to reinstate Salofaciolus. But by the kindly intervention of Salofaciolus, so characteristic of him, the Monophysite Patriarch was only banished. The Catholic Patriarch was thus restored; and for five years, 477—82, retained his see. Then, falling ill of a mortal sickness, he sent a deputation to Zeno, at the head of which was John Talaia, to procure the guarantee of the Government for a free election on the next vacancy at Alexandria. On the return of the embassy, Timothy Salofaciolus died, 482, and John was unanimously elected. But, by an unfortunate mistake, which had disastrous consequences, he contrived to give deep offence to Acacius. By the usual synodal letters he informed the sees of Rome and Antioch of his consecration; and wrote a similar letter, containing the news of it, for the Patriarch of Constantinople. But instead of posting it direct, he sent it under cover, to Illus, a former intimate of his own and now Master of the Offices; as if, by this means, it would reach the Emperor and the Patriarch with more effect. Illus, at this time, was at Antioch; and before the enclosure could reach Acacius, that prelate had learned, from another source, of the election of John. He took offence at the slight thus put upon him; and so did a kinsman of Salofaciolus, Gennadius by name, who had been made by him, in conjunction with Talaia, his *apocrisiarius*, or agent, at Constantinople. Together, Acacius and Gennadius determined to ruin John Talaia, and put Peter Mongus in his place. They represented to the Emperor that Peter, after all, was acceptable to the people at Alexandria, and not really at variance with the Faith: and they prevailed upon Zeno to suggest this course to Pope Simplicius. " If charges are to be made against John," replied the Pope, 15th July, 482, " by all means let his election stand over while they are investigated: but the appointment of a heretic, such as Peter Mongus, is not for a moment to be contemplated."[37] Irritated at this curt rejection of his plans, the Emperor was the more bent on giving them effect. He sent instructions for the banishment of John, and the installation at Alexandria of Peter Mongus. At the same time he addressed to the bishops of Egypt the *Henoticon*, 482, or *Instrument of Union:* which, drawn up as it was, by agreement between Acacius and Peter, was for the latter to sign as the price of his recognition in the see. It begins by setting forth the desire for reunion and the losses due to division. As the basis of union, the Nicene Creed is enough: it was reaffirmed at the Council of Constantinople and accepted by those who, at the Council of Ephesus, condemned Nestorius. The document then goes on to denounce Eutyches and to approve the Twelve Articles of Cyril; and, after an unexceptionable *résumé* of the Faith, it concludes by anathematising any who believe, or have believed, whether at Chalcedon or elsewhere, anything to the contrary thereof. But to approve the Twelve Anathematisms of Cyril, and to leave the authority of the *Tome* and of Chalcedon an open question was, while nominally retaining, really to reverse the settlement there attained. It was to put Leo second to Cyril and the Anathematisms above the *Tome*. The Church of the Byzantine Empire thus became officially Monophysite: and, as a result, though the political unity of the Empire may have been strengthened, it was a unity purchased at the price of alienation from the West. The relations between Rome and Constantinople were suspended by the Acacian Schism, 484—519; and were not restored till the accession of the House of Justin, 518—610.

§ 3. The Acacian Schism coincided with the reign of the Emperor Anastasius, 491—†518; who continued the general policy of Zeno.

Anastasius[38] was a guardsman, of genuine but unconventional piety, who conducted a Bible-class in St. Sophia. Much to the distaste of the Patriarch Euphemius, 490—6, the Empress Ariadne, †515, on the death of her husband Zeno, proclaimed him Augustus. But the people accepted her choice, with loud acclamations of " Reign as thou hast lived! " Euphemius contented himself with requiring from him a declaration of orthodoxy: which Anastasius readily signed.

The new Emperor put an end to the long domination of the Isaurians under Zeno; and then, in order to protect his capital against inroads of the Bulgarians, 493—502, he built the Long Wall which ran some forty miles west of Constantinople from the Sea of Marmora to the Black Sea, and is now represented by the Chataldja Lines, so famous in the Great War. At home, though " generous and open-handed himself," he " maintained a strict control of expenditure " : which " rendered him unpopular with the official classes, and did not endear him to the nobles and ladies accustomed to the pageantry of the Court."

Added to this, was the unpopularity of his religious policy. In sympathy Monophysite, he also found it politic to maintain the *Henoticon* of Zeno. For, since the western part of the Empire had now fallen into the hands of Goths in Italy, Gaul and Spain, and of Vandals in Africa, all of whom were Arians, he held it wiser to ignore the West, and to concentrate upon winning the good-will of the East, now largely Monophysite, in Syria and Egypt. By this means he might hope to consolidate the territories of his Empire. At a Council of Constantinople, 496, he obtained the confirmation of the *Henoticon*, and got rid of Euphemius. Macedonius II., 496—511, was appointed in his stead. He, too, was a Chalcedonian; but he did not scruple to accept the *Henoticon*. He could not, however, conceal his opinions for long; and, by a Council of 511, he was deposed in favour of Timothy, 511—8, an undisguised Monophysite. Three years before, a Monophysite monk, Severus[39] of Sozopolis in Pisidia, had arrived in Constantinople, and was received with honour by the Emperor. Severus was an advocate of inserting into the *Trisagion*[40]—" Holy God, Holy [and] strong, Holy [and] immortal, Have mercy upon us"—the clause " who wast crucified for us." The result was that the hymn would be taken as emphasising the deity of the Sufferer : whereas the sufferings belonged primarily to His humanity. The insertion was thus regarded, and probably intended, as a good piece of propaganda by Monophysites. In Antioch, where this hymn was taken as addressed to the Second Person in the Holy Trinity, the addition was not unorthodox. But in Constantinople, the *Trisagion* was customarily treated as addressed to the Trinity; and it might now carry a heterodox meaning, as if the Godhead had suffered in the flesh. Timothy seized his opportunity for a demonstration : and on Sunday, 4th November, 512, caused the *Trisagion* to be sung, at its usual place in the Liturgy, with the offending clause. A riot followed which all but brought about the abdication of the Emperor: but, in spite of his growing unpopularity, he managed to calm the tumult and to retain his throne. In the same year occurred the deposition of Flavian II., Patriarch of Antioch, 498—512, and a supporter of the *Henoticon* in favour of Severus, 512—8, " the leading theologian of the Monophysites and a bitter foe of Chalcedon."[41]

A rebellion in Thrace was the outcome of the Emperor's acquiescence in these proceedings.[42] Its leader was Vitalian, Count of the Federati, who were mostly Bulgarians and were stationed in Thrace. He appeared before Constantinople; and gave himself out not simply as the avenger of their grievances but as the representative of the prevailing religious discontent. Voicing the indignation of the orthodox at the new form of the *Trisagion,* and championing the cause of the deposed Patriarchs—Macedonius of Constantinople, his personal friend, and Flavian of Antioch—Vitalian succeeded in bringing the Emperor to terms. It was arranged that a Council should be held for promoting the peace of the Church: and that both should invite the co-operation of Pope Hormisdas, 514—†23. A fruitless correspondence between the Emperor and the Pope ensued:[43] and no reconciliation was in sight when Anastasius died at the age of 80 on 8th July, 518. His Patriarch Timothy had died three months before, on 5th April. He was succeeded by John II., 518—20: who no sooner appeared in his cathedral, 15th July, after the accession of Justin,[44] 518—†27, than the populace demanded the confirmation of the Council of Chalcedon, the expulsion of Severus from Antioch and reconciliation with the Roman see. Fresh overtures were made to Pope Hormisdas.[45] Ultimately, 26th April, 521, he dropped the demand that the names of Acacius and others[46] should be removed from the diptychs: and subject to acceptance of the right faith as held by the Roman See and expressed in the *Tome* of St. Leo, he empowered Epiphanius, who succeeded as Patriarch, 520—†36, in place of John, to act for him in receiving the churches into communion.[47] The *Henoticon,* without being formally revoked, was allowed quietly to disappear; and everywhere, except in Egypt, the Council of Chalcedon was received.

CHAPTER II.

JUSTINIAN, 527—†65:
VICTOR AND LAWGIVER.

For the "Genealogical Table of the House of Justin" see *L.R.E.*[2] II. ix.: as follows :—

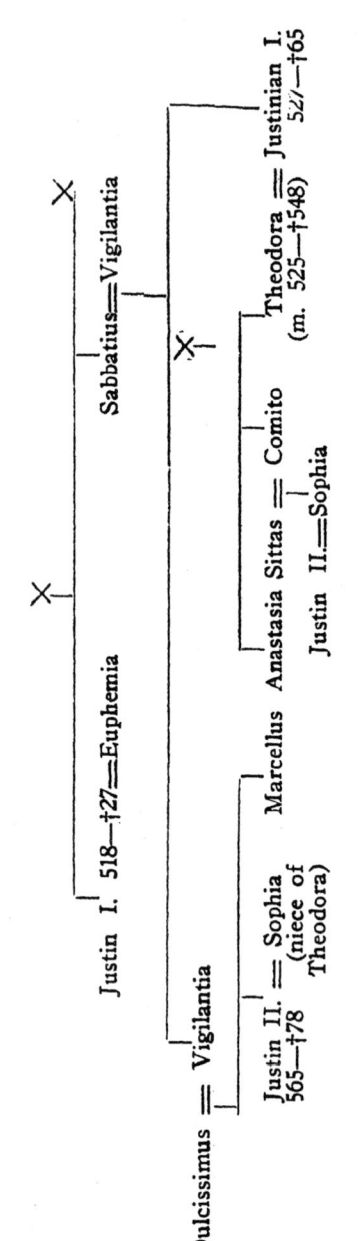

BISHOPS OF THE CHIEF SEES, 527—65.

ROME.		CONSTANTINOPLE.		ANTIOCH.	
Felix IV.	526—30	Timothy I.	511—18	Ephraim	526—45
Boniface II.	530—2	John II.	518—20	Domnus III.	545—59
John II.	532—5	Epiphanius	520—35	Anastasius I. (Sinait-	
Agapetus I.	535—6	Anthimus I.	535—6	icus)	559—70
Silverius	536—8	Menas	536—52		
Vigilius	538—55	Eutychius	552—65		
Pelagius I.	555—60				
John III.	560—73				

ALEXANDRIA.

Orthodox.		Monophysite.		JERUSALEM.	
				Peter	524—52
Paul	537—42	Timothy III.	519—36	Macarius II.	552
Zoilus	542—51	Theodosius I.	536—67	Eustochius	552—63/4
Apollinaris	551—70			Macarius II.[2]	
					563/4—75

CHAPTER II.

JUSTINIAN, 527—†65: VICTOR AND LAWGIVER.

§ 1. AT the opening of the sixth century, the condition of the Roman Empire differed considerably from what it was at the Council of Chalcedon. (i.) Constitutionally,[1] the Empire was governed in 451 by a *collegium* of Emperors living in East and West respectively, but each exercising a joint authority with the other over the whole. This unity found expression in the joint edicts[2] and in the consulship.[3] In 476, by the resignation of Romulus Augustulus, collegiate government disappeared for good; and the whole Empire reverted, in theory as in fact, to a single ruler, who henceforth exercised his authority from Constantinople.

(ii.) In extent, the Roman world was much reduced. True, that from the beginning of the barbarian invasions, each intruder was expected, and was proud, to regularise his position by formally accepting the theory that he ruled in the name of the Roman Emperor: so that the boundaries of the Empire continued to be almost as extensive as before. But in 450 there were territories actually under the authority of an Emperor which were lost by the sixth century. Thus Valentinian III. held Italy in his own power till his death in 455; and, from 425—50, under his mother Galla Placidia, the daughter of Theodosius I., no barbarian had set foot upon its soil. Fifty years later, large territories had been overrun. In 456 the Visigoths conquered Spain; and by 490 their kingdom extended northwards to the Loire. Mauretania was abandoned to the Moors. The Vandals, already masters of Numidia and Africa by the capture of Carthage, 439, acquired before 468 the Balearic Islands, Corsica, Sardinia and the westernmost corner of Sicily. The Ostrogoths established themselves in Pannonia, 454; and, by the fall of Ravenna, 493, in Italy and Sicily under

Justinian: Victor and Lawgiver

their great King Theoderic, 493—†526. The Franks became masters of northern France, 496, and the Burgundians of the south and east, 490. Such was the rapid advance of the German tribes, in the latter half of the fifth century. It was an Empire proportionately contracted which survived this advance. After 480, it consisted only of the Prefectures of Illyricum and the East. And this was the extent of the Roman Empire when the House of Justin, 518—602, gained possession of the throne.[4] The Empire over which it ruled for the greater part of the sixth century included Italy, Africa and part of Spain as well.

§ 2. Justin I.,[5] 518—†27, was, like Diocletian, an Illyrian peasant[6] and the founder of a new dynasty. He was a soldier, in command of the Guards, under Anastasius, 491—†518, his predecessor. Anastasius was unpopular, partly owing to his " strict control of the public expenditure,"[7] partly because he was a Monophysite. He maintained the policy of Zeno that was declared by the *Henoticon*, 482.[8] His aim was, by making terms between Chalcedonians and Monophysites, to keep his realm united, in face of the constant danger to his Eastern frontier from the might of Persia. But this policy involved the sacrifice of union with the West; and the continuance of the separation between Eastern and Western Christendom, known as the Acacian Schism, 484—519. Anastasius, moreover, as a Monophysite, favoured the Greens—one of the two factions of the world of sport who carried their partisanship into politics and theology. Justin, on the other hand, gave his patronage to the Blues,[9] and was orthodox: and, as he tells us in a letter to Pope Hormisdas, 514—†23, he attributed his promotion " first " to the favour of the Undivided Trinity, next to the good-will of the nobles and the senate, and also to the acclamation of the army.[10] Perhaps his long experience—for he was about sixty-six years of age—and his military reputation contributed to his elevation: but he was powerfully aided through funds placed at his disposal by the eunuch Amantius[11] with which he bribed his guardsmen. Everything, therefore, promised well for

Justin; but he was illiterate and unversed in affairs;[12] and from the first he looked for support to his nephew Justinian[13] who supplied his deficiencies. The reign of Justin—but for its putting an end to the schism and its reunion with the West[14]—is a blank. It is important mainly as the prelude to the epoch of Justinian. Power fell into his hands, when he became Consul, 521. He was created Augustus, April, 527; and, four months later, the death of his uncle, 1st August, left him sole master of the Roman world.

§ 3. Justinian ruled 527—†65. He was of Latin origin, born 483 at Tauresium (now Taor), near Scupi (now Skoplje in Serbia); and thus forty-four years of age at his accession. In person, he was rather above middle height, with a ruddy and smiling countenance, easy of access and with pleasant manners. In education, he was well read in literature : but a master in law and theology. In character, he was abstemious and devout : but his outstanding trait was an overmastering industry. One of his courtiers nicknamed him " The Emperor who never sleeps."[15] It might be thought that a prince of so masterful a spirit[16] would have listened to no council save his own. But he fell under the influence of his wife Theodora[17]—perhaps the most famous princess of antiquity. She was, by birth, of humble origin : small and pale, but beautiful, witty and fascinating. She followed the profession of an actress; and, though we are not bound to accept all the scandalous tales about her given c. A.D. 550 in the *Secret History* of Procopius, we need not doubt, in view of the degradation then incident to her trade, that her life had been notorious. It was probably this that led Euphemia, the empress of Justin, to oppose the marriage of her nephew with Theodora. But Justinian was madly in love : and induced his uncle to rescind,[18] in his favour, the law which put restrictions upon marriages with women of abandoned character. His choice was justified. Retaining all her charm and wit, and remaining, as before, a woman of energy and spirit, Theodora, in spite of her imperious ways, became a Christian lady, the rescuer and friend of the fallen.[19] From the Revolt of Nika,[20] 532, to her death in 548, she exercised an unbounded sway over her husband. But while he was orthodox and favoured the Blues, she had been brought up among the Greens and was a Monophysite. It was even said that, by thus dividing their interests, the Sovereigns gained the secrets of either party: and thus the Imperial pair—for Theodora was " partner in our counsels,"[21] and so more than Empress Consort—supported each other to maintain an absolute command of their subjects. Their portraits appear on either side of the sanctuary in the contemporary church (547) of San Vitale at Ravenna.

§ 4. The secular activities of Justinian exercised a direct influence on his ecclesiastical policy. His aim was twofold: to recover, under his immediate sovereignty, the lands lost to the barbarians of the West, and to reduce to order the administrative system under which his subjects should live. For the recovery of the West, he had to be orthodox, because he would have to gain the support of the see of Rome. For a uniform system of administration, he must needs bring the Church under the control of the law.

§ 5. For the recovery of the West, Justinian had to pursue a defensive policy in the East. Since 505, there had been peace between the Romans and Kavad I., King of Persia,[22] 488—†531. But owing to the growth of Roman influence in the Caucasian border-state of Lazica,[23] then subject to Persia, the situation became strained before the death of Justin. Justinian commanded his general, Belisarius, 505—†65, to build a new fortress at Dara, N.W. of Nisibis; and hostilities broke out 527. After a brilliant victory for the Roman arms at Dara, June, 530, and their defeat at Callinicum, on Easter Even, 19th April, 531, Belisarius was recalled; and on the accession of Chosroes I., 531—†78, " the endless peace " was concluded, 532, on terms disadvantageous to the Romans.[24] So ended *the first Persian War*, 527—32, of Justinian. A *second War with Persia*, 540—5, now jealous of his victories in the West, ensued in 540 and lasted for five years. It came to an end, 545, with a five-years' truce: which ripened into " the fifty-years' peace " of 562.[25] It was a peace, like the former, bought by the Romans with money: and did not last. But, nevertheless, Justinian's method of maintaining defensive war on his Eastern frontier by arms and gold alternately, permitted him to devote his attention to schemes of conquest in the West: where we now turn to the Roman restoration at the expense of the Vandals in Africa,[26] 533—34; of the Ostrogoths in Italy, 535—54; and, to a slighter extent, of the Visigoths in Spain,[27] 554.

Africa and Italy were governed respectively by Hilderic,[28] King of the Vandals, 523—30, and son of the Arian persecutor Huneric, 477—†84, and by Amalasuntha †535, daughter of Theoderic the Ostrogoth, as regent[29] for his grandson Athalaric, 525—†34. Both were unpopular: Hilderic, as a Catholic (he was the grandson of Valentinian III.) with his Arian subjects: and Amalasuntha, as a woman and a friend of Roman civilisation, with her barbarian nobles. No time could have been better for Justinian to intervene in the West. Further, the Catholics in Africa would welcome his intervention, for it would deliver them from their Arian oppressors; while the closing of the Acacian Schism would weaken the government of Amalasuntha because it had given her security that her Catholic subjects in Italy would have nothing to do with the Empire while it was practically Monophysite. Moreover, the Empire itself had recovered its strength. In 476 it was distracted by the rivalries of Zeno and Basiliscus, and too weak to come to the aid of the last Western Emperor: but it was now strong again in reliance upon the hoarded wealth of Anastasius,[30] 491—†518. Justinian found the moment favourable to reassert its claims upon the West.

His counsellors nearly dissuaded him from the attempt upon Africa: but the event proved his determination sound. In 530 Hilderic was overpowered by his cousin[31] Gelimer, 530—4: and Justinian took up his cause as soon as he had made up his quarrel with Persia by the recall of Belisarius and "the endless peace," 532. Belisarius embarked for Africa, 22nd June, 533, and landed at Caputvada (Ras Kapoodia) about 130 miles S.E. of

Carthage. He defeated the Vandals, 13th September, *Ad Decimum*, or ten miles from the city. Two days later he entered the capital of Africa: and secured the goodwill of the people by the disciplined behaviour of his troops. About the middle of December he won the final victory at Tricamaron, some twenty miles west from Carthage: which led to the surrender of Gelimer. Belisarius thereupon returned to Constantinople, 534: and, in the triumph which he was there accorded, he presented Gelimer, as a captive, to Justinian. But Africa, though conquered, was not yet won. It was the turn of the Berber tribes to resist. There was a revolt, 534—8, and a pacification, 539—43, by the Praetorian Prefect Solomon: and again both mutiny and revolt, 545. At last, order was restored, 546—8; the Berbers were reduced to subjection: and Africa became once more Roman. From east to west, it consisted of Tripolitana, Byzacena, Proconsularis, Numidia and Mauretania Sitifensis. But west of that, Mauretania Cæsariensis and Mauretania Tingitana, save for Septum (Ceuta) opposite Gibraltar, broke away. On the other hand, the Balearic Islands, Sardinia and Corsica, once part of the Vandal realm, were included in the lands recovered for the Empire: while S.E. Spain was won from the Visigoths, 554.

Belisarius[32] had but lately celebrated his triumph for the re-conquest of Africa when, May, 535, Amalasuntha was murdered by her nobles. She was the friend and ally of Justinian: and her death gave him a pretext for making war upon Italy. In the summer, Belisarius set sail from Constantinople. He took Sicily without difficulty; and, crossing the straits of Messina, May, 536, he made himself master of southern Italy by the capture of Naples and, 9th December, took Rome[33] unopposed. Then followed the siege of Rome, 537—8, by Witigis, King of the Ostrogoths, which the besiegers were forced to raise just before Easter, 4th April, 538. The deliverance of the city is commemorated in the *Secreta* of a Paschal Mass[34] in the *Leonine Sacramentary:* which cannot thus be much earlier than the middle of the sixth century.[85] Two other sieges of Rome ensued, and it was twice taken, in 546[36] and in 549,[37] by Totila, King of the Goths. Belisarius departed, 540, for the second Persian War, 540—5: but returned 544 till his recall 548. He was ill-supported by Justinian in Italy: and the war dragged on till the command was given, 551, to the Armenian eunuch Narses. Descending from the north by Ravenna and Rimini, he defeated and slew Totila at the battle of Taginae,[38] 552, Rome fell into his hands: and, at the foot of Vesuvius, on the slopes of Monte Lettere,[39] 553, he finally broke the power of the Ostrogoths. They agreed to abandon Italy:[40] which thus became, once more, an integral part of the Roman Empire.[41] But it was an Italy ruined and depopulated: and the beautiful but deserted churches[42] of San Vitale, 547, and San Apollinare in Classe, 549, which Justinian built about this time at Ravenna, mark both the magnificence of his achievements and the desolation that followed.

§ 6. The legal reforms of Justinian[43] went on contemporaneously with his conquests: for he was bent not only upon the recovery of Roman territory but on the revival of Roman institutions. The sources of law under the Empire were twofold: first, the Imperial ordinances or *Constitutiones* which took the place of the *Leges* of the Republic and the *Senatusconsulta* of A.D. 150 onwards; and, secondly, the writings of the great jurist Gaius who flourished in the age of the Antonines and Papinian, with his pupils Paul, Ulpian and Modestinus, who all held high place under the House of Severus. These writings, embodying as they did both *Leges* and *Senatusconsulta* of earlier times, represented a body of law which was from three to five centuries old in the time of Justinian, and were known as the *Jus vetus:* whereas the Imperial Constitutions, being more recent, were spoken of as the *Jus novum*. The whole, whether in ordinance or treatise, formed a mass of law which had become so confused and inaccessible as to be unworkable. Moreover, the acceptance of Christianity by the Empire led to changes in the law of marriage, in that of succession and in other branches of the law, which had rendered the older legislation, in many respects, obsolete. An attempt at reform had been made in the *Codex Theodosianus*[44] published 15th February, 438, under the authority of the Emperor Theodosius II. 408—50. But this reform dealt only with the Imperial Constitutions from the time of Constantine, and not with the writings of the jurists. Justinian resolved upon a complete revision[45] of the laws of the Empire. He took the simplest part of the task first, and began with the *Jus novum*. On 13th February, 528, he issued a commission[46] to John, an ex-Quaestor, and nine other eminent lawyers, chief of whom was Tribonian, †545, to review the *Constitutiones*, reducing them to order and removing inconsistencies. The commissioners accomplished their task in fourteen months: and, in April, 529, was published the *Code*[47] of Justinian which was re-issued in a second edition[48] of 16th November, 534. No Constitution was to be quoted in the Courts of Law except those contained in the *Codex*, and no other text was to be recognised than that there presented.

The next step was much more laborious: for it was now necessary to deal with the *Jus vetus* contained in the text-books of the authorised jurists. Justinian appointed a commission of sixteen lawyers, under the presidency of Tribonian: and gave them his instructions in a Constitution[49] of 1st December, 530. They took three years to accomplish their task; and the result of their labours is the *Digest*,[50] or *Pandects*, of Justinian, promulgated[51] 16th December, 533.

While the *Digest* was in progress, a third commission consisting of Tribonian and a professor of law from each of the great law-schools of Constantinople and Beyrout, was set to work on an elementary manual of Law: partly for teaching, but also for use as a law-book with the authority of the Emperor behind it. Based on the *Institutes* of Gaius, it dealt, in the same way, with the law of Persons, of Things, and of Actions: and is known as the *Institutes*[52] of Justinian. They were published 21st November, 533,[53] and became law, like the *Digest*, on 30th December.

Justinian had now systematised the law; but that did not relieve him from law-making. Many new laws were published between 534 and the end of his reign; most of them before the death of Tribonian. For the most part they are in Greek: and are addressed, if concerned with secular matters, to some civil official in high place: or, if with the affairs of the Church, to some important prelate. One hundred and seventy-four of these *Novellae Constitutiones post Codicem*[54] are extant. They are commonly called the *Novels* of Justinian.

Code, Digest, Institutes and *Novels* together make up the *Corpus Juris Civilis:* a monument to Justinian more lasting and imposing than all his conquests.

CHAPTER III.

JUSTINIAN, 527—†65:
THE THEOLOGIAN.

CHAPTER III.

JUSTINIAN, 527—†65: THE THEOLOGIAN.

As victor, Justinian enlarged the area over which he could direct the affairs of the Church. As lawgiver, he strengthened his hold upon them. But as theologian, he intervened to shape its doctrine. Three controversies gave him opportunity for such intervention—Theopaschitism, 519—33; Origenism, 531—43; and the *Three Chapters*, 544—53. The last two were stirred up by himself,[1] and were brought to an end by the Fifth General Council, at Constantinople, 553. And the course of all was largely controlled by Justinian's political necessities. In order to maintain the unity and integrity of his Empire, he was obliged to conciliate Monophysite feeling in the East; and, not without the secret aid of Theodora, he even went so far as to force concessions to it upon the West. Nevertheless, Justinian was a student of Christian theology for its own sake, apart from policy. It was this that induced him, at the end of his days, to go over to aphthartodocetism, and to try to enforce it upon his subjects.

§ 1. Theopaschitism is the heresy charged against those who wished to make an addition to the *Trisagion.*

Not to be confused with the *Sanctus*—" Holy, Holy, Holy, Lord God of Hosts," etc.—the *Trisagion* is one of the chants of the Liturgy. The legend of its supernatural revelation under Proclus, archbishop of Constantinople, 434—†46, probably marks the date of its insertion: and, since that date, it has been sung, in the Byzantine rite, at the Little Entrance, just before the lections.[2] In the Gallican rite it occurs just before and after the Gospel:[3] while in the modern Roman rite it is familiar among the Reproaches of Good Friday both in Greek and Latin and the *Preces* of Prime. It is actually mentioned for the first time, as an anthem chanted by the bishops of the Council of Chalcedon at the end of their first session, 8th October, 451, when Dioscorus and the leaders of the *Latrocinium* were deposed. " A just sentence ! " they exclaimed : and then, as they left the church, they broke out into the chant : " Holy God, Holy [and] strong, Holy [and] immortal, have mercy upon us ! "[4] The second mention of it occurs in connection with the Monophysite reaction at Antioch. In the tumults that accompanied the deposition of the Catholic patriarch Martyrius, 459—70, by his Monophysite rival Peter the Fuller, 470—1, Peter thought to give prominence to the One Nature by insisting on the deity of Him who suffered upon the Cross. In order to do this in striking fashion he inserted into the *Trisagion* a fresh clause : so that, as he used it, the hymn ran : " Holy God, Holy [and] strong, Holy [and] immortal, who wast crucified for us, have mercy upon us." So long as the hymn was held—as apparently at Antioch —to refer to our Lord, no exception could be taken to its orthodoxy, even when thus expanded : though the expansion was ingeniously calculated to please the Monophysites because it drew attention to the sufferings of one who was God. But at Constantinople it was customary to refer the *Trisagion* to the Trinity : and, in that case, the additional clause, since it attributed suffering to all Three Persons of the Godhead, was resented : and charged with Theopaschitism. " See the head of an enemy of the Trinity ! " cried the rioters of Constantinople, 6th November, 512, as they carried on a lance the head of a monk whom they had decapitated because, as they thought, he had prompted two great Officers of State to get the *Trisagion* sung in the Cathedral on the Sunday previous, with the objectionable addition of " Who wast crucified for us."

A few years later, 519, some monks from the province of Scythia[5] (now the Dobrudja), in the diocese of Paternus, bishop of Tomi (the present Constanza, in Rumania), appeared with a proposal for the adoption of the incriminated clause in a modified form. They were headed by their archimandrite, John Maxentius,[6] and among them was a Leontius, perhaps Leontius of

Byzantium,[7] 485—†543, *facile princeps* among the theologians of his day. They urged that to complete and safeguard the Chalcedonian definitions, so as to exclude Nestorianism on the one hand and Eutychianism on the other, it should be asserted that "One of the Trinity was crucified in the flesh";[8] and their cause, with that of Chalcedon, was taken up, in order to win support from the populace of Constantinople who were ardently Chalcedonian, by a relative of Leontius, the general Vitalian. He had raised a rebellion in 514—5 against Anastasius: and then was made *Magister militum* and *Consul* in 520 under Justin, in order to smooth the way towards the ending of the schism between East and West,[9] and reconciliation with Pope Hormisdas, 514—†23. On 25th March, 519, the papal legates arrived in Constantinople, and had a great reception.[10] The Scythian monks, supported by the Emperor and their fellow-countryman Vitalian, put their case to the legates:[11] but received no encouragement. Not to be put off, they started, early in May, to carry their cause to Hormisdas in person: and were now supported by Justinian who had hitherto, in opposition to his rival Vitalian, upheld the other side. The pope delayed his decision, so the Scythians had recourse to certain African bishops[12] then resident in Sardinia whither they had been banished by Thrasamund, King of the Vandals, 496—†523. Among them was the celebrated African doctor, Fulgentius of Ruspe, 468—†533. From him they obtained an opinion favourable to their cause;[13] and returned to Constantinople, August, 520. In a letter of 13th August to Possessor, an African bishop then resident there, Hormisdas condemned the conduct of the Scythians and belittled the importance of Fulgentius.[14] Afterwards he wrote to the Emperor Justin, 25th March, 521, that, in his view, further definition against Nestorians or Eutychians, could serve no useful purpose.[15]

We hear no more of the Scythian monks—but thirteen years later, in 532, the question was taken up, from the other side, by the Accometæ.[16] They were the monks of a house near Constantinople who owed their name of

"Sleepless" to the round of prayer which was kept up in their community, without intermission day or night: and they were so dyophysite as to be nearly Nestorian. They saw in the proposed addition, and the Pope's hesitation to condemn it, a challenge to the credit of the Council of Chalcedon. Justinian, on the other hand, who was convinced not only of its essential orthodoxy but of its religious value, thought that by adopting it, he might both dissociate himself from Nestorianisers and, at the same time, facilitate understanding with the Monophysites. So, after consultation with the section of that party which followed Severus, Patriarch of Antioch, 512—8, the Emperor put out an edict, 15th March, 533, condemning anyone who denied that "Jesus Christ, the Son of God, our incarnate God, who became man and was crucified, is one of the Holy and Consubstantial Trinity."[17] He eventually obtained its confirmation, 24th March, 534, from Pope John II.,[18] 533—†5, whose hesitation was overcome by the opinion of the African theologian Fulgentius Ferrandus,[19] a deacon of Carthage, disciple and biographer of Fulgentius of Ruspe. It was a victory for the Christological teaching of St. Cyril.

Thus the interpolation of the *Trisagion* was, in the end, disallowed: but the confession that "One of the Trinity was crucified in the flesh" was admitted to the language of orthodoxy. The addition, indeed, was no more than an extension of the language, used a hundred years before, in the *Tome* of Proclus, or of the term *Theotokos*. For Proclus, while making it clear that the Godhead is incapable of bodily suffering so that God the Word could not suffer in His Godhead, yet claimed the right to affirm that "One of the Trinity became incarnate."[20] Justinian emphasised the conclusion. "If One of the Trinity did not suffer in the flesh, neither was He born in the flesh, nor can Mary be said, verily and truly, to be His Mother."[21] Not only then was the phrase approved, under his auspices, by the Fifth General Council, 553; but it is embodied, at the opening of the Liturgy, in the hymn "Ὁ Μονογένης,"[22] which is attributed to Justinian himself:

Justinian: the Theologian

> "O Word immortal of eternal God,
>   Only begotten of the only Source,
>   For our salvation stooping to the course
> Of human life, and born of Mary's blood;
> Sprung from the ever-Virgin womanhood
>   Of her who bare Thee, God immutable,
>   Incarnate, made as man with man to dwell,
> And condescending to the bitter Rood;
>
> Save us, O Christ our God, for Thou hast died
>   To save Thy people to the uttermost,
>   And dying tramplest death in victory;
> One of the ever-blessed Trinity,
>   In equal honour with the Holy Ghost
> And with the eternal Father glorified."[23]

Thus theopaschite language has not only received the formal sanction of Pope and Council, but it has established itself in the devotional language of the Church. It is to the devout Emperor, the theologian Justinian, that we owe its vindication. It was a small thing that theopaschite language served as a useful barrier against Nestorianism: that was why the Accemetæ accused the Emperor himself of heresy for it. The great thing is that it protects truth of permanent value to religion and to suffering humanity. For if such language be true, and "One of the Trinity was crucified," then suffering (though, of course, not bodily suffering) has penetrated the innermost life of the Godhead—where there is thus eternal sympathy with all sufferers. Never have we felt the truth of this so acutely as since the Great War.

§ 2. Origen, 189—†254, the great teacher of Alexandria, based his teaching on the tradition of the Church, but considered himself free to speculate beyond its limits.[24] He used his freedom with fertility and daring; and such elements in his system as represent the excess of speculation over tradition are, in the main, what is meant by Origenism.[25] Attractive to some minds and equally repellent to others, it made him friends and enemies in his own generation,[26] in the age of Chrysostom,[27] and again in the reign of Justinian.

About 520 the monks of Palestine were sharply divided about Origenism.[28] In that year, four monks of the New Laura near Jerusalem were expelled for Origenism by their abbot, but secretly restored by his successor. Their convent became the centre of that allegiance. It excited the animosity of St. Saba, abbot of the Old Laura; and in 531 he went to Constantinople, to demand of Justinian the expulsion of the Origenists. The Emperor lent a willing ear; but, before any action was taken, St. Saba died, 532.

Five years later, two monks of the New Laura succeeded in establishing an influence with Justinian. He promoted them, 537, to important sees: Domitian to be archbishop of Ancyra and Theodore Ascidas to be archbishop of Cæsarea in Cappadocia, 537—†58. They were oftener at Court than in their dioceses: and continued to make influence for the Origenists in Palestine against the orthodox Sabaïtes. Controversy still went on between the rival Lauras; until, at length, Ephraim, Patriarch of Antioch, 526—45, was induced to intervene. In 541—2 he held a synod at Antioch, and condemned " the doctrinal propositions of Origen." But the condemnation remained without effect, until a Roman deacon, Pelagius, a papal *apocrisiarius* or nuncio, and a rival of Theodore at the Imperial Court, arrived from Constantinople at Gaza;[29] and, in response to request from the Sabaïtes, undertook to use his influence with the Emperor to clear the country of Origenists. He was as good as his word; and his intervention resulted, 543, in two important events. The first was the edict of Justinian or letter to Menas, Patriarch of Constantinople, 536—†52, in which the Emperor condemned the Origenists; and the second was the Home Synod at which Menas, supported by the prelates who then happened to be at Court, echoed, and gave spiritual authority to the Imperial condemnation.

Justinian's *Adversus Origenem*[30] or *Ad Menam* consists of three parts. The first enumerates the main errors of Origen; or, in other words, makes plain, with a view to its repression, what Origenism is. They are his overstatement of the Filial Subordination, his theory of the pre-existence and fall of the soul, his universalism and his doctrine of a plurality of worlds. In the second part, the Emperor confronts with extracts from the Fathers those passages of the *De Principiis* in which these erroneous speculations are set forth. And the letter concludes with a series of ten anathemas on all such as affirm that (1) human souls pre-existed, *i.e.*, were once spirits, then became degenerate and, in punishment, were sent down into bodies; or that (2) the soul of our Lord pre-existed and was united with the Divine Word before becoming Incarnate; or that (3) the body of our Lord was first fashioned in the womb of Mary and then the Divine Word was united to it and the pre-existing soul; or that (6) the sun, moon and stars are spiritual beings; or that (7) our Lord, in after ages, will be crucified for demons as He was for man; or that (9) the punishment of demons and wicked men is but for a time and then will come an universal restitution. Tenth and last, let Origen be anathema and all who hold or teach his doctrines.

These Imperial anathemas are repeated or expanded in a second series of fifteen, sometimes attributed to the fifth General Council; but more probably to be ascribed, because they are so clearly based upon the ten of the letter to Menas, to the Home Synod[31] held by him. Together these pronouncements had the desired effect. The evidence that Origen himself was condemned by the General Council of 553 is conflicting; but in the acts of the eighth session,[32] 2nd June, his name occurs among a list of heretics condemned in the eleventh canon. Conflicting as it is, the evidence is probably not sufficient to warrant a refusal to take the canon as it stands. But whatever that Council did, the practical measures that followed for the suppression of Origenism in Palestine ultimately took effect. They were aided by sharp divisions among the Origenists themselves. These lightened the task of Justinian's agent in the repression, Eustochius;[33] for, as Patriarch of Jerusalem, 552—64, he made an end of Origenism in the monasteries of Palestine. Yet no repression has obscured the fame of Origen; or deprived subsequent ages of a share in the benefits which, by his learning, courage and piety he conferred upon the Church of his day.

§ 3. *The Three Chapters*[84] is the name given to a melancholy controversy of 544—53, which arose out of the chagrin of Theodore Ascidas[35] at Justinian's abandonment of the Origenists, 543. Theodore planned to put the Emperor off the scent by trailing another theological enquiry across his path.[36] He contrived, in so doing, to avenge the Origenists by getting him indirectly to condemn the orthodoxy so dear to their enemies and, in particular, to Pelagius who had displaced him in the Imperial favour. Concerting his scheme with the Empress Theodora, he suggested to Justinian that he might get the Monophysites into a more conciliatory frame of mind if he were to condemn for their Nestorianism, Theodore, bishop of Mopsuestia, 392—†428, Theodoret, bishop of Cyrus, 423—†58, and Ibas, bishop of Edessa, 435—†57. The object of the plot was "not only to secure the condemnation of Theodore of Mopsuestia, whose writings were much disliked by the Origenists, but also to weaken the authority of the Council of Chalcedon by condemning the writings of those whom it had seemed to acknowledge as orthodox."[37]

It was a clever move: for something could be said, with truth, against all three. Theodore was the teacher of Nestorius, and Nestorianism his teaching in popular form.[38] When the writings of Nestorius were put under the ban, it was more than sufficient to circulate the writings of Diodore and Theodore, his masters in theology, instead. Theodoret had been a disciple of Theodore; and though, as the author[39] of the *Formulary of Reunion*[40] between Antioch and Alexandria, 433, he came to be the representative of an Antiochene or anti-Cyrilline orthodoxy, yet he had defended Nestorius and attacked Cyril: while some of his language had been by no means theologically sound. Thus he had spoken of Christ "as 'a man' who had been 'assumed'; of that 'man' as 'God-bearing' and as 'inseparably connected' with God the Word; and he had sometimes argued as if a human nature in Christ involves a distinct human personality."[41] As to Ibas, it was he who had translated the writings of Theodore into Syriac for circulation on the Romano-

Persian frontier: and in the Letter to Maris, 433, he had censured the Council of Ephesus, denounced the Twelve Anathematisms of Cyril and repudiated his bishop Rabbûla, a friend of Cyril, as a turncoat and a tyrant. Moreover, the recipient of the letter was a person whose place and influence, in the promotion of Nestorianism, would reflect suspiciously on Ibas. He is commonly known as Maris, bishop of Ardashir. But Mari means "My Lord"; and Ardashir is the Persian name of Seleucia-Ctesiphon. The letter was, therefore, in all probability, addressed to "My lord bishop of Seleucia-Ctesiphon," i.e., to the Catholicus Dadyeshu, 421—†56, the official head of the Nestorians in Persia.[42] So all these three—Theodore, Theodoret and Ibas—might not unreasonably be held to have been tainted with Nestorianism; though Theodore died in communion with the Church,[43] and Theodoret and Ibas had been reinstated at Chalcedon.[44] Theodore Ascidas had indeed exposed some blemishes in the good name of that Council.

Justinian fell into the trap. It was a case, like Origenism, only more important, for theological investigation: and he turned away from the one to the other. In 544 he published an edict[45] containing (1) a letter to the bishops with a Confession of Faith, and (2) the *Three Chapters*, or propositions, condemnatory of the incriminated writings. Here it should be noticed that, though this is the original meaning of *The Three Chapters*, yet, throughout the rest of the controversy, the term came to denote not the propositions themselves but the persons and writings designated in them; and *The Three Chapters* as denounced by the Council of Constantinople, 553, are "Theodore who was bishop of Mopsuestia and his impious writings, and also those things which Theodoret impiously wrote . . . and the impious epistle which Ibas is said to have written to Maris the Persian."[46] The edict of Justinian concluded with an express assertion of the authority of the Council of Chalcedon.

But, naturally enough, the edict was taken to imply a censure upon its authority; and was ill received. The patriarchs and bishops of the eastern part of the Empire yielded, though with reluctance. But the assent of Pope Vigilius, 538—†55, was not so easy to obtain. Vigilius belonged to one of the great Roman families. As nuncio at Constantinople, he had been brought into contact with the Empress Theodora; and had obtained his see by the aid of money received from her in return for a promise that, when he became Pope, he would do his best to undermine the authority of the Council of Chalcedon.[47] But he proved half-hearted about its fulfilment; and finding himself supported by the bishops of Africa, Dalmatia and Illyricum as well as by the African theologian Fulgentius Ferrandus, he refused his assent to the Imperial decree. It was, however, an inopportune moment for refusal. Belisarius was again in Italy, 544—8, and had recovered Rome from the Ostrogoths. Vigilius was thus in the power of Justinian, and of the imperious Theodora. " Put the Pope on shipboard," she ordered an emissary whom she dispatched to arrest him, " and bring him hither. If you do not do this, then, by Him that liveth for ever and ever, I'll have you flayed alive! " Vigilius arrived in Constantinople, 25th January, 547. At first, he remained firm; but, after a year of conferences, he consented to repudiate the *Three Chapters*. This he did in his *Judicatum*[48] of 11th April, 548. In § 1 he distinguishes between the guilt of Theodore of Mopsuestia, on the one hand, and, on the other, of Theodoret and Ibas : for while he anathematises Theodore " with *all* his impious writings," he anathematises only " the impious epistle which is said to have been written by Ibas to Maris the Persian, as contrary to the right faith " and " such writings of Theodoret as were written contrary to the right faith and against the *capitula* of Cyril,"[49] i.e., his *Twelve anathematisms* which never received œcumenical sanction. The remaining §§ 2—6 are devoted to maintaining the authority of Chalcedon[50] as above discussion. But the *Judicatum* created a bad impression. It was ill-received; and its author found himself deserted by Facundus,[51] bishop of Hermiane in the African province of Byzacena, by Dacius, archbishop of Milan, and by the bishops of Dalmatia and Illyricum. He was actually excommunicated, 550, by the episcopate of Africa.[52] Unable to maintain himself in isolation from the West, on 15th August, 550, Vigilius withdrew the *Judicatum;* and entered into a compact with Justinian that neither should take any further step either for or against the *Three Chapters* till a General Council should meet. At the same time he secretly pledged himself, under oath to Justinian, so " to act that the *Three Chapters* . . . may be condemned."[53]

Justinian now set himself to assemble the Council; but, impatient of the delay in getting it together, he listened to a suggestion of his evil genius Theodore Ascidas and put out, 551, his *Confessio rectae fidei adversus Tria Capitula*.[54] This lengthy pronouncement has three parts. In the first, there is an exposition of faith, of some interest. The Emperor states the doctrine of the Trinity in language very like that of the *Quicunque vult:* but he takes the retrograde step of accepting the ambiguous formula of St.Cyril, "One Nature of the Word [and that] incarnate "—Μία φύσις τοῦ Λόγου σεσαρκωμένη [55]—which led to Monophysitism: though Cyril himself, as Justinian is careful to explain, used "nature" (φύσις) in the sense of " person " (ὑπόστασις), and meant by the phrase " one Person of the Word incarnate." Justinian also comments on the misuse made by the Monophysites of the comparison of body and soul making but " one man " in favour of there being but one nature in Christ: whereas, when the holy Fathers employ the analogy of man to explain the mystery of Christ, their object is to show that just as " one man," not two men, is formed of the body and the soul,[56] so also " one Christ " is formed of the Godhead and the manhood, and must not be divided into " two Christs " or " two Sons."[57] The comment would serve as an excellent explanation of the thirty-seventh verse of the *Quicunque vult*. A third point of interest is that the Emperor, evidently relying upon the teaching[58] of Leontius of Byzantium, †543, affirms that, though our Lord's human nature never had an independent personality of its own, this was not because it had no relation to a person and was ἀνυπόστατος but because it was ever united to the Divine Person of the Word and was ἐνυπόστατος.[59] The second part of the *Confessio* consists of thirteen propositions which anathematise the contraries of the doctrines enforced in the exposition of faith; the eleventh, twelfth and thirteenth being formal condemnations of the *Three Chapters*. The third section concludes with answers to objections, as that the Council of Chalcedon had approved the letter of Ibas and that Theodore was not liable to condemnation because he was dead.

The publication of the *Confessio rectae fidei* was a breach of the compact with Pope Vigilius, and he forbade anyone to celebrate the Holy Eucharist in the churches where it was published. Theodore Ascidas braved his displeasure; and Vigilius proceeded to excommunicate him, together with the Patriarch Menas. For all his vacillation, Vigilius was not without courage, thus to come to Constantinople and, undefended, to resist the autocrat. But it cost him dear; and he had to take refuge in the basilica of St. Peter, close to the Palace of Hormisdas. Dragged from its altar, he fled across the Bosporus to the safer retreat of the church of St. Euphemia at Chalcedon: where, a hundred years before, the Council had met for which he was then making so brave a stand.[60] He justified his proceedings in an *Encyclical*[61] of 5th February, 552; but, at length, was persuaded to return to Constantinople, 6th January, 553. Here he received the profession of faith[62] of Eutychius, successor to Menas, † August, 552; in which the new Patriarch of Constantinople, 552—†65, accepted the first four General Councils and the *Tome* of St. Leo, and declared himself ready to submit the question of the *Three Chapters* to the forthcoming Council.

At last, the Council met,[63] 5th May, 553, with one hundred and fifty-one bishops in attendance. By far the larger portion were Easterns, and the Pope refused to take part in a Council so constituted. The Council proceeded without him. At the fourth session,[64] 12—13th May, they examined the case of Theodore of Mopsuestia. At the fifth,[65] 17th May, after discussing the question whether the dead should be condemned, they took up the case of Theodoret; and, at the sixth,[66] 19th May, that of Ibas. But, at this point, Vigilius intervened. He had declined to attend; but he would deal with the questions they were discussing by himself. Accordingly, he placed in the hands of Justinian his *Constitutum*[67] of 14th May, 553 : in which, while censuring the language of Theodore, he declined to visit him with a posthumous condemnation, or to touch the honour of Theodoret and Ibas. He concluded by forbidding any attempt on the Council of Chalcedon, and all further discussion of the *Three Chapters*.

Not a little displeased, Justinian at the seventh session,[68] 26th May, gave vent to his indignation. He made public the secret oath of Vigilius that he would aid in the condemnation of the *Three Chapters;* and then ordered his name to be removed from the diptychs on the ground that, by upholding the *Three Chapters,* the Pope had confessed himself a Nestorian and so was separated from the communion of the Church. It only remained for the bishops to take their cue from the Emperor and to condemn the *Three Chapters.* This they did at the last session,[69] 2nd June, 553; and they added fourteen anathemas which are in substance the same as those contained in Justinian's *Confessio rectae fidei.* The eleventh, as we have seen, contains, though out of the historical order, the name of Origen among heretics condemned by the Church. One hundred and sixty-four bishops appended their signatures to this document; and the Emperor set himself to obtain its recognition. The East acquiesced; and at last, under fear of exile, Vigilius gave way : at first, in a letter to the Patriarch Eutychius[70] of 8th December, 553, and, finally, in a second *Constitutum*,[71] 23rd February, 554.

It was a miserable dispute : and little to the credit of any of the parties concerned. The Pope was weak; and his surrender, at the end, so exasperated a number of Western churches as to lead them to actual breach with the Roman See.[72] The breach was not healed, in some cases, for a hundred and fifty years.[73] The Emperor was tyrannical : the Council subservient. But we must not judge too harshly Popes and Councils who lived under the Cæsaropapism[74] of Justinian. Nor must we overlook what is due to him. He imposed his will on Pope and Council alike, as on all his subjects. But his will was to maintain the balance of exact theological statement about the Person of the Incarnate; and, if possible, to open a way to re-union by inducing the Monophysites to accept the Chalcedonian Faith. Posterity has accepted it; and it was the fault not of the Emperor's theology, but of the political and racial antagonisms of the time, that not one Monophysite was attracted by it to rally to the Church.

§ 4. In the last year of his reign, Justinian is said to have adopted one of the varieties of Monophysitism[75] and to have prepared to enforce it upon his subjects. The statement has been doubted on the double ground that it rests on insufficient evidence and that the thing itself is improbable. The evidence is that of Evagrius,[76] 536—†c. 600, only; but, though slight, it is explicit. As to the improbability, even great men, when their faculties are enfeebled, may go back upon a life's purpose at the last. But it is a question whether Justinian in giving way to aphthartodocetism, did, after all, surrender the purpose of a life-time. He had been familiar with Monophysitism from the first. As a statesman he was aware both of its wide prevalence and of the intensity of conviction with which it was held. As a theologian, he would understand its attraction for the devout mind. There are two types of heresy: the religious and the rationalistic.[77] Nestorianism was of the rationalistic sort. It thought of Jesus as two persons, a man associated with God. It was repellent to Catholicism, and had been ousted from the Empire. But Monophysitism agreed with Catholicism in the religious view that it took of our Lord. It thought of Him as God who became man; and only differed from orthodoxy in so exalting His Godhead as to minimise His manhood. The probabilities then, political and religious, are in favour of the story of Justinian's capitulation to it being true.

(i.) As to the prevalence of Monophysitism, he had seen it growing from the first.

HIS ALL HOLINESS, THE ŒCUMENICAL PATRIARCH, BASIL III.

[see p. 297.]

Justinian: the Theologian

In the north,[78] it was not unknown at Constantinople. In 532, on the occasion of an earthquake, the crowd shouted: "Long live Justinian! but let him deliver us from those evil decrees of Chalcedon." About the same time, in 533, he arranged a conference[79] to find, if possible, common ground between the orthodox and the representatives of that milder type of Monophysitism who followed the lead of Severus, a former patriarch of Antioch, 512—8, now resident in the capital. They resulted in the edict approving some measure of theopaschite language.[80] On the death of Epiphanius, Patriarch of Constantinople, 520—†35, the Empress Theodora, ever watchful to maintain the unity of the Eastern Empire by conciliating the Monophysites in accordance with the policy of Zeno and Anastasius, brought the Monophysite Anthimus from Trebizond and installed him as patriarch, 535—6. A reaction followed. The Council of Constantinople, 2nd May—4th June, put Anthimus, Severus and others under its ban;[81] and the sentence was confirmed by Justinian,[82] 6th August, 536. But there were other conferences from time to time: in 548—50 and again 558—60; and, though the soil of Constantinople was unfavourable for Monophysitism to take root in, yet, to the end of his days, Justinian had to take notice of it, even at his doors.

In the south[83] of his Empire, Monophysitism had all things its own way. Paul, the Catholic patriarch of Alexandria, 537—42, and his successors, made valiant efforts to recover Egypt to orthodoxy. But national feeling there was intensely opposed to the creed as to the rule of the upstart capital; and shortly before the Mohammedan conquest, 640—7, whereas the Melkite, or Imperialist, Patriarch of Alexandria had but 200,000 Greeks and officials for his adherents, as many as six million acknowledged his Monophysite rival.[84]

The state of things in the East[85] was not dissimilar. At Antioch the orthodox Patriarch Ephraim, 526—45, was followed by a long series of Monophysite successors; while, in the hinterland, the Monophysites swept the field. Severus continued to direct the church life of Syria from his place of exile till his death, 539. John, bishop of Tella,[86] †548, brought over as many as 170,000 adherents to Monophysitism. And so threatening was the outlook that Justinian, in order to prevent Monophysite ordinations and so put a stop to their propaganda, shut up suspect bishops in prison. He reckoned without Theodora. She secured the consecration of James Baradai,[87] with authority over Syria, Mesopotamia and Asia Minor. For thirty-five years, 543—†78, he travelled, in the guise of a beggar, over those wide regions, setting up a rival hierarchy; and so laid the foundations of the Jacobite Church.

Palestine alone escaped the contagion; for, 19th September, 536, a synod of Jerusalem[88] adopted the decisions which had been taken at Constantinople earlier in the year; and the patriarchs maintained the tradition of orthodoxy.

(ii.) The varieties of Monophysitism rivalled its extent; and did not escape the notice of Justinian. There were two main divisions, the *Acephali* and the *Henoticians*. The *Acephali* consisted of those who would have nothing to do with the Church of the Empire, but organised themselves into autonomous Churches, as the Copts in Egypt or the Jacobites in Syria. The *Henoticians* included all who, like Theodora, were in sympathy with that policy of an elastic orthodoxy which had been inaugurated by Zeno in the *Henoticon* but abandoned by the House of Justin. These were political divisions. There were also religious divisions among Monophysites: especially such as originated with two bishops who were at one time joint-exiles in Egypt, Severus of Antioch and Julian of Halicarnassus. A monk raised the question whether the body of our Lord was liable to "corruption," or not;[89] and the two prelates give opposite opinions in reply. Severus recognised with St. Cyril the distinctness of the two natures in Christ, but laid stress on their unconfused union ($\mathrm{\mathring{\alpha}\sigma\acute{u}\gamma\chi\upsilon\tau o\varsigma\ \mathring{\epsilon}\nu\omega\sigma\iota\varsigma}$) and its consequences, especially in the one "energy" or "operation" of His will. He disliked the assertion of St. Leo and the Council of Chalcedon that our Lord is now "in two natures" (ἐν δύο φύσεσιν). But he accepted their theoretic distinction; and maintained the permanence of the characteristic attributes of each after the union. One of such attributes was the creatureliness of His body: which was, therefore, liable to " corruption." The Severians were consequently nicknamed *Phthartolatrae* or *Corrupticolae* by their opponents: and these were the followers of Julian who gave an opposite reply to the question above-mentioned. Reasoning from the union of natures (ἕνωσις φυσική), as defined by St. Cyril, Julian regarded our Lord's body as, from the moment of its conception, endowed with divine attributes. It was, therefore, incorruptible: not of itself liable to death, but liable only as and when He willed—in short, a glorified or even deified body, from the first. The Severians not unnaturally retorted upon the followers of Julian that they were *Aphthartodocetae* or *Phantasiastae*. They revived the old Docetism; and tended to deny that our Lord's Humanity was real.

Lines of thought consequential upon one or other of these two positions were adopted by further developments of Monophysitism. Thus the Severian Themistius, a deacon of Alexandria, c. 536, extended the principle of his master to our Lord's human soul. As His body was like ours, corruptible, so His soul was, like ours, of many things ignorant.[90] The Themistians were denounced as *Agnoetae* by their opponents who embraced not only Monophysites but orthodox and held that our Lord, from His conception onwards, was full of wisdom and did not really " grow in wisdom " as He did " in stature."[91] Julianists, as well as Severians, had their thoroughgoing logicians. These carried out the principles of Julian to the conclusion that our Lord's body, after its union with the Divine Word, was not only incorruptible but uncreate. This opinion had for its champion Gaianus, Patriarch of Alexandria, 535. His adherents were nicknamed *Aktistetae*,[92] and retaliated upon their adversaries by denouncing them as *Ktistolatrae*.

The objection of the Church to these and kindred theories of the Monophysites is that they " represent as an immediate [and] physical effect of Divine power what the New Testament treats as the necessary result of a continuous ethical process. . . . . They overlooked the mystery of the gradual advancement of Christ's humanity. . . . His assumption of Human nature in its weakness that it might pass over into indestructible strength."[93]

But such tendencies are congenial to a religious mind. They would be attractive in so far as their motive was to glorify Christ, and to assure men that He who stooped to suffer for our salvation was, from the first moment of His condescension, very God. And we need not be surprised at being told that Justinian, who would be influenced as a statesman by the policy, and as a theologian by the piety, of making terms with Monophysitism, went over to it, in the form of Aphthartodocetism, at the last.

CHAPTER IV.

CHURCH AND STATE UNDER JUSTINIAN.

CHAPTER IV.

CHURCH AND STATE UNDER JUSTINIAN.

THE general character of Justinian's ecclesiastical policy may be described in one word, as Cæsaropapism. " No Roman Emperor so nearly assumed the position of a temporal Pope."

§ 1. Thus, in dealing with theological disputes, none, as we have seen, was so interested in them, often for their own sake. But none was so assertive, as Justinian, of his right to intervene. His predecessors, it is true, watched carefully over the course of events at the General Councils of Ephesus, 431, and Chalcedon, 451; but they confined themselves to summoning these assemblies, to guiding their deliberations and confirming their decisions. Justinian went further. He took control at each step of the proceedings, simply to give effect to his will. In preparation for the fifth General Council, after *pourparlers*, 18th January, 552, with Pope Vigilius, 538—†55, which ended in favour of an assembly to be representative of Africa and the West as well as of Eastern Christendom, Justinian so summoned the Council as to exclude the Africans. They were opposed to the rejection of the *Three Chapters* on which he was bent. Not less rigorous than his domination over Councils was his tyranny over Popes. The Empress Theodora had promised the papacy to Vigilius, when a Roman deacon, in return for an undertaking on his part that, on his elevation, he would denounce the Council of Chalcedon, and so support her policy of uniting the East by favouring the Monophysites. Justinian allowed her, through her confidante Antonina, the wife of Belisarius, to depose and do to death Pope Silverius, 536—†8, in order to hasten the appointment of Vigilius. When Vigilius himself succeeded, the Emperor sent for him to Constantinople, 544; and, within the next ten years, forced him to do his will. After " judgments at least four times directly contrary to one another," the vacillating Vigilius twice refused, and twice consented to, the condemnation of the *Three Chapters*.

§ 2. So, too, in his treatment of all who were not orthodox and Catholic Christians, "Justinian was a resolute, though not always a consistent, persecutor."

Those who were Christians and accepted the Creed of Nicæa, but became either Nestorians or Eutychians, he punished with deposition, excommunication and, occasionally, with banishment. Such, for example, was the sentence upon Anthimus, Patriarch of Constantinople, 535—†6: when, in confirmation of his condemnation for Eutychianism by the Council of Constantinople, 2nd May—4th June, 536, the Emperor, 6th August, ordered his banishment from the city.[1]

There were heretics, however, who went further astray; and either repudiated the Creed of Nicæa as did the Arians; or, like Manichæans, Gnostics and Montanists, adopted errors savouring of heathenism.

The treatment of Arians by Justinian varied according to political exigencies. At first, he refrained from including them among heretics penalised by the *Code;* or, rather, he only mentions them to make an exception in their favour. The Goths were Arians; and they were, as yet, the masters of Italy. There would certainly have been reprisals, had the Emperor disturbed their coreligionists among his subjects. But after the recovery of Africa, 534, and, when contemplating the conquest of Italy, Justinian exchanged his tone of tolerance towards Arianism for one of rigour. The Vandals of Africa, who were Arians, were required to give back the goods of the Church which they had taken from the Catholics; they were forbidden to baptise, deprived of the public exercise of their worship, and disqualified for civil office. In the East, Justinian confiscated the goods of Arian officials and refused to employ any Arian in Government service: while, after the overthrow of the Goths in Italy, Arianism, in spite of its numbers, ceased to be of account.

He took sterner measures with the sects which had imported pagan errors into the Church.[2] Manichæans

Church and State under Justinian

were outlawed, and subjected to the penalty of death:[3] and, on one occasion at Constantinople, several of that persuasion were placed aboard old hulks and, when these had been towed out to sea, were burnt alive. The Montanists[4] of Phrygia, being required to submit to baptism, killed their wives and children, shut themselves up in their churches and burnt them over their heads: while in 551, John of Ephesus reduced conventicles of theirs to ashes, together with the relics of Montanus and his prophetesses, Maximilla and Priscilla. Gnostics were deprived of civil rights, and forbidden to meet for worship. Heretics in general were subjected to various disabilities. Their worship was forbidden.[5] Their churches closed. They were allowed three months within which to profess their conversion. Magistrates, on taking office, and soldiers, on enlistment, had to take oath before three witnesses that they were of the Orthodox Faith.[6]

§ 3. Similar rigours were inflicted on Samaritans, Jews and heathen.

Samaritans were ousted from their synagogues, and deprived of the right either to bring an action or to inherit and bequeath property:[7] while no Jew could take up a profession[8] or be heard in court against a Christian[9] or have a baptised slave.[10] In 529 Samaritans and Jews rose in revolt, and a terrible war desolated Syria. When it was over, some of them submitted to the formalities of baptism; but so alarmed was Justinian that, 15th June, 551, at the petition of Sergius, bishop of Cæsarea in Palestine, he thought it wise to restore some of the civil disabilities he had taken away.

In respect of heathenism, it is a simple matter to set down the severities decreed against it: but not so easy to be sure of the degree to which they were carried out. The laws of Justinian punish apostasy in a Christian with death.[11] They require all persons to be baptised, if they are to enjoy the common rights of citizens;[12] and, under this inducement, coupled with the missionary zeal of the Monophysite historian John, bishop of Ephesus, as many as seventy thousand converts were made, 542—6, in Asia, Caria, Phrygia and Lydia. The laws also deprive the heathen of the opportunity of education[13] and of all civil rights, and forbid the public exercise of their worship. But large numbers of heathen continued to exist: not only in the wild and remote districts of Greece, such as Mt. Taygetus, and of Asia Minor, but among the cultivated and official classes of Constantinople and other cities. Justinian dealt a final blow at educated paganism by the edict of 529 which closed the schools of Athens. Baptism or exile was the alternative it proposed to the professors of the University. Seven of them took refuge in Persia. The rest were baptised, and practised their ancient rites in private. But, whether among the educated or the vulgar, the Government, save for occasional barbarities, accepted conformity and made no inconvenient enquiries.

§ 4. By such enactments against heathenism and heresy, Justinian protected the Church against its adversaries. He also fostered its life by legislating for its welfare; and his ecclesiastical legislation is to be found first in the *Code* and then in the *Novels*.

(i.) Of the *Code*, the first thirteen Titles of Book I. contain laws relating as well to the doctrine and worship as to the administrative system of the Church. Title I. is headed *De Summa Trinitate et de Fide Catholica et ut nemo de ea publice contendere audeat;* and includes four laws of Justinian, in which he lays down the Faith as defined at the first four General Councils, and excludes " Nestorius the man-worshipper, Eutyches the insane and Apollinaris the soul-destroyer."[14] Title II. contains eight laws of Justinian, dealing chiefly with legacies to churches or charities and with the management of church-property. To Title III., *De Episcopis et Clericis*, belong fifty-five enactments, sixteen of which came from the hand of Justinian and provide for the election of bishops, the qualifications of clergy, the maintenance of discipline in Religious Houses and the observance of divine service. Title IV. covers fourteen of Justinian's laws, and is a miscellaneous collection *De episcopali audientia et de diversis capitulis quae ad jus curamque et reverentiam pontificalem pertinent*. Title V. deals with heresy, Title

VII. with apostasy, and Title XI. with the repression of paganism; and the contents of these three Titles we have already anticipated. Title XII. concerns Sanctuary; and Title XIII. manumission.

Taking these first thirteen Titles together, we observe that they manifest no intention on the Emperor's part to form a complete body of laws for the government of the Church, still less for its worship. Such matters were left to be dealt with by custom or by canon, as occasion arose. But Justinian makes no distinction, such as was made in the West, between the sphere of ecclesiastical and of civil authority. He dealt with each as he pleased; and to safeguard the Church, he bore heavily on rival forms of religion, whether heresy or heathenism. He failed, or rather was not fully willing, to put down heresy; but, except in certain remote regions, he succeeded in stamping out paganism.

(ii.) The *Novels* contain his *Constitutions* issued between the publication of the *Code* and the year of his death. They number 168, reducible to 153; and of these, 33 are devoted to matters ecclesiastical : most of them in Greek, save those intended for Thrace, Africa and Sicily, where Latin was spoken. Several groups may be distinguished among them. First, a group of eight, occupied with the temporal rights and relations of the Church and the clergy, as holders of property. A second group, of four, comprises constitutions which are local in their application. Thus, Novel 37 legislates for Africa, after its recovery from the Vandals.[15] Novel 3 for the great church of Constantinople; and limits the number of clergy to be employed there[16]—not more than 60 presbyters, 100 deacons, 40 deaconesses, 90 sub-deacons, 110 readers, 25 cantors, or 425 in all, exclusive of 100 ushers,[17] who did not rank among the clergy. Novel 40 permits Peter, Patriarch of Jerusalem, 524—†44, to dispose of lands belonging to the Church of the Resurrection so as to be better able to meet the expense of assisting pilgrims;[18] while Novel 11 erects the see of his birthplace, Justiniana Prima, now Skoplje, into a Patriarchate.[19] A third group, of thirteen, deals " with ecclesiastical organisation and discipline, the mode of choosing bishops and other clerics, their qualifications, the jurisdiction of bishops, the restrictions on the jurisdiction of civil courts . . . the rights, immunities and privileges of the clergy, the conditions under which a church or an oratory may be built, endowed and consecrated, the internal discipline of the monasteries and regulation of monastic life ";[20] and it is in one of these—*Sancimus igitur*,[21] of 18th March, 545—that the First Four General Councils are finally given that pre-eminence as the Civilian standard of orthodoxy which they retained, in spite of the rival standard set up by the Canonists, down to and, within the English Church, since the Reformation. A last group, of four Novels, is levelled against various forms of false doctrine; Novel 132 against heresy, with an appeal to return to the safe teaching of the Catholic Church:[22] Novel 45 against Jews and Samaritans;[23] Novel 109 against heretic women;[24] and Novel 42 against Eutychianism in the persons of Anthimus, Patriarch of Constantinople 535—6 and others.[25]

The whole series is characterised by the rigour usual to days when men had yet to learn the first principles of toleration; by a tendency to favour the Church, and by the assumption, on the part of the Emperor, of a right to complete control of its affairs. Justinian states his theory of the relation between Church and State in the preface to Novel 6 of 16th March, 535. " Among the greatest gifts of God," he says, " bestowed by the kindness of heaven are the priesthood and the imperial dignity. Of these, the former serves things divine; the latter rules human affairs and cares for them. Both are derived from the one and the same source, and order human life. And, therefore, nothing is so much a care to the Emperors as the dignity of the priesthood; so that they may always pray to God for them. For if the one is in every respect blameless and filled with confidence toward God, and the other rightly and properly maintains in order the commonwealth intrusted to it, there is a certain excellent harmony which furnishes whatsoever is needful for the human race."[26] To maintain this harmony he claims a universal and paramount right of legislating for the

Church; and the conclusion of Novel 137, of 26th April, 565, well illustrates the manner in which he exercised his right. He instituted, in fact, a control over the Church which was other than that of its own system of discipline. " We command that all bishops and presbyters shall offer the sacred oblation and the prayers in holy baptism not silently, but with a voice which may be heard by the faithful people, that thereby the minds of those listening may be moved to greater contrition and to the glory of God. Therefore it is right that to our Lord Jesus Christ, to our God with the Father and the Holy Ghost, be offered prayer in the holy oblation and other prayers with the voice by the most holy bishops and the presbyters; for the holy priests should know that if they neglect any of those things, they shall render an account at the terrible judgment of the great God and our Saviour Jesus Christ, and that we shall not quietly permit such things when we know of them, and will not leave them unpunished...."[27] True, as in the sequel of this Novel, the Emperor respects and even confirms the sacred Canons. But he admits no exclusive right of church or bishop to legislate on any topic. On the contrary, he prescribes all himself as in Novel 123, of 1st May, 546, concerning, for example, the ordination of bishops and clergy.[28] " We decree ... we command ... we do not permit" are recurrent phrases that give its tone. So, too, he defines the doctrine of the Church, as in the earlier Titles of the *Code:* and we are not surprised that, in the matter of the *Three Chapters,* the African bishops, with less to lose than Justinian's prelates nearer home, complained of his conduct in arrogating to the magistrate what belonged, as of right, to the spiritual rulers of the Church. But this is of the essence of Byzantinism or Cæsaropapism: and the East accepted, without demur, a sovereignty of the civil power over the spiritualty which was never even possible under the different political conditions of the West.

We have now taken a glance at the legislation with which Justinian attempted the maintenance of true religion and virtue. We must next see how it affected the hierarchy, the monastic orders, and the worship of the

Church, as well as the moral and social conditions of his day.

§ 5. The hierarchy was ranged under the five great Patriarchates of Rome, Constantinople, Alexandria, Antioch and Jerusalem. Of these sees, the bishops were officially styled Patriarchs; while two of them, the bishops of Rome and Alexandria, were commonly called Popes as well—by a name that eventually came to distinguish the bishop of Rome alone.

The Roman See was the first in Christendom, and its bishop had the primacy. Justinian's language is clear upon this point. In *Edocere volentes,* of 26th March, 533, he speaks of the bishop of Rome not only as " Pope and Patriarch " but as " Head of all the most holy bishops of God."[29] Addressing Pope John II., 532—†5, he lays stress on the importance of being in communion with the Apostolic See, and says " We have always made it our earnest endeavour to maintain the unity of your Apostolic See and the condition of the holy churches of God ";[30] while, to the same Pope, he speaks of the Roman See as " the summit of the chief pontificate,"[31] " the source of the episcopate,"[32] and " the venerable seat of the Apostle Peter."[33] Phrases of this sort are, no doubt, prompted, in part, by oriental courtliness; and they were used at a time when " Justinian wanted the assistance of the bishop of Rome in furtherance of his plans for the re-establishment of the Imperial power in Italy."[34] But they represent the status traditionally assigned in Christendom to the Roman See. It was that of an acknowledged but undefined pre-eminence; of primacy among colleagues but not of sovereignty over inferiors.

The See of Constantinople came next. Thus, the order of rank among Patriarchs is laid down in a *Novel* of 18th March, 545, which says that " the Pope of Old Rome is first among all bishops, but the most blessed Archbishop of Constantinople or New Rome has the second place."[35] If it be argued that more than the second place is claimed for the See of Constantinople because in *Omnibus rebus* of 530, " the Great Church of this our happy City and mother of all [churches] " is also hailed as " head of

Church and State under Justinian

all the other [churches],"[36] it should be noted that the words apply not to the See of Constantinople but to the Church of Saint Sophia. The See, however, was given an authority over Illyricum, in spite of ancient claims set out in the synod of Rome, 7—9th December, 531,[37] by Justinian's recognition of *Omni innovatione* of 14th July, 421, in which Theodosius II. assigned that region to Constantinople;[38] while the bishop of the capital was regularly addressed as Œcumenical Patriarch.[39] That title was also used in addressing Popes, though never assumed by them. Thus Hormisdas, 514—†23, and Agapetus, 535—†6, accepted it with equanimity. But no sooner had it been synodically assumed, 588, by John the Faster,[40] bishop of Constantinople, 582—†95, than it was indignantly denounced by Pope Gregory the great, 590—†604, as a challenge, on the part of an ambitious rival, to the pre-eminence of the Apostolic See. "It is clear," writes Gregory to the Emperor Maurice, 582—†602, " to every one who knows the Gospel that the care of the whole Church has been committed to the blessed Peter, chief of the Apostles . . . yet he is never called the Universal Apostle. . . . But John wishes to be called the Universal Bishop."[41]

A new and temporary Patriarchate of Justiniana Prima was created[42] in April, 535, to give distinction to Justinian's birthplace : but with this exception and those of the autocephalous churches of Cyprus and Mt. Sinai, the episcopate of the Empire was distributed among the five great Patriarchates. These were divided into provinces, each under a metropolitan, who was bishop of the capital or metropolis of the province. The province, in turn, was composed of dioceses, each usually conterminous with one or other of its cities whose pastors were bishops and suffragans of their metropolitan, the first among them having the title of the Protothrone. Some bishoprics, on the other hand, depended on the Patriarch only : and were thus extra-provincial or " autocephalous." Of their bishops, some ranked as metropolitans, though without suffragans; and others—a numerous class—as archbishops : for in the sixth century, the title " archbishop " had several meanings. It was sometimes the synonym of "autocephalous" which it tends to supplant; sometimes of "metropolitan," but only in Illyricum; sometimes it was given, as a title of distinction, to the bishop of any important city such as Amasia or Ancyra; and, in one instance, it is assigned to the prelate of quasi-patriarchal, or primatial, rank who held Justiniana Prima and is addressed, in his patent, as "not only metropolitan but archbishop."[43] As to the numbers of the episcopate, the Patriarch of Constantinople ruled in 535 over the twenty-eight provinces in Thrace, Asia and Pontus, enumerated as his a hundred years earlier by Theodoret,[44] bishop of Cyrus, †458. But it does not follow that there were twenty-eight metropolitans under his jurisdiction; for "Scythia" had none, while Bithynia had three, Nicæa and Chalcedon, out of honour to the Councils, held there, in addition to its old civil capital, Nicomedia. The number must have been about thirty metropolitans and four hundred and fifty bishops, all subject to the Patriarch of Constantinople.[45]

He was assisted by his Home Synod—a standing but irregular Council consisting of prelates who from time to time happened to be in the capital for business, in spite of Justinian's requirement of residence on their sees and of his prohibition to bishops against coming to Court,[46] 1st March, 528.

The duties of a bishop[47] were multifarious: pastoral and administrative, governmental and municipal. He was bound to inspect monasteries and hospitals. He was judge of his clergy and Religious. He was also arbiter between laymen, if invited by both parties. His election, therefore, soon became matter of moment to the State; and, the share of the people in it being eliminated,[48] the choice came to rest with the comprovincials, but, in practice, the will of the Emperor prevailed. Nor can we be surprised at the interest which the Government thus took in an episcopal election. A bishop was not only the spiritual leader of his flock but first among local magnates and an official of the Empire armed with statutory powers. Moreover, whereas other officials held their place only during the Emperor's pleasure, the bishop was elected to his See for life. Perhaps it was to curb the growing influence of a capable man so elected that translations from less to more important sees were forbidden; though they naturally, but only occasionally, took place for the advantage of the See of Constantinople.

The clergy consisted of priests, deacons, sub-deacons, readers and cantors. Deaconesses are mentioned, next after deacons, in this sequence; but they are expressly excluded from ranking as " clerics."[49] The privileges of the clergy were considerable. They are exempted from the burdens of municipal office. They enjoy an immunity from extraordinary imposts. They have a *forum*,[50] and even a prison, of their own. The conditions of admission to Orders are carefully prescribed, in respect both of age and of estate. No one is to be made priest under thirty-five years of age, deacon or sub-deacon under twenty-five, deaconess under forty, or reader under eighteen.[51] No woman could become a deaconess after a second marriage; and, in order to be admitted to that Order, she must be either a widow or a virgin: and she was, like a bishop, to remain unmarried. Clerics might live with their wives provided that they had married before they became sub-deacons. If a cleric lost his wife, he was to remain unmarried: unless he were of the order of Reader or Cantor. In that case, he might marry again provided that he was content to remain in these lower ranks of the ministry.[52] No women were permitted in the houses of the clergy, save such as were near relatives; and, in the house of a deaconess, no men at all.[53] The maintenance of the clergy was usually a charge on the revenues of the church to which they were ordained; though, where these failed, they might follow a trade.[54] Their duties were to perform the services of the church, and not to quit the church to which they were appointed at their ordination: whence the strict limitations of the numbers of the clergy at Constantinople,[55] 535, as has been already mentioned. Besides these regular ranks of the clergy, the bishop had a number of diocesan officials—from archdeacon, proto-presbyter or rural dean and syncellus or chaplain to steward, almoner, churchwarden and sacristan, and from registrar, chief constable, chancellor and advocate to notary librarian and archivist. But these officials varied both in number and dignity with the importance or the insignificance of his see. The chief bishops maintained *apocrisiarii* or *responsales*—as we should say, nuncios,— to represent them at court or in the more important churches: and for a Roman cleric so to serve at Constantinople was often a stepping stone to the papacy. Popes Vigilius, 538—†55. Pelagius I., 555—†60 and Gregory the Great, 590—†604, had so served.

§ 6. Next to the hierarchy, the factor of importance in the Church of the Empire was the Monastic Order. And this was recognised by Justinian in that monks were regulated with no less care than clerics in his legislation. Nor was such care unnecessary. In influence, the monks had proved themselves a power to be reckoned with for over an hundred years. Dalmatius, †440, an old abbot at Constantinople, had intervened effectively with Theodosius II., 408—†50, to the preservation of orthodoxy at the first Council of Ephesus, 431; while, at the second, 449, the Syrian abbot Barsauma, †458, had as effectively promoted its suppression. In Syria and Egypt monastic sympathies were with the Monophysites; in Jerusalem and Constantinople, with the Orthodox. As to numbers, in the diocese of Constantinople, there were sixty-eight monasteries of men and, across the water, at Chalcedon, there were forty. Not all monks, however, were collected in the monasteries: for there were two classes, solitaries as well as cœnobites.

The solitaries preserved the older tradition of monasticism, not only as monks, or μοναχοί dwelling alone: but also by individuality of preference for various modes of solitude. Thus some were Hermits, and dwelt in desert places; others were Stylites or Kionites, and lived on the top of a pillar: others, Dendrites, who took refuge in trees; others, recluses, who shut themselves up in a narrow enclosure. The Boskoi betook themselves to pastures where they could graze like cattle: the Hesychasts or Anchorites sought quiet retreats; and the Kelliotes retired to cells. These more or less fantastic types of ascetic were, however, the minority.

The majority were cœnobites. They both lived and worshipped in community : and they are the only sort of monks contemplated in the legislation of Justinian.[56] Their lauras or convents each had its archimandrite or hegumen, and each was autonomous. Such autonomy characterised the houses founded by St. Benedict, ?500—†550? after he left Subiaco, and founded his monastery at Monte Cassino, probably about 520. His Rule is concerned with the government of a single monastery only; and contains no provision for the grouping of monasteries into congregations or orders, as became the custom late in the West. It is remarkable also for other features characteristic of his time. He had himself tried, but he now abandoned, the old spirit of rivalry in austerities in favour of the little rule for beginners,[57] such as all could attempt in community : and it was during Justinian's conquest of Italy that Benedict was building up there the life which, for seven centuries afterwards, gave its monastic ideal to the West. With him also, work, whether manual or studious, formed part of the life; and its chief pre-occupation lay in the daily service of choir and altar. Here again there was a development by way of contrast with the older customs of the East; where work was but a pastime or a penance and common worship confined to the Sabbath and the Lord's Day. In a third particular, Western monasticism differed from Eastern at this epoch. The Benedictine house was governed by its abbot—in the Eastern part of Justinian's Empire every community was controlled ultimately by the bishop.[58]

Women had their share in the Religious life as well as men; and for them, it took two forms. There was the *Monastria* or *Ascetica,* who practised it at home, and the *Canonica* who lived in a community under a canon or rule. Their duties were discharged largely in procession and psalmody at funerals;[59] and their obligation was one of strict separation. Male and female ascetics were not only forbidden to dwell together in a double convent;[60] they might not visit each other's convent nor even be buried near each other.[61] Both had common privileges; among them, a *forum* of their own.[62] As to age for profession, a man might enter a community when his beard was grown; but women, who in that rough age needed protection, were sometimes admitted as girls. There are instances of children of twelve, or even of eight. The novitiate was fixed as of not less than three years' duration.[63]

§ 7. The worship of the Church receives much attention from the legislation of Justinian: and we may consider next the places where it was held, the sacraments there administered, and then briefly describe the Liturgy where it found highest expression.

(i.) Places of worship might be either " catholic," for general use, as a cathedral or parish church; conventual, for the use of Religious; or private oratories. In any case, they could only be put up with the consent of the bishop.[64] The founder retained the right of patronage;[65] and the building, as in our own country, faced eastward. As a rule, churches were small by comparison with the churches of the West in later days; and they varied in plan. Some were octagonal: as was San Vitale which Justinian built at Ravenna, 547. Others were rectangular as was the church of St. Mary at Jerusalem. Others took the form of a Greek cross, as did the Church of the Holy Apostles at Constantinople. But the general tendency came to be towards a polygonal plan, surmounted by cupolas, in imitation of the great church of Saint Sophia which Justinian's architects, Isidore of Miletus and Anthemius of Tralles, erected for him at Constantinople, 532—7. With justifiable pride, he provides for it as for "major ecclesia nostri imperii mater ";[66] and it became the model of innumerable sanctuaries as far as from Pessinus to Benevento. Concrete and brick are their usual materials; but their interiors were richly decorated with painting, mosaic and low relief, and sumptuously furnished. Their books were illuminated. Their book-bindings, diptychs and episcopal thrones, as that of Maximian, bishop of Ravenna, were of ivory. Their lamps and sacred vessels were of goldsmith's work. The vestments of their ministers and the hangings of their sanctuaries were resplendent in embroidery and jewels. No wonder that their churches impressed the beholder with a majesty not less serene, but more unearthly, than that of the Empire itself.

(ii.) The main use of these noble buildings was for the administration of the Sacraments; for Justinian required, in Novels[67] of 537 and 544, that the Sacraments must be administered in church. Baptism was bestowed at Christmas and Epiphany, at the Ascension of our Lord and the Assumption of our Lady, but most commonly at Easter. It was by trine immersion; and great reverence was paid to the baptisteries. There are two attached to Saint Sophia—and two in Ravenna—resplendent with mosaics —the " Arian baptistery," S. Maria in Cosmedin and the " Orthodox baptistery," S. Giovanni in Fonte. Confirmation was inseparable from Baptism: and was given to infants as to adults by the presbyter with unction blessed by the bishop. Communion also was given to infants, along with Baptism and Confirmation; it was repeated from time to time before years of discretion; and the Eucharist was celebrated frequently but not daily. Public penance ceased at Constantinople after the patriarchate of Atticus, 406—†26; but private confession and absolution were in use.[68] Extreme Unction was unknown. Orders were bestowed by the bishop, and by imposition of hands: not, as with Romans and Anglicans of to-day, at stated seasons, but at such times as he found convenient. Marriage—or coronation: so called because of its outstanding feature in the crowning of the bridal pair—was legal without the blessing of the Church; and divorce, though impossible by mutual consent,[69] was admitted for five specific reasons.[70] In this, the Civil Law imposed a declension from the Christian standard upon the churches subject to the Empire, far beyond that which was conceded to Jewish Christians by the qualifying clause added to our Lord's prohibition in the Gospel of St. Matthew; and the Eastern churches have been unable to maintain the indissolubility of Christian Marriage which is the ordinary requirement of the New Testament and of the churches of the West. The latter were independent of the

State and were never forced to compromise with the laxity of its heathen traditions.

(iii.) Greatest of all the Sacraments was, of course, the Eucharist; and the Liturgy is so named from the fact that the rites and ceremonies with which it was celebrated constituted, " par excellence," *the* Service.

Three types of Liturgy were in use in the Eastern part of the Empire of Justinian. The Alexandrian prevailed in Egypt and Abyssinia and is contained in the texts known as *St. Mark, The Coptic St. Cyril,* and *The Twelve Apostles.*[71] Its outstanding features are that the Great Intercession is made in the course of the Preface;[72] and that the cue from which the celebrant proceeds with the Thanksgiving, after the congregation has broken in with the *Sanctus,* is given by its word " full."[73] The West-Syrian rite prevailed in Antioch, Jerusalem and Cyprus, and is now contained in the texts of *the Greek* and *the Syriac St. James.*[74] Here the distinctive features are that the Great Intercession occurs between the Invocation and the Lord's Prayer;[75] and that the cue for the resumption of the Thanksgiving by the celebrant, after the *Sanctus,* is given by the word " Holy,"[76] in that hymn. A third type of Liturgy is derived from that of Syria or Antioch, and is known as the Byzantine Rite. It is found in the exarchates of Pontus, Asia, Thrace and Illyricum; and its prevalence there testifies to the influence of the once powerful, but since the time of St. Chrysostom, †407, much-reduced Patriarchate of Antioch. It is now represented in the three Orthodox Liturgies of *St. Basil, St. Chrysostom* and *the Presanctified:*[77] of which the first was in the sixth century, and the second is now the Liturgy normally in use throughout the Orthodox Church,[78] while the third[79] is used, except on Saturdays and Sundays, during Lent. Throughout the Empire the Liturgy was at first said in Greek; save in Syria where it was in Syriac and in Egypt, where it was in Coptic. But in these regions the majority were Monophysite. They celebrated their worship in the vernacular, all the more eagerly because the worship of the Empire was

Church and State under Justinian

conducted in Greek. By the year 520 the Byzantine Rite was universal throughout the Orthodox East.

As celebrated in the sixth century,[80] the Byzantine Liturgy enshrined an imposing worship. Outside the church sat the beggars, asking for alms as the faithful entered. Inside, appeared the *ambo* or pulpit, in the nave, from which the lessons were read, the anthems sung, and the sermon preached; the altar supported on columns, and surmounted by a canopy or *ciborium;* and behind it, facing west, the bishop's throne surrounded by the *synthronos* or seats of the presbyters, who could thus readily concelebrate with the bishop. The sanctuary, with its altar and *synthronos,* was separated from the nave by a light screen and veil: which afterwards developed into a solid "iconostasis" pierced only by the "holy doors."

The service began with the Mass of the Catechumens. It was introduced, not by the long preparation of the elements in the *Prothesis* which developed later, but by the Little Entrance at which, to the music of the *Trisagion,* the deacons carried in the Gospels attended by incense. Next, after the mutual salutation of celebrant and people, came the three lessons, all from the *ambo;* the Prophecy, or lesson from the Old Testament and the Epistle, both recited by a Reader; and the Gospel by a Deacon; all standing. After it, the salutation again and a homily. Then the Catechumens and others were dismissed; and the doors closed, before the Mass of the Faithful could begin. It opened with the Deacon's Litany and the Prayer of the Faithful: during which the elements were being prepared in the *Prothesis.* Then, after celebrant and people had saluted each other, they were brought in at the Great Entrance, while the anthem "King of Glory" was sung and, after 574, the Cherubic Hymn.[81] Another salutation and the Kiss of Peace was succeeded by the Offertory; and this by the Creed introduced at Constantinople, 511, by the Patriarch Timothy; and then the Diptychs of the dead and of the living were recited by the deacon. Now opened the culminating portion of the service in the *Anaphora,* or offering of the great sacrifice.

A custom was making way of reciting its solemn mysteries inaudibly; but Justinian, in 565, issued explicit directions that they must be so celebrated as to be heard.[82] The *Anaphora* begins with the Grace, the *Sursum Corda*, Preface or preliminary recitation of Thanksgiving by the celebrant, who was interrupted by the *Sanctus* of the people as if they could not but break in and take their part. Then he resumed with the recitation of the Institution, the *Anamnesis* in remembrance of Good Friday, Easter and Ascension, the *Epiclesis* or Invocation of the Holy Spirit, reminiscent of Pentecost, followed by the Great Intercession, salutation and Lord's Prayer. Thus the consecration was complete, and the sacrifice pleaded. The preparation of the elements for distribution came next by the Fraction and the Elevation of " Holy things for Holy People." Communion was then given, into the hand of the communicant. And the service ended with a thanksgiving: while, if any of the consecrated elements remained, they had to be consumed by the children present. Who so worthy to receive them as the innocents? As to minor accompaniments of the rite, we have mention of the fans manipulated by the deacons, and of the liturgical roll which served the celebrant for his altar-book.

(iv.) Next to the Liturgy, ranked the Divine Office in the worship of the Church. But it differs, in two respects, from the Liturgy. First, it was the service for the clergy, whereas the Liturgy was frequented by the laity. Next, while the Liturgy was reserved for Sundays and Holy Days, the Divine Office was recited daily, at any rate in the greater churches. " Let all clerics," orders Justinian in a law of 1st March, 528, " in every church, in their own persons recite Nocturns, Lauds and Vespers lest they be taken to be clerics simply for consuming the goods of the church; bearing the name of clerics, but withdrawing themselves from the service of our Lord God, which is the business of clerics."[83] Justinian is here requiring the older form of Divine Service, which in his time prevailed only throughout Egypt and Syria; for elsewhere Prime, Terce, Sext and None had established themselves between Mattins and Evensong, and the day had come to close with Compline. The Canonical Hours thus numbered seven, counting Nocturns and Lauds as one; and these were recited in the monasteries. But their obligation had reference to place: and not, as in the West, to persons. The monk was not bound to their recital outside his convent: nor the cleric to it beyond his church. The Psalter, of course, formed the staple of the Office; but hymnody found place there also. Its chief exponent was Romanus the Melodist, a deacon of Beyrout, afterwards attached to the churches of Blachernae and of Cyrus at Constantinople, probably c. 537—55. He was the poet of the *Kontakia,* so called from the roller (κοντός) like that of a map, to which the roll was attached for rolling up or unfolding. They were compositions in vogue from the fifth to the eighth century; and of the thousand such hymns ascribed to Romanus two are of special interest: the Christmas Hymn Ἡ παρθένος σήμερον [84] which, as late as the twelfth century, was sung with great ceremony at the Christmas Eve banquet in the imperial palace: and Εἰς ἁγίους πατέρας [85] which, from internal evidence, must have been written between the destruction of Antioch, c. 540, by Chosroes I., 531—†78, and the death of the Empress Theodora in 548.

(v.) Other forms of devotion were Litanies or Processions. According to an order of 1st May, 546, these were to be conducted by the clergy.[86] They were escorted by crosses, lights, incense and the carrying of the Gospels: and they took place either on occasion, to obtain some special grace, or regularly, on Friday evenings, to Blachernae. Masses for the dead were celebrated, according to an ordinance of 16th March, 539, on the third, the sixth and the fortieth day.[87] And popular devotion also expressed itself in prayer, either standing or kneeling; in the use of holy water; in miraculous healing by the aid of the sign of the cross, or of the Gospels, holy water and relics; in *ex-votos,* such as pictures or lamps, for recovery from illness or deliverance from disaster; in pictures, especially of our Lady; in doves, symbolic of the Holy Spirit, made of gold and silver, and suspended over altar or font; and in the use of crosses, whether small for reliquaries or portable for processions,[88] or large for setting up on sacred sites.

(vi.) Days and seasons had their place in the round of worship: for Christian devotion requires the sanctification of time as well as of persons, places and things. For fasting, Lent was the principal season. It consisted of thirty-six days, and so sanctified a tenth of the year. But Saturdays as well as Sundays were excluded from its reckoning, except that Easter Even was, of course, a fast. And abstinence from flesh was complete during Lent. Indeed, flesh could not even be bought. Of Feasts, and other days of observance, Sunday was, of course, the chief. It began over-night: and was a public holiday. The courts of law were closed: military exercises ceased: work on the land came to a standstill. Wednesday and Friday were set apart for fasting and good works; and bishops were ordered, 17th September, 529, on these days to visit the prisons.[89] The Feasts of our Lord were Christmas; which, coming originally from the West, had spread over the East in the fourth and fifth centuries: the Hypapante ($\dot{v}\pi\acute{a}v\tau\eta\sigma\iota\varsigma$), 542, or meeting of St. Mary with Simeon and Anna for the Presentation of our Lord in the Temple, so that it was His feast; not His mother's, as in the West where it commemorated her Purification: and the Exaltation of the Cross which was celebrated in the fourth century, long before the recovery of the Cross from the Persians by the Emperor Heraclius, 610—†41. Then there were Feasts of our Lady: her Annunciation, 25th March; her Falling Asleep, 15th August; her Nativity, and, 543, her Presentation in the Temple, 21st November; Blachernae being her peculiar sanctuary. Angels also enjoyed a widespread *cultus*, as Michael and Gabriel both mentioned, 20th April, 535, in an oath taken by all functionaries of the Empire;[90] as well as Patriarchs, Apostles and Martyrs. But bishops, abbots, founders and solitaries were celebrated locally only. Patrons of churches were usually John the Forerunner, Peter the Coryphæus, George the Standard-bearer, Mary the Theotokos and Michael the

Archangel. There was great devotion to relics, especially to the True Cross at Constantinople, with the Sponge and the Lance. They were used at the dedication of churches, and pilgrimages followed naturally upon the *cultus* of relics and souvenirs.[91] Sanctity was easily attained: for most of the Emperors and of the Patriarchs of Constantinople in the sixth century took rank as canonised saints.

§ 8. But the moral and social conditions of the time were not much elevated by this display of religion, whether official or popular. There were good people, of course. They would be found among the σπουδαῖοι and the φιλόπονοι who attached themselves to strong centres of religion and made them stronger. And Christian charity, by its orphanages and hospitals, provided, as now, on a lavish scale, for the helpless and the distressed. These institutions were placed under the control of the bishop, and were served by the clergy. Guilds of *parabolani*[92] risked their lives to tend the sick; and *copiatae*[93] gave their ministrations for the burial of the dead. The monasteries also practised charity on a large scale, and aided and sheltered numbers of the poor and needy. One convent, founded by Theodora, was situated in an imperial palace on the Asiatic shore of the Bosporus; and had five hundred penitents under its care; for the Empress herself had sounded the depths and knew from whence they had been rescued. Justinian's legislation itself reveals the shame and the misery which he tried alternately to suppress and to reform—castration,[94] prostitution,[95] sodomy,[96] betting and gambling,[97] blasphemy[98] among the laity: and, among the clergy, simony[99] and things much worse. The populace, in fact, remained half-pagan. What else could be expected when converts were made and baptised without, or even against, their will?

CHAPTER V.

THE SUCCESSORS OF JUSTINIAN, 565—610.

BISHOPS OF THE CHIEF SEES, 565—610.

ROME.	CONSTANTINOPLE.	ANTIOCH.
John III. 560—73	John III. (Scholasticus) 566—77	Anastasius I. (Sinaiticus) 559—70
Benedict I. 574—8	John IV. (the Faster) 582—95	Gregory I. (Sinaiticus) 570—93
Pelagius II. 578—90	Cyriacus I. 595—606	Anastasius I.[2] 593—8
Gregory I. 590—604	Thomas I. 607—10	Anastasius II. (Sinaiticus) 599—609
Sabinian 604—6		
Boniface III. 607		
Boniface IV. 608—15		

ALEXANDRIA.		JERUSALEM.
Orthodox.	*Monophysite.*	Macarius II. 544—74
Apollinaris 551—70	Theodosius I. 536—67	John IV. 574—c. 593
John II. 570—80	Peter IV. 567—70	Amos 594—601
Eulogius 580—607	Damian 570—603	Isaac 601—9
Theodore Scribo 607—9	Anastasius 603—14	
John III. (the Almoner) 609—19		

CHAPTER V.

THE SUCCESSORS OF JUSTINIAN, 565—610.

§ 1. JUSTINIAN died 14th November, 565, at the age of 87. He left behind him an undying fame, but an exhausted Empire. The exhaustion can be detected after the Plague, 542; but it had passed beyond remedy when, in his old age, the Emperor relaxed his hold on the government and, according to the poet Corippus,[1] *fl.* 546—66, became "cold to the things of this world and aflame only for love of the life to come."[2] All through his reign, Justinian had outrun his resources by the magnificence of his enterprises: and his successors had to face the consequences. There were three belonging to his house: Justin II., 565—†78, his nephew; Tiberius II., 578—†82, whom Justin had adopted as Cæsar; and Maurice, 582—†602, son-in-law to Tiberius. None of the three was strong enough to stem the tide of disintegration; for, in addition to the struggle with financial embarrassment, bureaucratic resistance and relaxation of military discipline—all legacies of Justinian's old age—each in turn had to contend with the pressure of enemies on the frontiers. Such was the geographical situation of the Empire that north and east were the frontiers in danger; and, while constant wars had to be waged with the Persians across the Euphrates, on the line of the Danube resistance had to be offered to invading hordes of Avars and Slavs. The result was a new departure in imperial policy. The West had to be left to take care of itself; and the greater part of Justinian's conquests in Italy were lost to the Lombards when, three years after the death of Justinian, they began to overrun the land. These were the disasters that thickened upon the dynasty of Justinian. They reached their climax in the ruin that ensued upon the usurpation of Phocas 602—†10.

§ 2. Justin II., 565—†78, was the nephew of Justinian

and married Sophia, the niece of Theodora. He abandoned the policy of his uncle in three respects. First, he failed to maintain such relations with Orthodox and Monophysite, as had been achieved by the respective sympathies of Justinian and Theodora; and in his edict[3] of 566 gave himself out as exclusively Orthodox. This weakened his hold on the oriental provinces, though, for the first six years of his reign, according to the monophysite historian, John of Ephesus († after 585), he did not persecute.[4] Secondly, he repudiated Justinian's policy of supporting arms by diplomacy, and buying off the Avars. It was a well-intentioned resolve; and, at first, made him popular. There was an air of the old Roman courage about it; and it also promised a remission of taxation. Thirdly, he allowed the imperial authority to be diminished, by yielding to the independence of the aristocracy, and by experiments in decentralisation. The cohesion of the Empire was too weak to run such risks with impunity. But Justin II. did not live to be seriously affected by the results of his unwisdom. In 574, he fell a victim to intermittent lunacy; and the government was carried on till his death by his masterful Empress Sophia in concert with Tiberius, *Comes Excubitorum,* or Commander of the Guards, whom she called to her aid as Cæsar.

§ 3. Tiberius II., 578—†82, succeeded: with his wife Ino, who became the Empress Anastasia. He was a good minister of war: and did much to strengthen the army: with money, with reinforcements of *Federati* and with a revival of discipline. In these endeavours, he was assisted by Justinian the great-nephew of Justinian I., and by Maurice, his successor both as *Comes Excubitorum* and on the throne. But, as emperor, Tiberius proved both imprudent and inefficient. He repeated the mistake of Justin by allowing his Patriarch to pursue the policy of exclusive Orthodoxy which further alienated his Monophysite subjects. He made a bid for popularity by remitting the duty on "political bread," and taking off one quarter of the taxes: and he enlarged the policy of doles but bestowed them not on the poor but on lawyers, doctors, silversmiths and bankers.[5] Moreover, he shared his power: and so imperilled public safety by compromising his authority. But he also died too soon to reap the effects of his unwisdom.

§ 4. It was Maurice, 582—†602, who, in a reign of twenty years, had to weather the storm, until he was overwhelmed by it. By his marriage with Constantina, daughter of Tiberius, he ranks as the last sovereign of the house of Justinian: and though greater as a general than as Emperor, no little glory[6] belongs to him: quite apart from his upright life and his truly Christian death.

Foreign foes beset him all his days. The Avars, a people of the same stock as Attila the Hun, advanced from Hungary: and made it their ambition to seize the fortresses that guarded the line of the Danube. They took Singidunum (Belgrade) 581, Sirmium (Mitrovitsa) 582, and Viminacium (Kostolats) 583; and then proceeded to harry Mœsia 586 and Thrace 591. In that year, Maurice, owing to successes in the war with Persia, was able to concentrate against the Avars forces sufficient to inflict a check upon them. But, 598, they overran Dalmatia; though, 601, they were defeated upon the Theiss. From that time, they figure less upon the scene. But, the Slavs, to whom the Avars appear to have stood as a caste of nobles to their retainers, accompanied their depredations: not as robbers, but as settlers. Already, in 571, a horde of 100,000 Slavs had settled in Illyricum and Thrace: and this was the first penetration southward of a race which afterwards came to dominate the Balkan peninsula. In 589, they harried Thrace. Then, 602, they suffered a severe defeat on the Danube from Priscus, one of the most distinguished of the generals of Maurice. But they made permanent settlement in Mœsia, Macedonia, and even in Greece: where Monemvasia, situated to the S.E. of Laconia and celebrated as the country of Malvoisie, was founded as a refuge from the invaders, much as Venice took its rise, 150 years earlier, as a place of safety from the Huns.

These invasions of Avars and Slavs rendered it difficult for the Romans to retain any but a slight hold on Italy. From 553—68, Italy had been Imperial: but, in the latter year, the Lombards, under their King Alboin, 561—†73, invaded the country by the route which had lain open to Alaric and Attila. Ticinum, now Pavia, became their capital: and by the end of the reign of Maurice, Italy was divided between the Empire and its foes. Imperial Italy covered three groups of territory: the northern, stretching along the Adriatic coast from Venetia to Picenum, and having for its centre Ravenna, the seat of the Exarchate of Italy: the central, mainly round Rome, but connected by a corridor, which ran through Todi, Perugia and Gubbio, with the Adriatic lands: and the southern, confined to the heel and the toe of Italy, but including Sicily. Elsewhere the land belonged to the Lombards: their northern conquests including Trent, Friuli and Lombardy, and their southern acquisitions consisting of the duchies of Spoleto and Benevento. The islands of Sardinia and Corsica belonged to the Exarchate of Africa; and it was owing to the rivalry between the Lombards and the Imperialists under the Exarch of Ravenna—a distant seat of government from Rome—that Pope Gregory the Great, 590—†604, became so independent of both as, in practice, to be ruler of Roman Italy. This was an immense step forward for the papacy in securing its supremacy over the West.

All the time that the northern frontier was thus violated, the successors of Justinian had been obliged to defend the Eastern frontier against the Persians. Rivalry for the possession of Armenia was the standing cause of war between Rome and Persia: and the desire of each, particularly of the Romans, to stand well with the Turks. The Romans obtained the silks of China through the Turks: and the Turks then lay to the north and east of Persia, and weakened that country in its conflict with the Empire, precisely as the Avars weakened the Romans in their contest with Persia. In 572 Justin refused to subsidise the Sassanids any longer for Lazica and the passes over the Caucasus: and Chosroes I., 531—†78, declared war. In 573 the Romans failed to take Nisibis; but, 574, the Persians made themselves masters of Dara; and, 589, they captured Martyropolis (Maiferkat). At this point, the Turks, and a civil war at home, intervened to call off the Persians: and Maurice was enabled to make an advantageous peace. He restored Chosroes II., 590—†628, to his rightful throne, and recovered Dara and Martyropolis. The Persians retained Nisibis: but Persarmenia passed into the possession of the Romans.

The peace between Rome and Persia continued for the last decade of the reign of Maurice: but it did not save him from disaster at home. He is described by Evagrius, 536—†600?, as "self-willed" and "moderate."[7] His self-will showed itself in extravagant expenditure upon the adornment of his birthplace[8] Arabissus in Cappadocia, in spite of his empty treasury and the economies forced upon him by the lavishness of Tiberius. His moderation is another name for his tolerance. He was no Orthodox persecutor, like Justin and Tiberius, but allied himself with John the Faster, Patriarch of Constantinople, 582—†95, who was much more intent upon the advancement of his see and his rivalry with Gregory the Great over the title Œcumenical Patriarch, in which Maurice supported him, than upon the suppression of Monophysitism. Such "self-will" and "moderation" were alike unacceptable to the opinion of the capital. In 599 Maurice gave further offence by refusing, on the ground of expense, to ransom twelve thousand Romans taken captive by the Avars; and again he offended the army, 601, by an order, also for reasons of expense, that the troops should winter across the Danube. A mutiny followed; and Maurice fled to Chalcedon: where he was murdered by the usurper Phocas. "Righteous art Thou, O Lord: and true are Thy judgments" were his last words.

The reign of Phocas, 602—†10, fell thick with disaster. To avenge his "father" Maurice, Chosroes II. renewed hostilities. In 606 he overran Syria: and in 608 the Persian host had crossed Asia Minor, and appeared before Chalcedon. They could be descried from Constantinople. But the city was delivered and the Empire revitalised by the arms of Heraclius, 610—†41.

It is now time to turn to the events and personages of

ecclesiastical history who stand out upon this dark background.

§ 5. The Orthodoxy of Justin II. and Tiberius II., by contrast with the tolerance of Maurice, had much to do with the effect of persecution in promoting the growth of Monophysitism. But it was the Patriarch even more than the Emperor who, at this time, directed religious policy.[9]

John III., otherwise Scholasticus, the barrister, was Patriarch of Constantinople 566—†77. He was born at Sirmin,[10] near Antioch. Here he was trained for the bar; for there was a flourishing school of law at Antioch, till Justinian closed it, 533, in order that legal studies should be carried on only at the capital. John took holy orders, and became agent of the church at Antioch. This would bring him into communication with Constantinople; and, perhaps, to the notice of Justinian. At any rate, the Emperor appointed him to succeed the Patriarch Eutychius, 552—65; whom he had banished for opposing his adoption of aphthartodocetism. Justinian died seven months afterwards; and, 14th November, 565, John Scholasticus officiated at the coronation of Justin II. Next year appeared the edict in which the new Emperor professed his orthodoxy, while deprecating quarrels about "persons or syllables."[11] John may have inspired the edict. For a time, he occupied himself in legal studies; and supplemented the *Digest of the Canon Law* which he had first prepared at Antioch by the *Nomocanon,* or collection of civil and ecclesiastical laws which he issued from Constantinople.[12] Then, as we are told by the Monophysite historian, John of Ephesus, " no sooner had the health of Justin failed and John was free to carry out his plans than he determined upon crushing the whole ' orthodox ' [sc. Monophysite] party."[13]

A few words must be said about John of Ephesus, 505—†85. He was born at Amida (now Diabekr); and brought up by Maron the Stylite in the tenets of Monophysitism. At the age of thirty, he came to Constantinople: and, 536, by the favour of Justinian and Theodora, was appointed bishop of the Monophysites, without a see. They gave him the task of converting the heathen: and to this work he devoted himself not only in Constantinople but in Asia, Phrygia, Lydia and Caria. Here, with the aid of Deuterius who succeeded him, " he began his labours in the mountains which overhang Tralles; in the territory of which city alone he converted many thousands from the error of idol-worship; and built for their use, twenty-four churches and four monasteries, all of which were entirely new."[14] For thirty-five years the mission of John and Deuterius continued; till they had covered the district with "ninety-nine new churches and twelve monasteries for their converts."[15] Then, it appears, John returned to Constantinople and became abbot of a monastery near the Golden Horn: till c. 571, he was deposed and imprisoned by the Patriarch John Scholasticus. At this date, his *Ecclesiastical History* begins. He wrote in Syriac. He regrets that his *History* is so ill-arranged. But that, as he says, was because he wrote "when the persecution was going on." His " papers and notes " were " concealed in various places," and he was often at a loss to know whether he had mentioned this or that episode before, or not.[16] But, on these very grounds, the *History* of John of Ephesus is " a valuable contemporary source for the reigns of Justin and Tiberius ":[17] and as it is written from the Monophysite side it supplements and corrects the *Ecclesiastical History* of the Orthodox Evagrius. This work covers the period 431—493; and is professedly a continuation of Socrates, Sozomen and Theodoret. As the author was born 536 and died 600, his work " has thus the full value of a contemporary authority "[18] for the period running from the end of the reign of Justinian to the closing years of Maurice.

To return to the persecution under Justin II. and John Scholasticus. It began, on the Saturday in Passion Week, 20th March, 571,[19] with an attack on the convents in the capital where Theodora had given a refuge to the persecuted nuns of Antioch and Asia Minor. He tried to make them receive communion at the hands of his clergy; and their refusal sums up the interpretation which the Monophysites, mistakenly but with conviction, read into the Chalcedonian doctrine. " We cannot," they protested, " communicate with the Synod of Chalcedon which divides Christ our God into two natures after the union, and teaches a quaternity instead of a Trinity."[20] John next proceeded to attack the leading bishops among the Monophysites. He arrested Paul, bishop of Aphrodisias and metropolitan of Caria, and deprived him of his orders as an opponent of Chalcedon.[21] He followed this up by the imprisonment of four distinguished bishops, all anti-Chalcedonian: John of Ephesus,[22] the historian; Stephen,[23] metropolitan of Cyprus; Paul[24] the Black, Patriarch of Antioch, 542—†78; and Elisha[25] a suffragan of Sardis; and he annulled their orders, in order to extend his own jurisdiction.[26] In all this John III. had the support of his sovereigns, Justin and Sophia:[27] and it is clear that, while constant contention had been going on for over an hundred years after the Council of Chalcedon between Orthodox and Monophysite—or, rather, between " Synodites " and " Orthodox," as the Monophysites would say—the final breach occurred under Justin II., and in consequence of the persecution directed by his Patriarch John III., Tiberius, as Cæsar, 574—8, refused to be party to it. Some of the Monophysites, in their attitude towards the Council, made a distinction between the position of Pope Leo and the tenets of St. Cyril with whom they agreed. " Tell me," said the Cæsar, when importuned by the Patriarch to countenance the persecution, " are these ' Distinguishers '[28] heretics? " " No," John was forced to reply, " they are not heretics; but they won't have anything to do with us." " Then, go and be quiet," retorted Tiberius, " I've quite enough to do with fighting barbarians, without fighting our own people as well."[29]

On the death of John, Eutychius was restored to the Patriarchate and held it for five years, 577—†82, until his death. He had spent the twelve previous years in exile at his old monastery of Amasia in Pontus: and, on his restoration, he wrote in support of the two natures in Christ[30] in defence of the impalpability of our bodies in the resurrection.[31] Gregory the Great was then residing at Constantinople, 582—5, as *apocrisiarius* of Pope Pelagius II., 578—†90: and contested this view. What then of " Handle me and see "?[32] he urged: to which, in the end, Eutychius replied with " Flesh and blood shall not inherit the Kingdom of God."[33] But the controversy left each side unconvinced by the other; and its main interest is that Tiberius II. took the plain man's view of the matter: and, after he had tried, in vain, to reconcile the disputants, ordered his Patriarch's book to be burnt.[34] Perhaps this rebuff turned the energies of Eutychius into another direction. In the fourth year of his restoration, 580, he took up the persecution of the Monophysites:[35] " ascribing," says John of Ephesus, " the ill-success of his books to the machinations of ' the orthodox.' "[36] He let loose upon them officials and soldiers, greedy for plunder, and threw them into prison for the sake of it. Tiberius was now Emperor; and Eutychius asked for his support. " Trouble me about such things no more," replied the Emperor, " I have as much as I can do with the wars I am engaged in. You must act in church-matters according to what you think right, at your own risk. Look to it yourself. I am free from guilt in this matter."[37] He gave him a free hand: but he must share the responsibility.

But in 582 that regime came to an end. Tiberius II. was succeeded by Maurice, 582—†602, and Eutychius by John IV., the Faster, 582—†95. John was too much concerned with vindicating against Pope Gregory,[38] 590—†604, his claim to the title of Œcumenical Patriarch, and both Emperor and Patriarch with putting the see of New Rome on a level with the see of Old Rome, to trouble about Monophysites; and the persecution died down. But its effects remained,—in the Monophysite schism that dates from this epoch. These effects, accentuated by other causes, have issued in the Armenians, Jacobite and Coptic Churches of to-day.

§ 6. The Church of Armenia[39] was the first of the churches which became Monophysite to adopt that creed. But this was due, in no small measure, to the political exigencies imposed upon Armenia by its geographical situation. The country lay between the rival empires of Rome and Persia; and was the battle-ground between them. At the time of the Synod of Chalcedon, 451, the Armenians were hard pressed by the persecuting edict,[40] 449, of Iazdgerd II., King of Persia, 438—†57, the object of which was to enforce Mazdäism on all his subjects. The Emperor Marcian, 450—†7, gave them no help; and they naturally took but little interest in his Council. After successive revolts, they secured their liberty under Balasch II., 484—†8; and meanwhile the Emperor Zeno, 474—†91, in order to conciliate opponents of the Council, had issued the *Henoticon*,[41] or "Instrument of Union," 482: under which the official religion of the Empire became virtually Monophysite. The Armenians, still in fear of Persia, made a bid for the support of the Romans; and at the Synod of Valarshapat (where now is the convent of Etchmiadzin) 491, under the Catholicus[42] Babken I., 490—†515, in conjunction with the bishops of Georgia, Iberia and Albania, they approved the *Henoticon* and denounced the Council of Chalcedon. This condemnation was re-affirmed, under the Catholicus Nerses II., at the Synod of Dvin, 525—7—a city on the left bank of the Araxes, to the S.E. of Valarshapat, and from the fifth to the tenth century the seat of the Catholicate. It was renewed, in the reign of Chosroes I., 531—†78, at a second Synod of Dvin, 551, under the Catholicus Moses II., 549—†79. Armenia, since 428, had been ruled by *marzbans* or Governors-General, appointed from the nobility, native or Persian, by the King of Persia. Between 564—72 they inaugurated a regular persecution, outraging Armenian women and enforcing conversion to Mazdäism. A revolt ensued, under the leadership of Vartan Mamegounian; and the Armenians sought the aid of the Emperor Justin II. who, 572, declared war against Persia.[43] The war proceeded with varying fortunes, until Maurice, then *Comes excubitorum*, took the field. He conducted a successful campaign, 577; and then invited the Catholicus Moses II., 549—†79, to a Synod of Constantinople, in the hope of re-union between the churches of Armenia and the Empire. At that time, as now, the

Armenians used unleavened bread and the unmixed chalice at the Eucharist; whereas the Byzantine Rite employed leavened bread[44] and infused hot water[45] into the chalice after the Commixture. " None of your leavened bread and hot water for me! " was the unceremonious reply of the Catholicus. Next year, Chosroes I. died: and was succeeded by Hormuzd, 579—†90. But a revolution broke out in Persia, and its strength was so reduced that Maurice, now Emperor, 582—†602, was able to make peace on advantageous terms with Chosroes II., 590—†628. He placed him upon the throne of his fathers; and, in return, received Persarmenia. The Armenians, however, were as unwilling as ever to yield up their independence to the Roman Empire, and to accept its orthodoxy. In 596, the Catholicus Abraham I., 594—†600, at a third Synod of Dvin, again repudiated the Council of Chalcedon; and when Chosroes II., in his turn, became a menace to the Romans, the repudiation was renewed, 616, to show that the Christianity of Armenia was different from that of the Romans and to secure his favour. It was different indeed. An hereditary priesthood and animal sacrifices long survived. " The Eucharist was long associated with the *matal* or animal victim; and only in the eighth century do we hear of an interval of time being left between the fleshly and the spiritual sacrifices, as the two rites were then called."[46] Thus the Armenian Church became settled in its adherence to Monophysitism; but the Synods which secured it in this allegiance can hardly be called free. They repudiated the Christianity of the Roman Empire because it was a matter of life and death to them to stand well with the Kings of Persia.

§ 7. In Syria, for an hundred years after the Council of Chalcedon, there had been constant contention between Orthodox and Monophysite; the Patriarchs of Antioch being sometimes of the one party and sometimes of the other. Best known of the Monophysite Patriarchs was Severus, who held the see from 512—8; when he was compelled to seek refuge at Alexandria. There he took sides against a fellow-exile Julian, bishop of Halicarnassus in Caria, ?—536. Julian maintained that, even before the Resurrection, the Body of Christ was incorruptible : or rather, not subject to decay at all. To this Severus replied that it shared in the infirmities common to all human bodies. The two parties denounced each other as *Aphthartodocetae* and *Phthartolatrae* respectively; and Severus continued to be the leader of the Monophysites of the latter persuasion until his death in Egypt, 539. An oration, attributed to Gregory of Nyssa, is really his;[47] and it is interesting as an early attempt to harmonise the Gospel-narratives of the appearances of our Lord after His Resurrection. Upon the death of Severus, a double succession of Patriarchs of Antioch ensued during the reign of Justinian, and has continued to the present day.[48] But the final breach between Orthodox and Monophysite took place under Justin II., 565—†78; and was the consequence of the persecution recorded by John of Ephesus. John was himself a Syrian, being born at Amida (now Diabekr). He wrote in Syriac; and was the first Syriac historian. From him we learn that the succession of the Monophysites and their organisation into a separate church in Syria was the work of James Baradai (Baradaeus) or Zanzalus, a monk of a monastery near Edessa, who came to Constantinople, c. A.D. 540, to plead the cause of Monophysitism. After remaining there fifteen years, he was consecrated bishop by the imprisoned Monophysite bishops in the capital, and sent to Syria to organise his sect. " He consecrated Sergius[49] to succeed Severus at Antioch, and appointed Paul the Black to succeed Sergius. He is said to have ordained two patriarchs, eighty-nine bishops and an enormous number of clergy. . . . He was a bishop with no fixed see. He died in 578; and, after his death, the Monophysites were driven from Antioch." His followers were nicknamed " Jacobites " by their opponents; and are so called to this day. But they adopted the name themselves, " tracing it, however erroneously, to the Apostle James, to whom also they ascribe their principal liturgy. " Their controversy with the Greeks, like the controversy of the East Syrians with the Greeks, was not only theological; it was largely tinged with national differences. Indeed, both were, to a considerable extent, contests between Syriac thought and Hellenistic culture."[50]

§ 8. At this point, we may pass for a moment from the West-Syrians to the East-Syrians;[51] for during the time that the churches of "the West" were becoming Monophysite, the "Nestorians" of "the East," beyond the frontier, were developing an independence of their own.

The independence of the Church in Persia had been attained in the fifth century. At the synod of Seleucia-Ctesiphon, 410, the bishop of that city assumed the title of Catholicus,[52] i.e. virtually, Patriarch. Fourteen years later, at the synod of Markabta of the Arabs, 424, the Church of Persia proclaimed its independence[53]—not so much in any spirit of schism as to escape from persecution and secure the protection of the King of Persia by letting it be seen that the Christianity of his subjects was distinct from that of his enemies the Romans. The ground was thus prepared for the spread of Nestorianism in Persia when, c. 435, it was driven from the Empire. Chief agent of its propagation was Barsumas (Barsōmā), 420—†92, metropolitan of Nisibis. By the *Henoticon*,[54] 482, of Zeno, 474—†91, the Roman Empire became officially Monophysite ; and Barsōmā took advantage of this to assure King Piroz, 457—†85, that the creed of the church in Persia[55] was different from that of the Romans. Thus he secured the independence which the church had claimed. Piroz was succeeded on the throne by Balas, 485—†8. No friend to Barsōmā, he appointed his rival Acacius as Catholicus, 485—†96. Barsōmā devoted himself, as metropolitan of Nisibis, to re-founding there the School of Edessa, which had been dispersed in 489, by order of Zeno; and under Narsai, †502, whom Barsōmā had appointed its Rector, it became both the well-spring of Nestorianism in Persia and the nursery of patriarchs, bishops and teachers.

Narsai was among its first teachers. He had already been teaching there for twenty years when he was among those who were expelled from Edessa to Nisibis in 457.

He was a poet and a homilist, called "the Harp of the Spirit"; and among his *Homilies*[56] are four which are of first importance for the history of the Eastern rite. No. xvii. is a "careful and detailed exposition of the Mass. . . . Nos. xxii. and xxi., in that order, describe the rite of Baptism," while No. xxxii., "On the Church and the Priesthood," contains some interesting liturgical references. In the service for Baptism, we notice the curious peculiarity that there was no anointing after Baptism. The absence of it was in accordance with original custom; and a post-baptismal unction seems to have been an innovation of c. 650.[57] As to the Eucharistic Liturgy, there are now three Anaphoras used by the East Syrians. The first is that of (1) the Liturgy of the Apostles Addai and Mari.[58] It has several early features: an undeveloped form of the invocation of the Holy Spirit[59] and the absence of the recitation of the Institution.[60] The other two are those of the Liturgies attributed to (2) Theodore the Interpreter[61] and (3) Nestorius.[62] All three are used with one common Pro-anaphora, and are all of the East-Syrian family, though the author of the third "must have had a Byzantine liturgy before him."[63] As to date, while the first must have been composed before A.D. 431, the two others are earlier than Narsai. His *Homily* brings out several features worthy of notice: the inclusion of the Creed[64] at a date earlier than had hitherto been suspected in any liturgy;[65] the absence of a veil or screen to shut out the act of consecration from the view of the people;[66] the silent recitation of the prayer of consecration;[67] and the early development of considerable ceremonial magnificence in vestments,[68] incense,[69] fans,[70] lamps,[69] bowing and genuflexions.[71] On the contrary, the singing is confined to Creed, Sanctus and Communion, and was, as yet, "a more popular than an artistic element of Christian worship."[72] There are also no examples of the litanies, now found in all Eastern rites.[73]

But to return from Barsōmā's nominee to his rival, Acacius, at a Council of February, 486, asserted the Two Natures in an ambiguous formula.[74] Barsōmā could accept it; and yet it could be offered as testimony to the orthodoxy of the Catholicus and his church. Acacius, on a visit to Constantinople, 491, both presented it and obtained its recognition: and there was thus friendly intercourse again between the churches of the Empire and of Persia. Acacius returned from his embassy to find Barsōmā dead: and was succeeded in the Catholicate by Babai, 496—†505, under whom there took place a Council, 497, permitting the clergy to marry.[75] Except for the requirement that bishops are to remain celibate, this is the rule of the East Syrians to-day. Babai was followed by the Catholicus Silas, 505—†23; who was not only married, despite the canon, but bullied by his wife. His rule was insignificant: and there ensued a long period during which the Catholicate was disputed between Elisha, the son-in-law of Silas, and Narses. It is known as "The Duality," 523—39; and was a time of confusion, from which the East Syrians were rescued by "the greatest and noblest of the patriarchs of the East,"[76] Mar Abha the Great, 540—†52.

Mar Abha[77] was a convert from Mazdäism, and became a professor in the School of Nisibis. In this capacity, he visited Jerusalem, Egypt, Greece and Constantinople, during the reign of Justinian. Here he was received into communion: for the Empire was once more dyophysite. On his return to Persia, 536, persecution again began to threaten the church: for Roman and Persian Christians were now alike dyophysite; and Justinian was again at war with Persia, c. 540, under Chosroes I., 531—†78. But this did not deter Mar Abha, as Catholicus, from setting on foot a programme of reform. At a synod of 540, he appears to have admitted the Council of Chalcedon,[78] and he caused the faith of Nicæa to be accepted "as expounded by Theodore."[79] He undertook a visitation[80] to re-inforce discipline, correcting schisms and abuses consequent upon The Duality. He put out pastorals *De recta fide*[81] and *De moribus*.[82] Then, returning to Seleucia-Ctesiphon (spring, 541), he devoted his days to correspondence, to teaching and to affairs: setting aside successive hours of the day for each. He set up an electoral college[83] to put an end to rivalries among candidates for the Catholicate and charged the college with the appointment so far as it could be kept independent of the nomination of the Crown. He busied himself with the revival and reform of monastic life.[84] But Mar Abha was a renegade from Mazdäism, and as such, liable to penalties to which converts from other religions were not exposed. His tenure of office was harassed by seven years of exile in Azerbaijan, 543—50, and by nine years of persecution. But this did not hinder him from carrying on the government of his church from his place of banishment, till his death, 29th February, 552.

He was followed, 552—604, in the last half of the sixth century co-incident with the successors of Justinian from Justin to Maurice, by four Catholici of lesser mould. First came Joseph, 552—†70, a good doctor but a poor patriarch:[85] of autocratic temper, who took bribes and was deposed. Then Ezekiel,[86] 570—†82: under whom the history of the East Syrians was uneventful because of a fresh outbreak of the Plague which had devastated the Roman Empire a generation before. Ezekiel was succeeded by Ishu-yahb I., 582—†96; under whom a Council affirmed the orthodoxy of Theodore of Mopsuestia,[87] for they had at last heard with indignation of the posthumous condemnation of the great teacher of "The East" by the Fifth Œcumenical Council, 553. The East-Syrians then differed from the church of the Empire not so much in doctrine as "over the names of doctors."[88] But they now considered themselves separate from the Romans. Then followed Sabr-Ishu as Catholicus, 596—†604. He was a saint and ascetic, formerly bishop of Lashom and greatly reverenced by Shirin,[89] the Christian wife of Chosroes II., 590—†628. His Catholicate was hardly a success; for the saint, like St. Chrysostom, was too severe a disciplinarian to be a wise ruler. Before its close, there set in the final phase of the long-drawn rivalry between Rome and Persia. Chosroes II. took up arms to avenge his "father" Maurice upon the usurper Phocas. He carried them to the shores of the Bosporus, till he was at length hurled back by the victories of

Heraclius. Both Empires then fell victims to the Arabs; and the East-Syrians, after being caught in the titanic struggle, settled down to the condition, only ended by the last Great War, of being a melet under Mahometan rule.

§ 9. Adjacent to Syria is Egypt; and we return to trace the dominance of Monophysite over Melkite among its people, the Copts.[90]

The growth of Christianity amongst the Copts begins to appear in the third century. There are Egyptian names[91] among the martyrs of the Decian persecution, 249—51. Origen, †254, himself a confessor in that persecution, was a copt. So also were Antony †356 and Pachomius †346, the founders respectively of the eremitic and the cœnobitic types of Egyptian monasticism. Moreover, the Scriptures were translated[92] into the three dialects of the Coptic tongue—Sahidic, the dialect of Upper Egypt; Middle Egyptian, the dialect of Memphis and the Fayum; and Bohairic, the dialect of the Delta—by the fifth century. Probably this rapid progress of the Gospel among the native Egyptians may be due to its offer of a religion based upon morality and provided with a clear doctrine of life after death—a religion such as would be congenial to their traditional temperament. Native Christianity also was predominantly monastic. The Copts were oppressed by the "Greek" landowners, and impoverished by Nubians and other invaders from the desert. The Roman Government was too weak to interfere. But the monasteries provided a refuge. A monk, Senoute[93] (Schnoudi, †451), maintained, for three months, twenty thousand men, as well as women and children[94] who had been rescued from the Blemmyes to the south. Thus Egypt was solidly Christian, and Upper Egypt monastic, by the fifth century. In the fourth, Athanasius, as archbishop of Alexandria, 328—†73, had as many as an hundred suffragans.[95]

The Christianity of Egypt, however, became the prey of divisions.[96] Dioscorus, patriarch of Alexandria, 444—51, was condemned by the Council of Chalcedon, 451, and banished by the Emperor Marcian, 450—†7; and Proterius, an orthodox prelate, was put in as his successor, 452—†7. The division between the parties represented by Proterius and his predecessor was outwardly one of religion: for the Council taught that in Christ there is one Person in two Natures, whereas its opponents held but one Nature of Christ [and that] incarnate. But the fundamental division went further. It was racial and political. The Proterians were the Court party; mainly of foreign extraction, and drawn from the various Greek-speaking races of the Eastern Roman Empire. As such, they were labelled by their opponents Melkites or Imperialists. The mass of the people were racially different from the Greeks and politically hostile to the Roman Government. Linguistically, also, they spoke not Greek but the vernacular. In religion, they were Monophysites.

These divisions, then, national as well as religious, produced a standing conflict for the patriarchal throne.

For thirty years, 451—82, from the Council of Chalcedon to the *Henoticon*[97] of Zeno, 474—†91, possession of it oscillated between prelates of orthodox Christology, appointed and supported by the Government, and intruders of anti-Chalcedonian opinions who succeeded from time to time in ousting them and seizing upon the Chair of St. Mark. Thus Proterius, 451—†7, the nominee of the Government, was murdered upon the death of the Emperor Marcian, and his place was taken by Timothy the Cat,[98] 457—60. Timothy had to pay for this intrusion by a long exile, 460—76, under the orthodox Emperors, Leo I., 457—†74, and Zeno; and during this period the orthodox Timothy Salofaciolus[99] occupied the patriarchal throne. With the temporary usurpation of the Emperor Basiliscus, 475—7, and his *Encyclical,*[100] 476, intended to make a bid for the support of the Monophysites, Timothy the Cat returned, 476—†7. But on his death, Timothy Salofaciolus was reinstated, 477—†82; and he was followed by John I. (Talaia[101]), 482, who, however, failed to maintain his authority, in the face of popular opposition and, on taking refuge in Rome, was made bishop of Nola.

A new period in the conflict now set in. Zeno put out the *Henoticon,*[102] 482, in order to conciliate the

HIS HOLINESS DAMIANUS, PATRIARCH OF JERUSALEM.

See p. 310.]

Monophysites throughout the Empire, not by repudiating but by belittling the Council of Chalcedon. This document was accepted by Peter[103] (Mongus) who had been elected by the Monophysites to succeed Timothy the Cat. He now received the Imperial recognition, and ruled as patriarch, 483—†90. With him began a succession of patriarchs, seven in all, who ruled for fifty-five years and were entirely devoted to the Monophysite cause. These were Peter (Mongus, or the Stammerer); Athanasius II., 490—†7; John I. (Mela), 497—†506; John II. (Niciota), 506—†17; Dioscorus II., 517—†9, nephew of Timothy the Cat; Timothy III., 519—†36; and Theodosius,[104] 536—8. By this time, an Orthodox reaction, after the pro-Monophysite policy of Zeno, †491 and Anastasius, 491—†518, had firmly established itself under the House of Justin, 518—610; and Orthodoxy was strenuously asserted by the rule of Justinian, 527—†65. He deposed Theodosius,[105] because of his Monophysitism, and appointed Paul,[106] 537—42. But Justinian had often to find his measures quietly modified through the Monophysite leanings of his Empress Theodora. She succeeded in getting a Council at Gaza to depose Paul, and to substitute Zoilus,[107] 542—†51. Then followed five Orthodox patriarchs till the Persian conquest of Egypt which ensued upon the fall of the House of Justin: Apollinaris, 551—†70; and John II.[108] 570—†80; Eulogius,[109] 580—†607; Theodorus Scribo,[110] 607—†9; and John III.[111] (the Almoner), 609—†19. Of these, the most interesting to us is Eulogius, the friend and correspondent of St. Gregory the Great. The Pope congratulated his brother of Alexandria on winning over the heretics, and told him that he was having equal success with our heathen forefathers in England.[112]

But the congratulations were scarcely justified: for these divisions proved fatal to the Christianity of Egypt. In the upper country, political and social life, together with commerce and literature, were maintained by the monks. But the minority of the population, not connected by the monastic institutions, were crushed by cruel burdens: and religious life was gradually sinking to a low ebb and distinguished by little spirituality. " In the year 616 the break-up of the Imperial power in Egypt began with the occupation of the country by the Persians on behalf of the Sassanian King Chosroes II., 590—†628. For ten years they held sway in Egypt. Whether the Copts welcomed their new masters is a matter of some doubt. That they hated the Byzantine domination is certain. Ever since Justinian had given the Melkite Patriarch the civil and military authority of a prefect, in the futile hope of coercing the Monophysites into orthodoxy, the Copts had been harried and oppressed by the Imperial power. The whole nation now looked to their own elected Patriarch, not so much as the champion of the Monophysite doctrine, but as the leader of the nationalists against the minions of Imperial bigotry and corruption. The wonderful victories of Heraclius, who drove out the Persians and re-conquered Jerusalem and the Holy Sepulchre, were a cause of rejoicing to Orthodox and Monophysite alike throughout the Eastern Empire; and it is possible that a wiser statesman than the Emperor might, amid the universal rejoicings of Christendom, have secured some kind of reconciliation. But Heraclius would extend no tolerance to heretics, with the result that, a few years later, when a sterner and more implacable enemy was at the gate, the Copts of Egypt were ready to welcome him. In 642 Egypt was ceded to 'Amr ibn al-'As, who had conquered it in the name of Islām." Whether the conquest was aided according to Arab tradition by the treachery of one called Mukaukis, supposed to have been the Coptic Patriarch: or, according to a modern authority, by none other than Cyrus[113] the Caucasian, whom Heraclius had appointed as the Melkite Patriarch, 630—†43, the Copts at any rate " welcomed their new masters as a change which, as they thought, could not in any case be for the worse."[114]

In doctrine, the Copts repudiate Eutyches as well as Nestorius: and this may be seen from the doctrinal formula with which the priest at the Elevation hails " the body and the blood of Immanuel our God. . . . This is the quickening flesh which thine only-begotten Son our

Lord and our God and our Saviour Jesus Christ took of the lady of us all, the holy Theotokos St. Mary; he made it one with his godhead without confusion and without mixture and without alteration. Having confessed the good confession before Pontius Pilate he gave it also for us on the holy tree of the cross by his own will himself for us all. I verily believe that his godhead was not severed from his manhood for one moment nor for the twinkling of an eye."[115] They were active as missionaries, in spite of the Arab invasion: for " during the sixth and seventh centuries the whole of Nubia was Christianised . . . from Assuan to the Blue Nile." Christianity had also penetrated into Abyssinia: which still remains Christian and Monophysite, though the Gospel perished in Nubia during the fifteenth century. The metropolitan of Abyssinia is a Coptic bishop appointed by the Patriarch of Alexandria, with three suffragans. But both the hierarchy and the numbers of Copts in Egypt are much reduced. There is now a Coptic Patriarch at Cairo, with twelve suffragans in Egypt and one at Khartum. Their flocks are a community of about 667,000. Some are wealthy; and the majority are better educated than the mass of their fellow-countrymen. Though they form only six per cent of the population, seventeen per cent of the children at school are Copts.

CHAPTER VI.

THE DYNASTY OF HERACLIUS, 610—95, AND THE FIRST ANARCHY, 695—717.

MOHAMMEDANISM AND MONOTHELETISM.

BISHOPS OF THE CHIEF SEES, 610—717.

Rome.	Constantinople.	Antioch.
Boniface IV. 608—15	Sergius I. 610—38	Macedonius 639—49
Adeodatus I. 615—9	Pyrrhus 638—41	George I. ?
Boniface V. 619—25	Paul II. 641—52	Macarius ?—681
Honorius I. 625—38	Pyrrhus² 651—2	Theophanes 681—?
Severinus 640	Peter 652—64	Thomas ?—685
John IV. 640—2	Thomas II. 665—8	George II. 685?—702
Theodore I. 642—9	John V. 668—74	
Martin I. 649—55	Constantine I. 674—6	
Eugenius I. 655—6	Theodore I. 676—8	
Vitalian 657—72	George I. 678—83	
Adeodatus II. 672—6	Theodore I.² 683—6	
	Paul III. 686—93	Jerusalem.
Donus I. 676—8	Callinicus I. 693—705	Zacharias 609—29
Agatho 678—82	Cyrus 705—11	Modestus 629—33
Leo II. 682—3	John VI. 711—15	Sophronius 634—8
Benedict II. 684—5	Germanus I. 715—30	* * *
John V. 685—6		John V. 705—?
Konon 686—7		
Sergius I. 687—701		
John VI. 701—5		
John VII. 705—7		
Sisinnius 708		
Constantine 708—15		

ALEXANDRIA.

Orthodox.	Monophysite.
John III. 609—19	Anastasius 603—14
George 620—30	Andronicus 614—22
Cyrus 630—43	Benjamin 623—62
Peter II. 643—52	Agatho 662—80
[Vacant 75 years.]	John III. 680—9
	Isaac 690—3
	Simon I. 694—701
	Alexander II. 703—26

THE DYNASTY OF HERACLIUS, 610—95.

See table in J. B. Bury, *Hist. Later Roman Empire*, ii. p. vi. (ed. 1889).

(1) Eudocia = Heraclius 610—†41 = (2) Martina (his niece).
| |
Gregoria=Constantine III. †641   Heraclonas
|
Constans II. 642—†68
|
Constantine IV. 668—†85 = Anastasia
(Pogonatus) |
            Justinian II. 685—95 and 705—†11
            (Rhinotmetus)

CHAPTER VI.

THE DYNASTY OF HERACLIUS, 610—95, AND THE FIRST ANARCHY 695—717: MOHAMMEDANISM AND MONOTHELETISM.

§ 1. THE usurpation of Phocas, 602—†10, came to an end with the accession to power of the dynasty of Heraclius, 610—95, son of an exarch of Africa. Five Emperors belonged to this house; and came to the throne in direct succession: Heraclius, 610—†41, its founder, who restored order at home and rolled back the tide of the Persian invasions; his son Constantine III., †641, who reigned but for three and a half months; his grandson Constans II., 642—†68; and his great-grandson Constantine IV. (Pogonatus), 668—†85. These had to stand the shock of the Saracen invasions. For no sooner were his great victories over Persia won, 622—9, than Heraclius had to see one province after another torn from his Empire by the Saracens, and Constans II. had to suffer some slighter reverses. But, at last, the storm was spent; and Constantine IV., by the naval victory off Syllaeum in Pamphylia, 678, gave the first check to the advance of Islām. All these sovereigns were rulers of character and ability. Heraclius exhibited the prudence of a statesman during the first ten years of his rule when he confined himself to the work of reorganisation, and he displayed the spirit of a great soldier when he took the field. Constans II. was a strong and independent ruler whose " foreign policy was, on the whole, successful." Constantine IV. acquired great prestige with the princes of Western Europe, as the successful defender of Christian civilisation against Mohammedanism: and no less favour with the Roman See. Unlike his predecessors, Heraclius and Constans, who each sought to impose his own doctrinal compromise, the *Ecthesis* (638) and the *Type*

(648), upon his subjects, Constantine left the question of Monotheletism to be decided by the Church. Fifth Emperor of this dynasty was Justinian II., 685—95, his son. He had all the energy of Heraclius: but none of the cool judgment which distinguished his father and grandfather. Like all of his house, he was a man of pure life. But his reign became a nightmare of oppression: and there ensued a period of twenty years' disorder, in the course of which five usurpers and Justinian II. himself, during a temporary restoration, 705—†11, endeavoured to seize or to keep the throne. It is known in the history of the Later Roman Empire as the "First Anarchy," 695—717. In the history of the Church, the epoch of Heraclius may be taken as the third period in ecclesiastical history since the Council of Chalcedon. The first may be reckoned from 451—518; and is occupied with the reaction against that Council representing the first phase in the Monophysite movement. The second period runs from 518—610, when Orthodoxy was dominant under the House of Justin; but concessions had to be made to Monophysitism. Thus, in the second phase of the Monophysite movement, 482—565, attempts were made under Zeno by the *Henoticon*, 482, and under Justinian by the condemnation of the *Three Chapters*, 553, to win its adherents back; but in vain. For in its third phase, 565—622, the Monophysites founded National Churches of their own in Armenia, Syria and Egypt. The third period in the history of the Church is that now before us when, owing to the Persian and Saracen invasions, under the dynasty of Heraclius, a reckoning had to be made with Mohammedanism beyond the Empire and with Monotheletism within.

§ 2. The renewal of war between Rome and Persia had had a direct effect upon the religious situation in the Roman Empire.

(i.) To begin with the progress of the Persian arms. Chosroes II., 590—†628, had recovered his throne by the help of the Emperor Maurice. On the murder of Maurice by Phocas, he made a pretext of avenging his death upon the usurper by renewing the old rivalries and

The Dynasty of Heraclius

invading the Empire. The Persians seized the Roman frontier fortress of Dara, 606, raided Mesopotamia and Syria, crossed Asia Minor and appeared for a time before Chalcedon, 608. Next year, Cæsarea in Cappadocia opened its gates. Such was their progress before the death of Phocas. After the accession of Heraclius, their attacks became much more serious. In 612 they entered Syria; and Antioch, Apamea and Emesa, with other important cities, fell one after another into their hands. Shahrbaraz conquered Syria in 613 and took Damascus. In 614, Palestine: where he took Jerusalem, and carried off the True Cross to Ctesiphon. In 616, Egypt. Meanwhile, Shahen overran Asia, 615, as far as Chalcedon: and, to cover his communications, fortified Ancyra, 619. As if these disasters were not enough, the Avars appeared before Constantinople from N. and W.; the Lombards made further conquests in Italy; and, between 621—31, the Empire lost its last foothold in Spain.

(ii.) For twelve years after his accession, Heraclius had to suffer these blows with what endurance he could. The disaffection of the nobles, the disordered state of the finances and the want of an efficient army made it impossible for him to move against the enemies of his country, until he had secured his power. But, at last, he was ready for war: and, answering to his own enthusiasm, the people gave it the character of a crusade. The Emperor took the field, supported by Sergius, Patriarch of Constantinople, 610—†38, who placed at his disposal the treasures of the churches, and sustained by the zeal of the populace for the recovery of the Holy Places and of the True Cross. In five campaigns, he completely shattered the power of Persia. In 623 he recovered Azerbaijan, and in 624 Armenia. In 625 he made himself master of Cilicia; and in 626 he broke the combined forces of Avars[1] and Persians who were besieging Constantinople. The fifth and last campaign was directed against the Persian frontier in Mesopotamia. Here, in 627, he captured Nineveh and, in 628, the Persian capital of Seleucia-Ctesiphon: whence he brought back the True Cross in triumph to Constantinople and restored it in person to Jerusalem, 629. Such an uninterrupted succession of victories has given Heraclius rank among the great military leaders of all time; with the peculiar glory that they were won in defence of his country and not out of the lust of conquest. Peace was made with Persia, 629.

(iii.) But part of the price of these victories was the imperious necessity for restoring religious unity to the Empire: and this meant that Heraclius would have to win over the Monophysites of Syria and Egypt, now once more its citizens. Supported by Sergius,[2] Patriarch of Constantinople, 610—†38, Cyrus,[3] bishop of Phasis, whom he made Patriarch of Alexandria, 630—†43, and Athanasius,[4] sixth Jacobite Patriarch of Antioch, 604—†31, he set himself, soon after setting out on the Persian campaigns, to find a formula of conciliation; and, to this end, put out the *Ecthesis*,[5] 638. The Empire was now apparently restored, and its prestige re-established throughout the East. Moreover, it was extended to the N.W. of the Balkan peninsula by the inclusion of Croats and Serbs; who were converted to Christianity probably about 678. But the finances were in a hopeless condition; and the separatist tendencies still unpacified. The doctrine, in which three of the Eastern patriarchs acquiesced, was contested by the fourth, Sophronius, Patriarch of Jerusalem, 634—†8.

§ 3. It was this situation that gave rise to the controversy concerning Monotheletism.[6] The problem of one or two "operations," or "wills," in Christ was not altogether new. The former position had been adopted by Severus, Monophysite Patriarch of Antioch, 512—8, who based it on the phrase [one] "theandric operation"[7] attributed to the Pseudo-Dionysius c. 500, and the latter by Leontius of Byzantium, 485—†543 : while about 600 the people of Alexandria were accustomed to speak of "one operation" and "one will" in the Saviour, though these expressions were distasteful to their Orthodox Patriarch Eulogius, 580—†607. It is probable that, but for the exigencies of politics, no more would have been heard of these discussions: but it was urgent to find a formula of union in the face of the common foes.[8] There is more than one account of the birth of the formula; but, according to Sergius, Patriarch of Constantinople, 610—†38, it dates[9] from the Armenian campaign of Heraclius in 623. At Theodosiopolis (now Erzerum), the Emperor met Paul, a follower of Severus, and tried without success to win him over to Monenergism.[10] In 626, he tried again, when in Lazica, to obtain the acceptance of "one operation" from Cyrus, bishop of Phasis. Cyrus could not make up his mind; and, at the command of Heraclius, he wrote to Sergius to ascertain whether or not he should admit in Christ, after the union, "one predominant operation."[11] Sergius reassured him:[12] and sent him authorities.[13] Then, 630, the Emperor took advantage of a vacancy at Alexandria to appoint Cyrus to that see, with instructions to attempt a union on this basis with the Monophysites of Egypt. Cyrus proved a skilful negotiator and the reunion was effected,[14] 633, being based on a series of nine propositions[15] which had been drawn up by the two parties. They avoided the Monophysite doctrine, but kept the Monophysite terminology; and the seventh proposition adopted the tenet of Monenergism, for it affirmed "that there was but one and the same Christ, working both the divine and the human actions by one theandric operation, as St. Dionysius teaches."[16] Both sides were satisfied. The Court had recovered the Monophysite population of Egypt, just at the time when the country had been re-conquered from Persia. And the Monophysites would say, not without good reason, that the victory was theirs:[17] for the recognition of "one operation" in Christ pointed directly towards "one Nature."

But this re-union was short-lived. Two monks, Sophronius,[18] a native of Palestine, and Maximus[19] the Confessor, 580—†662, both at the time in Egypt, declared their dissent. Sophronius, perceiving that there was force in the Monophysite claim to victory, begged Cyrus to denounce the nine propositions.[20] On his refusal, Sophronius went to put the same request before Sergius;[21] but the Patriarch managed to quiet his scruples, and the monk returned to his own country.[22] Shortly afterwards Sophronius was elected Patriarch of Jerusalem, 634—†8, —and, in a synodal letter,[23] announcing his accession to his fellow-patriarchs, he reasserted the doctrine of the two operations, though he nowhere speaks of two wills, in Christ. This letter is the most important document in the whole controversy, and a great theological treatise. Sergius, however, had forestalled its arrival in Rome by writing himself to Pope Honorius, 625—†38. After telling the Pope of the events just narrated up to the point of his interview with Sophronius, the Patriarch of Constantinople goes on to report that he has urged the Emperor simply to confess " that one and the same only-begotten Son of God, equally true God and true man, works both the divine and the human, and that from one and the same Incarnate Word all divine and human energy proceeds indivisibly and inseparably ":[24] and begs Honorius to concur in the policy of making no further mention of " one or two operations." The Pope accepted the suggestion: and sent two letters in reply: the first,[25] before he had heard from Sophronius: and the second after. In the former he, first, agreed in deprecating expression of opinion about the contested phrase. Secondly, he affirmed that Jesus Christ who is one Person worked in His two Natures, both divinely and humanly. Thirdly, he insisted that " We must hold the unity of Christ's will;[26] for, whilst the Word truly took our nature, He did not take our vitiated nature; He took our flesh, but not the law of the flesh which is repugnant to that of the Spirit. There was not, then, in Jesus Christ, a will tending in a direction differing from the law of the Spirit, or contrary to it: and the words ' I came down from heaven not to do mine own will, but the will of him that sent me,'[27] and ' Father, not what I will but what thou wilt,'[28] do not mark a will differing [from that of the Father], but merely the economy of the humanity which he had assumed."[29] In the second letter,[30] Honorius again deprecates the use of the controverted phrases; touches upon the true doctrine by reference to Leo's celebrated formula; and concludes that instead of speaking of one or two operations, we had better speak of " one operator and two operating natures."[31] He added that he was writing in the same sense both to Cyrus of Alexandria and to Sophronius of Jerusalem; and that the envoys of Sophronius had promised him that the Patriarch of Jerusalem would cease to speak of two operations on condition that the Patriarch of Alexandria would make no further mention of one.[32] Sergius was naturally encouraged by this reply: but, in order to parry the sudden declaration of Sophronius in favour of " two operations " he prepared the document, 636, which Heraclius promulgated as the *Ecthesis*,[33] 638. It is an Exposition of the Faith; and, after explaining the doctrines of the Trinity and the Incarnation, it comes to the subject of the operations and wills in the Incarnate. Deprecating " one operation " as tending to Monophysitism and " two operations " as suggestive of two *contrary* wills in Jesus Christ, it forbids the use of either phrase :[34] and then concludes by confessing " one will of our Lord Jesus Christ, the true God; for at no time did His rationally quickened flesh, separately and of its own impulse, and in opposition to the suggestion of the hypostatically united Logos, exercise its natural activity; but it exercised that activity at the time and in the manner and measure in which God wills it."[35] In the East the *Ecthesis* was generally accepted. This goes without saying, for it was an Imperial document.[36] But, upon the death of Honorius in the year of its publication, opposition to it began to gather in Rome and the West. Long years passed in the effort of the Byzantine Government to beat down the opposition, 638—78, and so to bind Orthodox and Monophysite of the East in united resistance to the Saracen invaders. At last, the invasions were brought to a standstill, 678; but not till after the loss of the Monophysite countries. Then there was no further need to buy their loyalty; and Old and New Rome united, at the Sixth Œcumenical Council, 680, in the final repudiation of Monotheletism.

§ 4. We must now give a brief sketch of the rise of Mohammedanism,[37] and trace the course of the Saracen invasions.[38]

(i.) In the year that Heraclius set out for the Persian Wars, Mohammed[39] took flight from Mecca to Medina, the City sc. of the Prophet,[40] 16th July, 622. This flight, or emigration (*hijra,*=hegira) marks the beginning of the Mohammedan era. Mohammed was born c. 570. About 594, he entered the service of a lady of means, by name Khadīja. She sent him into Syria on a commercial expedition which he discharged with success; and, on his return, he became her husband, ?595. After a time, he began to occupy himself with religious questions, and became conscious of a prophetic vocation, ?610. Among his first converts were his wife, his cousin Ali, and his friend Abū Bakr; and his teaching, as embodied in the earlier portions of the Koran, was directed against the polytheism and immorality — especially fornication, infanticide, theft, and lying—common among the surrounding tribes. It centres round three topics: (a) the unity and attributes of God, as in "The Chapter of Unity":[41]

'In the name of the merciful and compassionate God, say:
'He is God alone!
God the eternal!
He begets not and is not begotten!
Nor is there like unto Him any one!'

(b) The moral duties of mankind, and (c) the coming retribution:

'In the name[42] of the merciful and compassionate God,
When the inevitable [day of judgment] happens; none shall call its happening a lie!—abasing!—exalting!
When the earth shall quake, quaking! and the mountains shall crumble, crumbling, and become like motes dispersed!
And ye shall be three sorts;
And the fellows of the right hand—what right lucky fellows!
And the fellows of the left hand—what unlucky fellows!

And the foremost foremost.
These are they who are brought nigh,
In gardens of pleasure!
A crowd of those of yore, and a few of those of the latter day!
And gold-weft couches, reclining on them face to face.
Around them shall go eternal youths, with goblets and ewers and a cup of flowing wine; no headache shall feed therefrom, nor shall their wits be dimmed!
And fruits such as they deem the best;
And flesh of fowl as they desire;
And bright and large-eyed maidens like hidden pearls,
A reward for that which they have done,
And they shall hear no folly there, and no sin;
Only the speech " Peace, Peace ! "
And the fellows of the right, what right lucky fellows!
Amid thornless lote trees.
And tah'l trees, with piles of fruit;
And outspread shade,
And water poured out;
And fruit in abundance, neither failing nor forbidden;
And beds upraised!
Verily we have produced them [*sc.* the celestial damsels] a production,
And made them virgins, darlings of equal age [with their spouses] for the fellows of the right!
A crowd of those of yore, and a crowd of those of the latter day!
And the fellows of the left—what unlucky fellows!
In hot blasts and boiling water;
And a shade of pitchy smoke,
Neither cool nor generous!
Verily they were affluent ere this, and did persist in mighty crime; and used to say " What! when we

die, have become dust and bones, shall we indeed be raised? or our fathers of yore?"
Say "Verily those of yore, and those of the latter days, shall surely be gathered together unto the tryst of the well-known day."
"Then ye, O ye who err! who say it is a lie; shall eat of the Zaqqum tree and fill your bellies with it! a drink of boiling water! and drink as drinks the thirsty camel!"'

Mohammed's disciples called themselves Muslims, i.e., those who "surrendered themselves" to the new faith, as distinguished from the surrounding peoples who followed the hereditary cults; and the faith itself Islām= "surrender."[43] It was a monotheism which, as yet, he did not distinguish from the creed of the Jews and the Christians:

"Verily, those who believe and those who are Jews, and the Sabaeans and the Christians, whosoever believes in God and the last day and does what is right, there is no fear for them, nor shall they grieve":[44]

and though Mohammedanism differs from Christianity in that the one is the religion of a Book, and the other the religion of a Person, the one acceptance of a message[45] and the other union with a Saviour, yet they have this in common with one another and with Judaism, that all three being monotheistic religions and the first article of the creed of each being "I believe in one God,"[46] they are all missionary religions as well. The opposition of the people of Mecca led to the flight of Mohammed and the Muslims to Medina. Here for a year or more, they were in distress; and they began to relieve it by preying upon the caravans. Their first raids were upon the Jews; and then upon traders from Mecca, at the battle of Badr, 624. By this time, Mohammed had founded a community bound together exclusively by ties of religion; and was bent upon substituting monotheism for idolatry in Mecca. Early in 629, with about two thousand followers, he visited Mecca as a pilgrim. The inhabitants were impressed by his power, and began to go over to Islām;

The Dynasty of Heraclius 113

among them two of the aristocracy of the city: Khalid, afterwards the conqueror of Syria; and 'Amr ibn al-'As, of Egypt. In the autumn of that year, one of his detachments on the N.W. of Arabia came into conflict, for the first time, with the armies of Heraclius, and suffered a defeat at the battle of Mu'ta, a village to the east of the Dead Sea. But the Prophet recovered his prestige by, 630, the capture of Mecca. He died, 7th June, 632, while preparing another expedition against the Romans. Abū Bakr became the Khalifa or representative of the Prophet, 632—†4; and Omar his successor as Caliph, 634—†43, was the first to assume the title Amīr al-Mu'minīn or "Commander of the Faithful." In the autumn of 633, the Saracens began to invade Syria; at a time when Heraclius was stationed at Emesa. He set about collecting troops against them: and raids now gave way to campaigns for the conquest both of the Roman and the Persian Empire.

(ii.) Within three years[47] of the death of Heraclius, the reigns of the first two Caliphs sufficed not only to conquer Persia,[48] 636—40, and bring to an end the dynasty of the Sassanidae, 226—641, but to detach from the Roman Empire all its dependencies to the south— Syria, Mesopotamia, Egypt and North Africa. Thus in Syria[49] the Romans were defeated by the capture of Bostra, 623, and then at the battle of Ajnādain, 634, a village to the N.E. of Gaza in the direction of Jerusalem. Then followed the fall of Damascus, 635. Heraclius, worn out with campaigning, hurried south to Jerusalem in order to rescue the True Cross which he had brought back in triumph from Persia and replaced in the sanctuary six years before; and as he sailed home with the Sacred Relic he stood on the deck of his ship and took his leave of the East. "Farewell, Syria: farewell for ever." His forces were beaten at the decisive battle of the Yarmuk,[50] 636, a river which runs westward into the Jordan, just south of the Sea of Galilee. Jerusalem so vigorously defended by the Patriarch Sophronius, 634—†8, was obliged to open its gates, 637, to the Caliph Omar; and, 638, Antioch, Tripolis, Tyre, Cæsarea and fifteen other

I

towns surrendered. By 639 nothing was left in Syria belonging to the Roman Empire. In that year, Mesopotamia was lost to it by the capture, in succession, of the fortresses of Edessa, Constantine and Dara; and in July, 639, the conquest of Egypt[51] began with its invasion by 'Amr ibn al-'As. His first victories at Lycopolis (Assiut) and Heliopolis, six miles N.E. of Cairo, placed Upper and Middle Egypt in his power; and the Roman Government, unable to protect the Delta from the invaders, sent Cyrus, Patriarch of Alexandria, 630—†43, to make terms. In October, 642, he concluded a treaty which gave the Romans eleven months within which to leave the country; and by the evacuation of Alexandria, 29th September, 643, Egypt was lost to the Empire. So, too, were Cyrenaica and Tripolitana, 642—3; and the revolt of Gregory, Exarch of Africa, 646, facilitated the acquisition of Africa by the Saracens,[52] 647. Thus, within twenty years of their first attack on the Roman Empire, the Saracens had shorn away all its territories to east and south; and ruled from the Oxus to Carthage.

Then began the attack on the north. Mu'āwiya, the Governor of Syria, was the first to perceive the advantage which the Romans enjoyed, for the defence, by their command of the sea. He created a navy and surprised Cyprus, 648; destroyed Aradus, 649; and ravaged Cos and Rhodes, 654. Meanwhile, the Saracens had overrun southern Asia, 651, and Armenia, 652—4; but the barrier of the Taurus was still strong. Mu'āwiya therefore planned to support the land-attack on Asia by action at sea : and following along the coast of Lycia, he inflicted a defeat upon the Emperor Constans II., 642—†68, who was commanding in person, at the naval battle of Phœnix, 655. It was a tactical defeat, but a strategic success, for the Romans. A lull ensued, while Mu'āwiya had to secure his succession. He became Caliph 661—†79, the first of the thirteen Ommayad Caliphs of Damascus who ruled from 661—750. With his throne secure, in 663 he again took the offensive, harrying the coasts of Asia and, at last, appearing in the Bosporus, 668. In 669, the Saracens attacked Sicily and, 670, founded Kairawān, to the south

The Dynasty of Heraclius

of Carthage, in Africa. Then for five years, 673—8, they expended a supreme effort in striking at the heart of the Roman Empire, and laying siege to Constantinople by land and sea. The citizens destroyed the enemy vessels with the newly-invented " Greek-fire "; and manfully defended their city, till the besiegers sailed away. But the final blow was delivered by wind and weather. As the Saracen fleet made for home, it was caught in a storm off the coast of Pamphylia. Constantine IV., 668—†85, in hot pursuit, destroyed all that remained of it at the battle of Syllaeum, 678; while his generals inflicted so crushing a defeat upon the enemy, in his retreat by land from Constantinople, that only a shattered remnant reached Syria. Constantine IV. had thus administered the first check to the advance of Islām. The advantageous peace which he made with the Caliph, 679, created a great sensation throughout the West; and his alliance was sought by Western Kings and Castellans from Lombardy, France and, it would seem, England too. Never had the prestige of Rome stood so high, since the victories of Heraclius over the Persians. One effect of it was immediately to alter the religious policy of the Empire. Hitherto, under Heraclius and Constans II., the ruling idea had been to force Monotheletism on the subjects of the Empire in order to unite Monophysite and Orthodox in its defence. But the Monophysite regions were now permanently lost. The best defence would obviously be an alliance of Orthodox East with Catholic West, of New Rome with Old Rome, of Empire and Papacy: and this led to the condemnation of Monotheletism at the Sixth Œcumenical Council, 680.

§ 5. We return then to the history of Monotheletism[53] during the forty years from the *Ecthesis* of Heraclius to the victory of his great-grandson over the Saracens, 638—78.

(i.) The reaction against the *Ecthesis* began in Africa. In 645, Maximus the Confessor, 580—†662, held a colloquy[54] with Pyrrhus, ex-Patriarch of Constantinople, 638—41, and a Monothelete, in the presence of Gregory, Exarch of Africa; and, on the ground that will is a function of nature and not of person (for, otherwise there would be three wills in the Trinity, whereas there is but one),[55] obliged him to accept the doctrine of two wills, a human as well as a divine will, in Jesus Christ. Maximus was a person of influence. He had been secretary to the Emperor Heraclius. He was abbot of Chrysopolis (Scutari). He was also a great theologian. At his instigation, synods were held, 646, in the various provinces of Africa which sent letters[56] condemning Monotheletism both to Pope Theodore, 642—†9, and to Paul, the Monothelete Patriarch of Constantinople, 641—†52. Theodore, as requested, wrote to recall Paul to orthodoxy,[57] but, in the end, excommunicated him[58] because he persisted in his error.

(ii.) It was now the turn of the Emperor Constans II. to intervene: not simply in support of his Patriarch but in the interest of the unity of his Empire. He was only seventeen years of age; and he may well have been urged to this course: on ecclesiastical grounds by Paul: and by the Senate in pursuance of the policy, inaugurated by his grandfather, of conciliating Monophysite and Orthodox into common action against the enemies of their country. Constans therefore put out the *Type*[59] (=Decree), 648. It was unlike the *Ecthesis* in two respects. First, it deals with " will " whereas that dealt with " operation "; and so the *Type* marks the transition from the preliminary to the final stage of the controversy, from Monenergism to Monotheletism. Secondly, it was not a *symbolum* like the *Ecthesis* which Constans II. withdrew but simply a decree or edict. In spirit, it resembles the *Henoticon* of Zeno; for it does not enforce the doctrine of one or other side in the controversy, but seeks to go behind them both. Had the Emperor enforced the doctrine of one will in the *Type*, as Paul would probably have wished, he would have entered upon a line of action which might have had serious consequences in view of the strong partisanship of the populace of Constantinople in favour of two wills and of his personal unpopularity there. Constans contented himself, therefore, with a declaration in favour of the *status quo ante*.

The Dynasty of Heraclius

Under severe penalties, he requires, in the *Type*, " that our subjects . . . shall from the present moment onwards have no longer any permission to raise any sort of dispute . . . over the one will and energy, or over two wills and two energies . . . but everywhere shall be preserved the former customs, as before the disputes broke out, as if no such dispute had existed. . . Whoever dares to transgress this command is subject before all to the fearful judgment of Almighty God, and then also will be liable to the punishment for such as despise the imperial commands." It was a futile prohibition : not least because it gave the impression that, to the Emperor, one religion is as good as another—a doctrine acceptable enough to-day, but certain to provoke opposition in an Orthodox State.

(iii.) At Rome, it soon appeared that Constans II. was as good as his word. He was a strong and independent ruler : who took his own line, right or wrong. Pope Theodore, who had excommunicated his Patriarch, died 13th May, 649; and was succeeded by Martin I., 649—†55. Pope Martin was distinguished by a fine presence and physical strength, by courage and learning. He summoned the Lateran Synod,[60] of a hundred and five bishops mainly from Italy, Africa and the intervening islands, which sat 5th—31st October, 649. The Synod in its symbol or dogmatic formulary condemned Monotheletism and affirmed that " just as we believe in His two natures united without confusion, so we also believe in two natural wills [i.e., two wills each belonging to a nature], the divine will and the human ";[61] and, in its eighteenth canon,[62] repudiated both the *Ecthesis* and the *Type*. The Pope then circulated these decisions, by an encyclical to the rest of Christendom[63] and a letter communicating their terms to the Emperor.[64] The reply of Constans II. was characteristic. On the 13th June, 653, his emissary, Theodore Calliopas, Exarch of Ravenna, arrived in Rome, and carried off the Pope. He was brought to Constantinople, September, 654; and brutally treated till he died, 16th September, 655, an exile at Cherson and a martyr for the Catholic Faith; while Maximus the Confessor was horribly mutilated and died in banishment, 662.

The reason, though not the justification, for all this tyranny was that Constans II. was bent upon reviving the policy of Justinian. He would draw Italy and Africa closer into the frame of the Roman Empire. He would then present a compact resistance to the progress of the Saracens, more particularly by countering their recent successes in the West. The Balkans and Asia, for the time, were safe: but Africa had been invaded 647 and Sicily, 652. It was in pursuit of the same policy that Constans himself proceeded to the West, 662, partly to subdue the Lombards in Italy and partly to save Sicily and Africa. He left New Rome for Old Rome, where he was well received, 663, by Pope Vitalian, 657—†72 (the same who sent Theodore of Tarsus to be archbishop of Canterbury, 668—†90) and returned his courtesy by stealing the bronze tiles of the Pantheon (S. Maria Rotonda) to send them to Constantinople. The Emperor then made Syracuse his base of operations against the Saracens; and probably did much during his five years there, 663—8, to strengthen that hold of Byzantine civilisation upon southern Italy which was never relaxed till the eleventh century. But he was murdered in the baths of Syracuse: for as he was smearing himself with Gallic soap an assassin killed him with the soap dish. The new turn of events issued before long in the overthrow of Monotheletism.

(iv.) Constantine IV., 668—†85, had remained in Constantinople during the absence of his father, as his representative at the capital. On the news of his father's death, he left for Sicily to secure the situation. He came back with a beard. The populace hailed him with cries of [Beaver!] *Pogonatus:* and nicknames for Emperors, from this time onwards, became the vogue.

Within a few years, the political situation of the Empire underwent an entire transformation. The five years' siege of Constantinople, 673—8, ended in a great victory for the Romans, by land and sea, and in peace with the Saracens, 678. About the same time the Bulgars had settled in Mœsia, and, after collision with the

The Dynasty of Heraclius

Romans, had made peace in their turn, 679 : while the re-organisation of the Empire into *Themes,* which took place also about this period, served to consolidate its strength. Before the days of Justinian the civil and military authority had been divided; but, in some places, that great administrator had seen the advantage of uniting both powers under the same control. Maurice had extended the experiment, and made it general for defence of the frontiers. He had also created the Exarchate of Africa to keep the Berbers at bay, and the Exarchate of Ravenna for defence against the Lombards. The system now became general; and the provinces remaining to the Empire were grouped into *Themes,* each placed under a *Strategus* or General in command of an Army Corps, to whom the civil administration was subordinated. These commands were known as the *Themes* of Armenia, Anatolia, Opsikion (=*Obsequium,* so-called because the Imperial Guard were quartered there), Thrace and the Maritime Theme. The result of Bulgar and Slav infiltration was to rejuvenate the Empire; and of the administrative reorganisation to consolidate it. Constantine IV., therefore, had less to fear than his predecessors from the pressure of invaders north and east. What he needed was the cordial support of the West. His policy was to cut his losses, to concentrate and make good.

The ecclesiastical counterpart of this revolution was to win the support of the Roman See. His father had tried to beat down its resistance by persecuting Pope Martin precisely as Justinian had persecuted Pope Vigilius for the same reason : in either case, to conciliate the Monophysites of the East. But their countries were now lost to Mohammedan conquerors : and the need for conciliating their support was gone. The policy was reversed : and a doctrinal union with Rome was sought in order to obtain the political co-operation of the West. Moreover, the Church itself, and not the Emperor, for reasons of State, was to decide the course to be taken. Accordingly, 12th August, 678, Constantine IV. addressed a letter to the Roman See, proposing a conference.[65] The letter came into the hands of Pope Agatho, 678—†82. Rejoiced at the prospect of peace and unity, Agatho held a preliminary Synod at Rome,[66] Easter, 680, in order to collect Western opinion on the Monothelete question. Wilfrid, bishop of York, had been present at a Synod at Rome, October, 679, not in response to the summons, but on business of his own,[67] and the Pope regrets that, owing to distance, he had been unable to secure the presence of Theodore, archbishop of the great island of Britain (or rather, of Canterbury, 668—†90), " and philosopher, with others who still tarried in Britain."[68] But Theodore reassured the Pope by sending him an acknowledgment of the dogmatic decrees of the Lateran Council from his Synod of Hatfield,[69] 17th September, 680; and Agatho, on behalf of the West, sent the Emperor a letter[70] in repudiation of Monotheletism which is of great interest in that both in regard to its tone and contents and in the part which it played at an Œcumenical Council, it closely resembled the *Tome* of his great predecessor, St. Leo. The Pope informs Constantine IV. that he is sending three bishops as his legates, with others:[71] more in order to fulfil the will of the Emperor than from any special confidence in their learning. With people who live among the barbarians, and have to earn their living by the work of their hands, learning is hardly to be looked for. But what former Popes and the five great Synods have decided, this they hold in all simplicity.[72] From these envoys of his, and from testimonies of the Fathers which he has given them, his Majesty will have ample information as to what the Roman church believes. Let the Emperor, therefore, receive them graciously.[73] Agatho, however, might also add a word of explanation himself. This the Pope proceeds to do, in the form of a Symbol, at the end of which two natural wills and activities in Christ are asserted.[74] He explains the doctrine in detail; adduces in support passages from Scripture,[75] with their explanations from the Fathers; and does not forget to make it clear both that will is an affair of nature, not of person, and that the orthodox doctrine is " founded on the firm rock of this church of St. Peter, quae eius gratia atque praesidio ab omni errore illibata permanet."[76] There was also a

Synodal Letter from the Roman Council to the same effect.[77]

Upon receipt of these communications, Constantine IV. issued a rescript,[78] 10th September, 680, summoning the Council to meet at Constantinople. It became the Sixth Œcumenical Council;[79] and ultimately consisted of one hundred and seventy-four prelates including the three papal legates, George, Patriarch of Constantinople, 678—83, Macarius, non-resident Patriarch of Antioch and a staunch Monothelete, and Peter, monk and presbyter, who represented the church of Alexandria. They met in the domed Hall (in Trullo) of the Imperial Palace, the Holy Gospels being enthroned in the midst; the Emperor presiding, in person, at the opening and the last session, at other times by commission: though only to regulate the conduct of business and not to direct the decisions of the Synod. The Council held eighteen sessions, from 7th November, 680 to 16th September, 681. Its proceedings were tedious, taken up, as they were, with long discussions and the reading of lengthy authorities, including the weighty synodal letter of Sophronius of Jerusalem. But the bishops accepted the letters of Pope Agatho and the Roman Synod, on the ground that they agree[80] with the Council of Chalcedon, with the *Tome* of St. Leo, and with the synodal letters of St. Cyril against Nestorius and to John of Antioch; and, at the end of their long Symbol or Definition of Faith, accepted in the eighteenth session, they " expressed all in one brief phrase," thus :—" Believing that our Lord Jesus Christ, one of the Trinity also after the Incarnation, is our true God, we say that His two natures shone forth in His one Person, in which were both the miracles and the suffering throughout the whole incarnate life, not in appearance merely but in reality, the difference as to nature being recognised in one and the same Person; for, although joined together, each nature wills and operates the things proper to it. For this reason we glorify two natural wills and operations [where ' natural ' will means such a will as belongs to a nature, divine or human] concurring most fitly in Him for the salvation of the human race."[81] They also condemned the Monotheletes—Sergius, Cyrus, Pyrrhus, Paul, Peter: and "with these we decree that there shall be expelled from the holy Church of God and anathematised Honorius Pope of Old Rome, because of what we found written by him to Sergius, that in all respects he followed his view and confirmed his impious doctrines."[82] Whether Honorius was, after all, a heretic is another matter, though his condemnation was repeatedly re-affirmed by his successors;[83] for it seems not at all unlikely that he misunderstood the point at issue, and his language is quite unscientific.[84] The condemnation of Honorius may, or may not, affect the papal claim to infallibility,[85] but the condemnation of Monotheletism is of great moment. Monotheletism has been called "the ethical complement" of Monophysitism:[86] and its opponents did service to ethics by insisting that "will is an essential element of a complete nature."[87] They did service also to the fulness of Christ's human nature, for without a human will He could not have been our supreme example. Then by insisting that will belongs to nature and not to person, they secured the maintenance of belief in the Unity of the Trinity. But more than all this, they saved the verity of our salvation. If our Lord had no human will, then, since all the merit of His Passion turns upon His having voluntarily offered Himself for us, our redemption has not been accomplished. The question "was one for life and death. The denial of a human will in Christ was, in fact, a denial of His sacrifice."[88]

§ 6. The last seven years of Constantine IV. were years of peace: and, under the first decade of his son, Justinian II., 685—95, little of importance took place. He came to the throne at the age of sixteen: and was not a successful ruler. He provoked defeat from the Saracens, so that his foreign policy was a failure. In domestic affairs, he excited the resentment of his subjects by his financial oppression. So he prepared the way for his own downfall. But, till the crash came, his reign was uneventful; and, as we are now within five years of the end of the seventh century, we may take the opportunity

The Dynasty of Heraclius

of surveying the state of things, in church and society, under the House of Heraclius, whose sovereignty began and ended with that epoch. Valuable material for the survey is provided by the legislation of the Council in Trullo,[89] 692. Justinian II., in spite of his ungoverned impulses, was of pure life and orthodox faith. Knowing that questions of discipline had been passed over by the two Councils concerned with doctrine under his namesake, Justinian I. and his father, Constantine IV., he summoned this assembly to bring the Christian life again into order and to root out the remains of Jewish and heathen cults. It is sometimes called *Penthecte* or *Quinisext*, as thus intended to supplement the Fifth and Sixth Œcumenical Councils : more often The Council in Trullo : for it sat where the sixth sat in the domed Hall (Trullus) of the Imperial Palace; and, as it did not acquire the rank of œcumenicity, its place of session became its chief distinction. Its importance to us is that, in its legislation, we have a lasting picture of the life of the time.

(i.) The result of the Saracen conquests was to restrict the territory of the Orthodox Church; but also to consolidate it under the hegemony of Constantinople. The patriarchates of Alexandria, Antioch and Jerusalem were now under Mohammedan rule; and the Patriarch of Constantinople became as dominant in the Eastern Roman Empire as ever Rome had been in the West. Cyprus alone remained outside his jurisdiction. But the autocephalous church of Cyprus counted for little; for Justinian II., in consequence of the invasions, transferred the Cypriots, hierarchy and all, to Justinianopolis Nova in the province of the Hellespont. There the archbishop of Cyprus was to retain all his old rights—mainly, however, of rank and precedence, though he was still to be independent of Antioch and to be consecrated by his own bishops.[90] Of the territorial arrangements of Orthodox Christendom we still have an account preserved in the Τακτικὸν or list[91] of c. 650. They remained very much as under Justinian I., except for the loss of Mesopotamia, Syria, Egypt and Africa; and for the addition of the

Province of Lazica, the autocephalous diocese of Abasgia —both in the Caucasus—and two similar dioceses in Isauria. In all there were 424 dioceses in communion with the see of Constantinople: the total being made up of 1 patriarchate, 33 metropolitan sees, 356 suffragan bishoprics and 34 autocephalous sees called archbishoprics; and they covered the Balkan peninsula and Asia Minor.

(ii.) The sole supremacy of Constantinople in the Eastern Empire had, for a consequence, the intensification of the rivalry between New Rome and Old Rome. The primacy of the Roman See[92] was, of course, freely acknowledged by the churches of the Eastern Empire; but especially when they wanted its assistance, as by Councils of Africa,[93] 646, or by Sophronius,[94] Stephen, bishop of Dora,[95] c. 649, and Maximus the Confessor,[96] in the struggle with Monotheletism. It was as emphatically asserted by the Popes, who knew how to turn Oriental compliments into solid concessions: though they generally fell back, as had been customary since Pope Damasus, 366—†84, on the promise to Peter. Agatho thus claimed to have "strengthened his brethren,"[97] the bishops of the Sixth Œcumenical Council; and they hailed his support by informing Justinian II. that "Peter had spoken by Agatho"[98] and his letter. But, for all this deference on the one side and self-assertion on the other, the Patriarchs of Constantinople were as self-assertive in their turn.[99] They did not hesitate to reduce the power of the Roman See where they could, and to aggrandise themselves at its expense. Thus they supported Maurus, archbishop of Ravenna, 648—†71, who went so far as to excommunicate[100] Pope Vitalian, 657—†72; and, in an edict of 1st March, 666, Constans II. relieved Ravenna, as the see of the Exarchate, from dependence upon any ecclesiastical superior.[101] From 638—80 no name of a Pope was retained on the diptychs of Constantinople. The Sixth Œcumenical Council made no allowances for the orthodox intention of Pope Honorius; but seized upon his Monothelete language and condemned him as a heretic without hesitation: while there is a strong anti-

Roman bias discernible in the legislation of the Council in Trullo.[102]

(iii.) Coming to the higher hierarchy,[103] the patriarchal jurisdiction of Rome in Illyricum remained, so far as it was possible, under the Slav invasions. In 626 Honorius intervened at Nicopolis,[104] and 667, Vitalian in Crete.[105] But the Council in Trullo reaffirmed the pre-eminence of Constantinople;[106] and the principle, repudiated in the West, that ecclesiastical precedence should be regulated by the civil dignity of a city, received legislative confirmation.[107]

(iv.) As to the episcopate,[108] the system of bishops *in partibus* finds acceptance, as a natural consequence of the submergence of so many sees under the flood of Slav or Saracen invasion. Their incumbents lived at Constantinople, as did Macarius, Patriarch of Antioch, c. 650—80, who never visited his see. They retained their rank, and their right to confer orders,[109] and they increased the numbers but perhaps not the prestige of the Home Synod. Annual synods are required to be held in each province between Easter and Michaelmas.[110] Metropolitans are not to seize the goods of a bishopric during its vacancy.[111] Bishops are to be diligent in instructing their flocks;[112] and are not to live with their wives.[113] No digamist is to be consecrated to the episcopate.[114]

(v.) The clerical office[115] is the object of much solicitude on the part of the Council; which made many rules to secure its good order and dignity. Thus, while clerks in minor orders, such as Readers and Cantors, may marry after ordination, clerks in holy orders, *i.e.*, sub-deacons, deacons and priests, are forbidden to do so. They may, however, live with their wives, if married before ordination, though they are to refrain from intercourse before approaching the altar;[116] and they are not to abandon the married estate in order to enter Religion.[117] An age is fixed before which candidates may not be admitted to the various grades of the ministry:[118] 30 for the priesthood, 25 for the diaconate, 40 for a deaconess, 20 for subdeacons. Digamy is a bar to orders: so also is marriage to a concubine, a widow, a divorced woman, a prostitute, a slave or an actress.[119] The clergy are to have nothing to do with inns,[120] horse-racing,[121] theatres,[122] dice,[123] brothels.[124] They are to get up from a wedding-breakfast, and go as soon as the games begin :[125] a requirement which lets in a lurid light upon the lewd manners of the laity. They are not to take women into their houses :[126] they are to be properly shorn[127] and to wear clerical dress both at home and when on their travels.[128] Orders are not to be hereditary, as with the Armenians ;[129] nor given for money, for fear of simony.[130] In order to provide against clerical rapacity, it is required that the clergy are not to take fees for the administration of the Sacrament,[131] nor to lend at interest.[132] They are to abstain from conspiracy ;[133] to remain in the diocese to which they were ordained ; [134] and, if driven from it by invasion, to return to their post as soon as the invasion is over.[135] As to deacons, the old limit of seven to a city is removed ;[136] but a deacon is not to take precedence of priests, unless the deacon be officially representing his bishop at a synod.[137] So presumptuous was the deacon who would normally succeed to his bishop, and so humble a fellow the ordinary married priest or village pope.

(vi.) Monasticism[138] comes in for similar recognition and regulation. " Religion " being a state of penitence, anyone, however unworthy his previous life, may become a monk,[139] but he must be, at least, ten years of age.[140] If he marries, he is to be treated as unchaste.[141] Monks and nuns are not to wander from their own convents,[142] nor to be received at each other's houses.[143] Religious are not to make their self-sacrifice conspicuous ; as men do by their unkempt appearance in the streets,[144] or as women novices do by coquettishly dressing up in silks and jewels before assuming the habit at their profession.[145] The monasteries are not to be secularised.[146] They served as refuges for the failures of life. But this meant that they were not always centres of spiritual vitality; and that, as in the case of Theodotus, the General Logothete or Minister of Finance under Justinian II., and an ex-abbot, the monk, who saw the chance of starting again on a career, was apt to leave the monastery and take it. Otherwise, the failures made themselves at home there: and "the old boys," as monks were called,[147] gave the tone to monasticism in popular esteem. But Greek monasticism in the West meant the preservation of the Greek tongue and civilisation among the Latins or "barbarians":[148] and there are known to have been four such communities in Rome itself,[149] c. 676—8.

(vii.) If such was the tone of those who had left the world, Christian society,[150] as they found or left it, was not very different: half Christian but half pagan. Thus students in civil law are forbidden to indulge themselves in heathen usages by frequenting the theatres, or wearing strange clothes.[151] Actors and their plays, the exhibition of the chase and theatrical dances are equally forbidden.[152] So also are the remains of heathen superstition, the festivals of the Kalends, the Bota in honour of Pan, the Brumalia in honour of Bacchus, the assemblies of the first of March, public dancing by women, impersonation of women by men or of men by women, the wearing of comic, satyric or tragic masks and the invocation of Bacchus at the winepress;[153] feasts of the new moon;[154] soothsaying and amulets;[155] sham demoniacs;[156] mixed bathing;[157] pagan oaths;[158] indecent pictures;[159] and odious gallantry.[160] As to the cruelties of the age—blinding, slitting of the nose and cutting out of the tongue—the less said the better. Justinian II. himself was Rhinotmetus; and Stephen, his other finance-minister, took advantage of his absence to strip the Empress-mother, Anastasia, and give her a whipping like a little school-girl.[161] But we are not to suppose that all this means the decadence of society. Councils legislate for the exceptional. "From general prohibitions, which do not especially concern the clergy, we cannot draw many conclusions in regard to the morality of the age. In all ages men gamble, and women use arts to allure." In this, "the Emperors themselves set a good example. The sovereigns of the Heraclian dynasty seem to have led exceptionally irreproachable, almost severe lives. . . . No charges of sensual indulgence have ever been brought against them."[162] Nor, in the Quinisext, is there any prohibition of unnatural crime.[163] It must have been rare. And side by side with the follies and weaknesses of the time, society in the seventh century was deeply religious. Its religion was sometimes expressed in mechanical devotions; such as passing and re-passing relics so many times, reciting strings of Kyries: while kissing crosses and icons, coupled with talking, ogling and boredom at Mass, made up a perfunctory but sufficient attendance at church.[164] Such a populace forgot the place of missionary zeal[165] in the life of a Christian. But it was not overlooked by their rulers. Heraclius, in 641, urged the Pope to send missionaries to the Serbs and Croats to whom he had granted settlements in Illyricum. The army itself, in absorbing into its ranks the Slav invaders, converted them by the force of its own Christian spirit: or the numerous army chaplains took them in hand and sent them back, on leaving the colours, to be missionaries to their own people. Their proselytising zeal was supported by the local Greek clergy; and seconded by the Œcumenical Patriarchate, which appointed a Περιοδευτής or Inspector, to look after the converts in the European themes. And the importance of this office may be gauged from the fact that the two Patriarchs, Peter, 652—†64, and Constantine I., 674—†6, both held it at their election.

(viii.) But, as now, worship[166] and sacraments played a greater part than missions in the life of the ordinary Christian. Worship, as to-day, was largely conventional; for absence from church on three successive Sundays is visited with penalties.[167] On Sundays, there is to be no kneeling in church;[168] nor from Easter to Whitsuntide; an older prescription reaffirmed,[169] as if kneeling then were coming in: whereas it was still regarded as a constructive denial of the Resurrection, at such times. Honour is to be paid to the Cross; and so it is not to be used as a decoration in places where it would be trodden under foot[170]—as on the red-baize hassock, stamped with a black cross, so dear to the pitch-pine pew of a prim type of Anglicanism. Our Lord is to be represented, both on the Cross and elsewhere, not symbolically as hitherto, under the figure of the Lamb: but historically, by the crucifix.[171] This canon, no doubt, gave official recognition both to the cult of the Cross which had come in upon its recovery by Heraclius; and to a great change for the better, from symbolism to realism, which was coming over Byzantine art. Once more, women are not to talk in church[172]—it was a question not of their preaching but of their gossiping; and the psalmody, between the lessons at Mass, is not to be noisy nor unseemly.[173] Choirs even then were untuneful, and cantors liked showing off!

(ix.) In regard to sacraments,[174] preparation for baptism is to consist of learning the Creed and reciting it to the clergy on Thursdays.[175] Baptism is to be conferred on any child, though of unknown parentage,[176] thus indicating the opinion of its necessity; but it is only to be conferred in public churches.[177] The re-baptism of the earlier heretics is required.[178] Confirmation is not separate from Baptism, except in the case of heretics such as Nestorians, Eutychians and others who do not need to be baptised *de novo*.[179] Penance is not obligatory; but confessors are to receive careful training.[180] Marriage is forbidden with spiritual[181] and other[182] relatives: and with anyone betrothed to another;[183] mixed marriages are not allowed;[184] nor is desertion,[185] abortion,[186] or rape :[187] while careful provision is made for cases where re-marriage is allowable to a wife on the supposed loss of her husband, or to a husband on desertion by his wife.[188] Nothing is said of Unction or of Holy Order. Communion is not to be given to the dead;[189] nor for a fee,[190] nor by the laity to themselves, except in the absence of the clergy.[191] The rule of fasting before Communion, to which an exception was tolerated in Africa on the evening of Maundy Thursday, is made absolute;[192] and the Eucharist is to be given into the crossed hands of the communicant;[193] though, before long, the use of the liturgical spoon came in from Syria,[194] and communion was then given by intinction into the mouth.

(x.) We now come to the Liturgy,[195] as celebrated in the seventh century. For this, our information is drawn as to details from the Trullan canons,[196] but on the main outline of the service from the *Mystagogia* of St. Maximus the

Confessor, 580—†662 (where he expounds those elements of the rite in which the people take active part). The *Missa Catechumenorum* begins with the Introit or Little Entrance, when the bishop goes to his throne in the sanctuary, while the *Trisagion* is sung. There is an express provision that this anthem is not to include the Monophysite formula " who was crucified for us ":[197] for whereas the *Trisagion* was considered at Antioch to be addressed to the Son, so that the addition might then be compatible with orthodoxy; in Constantinople it would be heretical, for the hymn was there held to be addressed to the Trinity. Then follow the three lessons —prophecy, epistle and gospel—interspersed with chants, the *Antiphon* and the *Alleluia*, not to be sung noisily,[198] and the homily. The catechumens are then dismissed; but, by this time, the dismissals were rather theoretical and ideal than a matter of practice. The bishop then advances from his throne to the altar for the *Missa Fidelium*. It begins with the prayers of the faithful,[199] in the form of a litany, for church, clergy, prince and people. Then the Great Entrance. Perhaps, just before it the oblations of the laity were prepared, though these were not a matter of course; and it is not certain whether they were presented before, or during, the rite. But it was forbidden to present in the sanctuary joints of meat for the use of the clergy,[200] as did the Armenians, or grapes,[201] or milk and honey.[202] The chalice was to be mixed,[203] unlike that of the Armenians—they come in for repudiation from the Byzantines, as do the Romans, for fasting on Saturdays in Lent[204]—and the chalice was not veiled, for the liturgical fans were in use and rendered a veil unnecessary. Then followed the diptychs, the kiss of peace and the Creed: and then the Anaphora with Salutation, Sursum Corda, Preface, Sanctus, Recitation of Thanksgiving or Consecration, Elevation, Communion. This is to be received in the hand,[205] and not conveyed to the lips from vessels of gold or silver brought by the communicant.[206] The *Communio* was sung while the people communicated; and the service concluded with a *Troperium*, or hymn, of the Patriarch Sergius, 610—†38, first mentioned as having been added, A.D. 624.[207] The mass of an ordinary priest differed in no essential from the rite as celebrated by a bishop. Such was the Liturgy on Sundays. In Lent, its place was taken by the Liturgy of the Presanctified, except on Saturdays, Sundays and the Feast of the Annunciation.[208] Festal services and communion are required throughout Easter week.[209] There are to be no " love-feasts " in churches,[210] and no sort of trafficking in or near sacred places.[211] The ministering deacons are no longer to be limited to seven.[212]

(xi.) Passing from the services to the buildings[213] in which they were held, we find that they are not to be used as a dining room,[214] nor a bedroom,[215] nor a marketplace,[216] nor a shelter for cattle.[217] They consisted of a nave; and a sanctuary divided from the nave by a screen, and furnished with altar and synthronos. Here no layman was to be admitted.[218] And they were usually furnished with two sacristies, a *skeuophylakion*[219] and a *diakonikon*. But, owing to the impoverishment of the Empire, churches were built on a less magnificent scale under the dynasty of Heraclius than in the spacious days of Justinian I.

(xii.) Religious art,[220] however, maintained the same traditions of building and decoration in the seventh as in the sixth century. The Cross came to be treated not symbolically but realistically[221] by way of protest against Monophysitism. As to execution in art, the Heraclian epoch is a period of decadence, owing to the decline of all resources consequent upon the Persian and Arab wars.

(xiii.) Of Seasons we have already spoken. Saturday[222] and Sunday,[223] Holy Week[224] and Easter,[225] maintained, as of old, the weekly and the annual commemoration of our Lord's Death and Resurrection. Lent had its special observance.[226] Of Angels, St. Michael and St. Gabriel, and of saints, St. John Baptist and St. Stephen were the favourites; the Apostles being celebrated together on 30th June, and the Martyrs on the first Sunday after Pentecost. Pilgrimages[227] were common to Jerusalem and to Sinai. But they were attended with no little danger, since these sanctuaries were now in alien hands. The great saints of the age[228] were Sophronius, Patriarch of Jerusalem, 634—†8, Maximus the Confessor, 580—†662, and Anastasius of Sinai, *fl.* 640—700. Together with John Moschus, †619, they were also its authors and theologians.[229] Moschus wrote the *Pratum Spirituale,*[230] or account of the graces and miracles of contemporary ascetics: while the letter of his friend and pupil, Sophronius, on the two wills in our Lord, was given œcumenical authority at the Council of 680.[231]

§ 7. When Constantine IV. won his victory over the Saracens, 678, changes had broken over the Empire which seemed to promise it renewal of strength; and, at any rate, effected its transformation.[232]

Ethnographically, new peoples settled in the Balkan Peninsula. Croats and Serbs made a home in the North-West,[233] 610—41, and Bulgars to the North-East,[234] 679; while, c. 680, the Slavs penetrated the central districts.[235] They spread over Mœsia, Macedonia, up to the gates of Thessalonica, Thessaly, central Greece, Peloponnesus and even as far as the islands of the archipelago. Christianity made way among all these peoples; and they helped to re-invigorate the Empire.

Administrative changes were in process at the same time. For the Empire was reorganised into Themes,[236] where civil and military authority was concentrated in the same hands. So the Empire was consolidated, and better equipped both for the maintenance of order and for defence.

A cultural transformation was also going on under the Heracliad dynasty; and the Empire became Greek rather than Roman. This is first symbolised by the Imperial title Πιστὸς ἐν Θεῷ Βασιλεύς, which Heraclius adopted, 627; and Greek became the official language. Laws which had hitherto been promulgated in Latin, the language of Justinian's *Institutes* and *Code,* though not of his *Novels,* were now published in Greek. The titles of officials came to be Greek. Thus the *Comes sacrarum largitionum* became the *General Logothete;* the *Prefect* became the *Eparch,* and the *Magister militum* the *Strategus.* The title *Drongarius* was given to an admiral or a commander of the watch.[237] In the army, too, the word of command was now given in Greek, though the troops were recruited from among Armenians and Asiatics. It is true that the Empire was still called Roman, and its territories Romania : but ‘Pωμαῖοι meant " Greeks." And whereas writers of the fifth or sixth century affected a more or less classical Greek, authors of the Heraclian period write in vernacular Greek.

Closely connected with this process of Hellenisation is the ecclesiastical aspect which the Empire presented in the seventh century. Religious problems—Monenergism or Monotheletism—dominated Imperial policy : and religious questions engrossed public interest. Thus, the wars of Heraclius were crusades : and when Constans II. put out the *Type,* professing an indifference to theological niceties, he failed because he clearly opposed " the tendency of his age to look upon church matters as the vital interests of the world."[238] This zeal for religion is reflected in the high position occupied by the Patriarch of Constantinople : not merely because his rival Patriarchs of Alexandria, Antioch and Jerusalem had succumbed to extinction under Mohammedan rulers, but because he exerted an authority second, if not equal, to that of the Emperor himself. Literature and art, which hitherto had retained some flavour of the classical ideals, now became religious and popular : and Orthodoxy, driven in upon itself by the expulsion of Monophysitism into foreign lands, became the ally and the expression of nationality. Greek, in opposition to Latin, the Orient over against the Occident, the civilisation of the one in conscious superiority to the barbarism of the other, and the Pope of New Rome in rivalry with the Pope of Old Rome, are all phases of the new movement. Ecclesiastically, these tendencies prepared for the schism between East and West which took place in the ninth century; but they also served to give a sense of unity to the Empire which ultimately promoted its long-continued vitality. The Monarchy found its sources of strength in the combined forces of Hellenism and Orthodoxy.

But a collapse preceded the realisation of this new-found vigour.[239] Justinian II., by his blunders in foreign policy and by his tyranny at home, ruined, in the first ten years of his reign, 685—95, the advantages gained by his father. After defeats from Bulgars and Slavs, 689, and from Saracens, 692, he tried to force the decrees of the Council in Trullo upon the acceptance of Pope Sergius, 687—†701; and so was led into a rupture with the see of Rome.[240] Then followed the "First Anarchy," 695—717: during which Justinian II. and six usurpers contested the Empire with each other. Territories were lost to the Empire in rapid succession, and fell to the Moslems: Africa, 693—8, Armenia, 703, Cilicia, 711, Amasia, 712, Antioch in Pisidia, 713, Galatia, 714, Amorium, 716, and Pergamus, 717: while the Bulgars appeared before Constantinople and replaced Justinian, 705—†11. These losses by war were accompanied by social disaster: savagery[241] and treachery, superstition[242] and credulity, and a decline in morals which it was the avowed object of the Quinisext Council to restore.

A saviour of society and of the Empire was needed, if the transformation effected under the once vigorous Heracliad dynasty was to bear fruit. He was found in Leo the Isaurian: whose armies, drawn from the themes of Opsikion, Anatolia and Armenia, marched upon the capital. He became the founder of a new and vigorous dynasty, which lasted, over a "Second Anarchy," 802—20, from 717—867. The Isaurian Dynasty put new strength into the Empire; but plunged it into the long-drawn contest of *Iconoclasm,* and allowed the rivalries of Old and New Rome to drift into the *Schism* between East and West.

CHAPTER VII.

THE ISAURIAN DYNASTY, 717—867, INCLUDING THE SECOND ANARCHY, 802—20.

ICONOCLASM. SCHISM.

THE ISAURIAN DYNASTY, 717—867.

(H. B. George, 'Genealogical Tables,' No. xlvii.)

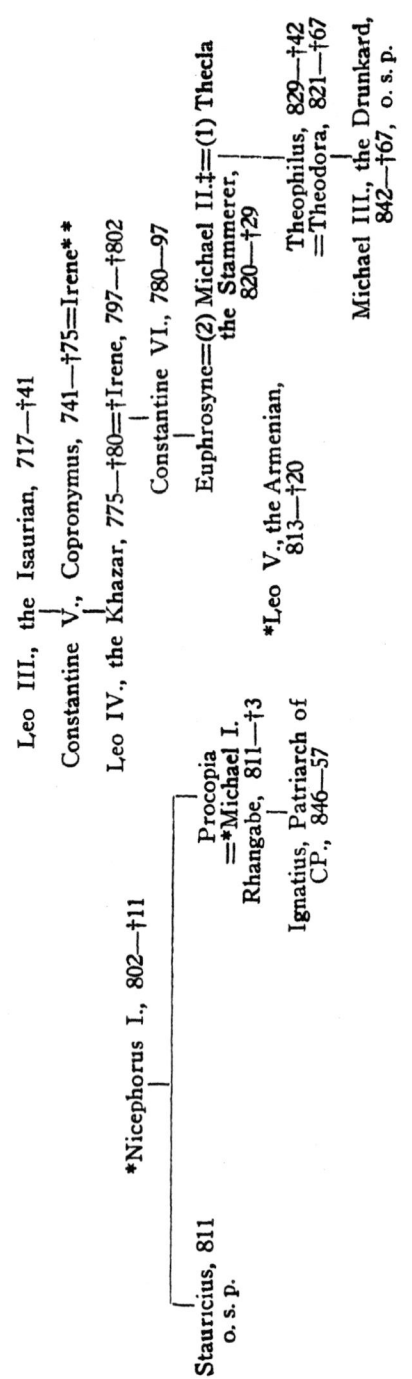

```
Leo III., the Isaurian, 717—†41
        |
Constantine V., Copronymus, 741—†75=Irene**
        |
Leo IV., the Khazar, 775—†80=†Irene, 797—†802
        |
Constantine VI., 780—97

Euphrosyne=(2) Michael II.‡=(1) Thecla
                  the Stammerer,
                    820—†29
                       |
              Theophilus, 829—†42
              =Theodora, 821—†67
                       |
              Michael III., the Drunkard,
                  842—†67, o. s. p.

*Leo V., the Armenian,
     813—†20

*Nicephorus I., 802—†11
        |
   -----------
   |         |
Stauricius, 811    Procopia
   o. s. p.      =*Michael I.
                   Rhangabe, 811—†3
                        |
                  Ignatius, Patriarch of
                     CP., 846—57
```

* Second Anarchy, 802—20.

† An accomplished and ambitious lady of Athens.

‡ Of Amorium (hence he and his son and grandson are sometimes classed as of "The Amorian Dynasty"). A. was a bpric. of Phrygia; and its ruins are now near the village of Hamza-Hadji in the vilayet of Konieh.

** Daughter of the Khan of the Khazars.

BISHOPS OF THE CHIEF SEES: 717—867.

ROME.		CONSTANTINOPLE.		ANTIOCH.	
Gregory II.	715—31	Germanus I.	715—30	Stephen III.	743—5
Gregory III.	731—41	Anastasius	730—54	Theophylact	745—68
Zacharias	741—52	Constantine II.		Theodoret	787— ?
Stephen II.	752		754—66	Job	814—45
Stephen III.	752—7	Nicetas I.	766—80	Nicholas I.	847—66
Paul I.	757—67	Paul IV.	780—4		
Stephen IV.	768—71	Tarasius	784—806	JERUSALEM.	
Hadrian I.	771—95	Nicephorus I.		* * *	
Leo III.	795—816		806—15		
Stephen V.	816—7	Theodotus I.	815—21	Theodore I.	752—67
Paschal I.	817—24	Antony I.	821—32	Eusebius, before 776	
Eugenius II.	824—7	John VII.	832—42	Elias II.	787—96
Valentine	827	Methodius I.	842—6	George	? —807
Gregory IV.	827—44	Ignatius	846—57	Thomas	807—29
Sergius II.	844—7	Photius	857—67	Basil	c. 829
Leo IV.	847—55			Sergius	842—58/9
Benedict III.	855—8			Solomon c.	858—63/4
Nicholas I.	858—67			Theodosius	867—79

ALEXANDRIA.

Orthodox.		Monophysite.	
		Alexander II.	
			703—26
Cosmas I.	727—67	Cosmas I.	726—7
		Theodore	727—38
		Michael I.	743—66
		Menas I.	766—75
Politian	767—801	John IV.	775—99
Eustathius	801—5	Mark II.	799—819
Christopher	805—36	Jacob	819—36
		Simon II.	836—7
Sophronius I.		Joseph	837—50
	836—59	Michael II.	850—1
		Cosmas II.	851—9
Michael I.	859—71	Sanutius I.	859—70

CHAPTER VII.

THE ISAURIAN DYNASTY, 717—867, INCLUDING THE SECOND ANARCHY, 802—20. ICONOCLASM. SCHISM.

§ 1. THE Isaurian Dynasty, 717—867, lasted for a hundred and fifty years. Its first two Emperors, Leo III., 717—†41, and his son, Constantine V., 741—†75, were vigorous rulers, intent upon reviving the Empire and, to that end, destroying the superstitions which were connected with the veneration paid to sacred Images or pictures. Their reigns, together with that of Leo IV., 775—†80, who continued the policy of his father and grandfather, cover the first period of Iconoclasm, which may be reckoned from 726—80. There followed a reaction in favour of Iconolatry under the Empress Irene, who survived her husband, Leo IV. and, after acting as regent for her son, Constantine VI., 780—97, eventually superseded him, 797—†802. She effected the first restoration of Images, which lasted for thirty-three years, 780—813. On her fall, the "Second Anarchy" set in, and continued for eighteen years, 802—20; the last of the usurpers being Leo V., 813—†20, who inaugurated a second period of Iconoclasm, which lasted for thirty years during the reigns of himself and of Michael II., 820—†9, and his son, Theophilus, 829—†42, "the last and most cruel of the Iconoclasts."[1] At his death, it fell, for the second time, to a woman to stay the persecution; and, in 843, his widow, the Empress Theodora, 821—†67, effected the second and final restoration of the Images. With the inglorious reign of her son, Michael III., 842—†67, who died without issue, the Isaurian Dynasty became extinct. The Iconoclastic Controversy entailed results disastrous to the Empire; "since a question of popular superstition produced the revolt of Italy, the temporal power of the popes, and the restoration of the Roman empire in the

West."[2] But the peace which followed it led to better things for the Church. There was an era of expansion issuing in the conversion of Bulgaria, 864, and the missionary activity of Cyril and Methodius, 863—85: but against this expansion has to be set the schism between East and West which resulted from the rivalries of Photius, Patriarch of Constantinople, 857—67, and 878—86 (†891) and Pope Nicholas I., 858—†67. Thus the year 867 marks an epoch not only in Byzantine history, but in the history of the whole Church.

§ 2. The restoration of the Empire under the first two sovereigns of the Isaurian dynasty must first be noted as a set-off to their Iconoclasm. They laid the foundation of the prosperity attained under the Macedonian dynasty, 867—1025, when the Eastern Empire reached its zenith.

Both were men of mark. Leo III., 717—†41, was born in Isauria but spent his youth at Mesembria (now Misivri, in Bulgaria) on the Black Sea. He became a soldier of fortune; and, 704, was promoted to be Spatharius, or aide-de-camp, to Justinian II., who entrusted him with a mission in Lazica. By 713 Leo had risen to be Strategus of the Anatolic Theme. In 716 he relieved Amorium (now Hamza-Hadji) in Phrygia Salutaris, when it was besieged by the Saracens; and entered Constantinople, 25th March, 717, to be hailed as Emperor. Only five months were allowed him to organise its defence before they should reach the Bosporus; and from 15th August, the Saracens laid siege to the capital for a whole year by land and sea. In August, 718, they were forced to retire. Their repulse by Leo III. was an epoch-making event; for from 718 onwards the Ommayad dynasty began to decline until, by their loss of Damascus, 750, and the transference of the Caliphate to the Abbasids at Bagdad, the centre of Saracen power was removed far away from the Roman frontiers. Constantine V., 741—†75, was born in the year of his father's triumph. He married, 732, Irene, daughter of the Khan of the Khazars; whose capital, at this epoch of their greatness (c. 600—950), was Itil at the mouth of the Volga, from whence they controlled the trade between the Caspian and the Euxine.[3] At the age of twenty-three, Constantine came to the throne; and, sharing his father's valour but disgracing it by cruelty, he carried further the successes of the Roman arms. Thus, in campaigns against the Saracens, he defeated them at Acroenus (now Afium Karahissar[4]) in Phrygia Salutaris, 739. In 745 he took the offensive in Syria; reconquered Cyprus, 746; and, 750, entered Armenia and penetrated to the Euphrates. The danger from Islām now being past, Constantine, in nine campaigns, 755—64, beat back the Bulgars; and simultaneously repressed a rising of the Slavs, 758, in Macedonia and Thrace. Numbers of them he transported, 762, to the theme of Opsikion. These victories endeared the first two Isaurian Emperors to their armies; they wrung unwilling tribute to the valour of these Iconoclast rulers from the fathers of the Seventh Œcumenical Council[5] at Nicæa, 787. But they also secured for them the support of the commercial classes who, though Iconophile, preferred to be ruled by the Iconoclast Emperors because they had rescued the Empire from anarchy and revived its prestige abroad.

But Leo III. and Constantine V. excelled in statesmanship[6] as in arms: and their domestic policy of reform and reorganisation—administrative, economic and social —was an additional reason for the support they enjoyed from the trading classes. Thus, they reduced the size and increased the number, of the Themes:[7] with the double result that better provision was made for defence and better security taken against the ambition of over-powerful governors. The military code of Leo III. restored discipline and efficiency to the army.[8] His agrarian code[9] maintained the distinction between the peasant proprietors ($\chi\omega\rho\tilde{\iota}\tau\alpha\iota$) who cultivated their own lands, and the peasants who worked on lands which did not belong to them but to the large estates ($\imath\delta\iota o\sigma\tau\acute{a}\tau a$) of rich owners, churches and abbeys. Peasants of the latter class were freemen; but were either tenants paying a rent ($\mu\iota\sigma\theta\omega\tau o\acute{\iota}$, *liberi coloni*) or labourers ($\dot{\epsilon}\nu a\pi\acute{o}\gamma\rho a\phi o\iota$, *adscripticii*), though in both cases (if the tenure was of over thirty years' standing) bound to the soil. Leo III. abolished both service and serfdom; and this would go a long way to embitter lords and abbots and prelates against the Isaurian Emperors for causes that touched their pockets as well as their religion. Again, the nautical code[10] protected maritime commerce against the Slavonic and Saracen pirates who infested the seas. But most important is the *Ecloga*,[11] promulgated by Leo III., 740, in the name of himself and his son. It touched not particular interests, like the military, the agrarian or the maritime code; but the general relations of life: and modified the civil and criminal law as hitherto fixed by Justinian. The modifications were twofold. First, it substituted Greek for Latin, in the domain of Law; for Latin, though the natural tongue of the Illyrian Justinian was even in his own day becoming unintelligible to the mass of his subjects, so that he issued most of his *Novels* in Greek and expressly recognises in one of them the necessity of using " the common Greek tongue."[12] Latin had become wholly unintelligible to the subjects of Leo III. But, secondly, the religion of the Empire had had very little influence on Justinian's legislation: and the *Ecloga* "may be described as a Christian law-book. It is a deliberate attempt to change the legal system of the Empire by an application of Christian principles."[13] Thus, in the field of civil law, marriage had been reckoned simply as a contract; dissoluble, therefore, like all contracts, by consent of the contracting parties: who, upon divorce, were free to marry again. The *Ecloga* asserts the indissolubility of marriage, on the Christian principle that it is a *consortium vitae;* and permits divorce in four cases only, and this as a concession to the weakness and wickedness of human nature.[14] Similarly, in view of the Christian principle of equality between the sexes, the *patria potestas* is modified and the mother is now given the same rights as the father. In the criminal law, it is the Christian spirit of humanity which inspires the *Ecloga*. The legislator modifies the barbarity of the laws of Justinian chiefly by the substitution of mutilation for death, as the usual penalty. This seems barbarous enough to us. But it was founded on Scripture: " If thine eye offend thee,"[15] etc. :

and, since death had hitherto been the penalty for so many crimes, the substitution of mutilation for death, as formerly of the exact equivalent, "an eye for an eye,"[16] for indiscriminate retaliation, like that of Lamech,[17] was at least a mitigation of barbarity. Amputation of the tongue for perjury,[18] of the hand for theft,[19] and of other offending members,[20] seemed to that generation appropriate punishments; while, like flogging for adultery[21] and whipping for fornication[22] (the women not being punished in either case), they were a great advance in human and Christian legislation.

§ 3. A religious reform was as much part of the general programme of restoration contemplated by the two first Isaurian Emperors as any other of their reforming projects. They proscribed pictures of our Lord, of His Mother and of the Saints, and so have gone down to history as Iconoclasts; whereas the majority of their subjects paid veneration to religious pictures and may thus be described as Iconolaters.

Images, whether in painting or sculpture, were slow to obtain recognition in the Christian Church; for art was so closely allied to idolatry that it had to be redeemed of its pagan associations before it could be adopted for Christian use.[23] Gradually, however, the *use* of images made its way among Christians. They were used either for adornment; or for instruction, to teach by an appeal to the eye what the unlearned could not otherwise apprehend; or, finally, to excite devotion by placing before men vivid representations of the Gospel scenes and characters. The *veneration* of images is another thing; but as late as c. 400 it had not made much progress. Vigilantius entered violent protest against the veneration of relics;[24] but says nothing against the veneration of images. But "adoration," in the technical sense[25] of salutation, was paid not only to the Emperor but to his images; the principle being well understood that the symbol, so far from being, as with us, distinct from the reality, embodied it;[26] and, therefore, the same honour that was paid to the original was paid to its representation and, through its representation, to the original. Thus it was not so much the direct influence of paganism as of the ceremonial of the Imperial Court which prompted veneration or "adoration" of things "august" or "sacred": and the impulse to such veneration would be part of the mental habits of the time. In some quarters, however, the old antipathy to anything suggestive of paganism remained. Thus in Spain, the Council of Elvira (Illiberris), 305, forbade pictures to be painted on the walls of churches.[27] Eusebius, again, bishop of Cæsarea, 314—†23, when asked by Constantia, the sister of Constantine I., for a picture of our Lord declined the request: alleging the prohibition in the second commandment, and fearing that, like the heathen, Christians might come to think that they carried God in a painting.[28] As late as 394, Epiphanius, bishop of Salamis, †403, if the story be true, says that he once entered a church and, finding there a veil "with an image of Christ or some saint" worked upon it, tore it to pieces, alleging the Scriptural prohibition.[29] But Epiphanius was a fanatical opponent of anthropomorphism: and, in this, cannot be taken as representing the feeling of the church of his day. A century later the use of images had become general. The veneration of sacred objects was becoming common too. Thus, the deacon Rusticus, a stubborn defender of the *Three Chapters,* deposed by his uncle Pope Vigilius, 538—†55, alludes to the adoration of the Cross.[30] Evagrius, 537—†600? relates a miracle which took place, c. 539, at Apamea, during an exposition and adoration of the Cross:[31] a rite which had become an established part of the ceremonies of Good Friday as far back as 380 in Jerusalem where it was seen by St. Etheria.[32] And one of the reproaches cast at the Paulicians was that they repudiated the adoration of the Cross. But the Cross then bore no image of the Saviour. And a new development took place, in the sixth century, of the Images of our Lord and His Mother, made without hands (ἀχειροποίητοι) i.e., of miraculous origin. They remind us forcibly of the ἀγάλματα Διοπετῆ, such as that of Artemis at Ephesus.[33] Such was the Image of our Lord, which He Himself was supposed to have sent to Abgar,

King of Edessa, and which saved the city from the attacks of Chosroes I., 531—†78;[34] or the veil of St. Veronica,[35] well accepted by this time. Zacharias, bishop of Mitylene, 536—†53, speaks of images of this kind, and of temples built to receive them.[36] St. Simeon Stylites, †596 (the younger), attests the veneration paid to images of our Lord and His Mother, by condemning the profanation of them which had taken place in a church :[37] Maximus the Confessor, 580—†662, at a conference held in 656, took part, with others, in such an act of veneration. They fell on their knees and kissed the Gospels, the Cross and the Image of our Lord and His Mother.[38] And Leontius, bishop of Neapolis in Cyprus, c. 600, answering the Jews who charged the Christians with idolatry, admits the fact that Christians adore the Cross and venerate Images with prostration and kissing, but maintains that such adoration is relative only and paid in intention to the persons represented.[39] In the eighth century the worship of Images in the East had reached an extreme point. When we read of people who chose not a living man but some special icon (εἰκών) to be the godfather of their child, and of priests who scraped the paint from an image, mixed it with the Chalice, and then gave it to the communicants as a magic medicine,[40] it is not difficult to understand that a reaction would come.[41] The Iconoclasts condemned as superstitious both the use of Images and their veneration.

Leo III., in promoting reform, had the support of several Orthodox bishops who had preached against images and relics—Constantine of Nacolia,[42] c. 720, Theodosius of Ephesus, c. 720, and Thomas of Claudiopolis,[43] c. 720. Pious people were shocked at the prevalent superstition. In Asia, whence Leo came, Jews and Mussulmans abounded. Their religions were strictly monotheistic, and incompatible not only with the use of images and pictures but with any sort of secondary adoration. The Paulicians, also, who thought all matter evil and so rejected outward things like pictures, were widely spread in the regions with which Leo was connected by birth : they, too, were opposed to Mariolatry and super-

CHRYSOSTOM, METROPOLITAN OF ATHENS AND ARCHBISHOP OF GREECE.

e p. 358.]

stition. So, indeed, was the Syrian as contrasted with the Greek spirit; and Leo, as a Christian of the non-Greek type, would be predisposed to view with distaste the superstitions current in the Empire to which he had attained. Political considerations would then come in to reinforce religious. These superstitions found their chief supporters among the monks. The numbers, wealth and immunities of the monasteries were a danger to the state. They withdrew taxes from its treasury, soldiers from its army, labourers from its fields, and functionaries from the public service. To put down the religion which they represented would be to bring them into discredit, and to settle two pressing difficulties together. Such were Leo's motives.

He found them shared by several classes among his subjects: and he might look for support from very different quarters, from classes not ordinarily in sympathy with each other but united in accord with the imperial policy. Thus the higher clergy were jealous of the influence of the monks; and, apart from their usual servility to the sovereign, would on this ground be behind Leo. The army was his, to a man: not merely because he was a successful commander, but because its ranks were made up of Armenians, Mardaïtes, Isaurians, Manichæans, Paulicians. It was, in short, not only non-Greek in temper, like Leo himself; but, owing to the hereditary character of the profession of arms, was actually a caste, and would follow where he led. The Monophysites, again, disliked Images: the more they laid stress on the one Nature of our Lord, the greater their tendency to look upon it as divine and the greater their hostility to any representation of Him in human form. And sensible men would be on the side of the Iconoclast Emperors: for these were neither puritans nor kill-joys. Indeed, the courts of Constantine V., 741—†75, and Theophilus, 829—†42, were more than lively. Nor were these Emperors irreligious. They were reformers who stood for enlightenment against superstition; and would, therefore, enlist the support of reasonable men.

§ 4. We come, then, to the events of the controversy

during the first period of Iconoclasm, 726—80: under the Emperors Leo III., Constantine V. and Leo IV.

Leo III., 717—†41, made no move against Images for the first few years of his reign; but he was advised by Constantine of Nacolia and his party that the worship of Images was the great hindrance to the unity of the Empire, that it ministered to superstition and was forbidden by the second commandment. John, bishop of Synnada, and, as metropolitan of Phrygia Salutaris, the ecclesiastical superior of Constantine, wrote to Germanus I., Patriarch of Constantinople, 715—30, to warn him of his suffragan's views: whereupon the Patriarch summoned him to his presence, expostulated with him and sent him back to his metropolitan with a letter in which he defends the use of Images on the ground that they showed forth His real Incarnation as opposed to the docetic doctrine[44] still common on that subject. Meanwhile, the Emperor had put out his edict, 725, for the destruction of Images; and in 726 began to enforce it. Greece[45] and Italy[46] were already disaffected because of the financial oppression they had to endure from the government of Leo: but, when the edict reached them, they broke out into rebellion, 727. In Greece it was easily suppressed: but in Italy it united Pope and people in opposition to the Imperial Exarch at Ravenna. At the same time, the Patriarch Germanus led the resistance to the Edict at Constantinople; and it could not be put into vigorous execution till his deposition by a *silentium*, or conference, of 7th January, 729. He was succeeded, 22nd January, by his chaplain, Anastasius, Patriarch, 730—†54, who immediately countersigned the edict, and gave it ecclesiastical sanction. Images were removed from the churches; and, the mosaics and paintings thus removed, their walls were whitewashed instead.

These measures provoked the opposition of men distinguished either for position or learning; and both in the letters of Germanus, Patriarch of CP., 715—30, and of Pope Gregory II., 715—†31, and in the orations of John of Damascus, ?676—†756?, the case for images was presented with an unanimity the more remarkable in proportion to the difference of circumstances which separated the three writers. The letters once attributed to Gregory are now seen to be spurious :[47] and we must, therefore, confine ourselves to the arguments of Germanus and John.

The letter of Germanus to Thomas, bishop of Claudiopolis[48] is important as the first formal document in the controversy. He refutes the objection (1) of Jews to images as contravening God's law, by retorting that they broke the same law by offering elsewhere those sacrifices which ought only to be presented at Jerusalem,[49] and (2) of Saracens, by reminding them of the cultus paid by themselves to the Kaaba, a cube of black stone at Mecca.[50] He explains that reverence to images was merely intended to stir the people up to an imitation of their lives who were thus represented.[51] Quoting St. Basil to the effect that a painting is an abridged history,[52] he refers to the fact that many Councils had been held and none of them had forbidden Images,[53] and to the miracles said to have been performed by them.[54] Statues must not be erected after the custom of the heathen;[55] but paintings and mosaics are quite legitimate.

John of Damascus held high office at the Court of the Caliph, and, like Cardinal Pole in his criticism of Henry VIII., was the more free to express his mind as he was out of the Emperor's power. He published his *First Oration*[56] *in defence of the Images, 727*; and it created such a sensation throughout the Empire that copies ran out, and a *Second Oration* appeared, 729. This did little more than repeat the arguments of the first: while a *Third Oration* is probably spurious. In the *First Oration*, John teaches, as to the *use* of Images, that it necessarily resulted from the Incarnation.[57] It is a testimony against the merely docetic view of our Lord's human nature. The Iconoclasts had adopted the Manichæan view of matter, abusing it as a vile thing;[58] and, of course, there is then but a step to docetism. Then, as to the *veneration* of images he quotes St. Basil to the effect that worship paid to images is paid to the original;[59] distinguishes between the adoration due to God alone and the honour due to whatever is associated with dignity,[60] religious or civil; and points out that the second commandment was abrogated by the Incarnation.[61] Iconoclasm, in fact, is a return to the bondage of Judaism from the freedom of the Gospel; and if its adherents observe the Law on this point, why do they not also observe Circumcision and the Sabbath?[62] Iconoclasts, too, are inconsistent. They adore the Cross, or the Holy Table and its vessels, why not then the sacred Images?[63] If I may adore the image of a cross to which He was affixed, why not the image of Him who was affixed to it?[64] He makes a weak attempt to get rid of the argument drawn by the Iconoclasts from Epiphanius's rending of the "idolatrous" curtain. One man's opinion, he says, is not to be set against the universal tradition of the Church; and he quotes as from Gregory Nazianzen the proverb "one swallow does not make spring."[65] He then endeavours to counter the historical argument by showing that some of the fathers[66]—as Basil and Gregory of Nyssa— approved of the use of pictures as a means for teaching the ignorant:[67] and answers the Emperor's contention that no Council had sanctioned the use of images, by retorting that none had condemned them, and silence in such a case was sanction. Lastly, Images are of apiece with sacraments; for they are channels of divine grace[68] —a conception peculiar to Greek theology. St. John of Damascus thus took the question of the use and veneration of Images down to fundamentals: and connected it with the possibility of matter being sanctified to spiritual use.[69] And to conclude his exposition, he declared with an emphasis impossible to a critic of the imperial policy who lived *within* the Empire, "that this is a question for Synods and not for Emperors":[70] "it is not the part of Emperors to legislate for the Church."[71]

While these arguments were being digested, Pope Gregory III., 731—†41 succeeded to the see of Rome. He was the last Pope to be confirmed by an Exarch of Ravenna, and the first, in the eighth century, to utter that cry for help from the other side of the Alps which brought the Franks into Italy. But he pursued, in the main, the same policy as his predecessor, steadily refusing to yield a point to the Emperor on the question of Image-worship, but also refusing to be drawn into any movement for the dismemberment of the Empire.[72] On 1st November, 731, the Pope convened a Council at Rome,[73] of ninety-three bishops, which excommunicated all who defiled or destroyed images of Christ or the Saints. The decree was communicated to Leo III. and his Patriarch, Anastasius; and, in wrath against the Papal decisions and the revolt of Italy, the Emperor attempted to retaliate by sending a fleet to administer punishment. It was wrecked in the Adriatic. Leo thereupon confiscated the estates of the Roman See in Sicily and Southern Italy, with their annual revenue of about £15,800; and withdrew the churches not only of these outlying portions of the Empire but of Illyricum itself from the jurisdiction of the Roman See.[74] The result of these measures was twofold: in the West, to sever the Popes from the Empire and throw them, for defence against the Lombards, into the arms of the Franks, i.e., ultimately of a Western Roman Empire; and to render the Patriarchate of Constantinople conterminous with the Roman Empire of the East. All this suited the centralising policy of Leo III.; but it changed the face of European history. He now let the contest lapse; and in Southern Italy he wisely refrained from enforcing his edicts. That district remained Greek in culture for four centuries.

Constantine V., 741—†75, however, resumed it; though not till his wars with the Saracens were over.[75] He was more of a theologian than his father, and carried both his opinions and his cruelty further. He was, in brief, a Byzantine prototype of our Henry VIII. Objecting not only to the veneration of Images but to the intercession of Saints, he summoned a Council to meet in the Palace of Hieria, opposite Constantinople, 753, which was to put down both, root and branch.[76] It consisted of 340 bishops. Rome, Alexandria and Antioch refused to send legates; and the patriarchate of Constantinople being vacant through the death of Anastasius, 754, the Council had for its presidents, Theodosius, bishop of Ephesus, and Pastillas of Perge.[77] They " carried out the Emperor's wishes exactly, and declared all images forbidden " by the second commandment[78] and the teaching of St. Paul.[79] " Pictures of Christ must be either Nestorian[80] or Monophysite,[81] since it is impossible to represent His Divinity: the only lawful representation of our Lord is the holy Eucharist.[82] It is blasphemous to represent by dead matter those who live with Christ. Image-worshippers are idolaters: Leo and Constantine are the glory of the Orthodox Faith, our rescuers from idolatry. With regard to the three great defenders of images "—Germanus, George, a monk of Cyprus (otherwise unknown to us) and John of Damascus—" the Trinity has deposed these three.[83] An Iconoclast, Constantine II., 754—66, was elected to the vacant see of Constantinople; and the government at once published the decrees of this synod, demanding that all bishops in the Empire should sign the acts and destroy images in their dioceses. Instead of pictures of saints, the churches were now decorated with those of flowers, fruit and birds. The Paulicians were well treated, but the monks were tortured and put to death " . . and " the Emperor, seeing in monasticism the mainstay of image-worship, made a great effort to abolish it altogether.[84] The monastic habit was forbidden, monasteries were turned into barracks, and the Patriarch was made to denounce his former state as a monk in his own church." On the death of Constantine Copronymus, his son and successor, Leo IV., the Khazar, 775—†80, " though he did not repeal the laws, was milder in enforcing them," at least in the earlier part of his reign. But towards its close he " renewed the active persecution of his father ":[85] though his wife, the Empress Irene, maintained, in secret, a devotion to Images.

§ 5. The first reaction,[86] in favour of Images, set in with the accession of her son, Constantine VI., 780—†97, then a child of ten years old. His mother was "an accomplished and ambitious Athenian lady."[87] As a woman and a Greek, she would be on the side of image-worship; but, at first, she could not effect its restoration. The army was fiercely Iconoclast, and had to be reckoned with. She had also to make peace with Harun Arraschid, 783, who had pene-

The Isaurian Dynasty

trated to the Bosporus, 782, and afterwards became Caliph, 786—†809. As soon, however, as she was free, she deposed the Patriarch Paul IV., 780—4, naturally a partisan of the late government; and appointed to succeed him, Tarasius, 784—†806, a secretary of state and a layman. She then renewed relations with Rome: and sent envoys to Pope Hadrian I., 772—†95, asking for a synod to undo the work of the Council of Hieria, and begging him either to come himself[88] or to send legates.[89] Hadrian misliked the promotion of a layman to the patriarchate, but expressed his approval of the orthodoxy of Tarasius in regard to Images. He repeats the arguments in their favour, lays stress on the authority of his see, and demands the restitution of Illyricum to his Patriarchate.[90] He sent two legates; and, though the other Patriarchs were too much harassed by their Mohammedan overlords to send their representatives, the monks of Egypt and Syria managed to send deputies who, in some sort, represented their Patriarchs too. Events were now in train for the Council; and it was opened by Tarasius, August, 786, in the Church of the Apostles at Constantinople. But it was at once dispersed by the soldiers.[91] The Empress-Mother, however, disbanded these troops and replaced them by others: and, for greater safety, the synod reassembled across the water, and so became the Second Council of Nicæa, 787. It is now recognised, by East and West alike, as the Seventh Œcumenical Council.[92] About three hundred bishops attended, under the presidency of Tarasius;[93] the Roman legates signing first and being named first in all lists of members. The Synod declared the lawful use of icons, and defended it by an appeal to Scripture, showing that there were images in the Temple, and by patristic testimonies.[94] In the fifth session an icon was set up in the hall of the synod. The Council of Hieria, 753, was declared at the sixth session not to be œcumenical, since neither the Pope nor any of the other Patriarchs were represented at it; and its arguments were refuted one by one.[95] At the seventh session, the Council drew up its *Definition:*[96] in which after the usual renewal of the condemnation of old heresies, it is declared that the holy icons are to receive "greeting and reverential worship" but not "the adoration which belongs to God alone.[97] The honour paid to them is only relative, and is given for the sake of their prototypes." There is nothing new in this. It is what the defenders of image-worship had said throughout the controversy. The Synod then anathematises the chief Iconoclasts; and, in opposition to the phrase of the other Council, declares—of Germanus, John and George—that "the Trinity has made these three glorious."[98] In the third of its twenty-two canons the Synod legislates in favour of the independence of the Church from the State.[99] Images were now restored in all the churches, and the first Iconoclast movement was at an end. There remained, however, a strong Iconoclast party, especially in the army: and they were ready to take advantage of any weakness in the position of the Empress-Mother. It was not long before their chance came. Elated by her victory, she entered, 790, upon a struggle for sovereignty with her son.[100] He was now of age: and began to show signs of impatience at his counting for nothing. After a long struggle, she dethroned him, and became the first Empress-regnant in Roman history, 797; but with fatal consequences as well to the Empire as to herself. For next year, the Caliph Harun Arraschid, whose armies had raided Romania almost every year, forced her to conclude a peace and pay tribute:[101] while the coronation of Charlemagne on Christmas Day, 800, as Western Emperor, was a still greater blow to the prestige of what had hitherto been "the Roman," and now was only the "Eastern Roman Empire."[102] By a *coup d'état* she was overthrown and her "general logothete." Nicephorus became sovereign in her stead.[103]

§ 6. A second Anarchy, 802—20, ensued; and a second period of Iconoclasm, 813—42, in part coincided with it and in part resulted from it. Nicephorus I., 802—†11, was a good financier and an able ruler. He was not a violent partisan in the matter of Images; but was bent on maintaining both the reforms of the Isaurian Emperors and the supremacy of the State over the

The Isaurian Dynasty 153

Church.[104] Indeed, the later stages of the quarrel about images anticipated very much the strife about Investitures in the Western Church: and centred upon a political rather than a doctrinal question. Nicephorus I., who was Patriarch, 806—15, and shared the name as well as the confidence of the Emperor, was a man of learning and moderation,[105] who supported the government; and the opposition was led by Theodore, abbot of the Studium,[106] 799—†826. In 809 the government dispersed and exiled the monks. They appealed to the Pope;[107] and readily acknowledged the claims of the Roman See provided that, at that price, they could secure the Church from its dependence upon the state. Michael I. (Rhangabe), 811—3, pursued the policy of his father-in-law;[108] but he was defeated by the Bulgars, 813, and forced to resign.[109] A military revolution of July, 813, set up the usurper, Leo V. (the Armenian), 813—†20, in his place: and the army persuaded him that the troubles of the Empire must be put down to the image-worshippers. Leo, therefore, invited the Patriarch Nicephorus to "re-open the question of the icons": but he refused, saying that it was already settled by a general council.[110] In 815 he was accordingly deposed by a Council,[111] in obedience to the Emperor's orders, and an Iconoclast, Theodotus I.,[112] 815—†21, set up in his place. This complaisant prelate then summoned a synod which undid the work of the Seventh Œcumenical Council, and renewed the acts of the Council of Hieria.[113] The persecution was renewed:[114] and the abbot Theodore was sent into his third exile. On the murder of Leo, the throne reverted to a connection of the Isaurian line, by the accession of the Armenian, Michael II.[115] (the Stammerer), 820—†9. His policy was to allow people to believe what they liked in private, but not to permit image-worship in public.[116] The persecution, however, was renewed under his son, Theophilus, 829—†42; perhaps at the instance of his friend, John the Grammarian, nicknamed by his enemies, John Lecanomantis,[117] who became the Patriarch John VII., 832—42. Monks were imprisoned; a bishop was scourged; image-worshippers were banished from Constantinople; and the painting of pictures was suppressed in the neighbourhood of the capital.[118] But a century of strife about images had now produced widespread weariness of the whole business; and, on the death of Theophilus, the final stage of the controversy was reached.

§ 7. It was the second, and final, restoration of Images, 843; and its events repeat the story of the first reaction with curious exactness. Theophilus left a son three years old, Michael III., 842—†67—afterwards known as Michael the Drunkard; and again the Empress-mother, whose name was Theodora, 821—†67, became regent for her son. We do not know the state of parties in Constantinople: but one of her co-regents, Theoctistus, the Logothete of the Course, persuaded her that, in order to secure his throne, the best way would be to effect the restoration of the Images.[119] The advice fell in with her own religious convictions. She summoned a Council, 843, which deposed the patriarch John and put an Image-worshipper, Methodius I., 842—†6, into his place. The Synod then received the decrees of the Seventh Œcumenical Council, and excommunicated all Iconoclasts; making, however, no mention of Theophilus out of respect for the Empress.[120] On 11th March, 843, being the first Sunday in Lent, the images were taken in triumph to St. Sophia, and restored to all the churches. The day is still kept as the Sunday of Orthodoxy. The honours of the long struggle are divided: for, while the theological justification of the use and veneration was accepted, the State remained victorious in securing its authority over the Church. As for Iconoclasm, " it was a merely negative doctrine . . . it might become, as it did, a fanaticism; it could never become a religion. Iconoclasm might proscribe idolatry; but it had no power of kindling a purer faith."[121]

§ 8. Disasters thickened upon the Empire during the later years of the controversy about Images. The fall of Irene was followed by " The Second Anarchy," 802—20, of Byzantine history; and, during this period, three events took place which impaired the prestige of the Empire. The first was the loss of imperial authority in the West.

The Isaurian Dynasty

Charlemagne, since his coronation at Rome on Christmas Day, 800, was anxious to get his imperial dignity regularised. The only constitutional way to do this was to obtain its recognition by the Emperor at Constantinople. In 803 hostilities broke out between them over Venice; and Charlemagne, possessed of its territories since 810, agreed to hand them back to their rightful overlord, the Emperor, in return for the acknowledgment of his own imperial title. By the treaty of 812, Michael I. (Rhangabe) agreed to his terms. The Emperor's ambassadors saluted Charles as Augustus at Aix-la-chapelle; and so there was again, in theory, one Empire with two colleagues for sovereigns, as in the days of Arcadius and Honorius, four hundred years before. Actually, there were for the first time recognised two Emperors, and a Western and an Eastern Empire; with a loss of prestige to the Roman Emperor at Constantinople who was now but one of two Emperors, with a territory in the West confined to Venice and a few towns in Southern Italy. A second blow to the prestige of the Empire was the succession of disasters inflicted upon it by the Bulgarians. In 807 the Emperor Nicephorus I. invaded their country; but Krum, King of Bulgaria, retaliated by the capture of Sardica (Sredec, or Sofia) in the spring of 809; and 26th July, 811, he defeated and slew Nicephorus on the field of battle. Not since Valens perished on the field of Adrianople, 378, had a Roman Emperor been overwhelmed by barbarians. The Bulgarians followed up their victory by the defeat of his son, Michael I., on 22nd June, 813, between Adrianople and Versinicia, and by laying siege to Constantinople. But, after the death of Krum, 815, they were annihilated by the Emperor Leo V., 813—†20, at Mesembria, now Misivri, on the Black Sea, 817. A third shock to the prestige of the Empire followed upon its losses to the Saracens: of Crete, 825, and Sicily, 827. But from this point a recovery set in. It was maintained under the rule of Theophilus, 829—†42; and was due to the enfeeblement of the Abbasid Caliphs at Bagdad, in spite of the defeat they inflicted on the Romans at Dazimon, now Tokat, to the N.E. of Asia Minor, on the road from Constantinople to Sivas, and the subsequent loss of Amorium, 24th September, 838. Sound administration, financial reform and skilful diplomacy distinguished the government of Theophilus; and in his reign, too, began the intellectual recovery which issued in the founding of the University of Constantinople, 850, by his brother-in-law, the Cæsar Bardas, 862—†6.

§ 9. Parallel to this recovery was the recovery of the Church.

(i.) The cessation of the controversy about Images led to the restoration of religious unity; though, unfortunately, by the forcible repression of heresy. The heresy of the Paulicians[122] was, in the ninth century, the main obstacle to religious unity. The sect is first mentioned under that name by Nerses II., Catholicus of Armenia, in an encyclical of 553; and the name is of Armenian formation, meaning "sons of Paulik," i.e., of little Paul, the diminutive—*ik*, carrying a touch of contempt. According to an anonymous account[123] of c. 840, the Paul in question was Paul of Samosata, bishop of Antioch, c. 260—70, and son of a Manichæan woman, Callinice. She sent him and her other son, John, as missionaries to Armenia. If this were the origin of the Paulicians, it would account for Manichæan and adoptianist elements in their creed. But, according to their own traditions, their founder, c. 660, was Constantine, a native of the region between the upper Euphrates and Erzerum; who based his teaching on the Gospels and the Epistles of St. Paul, to the exclusion of the rest of the Scriptures. Constantine was martyred, 684, by Simeon, whom the Emperor Constantine IV., Pogonatus, 668—†85, had sent to repress the movement. But Simeon was so impressed by the martyr's death that he was converted, himself became the head of the sect, and was, in his turn, put to death, 690, by the Emperor Justinian II., 685—95. About the middle of the eighth century Constantine V., 741—†75, transplanted, 752, many Paulicians from the neighbourhood of Erzerum to Thrace, in order that these "martial heretics" might defend the Empire from

Bulgars and Slavs. For the Paulicians have been described "as the left wing of the Iconoclasts";[124] and Constantine V. has been suspected of being himself a Paulician.[125] At any rate, they rejected, as he did, images, pictures, and crosses as idolatrous: and disliked monks and fasting. They were widely diffused throughout Asia Minor, from Armenia to Phrygia. They lived in peace under his rule: and contributed no little support both to his iconoclastic policy and to the defence of his Empire. In 801 their leader, Sergius, †835, took advantage of the tolerance of the Emperor Nicephorus I., 802—†11, to begin that ministry which put fresh life into the sect. Perhaps for this reason, or possibly to dissociate themselves from a sect denounced by the Church as Manichæan, Leo V., 813—†20, and Theophilus, 829—†42, abandoned the policy of their predecessors in the eighth century and set up a fresh persecution of the Paulicians. Leo V. provoked a rising at Cynoschora; whence many fled into Saracen territory to Argaeum (now Argoran), some twenty miles north of Melitene. From these regions the Paulicians, under their generals Karbeas and Chrysocheir, raided the Empire for fifty years; though Sergius condemned retaliation. The Empress Theodora, 842—†67, put to death 100,000 of them; and drove still larger numbers over the border to Argaeum, Tephrike (Devrik) and Amara near Manjilik.[126] At last, the Emperor Basil I., 867—†86, took Tephrike, 873; and the sect was temporarily repressed in the Empire, which once its sturdy warriors had done so much to uphold.[127]

(ii.) Meanwhile, missions not disconnected with politics, but untainted by persecution, effected conversions in the Empire and in neighbouring lands.

The Slavs of the Peloponnese were subjugated under Michael III., 842—†67, and the foundation of churches and monasteries[128] led to their rapid Christianisation under Basil I. and his successors; and some few converts were made among the Khazars,[129] c. 860, by Constantine "the Philosopher," who, at the end of his days, adopted the name of Cyril, and was sent there, c. 860, by the Emperor Michael III. and the Patriarch Photius,

857—67. His name is associated with that of his elder brother, Methodius : and brings us to the association of St. Methodius, 825—†85, and St. Cyril, 827—†69, in the conversion of Moravia. Moravia,[130] since the Great War, has become part of Czecho-Slovakia. Formerly, it belonged to Austria. It covers the basin of the Morava, whence its name, a tributary entering the Danube at Pressburg. It has a population of about two and a half million, 71 per cent of which is Slav and 27 per cent German : 95 per cent are Roman Catholics. The Slavs invaded and settled in the country about the end of the sixth century. About the end of the eighth, they assisted Charles the Great, 742—†814, to expel the Avars; and received part of the Avar country or what is now northern Hungary for their reward. They held it as a fief of the Western Empire. On the death of Charles, the Moravian princes took advantage of the dissensions among his sons to enlarge their possessions and to assert their independence. Teuton and Slav were forced into conflict; and in 845, Lewis, the German, 843—†76, was anxious to destroy the independence of Great Moravia under Prince Rostislav. The Prince found an ally, 853, in Boris, King of the Bulgars, 852—88; but the allies were defeated; and eventually Boris changed sides, and an alliance was negotiated between the German and Bulgarian Kings, 862. Thereupon Rostislav sent an embassy to the Court of Constantinople : and appealed for the help of the Emperor. He desired the Christianisation of his subjects, but also their independence of Germany. It was in answer to his appeal that Methodius and Cyril were dispatched on their mission to Moravia :[181] and they seem to have been at work in the country from 864—7.

Methodius and Constantine were the sons of an officer at Thessalonica. He gave them a good education; Methodius entered the public service, and then retired to a monastery on Mt. Olympus in Bithynia. Constantine found a patron in the Logothete of the Course Theoctistus,[132] who was all powerful with Theophilus and Theodora. The minister brought him to Constantinople where he became a pupil of Leo the mathematician and of the Patriarch Photius. The latter made him his librarian—no small tribute to his learning from a prelate so widely read as Photius—and the young priest took rank as third among these three eminent teachers of philosophy in Constantinople. His attainments stood him in good stead when he and his brother proceeded to Moravia. They began by preaching and teaching; and set up a seminary for the training of a native clergy. They also translated portions of the Scriptures and of the Service-Books into the vernacular; and in order that their translations might be written down, they invented an alphabet and employed the Glagolitic script based on Greek minuscules; though their names are popularly associated with the Cyrillic which superseded it. The Cyrillic is now used by Bulgars, Serbs and Russians; and is the Greek uncial alphabet, expanded by some necessary additions. It does not seem, at first sight, quite clear why the two brothers went out of their way to provide for their converts in Moravia a script which was not that in ordinary use in the Empire. But the Glagolitic characters had probably been devised for the Bulgars; and there are good reasons why they should have been favoured with a script of their own. They would be more likely to accept the Christian religion, if its Scriptures and Liturgy were presented to them in their own tongue and in letters that were *not* the ordinary Greek. It is interesting to note this example of the policy of the Orthodox Church: nationalism and the vernacular, leading to a federation of autocephalous churches which are at one in doctrine though they differ in usages. The Roman Church, on the contrary, maintained Latin everywhere as the language of worship, in the interests of a stricter unity. The clash of these opposing policies caused the apostles of Moravia to go and seek recognition, 868, from the Roman See. They had a great reception from Pope Hadrian II., 867—†72; by whom they were consecrated to the episcopate, and some of their disciples ordained priest. The Pope also seems to have expressed a qualified approval of the

Slavonic books, and to have authorised preaching and reading of the Scriptures in Sclavonic. These concessions would have encouraged Constantine: but he died, 14th February, 869, in Rome; and so he never returned to the mission in Moravia to see them recognised in practice. Methodius, however, went back to his labours in "Moravia," as archbishop of Sirmium in Pannonia. His province appears to have included part of what had previously belonged to the provinces of Salzburg and Passau. In 871, complaints on this account were made at Rome; nominally on behalf of the archbishop of Salzburg, but really in the interests of the German King and his Germanising ally, Swatopluk, 870—†94, nephew and successor of Rostislav. The complaints, however, were not immediately successful:[133] but Methodius was in an untenable position. "He was determined to celebrate Mass in Slavonic, yet he depended on the good-will of the Roman See."[134] Pope John VIII., 872—†82, indeed, continued to support him. He gave him leave to say Mass and other offices in Slavonic, 880; and a letter of recommendation to Swatopluk.[135] But after his death, the closing years of the life of Methodius were embittered by further disputes. He died, 6th April, 885. His disciples were forced to leave the country. The Latin language and literature supplanted the vernacular: and Moravia was absorbed into the organisation of the Western Church.

In 864 the disciples of Methodius and Cyril had better success in Bulgaria.[136]

This country[137] is now a Kingdom of S.E. Europe, lying to the N.E. of the Balkan peninsula. It is bounded on the W. by Serbia, on the N. by the Danube, on the E. by the Black Sea, and to the S. by the Rhodope Mountains from 6,000 to 9,000 feet high, through which the Struma (Strymon) on the West and the Maritza (Hebrus) on the E. run down into Turkey. Half way between the Danube and the Rhodope Mountains, and parallel to each, run the Balkans (Haemus), separating Bulgaria proper to the north from Eastern Roumelia on the south: they are from 7,000—8,000 feet. The population of the country in 1906 was about four million: three million of whom are Orthodox; 640,000 Moslem and 28,000 Roman Catholics; and these divisions show that whereas there were continuous efforts as in Moravia to draw the country within the orbit of Latin Christendom, they were unsuccessful: and Bulgaria was secured for the Orthodox Church. It is now an Exarchate, independent of the Œcumenical Patriarch, and not in communion with him. The Exarch lives in Constantinople; is elected by the Bishops, the Holy Synod and the General Assembly on which the laity are represented; and is titular metropolitan of a Bulgarian diocese. There are in Bulgaria itself eleven such dioceses,[138] each administered by a metropolitan and a diocesan Council. These dioceses contain 2,106 parishes; 78 convents of men with 184 monks; and 12 of women, with 346 nuns. Dioceses and parishes alike are governed under the authority of the Holy Synod, which consists of four metropolitans: and the laity take part in the election both of the bishops and of their parish priests.

Racially, the Bulgars are of Turanian origin, akin to Tartars, Huns, Avars, Petchenegs, Magyars and Finns. They made their appearance on the Pruth in the seventh century; and were governed by Khans (chiefs) and Boyars (nobles). Between the seventh and the ninth century they became absorbed in the Slavonic population; and, like the Franks in Gaul, they gave their name and a political organisation to the race they conquered. But they adopted its language, customs and local institutions. No trace of the Ugrian or Finnish element is to be found in the Bulgar tongue. The conquerors were completely assimilated by the vanquished. We have already seen what disasters Krum, King of the Bulgars, 802—†15, inflicted on the Empire; when he captured Sardica (Sredec, or Sofia) and made it his capital, 809; and then advanced to Constantinople. After his death, the Bulgars were driven back, 817, by Leo V., 813—†20; but they again became a power whose alliance was worth cultivating under their King Boris, 852—88 († 907). In alliance with Rostislav, Prince of Moravia, Boris took arms, for

162   *The Churches of Eastern Christendom*

Slavs against Teutons, to resist Lewis the German,[139] 843—†76. But when Carloman, †880, King of Bavaria and son of Lewis, rebelled against his father and was supported by Rostislav, Boris sided with Lewis in an alliance, 862, between Germany and Bulgaria. Caught between two foes, Rostislav sent for help to Constantinople : and the Emperor, Michael III., 842—†67, fearing that the Bulgars would throw themselves on to the side of Lewis and Latin Christendom determined, 863, to coerce Bulgaria. He invaded Bulgaria, and imposed terms on Boris : (1) that he should receive Christianity from the Greeks, and not from the Latins; (2) that his kingdom should submit to the ecclesiastical rule of Constantinople; and (3) that he should withdraw from the alliance with Lewis. Envoys, whom Boris sent to Constantinople, were baptised there : and when the peace was finally concluded, 864—5, Boris himself was baptised with the Emperor Michael III. for his godfather, and forced his subjects, after a revolt on their part, to be baptised too.[140]

The conversion of the Bulgars was followed by the organisation of the Church of Bulgaria.[141] Greek clergy[142] now poured into the country to teach the people and to set up the ecclesiastical arrangements; and the Patriarch Photius, 857—67, who was active in bringing about the conversion of Boris, addressed him a long letter in which he first explains the faith of the Church by reference to the Creeds of Nicæa and Constantinople and the Seven Œcumenical Councils, and then goes on to treat of Christian duty.[143] These Orthodox clergy were followed by Armenians,[144] probably of Paulician sympathies, 865. And, while the people were not unnaturally puzzled by the differences of opinion among their teachers and grew restive, the King resented the autocracy of Photius who would not let him have a bishop for Bulgaria but insisted on keeping the Bulgar nation in dependence upon himself. Accordingly, he turned for satisfaction to the West. In August, 866, his ambassadors appeared at Rome before Pope Nicholas I., 858—†67. They asked him to send a bishop and priests to their country; and submitted to him a hundred and six questions relating to the social and religious obligations which the acceptance of the Faith imposed upon them. At the same time, Boris sent an embassy to King Lewis, with a similar request for a bishop and priests. The King sent clergy, vestments, vessels and books : but his clergy returned as soon as they found that the Pope had been beforehand with similar aid. For Nicholas had sent two bishops as his legates, Paul, bishop, 861—77, of Populonia (Piombino, in Tuscany), and Formosus, bishop of Porto, 864—76; they were to attach the Bulgarians to the Western Church. And they carried with them not only sacred vessels, books[145] and vestments, but the *Responsa ad Bulgaros*,[146] 13th November, 866, of Nicholas I., in reply to the questions addressed to him.

The papal *Responsa* present a striking contrast at the outset to the letter addressed to King Boris by the Œcumenical Patriarch. Photius leads off with theological exposition; but Nicholas I. just opens with the statement that Christianity is (1) a religion of faith to be expressed in works; and then proceeds to the business in hand of answering the questions put to him. It would be tedious to go through them in detail. The questions remind us of those submitted by St. Augustine on behalf of his English converts : like his, they are often a little crude. But the answers of Nicholas I. are worthy to rank, for their wisdom and tolerance, with those of his predecessor St. Gregory the Great, 590—†604. And, indeed, he often refers to them; and evidently takes him for his model.

(a.) A good many of the *Responsa* concern the rules and customs of the Church; and are excellent examples of the exercise of that authority to " bind " and to " loose," i.e. to prohibit and to permit, which our Lord conferred upon His Church.[147] Thus (2) marriage between sponsors and their spiritual children is forbidden, just as by the Civil Law parents were not allowed to marry their adopted children; and (39) marriage within certain degrees of consanguinity is prohibited. The essence of marriage (3) consists solely in the consent of the parties to it, not in their cohabitation; nor in the ceremonies of the marriage rite. These, however, are carefully detailed; and the description of them is of unique interest. It is our earliest authority for the rites and ceremonies of Christian marriage. And it is evidence that what the Roman church did was simply to take over the marriage rites of pagan Rome " without the sacrifice; or rather, with the substitution of the [Nuptial] Mass for the pagan sacrifice." . . . " The acts which Pope Nicholas mentions are divided into two categories : those which precede, and those which accompany, the *nuptialia fœdera*. The first category contains (1) the betrothal, or espousal *(sponsalia)*, the expression of the consent of the couple to be married, and of their parents, to the projected marriage; (2) the *subarrhatio*, or delivery of the ring by the bridegroom to the bride; and (3) the delivering over of the dowry *(dos)* by written document, in the presence of witnesses. These are the preliminaries. The marriage ceremony itself comprises (1) the celebration of Mass in the presence of the newly married, who take part in the offering and are communicated; (2) the benediction pronounced while a veil is held above their heads; and (3) their coronation on leaving the church " : where the Pope requires that the crowns to be used should be those kept in the church for the purpose, as if otherwise they might employ crowns profaned by some heathen or superstitious association. Christian marriage also (51) requires the abolition of polygamy and (96) is indissoluble, except for the wife's adultery. Occasions of fasting and abstinence (5—9) receive a good deal of attention. In Lent (44—8) there is to be no hunting, for they will not want flesh to eat; no holding of law-courts, for they will put away quarrels; no feasting and no weddings; there is also to be abstinence from the use of marriage (9, 50), because there will then (9) be daily Communion; and the same rule holds, of course (63) for Sundays. Other *Responsa* enumerate the feast-days to be observed as holidays : viz., (10—12) Sundays, and other holy days. But the Sabbath is not to be kept; and (10) on the Lord's Day the reason for resting from labour is that men may be free for worship. Baptism is valid, in spite of its being administered by men (14—16) of in-

The Isaurian Dynasty

different character; provided only that it be bestowed (104) with water and in the name of the Trinity, or even of Jesus only; and the usual days (59) for Baptism are the first and last vigils of Eastertide, i.e., the eves of Easter Day and Whit-Sunday. Prayers for rain (59) are permitted; prayers may be stopped (74) on the approach of the enemy. The laity (61) are expected to observe the hours of prayer. In church (66), men must not wear turbans and (58) women must be covered. There is no reason why a woman (68) should not go to church, even on the day of her delivery, if she is strong enough and wishes to go. Fasting is imperative (65) before Communion; and, as nobody ever heard of people taking food before 9 a.m. (60) it is wrong to have even a " tiny bit " of breakfast earlier. People should not think (71) they suffer loss by receiving Communion from an unworthy priest. He is like a candle, burning to his own loss while he gives light to the darkness around him! The rebels who joined in the recent revolt against King Boris, and tried to turn him back from embracing Christianity (78) are to be admitted to penance, whatever the Greeks say. As for the last rites: for suicides (98) there is to be no burial in church, and no funeral Mass. But (99—100) Christians are to be buried in church, for then they will be prayed for: such prayers (88) being offered only for the faithful departed. The Pope is making provision for worship and discipline, by sending (37) the books needed; in particular, copies (14, 19—32) of the Civil Code as also (75—6) of the Penitential and the Missal. These latter must not be put into the hands of the laity; but both law-books and church-books demand official exponents. As to their demand for a Patriarch (which, in the eyes of Boris, was the most important question submitted to the Pope), Nicholas I. (72) declines to commit himself, until he has received the report of his legates, as to the numbers and unanimity of the Bulgarian converts. For the present, they may have a bishop. As the number of Christians grows, he will consecrate other bishops: who, eventually, will elect one of their number to be Patriarch, or, at least, Archbishop. As to his consecration (73) it will not be necessary for him to go to Rome for the purpose, because of the great distance; but he will be consecrated at home, though not enthroned nor empowered to consecrate person or thing except the Eucharist, until he receives the *pallium*. You are not to listen to (105) preachers without mission: and (106) as to the variety of opinions pressed upon you by Greek, Armenian and other missionaries, the Roman church is the safest guide because "it has been taught by St. Peter, whose confession of faith was divinely approved." You should be careful about listening to other preachers, so as to avoid dissensions: though what matters is not who preaches but whether the sermon is true. My legates and your future bishop will tell you what you ought to do; and, in doubtful cases, you will consult the Apostolic See.

(b.) The customs of heathendom also receive attention. Where they are not sinful, (49) they are to be retained. The Bulgarians had asked whether they should adopt the civilised habit of wearing drawers: the Pope replied (59) that it was not a matter of much importance either way. It was their custom for the King to sit at table in solitary grandeur: this (42), says Nicholas, is bad manners, though it is neither wrong nor irreligious. It is wrong, however, (62, 79) to use charms or amulets. Oaths (67) should henceforth be taken not on the sword but on the Gospel; and (33) the Cross should be substituted on the standards for the horse's tail.

(c.) Tolerant as he was of their customs when harmless, the Pope tried to mitigate such as were harsh and cruel. It is well enough to punish rebels, but (17) not their children; and to repudiate a Greek missionary who pretended to be a presbyter, but (14) not to cut off his nose and ears. Again, (40) in starting out for a campaign, it is wrong to kill off those who are unfit to share in it. Moreover (34—8) war is neither to be entered upon lightly, nor waged ruthlessly. It is to be preceded by prayers and Masses, confession and Communion, by the liberation of prisoners, the manumission of slaves and giving of alms to the needy; and to be suspended on holy days. There is to be (52) no mutilation: (on which point, " see the Civil Code "); no intercourse (65) with nursing mothers; justice (83—5) is to be tempered with mercy; and, above all, (86) no use of torture for extracting confessions from accused persons. The Pope enjoins (95) the right of asylum in churches; and lays it down that even parricides and fratricides who seek the refuge of the sanctuary should be treated with mildness. So also (97) should the slaves. Almsgiving (101) is part of Christian duty, but it is not to be indiscriminate. " Give to him that asketh thee " (*Mt.* v. 42) is to be balanced by " Give to the godly man, and help not the sinner " (*Ecclus.* xii. 4); and there are people who will let Christ's poor die of hunger, while they spend fortunes on actors!

(d.) There remain a few *Responsa* which strike us as falling below the high standard of good sense and sympathy which characterises most of them. They are such as reflect upon the faults of the Greeks. The Bulgarians are rightly enough warned against their doctrine (6) that it is wrong to take a bath on Wednesday and Friday; against (14—6) the missionary of Greek nationality who passed himself off as a presbyter, and baptised many; against (54—5) their notions as to the attitude proper to prayer, (77) their superstitious use of the *sortes biblicae,* and their refusal of penance (78), after the manner of Novatianists rather than of Catholics, to rebels who ask to be admitted to it; above all, against their pretensions (92—3) in favour of the see of Constantinople. It has attained its rank not because it is an Apostolic See like the three older Patriarchates of Rome, Alexandria and Antioch; but simply by Imperial favour. The Greeks, moreover, have no right to claim (94) that they are the sole originators and distributors of the Chrism. But there is a tone of asperity in all that the Pope says about the Greeks. Perhaps, there is some excuse for it. Rome and Constantinople were, at this moment, more embittered than usual: for the quarrel between Nicholas and Photius was ripening into an open breach.

" The prospect of an Archbishop " for Bulgaria "seems to have satisfied " King Boris. " He welcomed the papal legates: and, expelling all other missionaries from the kingdom, committed to them exclusively the task of preaching and baptising. . . . The Latin ecclesiastics worked for more than a year, 866—7, in the land which the Pope hoped he had annexed to the spiritual dominion of Rome."[148] But Photius resented their presence in a country converted by Greeks: and, in a letter of Lent, 867, to the three Eastern Patriarchs, he denounced the invasion of Bulgaria by the Latins.[149] On a change in the political situation, Photius was deposed, and his rival, Ignatius, recovered the Patriarchate, mainly by the help of the Roman See. But Ignatius proved as resolute as Photius to assert the jurisdiction of Constantinople over Bulgaria. At the Council of Constantinople, 869, which the Romans reckon as the Eighth Œcumenical Synod, Bulgarian ambassadors, Roman legates, and representatives of the Eastern Patriarchs were summoned,[150] 3rd March, 870, to the Imperial presence, along with the Patriarch Ignatius. The question " was raised to which church Bulgaria had belonged when it was a province of the Empire, and whether the clergy at the time of the Bulgarian conquest had been Greeks or Latins. It was answered that the province had been subject to Constantinople, and that the clergy found in it were Greeks. On these grounds, it was adjudged that Bulgaria ought to belong to the patriarchate of Constantinople. . . Ignatius in the same year consecrated an archbishop for Bulgaria, with ten bishops, and within a short time all the Latin clergy were ejected from that country."[151]

There was an interval of disaster, 856—60, before these conversions of Bulgaria and Moravia; when Michael III. escaped from the tutelage of his mother, Theodora, 821—†67, and her minister, Theoctistus, †856: and the Russians appeared before Constantinople,[152] June, 860. They, too, applied for a bishop and baptism, 866: but we hear nothing further of their conversion for a hundred years.

§ 10. The quarrel between East and West[153] under Michael III., 842—†67, darkened the last ten years of his

The Isaurian Dynasty

reign, and was the greatest disaster that had yet overtaken Christendom.

(i.) Nicetas, born 799, was the fourth[154] child of the Emperor Michael I. (Rhangabe). In 813, when his father was overthrown by the revolt of Leo V. (the Armenian), he was mutilated and banished. He received the tonsure and took the name of Ignatius. Afterwards, he founded new monasteries in the Islands of the Princes : where he presided as abbot, and gave shelter to many of the Image-worshippers who had been driven from the capital. He had little learning or knowledge of the world; and devoted himself wholly to the life of the cloister. The Empress Theodora was aided, in the restoration of the Images, by the Patriarch Methodius, 842—†6; and, on his death, she remembered the imperial birth and the piety of Ignatius; and advanced him to the Patriarchal Throne. Ignatius held the dignity, though without distinction, for about ten years : when, on the overthrow of his patroness, by the murder of her favourite minister, Theoctistus, †856, supreme power fell into the hands of her brother Bardas, who became minister of her son, Michael III., and Cæsar, 862—†6. Bardas was a patron of learning,[155] but a man of indifferent character : who divorced his wife to marry his daughter-in-law. For this, the Patriarch refused him communion on the Feast of the Epiphany, 858; and, in the autumn of that year, offended him again by refusing to force the veil on Theodora and her daughters against their will. On 23rd November, 858, Ignatius was seized and banished : but he refused to resign, and so remained Patriarch *de jure*. Disregarding the canonical obstacle that the see was not vacant, the Emperor and the Cæsar decided to procure the election of a more friendly patriarch : and their choice fell upon Photius, 800—†91.

Photius[156] was born c. 800. His father, Sergius, was brother to the Patriarch Tarasius, 784—†806; and, through his mother, he was connected with the family of Theodora.[157] His parents had suffered exile for the worship of Images : and early in the reign of Theodora, 842—67 he had become professor of philosophy at Constantinople. In this capacity, he soon proved to be a man of attractive personality, a stimulating teacher, and a scholar of encyclopædic learning. Most celebrated of his works is the *Bibliotheca*,[158] a collection of extracts from, and abridgments of, two hundred and eighty volumes of the classical authors. To this collection we are indebted for almost all that we possess of some of them. The works of historians and theologians are fully represented. But poets and philosophers are ignored: not because Photius was indifferent to these authors, but because he took it for granted that every educated man would be familiar with them:[159] a fine testimony to the general culture of his day. Besides the *Bibliotheca*, Photius undertook a *Lexicon* which was completed by his pupils, and intended to facilitate the study of old or sacred authors whose language and vocabulary had grown out of date: while, in his *Amphilochia*[160] he made a collection of some three hundred questions and answers on points of Scripture, addressed to Amphilochius, bishop of Cyzicus. But learning was not the only distinction of Photius. His family connections and his talents opened for him a career in the Imperial service. He became First Secretary of State, with the rank of a Protospatharius: and enjoyed the intimacy of the Cæsar Bardas, who was really responsible for his appointment as Patriarch. Photius was still a layman; but, within less than a week, he was promoted through all the inferior Orders: and on Christmas Day, 858, he was consecrated to the episcopate by his friend Gregory Asbestas, archbishop of Syracuse, 855—63; who had fallen out with Ignatius, the deposed Patriarch.

(ii.) The respective claims of Ignatius and Photius represent no mere personal rivalries, nor only a conflict between two types of churchmanship reflected, on the one hand, by the ascetic and devout Ignatius and, on the other, by the scholar and statesman, Photius. They brought out the opposition between two tendencies in ecclesiastical politics, which had already declared themselves under the late Patriarch Methodius, 842—6. He himself was a prelate who had suffered in the cause of

Image-worship, and had effectively assisted in its restoration by Theodora. But he had kept on good terms with her iconoclast husband, Theophilus, †842, and, by this practice of economy, had successfully maintained the Byzantine tradition in regard to relations between Church and State. He and his friends looked back to Tarasius, 784—†806, under Constantine VI. and to Nicephorus, 806—†15, under Nicephorus I., 802—†11, as the ideal patriarchs. They had both held high office as laymen before their consecration; and, like them, Methodius stood for " statesmanship in ecclesiastical administration " which deferred to the Emperor as supreme over the Church, and for the assertion of the Patriarchal and episcopal authority in dealing with the monks. There were monks, too, among his supporters. But the monks of the Studium took the opposite line. They stood for the independence of the Church over against the State; for the supremacy of the Roman See; and for the exemption of Religious from the control of the hierarchy. These parties continued under Ignatius and Photius; and, while the Court from the first revolution in the palace which led to the abasement of Theodora to the second which ended in the murder of her son, Michael III., supported Photius, popular feeling sided with Ignatius—not least because of the harsh treatment which he had received. But Photius succeeded in making anti-papalism a national enterprise : and so entered upon the controversy even with Nicholas I., one of the greatest of the Popes, with no small prospects in his favour.

(iii.) We come now to the events of the controversy : discreditable to either side, and disastrous to the unity of the Church.

Early in 859, Photius sent the customary Letters Enthronistic to the other Patriarchal Sees, announcing his accession. To Alexandria, Antioch[161] and Jerusalem he sent letters only; but the letter to the Pope was carried, together with a letter (now lost, but recoverable from the Pope's reply[162]) from the Emperor, by an embassy consisting of an Imperial Spatharius and three bishops. They presented rich gifts and were received, in the summer of

860, in the church of S. Maria Maggiore. Photius[163] enlarged upon his reluctance to accept the office. It was pressed upon him, he said, by the Emperor and the clergy. He declared his adherence to the Faith and to the Seven Œcumenical Councils, and concluded by asking the Pope for his prayers. He said nothing about his predecessor, nor about the circumstances of his own appointment. This omission, however, was made good by the Imperial Missive: in which Michael III. gave his own version of the events to the effect that Ignatius had voluntarily withdrawn after being deposed by a Council for neglect of his flock,[162] and invited the Pope to send legates to a synod which was to clear up some details of the Iconoclastic controversy. Nicholas may well have been suspicious. He "resolved to seize the occasion, and assert a jurisdiction which, if it had been accepted, would have annulled the independence of the Church of Constantinople."[164] On 25th September, 860, he dispatched two legates,[165] Rhodoaldus, bishop of Portus, 853—64, and Zacharias, bishop of Anagni, with powers to investigate and report, and with replies to the Emperor and to Photius. In *Principatum itaque*[166] addressed to the Emperor, the Pope begins by asserting the right of his See to be consulted; protests that this right has been violated by the deposition of Ignatius, "without reference to the Roman Pontiff"; and adds that the offence has been made worse by the election of a layman. He cannot consent to the consecration of Photius, until his legates have brought him their report upon the business; and he concludes by proposing "a bargain[167] in the interest of what he calls 'ecclesiastica utilitas.' "[168] Let the Emperor show his devotion to the Roman See by restoring to it the Vicariate of Thessalonica, together with its patrimony in Calabria and Sicily and the right to consecrate the archbishop of Syracuse. Ignatius, is the inference, will not stand in the way: and matters might be arranged. To Photius the Pope sent a brief note[169] only, censuring him for having accepted consecration to the episcopate without first having served in the inferior Orders; and declining to consent to it until his legates reported upon "his

behaviour and his devotion to 'ecclesiastica utilitas.'"
The inference again was "Let Photius show himself favourable to the papal wishes: let him, in fact, promote 'the deal'[170] which the Pope had suggested to the Emperor, and there would be no further difficulty about his acknowledgment as Patriarch."

The Emperor and the Cæsar were inclined, at first, to do business with the Pope on these terms. His proposals would have rid them of the party of Ignatius by ranging the Roman See against it. But they would have deprived the See of Constantinople of half its jurisdiction;[171] and Photius, not to be caught by the bait, succeeded in persuading Michael and Bardas to refuse them. So, on the arrival of the Roman legates, they were met by cajolements and threats. Photius prevented them from hearing the Ignatian side, and kept them quiet by costly presents: while the Emperor, by threatening to detain them in quarters where insects would make their life a misery,[172] induced them to take the part of Photius. Accordingly, at the Council of Constantinople,[173] May, 861, they concurred in affirming the deposition of Ignatius and sanctioning the appointment of Photius.

On hearing of these proceedings, the Pope, in the autumn of 861, repudiated the action of his legates. He received, with indignation, the minutes of the Council, with letters from the Emperor and the Patriarch. For Photius, in his communication,[174] assumed the independence of the See of Constantinople, and ignored the proposals for the return of Illyricum, Calabria and Sicily to the Roman See, on the ground that it was a question for the Emperor. Nicholas was hardly the man to take such a letter complacently; and, in March, 862, he determined to embrace the cause of Ignatius and to denounce Photius. In three letters[175] of 18—19th March, 862, addressed to the three Eastern Patriarchs,[176] to Photius[177] and to the Emperor,[178] he gave his judgment. The Patriarchs he informed that Ignatius had been illegally deposed and that a most wicked man had been intruded into his place; this the Roman See would never tolerate; and they must see to it that Ignatius be restored and Photius deposed.

To Photius and to the Emperor, he re-affirms, in terms stronger than before, the supreme authority of the Roman See.[179]

Not long afterwards, Nicholas was presented, for the first time, with the Ignatian case. For, in 862, Theognostus, exarch of the monasteries of Constantinople, arrived in Rome as an envoy from that party; and told the Pope about recent events from their point of view. He presented a *Libellus Ignatii*:[180] and implored the papal support. Nicholas was not slow to give it; for, April, 863, in the Lateran Council[181] he deposed and excommunicated Photius and reinstated Ignatius. Some time passed before he received from the Emperor, August, 865, a letter assuring him that all his efforts on behalf of Ignatius were in vain and requiring him to withdraw his sentence, but in November the Pope replied with *Proposueramus quidem*,[182] laying final emphasis on the privilege of the Roman See—bestowed upon it by Christ and not by synods—as the ultimate court of appeal in Christendom. In this correspondence the Emperor had spoken contemptuously of the language in which the Pope wrote as "a barbarian and Scythian tongue";[183] and the Pope had replied that this was only because he did not understand it. How ridiculous then for him to call himself the Roman Emperor![184] Tempers were rising: and the quarrel had almost reached its limit, when it was further inflamed by the contest between Rome and Constantinople for the control of the infant church of Bulgaria. Photius, at last, determined, with a resolution equal to that of Nicholas, to strike the final blow. At the Council of Constantinople,[185] Lent, 867, he condemned the Latins for the errors they had introduced into that country,[186] and went on to recount the complaints he had received of the tyranny of the Pope in the West.[187] These complaints emanated from Gunthar, archbishop of Köln, 850—64, and Theutgaud, archbishop of Trier, 847—†68, who, at the Synod of Metz,[188] June, 863, had supported Lothar II., King of Lorraine, 855—†69, in seeking a divorce from his Queen Teutberga in order to legitimate his marriage to his mistress Waldrada,[189] and the Pope had quashed the iniquitous decision at a Lateran Synod[190] of October, 863. It was such bold advocacy of the cause of what is right, as in the case of Teutberga, and such championship of the oppressed as in the support given to Ignatius, that won for the papal authority, as exerted by Nicholas, the tribute of men's consciences all the world over. But this did not prove that the papal claims were well founded; nor did it prevent the Emperor and his patriarch from taking action to resist them. A compact was concluded between East and West : whereby the Emperor Lewis II., 855—†75 (brother to Lothar) was to eject Nicholas from the papacy, while Michael III., in return, was to acknowledge him as Western Emperor. Lewis did his part early in 864 by advancing upon Rome;[191] and late in the summer of 867 the Council of Constantinople[192] met to carry out the rest of the bargain. They laid the pope under anathema; and they solemnly acclaimed Lewis as Basileus and Engelberta as Augusta.

The schism between Rome and Constantinople was now complete. The Pope had anathematised the Patriarch, 863; and the Patriarch had retaliated, 867, by excommunicating the Pope. But scarcely was the anathema returned, when events at Constantinople led to a reversal of the situation. By the murder of Bardas, †866, Photius had already lost a powerful friend; but by the assassination of Michael III., 24th September, 867, and the accession of his former boon-companion and murderer, Basil I., 867—†86, the forces that led to the elevation of Photius were dispersed. The new Emperor perceived well enough that public opinion sided with Ignatius; and that Photius enjoyed only the support of a minority in power. So Photius was sent into banishment, 25th September, and Ignatius reinstated, 23rd November, 867. The " Eighth Œcumenical " Council[193] at Constantinople, 869, ratified this settlement[194] and gave the victory to Rome. But it was only a temporary triumph. In 876 Photius was recalled to Constantinople by Basil I., and entrusted with the education of the Emperor's children. On the death of Ignatius,[195] 23rd October, 878, he was reinstated, 26th October, as Patriarch, 878—86; and in the next year at a Synod of Constantinople, November, 879 to March, 880, which was attended by the legates[196] of Pope John VIII.,[197] 872—†82, he was acknowledged, with their concurrence, as the " legitimate "[198] occupant of that see: though they insisted on recovering the papal jurisdiction over Bulgaria and on retaining the *Filioque*. John, however, disowned his legates for unconditionally recognising Photius,[199] and finally anathematised him.[200] But strong in the support of the Council, Photius simply ignored the papal excommunication. On the death of Basil I., his son, Leo VI., 886—†912, who had his own reasons for wishing to get rid of Photius because he had been all-powerful in Church and State during his father's malady, 779—86,[201] now finally deposed him. He was sent into exile at Bordi, in Armenia: where he died, 897—8[202] in extreme old age.

Quite as resourceful and resolute as his rival Nicholas I. and much more learned, Photius must be regarded as equally guilty with him of rending Christendom asunder by his love of power. Nicholas had the excuse of simply reasserting the traditional claims of his See. He believed himself to be the Pope of the whole world. Photius, with the contempt of an educated Greek for a Latin barbarian, meant that Nicholas should confine himself to the West; and that *he* should be his equal as Pope of the other half. He was the champion of the independence of the see of Constantinople: of Hellenic culture and of the sentiment of Byzantine nationality; and he acquiesced in the dependence of the Church upon the State. From his time onwards, the Churches of East and West drifted steadily apart; but the Empire acquired religious unity, political strength and intellectual distinction. It was thus prepared for the hundred and fifty years of prosperity which marked the zenith of its power under the Macedonian Dynasty, 867—1025, from Basil I. to Basil II.

CHAPTER VIII.

THE MACEDONIAN DYNASTY, 867—1056: ENDING WITH THE THIRD ANARCHY, 1025—81.

CONVERSION OF RUSSIA. SCHISM OF E. AND W.

THE MACEDONIAN DYNASTY, 867—1056.

From H. B. George, *Genealogical Tables*,[1] No. xlvii.

Basil I.[1] 867—†86
├── Leo VI., 886—†912, The Philosopher == Zoe, Regent 912—9
│   ├── Constantine VII., Porphyrogenitus 945—†59 [nominally fr. 912]
│   │   └── Romanus II. ==(1) Theophano (2)== Nicephorus II., Phocas,[3] 959—†63 / 963—†9
│   │   ├── Christopher 921—†34
│   │   ├── Stephen 924—†45
│   │   ├── Theophylact Patriarch 933—†56
│   │   ├── Constantine VIII. 924—†45
│   │   │   └── Zoe ==(2) Michael IV. the Paphlagonian, 1034—†41
│   │   │   ==(1) Romanus III. Argyrus, 1028—†34
│   │   │   ==(3) Constantine X. Monomachus, 1042—†54
│   │   │   1028—†50
│   │   │   ├── Mary ==Stephen
│   │   │   │   └── Michael V. Calaphates 1041—†2
│   │   │   └── Eudocia
│   │   ├── Basil II., Bulgaroctonus, b. 956, 976—†1025, o. s. p. [nom. fr. 963]
│   │   ├── Constantine IX. 1025—†8 b. 961 [nom. fr. 963]
│   │   ├── Theophano ==Emp. Otto II. 973—†83
│   │   ├── Anna == Vladimir of Russia bapt. 988
│   │   └── Theodora 1054—†6
│   │   └── Theodora == John I., Tzimisces, 969—†76
│   ├── Romanus I.,[2] Lecapenus, 919—44, †948
│   └── Helena
├── Alexander 912—3 o. s. p.
└── Stephen Patriarch 886—93

Jaroslav 1015—†54
└── Anna == Henry I. of France 1031—†60

[1] For Familia Basilii Macedonis Imp. see Du Cange, *Familiae Augustae Byzantinae*, No. xix, pp. 117—123 (Venetiis 1729), in *Corp. Byz.* xxiv.
[2] For Fam. R. I. Lec, see *Ib.* No. xx.
[3] For Fam. Phocae, see *Ib.* No. xxi.

CONTEMPORARY KINGS OF THE BULGARS.

Boris I. (843),	852—88 (†907).	Boris II.	969—76
Vladimir	888—93	Samuel	976—1014
Simeon	893—927	Gabriel Romanus	1014
Peter	927—69	John Vladislav	1015—8

BISHOPS OF THE CHIEF SEES: 867—1081.

ROME.
Hadrian II. 867—72
John VIII. 872—82
Marinus I. 882—4
Hadrian III.
    884—5
Stephen VI. 885—91
Formosus 891—6
Stephen VII.
    896—7
Romanus 897—8
Theodore II. 898
John IX. 898—900
Benedict IV.
    900—3
Leo V. 903
Christofer 903—4
Sergius III. 904—11
Anastasius III.
    911—3
Lando 913—4
John X. 915—8
Leo VI. 928—9
Stephen VIII.
    929—31
John XI. 931—6
Leo VII. 936—9
Stephen IX. 939—42
Marinus II. 943—6
Agapetus II.
    946—56
John XII. 956—64
Benedict V. 964—5
John XIII. 965—72
Benedict VI.
    972—3
Donus II. 973
Benedict VII.
    975—84
John XIV. 984—5
John XV. 985—96
Gregory V. 996—7
John XVI. 997—8
Sylvester II.
    999—1003
John XVII.
    1003
John XVIII.
    1003—9
Sergius IV.
    1009—12
Benedict VIII.
    1012—24
John XIX. 1024—33
Benedict IX.
    1033—44
Gregory VI.
    1044—6
Clement II. 1046—7
Damasus II. 1048
Leo IX. 1049—54
Victor II. 1055—7
Stephen X. 1057—8
Nicholas II.
    1059—61
Alexander II.
    1061—73
Gregory VII.
    1073—85

CONSTANTINOPLE.
Ignatius[2] 867—78
Photius[2] 878—86
Stephen I. 886—93
Antony II. 893—5
Nicholas I. 895—906
Euthymius I. 906—11
Nicholas I.[2] 911—25
Stephen II. 925—8
Tryphon 928—31
Theophylact 933—56
Polyeuctus 956—70
Basil I. 970—4
Antony III. 974—80
Nicholas II. 984—95
Sisinius II. 995—8
Sergius II. 999—1019
Eustathius 1019—25
Alexius 1025—43
Michael I. (Cerularius) 1043—58
Constantine III.
    1059—63
John VIII. 1064—75
Cosmas I. 1075—81

ANTIOCH.
Stephen IV. 870
Theodosius I.
    870—90
Simeon I. 892—907
Elias I. 907—34
Theodosius II.
    936—43
Theocharistus
    944—8
Christopher 960—9
Theodore I. 970—6
Agapius I. 978—96
John III. 997—1022
Nicholas II. 1025—30
Elias II. 1031—2
Theodore II.
    1033—41
Basil II. ?
Peter III. c. 1052—7
Theodosius III.
    1057— ?
Aemilian 1074—89/90

ALEXANDRIA.
Orthodox.
Michael I. 859—71
Michael II. 871—903
Christodulus 906—32
Eutychius 933—40
Sophronius II. ?
Isaac ?
Job ?
Elias I. c. 969
Arsenius ?
George or Theophilus
    c. 1019
Alexander II. or
    Leontius c. 1059
John IV. c. 1084

Monophysite.
Sanutius I. 859—70
Michael III. 881—906
Gabriel I. 913—23
Cosmas III. 923—34
Macarius I. 934—54
Theophanes 954—8
Menas II. 958—76
Ephraim 977—81
Philotheus or Theophilus 981—1005
Zacharias 1005—1032
Sanutius II. 1032—47
Christodulus
    1047—77
Cyril II. 1078—92

JERUSALEM.
Theodosius 867—79
Elias III. 879—907
Sergius II. 907—11
Leontius 911—27/8
Anastasius 927/8—37
Christopher I.
    937
Agatho ?
John VI. ? —969
Christopher
Thomas II. ?
Joseph II. ?
Alexander II.
    c. 975—1025
Agapius c. 983—995
Jeremias ? —1010
Theophilus ?
Arsenius before 1024
Jordanus ?
Nicephorus c. 1048
Sophronius II. c. 1059
Euthymius ?

CHAPTER VIII.

THE MACEDONIAN DYNASTY, 867—1056: ENDING WITH THE THIRD ANARCHY, 1025—81. CONVERSION OF RUSSIA. SCHISM OF E. AND W.

§ 1. WITH the Macedonian Dynasty, the Empire attained its zenith of power and glory, 867—1025. Basil I., 867—†86, the founder of the house, and his great-great-grandson, Basil II. (Bulgaroctonus), 976—†1025, under whom its fortunes reached their fullest expansion, were both remarkable men. But so also were three usurpers, who intervened: Romanus I. (Lecapenus), 919—44, Nicephorus II. (Phocas), 963—†9, and John I. (Tzimisces [Arm.=the Short]), 969—†76. All five were distinguished: as soldiers, for their energy, and, as statesmen, for their ability. In administration, the dynasty was further strengthened by the natural son of Romanus I., by name Basil Lecapenus[1] who for over forty years was the soul of the government, 944—88. Wise administration, however, was traditional with the Byzantine bureaucracy. It was the mark of a civilisation which distinguished the Empire from the barbarous kingdoms of the West. Trade throve under its protection; and sustained in prosperity a large middle-class, unknown in regions where there were only nobles and peasants. Hence the wealth of the Empire, far in excess of the resources of contemporary kingdoms: and the revenues thus put at the disposal of its military sovereigns for the upkeep of an army, inspired by religion and patriotism; for the maintenance of a navy, which secured for the Romans the command of the sea; and for conquest. In culture, the Emperor stood for Hellenism and Orthodoxy: in economics, for industry and commerce. They thus united, enriched and extended the Empire and made it the only great power in the world of their day.

But another force, peculiar to the Macedonian Dynasty,

added to its strength. This was the growth of the conception of legitimacy. Hitherto, succession to the throne had depended partly on birth but more often on election; and election had often been decided by the will of the army. But Basil I. and his son Leo VI. (the Philosopher) 886—†912, managed, though men of different type—the father a soldier and the son a pedant—to unite in creating a tradition in favour of the *Porphyrogeniti*, or princes born in the purple chamber, as the legitimate heirs of imperial authority. Not that this sentiment prevented military usurpers from seizing the opportunity offered by the long minority, 912—45, of Leo VI's son, Constantine VII. (Porphyrogenitus), 945—†59, and of the sons of Romanus II., 959—†63, viz., Basil II., a minor from 963—76, and Constantine IX., from 963—1025, to stir up revolution and so rise to power. But it forced a usurper to share his power with the reigning sovereign of the Basilian House: or rather, to cover his regency by entering into the imperial family and to secure his person being treated as sacrosanct by thus taking rank with the Augustus. Thus Romanus I. (Lecapenus) protected himself by the marriage of his daughter, Helena, to Constantine VII.: while Nicephorus II. (Phocas) and John I. (Tzimisces) legitimated their usurpation, during the minority of the sons of Romanus II., by marrying imperial ladies: the grim old warrior Nicephorus married Theophano, the young and beautiful widow of Romanus II., while the hardy soldier John married her sister, the princess Theodora. Further, so strong had the idea of legitimacy come to be, after the long and glorious reign of Basil II. (Bulgaroctonus), 976—†1025, that, in the Third Anarchy, 1025—81, which ensued upon his death, the only element of stability which survived centred upon his nieces, the Empress Zoe, 1028—†50, who had three husbands all legitimated in turn by marriage with her, and her sister and successor, the Empress Theodora, 1054—†6. Thus the Empire suffered little from princes disinclined to the burden of sovereignty, whether the studious but popular Constantine VII. (Porphyrogenitus) or the gay and pleasure-loving Romanus II.; nor from the long minority of Basil II.; nor from the opposition to Zoe and Theodora of ephemeral princes.

Moreover, the monarchy was well served by its admirals and generals. Romanus I. (Lecapenus) had won fame as an admiral. He could rely, when Emperor, on his friend John Kurkuas,[2] 920—42, who, as general, steadily advanced the borders of the Empire to the East. Constantine VII. was equally well served by Bardas Phocas[3] (who had held commands under Kurkuas) and his three sons, Nicephorus (afterwards Emperor), Leo and Constantine Phocas: and John I.[4] by Bardas Sclerus.[5] These were supported, at home, by able ministers: such as those of Constantine VII., viz., Basil "the Bird"[6] and Joseph Bringas, chief administrator of the Empire till 963: or Basil[7] (the natural son of Romanus I.) who ruled the Empire between the death of John Tzimisces and the attainment of his maturity by Basil II., 976—89.

In short, wars and diplomacy, legislation and administration, were well directed by the Emperors of the Macedonian Dynasty, or by the men who served or controlled their House: they were the sources of its strength. They succeeded, time after time, in surmounting difficulties such as arose from enemies on the frontiers, from agrarian and social unrest, from the feudal aristocracy. But, at length, the Empire was left a prey to Normans in the West and Turks in the East, during the Third Anarchy. For a hundred and fifty years, however, it was the supreme power of the civilised world.

§ 2. Its extent, under the Macedonian Dynasty, affords the best evidence of this supremacy.

(i.) The Empire was engaged in wars against three adversaries: the Saracens of the East, the Bulgars and the Saracens of the West.

(a.) In 823, Crete was seized by Mohammedan rebels from Spain; and half a century passed before Basil I., 867—†86, began to recover command of the sea in the Eastern Mediterranean. He put down the pirates,

880—1, from Africa, Crete and Cilicia, who raided the shores of Greece. Under Leo VI., 886—†912, the Saracens seized and plundered Thessalonica, 29th July, 904, and took twenty-two thousand prisoners; and another half century and more elapsed before Nicephorus II. (Phocas), 963—†9, recovered Crete, 961, which now became Christian. He took Cyprus also; and finally reasserted for the Romans the command of the sea. This was but a later episode in the long process of recovery by which the Empire, taking advantage of the anarchy that prevailed throughout the Musulman world in the tenth century, won back from the Saracens its former territories. A succession of great generals were the agents of these conquests: John Kurkuas, 920—†42, the friend of the Emperor Romanus I., 919—†44; Bardas Phocas, a Cappadocian noble entrusted with high command, 948, by Constantine VII. (Porphyrogenitus), 945—†59; and his three sons, Nicephorus, Leo and Constantine. Under their leadership, the Romans obtained possession again of Erzerum 928, Melitene 934, Edessa 944, Germanicia 949, Amida 957, Samosata 958; and so became masters once more of East Syria, Armenia and Iberia. In Cilicia, Nicephorus, now become Emperor and first of the three great Emperors of the Macedonian House to take the field in person, took Adana 964 and Tarsus 965; and 968 captured Antioch. In Mesopotamia, the campaigns of the Emperor John Tzimisces, 969—†76 secured Edessa and Nisibis, 974, for the Romans; and, in Syria, he captured Damascus and Beyrout, 976; while Basil II., 976—†1025, completed the series of victories by winning back Aleppo and Homs, 995, and annexing Armenia and Iberia, 1020. The authority of the Empire was thus fully re-imposed upon its ancient territories in the East.

(b.) A conflict with the Bulgars went on at the same time as the wars in the East; and the overthrow of Bulgaria is the outstanding military achievement of the Empire in the tenth century. During the ninth century the Romans had steadily retreated before the kingdom of Bulgaria; and Sardica (Sredec, or Sofia)

The Macedonian Dynasty

was taken by its pagan King Krum, 806—†15. Under the great Christian Tsar, Simeon, 893—†927, Bulgaria entered into rivalry on equal terms with the Empire. In 913 the Bulgars appeared before Constantinople; next year, they took Adrianople; and Simeon proclaimed the archbishop of Dorostolum (Silistria), Patriarch of the Bulgars and himself Emperor of the Romans. Nor were these pretensions unsupported, for his kingdom nearly reached to the Adriatic, including all Macedonia and Epirus, except the sea-coasts (923—34); and Bulgarian supremacy was recognised in Serbia. But Bulgaria declined in power under his son and successor Peter I., 927—†69; owing partly to a rebellion headed by Michael, the brother of Peter, and partly to the Bogomils.[8] Their name is a direct translation into Slavonic of "Massalians," the Syriac name of the sect known to the Greeks as "Euchites." They were also known in the East as "Pavlikeni," or Paulicians, and in the West, by the thirteenth century, as "Bulgari"; for, in 1223, the Albigenses are declared to be the local "Bougres." We may take this as testimony both to the influence of the sect in Bulgaria, and to the far-reaching infiltration, from east to west, of Bogomil tenets. The Bogomils were, in fact, the intermediaries for transplanting from east to west, and from ancient to mediæval times, the principles of adoptianist and Manichæan tendency which characterised respectively Paul of Samosata and the Gnostics, though their successors united them in one common heresy. Unorthodox, antisacramental and antisacerdotal, Paulicianism weakened the strength of Bulgaria by undermining the unity of its Church. Bulgaria, thus reduced by feudalism to heresy, invited the vengeance of the Roman Empire; and, in 967, the Emperor Nicephorus II. (Phocas), refused his tribute. With the aid of Sviatoslav, Grand Duke of Kiev, 945—†73, he attacked the Bulgars: and then turned against his ally. His successor, John Tzimisces, brought from his own country, Armenia, two hundred thousand Paulicians and settled them at Philippopolis. They were fine troops of his own nation, and would, as he thought, be a bulwark against the invading

Bulgars. But the colonists fraternised with the invaders, and so originated the Bogomil propaganda among them which we have mentioned above. Meanwhile, the Russians, under Sviatoslav, crossed the Balkans and sacked Philippopolis, 970, but were defeated at Arcadiopolis (now Lule Burgas). In the spring of 971, it was the turn of the Emperor John to retaliate. He took Peristhlaba,[9] the capital of Bulgaria, released Boris II., its King, 969—†76; besieged Sviatoslav in Dorostolum (Silistria); and forced him to evacuate the country. These two cities he named respectively Joannopolis, in commemoration of his victory, and Theodoropolis, in honour of his wife. Eastern Bulgaria, lost for three hundred years, was thus re-annexed to the Empire; its patriarchate suppressed; and Hellenism victorious to the Danube. But Western or Macedonian Bulgaria survived. It continued independent, and became a powerful state under its Tsar Samuel, 976—†1014. He took Dyrrhachium (Durazzo), subjugated the Adriatic coast, and forced his supremacy on Serbia. His Kingdom, sometimes called the Kingdom of Ochrida, and sometimes the Second Bulgarian Kingdom, entered upon a long rivalry with the Empire; and, after thirty years of warfare, 986—1018, it was overthrown by the Emperor Basil II. He inflicted a final defeat on the Bulgars, 29th July, 1014; and with horrible cruelty blinded his prisoners. Basil was saluted as " Bulgaroctonus," 1019, when he entered Constantinople in triumph. The only relic of the Kingdom of Bulgaria was the archbishopric of Ochrida, which remained autocephalous; and the Empire had now recovered its supremacy over the whole of the Balkan peninsula.

(c.) It had also recovered, by this date, its sovereignty over Southern Italy;[10] for the Romans reasserted their hold as the Saracens retired. In 712 the Saracens seized Corsica. During the ninth century they conquered both Sicily, 827—80; and Calabria, where they held Bari,[11] 841—71, and seized Taranto,[12] 871. But Basil I. re-established order in the Adriatic, by restoring the alliance with Venice and subduing the Croats. He then turned his attention to Apulia, where he re-occupied Bari,[13] 876, and Taranto,[14] 880. Calabria he recovered[15] in 885. And he organised these territories into the two new themes of Longobardia and Calabria. The feebleness of Leo VI. invited fresh attacks from the Saracens. They recovered Sicily, 902, and invaded Calabria. But the victory of the Romans at the battle of the Garigliano,[16] 915, gave them back their supremacy in Southern Italy for a hundred years; and in 1018 they imposed it once more by a victory at Canne[17] upon the rebels of Apulia. Southern Italy, with its Greek convents[18] and its Greek clergy[19] became again *Magna Graecia*. Attempts, however, were repeatedly made by the Western Emperors to dispossess their Eastern rivals of influence there. In 968, Otto I., 962—†73, attacked Bari[20] and was repulsed; but, for this insult, Byzantine pride was appeased by a treaty of peace, 972, and the marriage of Theophano,[21] daughter of Romanus II. to Otto II., 973—†83. The alliance did not prevent Otto from invading Calabria, but he was defeated at Stilo.[22] A fresh attempt was made by Henry II., 1002—†24, at unseating the Byzantine power in Apulia. He supported revolts there, 1022; but to no effect.[23] And at the close of the reign of Basil II., 1025, the Empire was as supreme in Southern Italy as in the Balkan peninsula,[24] and on its Eastern frontiers it had " attained its greatest extent and highest power."[25]

(ii.) But wide as were the limits of the Empire, its diplomacy reached far beyond them, and secured for it many vassal states. Thus, in North Italy, Venice became a faithful ally; and policed the Adriatic in return for commercial privileges bestowed in 992. In South Italy, the Empire entered into relations with the republics of Naples, Gaeta and Amalfi;[26] and with the Lombard princes of Salerno, Capua and Benevento.[27] To the N.W. of the Balkan peninsula Croatia[28] and Serbia[29] both became Christian in the reign of Basil I., 867—†86 and, while themselves seeking protection from the Bulgars, proved useful allies of the Empire against them. To the north of the Black Sea, Cherson both leaned upon the Empire and rendered it similar service against the

Khazars, Petchenegs (Patzinaks) and Russians of the neighbouring steppes. East of the Black Sea, the princes of Alania, Abasgia and Albania were vassals of the Basileus. Armenia, during the tenth century, withdrew from the Saracen into the Imperial orbit, whose armies it supplied with their best soldiers, until it was finally annexed by Basil II.[30]

§ 3. Missionaries worked hand in hand with diplomats: and the greatest achievement of religion in the tenth century was the conversion of Russia.[31]

The Russians began to appear on the horizon of civilisation, in the reign of Michael III., 842—†67. Their national life opens " with the settlement of a body of Scandinavians (traditionally under the leadership of one Rurik, 862—†79), in East Baltic regions from old Novgorod, about a hundred miles south of modern Petrograd, up to and even a little east and north-east of, the present Russian capital. . . . These Scandinavians, in the tradition, mostly came from the region of Upsala in Sweden. Both the name of *Rus*, and the fact of a Russian people and Russian states are due to them. With the coming of these ' Varangians,' this name of *Rus* (originally a Finnish description of the Swedes as *Rowers*) becomes famous in all the East." It was, in fact, " a Norman conquest of the East ";[32] and is assigned, by the *Chronicle of Nestor*,[33] A.D. 860, to the year 852. Rurik settled first at Ládoga; and began to build and to conquer on every side. " He went forward to the Ilmen, fortified a little town on the Volkhov, and called it Novgorod "[34] (Newtown). Then he pressed on southwards, by the river-route from the Baltic to the Black Sea, which followed up the Dvina and down the Dnieper, to Kiev on the latter stream. " From Kiev an ancient trade passed down the Dnieper and across the Black Sea, or along its shores, to the great markets of the Eastern Empire and, above all, to Constantinople itself. Within twenty-five years of the migration of Rurik, his successor, Oleg, 879—†912, took Kiev and made it his capital," c. 880. But before this, two of his nobles Askold and Dir had advanced down the Dnieper, penetrated into the Bosporus and laid siege to Constantinople with a fleet of two hundred ships, 865.[35] The Patriarch Photius was not merely an eyewitness of the raid,[36] but has left us some valuable information about it. It was planned, he says, after the Empire had broken a trade agreement; and it was embittered by an insult offered to Russian merchants. But it was an unofficial affair. Askold and Dir paid for their adventure. They were followed, captured and executed[37] 880—1, by Oleg, the successor of Rurik and guardian of his son Igor, 912—†45. The Grand Princes of Kiev were not going to be committed prematurely to a conflict with the Empire: but they did not forget the way to Constantinople. Four times in the tenth century, in 904—7, under Leo VI., in 935—41, and again 944, under Romanus I., and in 971 under John Tzimisces, they returned to the attack on the city—before the Russian people, as Photius had anticipated, acknowledged Christ for their God, the missionaries of the Church for their teachers and the Romans for their friends and brethren.[38]

The process of conversion took some time. The first Russian raid on Constantinople produced some converts; including, as it is said, though in a more than doubtful tradition, its leader Askold himself. But it is certain that, about this period, the first Christian bishop had been sent by the Emperor Basil I., 867—†86, to settle in, or to visit, Kiev. The bishopric continues to appear in the list of Byzantine sees, in the next generation under Leo VI., †912. The reign of Olga, †969, widow of Igor and regent, 945—64, for his son Sviatoslav I., 945—†73, shows another step on the road. In 957 she came on a state-visit to Constantinople. It is described[39] by the Porphyrogenitus, Constantine VII., 945—†59, who received her at his Court. She was baptised, with the Emperor for her godfather. She failed to win her son, or his warriors, to the Faith. "My retinue would laugh at me," pleaded Sviatoslav: and he took no notice of her prophetic reply, "If the Prince were once baptised, all his subjects would do the same."[40] But this proved true under his son and second successor, Vladimir, 980—†1015.

Vladimir has been called the Clovis of Russia, and by

Nestor, "a second Solomon." The latter description is as true as the other; for Vladimir, besides two wives and three mistresses of some standing, kept eight hundred concubines in three harems.[41] Unlike Solomon, he was also a great conqueror; for he won Peremyshl from the Poles; made extensive conquests in the direction of the Baltic towards Lithuania and Livonia; pushed down to the sea of Azov (where he would come on to the traderoutes leading to Persia and into contact with Mohammedans) and, attacking the Græco-Roman settlements in the Crimea, took Cherson, on the shores of the Black Sea. Nor was he insensible to the claims of competing religious movements going on among, and around, his own people. At first, he inclined to become a zealous restorer of the old heathendom; and he set up a new wooden image of the god Perún, "with a head of silver and a beard of gold,"[42] on one of the heights overlooking the Dnieper. There were images of other gods besides; and human sacrifices offered to them deluged the land in blood.[43] But the expansion of Russia under Vladimir, whether by conquest or commerce, brought him into contact with other and better creeds. Black Bulgaria of the Volga (the modern Kazan region) had become Mohammedan about A.D. 900; and Islām offered powerful attractions to so ardent a warrior and polygamist as Vladimir. But its prohibition of pork and wine was fatal to them. "We Russians," he said, "cannot live without drinking,"[44] and, disgusted by some of the habits of the Bulgarian Musulmans, "he spat upon the ground and said, 'It is abomination.'" The Roman Church on his Western borders had no attraction for him; whether from the failure of the Russians to appreciate its rites— "We saw nothing beautiful in them"[45]—or for other reasons such as the racial antipathy of the Slav to the Teuton, or the absence of any prospect of political advantage to be gained from the Western Empire. Then the Jewish faith confronted him, through his contact with the Khazars, a Judaised people to the south-east of his dominions. But theirs was now a waning power; and Vladimir, not ignorant of the dispersion of the Jews, is said to have asked " Do you wish that this evil should befall us too?"[46] Complete satisfaction was to be found only with the Eastern Roman Empire and the worship of the Orthodox Church. His envoys, in St. Sophia, hardly knew whether they were in heaven or on earth. " For there is no such spectacle on the earth, nor one of such beauty. We cannot describe it; we only know that there God dwells in the midst of men." And they promptly reminded him " If the Greek Faith were evil, Olga, thy grandmother, wisest of mankind, would never have received it."[47]

Such was the state of mind, according to Nestor, of the Grand Prince of Kiev, at the end of 987. Next year, he laid siege to Cherson; and succeeded in capturing this important centre of trade and Roman colony. It was just at the time when Basil II., 976—†1025, was putting out all his strength in the struggle with the Kingdom of Bulgaria; and the Russian alliance would be of first importance to him. At the price of marriage into the Imperial House and the conversion of himself and his people, Vladimir, in his turn, could attain the prestige of alliance with the mightiest and most civilised State of the day, when at the zenith of its power. Vladimir was therefore baptised A.D. 988, at Cherson, and married Anna[48] the sister of the Emperor Basil II. (Bulgaroctonus). As a wedding present to his bride, he gave the town back to her; and returning to Kiev, a true Russian Clovis, he " began to adore what he had burned, and to burn what he had adored." He had Perún thrown down, beaten with clubs, dragged at the horse's tail, and thrown into the Dnieper. Then he issued a proclamation: " Whosoever he be, who will not come to the river tomorrow to be baptised, be he rich or poor, will fall into disgrace with me." " A new people," he said, " was added to Christendom that day."[49] And what was done at Kiev, was adopted throughout the Russian land.

The organisation of the Church in Russia began to take shape in the reign of his son Yaroslav I., 1019—†54 : but, as all Russian history is either Before the Tartars [to c. 1240] or Under the Tartars [c. 1240—1480] or

After the Tartars [xvi.—xx. centuries], we may sketch its development down to the Tartar dominion in the thirteenth century. Organisation centred in the episcopate under the Metropolitan of Kiev; an office which was first held by Leo, 991—1004, a bishop sent from Constantinople. Until the fall of the Eastern Empire, all the Russian Metropolitans were appointed from Constantinople and consecrated there. Most of them also were Greeks, and men of little distinction. But there were two of Russian parentage; and with these began Russian theological literature. The one was the fifth Metropolitan of Kiev, by name Hilarion, 1051—†5, and author of a treatise *On Law and Grace;* the other the fourteenth, by name Clement, 1147—†54, and author of the *Epistle* to Thomas of Smolensk. To these works may here be added, for their special interest, an *Instruction* written by a lay-man, the Grand Prince Vladimir Monomachus, 1113—†25, and Abbot Daniel's account of his pilgrimage to Jerusalem, 1106—7. So early have we proof of Russian concern for education in the Faith and Russian piety towards the Holy Places. Other dioceses grew up round Kiev, and eight were founded under Vladimir, 980—†1015. Among these, was Chernigov, not far away to the N.E.; Bielgorod, fifteen miles to the S.W., on an estate of the Grand Prince, where the bishop was a sort of Domestic Prelate, or Court Chaplain, with the honorary title of Archbishop; and others in the dependent principalities: Vladimir in the principality of Volhynia to the west, Polotsk in the principality of that name to the north, Rostov in the principality of Vladimir-Suzdal to the north-east, and others. Eight more dioceses, of which one lapsed, came into being between the death of Vladimir and the Tartar invasion: so that there were fifteen suffragans of Kiev by the middle of the thirteenth century. For these sees, the secular clergy were, at first, eligible as bishops. But, before long, a tendency toward the present rule of taking bishops only from the regular clergy began to manifest itself. No doubt, this was due to the prestige of the monasteries both for learning and for piety.

The Monastery of H. Barlaam, Mt. Meteora.

See p. 361.]

Next to the establishment of the episcopate, the organisation of the Church in Russia depended upon the strengthening of Kiev, as a Christian centre, by the establishment of churches and monasteries. Vladimir himself built the Cathedral of the B.V.M. where the idol Perún had stood; it was consecrated, 996, and known, from its endowment by the Grand Prince, as the " Church of the Tithes." His son Yaroslav built and endowed the Church of St. Sophia, with a house for the Metropolitan: who now moved from Pereyaslavl, to Kiev, and Kiev became the residence of the Metropolitans until the see was moved, so as to be off the route of the Tartar invasions, first to Vladimir by 1299 and thence to Moscow, 1328. The generosity of the Prince was imitated by his Boyars, or nobles: so many churches in Kiev did they build that as many as sixty were destroyed by the fire of 1124. Of monasteries, the Pecherski Lavra at Kiev is the first in rank of all Russian monasteries. It is one of the oldest, being founded, 1055, by the hermit Antony, a Russian who had gone for training in the religious life to Mount Athos and was sent back by his abbot to plant it in his own country. The founder of Russian monasticism, he occupied a cave (pech) as a solitary. Then others gathered round him: and a monastic community grew up which became a centre of learning and devotion. The *Chronicle* of " Nestor " was compiled there: and monasteries grew up elsewhere, some of them serving as schools for clergy.

The clergy occupied a status of their own. They were exempt from the secular jurisdiction, and subject only to their own code. " This consisted primarily of the Byzantine Canon Law, which was made up of two sources: (a) the ecclesiastical legislation of the Emperors, and (b) the canons of Councils generally received: and, with them, as a supplement, the decisions of Church doctors and fathers reckoned to be authoritative, together with the patriarchal ordinances analogous to the papal decretals of the West."[50] When these two were combined, the compound term *Nomocanon*, c. 550, was adopted to be the title of the collection. After a first edition by John the Scholastic,[51] Patriarch of CP., 565—

†77, with additions by the Council in Trullo,[52] 692, and the Second Council of Nicæa,[53] 787, it was revised by the Patriarch Photius, †891; who produced a new *Nomocanon*,[54] 883. This has formed the basis of all subsequent Orthodox Canon Law. A series of epitomes reduced it to a more handy compass; and the great succession of commentators, Zonaras[55] 1120, Balsamon[56] 1170, and Matthew Blastares[57] 1330, took it as the basis of their expositions and codifications. The Photian *Nomocanon* only became available for the Church of Russia through the Serbian version made by archbishop Sabbas, 1221—37. This was adopted by the Russian metropolitan, Cyril, and by the Synod held at Vladimir in 1274. It was then supplemented from time to time by documents of local origin emanating from Russian Councils, Prelates and Princes; and also by new patriarchal decisions dealing with Russian affairs. But, except for an Ordinance of 1137 dealing with tithes, no legislative acts are extant which can, with certainty, be assigned to the pre-Tartar period of Russian history.

§ 4. We must now return to the home affairs of the Church of the Eastern Empire under the Macedonian Dynasty, 867—1056.

Basil I., 867—†86, had murdered his benefactor, Michael III., 842—†67; and usurped his throne. This made no difference at first to his friendly relations with the Patriarch Photius, 857—67, though he was connected with the family of the late Emperor. Photius also had many friends among the aristocracy; but he was unpopular because he had appeared to condone the vices of Michael : whereas Ignatius, whom he had displaced, had the support of the monks and the sympathy of the populace of Constantinople. Usurpers, if they are to maintain their authority, have to look round for influential friends; and, after two years' tenure of the throne, Basil may have felt that it would be rendered more secure if he could recover the good-will of the Roman See and conciliate the monks and the people of Constantinople. He therefore resolved to get rid of Photius. A Roman Synod in 863 had declared Photius to be deposed in

The Macedonian Dynasty

favour of Ignatius;[58] and Pope Nicholas I. had communicated its sentence to the Emperor Michael III.[59] The papal decision was disregarded;[60] and, when Nicholas I., in compliance with a request from Boris, King of Bulgaria, who had been baptised by Photius, sent Latin prelates[61] to instruct his people, Photius convoked a Synod at CP., Lent, 867, and, in a letter addressed to the Patriarchs of Alexandria, Antioch and Jerusalem, denounced the usages and doctrines of the Latins, and their intrusion into a country under his jurisdiction.[62] Later in the year, in a second synod, he excommunicated the Pope.[63] Soon afterwards, Pope Nicholas died, 13th November, 867; and was succeeded, in December, by Hadrian II., 867—†72. The negotiations of Basil with the Roman See occupied some time;[64] but they issued in a Synod at Constantinople, 869, which is reckoned by the Latins as the Eighth Œcumenical Council[65] of the Church. Only one hundred and two bishops could be assembled; for numbers of the Eastern episcopate had been consecrated by Photius, and many adhered to his cause. He was compelled to attend; and, of course, was condemned,[66] 29th October, 869. But his dignified resistance deprived his enemies of the triumph that they anticipated. Ignatius was, indeed, restored; and Pope Hadrian thought it a favourable moment for demanding that the estates belonging to the patrimony of St. Peter in the provinces of the Eastern Empire, which had been confiscated by Leo III., 717—†41, should be given back to him and that Bulgaria should be assigned to his authority. But no sooner were these demands made public than they served to unite Basil and Ignatius, with the clergy and people of the Empire, in an opposition to the papal claims as firm as that of Michael III. and Photius. Ignatius retained the Patriarchate till his death, 23rd October, 878; but, meanwhile, a majority of the episcopate remained attached to the cause of Photius, and it became clear to Basil that unity was only to be maintained within his dominions by his re-appointment. He had already been allowed to return from exile, 876. So Photius was reinstated, 26th October, 878, and another Synod which assembled at Constantinople, November, 879—13th March, 880, confirmed his reinstatement. It is the Eighth Œcumenical Council,[67] as reckoned by Eastern Christendom; and consisted of three hundred and eighty-three bishops. The Emperor Basil, Pope John VIII., 872—†82, and the Patriarch Photius, all alike, determined to temporise; and the Pope is said to have been willing to drop the *Filioque* and to restore the " Nicene " Creed to its original form, if he could have secured from the Easterns the recognition of his supremacy and from the Emperor the return of his patrimony and the jurisdiction over Bulgaria. Rome and the East continued at variance after the redintegration of Photius and until the death of the Emperor Basil, 1st March, 886.

With the accession of Leo VI.[68] 886—†912, we reach the last stage of the long story of Photius.[69] That prelate, by the Council of 879—80, had gained more than he expected. The Council had asserted the religious autonomy of Constantinople, and had placed its Patriarch on an equality with the Pope of Old Rome. Photius now aimed at supreme control of the State as well: and his opportunity arose, simultaneously with the Council, by the Emperor's decline in health and vigour, which followed upon the death of his favourite son, Constantine, †879. For seven years, 879—86, Photius ruled supreme both in Church and State; and, with the aid of his evil genius, the abbot Theodore of Santabaren, he organised a plot to make himself or, in default, one of his kinsmen, Emperor. He would thus have attained the goal of his ambition, and have given effect to those aspirations of Byzantine nationalism which he incarnated, by setting up a Pontifical State with its seat at New Rome equal to that of Old Rome itself. But Basil died before the dream came off; and Leo, resenting the long dominance of Photius, forced him to retire into a monastery. He then set up one of the Imperial Princes as Patriarch, his younger brother Stephen,[70] 886—†93; and, in order to win over to his adherence the partisans of Ignatius, he summoned them to Constantinople and told them that, if they hesitated to accept Stephen on the ground that he had been ordained deacon by Photius, they had better all refer themselves to the Pope. The letter of Leo to the Pope is lost; but we still possess that of Stylianus,[71] archbishop of Neocæsarea, written 886—7, to Pope Stephen VI., 885—†91. The object of the letter is to obtain from the new Pope the official pardon of the people of CP. If the friends of Ignatius were led to receive Holy Orders from Photius, it was due to the part taken by the papal legates Rodwald and Zacharias at the Council of May, 861, and Eugenius and Paul[72] at the Council of 879—80. The letter is thus an attempt to inform the Pope of all that had passed in reference to Photius before his accession, as well as of the reasons for his deposition: and it is probably an echo of the process with which Photius was threatened immediately upon the death of Basil. " You did right," replied Stephen, " in excommunicating Photius."[73] But, according to the Emperor, Photius had voluntarily resigned his see.[74] Probably this was the expression employed, in order to save appearances: and Photius died 891.

The relations of Leo VI. with the successors of Photius afford interesting glimpses into the ecclesiastical conditions of his time. Thus when Leo put in his brother Stephen, 886—†93, it is, perhaps, an indication of the Armenian origin of their dynasty; for in Armenia the Catholicus was usually a prince of the reigning house. And, fifty years later, Romanus I. appointed his third son Theophylact as Patriarch, 933—†56. Stephen was followed, after an interval of eight years, by Nicholas,[75] 901—7; and his deposition, consequent merely upon the family affairs of the Emperor, illustrates the helpless dependence of the Church upon the Crown. Leo VI. had had three wives in succession, Theophano †892, Zoe †896,[76] and Eudocia †900. They died without male issue; and Leo, anxious to avoid open violation of the laws of the Orthodox Church which forbade fourth marriages,[77] took to himself the beautiful Zoe Carbonupsina as a concubine. She gave birth to a son in the purple chamber, who thus became known as Constantine VII., Porphyrogenitus. He was baptised on the Epiphany, 906, by the Patriarch Nicholas, but on condition that the Emperor would not live any longer with his concubine. Leo kept his promise by marrying Zoe,[78] and creating her Augusta. The Patriarch, indignant at being so trifled with, degraded the priest who celebrated the uncanonical marriage and forbade the Emperor to enter the church. Leo paid mocking deference to the interdict by coming in—to the amusement of the populace—by a side door: and then, assuring himself of the good-will of Pope Sergius III., 904—11, he deposed Nicholas, the opponent of the tetragamy: and substituted Euthymius, 906—11. The new Patriarch recognised the tetragamy, on the pretext that the public welfare required the laws of the Church to yield to the exigencies of the State.

Leo's relations with the Roman See are also of interest. "The Νέα Τακτικά, which seems to date from about the year 900, represents the ecclesiastical provinces of Illyria, grouped with the other suffragan provinces of Constantinople";[79] and by the Διατύπωσις[80] Leo VI. incorporated into the Orthodox Church all sees of the Balkan peninsula which had hitherto been under the papal authority.[81] This does not seem, however, to have disturbed the union between East and West. Probably it was but nominal. They were culturally alien; and the West, at this date, was of little importance to the East for with Stephen III. began the twelve popes of the pornocracy,[82] 904—63. They rendered the Roman See of no account.

Leo's remaining distinction is the completion that he gave to the legislative activity of his father. "Their work represents a reaction in certain measure against the *Ecloga*" of Leo III. 717—†41, "and a return to Justinian. The aim of Basil" was to revive legal study, "and the revival could only be based on Justinianean lawbooks or their Greek representatives. These books were now treated somewhat as Justinian and his lawyers had treated their own predecessors. A handbook of extracts from the *Institutes, Digest* and *Code* was issued by Basil I. in 879 ('Ο πρόχειρος Νόμος, "the law as it is"),

The Macedonian Dynasty

to fulfil somewhat the same function as the *Institutes* ":[83] and " it was revised and republished by Leo VI. under the name of Ἐπαναγωγή τοῦ Νόμου, 886."[84] Then "a collection of all the laws of the Empire was prepared by two commissions, and completed under Leo VI. It was entitled the *Basilika*. In many points (in civil, but not in criminal, law) the principles of the *Ecloga* are set aside in favour of the older jurisprudence. Then the Justinianean ordinances on the subject of divorce were revived, and there remained henceforward a contradiction between the civil and the canon law."[85]

Constantine VII. (Porphyrogenitus) was born 905, and succeeded his father as Emperor, 912—†59. Throughout his life he personified the principle: *Le roi règne, mais il ne gouverne pas*. As a child, he was under the tutelage of his uncle Alexander, 912—†3, and Nicholas, once more patriarch, 911—†25; then, on his uncle's death, of his mother, the Empress Zoe Carbonupsina, till 919, when as a boy of fourteen he was declared of age. But power fell into the hands of the admiral Romanus Lecapenus. He secured the hand of Constantine for his daughter Helena; and, after being crowned by the Patriarch Nicholas, on 17th December, 919, he ruled for a quarter of a century as joint-Emperor, 919—44, with the legitimate sovereign. Nicholas had removed the name of the Pope from the diptychs;[86] but in 920[87] the differences between those who with Euthymius allowed, and those who with Nicholas condemned, fourth marriages, being composed in favour of the latter by the *Tomus unionis* of the Synod of CP., a reconciliation[88] was effected between Old and New Rome in terms which denied the validity of the fourth marriage of Leo VI. and so proclaimed Constantine VII. a bastard. This contributed, in the end, to the fall of the House of Lecapenus; and the House of Phocas rose to power upon its ruins. Constantine, now sole ruler, entrusted the defence of the realm to his general Bardas Phocas, and his three sons, Nicephorus, Leo and Constantine; and its administration to the Empress Helena and her favourite Basil " the bird." His books,[89] as under the intrusion of

Romanus I., remained his sole interest: and the chief ecclesiastical event of his reign was the baptism, 957, of Olga, princess of Kiev, which led to the conversion of her people a generation later.

He was succeeded by his son Romanus II.,[90] 959—†63, a gay and pleasure-loving youth, whom his father had allowed, 957, at the age of nineteen, to marry Theophano, a publican's daughter, and the evil genius of the Imperial House. Romanus II. left the management of affairs to Joseph Bringas. The minister committed to Nicephorus Phocas an expedition against the pirates of Crete: where the conquest of the island, 961, led to the conversion of its inhabitants by the Armenian monk Nikhon and his companions. Nicephorus returned from his victories to find Romanus II. dead, and Theophano a widow with two infant sons, Basil, b. 956, and Constantine, b. 961. He managed to get rid of Bringas; and, after receiving the crown from the Patriarch Polyeuctus,[91] 956—70, he legitimated his authority by marriage with Theophano,[92] and reigned as Emperor, 963—†9.

Nicephorus II.[93] (Phocas) regarded himself as prime minister, entrusted with the custody of the Empire and of the two sons of Romanus II., the legitimate sovereigns; but he was forced to become their colleague, in order to render his authority secure and his person sacrosanct. He was a great contrast to his predecessor; no youth, but in his fifty-second year, on his accession; not frivolous, but austere; trained not in the Court, but in the camp. Before he reached the throne he had already subdued Syria as far as the Euphrates; and, as Emperor, he rejoined his forces, now under the command of his nephew, John Tzimisces. In 968 they crossed that river, and threatened the power of the Caliph at Bagdad. In order to maintain the efficiency of his armies, Nicephorus had to impose heavy burdens both of taxation and of military service: and he looked with jealousy on the privileges of clergy and monks. Their numbers drew off from his recruits: and their estates from his sources of revenue. "He therefore prohibited, 963, the foundation of any new monasteries and hospitals, enacting that only those in existence should be maintained;[94] and he declared all testamentary donations of landed property in favour of the church void. He also excited the anger of the clergy, by forbidding any ecclesiastical election to be made until the candidate had received the imperial approbation. He was in the habit of leaving the wealthiest sees vacant and retaining their revenues; or, if the see was filled, of compelling the new bishop to pay a large portion of his receipts annually into the treasury."[95] These measures provoked the opposition of the spiritualty; and Polyeuctus, the Patriarch who had done much to place Nicephorus on the throne, resented but could not prevent them. The clergy, however, maintained their opposition. It was popular but unpatriotic: and particularly ungracious to Nicephorus. He lived only for his army; but, throughout his life, had strong sympathies with the cloister; and was the intimate friend[96] of Athanasius of Trebizond, the founder of the Great Lavra on Mount Athos. But for the charter, 969, of Nicephorus II. the Lavra might never have been founded.[97] Yet the clergy persisted in their opposition. In order to inflame the patriotism of his soldiers, the Emperor demanded that all Christians who fell in battle against the Moslems should be counted as martyrs. But Polyeuctus declined, in reliance on the canons of St. Basil. They also resisted his ecclesiastical policy in the East. Melitene had been devastated in the wars. At the Emperor's request the Jacobite Patriarch of Antioch issued an appeal to his flock to assist in the re-population of the city; and Nicephorus gave an undertaking that they should not be subjected to any vexations because of their differences with Chalcedonian orthodoxy. The Monophysites responded with alacrity to his invitation. As many as twenty-eight Syrian churches, besides numerous monasteries, sprang up in Melitene and the neighbourhood; and the Patriarch Mar Johannan (965—85), nicknamed Srigtā because he was clothed in a coat made of reeds, took up his residence in the convent of Barid. But the Orthodox archbishop of Melitene resented the invasion; and, with the support of the Patriarch Polyeuctus, contrived that Syrian bishops should be cited to Constantinople and forced into conformity.[98] Thus, in spite of his virtues and victories, Nicephorus made many enemies; among them, perhaps, his wife. She was still young; and he had given her but little of his time or affection. She and his nephew, John Tzimisces conspired to murder him,[99] 10th December, 969; and " so perished a brave soldier, an able general and, with all his defects, one of the most virtuous men and conscientious sovereigns that ever occupied the throne of Constantinople."[100]

The reign of John Tzimisces, 969—†76, though glorious in military annals, was uneventful in Church affairs. The Patriarch Polyeuctus at first refused him coronation, because he had murdered his predecessor; but afterwards consented; for John was willing " to abrogate the *Novel* of Nicephorus II. (Phocas) which ordained that no ecclesiastical decision, no promotion or nomination, could be made by the bishops without the Imperial consent."[101] " Closely connected with the efforts of the Emperor to strengthen his frontiers against the Bulgars was his importation of . . heretics . . from the eastern provinces of Asia Minor to increase the colonies of Paulicians . . . already established around Philippopolis ":[102] for these Armenians were his fellow-countrymen, and the best soldiers in his armies. But the Russian war was the great event of his reign. The Russians were forced, 972, to evacuate the country:[103] Bulgaria was annexed to the Empire, and the Patriarchate of Ochrida suppressed: Hellenism, *i.e.*, Orthodoxy, allied with Greek nationalism, became dominant up to the Danube, and the danger to the Empire threatened by the Slavs was brought to an end.

John I. was succeeded by his ward and colleague, Basil II., 976—†1025. He was of the age of 20 at his succession: and, though sociable and kindly in early days, afterwards became hard, suspicious and cruel. For twelve years the government continued in the hands of the eunuch Basil Lecapenus, a man of imposing presence and great ability, who had played a leading part in the revolution which placed Nicephorus II. (Phocas) on the throne,

The Macedonian Dynasty 203

and had carried on the administration during the wars of Tzimisces.[104] But in 989 Basil II. dismissed and banished his minister, and in the same year put an end to the revolts in Asia led by the two rival and veteran generals, Bardas Sclerus and Bardas Phocas.[105] To the year previous, 988, belongs his *Novel* I. reversing the anti-clerical legislation (*Novel* II.) of Nicephorus[106] and permitting the construction of churches and religious houses;[107] and also 988 the baptism of Vladimir which led to the conversion of the Russians.[108] Then followed the long series of Basil's conquests. In 1014 he overthrew the Kingdom of Bulgaria, which had been reconstituted during the first ten years of the Czar Samuel, 976—1014.[109] In 1020 he annexed Armenia and Iberia, having re-conquered the East,[110] because of the decline of the Caliphate of Bagdad. He then set out to expel the Saracens from Sicily,[111] but died 1025. His reign has been called " the culminating point of Byzantine greatness,"[112] and " the longest and most obscure of Byzantine history."[113]

§ 5. Great as was the might of the Empire under its three military sovereigns, 963—1025, there were then at work causes making for decay.

The first of these was feudalism. It had largely increased during the ninth and tenth centuries, through the powerful ($\delta\upsilon\nu\alpha\tau o \iota$) preying upon the poor ($\pi\acute{\epsilon}\nu\eta\tau\epsilon\varsigma$). A series of enactments remain to bear witness to the efforts of the legislator to check this danger. Thus *Novels* I.[114] (922) and III.[115] (934) of Romanus I. are intended to protect the poor man in the enjoyment of his holding against the rich man who would buy up his property, and add it to his own estate. If there has to be a sale, then a preference ($\pi\rho o\tau\acute{\iota}\mu\eta\sigma\iota\varsigma$, *praelatio*) must be given to the municipality as purchaser : so as to secure the chance of a fair price and to check the growth of *latifundia*.[116] Similar enactments occur in the legislation of Constantine VII.,[117] Romanus II.[118] and Nicephorus II.;[119] but their repetition only testifies to the continuance of the abuse, and to the growing accumulation of lands in possession of the great feudatories. The result was the feudal rebellion in Asia, 971, under Bardas Phocas,[120]

†989, the nephew of Nicephorus II. (Phocas) and, 976, under Bardas Sclerus,[121] †998. The latter menaced Constantinople itself,[122] 978, but was defeated by Bardas Phocas at the battle of Paukalia,[123] 24th March, 979. Then, 987, these two great lords united, in the interest of their order, to resist the Emperor[124] Basil II. But, 989, he put Phocas to death at Abydos; forced Sclerus to submission; and, 996, issued a fresh prohibition of the oppression of the poor man by the great.[125] These measures proved ineffective; and the feudal aristocracy showed themselves too strong for the imperial authority. The feeble sovereigns who succeeded Basil II. to the end of the Macedonian dynasty, 1025—57, made no head against them. There ensued the Third Anarchy, 1057—81; till, at last, order was restored, and the Empire given a fresh lease of life, by the feudal family of the Comneni,[126] 1081—1185.

The second cause of decay lay with the clergy and the Religious. They were as zealous as the nobles in the maintenance of the interests of their order. In the tenth century, as in the eighth, property was immobilised in their hands, to the loss of the State both in men and revenue. Nicephorus II. forbade, 963, the founding of new monasteries.[127] But the Church was too strong for their prohibition to continue; and, 988, the edict of Nicephorus was abrogated[128] by Basil II. Equally obstructive to the Government, at times, was the Patriarch of Constantinople. Though often but the puppet of the prince, the Patriarch could exert, on occasion, an influence as disturbing as that of any other " overmighty subject." Thus Nicholas I., though forced to resign by Leo VI., because of his opposition to the tetragamy, returned, on the death of Leo VI., and became guardian to his son Constantine VII.; under whom he directed imperial policy and, by the *Tomus unionis*,[129] settled the question of fourth marriages, and so won a triumph over the imperial authority. Similarly, Polyeuctus braved Nicephorus II. (Phocas), and had to yield; but, on the murder of Nicephorus by John I., he forced the latter, as the price of his recognition by the Church, to revoke all the legislation of his predecessors that had been detrimental to it. Nicholas and Polyeuctus thus successfully sustained the tradition of Photius; and it was the ambition of the Patriarch of Constantinople which led ultimately to a rupture with the see of Rome. After the breach between East and West under Photius, reunion was restored, 892, by the action of Pope Formosus, 891—†6. In a letter to Stylianus, archbishop of Neocæsarea, he recognised the status of those, if penitent, who owed their Orders to Photius.[130] But it was a lame reconciliation: and a latent conflict between Old and New Rome continued. The conflict was due not to secondary questions of doctrine or discipline; for these were all *ex post facto*. It was due rather to deeper causes. They were the contempt of Greeks for Latins, as for mere barbarians; the Latin claim to universal supremacy; and the ambition of the Patriarch of Constantinople to the Pope of the East. Thus the train was laid for the definite and final rupture, 1054, under Michael Cerularius, 1043—†58.

§ 6. But to understand the schism, we have first to see how it was bound up with the decline of the Macedonian dynasty, 1025—57 and with the Third Anarchy, 1057—81 which ensued.[131]

The decadence of the Empire, at this date, was due, first, to the failure of great rulers; and, next, to the advantage taken of the weakness of the Government by enemies on the frontiers.

Basil II. was succeeded by his nieces,[132] the Porphyrogenitae (legitimate), Zoe,[133] born 980; Empress 1028—†50; and Theodora, 1054—†6. For, after the short interval during which their worthless father Constantine IX. [b. 961], 1025—†8, became sole Emperor, these princesses occupied the throne for thirty years. Their legitimacy and popularity gave to the Empire a certain stability; but they were incompetent as rulers. Zoe was 48 at her accession: and developed into an old harridan as vain as Queen Elizabeth, but without either her cleverness or her character. She elevated three husbands, in succession, to her throne: Romanus III.[134]

(Argyrus) 1028—†34, a senator of sixty, who, in order to satisfy the Empress, had either to desert his wife or to lose his eyes; Michael IV. (the Paphlagonian) 1034—†41, an epileptic with whom she had a base intrigue before she poisoned her husband to put him in his place; and Constantine X. (Monomachus), 1042—†54, a patron of letters,[135] indeed, but a gouty libertine who did not scruple to appear in public, in the company of two Augustae—his old wife Zoe and his young mistress Scleraina.[136] Zoe was succeeded by her sister Theodora, a sour ascetic; and then followed six short reigns, mostly of usurpers, and of strife between the military and the bureaucratic party,[137] till the Empire was rescued from anarchy in 1081.[138]

Closely connected with this succession of incompetent sovereigns was the contraction of its frontiers—a second source of decadence. North, south and east, the enemies of the Romans took advantage of the feebleness of the government to press across every frontier. Thus, on the Danube, the Petchenegs (Patzinaks), a race of Turanian origin,[139] crossed the river, 1027, and by 1051 occupied the country up to the Balkans.[140] In 1040 Western Bulgaria rose in rebellion under Peter Deleanos (Deljan), 1040—†1,[141] a descendant of the Tsar Samuel, 976—†1014 :[142] Serbia also asserted its independence, in that year, under Stephen Bogislav,[143] 1040—50, and Venice broke away. On the south, the Normans[144] under Robert Guiscard,[145] Duke of Apulia and Calabria, 1059—†85, attacked the Roman Catapan[146] or governor of South Italy, George Maniaces. The governor managed to arrest their progress,[147] 1042. But, afterwards, a series of towns in Apulia were lost to the Empire :[148] 1055, Otranto; 1060, Troja; and 1071, Bari. Guiscard then built a fleet in order to carry the war across the Adriatic; and, sending his son Bohemund, Prince of Taranto and of Antioch, †1111, to intervene in Illyria, 1081, prepared to follow him thither with 30,000 men. In Asia, the situation was worse. The Seljūk Turks,[149] under the leadership of three remarkable sultans, Togrel Bey, 1038—†63, Alp Arslan, 1063—†72, and Malek Shah, 1072—†92, directed their assaults on the Empire. At first, they had to halt before the strong line of fortresses erected by Basil II., but Armenia, unfriendly to the Romans because of the persecution she had had recently to endure from Orthodoxy[150] could not be depended upon. In 1064 the Turks took its capital Ani.[151] Then they advanced, 1069, to Cæsarea in Cappadocia and to Iconium. The Emperor Romanus IV. (Diogenes), 1068—†71, made strong efforts to arrest this progress : but he suffered a dreadful defeat at Manzikert [Manazkert], 1071, to the north of Lake Van, and was himself taken prisoner. The Empire never recovered from this disaster; for Armenia, Cappadocia and the whole of the eastern portion of Asia Minor were lost; and these were lands from whence came its great Emperors of the "Macedonian" or better Armenian dynasty, as well as its best soldiers :[152] lands, too, (save part of Armenia) which belonged to the Romans from time immemorial and had never been shorn from the Empire before. Manazkert, in short, was a blow both to prestige and resources. Not long afterwards the Turks were in possession of Nicæa, 1078, by the invitation of a Byzantine faction;[153] and next year they held Chrysopolis (Scutari) whence they could look across the straits to Constantinople. Neither the Normans nor the Turks, however, were enemies more dangerous than those whom the Romans had vanquished before : but the Empire was more feeble.

§ 7. In the course of this decline, the final schism between East and West took place. Its causes were of long-standing : an alien culture and a growing contempt for each other. To Latins, the Greeks were " schismatics "; and to Greeks, the Latins were " barbarians." But its immediate occasion arose out of the ambition of Michael Cerularius who first came to the front as the minister of Constantine X. (Monomachus), 1042—†54.

The dangers of feudalism were soon to be manifested afresh by the revolts of military leaders. Thus the Catapan, George Maniaces, †1043, after being the hero of the resistance to the Normans in Sicily and Italy, made terms with the enemy, called them to his standard, and landed at Durazzo in order to contest the crown with Constantine.[154] A few years later, 1047, Leo Tornicius, a relative of the Emperor, raised a revolt. He was governor of Thrace; and Constantine wished to transfer him to Armenia, where danger was to be anticipated from the Turks. Leo considered this equivalent to disgrace, and marched on Constantinople.[155] In order to deal with such contingencies, it became a settled principle of imperial policy to strengthen the bureaucracy against the army; and effect was given to it in several ways. Constantine reduced the regular army, and substituted mercenaries: Normans, Scandinavians, one of whom was the adventurous Norseman Harold Hardraada,[156] Russians, and Anglo-Saxons. He placed the government in the hands of officials and learned men. Of the latter, were the polymath Michael Psellus,[157] 1018—†96, whom Constantine made first Secretary of State (Πρωτασηκρῆτις) and Professor of Philosophy in the University of Constantinople; Joannes Xiphilinus,[158] born in Trebizond, 1010—2, and an intimate friend of Psellus, who combined the chair of Law in Constantine's re-founded University[159] with the office of custodian of the laws (Νομόφυλαξ) until he became Patriarch, 1064—†75; and their friend Constantine Leuchudes, who had been the adviser of Michael V. (Calaphates=the caulker) 1041 —†2, was invested, 1043, with the administration when Cerularius became Patriarch, 1043—†8; then succeeded him and preceded Xiphilinus, as Patriarch, 1059—†63.[160] And, finally, Constantine founded, in the University, a school of Law, 1045, in order to supply trained functionaries for the government, so as to stabilise the administration and render it independent of palace revolutions and military uprisings.

One of such trained officials already was Michael Cerularius. His first appearance on the stage of history is in the year 1040, when he was the unwitting victim of a conspiracy against the Paphlagonian family of Michael IV., 1034—†41, and his brother and chancellor, John the Orphanotrophus,[161] into whose hands the actual government of the empire had drifted. Cerularius was a man of fine presence as well as of intellect and learning; and the conspirators, unknown to him, formed a plot to put him on the throne. The plot was betrayed, and he was sent into exile. But he returned, 1042, on the accession of Constantine X. (Monomachus): who had an equal distaste for the Paphlagonians and began his reign by putting out the eyes of John the Orphanotrophus. The new Emperor had never met Cerularius before; but he showed him marked favour; and is reported to have exclaimed when he first set eyes on him, " That's the man to be Patriarch." The see was still held by Alexius Studites, 1025—†43. Cerularius, for a time, became confidential adviser to the Emperor; and, on the death of Alexius, March, 1043, he was promoted to the Patriarchal throne. Once there, " he attempted to do for the patriarchate in the eastern church what his younger contemporary Hildebrand [Gregory VII., 1073—†85] did for the pontificate in western Christendom."[162] There were two limits on the ecclesiastical power of the patriarch. One of these was theoretical rather than practical: in the organisation of universal Christendom he held a subordinate position—second in dignity to the see of Rome.[163] The other limit was practical rather than theoretical: the patriarch was dependent on the emperor. From such subordination and dependence Michael Cerularius made an attempt to deliver the Byzantine pontificate, and was to a certain extent not unsuccessful.

" To break with Rome[164] was not difficult; the eastern and western churches were practically severed ";[165] and we have now to trace the course of events which led to the final breach.[166]

In the summer of 1053, the Normans were making rapid progress in Southern Italy. Pope Leo IX., 1048—†54, had taken the field against them, but he was defeated at the battle of Civitate,[167] 18th June, 1053: and kept in honourable captivity at Benevento till March, 1054. In spite of this, it looked as if the progress of their arms might end by transferring southern Italy from the Greek to the Latin Church. Michael Cerularius, though alarmed at this prospect, could take no overt action to prevent it;[168] for the Pope was in alliance with the Emperor Constantine X. (Monomachus), 1042—†54, who needed his support against the Normans. But he took advantage of the defeat and captivity of Leo IX. to open an attack through his friend Leo, archbishop of Ochrida; and, at the same time, closed the Latin churches and monasteries in Constantinople. Leo of Ochrida, accordingly, addressed a letter[169] to John, bishop of Trani, 1053—†9, in Apulia, warning him against the errors of the Latins. These were, in the eyes of Michael and Leo, § § 1, 2, the use of azyms or unleavened bread; § 3, the practice of fasting on Saturdays in Lent; § 4, the eating of things strangled and of blood; and § 5, the singing of Alleluia at Easter only; and the letter concludes with the request that the bishop would circulate it to his fellow-bishops and clergy of the West. It happened that Humbert, Cardinal-bishop of Silva Candida, 1057—†63, was at Trani when the letter arrived.[170] He translated it; and sent a copy to his friend and patron, Leo IX.; who was also informed of the seizure of the Latin churches and monasteries by Cerularius. The Pope at once sent a letter of remonstrance to the Patriarch —*In terra pax*,[171] of 2nd September, 1053. He enlarges, *more Romano*, § 7, on the privileges conveyed, through St. Peter, to the Roman See. Its faith cannot fail: whereas, § § 8—10, some of the Patriarch's own predecessors had been not only patrons of heresy, but heresiarchs. As to its authority, § § 13, 14, if the truth of the Gospel is not sufficient to assure us of it, at any rate the *Donation of Constantine*, c. 750, is enough;[172] and the Pope proceeds to quote it, without suspicion that it was a forgery, almost at full length. Never, he continues, § 21, had St. Paul cast any imputation on the faith of the Romans : it was with the Greeks that, in his day, heresies arose. You have shut up, § 29, the Latin churches and monasteries in Constantinople, and taken possession of them until they consent to worship after your manner. In Rome, we have been much more tolerant: we have never disturbed the churches and convents there devoted to your national rite. But then, § 32, by virtue of our Lord's own promise, the faith of St. Peter cannot fail. The exchange of letters, in such a tone, was most unfortunate at a time when the advance of the Normans was threatening the extinction of the last remnants of Byzantine possessions in Italy; and Constantine X. (Monomachus) put pressure on Cerularius to mitigate his zeal. Together, the Emperor and the Patriarch wrote to the Pope with a view to conciliation. Their letters are lost: but their contents can be recovered from the replies of Leo IX., of January, 1054. In *Quantas gratias*,[173] addressed to Constantine, he asks (87 l. 4) the Emperor's assistance against the Normans; says, (87 ll. 11—14) that he is daily expecting the arrival of the Western Emperor, Henry III., 1039—†56; begs (88 A l. 10) for the restoration of the patrimony of St. Peter; and (88 B ll. 10—19) remonstrates with him upon the arrogance of Cerularius. To the latter, in *Scripta tuae*,[174] the Pope is more outspoken. Welcoming (89 ll. 15—17) his professed desire for peace, he notes with regret that Cerularius (90 A ll. 26—7) was said to have come to the patriarchal throne as a neophyte, and not through the usual grades of the ministry; and censures him for attempting (90 A 31—4) to subject to himself the ancient thrones of Alexandria and Antioch, and for adopting (90 B 23) the title of Œcumenical Patriarch.[175] To the dishonour of Latin Christendom (91 A 31—4) he had calumniated all those who receive the sacrament in unleavened bread, and he concludes by reminding him that the (92 A 3—5) headship of the Roman church is incompatible with the independence of national churches.

Three legates were deputed to carry these letters to Constantinople. They were Humbert, Cardinal-bishop of Silva Candida; Frederick of Lorraine, who afterwards became Pope Stephen IX., 1057—†8; and Peter, archbishop of Amalfi, ?1048—?†63. They were received with honour by the Emperor. He was anxious to secure the good-will of the Pope: and proportionately annoyed at the indiscretion of his Patriarch. Humbert put forth a *Dialogus*[176] to state the points at issue between the Latin and the Greek church; in which "Constantinopolitanus" retails the topics of the letter to the bishop of Trani and "Romanus" replies to him point by point. To this, a Studite monk, Nicetas Pectoratus, made answer in a temperately written *Libellus*[177] which, in addition to the points raised, discussed the enforced celibacy of the Latin clergy. Humbert met it by a *Responsio sive contradictio*,[178] conceived in a style of violent abuse and ending with an anathema on Nicetas and all his adherents.[179] But, as he tells us in his *Commemoratio*,[180] he did not leave the controversy to be so decided: for the Emperor was induced to go, in company with the legates, to the monastery of the Studium; where Nicetas was compelled to anathematise his *Libellus* and all who should either deny the prerogatives or impugn the faith of the Roman See. The pamphlet was burnt, and its author was made to retract in the presence of the legates; while Humbert's *Dialogus* and *Responsio* were translated into Greek by the Emperor's order.

The pressing need for political alliance between Pope and Emperor will account for a good deal of the unanimity evinced by these proceedings. But Michael Cerularius was, unlike the prisoner Leo IX., a free agent; nor had he, like Constantine X. (Monomachus), a political ally to secure. He kept aloof. He declared that he could not, without the assent of his brother Patriarchs, settle the questions at issue between the two churches. At length, the legates, finding that they could make no impression upon him, on 16th July, 1054, entered St. Sophia; and laid on the altar, as it stood prepared for the liturgy, a sentence of excommunication.[181] They begin by acknowledging the orthodoxy of the City; but they charge the Patriarch and his adherents with tenets and practices like those of the most infamous heretics; and, in particular, with "contempt of, and injury to, the Apostolic See." They conclude by solemnly anathematising "Michael, pretended Patriarch, and neophyte" and his friends "with all heretics, yea with the devil and all his angels, unless they repent." They then left the church; and, shaking off the dust of their feet, they ex-

The Macedonian Dynasty

claimed, " The Lord look upon you and judge."[182] After charging the Latins of Constantinople to avoid the communion of such as should deny " the Roman sacrifice,"[183] they set out, 18th July, on their return, with rich gifts from the Emperor to the Pope. At this point Michael Cerularius expressed a desire to confer with them. But they suspected foul play; and, as the Emperor would only permit a conference, if held in his own presence, to which the Patriarch demurred, they continued their journey.[184] Michael, in his turn, at a Synod in Constantinople, 20th July, 1054, excommunicated the legates in language as emphatic as their own.[185]

It may be doubted how much of this was more than " common form " on either side. The points of the controversy were discussed for some time longer, both Leo IX. and Michael being anxious to win over their fellow-patriarchs, and Peter III., Patriarch of Antioch,[186] 1053—?, intervening as mediator.[187] But the breach was made: though contemporaries seem scarcely to have been aware that anything of lasting importance was taking place,[188] so accustomed were they to East and West each going its own way, save under stress of some passing need for political co-operation. But two elements in the situation were irreconcilable: the ambition of Michael to be Pope of the Eastern world, and the claim to universal sovereignty inherited by Leo IX. from the time when Damasus, 366—†84, asserted the Petrine privilege for his see[189] at the opening of the career of its rival, Constantinople. Thus, what looked like little more than another outbreak of the old rivalry became, at last, a standing schism.

§ 8. Michael had now succeeded in ridding himself of subordination to the see of Rome. It remained to " render his office independent of imperial interference "; and, like his younger contemporary, Hildebrand, 1073—†85, the adviser of Leo IX., to place the Church above the State. " He had a high ideal of " his " office." He held himself bound, according to Psellus, " to speak ' holy words ' to secular powers, to resist *tyrannies*, to exalt the humble and pull down the self-willed, to superintend education: it was the ideal of Ambrose and Chrysostom."[190] And it explains the coolness between Michael and Constantine X. (Monomachus). Soon after the death of the last Porphyrogenita, the Empress Theodora, †1056, the contest between the bureaucratic and the military faction was resumed; and in 1057 the latter set up Isaac Comnenus,[191] an illustrious general, who became emperor, 1057—†9. It is certain that Michael Cerularius lent his support to the conspirators against Michael VI. (Stratioticus)[192] 1056—†7, the nominee of Theodora: and it is probable that it was paid for at the price of those privileges which Isaac granted when seated on the throne. "We are told that he honoured the patriarch as a father, and he granted to the church a completer power in its own affairs than it had before possessed. The treasurer (σκευοφύλαξ) and the grand chancellor (ὁ μέγας οἰκονόμος) used to be appointed directly by the emperor; Isaac transferred these appointments to the patriarch. He rendered the church wholly independent of the palace; the entire ecclesiastical administration was to depend henceforward on the head of the church." But Cerularius "presumed too far, and he fell. He took upon himself, in accordance with his idea of the duties or privileges of the patriarchal office, to admonish the emperor like a father or censure him like a master. Moreover .. in mere external trivialities" he "gave proof of a dangerously autocratic spirit; he wore red boots like the emperor's, asserting that it was an ancient pontifical privilege. Things came to a crisis when on one occasion the emperor exhibited his impatience and the indignant patriarch cried 'It was I who gave you the empire, I, too, can take it from you'":[193] and the sequel was his arrest and death.

§ 9. But the party struggle continued.[194] The elevation of Constantine XI.[195] (Ducas), 1059—†67, marked a reaction in favour of the bureaucracy. It was interrupted by the reign of Romanus IV.[196] (Diogenes), 1068—71, the heroic but ill-fated victim of the disaster at Manzikert (Manazkert); but he was followed by Constantine's son, Michael VII. (Ducas, "Parapinaces"[197]), 1071—8, which ushered in the final triumph of the bureaucracy with Psellus, †1097, for prime minister and other pedants associated with him in the conduct of affairs. The consequences of a government of *literati* were as might be expected. The frontiers were driven in.[198] The population, undefended by the feeble government and crushed by taxation, detached themselves from the Empire or went over to the barbarians. Anarchy increased by the conflict of feudal families and military leaders, mercenaries and Norman *condotiere:* each fighting for his own hand. Michael VII. had to contend with the revolt of Nicephorus Bryennius in Europe,[199] and of Nicephorus Botaniates in Asia; while the latter, now Emperor, 1078—†81, had to hold his own, as best he could, against other pretenders.[200] At last, by the *coup d'état* of 1st April, 1081, the welter was brought to a close by Alexius Comnenus,[201] the best general of the Empire. His victory marked the triumph of the military aristocracy over the civilian party, and of the provinces over the capital. But Alexius saved the situation; for he founded a new dynasty[202] which gave the Empire once more a century of stable government under the Comneni and the Angeli, 1081—1204.

CHAPTER IX.

THE COMNENI AND THE ANGELI, 1081—1204.

THE CRUSADES.

THE COMNENI AND THE ANGELI, 1081—1204.

From H. B. George, *Genealogical Tables*,[4] No. xlviii.

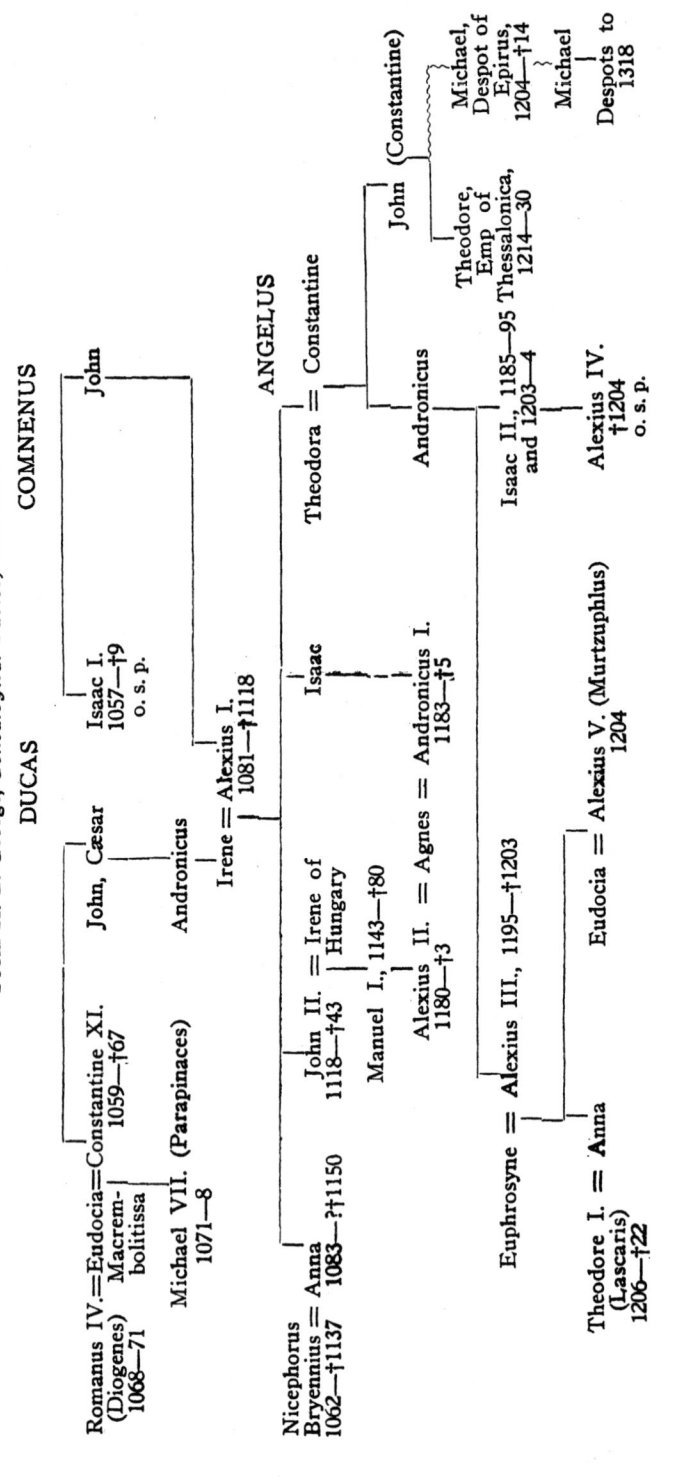

DUCAS COMNENUS

```
Romanus IV.=Eudocia=Constantine XI.        John, Cæsar        Isaac I.      John
(Diogenes)  Macrem-   1059—†67                                 1057—†9
1068—71     bolitissa                                          o. s. p.
            |                                |
            Michael VII. (Parapinaces)       Andronicus
            1071—8                           |
                                             Irene = Alexius I.
                                                     1081—†1118
                                             |
Nicephorus                                                            ANGELUS
Bryennius = Anna          John II.  = Irene of       Isaac          Theodora = Constantine
1062—†1137  1083—?†1150   1118—†43    Hungary                                 |
                          |                          |                        |
                          Manuel I., 1143—†80                                  |
                          |                                                   |
                          Alexius II. = Agnes = Andronicus I.                  |
                          1180—†3                1183—†5                       |
                                                              ┌────────────┬──────────────┐
                                                         Andronicus       John      (Constantine)
                                                              |            |               |
                                                ┌─────────────┴──┐    Theodore,     Michael,
Euphrosyne = Alexius III., 1195—†1203    Isaac II., 1185—95  Thessalonica,  Despot of
             |                           and 1203—4           Emp of           Epirus,
             |                              |              1214—30           1204—†14
             Eudocia = Alexius V. (Murtzuphlus)  Alexius IV.                    |
                      1204                      †1204                        Michael
                                                o. s. p.                   Despots to
                                                                             1318
             |
Theodore I. = Anna
(Lascaris)
1206—†22
```

RULERS, 1081—1204.

EASTERN EMPERORS.

Alexius I. (Comnenus), 1081—1118
John II. (Comnenus), 1118—43, his son
Manuel I. (Comnenus), 1143—80, his son
Alexius II. (Comnenus), 1180-3, his son
Andronicus I. (Comnenus), 1183—5 (usurper)
Isaac II. (Angelus), 1185—95 and 1203—4
Alexius III. (Angelus), 1195—1203, his brother
Alexius IV. (Angelus), 1203-4, son of Is. II.
Alexius V. (Ducas), Murtzuphlus, 1204

WESTERN EMPERORS.

Henry IV., 1056—1106
Henry V., 1106—25, his son
Conrad III., 1137—52, his nephew
Frederick I. (Barbarossa), 1152—90
Henry VI. (his son), 1190—7
Philip, 1198—1208, his brother

POPES.

Gregory VII. (Hildebrand), 1073—85
Victor III. (Desiderius, Abbot of Monte Cassino), 1086—7
Urban II. (Otto, bp. of Ostia), 1088—99
Pascal II. (Rainer, Abbot of S. Lorenzo), 1099—1118
Gelasius II. (Card. John of Gaeta), 1118—9
Calixtus II. (Guy, Abp. of Vienne), 1119—24
Honorius II. (Lambert, Bp. of Ostia), 1124—30
Innocent II. (Card. Gregory dei Papi), 1130—43
Cœlestine II. (Guy de Castro), 1143—4
Lucius II. (Gerard, Card. of St. Croce), 1144—5
Eugenius III. (Bernard, Abbot of S. Anastasius), 1145—53
Anastasius IV. (Conrad, Card. Bp. of Sabina), 1153—4
Hadrian IV. (Nicholas Brakespeare), 1154—9
Alexander III. (Roland Bandinelli, Card. of St. Mark), 1159—81
Lucius III. (Ubaldo, Bp. of Ostia), 1181—5
Urban III. (Uberto Crivelli, Abp. of Milan), 1185—7
Gregory VIII. (Card. Albert di Morra), 1187.
Clement III. (Paul Scolaro, Card. Bp. of Palestrina), 1187—91
Cœlestine III. (Card. Hyacinth), 1191—8
Innocent III. (Card. Lothario dei Conti di Segni), 1198—1216

PATRIARCHS OF CONSTANTINOPLE.

Michael I. Cerularius, 1043—58
Constantine III., Leuchudes, 1059—63
John VIII., Xiphilinus, 1064—75
Cosmas I., Hierosolymites, 1075—81
Eustratius, Garidus, 1081—4
Nicholas III., 1084—1111
John IX., Agapetus, 1111—34
Leo, Styppes, 1134—43
Michael II., Kurkuas (Oxeïtes), 1143—6
Cosmas II., Atticus, 1146—7
Nicholas IV., Muzalon, 1147-51
Theodotus II., 1151—3
Neophytus I., 1153
Constantine IV., Chliarenus, 1154—6
Lucas Chrysoberges, 1156—69
Michael III. (τοῦ 'Αγχιάλου) 1169—77
Chariton, Eugeniotes, 1177—8
Theodosius I., 1178—83
Basil II., Camaterus, 1183—7
Nicetas II., Muntanes, 1187—90
Leontius, Theotocites, 1190—1
Dositheus, 1191—2
George II., Xiphilinus, 1192—9
John X., Camaterus, 1199—1206

KINGS OF THE SERBS—*Dynasty of Nemanja.*

(Vulcan, 1089—1122)
Stephen Urus Neman I., 1122—36
Tichomil, 1136—51?
Stephen (Symeon) Neman II., 1151—95
Stephen (The First-crowned), 1195—1228

KINGS OF THE BULGARS.

Peter Deleanus, 1040—1
Tichomir, 1040
Alusianus, 1040—1
Constantine Bodin, 1073—82
Peter and John Asan, 1186—96
Joannitsa (Kalojoannes), 1197—1207

BISHOPS OF ALEXANDRIA, ANTIOCH AND JERUSALEM, 1081—1204.

ALEXANDRIA.

Orthodox.
John IV.   c. 1084
Sabas   ?
Theodosius   ?
Cyril II.   ?
Eulogius II.   ?
Sophronius III.
                    c. 1166
Elias II. (Alfterus)
                    c. 1180
Mark II.   c. 1195

Monophysite.
Cyril II.   1078—92
Michael IV.
             1092—1102
Macarius II.
             1102—29
Gabriel II. 1131—46
Michael V.   1146—7
John V.   1147—64
Mark III.   1164—89
John VI.   1189—1216

ANTIOCH.
Aemilian 1074—89/90
Nicephorus
             1089/90—?
John IV.   1098—1100
   ?   1137—55
Athanasius I.
             1157(?)—71
Theodore III. (Balsamon) 1185/91—1195

JERUSALEM.
Simeon II. c. 1094—9
Sabas I.   ?
James II.   ?
Arsenius II.   c. 1146
John VII.   c. 1156
Nicephorus II. c. 1166
Athanasius II. c. 1187
Leontius II.   ?
Dositheus I.   ?—1193
Mark II.   ?
Theophanes II. c. 1200

CHAPTER IX.

THE COMNENI AND THE ANGELI, 1081—1204: THE CRUSADES.

§ 1. THE Comneni[1] succeeded to an Empire seriously reduced[2] by the Third Anarchy. In Italy, it had lost Apulia and Calabria to the Normans on their capture of Bari, 1071, though Naples lingered on as a nominally imperial city till 1138. The Normans, after robbing the Empire of its Italian possessions, proceeded further to diminish its territory in the Balkan peninsula, by the invasion of Epirus, 1081—4, and the occupation of Dyrrhachium (Durazzo), 1081, and Korypho (Corfu), 1084. In the Balkans, also, Serbia asserted its independence, 1060, and was lost to the Romans. In Asia, there had been an advance in Armenia and Iberia (Georgia) under Basil II., who had also reduced Abasgia to a state of dependence: and under Constantine X. (Monomachus) Ani was won, 1045, and Kars, 1064. But the year which witnessed the capture of Kars saw the loss of Ani: and, with it, the first success of the Seljuk Turks against the Empire. In 1071, the fatal year of the loss of their last foothold in Italy, the Romans by their defeat at Manazkert, lost the greater part of Asia which now became the Seljuk Kingdom of Rūm, whose capital afterwards was fixed at Iconium. Ten years later the Turks captured Antioch, 1081; though in the previous year, 1080, at the south-east corner of Asia Minor, in the highlands of Cilicia, descendants of the old Armenian dynasty founded a new, or Lesser, Armenia. It maintained itself against the Turks, and owed a loose allegiance to the Emperors.

But the Comneni came of a vigorous stock. Their advent to power placed the State under the control of a military aristocracy: and they not only restored the authority of the Crown, but recovered considerable areas of the territories lost. The Turks were at Iconium, and there remained. In the Balkans, Slavonic peoples asserted their independence with the aid of Hungary. Across the Adriatic, there sprang up a dangerous rival in the commercial expansion of Venice. But in spite of these rivals, the Comneni restored the credit of the Empire; and in the times of distress that followed their extinction, men often looked back to its glories under their rule. Symbolic of their strength was the orderly succession, from father to son, of the first three sovereigns of their house; and the long reign of each, thirty-seven, twenty-five and thirty-seven years respectively. All of them were great soldiers. Alexius I., 1081—†1118,[3] the founder of the dynasty, was a diplomatist and administrator besides. He knew how to keep the enemies of the Empire beyond its frontiers as well as to re-establish order at home. In 1084 the Bogomils of Thrace revolted, and called to their aid the Petchenegs; but Alexius inflicted upon them so sanguinary a defeat,[4] 1091, that they disappeared for a generation; and, though they appeared again, 1121, they were once more routed by his son John, and after this vanished from history. In Asia, too, Alexius was equally successful. On the death of Malek Shah, 1092, the power of the Seljuk Turks showed signs of weakening. Alexius seized the moment to cross to Bithynia and to force a peace on the new Sultan of Iconium, Kilidj-Arslan I., 1092—†1106. He so inveigled the leaders of the First Crusade that they took Nicæa for him, 1097; and, pursuing their journey to Palestine, left him free to reconquer the coastland of Asia. On the death of Arslan, he took advantage of the occasion to impose a peace upon the Turks, after defeating them at Philomelium. At the death of Alexius, the Empire possessed in Anatolia Trebizond and the littoral of the Black Sea, all the coast as far as Antioch, and all the interior west of a line passing through Sinope, Gangra, Ancyra, Amorium and Philomelium. In Asia, as in the Balkans, the founder of the dynasty of the Comneni had gloriously restored the Imperial power. John II.,[5] 1118—†43, his son and successor, was a prince of no less distinction—" feared by his nobles, and beloved by his people."⁶ By training, frugal and abstemious; in character, beyond reproach; affable, generous and of prudent understanding, he was known by common consent as Kalojoannes, John the Excellent. His father had defended the frontiers: it was John's ambition to extend them: to carry the boundary of the Empire as far as Antioch and the Euphrates, and to impose his suzerainty on the Armenians of Cilicia, and on the Latin principalities which the Crusaders were setting up in the East. In 1120, he carried the Roman arms as far as Attalia; in 1130, to the Halys; in 1139, to Neocæsarea, and in 1142, on the eve of his death, he was planning the conquest of Syria. Manuel I., 1143—†80, his son, was the most famous of the Comneni. Like his father in ability and personal charm, he combined the culture of a Byzantine gentleman with the bravery of a crusading knight. He won back, for a few years, 1163—8, a footing in Italy for the Empire at Ancona. He reasserted its supremacy over Serbia, 1151. He twice forced a victorious peace upon Hungary, 1156 and 1168; and he formed the design of rivalling the exploits of Justinian and acquiring Italy and the Empire of the West. Part of this project was an alliance with Pope Alexander III., 1159—†81, against the Emperor Frederick I. (Barbarossa), 1152—†90, and the re-union of the churches of Old and New Rome. But the Pope thought twice before he would exchange his independence for that of a patriarch subordinate to a Byzantine Emperor; and events in Asia disillusioned Manuel. For eleven years, 1164—75, he had been obliged, while pursuing his ambitions in the West, to maintain a policy purely defensive against Kilidj-Arslan II., 1156—†92, the sultan of Iconium. At length, he recognised the peril from that quarter; and took the offensive. But it was too late; and the imperial forces suffered a terrible defeat at Myriokephalon, 1176, in Southern Phrygia. Manuel I., in fact, ruined his country by his grandiose imperialism.⁷ He was succeeded by his son Alexius II., 1180—†3, a child of ten years old: and the boy was murdered by Andronicus I., 1183—†5, the cousin of Manuel I. and the last of the Comneni, who secured his throne. Andronicus was a man of vicious life; but he made "a serious and resolute attempt to rescue the Empire from its decline, on the lines which had been followed by Basil II. and abandoned since his death; for he set himself to purify the administration and to remedy the economic evil which was ruining the Empire— the growth of vast estates."[8] But the time for reforms had gone by. Andronicus I. was dethroned by a revolt of the nobles who disliked his anti-aristocratic reforms: and Isaac II. (Angelus), 1185—†95, one of his opponents among the nobles, was elevated to his place. He, in turn, perished by his own vices, and the ambition of his brother Alexius III., 1195—†1203. " Their discord introduced the Latins to the conquest of Constantinople ":[9] and the Empire, restored by the Comneni, was broken to pieces.

§ 2. The Crusades[10] overthrew it: and we have now to trace the course of their contact with the Eastern Empire, and how they rendered permanent that breach between East and West which had been opened, almost unobserved to their contemporaries, by Pope Leo IX. and Michael Cerularius.

A Crusade, to those who took part in it, had a double significance. It was at once a " Pilgrim's Progress " and a " Holy War ": in either case, a *novum salutis genus*.[11] The pilgrimage was to the Holy Places: and the war for their recovery. In the fourth century, Constantine, †337, built great churches on the sacred sites of the Gospels: in particular, the Church of the Resurrection at the Holy Sepulchre;[12] and, 326, his mother, the Empress Helena, made a pilgrimage[13] to the Holy Land where she presided over the construction of Constantine's buildings (and erected others herself) on the Mount of Olives and at Bethlehem.[14] Her example spread far and wide; and in 333 a pilgrim went from Bordeaux who has left us an *Itinerary*,[15] marking all the stages *(mansiones)* from Bordeaux, *via* Constantinople, to Jerusalem. About 350, the Feast of the Exaltation of the Cross, on 14th September, is known to have been kept at Jerusalem;[16] and its " invention " was, at this date, ascribed to the days of Constantine.[17] This was early in the episcopate of

St. Cyril, 350—†86. Towards its close, the sacred sites were visited by St. Etheria, a relative of the Emperor Theodosius I., 379—†95, who travelled from his own country Gallaecia, and has left us, in her *Peregrinatio*,[18] a valuable account of all she saw, in particular of the Veneration of the Cross and the other rites of the church of Jerusalem. A year before Cyril died, Jerome, 385, settled at Bethlehem, whither he was soon followed by Paula and Eustochium, with other ladies of the Roman aristocracy. He used his influence in the West to encourage the habit[19] of going on pilgrimage; and in the sixth century the works of Theodosius[20] (530), and of Antoninus[21] the martyr (570), testify to its popularity.

But in the seventh century there came a check; when the East was overrun by Persians and Saracens. In 614 Jerusalem was taken by the Persians, and the True Cross carried off to Seleucia-Ctesiphon. In the true spirit of a crusader, it was recovered, and replaced in its shrine, by the Emperor Heraclius, 610—†41; but only to be rescued again and taken by him to Constantinople before Jerusalem was captured, 637, by the Mohammedans under the Caliph Omar. Its Holy Places were now in the hands of the Moslems; and pilgrimage became occasional only, as when Arculf,[22] bishop of Perigueux, spent nine months in Jerusalem, 670. It also became difficult; and, perhaps for that reason, it came to be imposed as a penance. Yet it was welcome, especially to our forefathers (as in the case of Willibald,[23] who spent seven years in pilgrimage, 722—9), for it not only provided the penitent with the means of satisfaction for his sins but it set his feet upon holy ground. Pilgrimage, therefore, continued to be popular in spite of its risks; and a protectorate of pilgrims was secured by the Franks. Envoys of Charlemagne, Emperor, 800—†14, went, 797—9, to Harun Arraschid, 786—†809, the Abbasid Caliph of Bagdad; who sent him the keys of the Holy Sepulchre[24] as a symbol of the site bestowed upon him.[25] Charlemagne thereupon lavished alms and hostels upon the pilgrims, as we learn from the *Itinerary*[26] of Bernard the Monk, 870; and his example was followed throughout the West where it became common to collect alms for the Holy Land. Pilgrimages. were now not difficult, with passports; and they were frequent throughout the tenth century. But in the eleventh century came a second check. The Fatimite Caliphs, who were of the Shiite sect of Mohammedans, whereas the Abbasids of Bagdad were Sunnites, began their rule in Egypt, 908; and Palestine fell under their authority, 969. At first, it made no difference to Christian pilgrims : but, 28th September, 1009, the Caliph Hakem ordered the destruction of the Holy Sepulchre and followed it up by ten years' persecution of Jews and Christians throughout the country. The Protectorate had thus fallen from the hands of the Western Emperor; and events now enabled the Eastern Emperor to assume it. In 1012 a Bedouin chief revolted against the tyranny of Hakem. He looked, for support, to the prestige of the great " Macedonian " Emperors, Nicephorus (Phocas) II., John I. (Tzimisces) and Basil II.; and ordered the Christians to rebuild the Church of the Holy Sepulchre. Under conventions of 1027 and 1036 between the Eastern Emperor and the Caliph, the rebuilding went on : till, at last, it was finished, 1048, under Constantine X. (Monomachus), by Nicephorus, the Patriarch of Jerusalem :[27] and the church with the Christian quarter was surrounded by a defensive wall. Thus the Byzantine Protectorate succeeded to the Frankish; but, after the Schism of 1054, it did not afford much assistance to Latin pilgrims nor conduce to good feeling between East and West. Thus, 1055, St. Lietbert, archbishop of Cambrai, was turned back by the Catapan of Cyprus;[28] and, 1056, Pope Victor II. had to write to the Empress Theodora to complain of the exactions of which pilgrims from the West were the victims at the hands of her officials. " They force every mounted man to pay three aurei, and every two travellers on foot the same; and sometimes they steal their horses too."[29] But, in spite of such obstacles, pilgrimages from the West were never more frequent than in the eleventh century : only pilgrims travelled under arms and in large numbers. Those, for instance, who set out, 1065, under the leadership of Günther, bishop of Bamberg, 1057—†65, amounted to as many as two thousand men.[30] A pilgrimage was, in fact, an expedition : and needed nothing but an enemy to turn it into a crusade. Moreover, a friendly route was now opened for these hosts by the conversion of Hungary,[31] 997—1038. It made the highway of the Danube available; and thus these large expeditions not only familiarised Europe with a knowledge of the way to the East but kept up an enthusiasm in the West for visiting the Holy Places.

It was not long after the pilgrimage of Günther that the enemy appeared whose advent turned the pilgrimage into the Crusade or Holy War. The Seljuk Turks had made themselves masters of Bagdad. After their victory at Manazkert, 1071, they seized and held the greater part of Asia Minor. In 1078 they conquered Jerusalem. They were at Nicæa 1081, and at Antioch 1084. These disasters coincided with the Third Anarchy at Constantinople : where the imperial power was paralysed till the accession of the Comneni. Accordingly, in 1073, Michael VII. (Parapinaces) wrote to Pope Gregory VII., 1073—†85, for assistance : promising, in return, the reunion of Eastern Christendom with the West. His letter appealed both to the generosity, and to the ambition, of Hildebrand. On 9th July, 1073, he replied to the Emperor welcoming his project of re-union.[32] He then took measures to send him assistance. On 2nd February, 1074, he wrote to William I., Count of Burgundy, 1057—†87, urging him, with others, to go to the aid of the Christians of CP. against the Saracens;[33] and followed it up, 1st March, by an encyclical to all the faithful, inviting them to hasten to the assistance of " the Christian Empire against the pagans who have now carried their devastation almost to the walls of Constantinople."[34] In a letter of 10th September, to William VIII., Count of Poitiers, 1058—†87, he speaks of the expedition as doubtful : for there is now a rumour from overseas that " the Christians have driven off the fierce attacks of the pagans."[35] By December 7th, the Pope's plans have matured in another direction. He now has in mind not the relief of Constantinople, but a Crusade whose objective is the Holy Places at Jerusalem; for he writes to Henry, King of the Romans [Henry IV., 1056—†1106] that he has fifty thousand men ready to start under his own command in order to deliver the Holy Sepulchre from the Turk; and that this will be a grand opportunity for reconciling the Orient with the Church.[36] Thus, among his other titles to greatness, Gregory VII. must be credited with this, that he conceived the idea of the Crusades; and not only gave it the sanction of the papacy but endeavoured himself to take the lead. But he was prevented from putting himself at its head because his energies were diverted to the strife about investiture;[37] and, as he was the ally of the Normans, he could not befriend the Eastern Empire. In a letter of 22nd January, 1075, to Hugh, abbot of Clugny, he regrets the alienation of Easterns from the faith.[38] It was left to another pope to re-kindle the ideal; and to the enthusiasm of the people to give it effect in the First Crusade.

§ 3. It began 1095 and ended with the capture of Jerusalem, 15th July, 1097.[39] Alexius I. (Comnenus), 1081—†1118, was hard pressed on all sides; by the Normans on the West, by the Petchenegs on the North, and by the Seljuk Turks to the East and South. In 1087 he asked aid of Robert, Count of Flanders, a pilgrim returning from Jerusalem through Constantinople; and Robert promised him five hundred knights.[40] But this was of small avail; and Alexius repeated his request to Pope Urban II., 1088—†99. In 1091, he was expecting from Rome an army to come to his assistance against the Petchenegs; and, 1095, on the eve of the Crusade, ambassadors from Constantinople appeared at the Council of Piacenza, 1st—7th March, and begged Urban II. and all Christians " to come to their aid against the pagans in defence of Holy Church."[41] But no mention was made of rescuing the Holy Places; and a Crusade, or expedition for this purpose, appears to have owed its initiation to the Pope alone. Urban II. was a French pope, and determined to preach the Crusade in France. In July, 1095, he crossed the Alps; and, 15th August, was received by Adhémar de Monteil, bishop of Le Puy-en-Velay, 1087—

†98. Summoning a Council to meet at Clermont-Ferrand,[42] 18th November, the Pope spent the autumn in travelling about central and southern France to make his plans known. On 27th November, he addressed the crowd of clerics and knights who had accompanied the bishops to Clermont, and stirred their zeal for the recovery of the Holy Places from the Turk. Loud cries of " Dieu le veult " testified to the enthusiasm which he invoked: and thousands took the cross. The 15th August, 1096, was fixed for the day of departure,[43] and Constantinople for the point of concentration; and, as the three kings of Western Europe—the Emperor Henry IV., 1056—†1106, Philip I., King of France, 1060—†1118, and William Rufus, King of England, 1087—†1100,— were all under excommunication, the leadership of the Crusade fell into the hands of barons and knights. At first, its success was threatened by the popular crusade which preceded it; for the multitudes excited by Peter the Hermit and others, who carried round the fiery cross which the Pope had enkindled, rushed off, 8th March, 1096, under his leadership, to Constantinople. They arrived 1st August, and Alexius treated them well; but the excesses they committed upon his subjects, increased the resentment of Greek against Latin, and no one was particularly sorry when they crossed the Bosporus, 6th— 7th August, only to perish miserably at the hands of the Turk. Meanwhile, the barons and knights had been organising better-disciplined forces. They converged upon Constantinople by different routes. Godfrey of Bouillon,[44] 1058—†1100, Duke of Lorraine, with his brother Baldwin, led the crusaders of Lorraine through Hungary to Constantinople, where he arrived, 23rd December, 1096. Raymond de St. Gilles,[45] Count of Toulouse, 1088— †1105[?9], with bishop Adhémar as papal legate, took the Provençals down the coast of Illyria and then due east, to Constantinople, which they reached 27th April, 1097. Bohemond[46] of Otranto, †1111, son of Robert Guiscard, with his nephew Tancred, 1096—†1194, brought the Normans by sea to Durazzo, and thence to Constantinople: where he arrived about the same time as

Raymond. Thus was gathered at Constantinople, in the spring of 1097, a great host of about one hundred and fifty thousand men. The majority, no doubt, took part for spiritual ends: but some were adventurers. There were prince-adventurers, bent on carving out kingdoms to inherit: like Bohemond, who became Prince of Antioch, 1098—1111; Baldwin, afterwards Count of Edessa, 1098—1100, and then King of Jerusalem, 1100—†1118; and Raymond, who set himself up as Count of Tripoli, 1102—5. And there were merchant-adventurers, who went with an eye to commerce, like the Genoese seamen: whose fleets supplied the Crusaders with provisions and munitions of war, and rendered help in the sieges of Antioch[47] and Jerusalem.[48] Thus jealousies among the leaders, and mixed motives among the rank and file affected adversely the progress of the Crusade: and so did the attitude of the Emperor Alexius. He had asked for auxiliaries; and received rivals. He might have tried to win them for allies; and, by frankly waging war in concert with them, have persuaded them to share the conquests on equal terms. But, even if they had not been ambitious to rule at his expense, this could hardly be expected to be the point of view of a Roman Emperor. He held that all the lands which the Crusaders would traverse were lost provinces of his empire. He therefore induced them to do him homage;[49] so that whatever they conquered, they would conquer in his name, and whatever they retained they would hold as his vassals. This done, he was glad to see the last of them;[50] for, during the winter of 1096—7, their presence had been that of unwelcome guests to the people of Constantinople. When they conquered Nicæa, 19th June, 1097, and afterwards defeated the field-army of the Turks before Dorylæum (now Eskishehr), 1st July, Alexius took advantage of their victories to recover all the coast-land of Asia Minor.[51] Meanwhile, the Crusaders passed on with good prospect of success. For, first, the way across Asia[52] lay open to them after the defeat of the Turks before Dorylæum; and they could count on, at least, the benevolent neutrality of the country-people, who disliked the military

The Comneni and the Angeli 231

rule of the Turk. And, secondly, circumstances further afield favoured the Crusaders: for on the death of Malek-Shah, 1073—†92, his empire fell to pieces. His son Barkiarok, 1092—†1104, ruled as Sultan at Bagdad; Kilidj-Arslan I., 1092—†1106, as Sultan of Rūm, at Iconium; while Syria became practically independent, and weak for lack of support from the main body of the Seljuk Empire. Thirdly, Syria was torn by dissensions within, and attacked by the Fatimite Caliph of Egypt from without. So, taking advantage of these misfortunes, the Crusaders pushed their attack upon Syria. They besieged and took Antioch, 21st October, 1097—3rd June, 1098,[53] and Bohemond set up a Principality there. Raymond proceeded, February—May, 1099, south, to the siege of Arca, which he afterwards included in his County of Tripoli; and Baldwin was already engaged in setting up the County of Edessa.[54] Disgusted with these exhibitions of self-seeking, the main body under Godfrey of Bouillon and his brother, Eustace of Boulogne, with Tancred and Robert Court-Hose[55] and the aid of Raymond, pressed on to the goal at Jerusalem, which had recently, 1098, been occupied by the Caliph of Egypt. Following the coast-road[56] they arrived before the city early in June. After a month's siege, the city was captured by assault, 15th July, 1099. There was a fearful massacre: but the end of the First Crusade was accomplished, now that the Holy Places were once more in Christian hands. They set up the Latin Kingdom of Jerusalem, 1099—1187, which was organised, at first, under Godfrey as Advocate of the Holy Sepulchre,[57] 1099—†1100, and then under his brother Baldwin I., as King, 1100—†18. Its natural counterpart was the Latin patriarchate: and Simeon, the last Greek Patriarch of Jerusalem having died in Cyprus,[58] Arnold de Rohez, chaplain to Robert Court-Hose, became the first Latin Patriarch of Jerusalem.[59] By all the events of the Crusade, the pressure on the Empire and the churches of Eastern Christendom had been relieved: but East and West were still further alienated from each other.

§ 4. The Second Crusade,[60] as commonly reckoned, is

that which took place, 1146—8, in the reign of Manuel I. In the interval which had elapsed since the First, expeditions from the West had poured into Palestine: and crusading was, in fact, almost continuous. But custom has included in the series of Crusades only those which were promoted after the news of some crushing disaster: and that which occasioned the Second Crusade was the fall of Edessa. It was a vassal state of the Kingdom of Jerusalem, and the furthest outpost of Christendom against Islām: and it was captured on Christmas Day, 1144, by Imād-ed-Dīn Zengī, one of the regents (Atābegs) whose rise to power marked the decline of the Seljuk house and who founded dynasties on its ruins. The Zengīds, 1127—1250, were Atābegs of el-Mosīl and eventually of all Mesopotamia and trans-Jordanic Syria. On the death of Zengī, 1146, an attempt was made by Joscelin II. (de Courtenay), the Count of Edessa, to recover his city; but without success. Meanwhile, news of its fall had been brought from Antioch, November, 1145, to Pope Eugenius III., 1145—†53. In *Quantum praedecessores* of 1st December, 1145, he urged upon Louis VII. of France, 1137—†80, to hasten to the aid of " the Church in the east."[61] His appeal found support in the eloquence of St. Bernard, 1091—†1153, both at Vézelay, 31st March, 1146, where Louis VII. and his nobles took the Cross: and at the Diet of Speier, 25th December, 1146, where his example was followed by the Emperor Conrad III., 1137—†52, and his princes and knights in large numbers. So the Second Crusade was begun under auspices more favourable than those of the First. Its leaders were kings and not knights: and " its armies would no longer be penetrating into the wilds, but would find a friendly basis of operations ready to their hand in Frankish Syria."[62] On the other hand, there were omens of disaster. The armies of the Crusaders, though better disciplined, were smaller than before, and embarrassed by a following of non-combatant pilgrims. The sympathies of the Emperor Manuel I. were alienated by the conduct of the Germans in their passage through Thrace, where they plundered at large, till he had to send troops against them to protect his subjects.⁶³ He demanded that Louis VII. and Conrad III. should do homage to him for their future conquests; and was only too glad to see the last of the Germans when they had crossed the Bosporus to suffer a considerable defeat before Dorylæum.⁶⁴ The armies of Louis VII. preserved better discipline, and the Emperor received him with courtesy. The French then crossed the Bosporus in their turn; and, making a detour to Attalia,⁶⁵ found a Byzantine fleet to transport them to Antioch. But, when they reached Jerusalem, both Conrad and Louis had lost the greater part of their armies; and, though re-inforced by its King, Baldwin III., 1144—†62, and his troops, they found an advance upon Edessa impossible. The three kings therefore, resolved, after some deliberation, to attack Damascus. But the attack was impolitic: for Damascus was the one ally which could enable the Crusaders and the Franks of Palestine to hold their own against Nūr-ed-Dīn, 1146—†74, the successor of Zengī in Northern Syria and Edessa. It was also unsuccessful: and the Second Crusade at once collapsed. Emperor and King of France went home, 1148—9: and the ignominious failure of a Crusade led by the two chief monarchs of Europe brought the whole Crusading movement to shame. Manuel I. alone had any gains to show: for he occupied Ancona, 1151: and so the Byzantine power set foot again in Italy.

§ 5. A generation passed between the failure of the Second Crusade and the dispatch of the Third, 1189—92. In the East, the immediate result of the failure was that Nūr-ed-Dīn renewed his attacks. Having taken the city of Edessa, he now conquered the County, 1150. He defeated and killed Raymond of Antioch, †1149, and overran the eastern parts of his Principality. Baldwin III. of Jerusalem attempted to check these advances, partly by renewing the old alliance with Damascus, and partly by drawing closer to the Emperor Manuel I. Baldwin and his brother, Amalric I., 1162—†73, married, respectively, Theodora the niece, and Mary the great-niece of the Emperor: and Manuel took for his second wife

Mary the daughter of Raymond of Antioch. In this, and other ways, the Frankish kingdoms, relying upon the support of the Eastern Empire, succeeded in prolonging their resistance to Nūr-ed-Dīn. But he was a formidable adversary. Unlike his father, he was definitely animated by a religious motive; and, leaving Moslem rivals alone, he confined his attention to the Franks and attacked them in the spirit of a holy war. For this purpose, he seized Damascus, 1154, their ally in Syria; and then pursued the contest in Egypt. Baldwin III. had taken Ascalon, 1153, in an attempt to close the way into Egypt against Nūr-ed-Dīn. But the conflict was renewed in Egypt itself between Nūr-ed-Dīn's Kurdish lieutenant Shirguh[66] and Amalric I., the brother and successor of Baldwin. They each supported rival viziers of the now decadent Caliphs of Egypt: and, in the end, Shirguh won and, January, 1169, became vizier himself. He died in March: and was succeeded by his nephew Salāh-ed-Dīn Yusuf ibn Ayyūb. On the death of the Caliph,[67] Saladin became sole ruler of Egypt, and the founder of the dynasty of the Ayyubīds,[68] 1169—1341. Thus the divisions of the Mohammedan world between Sunnite in Bagdad and Shiite in Egypt dissolved into a Sunnite supremacy[69] centred in Egypt: and the Frankish kingdoms were faced, at last, with a united foe. Saladin,[70] 1171—†93, acquired Damascus, 1174, and Aleppo, 1183. With Northern Syria and Egypt thus united under a single hand, the hour of the kingdom of Jerusalem had struck. Saladin, in the spirit of a crusader—for he, too, was bent on a *jehad* or holy war for the recovery of the city— advanced upon it from the north. At the battle of Hittin, 4th July, 1187, he completely defeated the Franks: and the way south lay open before him. After a fortnight's siege, Jerusalem capitulated, 2nd October: and by the end of the year, 1189, nothing was left to the Franks except Tyre, Antioch, Tripoli and the fortress of the Knights Hospitallers at Margat. This was the disaster that called for the Third Crusade, 1189—92; and those who embarked upon it had to face for the first time the resistance of a united Mohammedan world.

Conrad Marquis of Montferrat,[71] 1183—†92, the brother-in-law of the Emperor Isaac II. (Angelus), 1185—95, was as much as any man responsible for it. He defeated Saladin under the walls of Tyre, 1st January, 1188:[72] and sent out appeals for succour to the West. They were endorsed by the papacy;[73] but the impetus this time came from the lay-power, and the Crusade was led by the three strong monarchies of Germany, France and England. In Germany, the Emperor Frederick I. (Barbarossa), at a Diet at Mainz, 23rd March, 1188, took oath to make expedition to the Holy Land;[74] while Philip Augustus, 1180—†1223, of France, and Henry II., 1154—†89, of England, began a scheme of taxation for its support known as "the Saladin tithe."[75] The Emperor Frederick I. (Barbarossa), 1152—†90, set out[76] from Ratisbon, 11th May, 1189. He had accompanied his uncle, Conrad III., on the second Crusade; and he now marched through Hungary, with carefully disciplined forces, to Constantinople. But he had to encounter opposition and treachery from Isaac II. He not only shared the old grudge of all Eastern Emperors against the "upstart" Emperor of the West; but, in order to secure for himself the patronage of the Holy Places and religious supremacy in the Levant, he had actually allied himself with Saladin. Terms, however, were arranged at length: and Barbarossa crossed the Bosporus, passed through Philadelphia and Iconium,[77] and died from a chill after bathing in the river Calycadnus—a petty torrent in Cilicia. Of his fine army, only a thousand men, under his son Philip of Swabia, won their way through to join the French and English before Acre, October, 1190. At this time, Philip Augustus and Richard I., 1189—†99, were on their way, but wintered in Sicily, 1190—1. After long delays, of which Richard made use to seize Cyprus and sell it to Guy of Lusignan,[78] the founder of the Latin kingdom there, the two kings, in spite of dissensions, succeeded in capturing Acre, 12th July, 1191. Philip thereupon departed home, on plea of ill-health: but Richard remained for a further year, now fighting and now negotiating with Saladin, until he too departed,

October, 1192. The net result of the Crusade, from the point of view of its purpose, was to preserve the kingdom of Jerusalem, in an attenuated form, as a strip of coastland from Jaffa to north of Tyre, to which it was the object of later Crusaders to annex Jerusalem itself by a "corridor" connecting it with the coast. From the point of view of relations between East and West, the treatment of Frederick Barbarossa by Isaac II. was to intensify further the resentment of Latin against Greek. And this led, within twenty years, to the overthrow of Constantinople by the Fourth Crusade.

§ 6. The Fourth Crusade,[79] 1202—4, directed against Constantinople, was really the work of Philip of Swabia: though sanctioned, with reluctance, by Pope Innocent III., 1198—†1216. It may be regarded as a phase of the struggle between the Popes and the Hohenstaufen fought out in the East: a phase in which the Imperialists won. In it, the lay motive was supreme.

In the year after Richard Cœur-de-Lion left the Holy Land, Saladin died, 1193. A civil war ensued for his inheritance between his brother Malik-al-Adil and his sons. The former secured Egypt: and Mohammedanism was weakened against attacks from the West because its forces were no longer directed, as under Saladin, by a single and capable hand. About the same time, Henry VI., 1190—†7, succeeded as Western Emperor. He was the ablest since Charlemagne: and he aimed at the sovereignty of the East. But, for subsidiary reasons also, his energies were directed against Constantinople. As the son of Frederick I. (Barbarossa) he had neither forgotten nor forgiven the insults and treacheries with which Isaac II. (Angelus) had opposed his father. As master of Central Italy and, since Christmas, 1194, King of Sicily, he had inherited the aggressive policy of the Normans against the Eastern Empire. The Basileus, Alexius III., 1195—†1203, had recently deposed and blinded his brother Isaac II. In spite of that, he could rely on the support of the Pope. But for that reason, as also to create for himself a claim upon the Eastern Empire, Henry VI. had arranged that Irene, the widow of Roger of Sicily and daughter of Isaac II., should marry his brother Philip of Swabia [Emp. 1198—†1208]. To enforce this claim, though ostensibly to take the Cross, Henry VI. held a Diet at Bari, 31st May, 1195; and started upon a Crusade by way of Constantinople, which, however, came to nothing. His aim was the absorption of the East and the creation of but one Empire. But he died in Sicily, in the autumn of 1197, before he could carry it into effect.

"The true heir of Henry VI. was Pope Innocent III."[80] Cardinal Lothario dei Conti di Segni was born 1161; and was only thirty-seven at his election. But he was chosen in order to put the vigour of youth into the cause of the papacy: and he began at once. On the death of Henry VI., he took up his project of universal supremacy but with this difference, that it should be the supremacy of the spiritual power. On 21st February, 1198, he wrote to the Patriarch of Jerusalem, and promised him assistance.[81] He then turned his attention to relations with Constantinople. On the one hand, he could not ally himself with a schismatic Emperor. On the other, he could not suffer his rival Philip of Swabia to become supreme at Constantinople. He therefore resolved to induce the Basileus Alexius III., 1195—1203, to promote the reunion of the Orthodox Church with the Apostolic See and then to use him for the purposes of the Crusade. Accordingly, 15th August, 1198, he sent two legates to Constantinople with letters to Alexius III.,[82] and to the Patriarch George II. (Xiphilinus)[83] 1192—9: proposing the re-union of East with West, and on these terms, a joint Crusade. Alexius III. felt insecure on his throne; and he sent a reply consenting to re-union and promising co-operation in the Crusade, on condition that Cyprus might be assigned to him. But he was really playing for delay. Meanwhile, the Pope sent letters to all Christian Princes in favour of the Crusade; and designated Fulk, †1201, the parish priest of Neuilly, near Paris, to preach it. There took the Cross at his preaching, Theobald, Count of Champagne, Louis, Count of Blois, and Baldwin VIII., Count of Flanders: all of the lesser nobility only, for kings were indifferent. The Emperor Philip had his own plans; while Philip Augustus of France was excommunicate and John of England a miscreant. In 1200 the leaders elected Theobald as their chief : and decided to go by sea, in Venetian ships, with Egypt as their first objective. For Egypt, and not Jerusalem, was now the true point of attack. Strategically, Jerusalem was best reached from Egypt. By the division of the dominions of Saladin, Egypt, under his brother, was the focus of Mohammedan power. And motives of trade impelled the Italian cities to Egypt: for, from it, they could reach the Red Sea and the commerce of the Indian Ocean, whereas the old trade-route with the East through Constantinople was now closing down. Accordingly, they sent envoys to Venice, of whom Marshal Villehardouin was one, to bargain for ships with the Doge Enrico Dandolo (b. 1105 : Doge 1192—†1205). A treaty was concluded, March, 1201, by which the Venetians were to provide the Crusaders with transport to Egypt, on payment of 85,000 marks, and on condition that half their conquests were to go to the Republic. The fleet was to sail a year from midsummer. On 8th May, the Pope was induced to confirm the treaty : but he made it a condition that the Crusaders " should do no injury to Christians, save in the case of being unjustly opposed."[84] He evidently had reason to fear that, according to the project of Henry VI. of which his brother Philip of Swabia was now the depositary, the Crusade would be diverted to an attack upon Constantinople.

Nor was Innocent III. mistaken. Two days before the treaty, Theobald died, 8th May; he was succeeded in the leadership of the Crusade by Boniface II., Marquis of Montferrat, 1192—†1207; and while Philip, as the son-in-law of Isaac II., had a claim on the succession, Boniface, as belonging to a family which had served and been ill-rewarded by the Eastern Empire, had an interest in Constantinople. They both wanted a Ghibelline crusade for its acquisition : whereas the aim of Innocent III. was no such laicised lust of gain but a crusade for the recovery of the Holy Places. For this he relied on the support of the Guelphs and the aid of the usurper, Alexius III. Innocent and the Hohenstaufen had now transferred their rivalries to eastern soil.

In the spring of 1201, Alexius, the son of Isaac II., escaped from captivity at the hand of his uncle, Alexius III. : and came to the West to seek reinstatement. He first went to Rome, and promised the Pope that, if restored, he would see to the re-union of Eastern Christendom with the Apostolic See. He then went on to Germany : where, on Christmas Day, 1201, at Hagenau, he met his brother-in-law, the Emperor Philip, and Boniface of Montferrat; and induced them to set out for the restoration of his father, Isaac II. Thus, before the concentration of the Crusaders at Venice, to take place at midsummer, 1202, there was already a pact[85] in existence to shift its course to Constantinople. But Innocent was aware of it, and, 16th November, 1202, he wrote to Alexius III. warning him of the aims of his nephew, Alexius, and Philip of Swabia. He undertook, however, to keep Philip quiet by means of his rival Otto (afterwards Otto IV., 1208—†18), of Brunswick, Ghibelline by Guelph.[86] Meanwhile, the Crusaders had concentrated, according to plan, at Venice : but, in November, they found themselves unable to pay the 85,000 marks in full. They could only find 49,000; and, in discharge of the balance of 36,000, they agreed to divert the Crusade to the conquest of Zara. Whether there was any further compact between Philip of Swabia and Venice to direct the Crusade, afterwards, upon Constantinople, we do not know. But the Venetians, at any rate, were not sorry to acquiesce in the plan, not only because Alexius III. had given privileges to their rivals of Pisa,[87] but also because they had already gone back secretly upon their promise to transport the Crusaders to Egypt. During the months which elapsed between the treaty of March, 1201, and the concentration of 24th June, 1202, the Republic made a compact, 13th November, 1202, with the Sultan of Egypt by which, in return for an undertaking that the Crusade should not attack Egypt, they received important concessions : a quarter in

Alexandria, and a safe conduct for all pilgrims visiting the Holy Sepulchre under Venetian protection—a privilege of great pecuniary value. Zara was easily won, 24th November, 1202: and, 1st January, 1203, as the Crusaders lay encamped before it, an envoy of Philip appeared with the proposal that they should next turn their energies to the restoration of the young Alexius who, on his part, promised (1) to bring back the Eastern Empire to the obedience of the Roman See, (2) to pay the Crusaders 200,000 marks in silver, (3) to take part in the Crusade himself, and (4) to maintain 500 cavalry in Palestine in perpetuity. Thus the taking of Constantinople would not be a substitute for the legitimate object of the Crusade, but a step towards its attainment. Some of the Crusaders, like Simon de Montfort,[88] 1150—†1218, saw through the trick, and sailed away to the Holy Land. But, on the arrival of Alexius at Zara, 7th April, the main body took ship, 24th May, for Corfu, on their way to Constantinople. Innocent III., however, had been informed of the pact of Zara with as much precision as he had formerly been kept aware of the pact of Hagenau. On 20th June, he wrote to Boniface of Montferrat, Baldwin of Flanders, and Louis of Blois, forbidding them to proceed to Constantinople and commanding them to hold course direct for the Holy Land.[89] But the die was cast: it was too late. The intrigue of Philip of Swabia had triumphed, and the Crusaders were well on their way to Constantinople instead.

It was 23rd June when their fleet arrived at St.Stefano, within sight of Constantinople. Next day they landed and re-victualled at Chalcedon on the Asiatic shore; and, afterwards, they effected a concentration at Scutari. On 7th July, after communicating and making their wills, they crossed the Bosporus and made for the suburb of Galata on the left bank of the Golden Horn. Alexius III. retired within the walls; and, while the Venetian galleys sailed into the harbour, the army advanced up the left bank of the Golden Horn, re-built and crossed the Galata bridge and encamped on a hill opposite the Palace of Blachernae to the N.W. of the City. A general assault

THE CATHEDRAL OF THE ASSUMPTION, MOSCOW.

See p. 374.]

The Comneni and the Angeli

took place, 17th July; and the Venetians made good their footing on part of the walls. Alexius III. replied by a sortie: but he was driven in, and took flight in the night. Next morning, 18th July, the citizens drew Isaac II. from his prison, and reinstated him on the throne. Communications were then established between the blind old Emperor and his son Alexius, who entered the Palace of Blachernae supported by his brother-in-law, Philip of Swabia. Alexius averred that, if the Crusaders entered the City, he could not answer for their safety: and they retired to Galata while, 1st August, Alexius was crowned as Alexius IV., joint-Emperor with his father. He now paid over the 200,000 marks which he had promised: and of this sum, 36,000 marks were assigned to the Venetians in discharge of the debt which the Crusaders owed to them under the pact of March, 1201. But, as Michaelmas, the date assigned for the departure of the Crusade to the Holy Land, approached, the Crusaders began to get impatient. They had not yet been put into possession of the City: and Alexius IV. begged for a delay. It was granted: for he had yet to make himself master of his Empire, before he could fulfil his engagements. He then went off to chase Alexius III. out of Adrianople. During his absence, Latins and Greeks fell out; and, on his return, 11th November, the breach between himself and the barons declared itself. He could neither discharge his obligations to his allies, nor control his own people. The Emperors, in short, were powerless. At this point, Alexius (Ducas), nicknamed Murtzuphlus because of his shaggy and meeting eye-brows, raised a tumult. He got himself proclaimed, 5th February, 1204, as Alexius V.: and took in hand the defence of the City. A second siege thus became necessary, and both sides began to prepare for it. The barons and the Venetians, on their part, entered into a compact, March, 1204, for the division of the spoils: by which a fourth part was to go to the new Latin Emperor whom they should elect; and, of the remaining three-fourths of the Empire, and its territories, some, chiefly the coasts and islands, were to be assigned to the Venetians and the remainder divided, in the form of fiefs, among the barons. The Venetians also reserved to themselves the Church of St. Sophia and the appointment of the Patriarch. On these lines, the Latin Empire, 1204—61 was afterwards organised. Thus agreed, the besiegers pressed forward to the attack. A first assault was delivered, 9th April, but it was beaten off with loss. On Palm Sunday, 11th April, the Crusaders confessed and communicated; and, on Monday, made the next assault. Alexius V. (Murtzuphlus) conducted the defence : but eventually fled towards the Bucaleon at the east of the promontory and thence, by the Golden Gate, to the S.W., into the open country. On the 13th, Wednesday in Holy Week, the Crusaders entered the City to find it deserted: and with carnage, rape and plunder, completed its destruction. On 16th May, they set up Baldwin IX., Count of Flanders, as Emperor, 1204—5; and proceeded to parcel out the Empire as arranged. The whole undertaking was in direct violation of the policy of Innocent III. The Crusaders had turned to their own profit the resources that he had intended for the prosecution of the Crusade, and, by their conduct at the taking of CP., rendered the breach between Greek and Latin irreparable.[90] But he could only accept the *fait accompli*. Congratulating himself that the schism of the Greeks was at an end and that their Emperor was now the true servant of the Church, he wrote, 13th November, 1204, to "the Clergy of the Crusading Army at Constantinople" that God had transferred the Empire of the Greeks to the Latins,[91] and so opened the way to the conquest of the Holy Land. Thomas Morosini, a young Venetian noble was elected Patriarch, 1205—†11, by the Canons of St. Sophia, and confirmed by the Pope; and, in spite of the papal efforts to gain over the Orthodox clergy, none but Venetians were appointed to fill their benefices and discharge their functions. The lay powers had diverted the Crusade to their own ends: and the Pope, in acquiescing, found his power diminished rather than increased by the sordid taint of a political and commercial enterprise.

CHAPTER X.

THE RIVAL EMPIRES: 1204—61.
LATIN AT CONSTANTINOPLE: GREEK AT NICÆA.

THE COMNENI AND THE PALAEOLOGI, 1204—61.

From H. B. George, *Genealogical Tables,* No. xlviii.

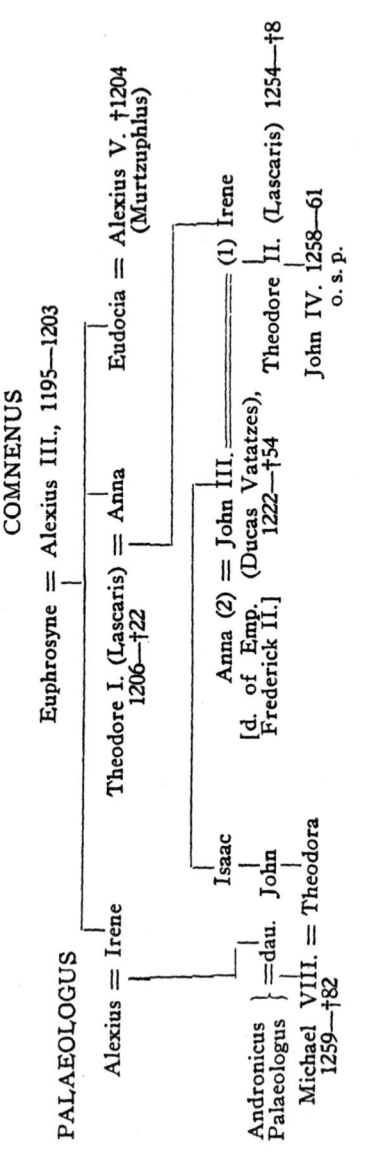

COMNENUS

Euphrosyne = Alexius III., 1195—1203

```
                    |
    ┌───────────────┴───────────────┐
Theodore I. (Lascaris)          Eudocia = Alexius V. †1204
   1206—†22      = Anna                    (Murtzuphlus)
        |
   ┌────┴──────────────────────┐
Anna (2) = John III.        (1) Irene
[d. of Emp.  (Ducas Vatatzes),
Frederick II.]  1222—†54
        |
   Theodore II. (Lascaris) 1254—†8
        |
   John IV. 1258—61
        o. s. p.
```

PALAEOLOGUS

Alexius = Irene
|
┌────┴────┐
Isaac   John
|
Andronicus } = dau.
Palaeologus }
|
Michael VIII. = Theodora
1259—†82

See Maps lxxiii., lxxiv. in R. L. Poole, *Hist. Atlas of Modern Europe.*

EMPERORS AT NICÆA.

Theodore I. (Lascaris) [son-in-law of Alexius III. (Comnenus)], 1206—†22
John III. (Ducas: Vatatzes) [his son-in-law], 1222—†54

Theodore II. (Lascaris) [his son], 1254—†8
John IV. [his son], 1258—61
Michael VIII. (Palaeologus) [his second cousin once removed], 1259—†82

EMPERORS AT CP. [LATIN].

Baldwin I. [IX. Count of Flanders], 1204— †5
Henry, 1206—†16, his brother
Peter [Courtenay], 1216—†8, his brother-in-law
Yolanda, his wife, 1218—9
Robert II., 1221—†8, son of Peter and Yolanda

Baldwin II. [b. 1217—†1273], 1228—61, his brother
John of Brienne, Co.-Emp., 1231—7
*Anseau de Cayeux, 1237—8
*Narjot de Toucy, 1238—40

* Regents.

EMPERORS AT TREBIZOND.

Alexius I. (Comnenus), 1204—†22 [grandson of Andronicus I., 1183—†5]
Andronicus I. (Gidon), 1222—35

John I. (Axuchus), 1235—8
Manuel I., 1238—63, and 16 more to 1462

SERBIA.

Stephen, 1195—1228
Radoslav, 1228—34

Vladislav, 1234—40
Stephen Uros I., 1240—72

BULGARIA.

Joannitsa (Kalojoannes), 1197—1207
Boris, III., 1217—8
John Asan II., 1218—41
Kaloman I., 1241—6

Michael I., Asan, 1246—57
Kaloman II., 1257—8
Mytzes, 1258—?
Constantine Asan Tech, 1258—77

POPES.

Innocent III. (Segni), 1198—†1216
Honorius III. (Savelli), 1216—†27
Gregory IX. (Ugolino), 1227—†41

Cœlestine IV. (Castiglione), †1241
Innocent IV. (Fieschi), 1241—†54
Alexander IV. (Rinaldo, bp. of Ostia), 1254—†61

ORTHODOX PATRIARCHS OF CP.

John X. (Camaterus), 1199—1206
Michael IV. (Autorianus), 1206—12
Theodore II. (Irenicus: Copas), 1212—5
Maximus II. 1215

Manuel I., 1215—22
Germanus II., 1222—40
Methodius, 1240
Manuel II., 1244—55
Arsenius, 1255—60 and 1261—7
Nicephorus II., 1260—1

LATIN PATRIARCHS OF CP.

Thomas Morosini, 1204—11
Gervasius, 1215—19 (?20)
Matthaeus (? Mathias), 1221—6
John Halgrin, 1226—7

Simon, 1227—32
Nicholas I. (of Piacenza), 1235—51
Pantaleon Giustiniani, 1253—61

BISHOPS OF OTHER SEES: 1204—61.

ALEXANDRIA.
Orthodox.
Nicholas I.   c. 1210
Gregory I.   ?
Nicholas II.   c. 1260

Monophysite.
John VI.   1189—1216
Cyril III.   1235—43
Athanasius III. 1251—61

ANTIOCH.
Simeon II.   1206—35
David   c. 1242—7
Euthymius I.   c. 1258—73

JERUSALEM.
Gregory II.   ?
Athanasius III.   ?

CHAPTER X.

THE RIVAL EMPIRES: 1204—61. LATIN AT CONSTANTINOPLE: GREEK AT NICÆA.

§ 1. No sooner had the Franks and Venetians conquered Constantinople, than there existed four, and for a time five, potentates with the imperial title: two Latin, the Western Empire and the Empire of Constantinople: and three Greek, the Empires of Nicæa and Trebizond: and, from 1222, the Empire of Thessalonica. The conquerors divided the spoil by an Act of Partition,[1] which assigned a quarter of the Byzantine territory to the Latin Emperor, three-eighths to Venice, and the remaining three-eighths in fiefs to the Crusaders. But these possessions had yet to be won: and the partition was never carried out as designed.

The Latin Empire, 1204—61, consisted of Constantinople itself, southern Thrace, the south coast of the Propontis and Bithynia as far as the river Sangarius, with some of the islands: but this share was soon reduced by the advance of the rival Empire of Nicæa.

Venice acquired Crete,[2] which she held, 1206—1669: footholds in the Peloponnesus, Euboea and the Cyclades: and, nearer CP., Rodosto, Gallipoli, Heraclea and an important quarter in CP. itself.

Of the other Latin states, the Kingdom of Thessalonica[3] was founded by Boniface, Marquis of Montferrat, in 1204: and took in Thessaly. But it was conquered, 1222, by the Greek Despot of Epirus and became part of the Greek Empire of Thessalonica, 1225—37, which, 1244, was made subject to the Greek Empire of Nicæa. Fiefs of Thessalonica were the Signory, then Duchy, of Athens, founded by the Burgundian Otto de la Roche,[4] and the Principality of Achaia[5] (Morea) by Geoffrey I. of Villehardouin, 1209—†18.

Of the Greek states which emerged from the disaster, one was in Europe, the Despotate of Epirus. It was founded by a bastard of the House of Angelus, Michael I.,[6] 1204—†14, and extended from Naupactus to Durazzo. Afterwards it became the Greek Empire of Thessalonica 1225—37; and was merged into Serbia, when that country was at its zenith a century later. The other two Greek states were in Asia. To the East lay the Empire of Trebizond, founded at the time of the Latin conquest of Constantinople (though not in consequence of it) by Alexius[7] (Comnenus), a grandson of the Emperor Andronicus I. It maintained an independent existence till 1461. But the true successor of the Eastern Roman Empire was the Empire of Nicæa.[8] It was founded by Theodore I. (Lascaris), 1206—†22, the son-in-law of Alexius III. and the only general of his who put up a good fight to the last at the taking of Constantinople. He gathered round him at Nicæa the aristocracy and the higher clergy of the Empire. This Greek Empire gradually pushed back the Latin Emperors across the Bosporus, and recovered from them the islands of Samos, Chios, Cos and Lemnos. Then it advanced into Europe: absorbed the Empire of Thessalonica, 1244; made head against the Bulgars to the north and Epirus on the west; until Epirots and Latins were defeated at Pelagonia, 1259, and the Greeks once more ruled at Constantinople, 1261. The contrast between the Latin and the Greek Empires which resulted from the Latin conquest of Constantinople can hardly escape notice. The Latin Empire, in spite of the capacity of its first two sovereigns, lasted just over half a century: its feebleness at the start ensured it but a short-lived career. For the Greeks, on the other hand, their consciousness of defeat by a foreigner roused a new sense of nationality: and their one ambition was to rescue Constantinople from the domination of the hated Latins.

§ 2. This was not beyond hope. The Latins had set up a feudal state, and their Emperor was little more than the first of his barons. Baldwin I., 1204—†5, fell out with the King of Thessalonica. His successor, Henry, 1206—†16, succeeded in imposing his authority on Thessalonica, 1209; and in getting his suzerainty accepted by the feudatories of Greece at the Diet of Ravennika,[9] 2nd May, 1210 (? near Zeituni) in N. Greece. But Athens and Achaia remained practically independent: and, while little support was to be expected from the greedy Venetians, the Greeks remained hostile, and looked only for a deliverer whether from Epirus or from Nicæa. As if this danger were not enough, the Latins overlooked another threatening from the Bulgars. The Tsar Joannitsa [Kalojoannes], 1197—†1207, offered them his alliance against the Greeks. They were foolish enough to reject it: and so threw the Bulgars into the arms of the Greeks at Nicæa. Nevertheless, immediately after the Latin capture of Constantinople, it looked as if the Latins would triumph. Central Greece and Peloponnesus were quickly overrun. In Asia, Henry beat the Greeks at Poimanenus,[10] 6th December, 1204, and threatened the young Empire of Theodore at Brusa. Theodore, however, was saved by the Bulgars under Joannitsa: who inflicted a severe defeat upon the Latins, 1205, in which Baldwin was taken captive,[11] and then proceeded to lay siege to Thessalonica where, happily for the Latins, he died, 1207. Theodore took advantage of this diversion to re-establish and consolidate his power. He found a rival in Baldwin's brother, Henry, 1206—†16: for he made peace with the Bulgars, enforced his authority upon his feudatories, and took the offensive against the Greeks both of Trebizond, 1206, and of Nicæa, 1212. But Henry died 1216. Both Greeks and Bulgars now had their hands free; for, under the feeble princes who succeeded Henry in Constantinople, the state founded there by the Crusaders entered upon its decline.

§ 3. The Empire of Nicæa, meantime, was making steady advance. Theodore I. (Lascaris),[12] 1206—†22, began by making himself master of N.W. Asia. He defeated the Emperor of Trebizond, Alexius I. (Comnenus), so jealous of his fortunes. He drove back the Seljuk Turks of Iconium, 1211. He reconquered the coasts of Asia Minor. On the death of Henry, he gave the Latins no rest: and when he bequeathed his throne to his son-in-law, John III. (Ducas: Vatatzes), 1222—†54, he had re-united under his rule all Western Asia, from the Sangarius to the Meander, save for a fragment of Bithynia still left to the Latins. John Vatatzes was a good general and a capable administrator: and during his long reign he completed the work of his father-in-law and gave to the Greek territories of Asia, by good farming (not by commerce, for at first he had no ships and the Empire no longer enjoyed the command of the sea), a final interval of prosperity. Its symbol was the tiara which he presented to his wife, the good Empress Irene, †1241, out of the profits of his eggs! But farmer John also extended his power to Europe. Theodore, Despot of Epirus, 1214—30, had enlarged his realm at the expense both of Latins and Bulgars. From the Latins,[13] he took Thessalonica, 1222: and had himself crowned Emperor of that realm. Pushing on to Philippopolis and Adrianople, through Bulgaria, he inflicted a defeat at Serres,[14] 1224, on the feeble forces of the Latin Emperor, Robert de Courtenay, 1221—8; but failed of his ambition to take the City. His ambitions had been closely observed by the King of the Bulgars, John Asan II., 1218—†41, an active and intelligent prince.[15] He offered his alliance to the Latins; and, on the death of Robert, 1228, proposed himself as guardian to Baldwin II., a child of seven, during his minority. But the Latin clergy, rather than have an Orthodox regent, procured the appointment to that office of John de Brienne (Co.-Emp., 1231—7); a brave knight but an incapable ruler. The King of the Bulgars took offence, and began to make overtures to the Greeks of Nicæa. He defeated the Greek Emperor of Thessalonica at Klokotinitza,[16] 1230: and, 1234, made alliance with John III. (Vatatzes). In the ten years preceding this addition to his strength, John[17] had considerably enlarged his dominions. Defeating the Latins at Poimanenus, 1224, he seized their last strongholds in Asia; recovered from them the islands of Samos, Chios, Lemnos and Cos, and, 1233, forced Leo Gabalas, the Greek Prince of Rhodes, to become his vassal. He also crossed to Europe, where he occupied Adrianople in an attack on the Emperor of Thessalonica; and he even struck at the

Venetians in Crete. The alliance with the Bulgars enhanced his power : and, 1236, the allies began to meditate a joint assault upon Constantinople. But, by this time, the West became aware of what was at stake : and the assault was warded off by the maritime cities of Italy in conjunction with the Prince of Achaia. The Bulgar-Nicene alliance collapsed upon the death of John Asan II. in 1241 : but the victories of John III. (Vatatzes) continued. He ousted the Latins from their last possessions in Anatolia. He married Anna, the daughter of the Western Emperor Frederick II., 1214—†50, who, out of hatred for the papacy, abandoned Constantinople to the Greeks. He enlisted the support of the Sultan of Rūm against the Franks, and at the same time profited by the Mongol invasion of the Sultanate to increase his dominions at the expense of the Turk. Then he intervened in Europe. He forced John Angelus, Emperor of Thessalonica, 1237—†44, to renounce the imperial title, and acknowledge himself, as Despot only, the vassal of the Emperor of Nicæa, 1243. Three years later, 1246, he took possession of Thessalonica and expelled the Despot Demetrius, 1244—†6.[18] Then, after recovering a large part of Macedonia from the Bulgars, and wresting Bizya and Tzurulon, to the S.E. of Thrace, from the Latins, he imposed his suzerainty, 1254, upon the last Greek sovereign of Europe who remained independent, Michael II., the Despot of Epirus, 1237—†71. Thus John III. (Vatatzes) bequeathed to his son, Theodore II., an Empire, rich, prosperous and powerful. It encircled, on every side, the remnants of the Latin Empire: and nothing remained but to regain possession of Constantinople.

Theodore II., 1254—†8, forced a peace upon the Bulgars, 1256, who had taken advantage of the death of his father to try to avenge their defeats at his hands : but he died too soon[19] to deal with the Despot of Epirus who had renewed hostilities. Michael II., allying himself with Manfred[20] King of Sicily, 1255—†66, and Guillaume II. de Villehardouin, Prince of Achaia, 1245—†78, and relying upon the support of the Albanians and

the Serbs, began to menace Thessalonica. By this time
Michael VIII. (Palaeologus), 1259—†82, had made himself master of the Empire of Nicæa. He took the field
against the combination. Overrunning Macedonia and
invading Albania, he inflicted a crushing defeat upon the
allies in the plain of Pelagonia,[21] 1259, which put an end
to the Despotate of Epirus. Then he turned south to
possess himself of Constantinople. The Venetians might
have assisted in its defence; but, by the Treaty of
Nymphæum,[22] January, 1261, Michael VIII. gave equal
privileges to their rivals, the Genoese: and thus, by playing off one set of greedy adventurers by another, he
easily overwhelmed the last remnants of the Latin Empire
and entered Constantinople, 15th August, 1261.

§ 4. It is now time to look at the affairs of the Church,
so far as they can be discerned against the dark background of these years of strife. They are mainly concerned with attempts at re-union of East to West. The
schism of 1054 was not, at first, taken seriously enough
to be regarded as final: for similar breaches of communion had happened before. So when East and West
were once more brought into contact by the Crusades,
1095—1204, and again by the rivalry of Greek and
Latin Empires, 1204—61, attempts at re-union were inevitable, if only because the two sections of Christendom
were confronted by each other and by a common foe.

The first of such attempts dates from the Council of
Bari,[23] 3rd—10th October, 1098. Bari was the last city
in Apulia to be held by the Eastern Empire, and had been
taken by the Normans, 1071. But southern Italy retained
its Greek traditions: and Urban II., with a view to reconciling Greek and Latin differences, arrived at Bari for a
Council, 3rd October, 1098. The Acts are lost: but we
know that the Council was attended by 185 bishops, and
chief among them Anselm, archbishop of Canterbury,
1093—†1109. Anselm defended the *Filioque*[24] and the
use of unleavened bread in the Eucharist to the satisfaction of the Council. His arguments are contained in his
De processione Spiritus sancti contra Graecos[25] and
De azymo et fermentato.[26] The bishops, many of whom

must have been Italo-Greeks, under strong Norman pressure, admitted the papal jurisdiction and accepted both the Double Procession and the use of azyms. But it was scarcely a free Council: and had little permanent effect. Upon the conquest of Constantinople by the Latins, Pope Innocent III. in *Diversis aliis* of 15th May, 1205, wrote to commend his legate Benedict, Cardinal of Santa Susanna, to the Emperor Baldwin I.; and singled out the *Filioque* and the use of unleavened bread at the Eucharist as the two points of Western belief and usage with which Easterns were at variance.[27] He bade the legate to try to win over the Greeks to such worship and purity of faith as were in accordance with the customs of the holy Roman church.[28] Benedict interpreted his instructions leniently: but the greater part of the Greek clergy declined his advances. Deep resentment had been aroused by the harsh and vile deeds of the Latins at the taking of Constantinople: though Innocent would reply that the perpetrators of them were under his excommunication. But national feeling ran high: and Michael Acominatus, archbishop of Athens, with other prelates, preferred to abandon their sees rather than acknowledge the papal authority. They took refuge with the Emperor Theodore I. (Lascaris): and the Court of Nicæa, with the Patriarch John X. (Camaterus), 1199—†1206 as its ecclesiastical chief, became the centre of opposition to re-union with Rome. The legate, however, succeeded in winning over a few Greek bishops, with whose help he began to organise an Uniat church. But his efforts were rendered abortive by the zeal of the Spaniard Pelagius, Cardinal bishop of Albano, 1211—†40; who, 1213, endeavoured to bring about re-union by main force. The effect was only to increase the numbers of Greek clergy, who found refuge at Nicæa.

Political necessity,[29] however, induced John III. (Vatatzes), 1222—†54, to re-open the question of re-union[30] with Pope Gregory IX. 1227—†41. He was alarmed at the choice of the warlike John of Brienne to be Regent of the Latin Empire, 1231—7, and at the close relations with the West maintained by his Greek rival in

Europe, the Emperor Manuel of Thessalonica. John therefore caused his Patriarch, Germanus II., 1222—40, to approach the Pope by letter,[31] to which Gregory replied,[32] 26th July, 1232. The correspondence exhibits the tension of feeling on either side.

Germanus begins by a prayer to our Lord for unity,[33] and hopes that re-union will be the work of the Pope, as he has attained to the primacy of the Apostolic See.[34] He deplores the schism within the Church; but it is the work of the Latins not of the Greeks, for the Latins it is who have set up contrary doctrines, made light of canons, and erected barriers between brothers formerly at one.[35] They have been brutal in war; they have devastated cities and closed churches; they have preferred rather to break up divine service than to let God's praises be told in the Greek tongue. In Cyprus there have been actual martydoms at their hands.[36] The Pope, he trusts, will not take this plain-speaking amiss;[37] but make the first advances towards re-union. He will find the Greeks ready to meet him. And Germanus followed up his appeal by a letter to the Cardinals,[38] in which he makes much of the extent of the Orthodox Church including, as it does, Ethiopians, Syrians, Iberians, Lazi, Alans, Goths, Khazars, Assars, Russians and Bulgars.

Pope Gregory IX., in reply, observes that, without doubt, Peter received the primacy among the Apostles. All questions of faith, therefore, are to be referred to the See of Peter.[39] The Greeks separated from this centre of unity, and have received their punishment by being enslaved to the State. No one can mistake the decadence of the Greek Church. Its faith is inactive, and its love has grown cold.[40] Let the Patriarch put aside his prejudices, and he will see that the bishop of Rome is made all things to all men that by all means he might save all; that he is a wall of strength to his colleagues of the episcopate in their conflict with heretics, schismatics and tyrants; and, above all, that he is the champion of the Church's liberty.[41] The Greek Church, on the contrary, has lost its liberty; and has allowed the dignity of the priesthood to be trampled under foot.[42]

The tone of these letters was far from promising: but Gregory IX. sent four friars as his envoys; and, after their departure, he wrote a second letter[43] to the Patriarch Germanus—*Cum iuxta testimonium,* of 18th May, 1233—in which he laid stress on two points: (1) on the figure of the "two swords," both given to the Church, which has retained the spiritual sword but passed on the temporal to the State, to be used at the Church's direction; and (2) on the unity of the Eucharistic mystery as celebrated both by Greeks and Latins, though the former use leavened and the latter unleavened bread.

On 15th January, 1234, the papal envoys[44] arrived at Nicæa; and, 16th January, were honourably received by the Patriarch, to whom they presented the Pope's first letter. Next day, 17th January, they had an audience of the Emperor: and then followed, 19th—27th January, seven conferences with the Greeks. The first six were taken up with the *Filioque.* The Greeks declared, 20th January, that *they* had never added to the Creed. " What, then," asked the Latins, " about the additions to the Creed of Nicæa which were made at Constantinople?" "Those were not additions, but expansions ": or as we might now put it, developments not accretive but explanatory. "Then that is precisely the case," retorted the Latins, " with the *Filioque.*" At the seventh conference, 26th January, it was agreed to pass on to the question of the bread, whether leavened or unleavened, in the Eucharist. But the Patriarch announced his intention of putting off the discussion till the middle of March, when it could take place before himself and his colleagues of Alexandria, Antioch and Jerusalem. The papal nuncios replied that they had no power to treat with a Council, only with the Patriarch himself; and set out on their return to Constantinople. But the Emperor, John III. (Vatatzes), intervened. His political necessities made him much more alive than his ecclesiastics to the need of re-union. " On what terms," he asked the envoys, 27th January, " could it be secured?" " It would soon be achieved," they replied, " if the Greeks were (1) to confess the same faith as the Roman church: they would not then be asked to *sing* the *Filioque;* and

(2) to obey the Roman church as before the schism." "But would the Pope," enquired the Emperor, "accord to the Patriarch his rights?" To which the envoys could only say: "If he submits to his mother, the Roman church, he will probably receive much better treatment than he expects." They then took their leave, and returned to Constantinople.

Toward the middle of March, they received from the Patriarch a summons to Lescara, where the Emperor had a country house in Bithynia, and the Council was to be held. At first, they demurred: but afterwards, on the advice of the Latin Emperor, John of Brienne, they consented, in the interest of unity, to go. They went first to Lescara, 13th April; then, 14th April, to Nympha in Bithynia: where, 17th April, the Monday in Holy Week, they were received by the Emperor, John III. (Vatatzes). The Patriarch of Antioch arrived later: those of Alexandria and Jerusalem not at all. At the first session of the Council, on Easter Monday, 24th April, 1234, Germanus proposed for discussion the question of the *Filioque:* but the Latins demanded that he should keep to his promise and begin with the question about the Eucharistic bread. On the 26th, at the second session, the Latins observed that the Greeks evidently held them for heretics in this matter: for they washed the altars where the Latins had celebrated, erased the name of the Pope from the diptychs, and annually pronounced against him a sentence of excommunication. The Greeks repudiated the last accusation as unfounded. As to the rest, let the envoys only remember what the Crusaders had done to the churches and their ornaments at the taking of Constantinople. To this, the nuncios replied that these outrages were the work of laymen under excommunication. In regard to the diptychs, if the Patriarch said "The Pope began it, by erasing *my* name from his diptychs," the simple answer was "That is not true: for your name was never there: and, if you are thinking of the names of your predecessors, certainly it was not the Pope who made the first erasure." They then announced their intention of departing, and demanded a safe-conduct from the Emperor; but, at his especial request, they waited for a third session, on the Friday in Easter Week, 28th April, at which the Greeks produced their long-promised declaration against the use of unleavened bread. Again, the envoys desired to take their leave: when, 4th May, the Emperor suggested a compromise: the Greeks would admit the use of azyms if the Latins would abandon the *Filioque*. The Pope, they replied, would not modify the faith by one iota! The Emperor was greatly disappointed. A week later, at the final session of Thursday in the second week after Easter, 11th May, the question of the *Filioque* came up once more; and the Latins, wearied of the long discussion, propounded at last two questions, to be answered with "Yes" or "No." (1) "Do you believe that the Holy Spirit proceeds from the Son, or not?" The Greeks answered "No": and they said "No" again to the second question. (2) "Do you believe that the Sacrament of the Altar may be celebrated either with unleavened bread or with leavened?" "Heretics!" cried the nuncios, as they rose and left the Council. "*You* are the heretics," came the reply: and so these futile conferences came to an end.

Each side had manifested its tenacity: but, on the whole, it was the Greeks who, at this date, seemed the more unwilling to make efforts for re-union: not their statesmen, but their theologians. Exasperated, beyond measure, at all they had suffered from the Crusaders, they were in no mood to discuss it reasonably: and it was the Latins who, though they probably did not know it, were, on the main question—that of the *Filioque*—in the wrong. Not as to the doctrine: for, as the envoys pointed out by references[45] to St. Athanasius[46] and St. Cyril of Alexandria,[47] there was Eastern as well as Western authority, in favour of the Double Procession of the Holy Spirit: and it is "a mistake to describe the doctrine as merely Western."[48] The history and the meaning of it, and an enquiry into the misunderstandings of either side—how the Greeks thought its assertion meant a denial of the Unity, and the Latins read into its

s

repudiation a denial of our Lord's equality with the Father in godhead and so of the Trinity—may be deferred till we come to later Councils concerning re-union, the Council of Lyons, 1274, and the Council of Florence, 1439, at which the doctrine was discussed again. But whether the doctrine contained in the *Filioque* be true or not, the Latins had no right to insist on its retention in the Creed: when, though they were probably unaware of the fact, it got there by accident.[49] And they did so insist: though characteristically enough, they told the Greeks: "You need not *sing* it!" Still, they were accommodating, and desirous of unity. The Greeks were not.

CHAPTER XI.

THE RESTORATION OF THE EMPIRE AND ITS DOWNFALL: 1261—1453.

THE PALAEOLOGI : RE-UNION AND ITS REPUDIATION.

THE PALAEOLOGI, 1261—1453.

From H. B. George, *Genealogical Tables,* No. xlviii.

```
Michael VIII. = Theodora
1261—†82
   |
Andronicus II. = Anna (d. of Stephen IV. of Hungary and g.g.d. of Theodore I. [Lascaris])
1282—1328
   |
   Michael †1320
   |
Agnes of = (1) Andronicus III. (2) = Anne, d. of Amadeus V. of Savoy
Brunswick      1328—41
   |                  |
   |        John V. 1341—91 = Irene (Helena) Matthew      John VI. (Cantacuzene) 1347—54 (†1383)
   |                                |                              |
   |                                |                        Theodora
   |                                |                        = Orchan
   |                         Manuel II. 1391—†1425
   |                                |
Andronicus IV. 1376—9    John VIII. (2) Theodore,  (4) Constantine XIII. (Dragases)
   |                     1425—†48    Despot of              1448—†53
John of Selymbria                    Selymbria
                                     †1458
```

OTTOMAN SULTANS.

Ertoghrul, 1231—†88
Osman I., 1288—†1326, his son
Orchan, 1326—†59, ,, ,,
Murad I., 1359—†89, ,, ,,
Bayazid I. 1389—†1403 ,, ,,
[Anarchy, 1403—13]

Mohammed I., 1413—†21, his son
Murad II., 1421—†51, his son
Mohammed II., 1451—†81, his son

SERBS.

Stephen Uros I., 1240—†72
,, Dragutin, 1272—81 †1316
,, Uros II. Milutin, 1281—†1320
,, Constantine, 1322
,, Uros III. Decanski, 1322—†31
,, Dusan Uros IV., 1321[31]—†55

POPES.

Urban IV. (Pantaleon, Patriarch of Jerusalem), 1261—4
Clement IV. (Guy Foulquois, Archbishop of Narbonne), 1265—8
Gregory X. (Tebaldo, Archdeacon of Liége), 1271—6
Innocent V. (Peter of Tarantaise), 1276
John XXI. (a Portuguese), 1276—7
Nicholas III. (Orsini), 1277—80
Martin IV. (Simon de Brion), 1281—5
Honorius IV. (James Savelli), 1285—7
Nicholas IV. (Jerome, bp. of Palestrina), 1288—92
Cœlestine V. (Peter Morrone), 1294
Boniface VIII. (Benedict Gaetani), 1294—1303
Benedict XI. (N. Bocasi), 1303—4
Clement V. (Bertrand de Goth, Abp. of Bordeaux), 1305—14
John XXII. (James d'Euse), 1316—34
Benedict XII. (James Fournier), 1334—42
Clement VI. (Peter, abp. Rouen), 1342—52
Innocent VI. (Stephen Aubert), 1352—62
Urban V. (Wm. Grimoard), 1362—70
Gregory XI. (Peter, nephew of C. VI), 1370—8
The Great Schism, 1378—1415
Martin V. (Colonna), 1417—31
Eugenius IV. (Gabriel Condulmier), 1431—47
Nicholas V. (T. de Sarzana), 1447—55

PATRIARCHS OF CP.

Arsenius, 1261—7
Germanus III., 1267
Joseph I., 1268—75
John XI. (Beccus), 1275—82
Joseph I.,² 1282—3
Gregory II., 1283—9
Athanasius I., 1289—93
John XII., 1294—1303
Athanasius I.,² 1303—11
Nephon I., 1311—15
John XIII., 1316—20
Gerasimus I., 1320—1
Jesaias, 1323—34
John XIV., 1334—47

Isidore I., 1347—9
Callistus I., 1350—4, 1355—63
Philotheus, 1354—5, 1364—76
Macarius, 1376—9, 1390—1
Nilus, 1380—8
Antonius IV., 1389—90, 91—7
Matthias, 1397—1410
Euthymius II., 1410—6
Joseph II., 1416—39
Metrophanes II., 1440—3
Gregory III., 1443—50
Athanasius II., 1450
Gennadius II., 1453—9

BISHOPS OF THE CHIEF SEES: 1261—1453.

ALEXANDRIA.

Orthodox.
Athanasius III.
    1276—1308
Gregory II. c. 1320
Gregory III. ?
Niphon c. 1367
Mark III. ?
Nicholas III. ?
Gregory IV. ?
Philotheus I. 1437—50

Monophysite.
John VII. 1262—9
Gabriel III.
    1269—71
John VII.² 1271—93
Theodosius II.
    1294—9
JohnVIII. 1300—20
John IX. 1320—6
Benjamin II.
    1327—39
Peter V. 1340—8
Mark IV. 1348—63
John X. 1363—9
Gabriel IV.
    1369—78
Matthew I. 1378—1401
Gabriel V. 1401—18
John XI. 1418—41
Matthew II. c. 1450

ANTIOCH.

Euthymius I.
    c. 1258—73
Theodosius IV.
    1275—83/4
Arsenius
    1283/4—1285/90
Cyril II.
    1285/90—1308
Dionysius I.
    ?1309—?16
Cyril III. ?
Dionysius II. ?
Sophronius ?
Ignatius II.
    c. 1344—59
Pachomius I.
    1359—68
Michael I. 1368—75
Pachomius I.²
    1375—7
Mark I. 1377—8
Pachomius I.³
    1378—86
Nicon 1387—95
Michael II. 1395—1412
Pachomius II. 1412
Joachim I. 1424—5
Mark II. 1426—7
Dorotheus I.
    c. 1434—51
Michael III.
    c. 1451—6

JERUSALEM.

Thuddaeus c. 1298
Sophronius III. ?
Athanasius IV. ?
Gabriel Brula ?
Lazarus c. 1332—67
Sophronius IV.
    ?—1387
Dorotheus I. ?
Theophilus II. c. 1419
Theophanes II. c. 1430
Joachim c. 1439
Theophanes III.

CHAPTER XI.

The Restoration of the Empire and its Downfall: 1261—1453. The Palaeologi: Re-union and its repudiation.

§ 1. THE Empire, as restored in 1261, was much inferior, both in extent and resources, to what it had been before the Latin conquest. Thus, in extent, the frontier under the Comneni, about 1150, ran on the south and west coasts of the Black Sea from Trebizond to Varna. It followed the Danube westward to Belgrade; thence across to the Adriatic at Durazzo; and so included the Balkan peninsula, south and east of these limits, with the western half of Asia Minor, the lands round the gulf of Alexandretta, and the islands of the Ægæan with Crete and Cyprus. But, by the accession of Michael VIII. (Palaeologus), 1261—†82, the Empire had been much reduced. In Asia, indeed, its territorial losses had been less than might have been expected; for Theodore I. (Lascaris), 1206—†22, and his son-in-law, John III. (Ducas Vatatzes), 1222—†54, had kept back the Turk. And only two districts had become Turkish: the Pisidian coast, with the seaport of Attalia (Adalia) on the south, and on the north the coast of Paphlagonia with the seaport of Sinope. But in Europe the losses were more serious: and four regions of the Empire were lost to it for good. A strip along the southern slope of the Balkans with northern Thrace and Macedonia had fallen to Bulgaria; and become completely Slavonised. The modern Albania, then the Despotate of Epirus, which stretched along the coast of the Adriatic from above Durazzo to Naupactus (Lepanto) on the gulf of Corinth, maintained itself in opposition to the Empire by alliance with the Latin principalities of southern Greece. Greece itself was divided between the Dukes of Athens, of the house of Brienne; and the princes of Achaia, of the house of Villehardouin. And the islands of the

Ægæan were divided between Venice and Genoa. Thus the restored Empire consisted only of two remnants of territory: in Asia, of the possessions of the former Empire of Nicæa: and in Europe, of Constantinople with Thrace and that part of Macedonia of which Thessalonica was the principal city, together with the islands of Rhodes, Lesbos, Samothrace and Imbros. Moreover, it had to confront powerful rivals. Immediately to the north, lay the Second Bulgarian Empire, 1186—1241, of the thirteenth century. To the west, the Serbian Empire of the fourteenth, reached its furthest limits, under Stephen Dusan, 1331—†55, from Belgrade in the north to Thermopylae on the south, and from the Strymon (Struma) on the east to the Adriatic on the west; while about the same time the Turks had acquired all Asia, and first crossed into Europe, 1353.

More fatal than diminution in extent was the loss of vitality to the Empire, and its growing enfeeblement. During the Latin conquest, it lost the tradition of administrative efficiency. A pathetic illustration of this is the attempt of John III. (Ducas Vatatzes) to raise revenue by poultry-farming. The same period saw a steady decline in commerce. The old empire had been wealthy because, for centuries, Constantinople had continued to be the mart of the world's trade. Caravan routes converged on it from Persia and Syria. Sea-borne commerce flowed to and from it; and the products of the Black Sea and of Egypt and the East were unloaded at its quays. But the Crusades put an end to this. They showed the West how to trade direct with Syria and Egypt. The Latin conquest of Constantinople delivered the final blow to its supremacy at sea; for, when the Italian republics became the middlemen between East and West, the Emperors found that they had no navy with which to repel these greedy rivals.

The incapacity of the Palaeologi did as much as reduction of territory and commercial decline to ruin their empire. Michael VIII., 1261—†82, was a wily intriguer; but neither soldier nor statesman. He disbanded the native Greek troops, and would not employ Greek generals: in

The Restoration of the Empire and its Downfall

spite of the long traditions of efficiency in the Byzantine army. He dispersed the Bithynian levies, though they were his only means of securing the frontier against the Turk. He barely held his own in Europe against Franks and Bulgars. On the seas, he could hardly keep in check the navies of Venice and Genoa; and in Asia he failed to stem the advance of the Turk. Andronicus II., 1282—1328, his son, spent his time in making and unmaking Patriarchs: of whom there were nine during his reign. He took into his service Roger de Flor and the mercenaries of the Grand Company, nominally to drive back the Turk in Bithynia; but they turned against him and plundered his subjects. And, as if war with his mercenaries were not enough, he went to war also with his grandson, Andronicus III., 1328—†41, in order to exclude him from the throne. By the time of his death he had lost one third of his already diminished Empire. Andronicus III. lost the whole of his Asiatic provinces to the Turks: who reached the Bosporus, 1338. His son, John V., 1341—†91, was a minor at his accession: a misfortune which gave to the usurper, John VI. (Cantacuzene), 1347—54, the opportunity to emulate the career of Michael VIII. and seize the supreme power. He maintained it not simply by the usual expedient of legitimatising his claim through the marriage of his daughter Irene (Helena) to the sovereign whom he had displaced but by calling in the enemies of the Empire, both Serbs and Turks, against his opponents headed by the Dowager Empress Anne of Savoy. By such treachery to his country, he lost Macedonia and Thessaly to the Serbs under Stephen Dusan; and Thrace itself to the Turks. Only Constantinople, Adrianople, Thessalonica and part of the Peloponnese remained.[1] In 1365, John V. lost the battle of Adrianople to the Turk: and became a vassal of the Sultan Murad I., 1359—†89. His capital might have fallen, then: but for the defeat of the Turks by Timour (Tamerlane) at the Battle of Ancyra (Angora), 1402; and their long struggle first against the Mongols and then against anarchy among themselves. But after their civil war, 1402—13, the Turks recovered.

In 1430 they captured Thessalonica: and the Greeks, at last, began to take alarm. The Emperor John VIII., 1425—†48, after the example of his grandfather John V. and his father Manuel II., went to the West to beg for assistance. His concessions led to the re-union effected at the Councils of Ferrara, 1438, and Florence, 1439. But no practical help was forthcoming: and only the heroism of his brother Constantine XIII., 1448—†53, at the fall of Constantinople, made amends for the disasters which the Palaeologi, by their feebleness and their feuds, brought upon their Empire.

§ 2. We must now return to the reign of Michael VIII.,[2] 1261—†82; the chief event of which, from the point of view of the ecclesiastical historian, was the hollow re-union effected at the Council of Lyons,[3] 1274.

Michael VIII. was born 1224, the son of Andronicus Palaeologus and Irene Angela, and great-grandson of the Emperor Alexius III. (Angelus), 1195—†1203. His birth gave him rank at the petty court of Nicæa; but, at the same time, exposed him to the suspicions of the Emperor John III. (Ducas Vatatzes), 1222—†54. Under his son and successor Theodore II. (Lascaris), 1254—†8, Michael became Governor of Dyrrhachium (Durazzo); and then, on his return to Court, so established himself in the Emperor's confidence that Theodore, foreseeing his own death, commended to his care his son John IV., 1258—61, a child of nine. The boy was under the guardianship of the Patriarch Arsenius, 1261—7, and the Grand Domestic (Commander-in-chief) Muzalon. They were detested at Nicæa as the friends of the Latins. Michael took advantage of this to murder Muzalon and to take his place as guardian to the little Emperor John. They were crowned together at Nicæa, 1st January, 1260. His accession to power, as the leader of a nationalist party, at once roused the apprehension of Baldwin II., 1228—61(†73): who still ruled at Constantinople over the shadow of the Latin Empire. War ensued: and Michael was on the point of attacking the capital when the ambitions of Michael II., Despot of Epirus, 1237—†71, crossed his path. The Despot, counting upon the support

of the natural son of the Emperor Frederick II., 1214—
†50, Manfred, King of Sicily, 1258—†66, and of William II. of Villehardouin, Prince of Achaia, 1245—†78, set out to seize the throne at Constantinople. But he was defeated by John Palaeologus, brother of Michael, at Ochrida, and Michael laid siege to Constantinople. The Emperor Baldwin succeeded in making good his escape on board a Venetian galley, and, 25th July, 1261, the Greeks recaptured their city.

It was a very different city from what it had been before the Latin conquest. Fire and pillage had destroyed its ancient splendour. Commerce had deserted its quays. The wealthy families had abandoned their palaces rather than live in contact with the hated Latins. Michael's first care, therefore, was to repair its ruins and to recall its inhabitants. He then had himself crowned in St. Sophia; but this time the boy prince was not crowned with him. Instead of that, Michael committed the horrible crime of putting out the poor child's eyes, and imprisoning him, December, 1261, in a distant fortress. But, so far from securing his power, this act of cruelty excited such horror against him that the rest of his reign was spent in efforts to retain his throne. At home, the Patriarch Arsenius, hitherto his best friend, excommunicated him: and was deposed[4] in favour of Germanus III., 1267, an advocate of union with the Latins, and then of Joseph I., 1268—75, who absolved the Emperor but was anti-Latin. Abroad, he had to face the hostility of the West. On his western frontiers, the Despot of Epirus and the Prince of Achaia, encouraged by Pope Urban IV., 1261—†4, obtained some successes against the Greeks; and Michael had to buy them off by promising the Pope to use all his efforts for the re-union of the Orthodox Churches with the Roman See. In 1262, he sent an embassy to Urban: urging the Pope to recognise him as the legitimate Emperor at Constantinople, and adding that then religious union would be easy. But Urban put union first, and political alliance second; and, 28th July, 1263, sent four Franciscans with a letter to Michael exhorting him to work for the union of the churches, and promising him peace and the friendship of the West. Michael, however, went on attacking the Latins in the East: and in May, 1264, the Pope renewed the crusade against him. Michael received a check in Messenia: and this was sufficient to renew his interest in re-union. So he sent Nicholas, bishop of Crotona in Calabria, to the Pope; with a letter recognising the primacy, and asking for envoys to treat of union. On 22nd June, 1264, Urban sent two more Franciscans, Gerard and Rainer, to Constantinople to act with the Bishop. But, before these transactions could bear fruit, Pope Urban IV. died, October, 1264.

Urban was succeeded by Clement IV., 1265—†8; and during his pontificate, the situation in the West became much more threatening to the interests of the Eastern Empire. Clement himself was occupied, at first, with the maintenance of the Guelph cause against the Ghibelline supporters of Manfred,[5] King of Naples and Sicily. But, February 12th, 1266, Manfred was defeated at Benevento by Charles, Count of Anjou,[6] the brother of St. Louis, King of France, 1226—†70; who became King of Naples and Sicily, 1266—†85, and by the treaty of Viterbo, 27th May, 1267, induced Baldwin II. to surrender to him his rights over the Latin Empire of Constantinople. He at once proceeded, in concert with John, †1296, the natural son of Michael II., Despot of Epirus, and himself Despot of Thessalonica, to assert them by attacks upon Michael VIII. The Pope, well aware how Michael stood in fear of this new "crusade," wrote on 17th May, 1267, to the Eastern Emperor insisting on union between the Churches first and promising help against Charles, if this should be taken in hand. But Clement IV. died, 28th November, 1268; and for three years the Roman See remained vacant. At last, it was filled by the election of Gregory X., 1271—†6. He regarded re-union with the Greeks and the recovery of the Holy Land as the twofold aim of his life: the first being, in his view, necessary to the second. And as both Pope and Emperor were equally afraid of Charles of Anjou, the way was open to joint action in favour of re-union. Gregory, on his side, began by a bull[7] of 1st April, 1272, in which he convoked a General Council to meet, 1st May, 1274; its objects being to treat, and in this order, of (1) reform, (2) re-union, and (3) the recovery of the Holy Land. Michael, in his turn, set on foot a propaganda among the clergy of his Empire, emphasising the benefit that would accrue to the Empire by re-union, and how it could be purchased at the trifling cost of acknowledging the primacy of the Roman See and consenting to name the Pope on the diptychs. But these were no trifling concessions in their eyes: and were steadily resisted by the Patriarch Joseph I., 1268—75. The Pope, nevertheless, proceeded: and, 24th October, 1272, he invited the Emperor and the Patriarch to a General Council to meet at Lyons.[8] The Emperor responded, May, 1273, by a new embassy to Rome: saying that union would soon be effected, and asking the Pope for safe-conducts[9] for the envoys whom he would be sending to the Council: Gregory X. called, 20th November, 1273, upon the King of the Two Sicilies to respect the imperial ambassadors;[10] and Charles was obliged to do so, for fear of a Ghibelline rising in his newly-acquired realm. Meanwhile, Michael's propaganda among the Greek clergy continued. The chartophylax, John Beccus,[11] went over to the cause of union; and, encouraged by his learning, the clergy, in considerable numbers agreed to support the union in the triple basis of the primacy of the Pope, the recitation of his name on the diptychs and the right of appeal to Rome. But a large section had its misgivings: and the Patriarch, Joseph I., 1268—75, remained obdurate.

The Council of Lyons, reckoned by the Latins as the Fourteenth[12] General Council, opened for its first session[13] on 7th May, 1274—the Monday in Rogation week; and, a month later, at its third session, 7th June, the envoys of the Eastern Emperor were received:[14] Germanus III., who had been Patriarch, 1267, Theophanes, archbishop of Nicæa, and George Acropolites, the Grand Logothete. They brought with them dispatches from the Emperor; and these were read out by the Pope,[15] at a fourth session on 6th July, the Octave of St. Peter and St. Paul. The Grand Logothete repudiated the schism:[16] and the union thus effected was proclaimed by a solemn *Te Deum*. Letters from the Serbs and the Bulgars added their consent to it. The seventh and last session followed on 17th July: and following this happy event, the Pope, on 1st May, 1275, arranged with Charles of Anjou for a truce between himself and the Eastern Empire.

But it was now to be seen whether Michael VIII. could make good his share of the bargain. On 16th January, 1275, the Emperor was present at a service during which the Pope was proclaimed as Supreme Pontiff and commemorated on the diptychs; and on 26th May, Beccus became Patriarch as John XI. in place of Joseph I. who still maintained his opposition. In this he was supported by the Princess Eulogia (the Emperor's sister) and the majority of the people; and the Emperor was obliged to defer the publication of the union effected at Lyons. Gregory X. died during these proceedings, 1276; and was succeeded by three popes of the Angevin party, of whom the last, John XXI., 1276—†7, sent an ultimatum to Michael VIII. He was to swear to the union himself and to obtain a similar oath from the Greek clergy. But in spite of pressure from the Court and the Patriarch, John XI., it was refused. On the death of John XXI., his successor, Nicholas III., 1277—†80, who was anti-Angevin, took up the negotiations: and wrote both to Michael and to Charles. On 7th October, 1278, he summoned the Emperor once more to confirm the union;[17] and on 18th October he forbade the King of the Two Sicilies to attack Constantinople.[18] And he followed this up by a new ultimatum[19] to Michael in which he was required (1) to send a fresh statement of his adherence to the confession of Lyons, (2) to compel the Patriarch and the clergy to swear to it, (3) to introduce the *Filioque* into the Creed, (4) to renounce all usages which the Pope might deem contrary to the faith, (5) to receive papal envoys and assist them to visit the churches of the Empire and see that all is done there as agreed, (6) to accept a permanent nuncio at Constantinople, (7) to require his subjects to seek absolution from the envoys for their adherence to the schism, (8) the envoys, on their part, to confess and absolve all returning from the schism, and (9) to excommunicate the enemies of the union: finally (10) the creed or confession of Lyons once accepted, the Patriarch and clergy to seek confirmation in their office from Rome. It would have been difficult for the Emperor, had he and his subjects been never so willing, to get these demands accepted quickly. The Patriarch, indeed, did his best. He announced his acceptance of the *Filioque* in the Creed: but this led to fresh disturbances. And before answer could be made to Rome, a new pope had succeeded—the Angevin, Martin IV., 1281 —†5. As if anticipating this change in his favour, Charles was already attacking Epirus; and Michael was once more sending embassies to Rome. But the pope cut him short. In July, 1281, he entered into alliance against Michael with Charles of Anjou and Venice, excommunicated the Emperor,[20] 18th November, and gave out that the Crusade would start against him in April, 1283. The allies endeavoured to set up the Latin Empire again, but they were defeated at Belgrade;[21] and Michael took his revenge by reinforcing the rebels in Sicily with Byzantine gold.[22] They rose, and massacred the adherents of the Angevins in the Sicilian Vespers, on 30th March, Easter Even, 1282. The Emperor died 11th December. The nightmare of the Angevin assault on the Empire was gone. But the schemes of re-union—never really religious, but only political—were dispelled too.

§ 3. Three princes of the House of Palaeologus succeeded its founder, Michael VIII.; and their reigns covered rather more than the century which followed his death. They were his son Andronicus II., his great-grandson Andronicus III., and his great-great-grandson John V. [VI.]. The first and the last of these reigned for about fifty years; and it was during the reign of John V. [VI.] that the Turks established themselves in Europe. Then ensued rather more than half a century during which, though the danger to the Eastern Empire was deferred owing to Timour's defeat of the Turks at Angora, 1402, its rulers Manuel II. and John VIII. visited the West in person in order to secure assistance, the price of it being the Union of East and West effected at the Council of Florence, 1439. Its repudiation was speedily followed by the Fall of Constantinople, 1453. For ecclesiastical history, the interest of this period is to note the terms on which this union was negotiated, and the hollowness of an agreement in doctrine and polity when necessitated only by political exigencies.

§ 4. Andronicus II.,[23] 1282—†1328, was in his twenty-third year when he succeeded to the throne; but, unlike his father, he was feeble and inept: and given to devotion and theological disputation when he should have been bestirring himself for the defence of his country. One of his first acts was to annul the measures taken by Michael VIII. for the re-union of East and West; and to substitute for John XI. (Beccus), 1275—82, the Patriarch who had carried them through, their opponent Joseph I. as Patriarch, 1282—3. Such depositions and substitutions became a pastime with Andronicus; and the Patriarchate was vacated and filled as many as nine times during his reign. For this repudiation of the union the Emperor was at length excommunicated,[24] 3rd June, 1307, by the first of the Avignonese Popes, Clement V., 1305—†14. But, by this time, dangers more serious than a papal excommunication had beset Andronicus. His armies were beaten by Osman I., 1288—†1326, the founder of the Ottoman Empire; who gradually conquered most of the Roman possessions in Asia, 1301—3. In this extremity, the Emperor called to his aid the Catalans,[25] a " Grand Company " of adventurers, chiefly from Spain, under the command of Roger de Flor, or Roger Blum, the son of a German noble at the court of the Western Emperor, Frederick II. Roger thrust back the Turks in 1304 at Cyzicus; in 1305, near Philadelphia; and, again, in the mountains of the Taurus. For these services, he was rewarded with the rank of Cæsar. But his mercenaries treated the subjects of the Empire with as much rapacity as the Turks; and he was assassinated, 28th March, 1305, by order of the Emperor. In revenge, the Catalans turned their arms against the Empire; and, after devastating Thrace and Macedonia, passed over

The Restoration of the Empire and its Downfall

into the Peloponnese; parts of which they seized and settled in at their pleasure. Domestic troubles followed these disastrous wars. For Michael, the son of Andronicus, who had been co-regent with his father as Michael IX., 1295—†1320, had two sons, Andronicus and Manuel: who both fell in love with the same woman without knowing that they were rivals. Manuel was unwittingly slain by his brother. Their father died of grief; and the Emperor was so exasperated against his grandson that he endeavoured to exclude him from the succession. The result was a series of three civil wars, 1321—8: which ended in the abdication of Andronicus II. in favour of his grandson. Such wars, though they wasted the resources of the Empire, were yet so common under the later Palaeologi that their quarrels positively invited the overthrow of the Empire long before the end came.

§ 5. Andronicus III., 1328—†41, had no sooner attained the throne than he had to defend himself against the advance of the Turks in Asia under their Sultan Orchan,[26] 1326—†59. They took Brusa and Nicomedia, 1326; defeated him at Philocrene, and captured Nicæa, 1330. By 1338 they had reached the Bosporus, and two years later, had completed the conquest of Bithynia. Andronicus, however, prevented them from crossing into Europe; though they were now able to establish themselves as a maritime power. Accordingly, the Venetians, alarmed for the safety of their coastal settlements, made a league against the Turk with Pope John XXII., 1316—†34, the Emperor Andronicus III., the Kings of France, Naples and Cyprus, and the Grand Master of the Knights of St. John at Rhodes. It led to little; and Andronicus, after the manner of Eastern Emperors in distress, turned to projects of re-union with the West. He would, however, have sympathies with the West; because of his alliances,[27] through marriage, with its princely houses. His first wife was Agnes (m. 1318, d. 1324), daughter of Henry the Wonderful †1322, Duke of Brunswick-Grubenhagen; while his second marriage, 1326, was with Anne, daughter of Amadeus V., Duke of Savoy, †1323.

In 1339 there came to Constantinople a Greek monk

from Calabria, Barlaam[28] by name. He was a scholar of distinction, who at Avignon had taught Greek to Petrarch, 1304—†74; and afterwards became bishop of Hieracum, now Gerace,[29] in Calabria, 1341—†8. The Emperor made him his envoy; and sent him on a secret mission to Pope Benedict XII., 1334—†42, at Avignon. Barlaam urged,[30] with truth, that the Emperor was not less desirous than the Pope of the re-union of the churches. There were two ways of securing it: by force, or by persuasion. Force was no good. It had already been tried. The Latins had subdued the Empire, but not the minds, of the Greeks. Persuasion should now be attempted. A handful of theologians on either side could probably come to an agreement; but what would be the use of it? A nationalist reaction at Constantinople would be the certain result. But the Greeks accept the Œcumenical Councils; and, if they repudiate the Council of Lyons, 1274, it was because the Greek emissaries there had been appointed by the Emperor and not by the four Patriarchs of the East. Let the Pope send a legate to convene, through these four Patriarchs, a really genuine Œcumenical Council. The need, at the moment, is great. The Turk has occupied four of the chief cities of Anatolia. The Christians there want to return to their allegiance, and their religion. But the resources of the Emperor are unequal to delivering them. So the Roman legate should be accompanied, or preceded, by armies from the West. If the Latins are once more suspicious of thus putting rescue before re-union, then let them take account of such considerations as these: (1) That an Œcumenical Synod alone can consummate the union so ardently desired; and that, if it is to be really Œcumenical, then the Patriarchs of Alexandria, Antioch and Jerusalem, together with many bishops, now groaning under the Mohammedan yoke, must first be set free; (2) That the Greeks have been alienated by the memory of ill-usage from the Latins, and that what is wanted to remove their ill-will is a great act of generosity on the part of the Pope and the West, such as would alone provide effective support to the arguments of the Emperor and the friends of re-union; (3) That, if some difference of doctrine or worship between Latins and Greeks should still remain, then, let it be remembered, Armenians and others are equally concerned: and that, as the Turks are the common enemy of the Christian name, it will be the glory of the Franks to strike a blow in the common defence of our religion; (4) That, should the subjects of the Eastern Emperor, still be treated simply as schismatics, common prudence would require that the Western Powers should support his Empire as the bulwark of Europe against the Turk, and join the Greeks against the Turks rather than have ultimately to fight the Turks reinforced by the troops and treasures of the Greeks. Barlaam was a skilful as well as a prophetic advocate: but he made no impression on the West. " The Kings of France and Naples declined the dangers and glory of a crusade: the pope refused to call a new synod to determine old articles of faith: and his regard for the obsolete claims of the Latin emperor and clergy engaged him to use an offensive superscription: ' To the *moderator* of the Greeks, and the persons who style themselves the patriarchs of the Eastern churches.' "[31] After all, what more could have been expected. Benedict XII. was " a dull peasant .... immersed in sloth and wine."[32] It was he whose personal habits gave rise to the jest: *Bibamus papaliter!*[33]

On his return to Constantinople, Barlaam came into prominence again as the chief opponent of the Hesychasts. Hesychasm,[34] or Quietism, was a system of mysticism defended at this time by the monks of Mount Athos; and may be regarded, in one of its aspects, as " a reaction of the national theology of the Greeks against the invasion of Western Scholasticism."[35] Its advocates defended the theory that it is possible by asceticism, detachment and a peculiar method of contemplation to see " the uncreated light " of God, which they identified with " the light of Mt. Tabor " that appeared at the Transfiguration. It was not the divine Essence (οὐσία) but the divine Operation (ἐνεργεία) that they thus perceived: and the process was one of auto-suggestion. Hesychasm thus rested on two assertions: (a) that such contemplation is "the chief end of man," and (b) that there is a distinction between the divine Essence and the divine Operation, i.e. between God and His attributes. Its father was Symeon,[36] the New Divine (ὁ Νέος Θεολόγος) 1025—†92, a monk of the Studium; and, on the point of the distinction between God and His attributes, it raised the issue not only between Mysticism and Scholasticism, or between Platonist and Aristotelian, but between Greek and Latin, i.e. between a nationalist Orthodoxy and hopes of re-union with the West. Its leader was Gregory Palamas,[37] a monk of Athos: and archbishop of Thessalonica, 1349—† c. 60. He denied the identification of God's essence and His attributes; rejected the *Filioque:* and was vehemently anti-Latin. Its chief opponents were (1) Barlaam; who wrote[38] in defence of the *Filioque,*[39] of the papal primacy,[40] and of re-union;[41] (2) his friend and successor Gregory Akindynos;[42] and (3) Nicephorus Gregoras,[43] † after 1359, the most distinguished man of letters in the Greek world of that age.

Barlaam proceeded to argue against the possibility of "an uncreated light" which was *not* God's essence; and also to make fun of the method of contemplation which he called Ὀμφαλοψυχία. He then demanded of the Patriarch John XIV. (Aprenus)[44] 1334—†47, a synod to settle the question. John was at heart on the side of Barlaam: and he procured the synod,[45] 11th June, 1341. But it was presided over by the Emperor Andronicus III.: who was on the side of the Hesychasts. Two questions were submitted to the synod: (1) whether the light of Mt. Tabor was created, or not? and (2) whether a prayer in use with the Hesychasts[46] was open to the charge of ditheism, or not? In either case, the answer was in the negative: and so in favour of the Hesychasts. They owed their victory[47] to nationalism and to the influence of the monks at Court. Barlaam, after his condemnation, returned to Calabria; and the later stages of the controversy, 1341—51, belong to the next reign: for Andronicus III. died 15th June, 1341.

§ 6. He was succeeded by his son, then a child of nine,

as John V., 1341—†91. "Orphan and Emperor"[48] by the death of his father, John V. reigned, at first, under the guardianship of his father's friend and comrade, John Cantacuzene. This man belonged to one of the great families of Byzantine nobles,[49] and gives us in his *History*[50] of his own time, 1320—56, a picture of his wealth. "His pastures were stocked with 2,500 brood mares, 200 camels, 300 mules, 500 asses, 5,000 horned cattle, 50,000 hogs and 70,000 sheep: a precious record," says Gibbon, "of rural opulence in the last period of the empire, and in a land, most probably in Thrace, so repeatedly wasted by foreign and domestic hostility."[51] The *History* of Cantacuzene is anything but impartial; yet, if checked by the *Roman History*,[52] of his contemporary, Nicephorus Gregoras, 1295—† c. 1359, which covers the period 1204—1359, it is an invaluable record of this fateful epoch. It was to the loyalty of so powerful a friend that Andronicus III. owed his success in the Civil Wars over his grandfather; and he rewarded it by making him "Grand Domestic," and finally by naming him guardian of his son and regent of the Empire. This disposition, however, was far from acceptable to the Empress-Mother, Anne of Savoy. She considered herself the natural guardian of her son John V.; and she was encouraged to assert her claim by the Admiral Apocaucus and the Patriarch John XIV. Taking advantage of a temporary absence of Cantacuzene from the capital, they charged him with high treason, sentenced him to death and deprived him of his estates and emoluments. John Cantacuzene had now no choice but to consult his safety by taking up arms not against his young ward the Emperor but against his powerful counsellors. He proclaimed himself Emperor; and, 21st March, 1342, was crowned with great solemnity, together with his wife Irene, at Adrianople, by Lazarus, Patriarch of Jerusalem. He also obtained the support of Stephen Dusan,[53] King of the Serbs, 1331—†55; and of the Turks under their Sultan Orchan, 1326—†59, to whom he gave his daughter Theodora in marriage, January, 1347. For six years, 1341—7, the Empire was desolated by civil war. At last, after effecting a reconciliation with the Empress-Mother and by the aid of Latin mercenaries, he possessed himself of Constantinople, 7th February, 1347. The Admiral Apocaucus was slain in the siege; and Cantacuzene, now sole master of the Empire, consented to legitimatise his authority, after the manner of Byzantine usurpers, by stipulating that, until the boy of fifteen should come of age, according to the law of the Empire, at twenty-five, he himself should be recognised as the sole ruler. As a guarantee of good faith and future harmony, he gave his daughter Helena in marriage, 25th May, 1347, to his young colleague; with whom he had just been crowned, 13th May, for the second time, in the Church of Blachernae by the new Patriarch, Isidore I., 1347—9. There were now two Emperors, John Palaeologus and John Cantacuzene; and three Empresses, Anne, mother of John Palaeologus; Irene, wife of John Cantacuzene, and their daughter Helena, whom John Palaeologus had recently married.

§ 7. John Cantacuzene now reigned as John V., 1347—54; and it was during this interval that the controversy in respect of Hesychasm was finally settled. He and his Patriarch Isidore represented a nationalist reaction, and sided with the Hesychasts: while the Empress-Mother, true to her Western affinities, took sides with their opponents, the Barlaamites, who thus came to be associated politically with the claims of legitimacy against usurpation. After the synod of 11th June, 1341, which condemned Barlaam, a second[54] was held, without the presence of the Patriarch John XIV., his secret sympathiser: it condemned Gregory Akindynos, the successor of Barlaam as leader of the opposition to Hesychasm, representing Gregory and his adherents as Latinisers who were bent upon the elimination of Orthodoxy. At last, John XIV. made up his mind openly to withstand the Hesychasts; and, in a third synod at Constantinople, 1345, he excommunicated their leader Gregory Palamas, afterwards archbishop of Thessalonica, 1349—†60, and deposed Isidore Buchiram, bishop-elect of Monemvasia (Malvoisie). But the triumph of John Cantacuzene reversed the situation : and a fourth synod,[55] 2nd February, 1347, deposed John XIV. and the presbyter Gregory Akindynos. They then appointed the bishop of Monemvasia as Patriarch, under the title of Isidore I., 1347—9, whom the third synod had excommunicated. The opponents of Hesychasm retorted by a fifth synod, July, 1347, in which they refused to acknowledge Isidore,[56] and excommunicated Gregory Palamas, Nicephorus Gregoras taking the lead in opposition to the Hesychasts. Isidore I., however, held the Patriarchate for two years, February, 1347—April, 1349 :[57] and was succeeded by Callistus I.[58] 1350—4, a monk of Mt. Athos, who was also an Hesychast. A sixth synod[59] was held, 27th May, 1351 : at which the Emperor John Cantacuzene presided, and the question lay between Nicephorus Gregoras and Gregory Palamas. The Synod put forth a doctrinal statement or *Tome*,[60] which gave the final victory to Hesychasm : while its opponent Nicephorus Gregoras was condemned and imprisoned till the downfall of John Cantacuzene.[61] The usurper withdrew to Mount Athos : where, as the monk Joasaph, †1383, he divided his time between writing his *History* and contemplating " The uncreated Light." From this time Hesychasm was identified with Orthodoxy : Gregory Palamas became a Doctor of the Church : and the *Tome* a " faultless canon of the true faith of Christians."

Besides Hesychasm, the business of re-union excited the interest of John Cantacuzene. As soon as he became master of Constantinople, February, 1347, he sought to dispel the distrust he had excited by giving his daughter in marriage to the Sultan. So he sent an embassy to the Pope to persuade him that, far from favouring the Turks, he was still prepared to fight them, if only the Pope would send him the assistance of the West. Three years elapsed before Clement VI. sent him two Dominicans with instructions to negotiate the religious union. To these overtures, Cantacuzene replied, by protesting his zeal for the union of the churches but declaring at the same time that only an Œcumenical Council could bring it about. The pope, in his turn, lamented that the existing condition of Christendom made it impossible to assemble such a Council. And in this conclusion—perhaps not unwillingly reached on either side—the Pope and the Emperor acquiesced.[62]

§ 8. John V. (Palaeologus), by the abdication of John Cantacuzene, became John VI.; and "after his enfranchisement from an oppressive guardian, he remained thirty-six years," 1355—†91, "the helpless and, as it should seem, the careless spectator of the public ruin."[63] Scarcely was he secure in his throne, when the Turks—to whom his predecessor had given, in return for their aid, a foothold on the European side of the Dardanelles—began to advance to the conquest of Europe. The Emperor saw no hope of safety but in submission to the Pope. In 1355 he sent two envoys to Pope Innocent VI., 1352—†62, at Avignon "with a document[64] in which he pledged himself to recognise the Pope as head of the Church, to obtain like recognition from his subjects, to receive the pontifical legates with all respect, and to send his son Manuel to Rome as a hostage. In return he claimed prompt aid for Constantinople, of which the Pope would bear the cost for six months." Innocent VI. "replied by a gushing letter,[65] writing also to the Patriarch Callistus[66] and the principal bishops, and sent two nuncios to Constantinople."[67] But no aid arrived: and the project dropped.

Meanwhile, the Turkish advance went on. In 1356 they captured the little fortress of Tzympe, near Gallipoli; and, in 1358, Gallipoli itself.[68] This was in the last year of the Sultan Orchan. His son and successor, Murad I., 1359—†89, pushed inland with large forces. In 1361 he captured Adrianople. Thence, he got possession of Philippopolis, 1362, and came into collision with a federate army of Slavs—including Serbs under their Tsar Uros V., 1355—†65, Bosnians and Wallachians. They were marching to the recovery of Adrianople; but were defeated by a far inferior force of Turks on the banks of the Haemus, now the Maritza. After this Murad made Adrianople his capital,[69] 1365; and, taking up his residence there, he used it as a base of operations against

Slavs and Hungarians to the north. While so engaged, he made peace with the Emperor, John VI., who paid him tribute. The Emperor, aware that his turn would come as soon as the Sultan had disposed of the Serbs and their allies, resolved once more to implore the assistance of the West. In pursuance of this aim, he made overtures to Pope Urban V.,[70] 1362—†70; and promised re-union with the Latins, if the Pope would send him aid. He went twice to Rome, 1369—70; and, though the Pope's promised reinforcements never appeared, nevertheless, John VI. kept faith; and, 18th October, 1369, in the presence of four cardinals, accepted the Double Procession of the Holy Spirit, the primacy of the Roman Church and its authority in matters of faith, with the right of appeal thereto.[71] Disappointed in Rome, the Emperor went on to Venice. Here, however, he not only failed to obtain assistance, but was arrested for debt. He sent messengers to his son Andronicus, whom he had left at Constantinople as regent in his absence, and implored his assistance. Andronicus turned a deaf ear. But his younger brother, Manuel, then governor of Thessalonica, informed of his father's misfortunes, at once sold all that he had, hastened to Venice, and released him. The Emperor returned at once to Constantinople, 1370; though not without fears of the vengeance that the Sultan might take. In order to appease him, he sent his third son, Theodore, as a hostage to Adrianople; and, while Andronicus was deprived of his authority, the filial devotion of Manuel was rewarded by his promotion to be co-emperor with his father.

Andronicus determined to take his revenge. He made friends with Saudshi, a son of the Sultan who also had quarrelled with his father : and, 1385, the two undertook to murder their respective fathers, and to seize the supreme power. The Sultan discovered the conspiracy : and summoned the Emperor to join him in dealing with it. Saudshi was taken in the city of Didymoterchos (Demotika), then blinded and put to death; while Andronicus and his son John of Selymbria were also seized and sentenced to be deprived of their sight. The operation, however, was unskilfully done. They were only partially blinded; but imprisoned. The progress of the Turkish arms, in the meantime, continued. They passed on into Macedonia, 1373—4. In 1375 the King of the Bulgars, John Shishman III., 1365 —†93, became the vassal[72] of the Sultan Murad, who took Sophia, 1385. But a check ensued. Lazar I., Prince of the Serbs, 1372—†89, won important successes over the Turkish invaders of Bosnia. These emboldened the other Slavs of the Balkan peninsula; and the Bulgars revolted. The rest of the confederacy hastened to their aid under Lazar of the Serbs; who was supported by Bosnia, Croatia, Herzegovina and Wallachia, together with some Bulgars who had escaped from the wreck of their country and some Hungarian auxiliaries. The battle was joined, 15th June, 1389, at Kosovo-polje[73]—" the field of the blackbirds "—near Pristina, where the independence of the Slavonic kingdoms was finally crushed. But the Sultan Murad was murdered by a Serbian: and the operations had to be continued by his son and successor, Bāyāzid I.

Bāyāzid I., 1389—†1403, took advantage of the dissensions within the House of the Palaeologi; and, entering into secret negotiations with Andronicus and his son John while they were still in prison, he concerted with them and the Genoese at Pera a plan for dethroning John VI. Surprising the Emperors John and Manuel in one of their palaces outside Constantinople, he handed them over to the custody of Andronicus, who threw them into the prison from which he had just escaped. John VI., however, made terms with the Sultan. He agreed to take the oath of allegiance to him, to pay him tribute and to support him in his wars with 12,000 horse and foot; and, in return, Bāyāzid, having ascertained that the Greeks preferred Manuel to Andronicus, required the latter to set his father and brother at liberty: and to submit to such dispositions as he should see fit to impose for the prevention of further dissension in the imperial house. Accordingly, it was arranged that John VI. and Manuel

The Restoration of the Empire and its Downfall 283

should reign at Constantinople; while Andronicus and his son John should hold, as a fief of the crown, the towns of Selymbria, Heraclea and Rodosto on the sea of Marmora together with Thessalonica. John VI. then sent his son Manuel, as a hostage, to Bāyāzid, at Nicæa; and both had to submit to the humiliation of being compelled to assist in person at the reduction of Philadelphia, 1390, the last possession in Asia of the Roman Empire. In alarm for the future, Manuel urged his father to strengthen the fortifications of the capital, and John VI. began the task. But it was discovered and forbidden by the Sultan: and in 1391 the aged Emperor died of shame and distress at being thus treated as the impotent vassal of the Turk.

§ 9. Manuel II., 1391—†1425, at the court of the Sultan, no sooner heard of the death of his father than he made his escape and hastened to Constantinople to secure his throne. His flight enraged Bāyāzid, who invested the city, 1391—5. In this extremity Manuel implored the assistance of the West; and a powerful army, composed of Hungarians, Germans and French, approached the Turkish frontier and forced the Sultan to raise the blockade. But, 25th September, 1396, they suffered a disastrous defeat at Nicopolis (Nikopol) on the Danube;[74] and the Sultan drew the investment of Constantinople closer. Alarmed, however, by the westward progress in Asia of the Mongols under Timour, 1370—†1405, the Turks at last became disposed to treat; and Bāyāzid and Manuel came to terms. Manuel turned the goodwill of the Sultan towards his nephew John VII. to his own advantage. He made over to him the government of Constantinople, reserving for himself the control of the Peloponnese. Proceeding thither, he set out, 10th December, 1399, thence for the West; and sought assistance from the French. On 3rd June, 1400, he entered Paris. It was the epoch of the Great Schism in the papacy, 1378—1415; centred, at that moment, in the rivalry between Benedict XIII., 1394—1423, at Avignon, and Boniface IX., 1389—1404, at Rome. Boniface issued an encyclical, 27th May, to the princes of Europe, inviting them to go to the aid of Constantinople: but there was no response. Fêted, but not assisted in Paris, Manuel went on to England; and he was received in London, 21st December, 1401, by Henry IV. He gave him three thousand marks with which to hire mercenaries: but no effective aid. So the Emperor turned homewards. He stayed in Paris, February, 1401—November, 1402. In April, 1403, he set sail from Venice; and arrived at Constantinople, 15th June: where the good news awaited him that, for the present at any rate, the danger was over. For at the battle of Angora, 20th July, 1402, the Turks had been annihilated by Timour;[75] and the Sultan Bāyāzid, with his son, Musa, fell into the hands of the conqueror. Dissensions followed among Turkish claimants for the throne, till at last they came to an end by the accession of Mohammed I., 1413—†21. Manuel had anticipated his success and had rendered him assistance. By way of recompense, the new Sultan assigned him places on the Black Sea, Thessalonica and its territories, with districts of the Peloponnese. Still feeling too dependent, however, the Emperor looked to the West for aid; and sent an embassy to Pope Martin V., 1417—†31, which was received at the Council of Constance,[76] 19th February, 1418. The Turks began to move again under Murad II., 1421—†51, who laid siege to Constantinople,[77] 1422: and when Manuel sent a second embassy, this time to go the round of the Western courts, Martin V. responded. He proposed that a Council should be held in Italy with a view to the union; and offered 100,000 florins to defray the travelling expenses of the Greeks, 1423. In 1425 he authorised marriages between Greeks and Latins; and granted indulgences to those who would go to the aid of the Greeks. He even nominated a legate for Constantinople, and sent two nuncios to inform the Emperor of his intention to establish a legation. But Manuel had just made terms with Murad II. He let the Pope know that no union was possible before the Œcumenical Council, 1425, should meet. Manuel, indeed, never genuinely wished for re-union; and only negotiated with the West in order to ward off the Turk. His secretary, George Phrantzes, 1401—†77, who wrote in his *Chronicle* the history of 1258—1476, reveals his real mind. " Propose a Council," he said, as he lay dying, to his son and successor, John VIII.; "open negotiations, but protract them interminably. The pride of the Latins and the obstinacy of the Greeks will never agree. By wishing to achieve the union, you will only strengthen the schism."[78]

§ 10. Nevertheless, when John VIII.,[79] 1425—†48, succeeded, the tide of Turkish aggression—after an interval of ten years of peace—moved so fast that reunion was actually, though but temporarily, achieved at the Council of Florence, 1439.

In the year of his accession, John concluded a fresh peace with the Sultan Murad: who was then engaged in wars on both his European and his Asiatic front. The Emperor was thus left for some years in peaceable possession of Constantinople and its immediate neighbourhood: while the other scraps of the Empire, in Greece, on the Sea of Marmora and the Black Sea, were governed by his six brothers,[80] fourth among whom was Constantine, Despot of the Peloponnese and afterwards the last Emperor of the Romans. But the peace with Murad did not include the brothers: and one by one their principalities were absorbed by the Turks, while they themselves took refuge at Constantinople. John still hoped that the Empire could be restored by the help of the western powers; and, following the practice of his father, Manuel II., and his grandfather, John V. [VI.], he promised to unite the Orthodox Church with the Roman, if the pope would rouse the sovereigns of Europe in his defence.

The papacy was just recovering from its contest with the reforming Councils; Pisa, 1409, Constance, 1415, and Basel, 1431: Eugenius IV., 1431—†47, having successfully ignored his suspension,[81] 24th January, 1438, by the last of the three. By the Council of Ferrara,[82] 1438, he hoped to win back all the prestige which the papacy had lost. "The union of the Greek Church was to reinstate the papacy in its position in the eyes of Europe: the Pope was again to appear as the leader of Christendom in a great crusade for the protection of Constantinople."[83]

Purgatory, the use of leavened or unleavened bread in the Eucharist, and the *Filioque*, were the points nominally in dispute between East and West: but the real disagreement was upon the papal claim to supremacy. Greek nationalism and Greek contempt for the "barbarous" Latins steeled their minds against any real union; but they were ready to sacrifice their traditions to the pressing need for present aid.

The Emperor John VIII., his brother Demetrius, the Patriarch Joseph II., 1416—†39, and twenty-two bishops were accordingly conveyed in the papal galleys, at the Pope's expense: and set sail for Italy, 24th November, 1437. They reached Venice, 8th February, 1438; where they were magnificently received by the Doge. On 28th February, they left for Ferrara, and entered the city, 7th March. The Council had opened, 5th January; and, 8th February, the Pope had commended to its deliberations the work of union with the Greeks. A good deal of time was spent by them, after their arrival, in manœuvring for their rightful precedence; but, as they were dependent upon the Pope for money, they had to be content with rather less than they thought their due. The first session[84] took place, in the Cathedral, 9th April: the Greek Church being represented not only by the Emperor and the Patriarch of CP., but by delegates of the other three Eastern Patriarchates: Alexandria, by Antony, metropolitan of Heraclea, and the protosyncellus, Gregory Mammas,[85] †1459, of CP.; Antioch, by the archbishops Mark of Ephesus,[86] †1443, and Isidore of Moscow, †1463; Jerusalem, by Dositheus, bishop of Monemvasia. The session, however, was scarcely more than formal: and, though progress was slow, the Greeks were at last induced to consent to the appointment of commissioners on either side, who were to begin the discussion of the points of difference. They themselves appointed Mark of Ephesus and Bessarion[87] 1395—†1472, archbishop of Nicæa; while the Latins put forward Julian, Cardinal Cæsarini, 1398—†1444. The discussions began, 4th June, with the point of Purgatory;[88] and Mark, for all his conservatism of Greek tradition, was fain to admit that the differences on this point were not serious. Long delay followed till the second session,[89] 8th October : when they took up the question of the *Filioque*. But, before it was discussed on its merits, the old but preliminary question was raised by Mark of Ephesus whether it was permissible to make an addition to the Creed.[90] Long disputes ensued till the end of November: when the Cardinal cut them short by proposing that the truth of the doctrine of the Double Procession should now be considered.[91] But its consideration was interrupted by the transference of the Council to Florence, 10th January, 1439. The plague had made Ferrara a dangerous place to remain in : and to this was added the Pope's inability to feed his guests there, because the surrounding country had been ravaged by war.[92]

At Florence,[93] the Pope was determined to proceed more speedily: and, 26th February, it was agreed to confine the discussions to forty members on either side.[94] On 2nd March the debate began: between John[95] of Montenegro, a Dominican theologian, and Mark of Ephesus. On the 17th John said explicitly that the Latins recognised the Father as the one cause of the Son and of the Holy Ghost.[96] As this was the only theological point at issue, and the Greeks were able to produce a passage in which it was admitted by St. Maximus the Confessor, 580—†662, one of the chief opponents of Monotheletism and the most distinguished theologian of his day,[97] there was a prospect of agreement. " If the Latins will accept this," exclaimed the friends of the union, " what hinders us from agreement? " But Mark of Ephesus had first to be propitiated : and " the discussion passed from being one between Greeks and Latins to one between two parties among the Greeks ":[98] between Bessarion and Isidore on the side of union, and Mark the exponent of Greek traditionalism. Mark was supported by the Patriarch Joseph : who, though absent from the discussions through illness, threw his ecclesiastical authority on to the side of Mark. The Emperor, however, had had enough of theology; he wanted armed support, and was anxious to be off. At last, he turned to the Pope, and demanded to know what succours he would give.[99] Eugenius promised, 1st June, three hundred troops and two galleys for the constant defence of Constantinople; and twenty galleys for six months, or ten for a year, in time of need. He also undertook to preach a crusade and rouse the West for the defence of the Greeks.[100] Satisfied with this promise, the Emperor hastened to bring matters to a conclusion,[101] and silenced Mark; while, on the death of the Patriarch, 10th June, a paper was found subscribed by him, approving whatever seemed good to his spiritual sons, and acknowledging the supremacy of the Roman Church.[102] Joseph lies buried in the Church of Santa Maria Novella.

Fortified by his declaration, the Emperor urged on the work of union: and the Pope proceeded, 9th June, 1439, to submit to the Greeks for their consideration the further points of difference between the two churches—purgatory, the papal primacy, unleavened bread and the words used in consecration.[103] Purgatory had been dealt with at Ferrara; and a formula satisfactory to both sides was soon found. The use of leavened or unleavened bread was left open. On the use of the Invocation of the Holy Spirit or of the Words of Institution as the " form " of consecration, the Greeks were ready to admit that the Words of Institution by themselves effect a valid consecration; but they demurred to the incorporation of this admission into the Articles of Union; and it was agreed that the admission by itself was enough. There remained the question of the papal supremacy; so inconsistent, as the Greeks had always held, with the independence of their Church. There were stormy discussions about it. At first, the Greeks would only accept the supremacy 21st June, with two provisos: (1) that the Pope should not convoke a Council, without the Emperor and the Patriarch, and (2) that, in case of an appeal to the Pope against the Patriarch, the Pope should send commissioners to try the case on the spot,[104] without summoning the Patriarch to the Council. Next day, Eugenius IV. announced that he intended to keep all his prerogatives intact; that he had the power of summoning

CHURCH OF ST. BASIL THE BEATIFIED, MOSCOW.

See p. 386.]

a Council whenever necessary; and that all Patriarchs were subject to his will.[105] " Then see to our departure,"[106] ordered the Emperor. The observances of St. John Baptist Day gave time to think : and, on 26th June, Bessarion and his friends submitted a proposal couched in vaguer terms : " We recognise the Pope as Sovereign Pontiff, Vicegerent and Vicar of Christ, Shepherd of all Christians, Ruler of the Church of God : saving the privileges and rights of the Patriarchs of the East."[107] This was accepted by the Pope.

Nothing now remained but to draft the decree, which should embody the various conclusions reached. A committee of twelve[108] was appointed for the task : and, 5th July, it was signed separately by the Latins and the Greeks.[109] It bears the signatures of one hundred and fifteen Latin prelates and abbots, and of thirty-three Greek ecclesiastics. But Mark of Ephesus did not sign; and a majority of the Greeks signed with reluctance. They knew what reception awaited the decree when they got home. At the same time, they felt it useless to entreat for papal aid without paying the price by acknowledging papal supremacy. But the circumstances of the time were such that the Pope was as anxious for the union as the Greeks themselves. He accepted vague conditions and agreed readily to compromises. On 6th July the decree was published in the Duomo of Florence as the Bull *Laetentur coeli*.[110] It was a signal triumph for the papacy : and it was followed by another, less conspicuous indeed but which added strength to the papal cause. On 22nd November, 1439, appeared the Bull *Exultate Deo*,[111] in which the Pope expounded the doctrine of the sacraments in the *Decretum pro Armenis,* and so reconciled another of the ancient churches of the East to Western Christendom. " Jacobites,[112] Syrians, Chaldæans and Maronites in succeeding years made illusory submission."

But it was a sorry reception that the union received at Constantinople. The Emperor left Florence, 26th August, 1439; and, when he and his prelates reached home, 1st February, 1440, his people could not be induced to acquiesce in what had been done. Mark became a national hero. When the new Patriarch, Metrophanes II., 1440—3, gave the blessing, the congregation turned away that they might not be defiled by one tainted with Latinism. In 1443 the three Patriarchs of Alexandria, Antioch and Jerusalem put out an encyclical in which they repudiated the Council of Florence as a new *latrocinium*, and declared their brother of Constantinople a matricide and a heretic![113]

§ 11. It was evident now that the end of the Eastern Empire[114] could not long be delayed. After his return home, the Emperor John VIII. continued to negotiate with Eugenius IV.: who, moved by the fear of a Turkish invasion of Italy, stirred up Ladislas VI., King of Poland, from 1434 and of Hungary, 1439—†44, to break the peace he had concluded, July, 1444, with Murad II. and to invade his dominions. He paid a dreadful penalty by his defeat and death at the battle of Varna, 10th November, 1444: but Murad refrained from taking vengeance on the Emperor. Yet he invaded the Peloponnese, and ravaged the dominions of his brother Constantine, 1446. Constantine was saved from extinction by another onslaught of the Hungarians, which, however, ended in disaster by their defeat at the battle of Kosovo, 18th October, 1448. Constantine was forced to pay tribute: the peace between him and the Sultan Murad II. being concluded by the historian, George Phrantzes. On 31st October, John VIII. died.

§ 12. He was succeeded by his brother as Constantine XIII. (Dragases[115]), 1448—†53: who was soon confronted by the ambitions of the new Sultan, Mohammed II., 1451—†81. The crushing blows dealt by his father Murad at the Hungarians left the northern frontier of the Turks secure: and Mohammed made no secret of his intention to complete his hold on the Balkan peninsula by the capture of Constantinople.[116] In November, 1452, the Cardinal Isidore of Kiev arrived there with two hundred soldiers sent by Pope Nicholas V., together with a letter demanding the ratification of the union of the churches: and on 12th December a service was held in St. Sophia to commemorate their reconciliation.[117] On

26th January, 1453, fresh reinforcements arrived under Giovanni Giustiniani, a Genoese noble of great reputation as a soldier, with seven hundred men. He was named by the Emperor commander-in-chief : and put the city in a state of defence. The siege began 6th April. On the night of 28—29th May, the last Mass was said in St. Sophia—Emperor and nobles, Patriarch and Cardinal, Greeks and Latins, all present—they made their last communion: for they knew that the assault was to be delivered at dawn. Then Constantine mounted his horse: and rode out to the defences. He perished, sword in hand, in the breach by the Gate of St. Romanus. " God forbid," cried the last Emperor of the Romans, " that I should live an Emperor without the Empire! I will die with my city ! "[118]

CHAPTER XII.

THE ANCIENT PATRIARCHATES WITH CYPRUS AND SINAI.

BISHOPS OF THE CHIEF SEES: FROM 1453.

Constantinople.

Gennadius II. 1454—6
Isidore II. 1456—63
Sophronius I. 1463—4
Joasaph I. 1464—6
Mark II. 1466—7
Dionysius I. 1467—72
Symeon 1472—5
Raphael I. 1475—6
Maximus III. 1476—82
Symeon² 1482—6
Nephon II. 1486—9
Dionysius I.² 1489—91
Maximus IV. 1491—7
Nephon II.²1497—8
Joachim I. 1498—1502
Nephon II.³ 1502
Pachomius I. 1503—4
Joachim I.² 1504—5
Pachomius I.² 1505—14
Theoleptus I. 1514—20
Jeremias I. 1520—2
Joannicius I. 1522—3
Jeremias I.² 1523—7
Dionysius II. 1537
Joasaph II. 1555—65
Metrophanes III. 1565—72
Jeremias II. 1572—9
Metrophanes III.² 1579—80
Jeremias II.² 1580—4
Pachomius II. 1584—5
Theoleptus II. 1585—6
Jeremias II.³ 1586—95
Matthæus II. 1595
Gabriel I. 1596

Theophanes I. 1596—7
Matthæus II.² 1599—1602
Neophytus II. 1602—3
Raphael II. 1603—7
Neophytus II.² 1607—12
Cyril I. (Lucar) 1612
Timothy II. 1612—21
Cyril I.² 1621—3
Gregory IV. 1623
Anthimus II. 1623
Cyril I.³ 1623—30
Isaac 1630
Cyril I.⁴ 1630—4
Cyril II. 1632
Athanasius III. 1634
Cyril I.⁵ 1634—5
Cyril II.² 1635—6
Neophytus III. 1636—7
Cyril I.⁶ 1637—8
Cyril II.³ 1638—9
Parthenius I. 1639—44
Parthenius II. 1644—5
Joannicius II. 1646—8
Parthenius II.² 1648—51
Joannicius II.² 1651—2
Cyril III. 1652
Athanasius III.² 1652
Paisius I. 1652—3
Joannicius II.³ 1653—4
Cyril III.² 1654
Paisius I.² 1654—5
Joannicius II.⁴ 1655—6
Parthenius III. 1656—7
Gabriel II. 1657
Theophanes II. 1657
Parthenius IV. 1657—62

Dionysius III. 1662—5
Parthenius IV.² 1665—7
Clemes 1667
Methodius III. 1668—71
Parthenius IV.³ 1671
Dionysius IV. 1671—3
Gerasimus II. 1673—5
Parthenius IV.⁴ 1675—6
Dionysius IV.² 1676—9
Athanasius IV. 1679
James 1679—83
Dionysius IV.³ 1683—4
Parthenius IV.⁵ 1684—5
James² 1685—6
Dionysius IV.⁴ 1686—7
James³ 1687—8
Callinicus II. 1688
Neophytus IV. 1688—9
Callinicus II.² 1689—93
Dionysius IV.⁵ 1693
Callinicus II.³ 1694—1702
Gabriel III. 1703—7
Neophytus V. 1707
Cyprian 1708—9
Athanasius V. 1709—11
Cyril IV. 1711—3
Cyprian² 1713—4
Cosmas III. 1714—6
Jeremias III. 1716—26
Callinicus III. 1726
Paisius II. 1726—33
Jeremias III.² 1733
Seraphim I. 1733—4
Neophytus VI. 1734—40

Paisius II.² 1740—3
Neophytus VI.²
    1743—4
Paisius II.³ 1744—8
Cyril V. 1748—51
Paisius II.⁴ 1751—4
Cyril V.² 1752—7
Callinicus IV. 1757
Seraphim II.
    1757—61
Joannicius III.
    1761—3
Samuel 1763—8
Meletius II.
    1768—9
Theodosius II.
    1769—73
Samuel² 1773—4
Sophronius II.
    1774—80
Gabriel IV. 1780—5
Procopius 1785—9
Neophytus VII.
    1789—94
Gerasimus III.
    1794—7
Gregory V. 1797—8
Neophytus VII.²
    1798—1801
Callinicus V.
    1801—6
Gregory V.²
    1806—8
Callinicus V.²
    1808—9
Jeremias IV.
    1809—13
Cyril VI. 1813—8
Gregory V. 1818—21
Eugenius II.
    1821—2
Anthimus III.
    1822—4
Chrysanthus
    1824—6
Agathangelus
    1826—30
Constantius I.
    1830—4
Constantius II.
    1834—5
Gregory VI.
    1835—40
Anthimus IV.
    1840—1

Anthimus V.
    1841—2
Germanus IV.
    1842—5
Meletius III. 1845
Anthimus VI.
    1845—8
Anthimus IV.²
    1848—52
Germanus IV.²
    1852—3
Anthimus VI.²
    1853—5
Cyril VII. 1855—60
Joachim II.
    1860—3
Sophronius III.
    1863—6
Gregory VI.²
    1867—71
Anthimus VI.³
    1871—3
Joachim II.²
    1873—8
Joachim III.
    1878—84
Neophytus VIII.
    1884—94
Anthimus VII.
    1894—7
Constantine V.
    1897—1901
Joachim III.²
    1901—
Germanus V. —18
[Dorotheus, metropolitan of Brusa, locum tenens
    1918—21]
Meletius IV.
    1921—3
Gregory VII.
    1923—4
Constantine VI.
    1924—5
Basil III. 1925—

ALEXANDRIA.
Orthodox.
Athanasius IV. ?
Philotheus II. c. 1523
Gregory V. ?
Joachim I. c. 1564
Silvester c. 1574

Meletius Pigas
    1592—1602
Cyril Lucar
    1602—21
Gerasimus I.
    1621—36
Metrophanes
    1636—9
Nicephorus
    1639—43
Joannicius 1643—65
Joachim II.
    1665—70
Paisius 1675—85
Parthenius I.
    1685—9
Gerasimus II.
    1689—1710
Samuel 1710—24
Cosmas II. 1724—37
Cosmas III.
    1737—46
Matthew 1746—66
Cyprian 1766—82
Gerasimus III.
    1783—8
Parthenius II.
    1788—1805
Theophilus
    1805—25
Hierotheus I.
    1825—45
[Artemius]
    1845—7
Hierotheus II.
    1847—58
Callinicus 1858—61
James 1861—66
Nicanor 1866—70
Sophronius IV.
    1870—99
Photius 1900—25
Meletius 1925—

Monophysite.
Matthew II. 1450
Gabriel VI. ?
Michael VI. ?
John XII. ?
John XIII. ?
Gabriel VII.
    1526—69
John XIV. 1570—85
Gabriel VIII.
    1585—1602

Mark V. 1602—18	Macarius II.	JERUSALEM.*
John XV. ?	?1543—50?	Theophanes III. ?
Matthew III. c. 1637	Michael VII.	Abraham c. 1460—8
Mark VI. 1645—60	1576—92/3	James III. ?—1482
Matthew IV.	Joachim V. 1581—92	Mark III. ?
1660—76	Joachim VI.	Gregory III. 36 years
John XVI. 1676—1718	1593—1604	Dorotheus II.*
Peter VI. 1718—26	Dorotheus IV.	1493—1543
John XVII.	1604—12	Germanus I.
1727—45	Athanasius II.	1543—79
Mark VII. 1745—70	1612—20	Sophronius V.
John XVIII.	Ignatius III.	1579—1608
1770—97	1620—34	Theophanes IV.
Mark VIII.	[Cyril IV. 1620—7]	1608—45
1797—1809	Euthymius II. 1634	Paisius 1645—61
Peter VII. 1809—54	Euthymius III.	Nectarius 1661—9
Cyril IV. 1854—61	1634—47	Dositheus III.
Demetrius II.	Macarius III.	1669—1707
1862—75	1647—72	Chrysanthus
Cyril V. 1875—	Cyril V. 1672	1707—31
	Neophytus 1672—82	Meletius 1731—7
ANTIOCH.	Cyril V.² 1682—1720	Parthenius 1737—66
Michael III.	[Athanasius III.	Ephraim 1766—71
1451/6(?)	1685—94]	Sophronius
Mark III. 1456—7/8	Athanasius III.²	1771—5
Joachim II. 1458—9	1720—4	Abraham 1775—87
Michael IV.	Sylvester 1724—66	Procopius 1787—8
1470/4—84	Philemon 1766—7	Anthimus 1788—1808
Dorotheus II.	Daniel 1767—91	Polycarp 1808—27
c. 1484—1500	Anthemius 1791—1813	Athanasius V.
Michael V. 1523/4—9	Seraphim 1813—23	1827—45
Dorotheus III.	Methodius 1823—50	Cyril II. 1845—72
?—1530/1	Hierotheus 1850—85	Procopius II.
Joachim III.	Gerasimus 1885—91	1872—5
1530/1—4	Spyridon 1891—8	Hierotheus 1875—82
Michael VI.	Meletius II.	Nicodemus 1883—90
1534—42/3	1899—1906	Gerasimus 1891—7
Joachim IV.	Gregory II. 1906—	Damianus 1897—
1542/3—75		

* From Ἡ ἐκκλησία Ἱεροσολύμων 1517—1900 (Athens, 1900).

CHAPTER XII.

THE ANCIENT PATRIARCHATES WITH CYPRUS AND SINAI.

§ 1. THE Churches of Eastern Christendom[1] are, at present, as they have been since the fifth century, either Orthodox or Heretical. The Heretical Churches may conveniently be enumerated here, and then left for detailed treatment later on. They are either Nestorian, as are the East Syrians (Assyrians) who, as the Church of Persia, declared themselves independent of the Churches of the Roman Empire, 424; or Monophysite: as are the Churches of Armenia, whose separation dates from 491; of West Syria (Jacobites), from 543; of Egypt (Copts), from 476; and of Abyssinia, founded 357. These have no intercourse with the Orthodox Church: which, since the Great War, has come to consist of eleven different Churches, all professing the same faith, all using the same liturgy (though in different languages), and all, except Bulgaria, in communion with one another and with the Patriarch of Constantinople. We shall devote a chapter to their creed and another to their rites. We are now concerned with their external history. Politically, except for Russia, it turns upon their subjection to, and deliverance from, the Turkish yoke: constitutionally upon their relation to, and growing independence of, the Œcumenical Patriarchate. These processes are now complete: and Orthodox Christendom to-day consists of eleven independent but inter-related Churches.[2] They are (1) the " Great Church " of Constantinople, with the three other ancient Patriarchates of (2) Alexandria, (3) Antioch, (4) Jerusalem. To Antioch and Jerusalem respectively were once subject (5) Cyprus and (6) Mt. Sinai: though Cyprus became autocephalous in virtue of the eighth canon of the Council of Ephesus, 431, and the Monastery of Mt. Sinai in 1782. Then (7) the Church of Russia became autocephalous, 1589, and Moscow, the fifth Patriarchate, 1591. And, finally, the Churches of the Balkan peninsula which secured their independence of the Œcumenical Patriarchate (8) Greece in 1850, (9) Bulgaria in 1870, (10) Serbia, or, as it now is, Jugo-Slavia, in 1879, and (11) Rumania in 1885. The Churches of Georgia, once absorbed, 1802, by the Russian Church, and of the Ukraine hitherto part of it, declared themselves autocephalous in 1919; but, owing to the disturbed state of Russia, their declaration is still awaiting confirmation. On the other hand, the Church of Jugo-Slavia has now, under Demetrius, Patriarch of Belgrade since 1920, absorbed the formerly independent Churches of Carlowitz,[3] 1765 (once the centre of the Serbs in Hungary), Czernagora[4] (Montenegro) and Bosnia, 1880, and Herzegovina; while the Church of Rumania has similarly absorbed the Churches of Hermannstadt[5] 1864 (once the centre of the Rumans in Hungary) and Czernowitz,[6] 1873 (once the metropolis for the Ruthenians of Bukovina, and for Dalmatia).

The Orthodox Church, in the realm of faith, is apt to be static: but, in the realm of order, by its policy of adjusting and readjusting its constitution to the shifting frontiers of rival nations, it has proved itself a living and progressive Church. The principle, on which it has acted, is that ecclesiastical divisions should conform to civil:[7] a principle first known to have been asserted when the Emperor Valens, 364—†78, erected part of Cappadocia into a province. Anthimus, bishop of Tyana, which thus became a civil metropolis, claimed corresponding rank; and succeeded in asserting his claim, in spite of the opposition of his ecclesiastical superior, St. Basil, Exarch of Cæsarea in Cappadocia, 370—†9. The principle was accepted by the Council of Chalcedon, 451,[8] and reaffirmed by the Council in Trullo,[9] 692. It thus became the governing principle of Eastern policy. "The Latin Church," on the other hand, "with a certain superb indifference to political changes, maintained the opposite principle."[10] "It has not seemed fitting," wrote Pope Innocent I. in reply to Alexander, bishop of Antioch, c. 415, "that the Church of God should change her course to suit the fickleness of worldly needs."[11] Characteristic difference of spirit! But the Eastern way is not less characteristic of a living church than the Western: and the West has sometimes copied it, " as when Paris, for many ages a suffragan of Sens, became at last, in 1622, an archbishopric . . . while London," on the other hand, in conformity with the principle laid down by Innocent, " continues in that subjection to Canterbury which was natural while Essex was a dependency of Kent."[12]

§ 2. The Turkish Empire[13] was the new political entity within whose bounds the Churches of Eastern Christendom had to live as best they could. Its rise, zenith and decay, directly affected the power and prestige of the Orthodox Patriarchate: for the Church of Constantinople was more closely bound up with the State than any other Church.

The period of the expansion of the Turkish power is covered by the seventy years, 1450—1520, which elapsed between the fall of Constantinople and the outbreak of the Reformation in Germany. Mohammed II., 1451—†81, completed the conquest of the Balkan peninsula and its adjacent islands. His armies overran Moldavia, 1456; Serbia, 1459; the Peloponnese, 1460; Bosnia, 1463; and Herzegovina, 1483. The Ægæan Islands fell to his Empire, 1457—62, and the Ionian Islands, 1479. He acquired the Crimea by 1476; and even got a footing on the soil of Italy for a year, when he held Otranto, 1480—1. His grandson, Selim I., 1512—†20, obtained possession of Kurdistan, 1515; and, on the capture of Egypt, 1516—7, with the Holy Places, proclaimed himself Caliph. This gave a religious sanction to Turkish militarism: and powerfully assisted the further expansion of the Empire.

It reached its zenith, 1520—1614. Under Suleiman the Magnificent, 1520—†66, the Turks took Belgrade, 1521; and Rhodes, 1522, whence they expelled the Knights Hospitallers to Malta. By the defeat of Louis II., King of Hungary and Bohemia, 1516—†26, at Mohacz,[14] 1526, they made themselves masters of two thirds of Hungary and threatened the eastern frontiers of the Habsburg Empire. In September—October, 1529, they appeared before Vienna with 120,000 men and 400 guns; but were forced to retire with the loss of 40,000 men. This was the first check to their arms, but it proved only a temporary repulse; for, in 1532, the Turks advanced again in Styria and Austria; and it is worth while noticing that their three threats to the power of the Habsburgs, in 1526, 1529, and 1532, mark the points at which the Reformation in Germany owed its safety to the intervention of the Turk.[15]. A fourth epoch of Reforming expansion was 1541, when the Turk, advancing again,[16] took Buda-Pesth. Thenceforward a protracted struggle ensued, under Suleiman I., Selim II., 1566—†74, and their successors to Ahmed I., 1603—†17, for Turkish hegemony in Europe; but it issued in the Turks being confined to its S.E. territories. They suffered a second check—this time at sea—when they were defeated at the battle of Lepanto, 1571, by Don John of Austria, a natural son of the Emperor Charles V., 1519—56. " Fuit homo missus a Deo, cui nomen erat Ioannes " was the comment of Pope Pius V., 1566—†72. But Don John's victory led to little result;[17] and the struggle went on till 1606: when, by the Treaty of Sitvatorok,[18] a period at last was put to the Turkish advance. By this treaty the Emperor Rudolph II., 1576—†1612, and the Sultan Ahmed I., 1603—†17, recognised each other as equals, whereas, since 1547, the Emperor had been tributary; and large parts of Hungary and Transylvania were set free from the Turkish yoke.

The Peace of Sitvatorok anticipated the settlement made at the end of the seventeenth century: for then set in the period of the decline of the Turkish power which has continued until to-day. The decline began, 1686, with the loss of Buda-Pesth; and this was followed by the treaty of Carlowitz, 1699, when the Turks ceded Hungary and Transylvania to Austria. The agreement had scarcely been reached when a second and more powerful rival appeared on the Turkish horizon. The rivalry between Russia, seeking an economic outlet by way of the Bosporus and the Dardanelles, and Turkey holding Constantinople, became inevitable. It increased during the eighteenth century, till the Turks had to abandon the Crimea to Russia, 1784. By the Treaty of Jassy, 1792, Russia moved her frontier forward to the Dniester; by the Treaty of Bucharest, 1812, she advanced it again to the Pruth; and, but for his preoccupation with resistance to France during the Napoleonic Wars, the Tsar would have been seated on the throne of Constantinople long before 1815. From that time forward, the reciprocal jealousies of European powers kept the Sultan in possession; but they could not save him, during the nineteenth century, from the loss of one province after another. In reliance upon Russia, the Balkan nations, in turn, declared their independence. Greece became an independent kingdom, 1832; Rumania, 1881; Serbia, 1882; and Bulgaria attained its autonomy, 1885. And just as the earlier phase of Turkish expansion enlarged the area and the authority of the Œcumenical Patriarchate, so this last phase of shrinkage and retreat, ending as it did in the emancipation of the Balkan nations, has encouraged Philetism and diminished the range of the Patriarch's authority by the creation of National Churches: fully in communion with him but not directly under his control.

§ 3. This alternation of expansion and contraction in the powers of the Patriarchate, and in the area over which they have extended, since 1453, is the next topic for our consideration. By the conquest of Constantinople, the Œcumenical Patriarch experienced an immediate gain, but ultimate loss. Nevertheless, he remains to-day the centre of communion for all Orthodox Churches.

(i.) The immediate gain lay in the addition of secular to spiritual jurisdiction.

Athanasius II. resigned the Patriarchate, 1450; and, at the fall of the city, the see was vacant. Within a few days, Mohammed II. summoned the clergy of Constantinople to his presence, and wished to see their Patriarch. "Why is he not here? Why does he not pay me the accustomed reverence?" The clergy explained that they were without their chief; and the Emir,[19] foregoing his wrath, commanded them to proceed to an election, hoping thus to give confidence to the Christian population and to induce them to return to the city. The clergy elected George Scholarius,[20] who had been a member of the judicial bench under the Empire and had accompanied the Emperor, John VIII. (Palaeologus), 1425—†48, to the Councils of Ferrara and Florence, 1438—9. Here he took up the cause of Re-union : but, on his return, he was won over to the reaction headed by Mark, metropolitan of Ephesus. George was now consecrated, according to custom, by the metropolitan of Heraclea, in the Church of the Holy Apostles : and took the title of Gennadius II., 1453—6. The Emir invested him with the crozier, confirmed him in the rights and privileges of his see, and assigned him the Church of the Holy Apostles and its precincts for his residence; but this was so deserted that Gennadius presently obtained a grant of the Church of our Lady Pammakaristos in exchange.[21] Here the Patriarchate had its centre, 1456—1586. A Greek population returned, and settled in that region of the city. But factions among them were fatal to the authority of the Patriarch; and Gennadius II. resigned in 1456. He died about 1468.

To understand the position of the Patriarch under the new regime,[22] it must be remembered that the Turk distinguished not only between Moslems and unbelievers, but between two kinds of unbelievers as well. The first are *Kaffirs,* i.e., heathen pure and simple : and their only privilege is to choose between Islām and extermination. Jews and Christians, however, are, like the Moslems, " People of the Book " : each having a revelation contained in their own scriptures. So Christians were treated as *Rayahs* (Flock) : who are thus entitled to protection, though they must be kept in their place. They must pay taxes, wear a distinctive dress, display no outward signs of their creed upon their churches, as by mounting the cross upon them or ringing church bells. Otherwise, they are free to practise their religion. But religion, with the Turk, means nation *(millet);* for he makes no distinction between religion and nationality. So the *Rayahs* were organised according to their nations. Chief among these were the Orthodox or Roman nation *(Rum millet)*; and at its head was placed the Orthodox Patriarch, with secular jurisdiction added to his spiritual authority. So he acquired greater power after the conquest than he had before it. Thus, instead of merely enjoying ecclesiastical precedence above his brother Orthodox Patriarchs of Alexandria, Antioch and Jerusalem, he now exercised over them secular authority as well;[23] since he became responsible to the Turkish Government for their affairs, and they could only approach the Government through him. Not unnaturally, it became a temptation, under cover of his secular authority over them, to bring them ecclesiastically under his jurisdiction : and, in the Balkans, his spiritual authority reached its height when in 1767 he succeeded in bringing under his immediate jurisdiction the three archbishoprics of Ochrida, Ipek and Tirnovo, and so incorporating the three autocephalous churches of Bulgaria, Serbia and Rumania into the Patriarchate. At the opening of the nineteenth century, the Patriarchate included the whole of the Balkan peninsula; and in Asia it reached on the north to Trebizond, and in the southeast to the Taurus. The reduction of these wide territories began with the declaration of the independence of the Church in Greece, 1833 : where there were, under the Metropolitan of Athens, 12 sees.[24] In 1911 there were left to the immediate jurisdiction of the Patriarch, 74 sees in possession of metropolitans, mostly without suffragans, and 20 sees[25] dependent upon 5 metropolitans.[26] Further reductions in the Patriarchate have ensued since the Great War : and by the Treaty of Lausanne, 1923, the Œcumenical Patriarch is stripped of all but his spiritual jurisdiction.

(ii.) To what, then, may we attribute this ultimate loss of his authority?

Primarily, to his complete dependence upon the Turk. Gennadius II. was the first of a long line of Patriarchs content to receive spiritual investiture from the Sultan, and a *berat* confirming and defining their powers. The line came to be a series of puppet prelates who, for all the dignity that surrounded them, were the creatures of the Sultan, made and deposed at will. No doubt this was due, in part, to the factiousness of their flock: among whom one party, as soon as the Patriarch was appointed by the influence of their opponents, set about intriguing for his downfall in favour of their own man. Money also came to play a sinister but important part in the appointment of a Patriarch. The first four patriarchs[27] were untainted by it: but, in opposition to the fourth, named Mark II., 1466—7, a junta of immigrants from Trebizond offered the Sultan[28] 1,000 florins[29] to displace him in favour of a fellow-countryman of theirs, one Simeon,[30] a monk. But Simeon was outdone by the Sultan's stepmother who offered him 2,000[31] in the interest of a favourite, Dionysius,[32] metropolitan of Philippopolis. Then the Patriarchate was bought for 2,500 by Raphael, a drunken Serb.[33] By 1572 the regular payments had become an investiture fee[34] of 2,000 florins, and an annual tribute[35] of 4,000.[36] It is obvious that to procure the Patriarchal throne, and to hold it, money was the first requisite. The Greeks were traders: and possessed it in plenty. And, as the Patriarchate had considerable emoluments, each party among them was as ready to offer bribes as the Turk to receive them. Vacancies could be arranged: and the tenure of each Patriarch was precarious and short-lived. So rapid were the changes that many Patriarchs secured the throne, lost it to a rival, and regained it: while some lost and recovered it as many as five or six times. Out of 159 Patriarchs who held office between the fifteenth and the twentieth century, the Turks have on 105 occasions driven Patriarchs from their throne; there have been 27 abdications, often involuntary; 6 Patriarchs have suffered violent deaths by hanging, poisoning or drowning; and only 21 have died natural deaths while in office. No succession of rulers could maintain its prestige under such conditions; nor is it matter for surprise that few of the Œcumenical Patriarchs have been men of any distinction. Not less undistinguished have been their surroundings: for, since they were expelled from the Church of the Pammakaristos, 1586, they have had to be content to set up their throne in the insignificant Church of St. George, 1601—1924, situate in the Greek quarter of the city called, after the old lighthouse, the Phanar. Thus the Patriarchate, enslaved by the Turk, degraded by simony and made the sport of intrigue by its own people, has come to be regarded by many of the Orthodox as an agent of the Turkish government and identified with its oppression.

But the Patriarchate has also come to be identified, by such of the Orthodox as are non-Greek, with the cause of Hellenic nationalism. The Phanariot Greeks,[37] alone of the subject races of the Porte, possessed wealth. They could buy the Patriarchate for a favourite; while he, in his turn, recovered what was spent in purchasing his office from the Greek bishops whom he placed out in the sees of his wide jurisdiction. Then they passed on their outlay to their clergy: and these got it back from their Bulgar, Serb, or Rumanian parishioners.[38] A widespread hostility has thus pursued the Phanariot clergy among the non-Greek Orthodox: and the revolts which the Phanar puts down to Philetism have issued in the enforced recognition of national churches, as a refuge from Phanariot oppression.

(iii.) But, when the worst is thus told, we must not forget that the Patriarchate owes its loss, whether of character or territory, to long association with the Turk, and to five centuries of subjugation to his oppression. There have been good men among the Orthodox Patriarchs of Constantinople. Joasaph I., 1464—6, was deposed because he refused to sanction the marriage of a Christian girl to a Moslem courtier.[39] Maximus III., 1476—†82, suffered mutilation in a similar cause.[40] Gregory V., 1818—†21, in the War of Greek Independence, died a martyr to the cause: being hanged over the gateway of the patriarchate.[41] Confessors and martyrs have been numerous during the centuries of Turkish misrule. They have resisted every inducement to abandon their religion:[42] and to them, as to all the Orthodox, the Œcumenical Patriarch is still their spiritual father and their centre of communion.

§ 4. Next to him ranks the Orthodox Patriarch of

x

Alexandria.[43] As the great majority of Egyptian Christians are Copts, his flock is a small one, and is said to number not more than 50—60,000 souls.[44] But his jurisdiction extends over Egypt, Libya, Arabia and Nubia: and he has the title of " All-Holiness " and " Œcumenical Judge." During the seventeenth and eighteenth centuries he lived at Cairo:[45] but he has now returned to Alexandria.[46] The dioceses of his Patriarchate were, since 1672, reduced to four: Ethiopia, Cairo, Damietta and Reshid, but in 1913 numbered seven—with 5 monasteries, 31 parishes and 55 churches. Their bishops have the title of Metropolitan. They do not reside in their dioceses: but form the synod of the Patriarchate,[47] or its court.

§ 5. Third in rank is the Patriarch of Antioch:[48] but his territories have suffered repeated loss. The growth of the Patriarchate of Constantinople was largely at the expense of the Patriarchs of Antioch: and ended by taking away from them all Asia Minor. Cyprus established its independence, 431—88. Jerusalem took away Palestine, and became a Patriarchate, 451. The Church in Persia asserted its independence, 424, and became Nestorian after the Council of Ephesus, 431, drawing away numbers of East Syrians from their allegiance to Antioch. In the sixth century, West Syria became preponderatingly Jacobite;[49] and there are now Uniates in large numbers throughout these regions—seven communities of them, in fact, each of which represents a fraction of the ancient church of Antioch.[50] There are, moreover, as many as seven Patriarchs of Antioch: the Orthodox Patriarch, who lives at Damascus; the Titular Patriarch of the Latin rite, who resides at Rome; the Jacobite Patriarch, at Mardin; and four Patriarchs in charge of Uniate churches—Maronite, Greek or Melkite[51] Armenian and Syrian. It will not, then, be a matter of surprise that, though the jurisdiction of the Orthodox Patriarch extends over Syria, Cilicia, Mesopotamia, Isauria and other Asiatic provinces,[52] his flock is estimated at not more than 200,000 to 250,000 souls,[53] and his dioceses at not more than twelve. His bishops have each the title of metropolitan:[54] and with two or three titular bishops, form the Patriarchal Curia. From 1724—1899, all the Orthodox Patriarchs of Antioch have been Phanariot Greeks, in spite of the fact that the great majority of the people speak Arabic.[55]

§ 6. The Church of Jerusalem[56] is the fourth of the ancient Patriarchates in the East. Its bishopric dates back to St. James, the Lord's brother;[57] and its prestige was enhanced by the discovery of the Holy Places in the reign of Constantine, 323—†37. They became centres of pilgrimage. The Emperor erected famous buildings on their sites; and, about 380, St. Etheria, a kinswoman of the Emperor Theodosius, 379—†95, made the pilgrimage to visit them, and has left us an account of the worship of the Church of Jerusalem as she saw it.[58] Already, the Council of Nicæa, 325, had assigned an honorary precedence to the bishop of Jerusalem, without withdrawing him from the authority of his metropolitan, the bishop of Cæsarea.[59] It was over this question of precedence[60] that Acacius, metropolitan of Cæsarea, 340—†66, succeeded in deposing St. Cyril, who was bishop of Jerusalem, 348—†86, at the time of Etheria's visit. His successors were strong enough to maintain their authority thus vindicated; until Juvenal, who was bishop of Jerusalem, 420—†58, "made up his mind to get precedence turned into jurisdiction, and to be content with nothing short of power in proportion to the reputation of his see."[61] His contention was that the see of Antioch ought to be subject " to the Apostolic See of Jerusalem."[62] The matter was, at length, referred to the Council of Chalcedon, 451; and, after long negotiations, was settled between Antioch and Jerusalem by consent.[63] " The Patriarchate of Antioch kept Phœnicia I. and II. and Arabia, provinces of which the metropolitical sees were respectively Tyre, Damascus and Bostra. Juvenal was henceforth to support the dignity of a Patriarch with the three Palestines, whose metropolitans had their sees respectively at Jerusalem, Scythopolis and Petra. Afterwards, at the fifth General Council, 553, 'Arabia' was transferred from Antioch to Jerusalem; and the newest Patriarchate of the Church then came to include all the territory from Lebanon to Sinai."[64] It now contains thirteen[65] dioceses, besides that of Jerusalem; all of whose bishops are metropolitans. They are the dioceses of Cæsarea, Bethshan (Scythopolis), Petra, Acre, Bethlehem, Nazareth, Lydda, Gaza, Jaffa, Nablus, Samaria, Tabor and Philadelphia.[66] And " its boundaries extend beyond the present boundaries of Palestine into regions under French protection in the north, and to those beyond the Jordan and the Dead Sea in the east, and include the Peninsula of Sinai, excepting the Monastery of St. Katharine and the adjacent communities under the autocephalous church of Mount Sinai."[67] There is an Orthodox population of about 60,000.[68]

The importance of the Patriarchate, however, greatly exceeds its limited size and its scanty flock.

For, (1) " since the days of Constantine, for 1,700 years, Jerusalem has been one of the chief centres of Christendom; and the Patriarch of Jerusalem, with the Brotherhood of the Holy Sepulchre which has grown up around him and of which he is the official head, has . . . been the . . . principal guardian of the Holy Places to which pilgrims and worshippers from all the nations of Christendom have continuously resorted."[69]

(2.) " On the division between East and West, as one of the four Patriarchs, he became one of the Four Heads of the Orthodox Eastern Church. . . . The Four Patriarchs still continue the most venerable authority which the Church possesses," and are officially recognised as " the most Holy, Patriarchal and Apostolic Sees upon which sacred four as upon a four-square base is founded the assembled unity of the one Holy and Catholic Church of Christ."[70]

(3.) " Besides the Monastery of the Holy Sepulchre, the Patriarchate has many other monasteries throughout the Holy Land." There are 34 in Jerusalem and the neighbourhood; and, further afield, 18, excluding the famous Monastery of Mar Saba.[71] Before the Great War, 1914—18, it maintained, " generally with the help of local endowments, similar institutions in Constantinople, Moscow, Athens, Cyprus, Crete, the Peloponnese, Tiflis, Smyrna, Samos, Adrianople and other places "— not to mention schools throughout Palestine, a Theological College and a hospital with other charitable works in Jerusalem. The expenses of all these institutions were in great part met out of the revenues of the Patriarchate : and these were derived either from rents of estates in Russia, or from gifts of donors in past ages, or from the lavish contributions of pilgrims, mainly Russian, who have flocked to the Holy Land in increasing numbers during the last two generations.[72]

But, since the War, the Patriarchate has fallen on evil days. Its income, derived in the main from Russian sources, has dried up since the Revolution in Russia, 1917. Its estates, in Bessarabia, have been transferred, with that province, to Rumania; and there is hope that their revenues may again be available for the Patriarchate. But, at present, they are diverted elsewhere; and meanwhile the flow of pilgrims and oblations from Russia has ceased. Thus the Patriarchate is heavily in debt; but it is also weakened by dissension at home. The laity and the parochial clergy are nearly all Arab-speaking. But the Fraternity of the Holy Sepulchre is Greek. It is a powerful corporation consisting of 7 bishops, 44 archimandrites, 26 priests, 11 deacons, 52 monks not in Holy Orders, 23 attendants at the Holy Sepulchre, 82 residents (including 50 at Mar Saba) in other Monasteries of Palestine, besides 21 Patriarchal representatives at various centres in Palestine and 12 in other countries—or a total of 278 all told.[73] The Brotherhood regards itself, and by other Greeks is regarded, as an outpost of Hellenic nationalism.[74] And this explains the divisions in the Church of Jerusalem between the Patriarch, with his Synod on the one side and his flock on the other; or again, between the Fraternity, or Synod, as representative of militant Hellenism in possession of the Holy Places, and Christians of foreign connexion : such as the Latins who dispute the claim to the Sacred Sites, or the Orthodox of Slav affinities and, in particular, Russia which, as it pays the piper, has been disposed to call the tune.

These difficulties led to a dispute between the Patriarch Damianus and the Fraternity. It has been the desire of Damianus to give the Orthodox Arabs of his patriarchate a greater share in ecclesiastical administration.[75] His Synod accused him of not making a sufficiently resolute resistance to the laity: who, taking advantage of the Turkish Revolution of 1908, demanded that the Patriarchate should be turned into a wholly local institution, its endowments treated as local endowments, and administered by a Council on which the laity were to be predominant. The Synod then proceeded to depose him. At this point, intervened Lord Allenby's campaign and the capture of Jerusalem, 1917. Palestine passed under British control; and the case was referred by the High Commissioner to a Commission of Inquiry. They reported, 24th March, 1921, that, in the Orthodox Church, "there is no ecclesiastical authority empowered to adjudicate on the dispute,"[76] and trusted that a reconciliation might be effected. They went on to recommend that, in the interest of the Patriarch himself, his appointment should still be confirmed by the Government, as it had formerly been confirmed by the *berat* of the Sultan;[77] and that, in the interest of the local community, no restriction should be placed, so far as nationality goes, upon admission of members to the Fraternity.[78] This recommendation will, if acted upon, open the office of Patriarch to Arabic-speaking Orthodox of Palestine, and so tend to re-establish the Patriarch in the affections of his flock. A second recommendation may, if adopted, have similar results: for it is proposed to reconstitute the local bishops in the Trans-jordanic dioceses, and no longer to leave their populations to the ministrations of the Superior of the monasteries as representing the Patriarch.[79] And a third looks forward, as soon as the efforts of the Commission to set in order the finances of the Patriarchate have taken effect, to the re-opening of the Theological School of the Monastery of the Holy Cross—hitherto "one of the most valuable institutions of the Patriarchate."[80]

§ 7. Next in rank to the last of the four Eastern

Patriarchates is the autocephalous Church of Cyprus.[81] Its history falls into four periods: (i.) from the conversion of the island to the extinction of the Byzantine supremacy, 1191; (ii.) the Latin domination, 1191—1571; (iii.) the Turkish yoke, 1571—1878; and (iv.) finally the British occupation, 1878—1924.

(i.) The Gospel was first preached in Cyprus, A.D. 46, by St. Barnabas, "a man of Cyprus by race,"[82] and St. Paul: who were sent on their mission of evangelisation by the church of Antioch.[83] Little is known of the further progress of the church in Cyprus till A.D. 325: when, at the Council of Nicæa, it was represented by St. Spyridon, bishop of Trimythus,[84] and two other bishops: Cyril of Paphos, and Gelasius of Salamis (Constantia).[85] Spyridon was a shepherd, who kept his sheep after he became a bishop; and Trimythus was the scene of the battle between Isaac II. (Comnenus), 1185—95, and the Crusaders under Richard Cœur de Lion, 1189—†99, when the Byzantine was exchanged for the Latin supremacy. Gelasius had a well known successor in Epiphanius, bishop of Salamis, 367—†403, and metropolitan, a sleuth-hound of heresy and the enemy of Origenism. One of his successors was Rheginus who, at the seventh session of the Council of Ephesus, 31st July, 431, secured the liberation of the church of Cyprus from dependence upon Antioch.[86] The island was, at that time, in the civil Diocese of the East; and was administered by a Consular sent from Antioch. Alexander, bishop of Antioch, 413—†21, accordingly claimed similar rights over the church of Cyprus; and contended, in a letter to Pope Innocent I., 402—†17, that they had formerly been exercised by his predecessors but had lapsed during the schism in the church of Antioch, which he has the credit of bringing to a close. The Pope, in his reply,[87] assumed that the facts were as stated by Alexander, and ordered that the bishop of Antioch should not only consecrate the metropolitan of Cyprus, but should be consulted before the appointment, in the island, even of a simple bishop. "The bishops of Cyprus," he said, "who, to avoid the tyranny of the Arians, have taken upon themselves to perform their ordinations without consulting anyone ought to return to the observance of the canons,"[88] that is to say, in their " dependency upon Antioch."[89] But they took no notice of these admonitions: for, after all, the Pope's advice was contingent upon the information supplied to him by Alexander being correct. At length, on the death of Troïlus, metropolitan of Salamis, an opportunity occurred for John, Patriarch of Antioch, 428—†41, to reassert the claims of his see. Exerting his influence with Flavius Dionysius, Count of the East, he persuaded him to write, 21st May, 431, to Theodore, Consular of Cyprus,[90] and to the clergy of Salamis,[91] forbidding them to proceed to the election of a successor till the Council of Ephesus had given its instructions. They took no notice, and elected Rheginus: who at once proceeded to Ephesus, with three of his suffragans, and laid the case before the Council. Rheginus was an ardent anti-Nestorian:[92] and the Council, nothing loath to aid him in his revenge upon John of Antioch, the friend of Nestorius, gave willing attention to his case.[93] They inquired (1) whether any bishop of Antioch had ever been known to consecrate a bishop in Cyprus, to which Zeno, bishop of Citium, answered by an emphatic No; (2) whether it was certain that no such right had existed when the sixth canon of Nicæa reserved all its rights to the see of Antioch; and (3) whether the last three metropolitans —Epiphanius, Sabinus and Troïlus—had been consecrated by the insular bishops. To these two questions, Zeno replied again, with an equally emphatic Yes. It was a case of Zeno *versus* Alexander; of testimony taken for granted, and not cross-examined, on either side. A modern tribunal would have refused a decision. But not so a Pope or a Council. The Synod reversed the Pope's decision; and gave a contingent judgment in favour of the Cypriot claims " according to the canons of the holy fathers and ancient custom."[94] But, conditional as it was, the decision held its ground until Peter the Fuller, Monophysite Patriarch of Antioch, 468—488, made a last effort to vindicate the supremacy of Antioch. He claimed it, however, not on the ground of ancient custom:

but on the plea that, as Cyprus had originally received the faith from Antioch, which was an Apostolic foundation, it ought therefore to be subject to that see. There is little doubt that the renewal of the claim would have succeeded; for Peter the Fuller was a leader of the Monophysites and the Emperor Zeno, 474—†91, who had but recently put out the *Henoticon*, 482, in order to conciliate that powerful party, would find it convenient to acquiesce. But Anthemius, metropolitan of Salamis, was equal to the occasion. He opportunely discovered near Salamis the relics of St. Barnabas, the Apostle of Cyprus. No one could now doubt that the Church of Cyprus had as good a claim to be apostolic as the Church of Antioch. Hastening to Constantinople with the relics, he displayed them before the Emperor, and besought his protection. Zeno referred the matter to Acacius, Patriarch of Constantinople, 471—†89, and his Synod. They decided in favour of the Cypriot claim to independence : and from that time forward, the Church of Cyprus has been reckoned as autocephalous. Its archbishop has the title of Exarch, and ranks next to the Patriarch of Jerusalem in the Orthodox Hierarchy. And he still enjoys privileges granted him by Zeno—to sign in red ink, to wear vestments of silk and purple, to carry the sceptre instead of the pastoral staff, and to be addressed as Your Beatitude.[95]

On the conquest of Cyprus by the Saracens, 632—47, the bishops, with their clergy and faithful, took flight in a body to the mainland. Here Justinian II., 685—95, gave them a settlement by the Hellespont, in a city which he built for them and called Nea Justinianopolis : where the archbishop was to have the same rights as in his own island city of Constantia.[96] But under the usurper Tiberius III., 695—8, the exiles were enabled, by his vigorous policy against the Saracens, to return home. Cyprus, however, was not freed from the Saracen yoke till 964; when it was recovered by the great Emperor Nicephorus II.[97] (Phocas), 963—9. It remained part of the Eastern Roman Empire for two centuries more. And to the first half of the twelfth century belongs the foundation of its three most celebrated monasteries : Kykko,[98] belonging to the diocese of Kyrenia, and situate toward the centre of the western part of the island: Machaera,[99] in the archdiocese of Nikosia; and Enclystra,[100] in the diocese of Paphos. At the monastery of Kykko is preserved the icon of our Lady, traditionally said to have been painted by St. Luke.[101]

(ii.) In 1191 began the Latin domination.[102] It was marked, as elsewhere, by the harsh treatment which the Latins meted out to the Greeks; and by the rivalries of the two hierarchies,[103] and the two communions. In 1489 the Venetians came into possession of the island. Their treatment of its inhabitants was harsher still; and the islanders welcomed with relief the Turkish conquerors.[104]

(iii.) But, under the Turkish domination,[105] 1571—1878, they found themselves worse off than ever. The Turks began with bloodshed. They massacred 20,000 of the inhabitants,[106] at the siege of Nikosia, 9th September, 1570; and, after the capitulation of Famagusta, 1st August, 1571, they took its heroic defender, Marc' Antonio Bragadino and flayed him alive.[107] They showed no consideration to the Latin hierarchy: but they gave favourable terms to the Orthodox. For they granted them free enjoyment of their religion, with the undisturbed possession of their churches; the right of ransoming monasteries and churchlands, seized by the conquerors; permission to acquire, to hold and to transmit property; and supremacy over all other Christian communities in the island.[108] For two hundred and fifty years these conditions continued. But on the outbreak of the Greek War of Independence, the Turks began to be nervous about their hold on the island: where there were 80,000 Christians to 20,000 Moslems. On a charge of aiding and abetting the rebels, the Turks, in July, 1821, put to death the archbishop of Nikosia, with the three metropolitans of Paphos, Kition (Larnaka) and Kyrenia; and then carried massacre and confiscation throughout the island.[109] But, when "order was thus restored," they allowed the hierarchy to be reconstituted, December, 1821, by the Œcumenical Patriarch:[110] and things went on as before.

(iv.) At last, by the treaty of Berlin, 1878, the Turkish yoke was broken; and, 10th July, Cyprus was incorporated into the British Empire. The Church of Cyprus[111] has now its chief see at Nikosia, and its head has the title of the Most Blessed Archbishop of Nova Justiniana and all Cyprus : and there are three suffragan sees of Paphos, Kition and Kyrenia, all of whose bishops are metropolitans. There are about 900 priests : and a population of 206,000, of whom 158,000 are Orthodox and 48,000 Moslem. On the death of the last archbishop, Sophronius, 1865—†1900, there followed prolonged dissensions over the election of his successor. The bishop of Paphos died soon after him : and the other two bishops, both named Cyril, of Kition and Kyrenia respectively, became the rival candidates for the archbishopric. But to this neither of them could be canonically elected; for lack of the necessary *quorum* in the synod. The contest was sharp : for Cyril of Kition was a Philhellene and had the support of the nationalist party, while Cyril of Kyrenia enjoyed the favour of the British Government. The Œcumenical Patriarch several times endeavoured to mediate : but he was warned off on the ground that he had no authority in an autocephalous church : and, for ten years, the deadlock continued. At last, in January, 1910, it was removed by the appointment of Cyril, bishop of Kition, to the archbishopric; and the two vacant sees of Paphos and Kition were filled. The archbishop then called an assembly to consult together on the subject of drawing up rules by which the Church of Cyprus should hereafter be governed; and it was left to the Holy Synod to appoint a committee and empower it to draw up Canons for the Church of Cyprus. The committee completed and published its work in May, 1914, under the title *Canons of the Most Holy Apostolic Church of Cyprus:* and these, under the authority of the Holy Synod, are now in force. They consist of 138 articles. In the first, it is defined that the Church of Cyprus is governed by the Canons and Traditions of the Holy Orthodox Church. Others treat of the Holy Synod, its governing body : which is composed of the three metropolitans of Paphos,

Kition and Kyrenia, under the presidency of the Archbishop of Nea Justiniana (=Justinianopolis) and all Cyprus. Others make elaborate provision for the due conduct of elections to the archbishopric and to bishoprics.[112]

§ 8. It only remains to notice the Monastery of St. Catherine on Mount Sinai: for, as Cyprus had once some sort of connexion with Antioch, so the monastery was at one time dependent upon Jerusalem and is now an autocephalous church.[113] Sinai was a place of pilgrimage since the fourth century; and the Monastery of St. Catherine became very rich, with as many as fourteen *metochia* or daughter-houses in various parts of the Orthodox world. Since the tenth century the Hegumen (abbot) has held the diocese of Pharan (now extinct) in Egypt, has always been in episcopal orders, and has borne the title of Archbishop of Mt. Sinai. Thus he was at one time dependent upon the Patriarch of Alexandria; but also upon the Patriarch of Jerusalem, by whom he has always been consecrated. But chiefly because of his distance from other centres, he succeeded, after long disputes, in obtaining his independence of any other authority, 1575—1782. From that time the Monastery and its dependencies have had the rank of an autocephalous church. The Archbishop-abbot is elected by the Convent of St. Catherine and its daughter-house at Cairo where he lives. His authority is limited by the council of monks who share in the government of his church: but he owns no superior save Christ and the Seven Œcumenical Councils.

CHAPTER XIII.

THE CHURCHES OF THE BALKAN PENINSULA:
(I.) BULGARIA.
(II.) JUGOSLAVIA.

CHAPTER XIII.

THE CHURCHES OF THE BALKAN PENINSULA:
I. BULGARIA. II. JUGOSLAVIA.

THE Churches of the Balkan Peninsula may occupy our attention next after those of the Four Eastern Patriarchates, and their offshoots. They are the Churches of Bulgaria, Jugoslavia, Rumania and Greece. As part of the Œcumenical Patriarchate they all fell, with it, under the yoke of the Turk; and it is convenient to take them together and in this order, because it was in this order that their several countries began to emerge into nationality in conflict with the ruling power at Constantinople, whether Roman or Turk.

I. BULGARIA.[1]

It was in the last quarter of the seventh century that the Bulgars settled in Mœsia. So we learn from Nicephorus, Patriarch of Constantinople, 806—†15, in his *Breviarium*[2] which covers the history of 602—709. They were a Finnish, or Tartar, race who found the country which they occupied peopled by Slavs; and in time adopted their language. The country lay between the Danube and the Balkans: and corresponds roughly to the Bulgaria which attained its independence at the Treaty of Berlin, 1878. There are seven periods distinguishable in the history of its people.

§ 1. The first extends from the settlement of the Bulgars to their conversion, 679—864. It is mainly taken up with campaigns against the Roman Empire, then ruled by the Isaurian dynasty, 717—867. At first, their hostility was not very formidable: for the Bulgarian monarchy was elective, and their strength was wasted in civil war. But with the accession of the Sublime Khan Krum, 802—†14, it became more dangerous. He succeeded in establishing an hereditary monarchy: and from his capital at Pliska, to the N.E. of Shumla, his rule extended north of the Danube into what is now Rumania and perhaps even into Transylvania.³ But his ambition was to extend it, in the opposite direction, into Macedonia; and this brought him into rivalry with the Romans—fortunately, for him, at the time of the Second Anarchy, 802—20, in the Empire. Sardica (Sofia) was at that time the outpost of the Empire towards Macedonia: and Krum took it, 809. The Emperor Nicephorus I., 802—†11, perceived the peril: and advanced to meet him. But Krum defeated and slew him, 811. It was a dreadful disaster: for never since Valens fell before the Goths at Adrianople, 378, had a Roman Emperor perished on the field. Krum followed up his victory by the defeat of Michael I. (Rhangabe), 811—†3, at Versinicia, near Adrianople, 813: and advanced to the siege of Constantinople, just as eleven hundred years later the Bulgars appeared before the lines of Chataldja. But he was driven off, and completely defeated at Mesembria by Leo V., 813—†20: and there ensued a thirty years peace, 820—50. Bulgaria and the Empire confronted each other in stale-mate: and the frontier between them was marked by a rampart and trench, known as the Great Fence, which ran from Develtus to a fortress between Adrianople and Philippopolis, and thence turned northwards towards the Balkans.

Toward the end of this truce, the Western Empire advanced its borders as far south as Croatia: and the Bulgars, under their King Boris I., 852—88 (†907) became a power worth cultivating. Boris allied himself with Rostislav, Prince of Moravia, and took arms, for Slav against Teuton, against Lewis the German, 843—†76. But, when Carloman, King of Bavaria and son of Lewis, rebelled against his father and was supported by Rostislav, Boris changed sides and stood by Lewis, 862: and thus was concerted an alliance between Germans and Bulgars which anticipated their alliance in the Great War. Rostislav was now caught between two fires: and sent for help to Constantinople. It was readily given: for the Emperor Michael III., 842—†67, was not unwilling to aid in the destruction of a dangerous neighbour; and he also feared that the Bulgars, by their alliance with the Germans, would be drawn into the orbit of Latin Christendom. This would be to reverse the policy of the Emperor Leo III., 717—†41 : for not much more than a century earlier, he had taken Eastern Illyricum from the Latins, and transferred it, from being a papal vicariate under the archbishop of Thessalonica, to the Patriarchate of Constantinople.[4] Michael felt that it would be intolerable to have Latin Christendom so near to Constantinople as Sofia : and determined to coerce Bulgaria. He invaded the country, and imposed terms on Boris : (1) that he should become a convert to Christianity, and receive it from the Greeks and not from the Latins; (2) that his kingdom should submit to the spiritual authority of Constantinople; and (3) that he should withdraw from the alliance with Lewis. The treaty was concluded, 864; and Boris was baptised with Michael for his godfather. After some resistance, he succeeded in compelling his subjects to receive baptism also.

The conversion of the Bulgars was followed by the organisation of their Church.[5] It was the work of the Patriarch Photius, 857—67; a learned but masterful prelate, who was at this time engaged in a controversy with the equally masterful Pope Nicholas I., 858—†67. Photius declined[6] to let Boris have an archbishop for his country; for it was part of Byzantine policy to keep church and nation in dependence upon Constantinople. Boris, therefore, turned for satisfaction to the Pope. He, too, made no response to the request for an archbishop : but he claimed that the Bulgarians, having settled in Eastern Illyricum, belonged to his Patriarchate, and sent two bishops, Paul and Formosus, as his legates, with instructions to attach them to the Western Church. The legates carried the *Responsa ad Bulgaros* of 13th November, 866, in reply to questions they had addressed to him. But the Patriarch of Constantinople was on the watch : and in Lent, 867, he denounced the intrusion of the Latins[7] into a country claimed by the Eastern Empire and attached to the Patriarchate of Constantinople. By the murder of the Emperor Michael and the accession of the Macedonian

Y

Dynasty, Photius was deposed in favour of Ignatius. But Ignatius, as Patriarch, 867—78, proved as resolute to assert his jurisdiction over Bulgaria. At the Council of Constantinople, 869, which East and West unite to reckon as the Eighth Œcumenical Council, it was adjudged not only that Eastern Illyricum had been transferred from West to East but also that the clergy at the time of the conversion of Bulgaria had been Greeks; and that on both these grounds the country ought to belong to the Patriarchate of Constantinople.[8] Ignatius then consecrated the Moravian Gorazd, a disciple of St. Methodius, as archbishop of Bulgaria:[9] and dispatched him, 870, with ten bishops to inaugurate the administration of the Church in that country. Boris, in return, sent his son Simeon to be educated at Constantinople. Churches and monasteries were founded by Clement, the fellow-countryman and co-disciple of Gorazd, who succeeded him as archbishop,[10] †916: and both Slavonic books and the Slavonic liturgy were introduced into Bulgaria, 870—86.

§ 2. The second period is that of the *First Bulgarian Empire*, 893—972, contemporary with the Macedonian Dynasty, 867—1025. The Bulgars under Boris's younger son Simeon, 893—†927, the first of the sovereigns to assume the title Tsar, resumed the struggle with the Romans and met them on equal terms. In 913 they appeared before Constantinople, and next year they captured Adrianople. In 917 they inflicted a crushing defeat on the Romans at Anchialus: and the Tsar Simeon, in a personal conference with the Emperor, imposed, 923, conditions of peace. Among them was a subsidy, and an independent archbishopric for the Church of Bulgaria. The archbishopric had its seat at the new capital, Great Prêslav. Simeon was succeeded by his second son, Peter, 927—†69. He married Maria, the grand-daughter of the Byzantine co-Emperor Romanus I. (Lecapenus), 919—44, and so secured the recognition both of his title Tsar and of the autonomy of the Bulgarian Church. But he failed to maintain his power: and Bulgaria, during his reign, was weakened partly by the revolt of the Serbs, who, 931, recovered the independence of which they had been deprived, 924, by his father, and partly by the spread of the Bogomil heresy. These misfortunes were accentuated, 963, by the revolt of Shishman, a noble of Tirnovo, who succeeded in detaching Western Bulgaria, including Vidin and Sofia, and in establishing a rival kingdom there.

§ 3. With these events, began the third period in the history of Bulgaria, when the Romans recovered their supremacy, 963—†1186. It was the epoch of the great Macedonian Emperors, Nicephorus II. (Phocas), 963—†9, John I. (Tzimisces), 969—†76, and Basil II. (Bulgaroctonus), 976—†1025 : when the power of the Eastern Roman Empire reached its zenith. In 966, the Emperor Nicephorus, taking advantage of the decline of Bulgaria, refused the tribute imposed by the Tsar Simeon; made alliance with Sviatoslav, Grand Duke of Kiev, 945—†73, and attacked the Bulgars. Sviatoslav was called off to deal with the Patzinaks; but, attracted by the riches and fertility of Bulgaria, he returned—this time on his own account. He captured Great Prêslav, the Bulgarian capital, and the Tsar, Boris II., 969—†76 and then, crossing the Balkans, he took Philippopolis, 970; and challenged the Romans either to pay him compensation or to quit Constantinople. The warlike Emperor, John I., immediately took up the challenge; for the security of his northern frontier. He completely defeated the Russians at Arcadiopolis (now Lüle Burgas), 971; and, marching north, besieged them in Great Prêslav, whence he released the Tsar; and, after besieging Sviatoslav in Dorostolum (Silistria), compelled him to evacuate the country. John then made peace with the Russians, July, 972 : and, at the same time, settled accounts with Bulgaria, by dividing it into two. Eastern Bulgaria was incorporated into the Empire : and lost its ecclesiastical independence. Western Bulgaria, with its capital at Sofia, became the kingdom of the House of Shishman, under the Tsar Samuel, 976—†1014. He removed the capital to Ochrida, 981, which thus became the seat of an autocephalous archbishopric;[11] and for some years, 985—96, he recovered ground in the struggle with the Romans. But his fortunes declined in the last twenty years of the long drawn out conflict until, in 1014, the Emperor Basil II. defeated him at Seres and, in 1016, took his capital Ochrida. Western Bulgaria thus came to an end, and remained a Byzantine province, 1018— 1186. The archbishopric of Ochrida lost its independence; and was handed over to be ruled by a Greek archbishop and clergy.[12] In charters of the year 1020, Basil II. confirmed the status of the archbishop, and his residence at Ochrida. " He maintained intact the rights and area of its jurisdiction, as it had been in the times both of Peter and Samuel : which, therefore, included thirty[13] bishoprics and towns, such as Ochrida, Kastoria, Monastir and Skoplje (Usküb) in Macedonia; Sofia and Vidin in Old Bulgaria; Belgrade, Nish, Prizren and Rasa in what is now Jugoslavia; Canina (above Avlona), Cheimarra Butrinto, and Joannina in South Albania and Northern Epirus; and Stagi (the modern Kalabaka) in Thessaly. . . In 1020 these thirty bishoprics contained 685 ecclesiastics and 655 serfs."[14]

§ 4. During the fourth period of their history, the Bulgars recovered from their overthrow by Basil II. (Bulgaroctonus), and established the *Second Bulgarian Empire*, 1186—1241. It reached the height of its power under John Asan II., 1218—†41; who knew how to profit by the rivalry between the Greek Emperors at Nicæa and the Latin at Constantinople, 1204—61. The discontent of the Bulgars under the Roman yoke broke out occasionally as in 1040 and 1073 : but they failed to recover their independence till 1186. Angered by the taxes which Isaac II. (Angelus), 1185—†95, imposed to furnish his wedding festivities, they rose in rebellion under the leadership of Peter and John Asan. They assembled in the church of St. Demetrius at Tirnovo; and, while Peter assumed the title of " Tsar of the Bulgars and the Greeks," Basil was proclaimed as archbishop. The younger brother, however, acquired the first place : and reigned as John I., 1186—96. He secured the support of the Serbs under Stephen Nemanja in 1188, and of the crusaders under Frederick Barbarossa in 1189; and, advancing to Sofia, his forces took the city, carried off the relics of their national patron, St. John of Rila, and returned with them in triumph to Tirnovo. But both John and Peter were assassinated; and the government fell into the hands of a third brother, Kalojan, 1197—1207. He extended his dominions at the expense of his neighbours. From the Romans he took Varna to the N.E.; and, making the most of a fratricidal war between the two sons of Nemanja, he seized from the Serbs Nish, to the N.W. and Skoplje (Usküb), to the S.W. Bulgaria thus became the leading power of the Balkans. But it was menaced by Hungary on the north and by the Latin Emperors of Constantinople to the south. Kalojan, therefore, thought it prudent to approach Innocent III. for help. He begged the Pope to send him an imperial diadem like that of his predecessors the Tsars Peter and Samuel and a patriarch.[15] But Innocent put off the king with a royal crown, and his archbishop with the title of primate,[16] though he also provided the latter with two metropolitans[17] and four bishops[18] to complete the Bulgarian hierarchy. The Latins at Constantinople, less prudent than the Pope, made an enemy of Kalojan instead of a friend; and he avenged himself, 14th April, 1205, at Adrianople, where he defeated and brutally murdered the first Latin Emperor, Baldwin I., 1204—†5. But he did not long survive his victim: for he was assassinated by his nephew Boril, 1207; and, after a decade of turmoil, the kingdom passed to his son John Asan II., 1218—†41. He was an enlightened ruler who encouraged agriculture and commerce; and built schools and monasteries. But he was also a successful warrior. At the battle of Klokotinitza, 1230, he overthrew the vigorous Greek Empire of Thessalonica which had risen on the ruins of the Latin kingdom of that name: and an inscription in the Church of the Forty Martyrs at Tirnovo records how he had " captured the Emperor Theodore," 1223—30, " and conquered all the lands from Adrianople to Durazzo." The alliance of John Asan II. was now worth having; and, as the price of his aid against the Latin

Emperors of Constantinople, he obtained from the Emperor John III. (Ducas Vatatzes), 1222—†54, and the Œcumenical Patriarch, the recognition of the autonomy of the Bulgarian Church and the revival of its autocephalous archbishopric, 1236. Its seat had formerly been at Ochrida; but this city had been included in the dominions of Theodore, his defeated rival. John Asan II. now obtained the transference of the archbishopric to Tirnovo: and here it remained till the Turkish conquest once more placed the Church of the Bulgars under the control of the Greeks. But the alliance between John Asan II. and the Emperor John III. was not to last. They were defeated, 1236, in their joint assault upon Constantinople; and the Tsar, who had no wish to see the Greeks re-established there, began to draw off. He spent the rest of his days in playing fast and loose with one ally after another, till his death in 1241. With the third of his successors, who was murdered by one of his nobles, the dynasty became extinct, 1258. Bulgaria was reduced to a shadow of its former greatness.

§ 5. The fifth period of its history may be reckoned from 1258—1393; and is the record of its disappearance before the Serb and the Turk. Early in the fourteenth century the Serbs entered upon a period of expansion under Stephen Uros II., 1281—†1320; and the Turks advanced to the N.W. of Asia Minor, where they took Brusa, 1326, and made it their capital. These events were menacing alike to the Bulgars and the Romans. Accordingly, in 1326, Michael (Shishman I.), 1323—†30, the founder of the last Bulgarian dynasty, made a compact with the Emperor Andronicus III., 1328—†41. He promised to help him in the civil war against his grandfather; and Andronicus in return undertook to assist Michael against the Serbs. But in 1330 the Serbs, under the greatest of their sovereigns, Stephen Dushan, 1331—†55, inflicted a crushing defeat upon the allies at Velbuzd (Küstendil) in Macedonia; and set up a Serbian Empire in the Balkans, stretching from the Danube to the gulf of Arta, and including Bulgaria as a vassal state, 1331—65. Meanwhile, the Turks had crossed, 1356, from Asia into

Europe: where Adrianople became their capital, 1361. Five years later Bulgaria was invaded by the Hungarians. They called in the Turk: and this was the beginning of the end. For, in 1382, the Turks took Sofia; and, after extinguishing the Serbs at Kosovo, 1389, in 1393 they destroyed the Bulgarian capital Tirnovo, and exiled its last patriarch Euthymius. Next year, the Œcumenical Patriarch temporarily entrusted the metropolitan of Moldavia with the administration of the Church of Bulgaria: and, when in 1398, Vidin opened its gates to the Turk, there was an end for 500 years both of national independence and of ecclesiastical autonomy.

§ 6. From 1393—1767 extends the sixth period of Bulgarian history. It can be summed up in a sentence. The control of the Bulgarian State passed to the Turks, and of the Bulgarian Church to the Greeks. For the Bulgars were placed ecclesiastically under the Græco-Bulgarian archbishopric of Ochrida; and as all ecclesiastical posts had to be bought of the Turks, the higher preferments fell into the hands of the Phanariot Greeks, since they alone had the money to pay for them. At last, on 16th January, 1767, the autocephalous archbishopric was abolished. The religious control of the Greeks became as complete as the political control of the Turks. Greek became the language used in church and school: and the mutual hatred of Greek and Bulgar became even more intense than their common detestation of the Turk.

§ 7. In the seventh and last period of their history, since 1767, the Bulgars recovered their independence. About that time Russia had begun to exert a strong influence in the Balkans; and the Slavonic peoples subject to Turkey became aware of support in reserve. Between 1800—50 an intellectual renaissance took place in Bulgaria, and with it came the recovery of national ideals. " Open schools," it was urged, " before building convents; and write manuals of literature before teaching the catechism." So schools were opened to inculcate the new aspirations; and printing presses were set up to promote them: in 1839 at Thessalonica, in 1840 at Smyrna, and in 1843 at Constantinople. After the Crimean War, the

Porte, under pressure, promised religious reforms tending to the appointment of Bulgarians to bishoprics and to the recognition of the Bulgarian language in church and school. But the promises remained unfulfilled. Thereupon the Bulgars took matters into their own hands. They were led by Hilarion, bishop of Macariopolis, and Auxentius, bishop of Durazzo. On Easter Day, 3rd April, 1860, Hilarion omitted the name of the Œcumenical Patriarch in the Liturgy. In the autumn, he and his friends refused to recognise Joachim II. as Œcumenical Patriarch, on his accession, 4th October, 1860; demanding, instead, a national hierarchy independent of Constantinople. The immediate reply of the Patriarch was their excommunication, 4th February, 1861, by a Synod of Constantinople consisting of the Four Orthodox Patriarchs with twenty-one metropolitans and bishops. But Russia, afraid of a Bulgar movement which then sprang up for re-union with Rome, put pressure on the Œcumenical Patriarch; and induced him to modify his unyielding rigour. Accordingly, 9th March, 1861, Joachim offered a compromise, in fifteen articles. The Bulgars declined it in a document of eight. Thereupon, the Patriarch, who still enjoyed civil authority over his *millet*, had three of the leaders—Hilarion, Auxentius and Païsius of Philippopolis—imprisoned in different towns of Asia Minor.

The ecclesiastical situation was now so strained that the Porte thought it time to step in. On 30th July, 1862, with a view to reconciliation, it appointed a commission to examine the eight articles: but, owing to the opposition of the Patriarch, the commission had no result. A year later, Joachim II. was deposed, 21st July, 1863; and replaced, 2nd October, by Sophronius III., 1863—6. No progress, however, was made under his rule. A conference, held in July, between equal numbers of Greek and Bulgar bishops led to no result; save that the Bulgars pressed their claims further. They began by refusing either to recognise Greek bishops or clergy on their appointment, or to pay ecclesiastical dues; and they next proceeded to expel the Greek bishops of Vidin, Rustchuk,

Tirnovo and Monastir. The Turks, meanwhile, for fear of Russia, refrained from lending the support of the secular arm to Greek nominees: but they got rid of Sophronius III., 16th December, 1866, and put into his place Gregory VI., 1867—71, who had been Patriarch, 1835—40, in the hope that he might find a way out of the deadlock. In August, 1867, Gregory made his attempt by submitting to the Grand Vizier a proposal to appoint an Exarch of all Bulgaria: who should live in Constantinople but exercise authority within the vilayet of the Danube, or Old Bulgaria. But this was too restricted a sphere to please the Bulgarian nationalists: who also wanted their Exarch to live in Bulgaria. The Turks, on the other hand, thought an Exarch of Bulgaria too reminiscent of the ancient Bulgarian Empire; and, if there was to be an Exarch at all, desired that he should live at Constantinople, under the eye of their government and not far away from its control in the heart of Bulgaria. In the end, the Œcumenical Patriarchate repudiated the plans both of Turks and Bulgarians; and stood upon its rights, though professing a readiness to have the question of its relations to the Church of Bulgaria determined by an Œcumenical Council of the Four Patriarchates. This proposal was welcomed by the Bulgars: but rejected by Russia, for she would then have no say in the matter. The Russian objection was fatal to the scheme; and the Porte fell back, 1869, on an attempt to procure an arrangement between the parties. They were to be represented at a conference by three Greek and three Bulgar bishops. But they came to no decision: and, at last, the Sultan decided the dispute over the heads of the parties to it. By a Firman, of 11th March, 1870, he set up a Bulgarian Exarchate,[19] independent of the Œcumenical Patriarch. The Exarch was to have authority over all the bishops of Bulgaria itself, and over all Bulgarians beyond its boundaries. Gregory VI. replied, 20th June, by a dignified protest, and then sent in his resignation. He was succeeded, 17th September, 1871, by Anthimus VI., reinstated for the third time. In 1872, Anthimus, bishop of Vidin, was elected the first Exarch: and on the Feast of the Slavonic Apostles, St. Cyril and St. Methodius, 23rd May, he proclaimed the independence of the Church of Bulgaria. Anthimus VI. retorted by excommunicating the Bulgarians for Philetism, in a Council held at Constantinople, 10th, 24th and 28th September: but, as this decision was not approved by the Patriarch of Jerusalem, nor by the Churches of Russia, Rumania and Serbia, it had no practical effect. Thus, at the cost of a breach with the Œcumenical Patriarchate, though maintaining communion with the rest of Orthodox Christendom, the Bulgarians recovered the independence of their Church: and that autonomy of which the Greeks robbed them when, with the aid of the Turks, they absorbed the archbishopric of Tirnovo, 1393, and of Ochrida, 1767, they won back from the Greeks in 1870, the Turks assisting again.

Ecclesiastical autonomy led on to national independence. In 1878, by the Treaty of Berlin, Northern Bulgaria, between the Danube and the Balkans, received the status of an autonomous Principality: which, 28th April, 1879, legalised Orthodoxy as its official religion. Then Eastern Roumelia, in 1885, was joined to Northern Bulgaria and recognised as autonomous. At the same time, Prince Alexander of Battenberg, who had been Prince of Bulgaria since 1879, abdicated, 1885: and made way for Ferdinand of Coburg, who was elected, 7th July, 1887, and confirmed by the Sultan. Ungrateful to Russia, its liberator, in the Russo-Turkish War of 1877—8, Bulgaria, under his guidance, drifted away towards Austria and Germany. On 16th March, 1896, Ferdinand obtained the status of an independent prince under the suzerainty of the Sultan. But, after the revolution of the " Young Turks " in July, 1908, he renounced the Sultan's suzerainty, and proclaimed himself Tsar. In co-operation with M. Venizelos, on 30th September, 1912, he formed the Balkan League between Serbia, Montenegro, Greece and Bulgaria, with a view to joint action against the Turks. In the First Balkan War, 1912—3, the allies defeated the Turks at Kumanovo, 23rd October, 1912;

The Churches of the Balkan Peninsula 331

captured Adrianople, 26th March, 1913; and advanced to the lines of Chataldja before Constantinople. Then they quarrelled over the spoil. Anticipating a treacherous attack from Bulgaria, Serbia and Greece entered into a convention, 2nd June, 1913, each to assist the other in case of need. The need arose, and the Bulgarian attack was delivered. But in this Second Balkan War, the Bulgarians, on 1st July, 1913, were badly beaten by the Serbs on the Bregalnitza, a tributary of the Vardar; and forced to accept the disadvantageous peace of Bucharest, 10th August, 1913. The Bulgars got nothing: but were thrown into the hands of Germany and Austria, who were disgusted not only at seeing their two protégés—first Turkey and then Bulgaria—destroyed in turn, but also at finding their own hopes of reaching the East, *via* Salonika or Constantinople, completely shattered by the victorious Serbs. They sought revenge by an attempt at the annihilation of Serbia which led to their own annihilation in the Great War of 1914-18. Bulgaria was the first of the satellites of Germany to give in. She lost the Dobrudsha to the Rumanians, and Strumitza to the Serbs. But she retained her independence as a nation, and the Church of Bulgaria remains, as in 1870, an autonomous Church out of communion with the Œcumenical Patriarch, but in communion with the rest of the Orthodox world. The Exarch resides at Ortakeuï on the Bosporus: and claims jurisdiction over all Bulgars, whether domiciled in Bulgaria or not. He employs a co-adjutor, one of his own suffragans, to look after his own see. Of such sees[20] there are eleven in Bulgaria itself, all ruled by metropolitans: (1) Lovetch, (2) Philippopoli, (3) Rustchuk, (4) Samokof, (5) Sliven, (6) Sofia, (7) Stara-zagora, (8) Tirnovo, (9) Varna, (10) Vidin, (11) Vratza: though Lovetch and Samokof are to disappear shortly. There are also twenty-one sees in cities outside Bulgaria for the benefit of Bulgarian flocks. Seven of these are in Macedonia, and are provided with bishops: (1) Usküb, (2) Ochrida, (3) Veles, (4) Nevrokop, (5) Monastir, (6) Strumitza, (7) Dibra. The remainder are not all as fully organised: viz., (8) Castoria,

(9) Drama, (10) Melnik, (11) Moglena, (12) Polianino, (13) Salonika, (14) Seres, (15) Vodena, (16) Adrianople, (17) Demotica, (18) Enos, (19) Maronia, (20) Ortakeuï, (21) Xanthi. The clergy are paid, in part by the State, and in part by fees: 1 franc for a baptism, 15 for a marriage, 6 for a funeral, and so forth. There are two seminaries: one at Sofia for Bulgaria, and another at Constantinople for Macedonia and Thrace. But they contain only 280 students, and the level of their education is low. What wonder if, with a clergy insufficient in numbers and poorly educated, the Church has but little influence among the masses and is treated by the official world with an indifference bordering on contempt.

II. JUGOSLAVIA.

Jugoslavia[21] is the name now given to the lands of the southern Slavs, included in " the kingdom of the Serbs, Croats and Slovenes." " It came into being in the closing months of 1918 as a result of the collapse of Austria-Hungary and the voluntary union of its Jugoslav territories with the former kingdoms of Serbia and Montenegro; the triune kingdom of Croatia-Slavonia-Dalmatia (of which the first two enjoyed special autonomy under the kingdom of Hungary . . . while the third was one of the seventeen provinces of the Austrian Empire); parts of the Banat, Bacska and Baranja (which were portions of Hungary proper); Slovenia (consisting of portions of Carniola, Carinthia, Styria and Istria); and Bosnia-Herzegovina (which was from 1878—1918 under the joint administration of Austria and Hungary)."[22] The population of Jugoslavia amounted at the census of 1921, to 12,162,000. In religion, while Croats and Slovenes are Roman Catholic, Serbs and Montenegrins are Orthodox; and within the Patriarchate of Belgrade are now included five churches—Serbia, which became independent, 1831; Montenegro (or Czernagora), in 1763; Carlowitz, for the Banat, Croatia and Slavonia, in 1765; Bosnia, 1880; and Herzegovina, 1880. It is this group of churches whose fortunes we have now to trace in connexion with the history of Serbia:[23] a history which, like that of Bulgaria, falls naturally into seven periods.

§ 8. The first extends from the sixth to the twelfth century, and may be described as the period of the settlement followed by foreign domination. We have no contemporary records of the settlement of the Slavs in the N.W. of the Balkan peninsula, i.e., in Serbia, Croatia and Dalmatia. The earliest account is contained in the *De administrando Imperio*,[24] written 948—52, by the Emperor Constantine VII. (Porphyrogenitus), 912—†59. He accepts the tradition that the Slavs first occupied these lands in the reign of Heraclius, 610—†41. But their penetration had already begun in the sixth century; and " what occurred under Heraclius was simply the recognition by the Imperial Government of a *fait accompli.*"[25] It was further recognised in the legislation of the Isaurian Emperor Leo III., 717—†41 : for Slavonic settlements raised an agrarian question with which he dealt in his Agrarian Code, and Slavonic piracy demanded increased securities for maritime trade with which he dealt in his Navigation Code.[26] If we know nothing precise as to the settlement of the Slavs, we are in equal uncertainty as to the incidents of their conversion.[27] It is commonly assigned to the brothers St. Cyril, †869, and St. Methodius, †885 : but the field of their personal activity was Moravia, 863—8. Methodius, on the death of his brother, went to Blatno on the Platten See in Pannonia (where Kocel, prince of the Slavs of those regions, held his court)—an ancient see which was now reconstituted. Here he exercised missionary influence on the neighbouring Croatia. But it was the indirect influence of Cyril that effected the conversion. By framing a Slavonic alphabet and translating the Gospels into Slavonic, he affected, as no other single man has ever done, every Slavonic people. Within a century, Serbia, Croatia and Dalmatia were not only Christian, but Orthodox lands : for the Eastern form of Christianity was proclaimed as the State-religion by Prince Mutimir, †891.

This Prince was one of the chiefs of the various Serbian districts or *zupe,* who were thence styled *zupans.*

There was little cohesion among them, beyond the fact that they acknowledged the more or less nominal overlordship of one of their number as *Veliki Zupan*, or Great Chief. The result was that the Serbs and other Slavs lived under foreign domination, alternately Byzantine and Bulgar. The Byzantine supremacy was effective under Basil I., 867—†86, the founder of the Macedonian dynasty; again, under his successors, John I. (Tzimisces), 969—†76, and Basil II. (Bulgaroctonus), 976—†1025; and once more under Manuel I. (Comnenus), 1143—†80. The Bulgar supremacy became effective, though only over Eastern and Southern Serbs, during the First Bulgarian Empire of the Tsar Simeon, 893—927; then, fifty years later, under the Tsar Samuel, 976—†1014; and, finally, during the Second Bulgarian Empire which reached its zenith under John Asan II., 1218—†41. A similar subjection to extraneous authority is reflected in the religious situation. For, after the conquests of Basil II., i.e., from about the middle of the eleventh century, all the Serb lands (except Dalmatia, Croatia and W. Bosnia, which were Latin), including E. Bosnia and Hum (since 1448 called Herzegovina), were not only Orthodox but completely under the control of the Greek hierarchy. But the wealth, the order and the Hellenism of the Church thus administered proved uncongenial to the Serbs; and, consequently, great progress was made by the Bogomils in Serb as in Bulgar lands.

§ 9. The second period, 1168—1371, covers some two hundred years of independence, under the Nemanja dynasty. About 1200 the times were favourable to Slav freedom; owing, first, to the decline of the Empire during the Latin rule at Constantinople, 1204—61, and, then, to the collapse of the Second Bulgarian Empire after the reign of John Asan II., 1218—†41. The Western lands of Bulgaria fell, on his death, to the Serbs: but, on the other hand, Hungary, which had been converted to Christianity under St. Stephen, 996—†1038, was becoming a menace to Serbia. The Hungarians, in 1102, absorbed the Serb territories of Croatia, Slavonia and the interior of Dalmatia, and exercised a supremacy over

Bosnia. This, however, was set off by the friendliness of Venice. For Venice was a sea-power with no interests running counter to those of a land-power like Serbia: and trade sprang up to the benefit of both countries through the Serbian port of Dubrovnik, better known to the West as Ragusa. The founder of the dynasty, which took advantage of this favourable turn of events to establish its power, was Stephen Nemanja, 1151—95. He extended Serbian territories at the expense of the Roman Empire. At home, he retained the traditional title of Veliki Zupan, or Great Chief, but converted the aristocratic federation, as far as possible, into a single state: whose head, in the next generation, took the more appropriate name of King. Further, in order to strengthen his position with the majority of his people, he embraced the Orthodox Faith: and endeavoured to promote ecclesiastical no less than political unity. For this purpose, he persecuted the Bogomils who took refuge in Bosnia: where, however, they renounced their errors, 8th April, 1203, in the presence of a legate of Pope Innocent III. Nemanja, at length, at the instance of his youngest son, St. Sava, retired to Mount Athos and abdicated in favour of his second son, Stephen, leaving to him, as Great Zupan, the bulk of his dominions: and to his eldest son, Vukan, his native Zeta, or Montenegro. When Stephen Nemanjic, 1195—1228, succeeded, a quarrel broke out between the King and his elder brother, who felt that the throne ought to have been his. The quarrel was immediately turned to account by Kalojan, 1197—†1207, who gave himself out as "Tsar of the Bulgars and Wallachs," and proceeded to extend his dominions at the expense of his neighbours. He seized a large part of Eastern Serbia, including Belgrade to the north, Nish in the centre, with Prizren and Skoplje (Usküb) to the south: while Serbia lay dismembered, owing to the disunion of her reigning family, and the intervention of foreigners which it produced. But in 1207, St. Sava returned from Mount Athos to Serbia and managed to effect a reconciliation. He persuaded Vukan to recognise the right of Stephen to the position of

Great Zupan: and, after Serbia had been proclaimed a kingdom, 1217, he journeyed to Nicæa and obtained, with the consent of the Emperor Theodore I. (Lascaris), 1206 —†22, the recognition by the Œcumenical Patriarch of the autonomy of the Church of Serbia, and his own consecration, 1219, as " Archbishop of all the Serbian lands." On his return home, St. Sava crowned his brother Stephen, 1222, in the church of Zica, which the " first-crowned " King and his eldest son had founded, and which remains to this day the coronation church of the Serbian kings. On the death of Stephen, his son Radoslav, 1228—34, succeeded. But he turned out a weakling; and resigned in favour of his more virile brother, Vladislav, 1234—43, who was also crowned, though with reluctance, by St. Sava. Two years later St. Sava died, 1236. He is revered by the Serbs as the founder both of their first dynasty and of their national church: and he became the Patron Saint of Serbia.

The century which followed the death of St. Sava saw a steady rise in the fortunes of Serbia. An economic development and a strengthening of the internal administration marked the reign of Stephen Uros I., 1240—72, the son of Vladislav: but he was deposed by Stephen Dragutin, 1272—81, and he, in turn, by Stephen Uros II. (Milutin), 1281—†1320. Milutin exploited the mineral wealth of his country: extended his kingdom northward so as to make the Danube and the Save its boundaries in that direction, and gained a sea-board on the Adriatic. He was succeeded by his son Stephen Uros III. (Decanski), 1321—31, who won the hegemony of the Balkans at the battle of Velbuzd (Küstendil), 1330, where he defeated a league of Bulgars and Romans against him. But he was deposed by his son Stephen Uros IV. (Dushan) who became King in 1331. Between 1331—44 Dushan subjugated all Macedonia, Albania, Thessaly and Epirus; maintained good relations with Ragusa and Hungary, and, by alliance with a Bulgarian princess, succeeded in keeping Bulgaria a Serbian dependency. In 1345 he proclaimed his country an Empire. Its boundaries stretched from the Danube on the north to the gulf of

THE LATE PATRIARCH TIKHON.

See p. 414.]

Arta and the channel of Eubœa on the south; and in 1346 he had himself crowned "Emperor of the Serbs, Bulgars and Greeks." At the Synod of Seres, 1351, he procured the elevation of the Serbian archbishopric into a Patriarchate with its seat at Pec (Ipek): whereupon the Church of Serbia lay under the anathema of the Œcumenical Patriarch till 1375. Dushan was a legislator as well as a military commander; and his Code of 1349—54 bestowed special privileges on the nobles and the Orthodox Church, while Skoplje (Usküb) became his capital. But, as so often in the history of the Balkan States, the rise of an Empire depended upon one man; and chaos supervened at the death of Dushan, †1355.

§ 10. His death was followed by the third epoch of Serbian history, 1371—1459, which is marked by the extinction of the independence of the Serbs. For in 1354 the Turks landed in Gallipoli. They advanced to Adrianople, 1361; and ten years later, by the defeat of the Serbs on the Maritsa, brought the dynasty of Nemanja to an end. In the face of these disasters, the Orthodox at last perceived the importance of reconciliation : and in 1375 the Œcumenical Patriarch gave his recognition to the Patriarchate of Pec (Ipek). But the advance of the Turks continued. On the fatal field of Kosovo, 1389, they destroyed the independence of Serbia. After the defeat of the Hungarians at Nicopolis, 1396, and again at Varna, 1444, followed by the overthrow of Constantinople, 1453, they became masters of the whole of Serbia, 1459; of Bosnia, 1463; of Herzegovina, 1478; and of Montenegro, 1496. The Patriarchate of Pec was abolished; and from 1459—1557, it was placed under the archbishopric of Ochrida. The Serbian Church fell once more, by the assistance of the Turks, under the yoke of the Greeks.

§ 11. The fourth period covers three hundred years of Turkish domination, 1496—1796. In 1521 the Turks captured Belgrade from the Magyars; and, after the defeat of Louis II., King of Hungary and Bohemia, at Mohacs, 1526, extended their rule over two-thirds of Hungary. But about the middle of the century, Mohammed Sokoli Pasha, a Serb-Moslem, rose to the office of Grand Vizier. He so used his authority in the interest of his fellow-countrymen that the Church of Serbia, which had been merged in the Græco-Bulgarian archbishopric of Ochrida, recovered its independence. The Patriarchate of Pec (Ipek) was restored 1557. It became the centre for the Serbs of their national life: from which monasteries were restored, books printed and priests educated. In 1571 the Turkish advance suffered its first check from Western Christendom at the naval battle of Lepanto: but the defeat was without effect on land. In 1683 the Turks advanced to Vienna. The Austrians, however, made reprisals, the Serbs assisting. On the Austrian retirement, the Turks took vengeance on the Serbs. So severe was the pressure that in 1691 the Patriarch, Arsenje III., abandoned Pec (Ipek) with large numbers of his flock and settled in Slavonia and Hungary at the invitation of the Emperor Leopold I. The Patriarchate thus fell once more into the hands of the Greeks. Austria, being Roman Catholic, had no real sympathy with the Orthodox Serbs: who now found themselves between the hammer and the anvil, Austria to the north and the Turks to the south. Thus the Serbian Church fell a prey to the Phanariot Greeks. In 1737 they began to deal with it after their usual manner.[28] The Œcumenical Patriarch managed to secure the nomination to the see of Pec (Ipek), and at once put it up to auction. This provoked resentment, and revolts on the part of the Serbs: till in 1766 the Turkish Government stepped in. They abolished both the Archbishopric of Ochrida and the Patriarchate of Pec (Ipek).[29] Serbian bishops and clergy were replaced by Greek. Sees were sold to the highest bidder. Greek was substituted for Slavonic in the service-books. Greek alone was tolerated in church and school: and the Serbs became the victims at once of a grasping hierarchy and of fiscal oppression. Montenegro, indeed, secured its independence, 1796, under its Prince-Bishop, Peter I.: but other Serbian lands lay at the mercy of Turkish officials and Greek ecclesiastics.

§ 12. The fifth period of Serbian history records the

liberation of the country, 1796—1830. It was slow of attainment, owing to the inaccessibility of the country and to its dissensions. There were two revolts, led by Karageorge, 1804—13, and by Obrenovic, 1815—30. But they made little progress: for, as long as Napoleon was not disposed of, it was impossible for Russia to help the Serbs against the Turks. The intervention of Russia, however, became gradually effective: and in 1826 the Turks recognised a Russian protectorate over Serbia, and the Convention of Akerman secured them the right to erect churches, schools and printing presses. The Convention was enforced by the Russian war against the Turks, 1828—9; and, at its conclusion in 1830, Milos Obrenovic became Prince of Serbia, though tributary to the Sultan.

§ 13. His accession ushered in the sixth period, of an independent Serbia, 1830—1903, under the dynasty of Obrenovic. Under Prince Milos, 1817—39, and again, 1858—60, the Church of Serbia[30] obtained its emancipation, 1830, with the Metropolitan of Belgrade for its ecclesiastical head. Milos was followed by Michael Obrenovic III., 1840—2 and 1860—8; an able ruler who was murdered in 1868, soon after the last Turkish soldier had been withdrawn, 1867, from Serbian soil. Then came Milan Obrenovic IV., 1868—89, a lover of pleasure. In his time the Treaty of Berlin, 1878, bestowed complete independence on Serbia and Montenegro; but Austria was to administer Bosnia and Herzegovina, though they were mainly Serb, and to hold the province of Novi-Bazar. This was the ancient Rascia and the cradle of the Serb race; and it was all the more irritating to aspirations for national unity that, as it lay geographically between Serbia and Montenegro, the Austrian occupation of it kept the two kindred countries apart. But in Serbia itself the growing consciousness of nationality and independence received further encouragement. On 1st November, 1879, the autonomy of the Serbian Church was recognised by the Œcumenical Patriarch, and in 1882 Serbia received the status of a kingdom. Zealous for their own independence, they grudged that of their neighbour Bulgaria; and in 1885 they declared war on Bulgaria, recently united as a kingdom, but only to incur the just penalty of a defeat at Slivnitza between Nish and the Bulgarian border. Shortly afterwards, King Milan abdicated, 1889, aware of his unpopularity. He was succeeded by his son Alexander, 1889—†1903: who, with Queen Draga, was foully murdered. The crime was political: for its purpose was to put an end to the Obrenovic dynasty which had become wholly pro-Austrian, and so wholly out of sympathy with the aspirations of Slavdom. These aspirations could only be attained in reliance about the great Slav Empire of Russia, and in the teeth of its rival Austria-Hungary.

§ 14. The last period of Serbian history[31] is that of our own generation: and is concerned with the development of Serbia into Jugoslavia under the dynasty of Karageorge, 1903—24. It began with a movement for Serbian expansion and unity, 1903—8, which naturally excited the hostility of Austria. The movement had a large measure of success in Bosnia, Herzegovina, and Old Serbia, i.e., northern Macedonia: when its prospects became still brighter by the revolution of the "Young Turks" at Constantinople in July, 1908. In October, Ferdinand of Bulgaria renounced the Turkish suzerainty and declared himself Tsar. Austria retaliated by annexing Bosnia and Herzegovina; but foolishly withdrew its garrisons from the *sandjak* of Novi-Bazar, thus leaving the way open between Serbia and Montenegro to make the next move in concert with each other. All the Balkan states were now on the tiptoe of expectation: and, in 1909, an alliance was mooted between Greeks, Bulgars and Serbs for common action, in self-defence against a possibly rejuvenated Turkey. The alliance developed, 30th September, 1912, into the Balkan League. It was concerted by the Tsar Ferdinand and the Greek statesman Venizelos: and the parties to it were Serbia, Greece, Bulgaria and Montenegro. Its immediate result was the First Balkan War, 1912—3. On 8th October, 1912, Montenegro declared war on Turkey, and, 23rd—24th October, the League inflicted a crushing defeat on the

Turks in northern Macedonia at Kumanovo. King Peter of Serbia entered Skoplje (Usküb), the capital of Stephen Dushan in the fourteenth century. On 9th November, the Greeks entered Salonika and, 26th March, 1913, the Serbs and Bulgars captured Adrianople. So rapid were these blows that, on the intervention of the Powers, the Turks admitted their defeat: and, 30th May, by the Treaty of London, a peace was made. At the suggestion of Austria, the treaty contained a provision for an independent Albania. But this deprived Serbia of an important part of the fruits of victory. It cut the Serbs off from the sea, and was resented. As Bulgaria was also to have central Macedonia contingently upon the Serbs acquiring access to the sea, the Bulgars were equally discontented. Two consequences followed. One was the dissolution of the Balkan League, to the entire satisfaction of Germany and Austria: for the continued existence of the League would have blocked the route of Germany to the East, by way whether of Salonika or of Constantinople. The other result was the Second Balkan War, 1913. On 2nd June, a Convention was signed between Greece and Serbia for common action in case of a treacherous attack by their *quondam* ally Bulgaria. Nor was this compact without foresight. On 30th June—1st July, the Bulgars did attack the Serbs; but they were badly beaten at the battle of Bregalnitza. It avenged Slivnitza (1885) on the Bulgars, just as Kumanovo (1912) avenged Kosovo (1389) on the Turks: and it issued in the Treaty of Bucharest, 10th August, 1913. The Treaty had results, some of which were not foreseen. First of all, Serbia retained northern and central Macedonia. The north was Serb; but the Bulgars had also hoped to obtain central Macedonia. Their disappointment alienated the Bulgars; and disposed them, later on, to look for other alliances among the foes of Serbia. Secondly, Serbia and Montenegro joined hands and Skoplje (Usküb), the old capital of Stephen Dushan, became once more a Serbian city. Thus the victories of Kumanovo and Bregalnitza so strengthened the Slav block in the Balkan peninsula as to threaten a final check to German and Austrian plans for a route to the sea and then further onwards to the East. The Central Powers of Europe had only to find a pretext for the attack on Serbia, which led to the Great War: and then to beckon to Bulgaria and Turkey who were both smarting under Serbian successes at their expense. The rest we know—till the armistice of 11th November, 1918. On 6th November, 1921, the Prince Regent of Serbia became King of the Serbs, Croats and Slovenes: and in 1920 Belgrade took rank as a Patriarchate, with four metropolitans and twenty-two bishops under its jurisdiction. The metropolitical sees are those of Belgrade for Serbia, Cetinje for Montenegro, Serajevo for Bosnia, and Skoplje (Usküb) for Macedonia, and the twenty-two bishoprics are those of Nish, Timok, Zica, Sabatz, Shtip, Bitolj, Ochrida, Pasko-Presrend, Pozarevatz, Kotaron, Pec (Ipek), Nixe, Dalmatia, Herzegovina, Banlajuka, Zvornik, Sremski Karlovitz, Bacska, Budimska (Buda-Pesth), Karlovatska, Temesvar and Vratza.[32] In 1921, Mgr. Dmitrye, metropolitan of Belgrade, was enthroned as Patriarch, by friendly arrangement with the Œcumenical Throne. Among the bishops is Dr. Nikolai Velimirovic, so well known in England during the War. He occupies the ancient see of Ochrida. For the training of the clergy there are two Theological Schools at Belgrade and Zagreb (Agram); and six seminaries in Belgrade, Serajevo, Karlovitz, Prizren, Cetinje and Bitolj. The maintenance of the clergy is still under the consideration of the Ministry of Public Worship: but the State is not to pay their salaries, and the best of the clergy see the wisdom of this decision. The younger generation of theological teachers and students—most of them educated at Oxford during the War—are already exerting an influence upon the religion of the country with marked effect.[33]

CHAPTER XIV.

THE CHURCHES OF THE BALKAN PENINSULA: *(continued)*.

    (III.) RUMANIA.
    (IV.) GREECE.

CHAPTER XIV.

The Churches of the Balkan Peninsula:
III. Rumania.   IV. Greece.

III. Rumania.

Rumania[1] is the third of the Balkan states to demand our attention. Before the War, it consisted of Wallachia and Moldavia : two districts lying the one to the south of the Transylvanian Alps and the other to the east of the Carpathians. They were formerly autonomous provinces of the Ottoman Empire : but, since 23rd December, 1861, they had become, with the Dobrudja, an independent Principality. In area and population the Principality, before 1914, covered 53,689 square miles and had 7,516,418 inhabitants. But, since the War, the kingdom, as it became in 1881, has been more than doubled in size and resources. It now includes an area of 122,000 square miles, and has a population of 17,500,000. The territories gained are Bessarabia, from Russia : and, from the Austro-Hungarian Empire, those districts of it which might once have been described as *Rumania Irredenta,* viz., parts of Transylvania, Bukovina and the Banat. The chief towns of the country are Bucharest, the capital; Jassy, the capital of Moldavia; with Galatz, Braila, Ploësti and Craiova. The kingdom of to-day corresponds, as nearly as possible, both in situation and extent, to the ancient Dacia : and its history falls into four recognisable but very unequal periods.

§ 1. The first of these extends to the thirteenth century : and is the period of the formation of the Rumanian nation. The Dacians established themselves on either side of the Danube : some to the north of that river in the province of Oltenia which lies south of the mountain ranges, and in the Banat and Transylvania parts of Hungary to the north of them : and others south of the Danube, in the Roman province of Mœsia which lay between the Danube and the Balkans. Between A.D. 101—6, the Emperor Trajan, 98—†117, brought Dacia beyond the Danube under Roman rule. He introduced there a garrison of 25,000 men and many settlers besides. Two consequences followed. A large population of Roman origin came to be established beyond the Danube: and this conquest and settlement of Dacia so changed the situation on the northern frontier that, in the Roman Empire, " the military centre of gravity was shifted from the Rhine to the Danube."[2] It was a change that prepared the way for the transference of the seat of government from Rome to Constantinople; and, ultimately, for the inclusion of the Latin people, who came to be known as Rumanians, into the Orthodox Eastern Church.

About a hundred and fifty years after Trajan's conquest of Dacia, the lands on either side of the Danube fell a prey to the incursions of the Goths: and the Emperor Decius, 250—†1, was defeated and slain[3] by them in the Dobrudja. In 255 Dacia was lost to the Empire by its abandonment to the Goths:[4] and the Emperor Aurelian, 270—†5, wisely recognised the situation by evacuating Dacia,[5] north of the Danube, 271. He withdrew the legions across the river into Mœsia. But the Roman colonists remained to the north of it: only they moved for safety from the Goths into Transylvania. From the third to the eighth centuries a succession of barbarian invaders swept over eastern Europe: Goths, 271—375, Huns, 375—453, Gepids,[6] 453—66, and Avars, 566—799. But the Daco-Rumanians withstood the flood that passed over them. They preserved their identity by retiring further into the mountains. About 679, on the heels of the Avars, came the Slavs. They occupied the Balkan lands south of the Danube; and so cut off the Rumanians from the Roman Empire. But parts of the Rumanian country became subject to the Bulgars: and, on the conversion of the Bulgars, 864, the Slavonic language was introduced into their churches and so into the churches of their subjects the Rumanians. Hitherto the Rumanians had preserved their Latin tongue, in worship as in ordinary life: but they now had to exchange it, in worship, for another, and were so far severed from the Latin world. The ninth century is the epoch of the coming of the Hungarians. This put an end to the domination of the Bulgars in Rumania, and, for a while, the *Terra Blachorum* in S.E. Transylvania, enjoyed autonomy as " former colonists of the Romans." But these happy relations did not last. Hostility arose between the Rumanian nobles and the Magyars : until, as well for this reason as in order to escape persecution from the Catholic Kings of Hungary, the Rumanians migrated south and east of the mountain-ranges.

§ 2. The effect of this migration was the foundation of the Rumanian Principalities. It took place c. 1300 : at a time when the tide of Tartar invasion of eastern Europe, 1241—1345, was beginning to ebb, and it was accomplished contemporaneously with the Serbian Empire of Stephen Dushan, 1331—†55.

Thus, in Wallachia, Rudolph the Black crossed the mountains, 1290, and established himself at Kimpolung. He gave to the flat country of Wallachia the name of Muntenia (land of the mountains) in memory of his former home. Wallachia attained its independence, 1330, under Ivanko Basaraba. He allied himself with the Bulgars against the Serbs : but managed to extricate himself from the defeat suffered by his allies at Velbuzd (Küstendil) at the hands of a league of Serbs and Romans. He then routed the Hungarians, and succeeded in delivering his Principality from their domination.

It was next the turn of Moldavia to win its freedom. In 1345, Dragosh, leader of another colony of Rumanians, from the N.E. of Transylvania, founded the province, at first under the suzerainty of the Crown of Hungary : but in 1349 he threw off its overlordship, and rendered the country independent.

But in neither province could the liberties thus won be maintained. Politically, owing to the method of succession to the throne, half-hereditary and half-elective, Wallachia and Moldavia became the prey of internal dissension; and this led ultimately to their absorption into the Ottoman Empire. Similar consequences followed in the ecclesiastical sphere. By an arrangement dating from the time of the First Bulgarian Empire, 893—972, both provinces had been ecclesiastically dependent upon the archbishopric of Ochrida : whence Old Slavonic held its ground as the language of worship in the churches of Rumania. In Moldavia, Alexander the Good, 1401—33, recognised the Œcumenical Patriarch : but the authority of Ochrida remained in both provinces, in Wallachia till the end of the fifteenth century and in Moldavia till the end of the seventeenth : when the Rumanian language replaced the Slavonic in the celebration of the Liturgy.

§ 3. In the third period, from the sixteenth to the nineteenth century, both provinces fell, and remained, under the power of the Turk : Wallachia from 1460 and Moldavia from 1529. Their history is a long series of treacherous risings of the *boyars* or nobles against their Princes : until, at last, the Turks dared no longer entrust the government to native *Hospodars* but sold it, in 1712—6 to the Phanariot Greeks.[7] The transfer was a change from anarchy to oppression.

§ 4. In the nineteenth and twentieth centuries, the Rumanians set themselves to effect their deliverance : and, like other Balkan nations, in their struggle for liberty, they looked to Russia for aid. On 2nd September, 1829, by the Peace of Adrianople, which concluded the Russian War against Turkey, it was arranged that Wallachia and Moldavia were to have the status of self-governing states under Russian protection, and to elect their princes for life. In 1831 a *Règlement organique* provided for this *régime:* but, after the Crimean War, the principalities were put back under the Sultan. National aspirations, however, after unity and independence, proved too strong for so retrograde a measure to endure. On 23rd December, 1861, they became, with the Dobrudja, an independent realm : and their union was finally effected, 1864. In that year, also, the Church declared itself independent of any foreign bishop. But it paid the price of enfranchisement by loss of property, and by servitude to the State. For the monasteries were sequestrated on the pretext that many of them were in foreign hands, as were the estates in Rumania of the Fraternity of the Holy Sepulchre at Jerusalem: while, in 1872, the State made laws for the election of bishops by the Senate, the Chamber of Deputies and an ecclesiastical Synod. Shortly after the declaration of independence, Charles of Hohenzollern-Sigmaringen, became Hereditary-Prince, 1864: and, after he had declared himself King, 1881—†1915, the Œcumenical Patriarch, Joachim III., was induced to recognise the independence of the Church of Rumania, 13th May, 1885. Charles was succeeded by his nephew, Ferdinand I., 1914—†27: and Ferdinand by his grandson, Michael I., a child of six. Of the seventeen and a half million of his subjects, there are about nine and a half million Orthodox.

As to organisation, the Rumanian hierarchy consists of two Metropolitans, of Bucharest and Jassy: with eleven suffragan sees: (1) Kisinev, for Kisinev and Hotin districts, with Bessarabia proper; (2) Cetatea Alba, for Southern Bessarabia; (3) Roman, (4) Husi and (5) Galatz, in Moldavia; (6) Buzeu, (7) Arges and (8) Ramnicu-Valcii, in Wallachia; (9) Caransebes, for the Banat; (10) Arad and (11) Oradia-Mare.[8] There is now an archbishop of Transylvania and of Bukovina.

As to the religious situation in general, it is the product of the fate that befell the Rumanian Church during the first half of the nineteenth century. At its opening, the country was penetrated by the philosophic materialism of the West, which reached it chiefly through France: and in 1860, Cuza-Voda, the last prince of Rumanian nationality, abruptly secularised such ecclesiastical properties as had escaped absorption, on the pretext that their revenues were going out of the country to Greece and Constantinople where, especially during the War of Greek Independence, they had been diverted to propaganda, sometimes directed against Rumanian interests. Thus, the Church, impoverished and helpless, was " put under Government control and became a department of the State under the Ministry of Education. Lay schools were built and two Universities were founded, and the interest and outlay occasioned by these new institutions caused the Church to be little by little crowded into the background, and the clergy began to settle down into ill-paid drudgery, disdainfully tolerated by the ' enlightened ' Government as a necessary concession to the superstitions of the people. The masses of the clergy had never been either educated or conscious of the high calling entrusted to them; and, though the Ministry provided them with two seminaries, and later with two Faculties of Theology, the professors in the institutions being mostly secular and openly indifferent to the Christian Faith, the latter state of the priests became worse than the first.

" From being a Government department, the Church soon became a political instrument, and the election of the higher clergy was decided by party interests. . . . The lower ranks of the clergy were miserably underpaid and overworked . . . . . the students wise in doctrine and theology, but barren in spirit. . . .

" To-day, many of the laymen and many of the clerics . . . . are deeply dissatisfied . . . and some members of the well-educated classes, especially among women . . . turn to the Roman Catholics.

" The peasants, who form the bulk of the population, are fanatically attached to their religion, and do not consider as Christians those of another Faith. They conscientiously follow every precept of the Church, and consider it a greater sin not to keep the forty days' fast before Easter than to steal a neighbour's goods. They love the ceremonial of their Church without understanding it, and they piously dream through the two-hour-long Sunday service, in which no sermon is preached. . . .

" They may be unfortunate enough to have an unworthy priest in their village whom they thoroughly despise on week-days, but on Sundays they respectfully listen to the Mass held by him, and kiss his hand when he presents to them the Cross, and anoints their foreheads at the end of the service. God is to them a very shadowy conception : Jesus Christ is worshipped rather from a distance . . . ; but they feel at home with their Saints—SS. Nicholas and Dmitri, Basil and Grigori, and especially the Holy Virgin. They burn candles before their shrines: pray to them in distress: take the clothes of the sick to the holy images to be blessed by the priest: and very scrupulously keep the feasts of the Saints."[9]

IV. GREECE.

The Kingdom of Greece,[10] at its inauguration in 1832, included three divisions of territory. There was, first, continental Greece, bounded, on the north by a line running from the Gulf of Arta on the west to the Gulf of Volo, on the east, and on the south by the Gulf of Corinth. Then there was the Peloponnese. And, finally, the islands of the Ægæan Sea. These consisted of three groups: Eubœa (Negropont), with the northern Sporades lying N.E. of it; the Cyclades (about 220 in all), to the S.E.; and the southern Sporades (about 40 in number) lying off the S.W. of Asia Minor. In 1864, Greece acquired the Ionian islands—Corfu, Santa Maura, Ithaca, Cephalonia, and Zante, together with two little islands that lie between Cape Malea and Crete, *viz.*, Cerigo (Kythera) and Cerigotto (Anti-Kythera). So Greece remained—a small kingdom—till the addition of Thessaly in 1881. This settlement, with a slight strategic modification in 1898 in favour of Turkey, lasted till 1913—the year of the expansion of Old into New Greece after the Balkan Wars of 1912—3. New Greece included Epirus and Macedonia: which together stretch from the Ionian Sea opposite Corfu to the Ægæan Sea opposite Thasos, and take in the important towns of Salonika and Kavalla. It also included the islands of Thasos, Samothrace, Lemnos, Mitylene, Chios, Samos and Crete. On the other hand, Greece, in 1912, had lost to Italy " the thirteen southern Sporades (Rhodes, Kos, Kalymnos, Leros, Nisyros, Telos, Syme, Chalke, Astypalaia, Karpathos, Kasos, Patmos and Leipso), known colloquially but inaccurately as the *Dodekânesos:* for the real *Dodekânesos* (a term first used by Theophanes early in the ninth century) excluded Rhodes, Kos and Leipso, but included Ikaria (which, at this time declared its independence) and Kastellorizon."[11] By these acquisitions,

Greece more than doubled its population: for, whereas in 1907 the population stood at 2,631,952, in 1921 it had increased to about 7,900,000. The country also increased considerably, though not proportionately, in extent: for, as the result of the wars with Turkey (17th October, 1912—30th May, 1913), and with Bulgaria (30th June— 10th August, 1913), Greece acquired 5,134 square miles of territory; and the kingdom now covers a total area of about 65,000 square miles.[12] After the Great War, 1914—8, Greece seemed to be on the eve of a still greater expansion: for, in August, 1920, by the Treaty of Sèvres, Eastern Thrace, including Adrianople and the peninsula of Gallipoli, together with the islands of Imbros and Tenedos off the mouth of the Dardanelles, were ceded to her; while Smyrna and a large tract of country behind it were placed under Greek administration. But disasters ensued at the hand of the Turk: and Smyrna was evacuated, 8th September, 1922. By the Treaty of Lausanne, 1923, the districts claimed by Greece were handed back to the Turks. Nevertheless, Greece, though she has suffered severely in resources, is now a kingdom of much larger territory and population than when she attained her independence nearly a hundred years ago.

§ 5. The history of Greece, from her loss to her recovery of independence,[13] falls conveniently into three periods: (1) the period of direct administration by the Turk,[14] 1460—1684; (2) the Venetian conquest of the Morea,[15] 1684—1718; (3) the Turkish restoration[16] and decline,[17] 1718—1800, till modern Greece,[18] 1821—1924, emerged into being.

(i.) Soon after the capture of Constantinople, 1453, the Turks made themselves masters of continental Greece. In 1460 they took possession of the Peloponnese, except for a few Venetian colonies: but these became Turkish in 1540. Greece was divided into six *sanjaks* or military districts. In each *sanjak,* a number of fiefs was apportioned to Turkish settlers, who were bound in return to furnish mounted men for the Sultan's army. The local government was left in the hands of the *archontes* or primates in each community: and the country, as a whole,

The Churches of the Balkan Peninsula

lay passive under the Turkish domination, and subject to oppressive taxation. Chief of its burdens was the land-tax: which fell on all, without distinction of religion or race. The tax consisted of a fixed proportion of the annual produce, varying from a tithe to a third of the whole crop. But what made it oppressive was its mode of collection. The farmer might not put his sickle into the harvest until the tax-gatherer was on the spot to claim his share: and the effect was to produce stagnation in agriculture and poverty throughout the countryside. But there were other imposts which fell upon the Greeks as *rayahs* or infidel subjects of the Sultan: the *haratch,* or poll-tax, which produced nearly two-thirds of the revenue of the Ottoman Empire in the form of tribute from its Christian subjects, and the tax on imports and exports—a duty of 5 per cent in the case of Christians, but of $2\frac{1}{2}$ per cent only, if the goods belonged to a Mohammedan. But worst of all imposts was the tribute of Christian children. Officers of the Sultan visited towns and villages every fourth year. All the boys, between six and nine years of age, were paraded before them: and they took a fifth of their number to be trained at Constantinople for enlistment into the Corps of Janissaries, i.e., Yeni-Asker, or New Soldiery. This tribute came to an end in 1676, with the gradual weakening of the central government. As this weakness increased, the Greeks became exposed to further oppression by Turkish residents, or by their own magistrates and clergy. For the Turkish rulers not only treated the Greek clergy with favour and so induced them to acquiesce in their dominion, but often made them the instruments of keeping their own people down. Entirely free from such complicity, however, were the humblest class of the clergy, the village priests. They were ignorant and unlearned, and peasants like their people. They shared their labours and misfortunes: were identified with their interests: and uniformly deserved and retained the respect of their flocks. So the country clergy, for all their rusticity, strengthened the mass of the people to persist in their loyalty to the Christian Faith, and kept alive the spirit of patriotism till the dawn of a better day.

(ii.) The Turks, in spite of their conquests, had an ancient rival in Venice for supremacy in the eastern Mediterranean; and, although by 1570, they had completed the subjugation of the Ægæan islands, Venice kept hold of Crete till 1669, and never lost Corfu till its cession to France in 1797. In 1684, the year after the Turks had been busy with the siege of Vienna, the Venetians took advantage of their entanglements to attack the Morea. By 1687 they had nearly obtained possession of it. In the same year they even captured Athens, though they had to abandon it again: and were brought to a standstill, 1688, in their attack upon Eubœa (Negropont). But the success of their arms was recognised by the peace of Carlowitz, 1699, by which the Morea became a possession of Venice. Their administration, which lasted, 1684—1718, proved, on the whole, to the benefit of the people. They introduced a Catholic clergy, under a hierarchy of four bishops headed by the archbishop of Corinth: and the influence of this foreign priesthood, in setting up higher standards both of education and of morality, produced a sensible effect on the Greek clergy. Moreover, the Venetians by their attempts to co-operate with the native magistrates, and the mildness of their administration improved the spirit of their subjects. But they failed to make their government popular: and when, in 1715, the Turks with a large and disciplined army set themselves to recover the Morea, the Venetians found themselves unsupported by the Greeks. The peninsula was rapidly recaptured; and by the peace of Passarowitz, 1718, again became a Turkish dependency.

(iii.) The Turkish Restoration in Greece, 1718—97, continued for the greater part of the eighteenth century. But, 1764, Russian agents began to appear in Greece, with promises of speedy deliverance from the Turks. In 1774 a concession embodied in the treaty of Kutchuk-Kainarji between Russia and Turkey, allowed to Greek traders the privilege of sailing under the Russian flag. This marks an important step in the rehabilitation of Greece as an independent power. For Greek commerce spread rapidly throughout the Levant; and with it a growing sense of the vitality of the Greek people and of Hellenic unity. Such unity had for its basis all along the sense of a common religion in Orthodoxy: but it was further strengthened at this period by a literary revival, by the growing sentiment of nationality, and by a desire for freedom due to the French Revolution. At the first sign of weakness in the Turkish dominion, the Greek nation, c. 1800, was ready to rise.

§ 6. And so came into being modern Greece, 1821— 1924. Another clause in the treaty of Kutchuk-Kainarji, 1774, granted to Russia a vague protectorate over the Orthodox subjects of the Porte; and, in pursuance of her policy of extension towards the Balkans, Russia, in 1781, concerted with Austria what is known as "the Greek project." This was an arrangement between the two Powers by which they were to divide the Ottoman dominions, and to restore the Empire at Constantinople under a Russian prince. The project came to nothing, because the attention of its authors was distracted by the French Revolution, 1789—99, and the Napoleonic Wars, 1799—1815. But Russian intrigue went on; and, in the year of Napoleon's downfall, there was formed the Philiké Hetaerea, or "League of Friends"; which was a revolutionary organisation of Greek nationalists with centres at Moscow, Bucharest, Trieste and throughout the Levant. In 1821, Prince Alexander Hypsilantis, a Phanariot in the Russian service and president of the League, entered Moldavia from Russian territory at the head of a filibustering expedition: while Germanos, archbishop of Patras, collected a force of insurgents at the monastery of Megaspelaion near Kalavryta in the Peloponnese, and unfurled its altar-cloth as the standard of revolt. The assembled patriots took an oath to deliver their country from the Turks or to perish in the attempt; and, meanwhile, the Christians attacked and murdered the Mussulmans—many of them renegade Greeks—in every part of the peninsula. But the Hetaerists were mostly civilians, and indifferently led: so that the rebellion fell into the hands of the Klephts or brigands, and drifted into anarchy. At last, John Capo d' Istria was elected President of the Greek Republic, 18th January, 1828. He was a Corfiote Count, with a Venetian education and a career in the diplomatic service of the Tsar. His accession to power did not conciliate the factiousness of Greek patriots: and the disorder which continued led to the intervention of the Great Powers. On 20th October, 1827, at the battle of Navarino, a combined force of British, French and Russian ships annihilated the Turkish fleet: and this victory led to the Protocol of London, 22nd March, 1829, by which continental Greece, south of a line extending from the gulf of Arta to the gulf of Volo, together with the Peloponnese and the Cyclades were constituted a principality, to be tributary to the Sultan but ruled by a Christian prince. On 14th September, these territorial limits were confirmed by the Treaty of Adrianople, and Greece was declared an independent monarchy. Independence thus achieved, there ensued a reaction against the enthusiasts, and a temporary reduction of Greek territory. Count John Capo d' Istria, moreover, failed to retain his authority, and was assassinated, 9th October, 1831, because of his Russian sympathies and his arbitrary methods of government. A fresh intervention of the Great Powers became inevitable; and by the Convention of London, 7th May, 1832, the Greek kingdom was committed to Otto of Bavaria and placed under the joint protection of Great Britain, France and Russia. Athens became the capital in 1834: but it also became the scene for the rivalries of factions, claiming the support of Britain, France and Russia respectively. During the Crimean War, the Greeks, as a whole, displayed their sympathies with Russia: and the Piraeus was blockaded by the combined fleets of Britain and France. The indignity and inconvenience only served to increase the difficulty of the king: for Otto was unpopular because of his despotic rule. At a National Assembly, held in 1862, he was deposed: and the throne was offered to, and accepted by, George, Prince of Schleswig-Holstein-Sonderburg-Glücksburg, and brother of Queen Alexandra.

King George I., 1863—†1913, understood the part of a constitutional monarch. He was patient, not arbitrary; and he loved his adopted country. He steered it through many difficulties; and lived to see large acquisitions to its resources. In 1864, the Ionian islands, which had been British since 1815, were handed over to Greece. In 1881 she profited by the diplomatic arrangements consequent upon the Russo-Turkish War, 1877, and the Treaty of Berlin, 1878, so far as to obtain the addition to her dominions of Thessaly and, with it, a population of 300,000 new citizens. The acquisition of Crete followed in 1897; and, though in that year Greece suffered defeat from Turkey and some rectification of the frontier took place in favour of the Sultan, still King George lived to see Epirus and Macedonia added to his realm after the Balkan Wars of 1912—3. But in the moment of victory and in the year of his jubilee, he was assassinated at Salonika: which he had but just entered in triumph.

His son Constantine, the brother-in-law of the German Emperor, William II., played a sorry part in the Great War, by opposing M. Venizelos, his minister: who had engineered the Balkan League, had won for Greece her great expansion, and would have had her enter the War on the side of the Western Allies. Had she done so, she would have shared in the ultimate victory. Venizelos was not strong enough to carry this daring policy into effect: but he succeeded in inducing Great Britain and France to drive King Constantine into exile, 12th June, 1917. He was succeeded by his son Alexander: who died, 25th October, 1920, from the effects of being bitten by a monkey. By that time, a strong anti-Venizelist and militarist reaction had taken place in Greece: and Constantine, restored in December, 1920, placed himself at the head of his armies and, encouraged but not helped by Mr. Lloyd George, attacked the Turks from Smyrna as his base, in the hope of securing for Greece the Asiatic territories mandated to her by the Treaty of Sèvres. But the Greek forces were badly led, and the strength of the country exhausted. They were driven by the Turks into the sea, because the Great Powers were too divided or too supine to come to their assistance. Constantine returned home, but only to be forced into exile again, September, 1922. He died in 1923: and was succeeded by his son, King George II. But he was deposed, and a Republic proclaimed, March, 1924. Greece is now left to face the situation as best she may: basely deserted by the Christian Powers of Western Europe, who should have supported her armies inasmuch as they sent her against the Turk: deprived of many of her sons after ten years of warfare, 1912—22: ruined in resources: and crowded with destitute refugees.

§ 7. Against this lurid background we have now to picture the rise and the present condition[19] of the Orthodox Church of Greece.

It became autocephalous with the independence of the nation: for, at the Synod of Nauplia, 15th June, 1833,[20] a decree was signed by thirty-four bishops in which they proclaimed the Church of Greece to be free from exterior control, and vested its government in the Holy Synod. This was to consist of the metropolitan of Athens, as president, and four other prelates who were to be nominated by the Crown and to be resident in Athens during their term of office. A Royal Commissioner attends the meetings of the Synod, and its members occupy five seats of marble in the Cathedral of the Metropolitan at Athens. As in similar cases, the Œcumenical Patriarchate was slow to recognise this movement for independence: but by a Synodal Tome of 11th July, 1850, recognition was eventually given. When the Ionian islands, 1864, Thessaly, 1881, and Crete, 1897, were politically united to Greece, the bishops and churches of these territories were similarly transferred to the Church of Greece. But the Œcumenical Patriarchate, in token of its ancient privilege and as a symbol of unity throughout the churches of the Orthodox communion, reserves the ancient right of consecrating the Holy Oil on Maundy Thursday, and of sending it to each.

The hierarchy of the Church in Greece has greatly increased, with the expansion of the country. In Old Greece, there are now thirty-three bishoprics under the jurisdiction of the Metropolitan of Athens: Ægion on the Gulf of Corinth, with Kalavryta to the south of it, being counted as one bishopric. Thus continental Greece has (1) Livadia, (2) Amphissa, (3) Mesolongi, (4) Arta, (5) Naupaktos, (6) Lamia. In Thessaly there are (7) Trikkala, (8) Karditsa, (9) Larissa, (10) Volo; and in Eubœa (11) Khalkis and (12) Kymé. To the Peloponnese belong (13) Nauplia, (14) Ydra, (15) Corinth, (16) Tripoli, (17) Demetsana, (18) Patras, (19, 20) Ægion with Kalavryta, (21) Pyrgos, (22) Kyparissia, (23) Kalamata, (24) Gytheion, (25) Sparta. The Ionian Islands have bishoprics at (26) Kerkyra (Corfu), (27) Leukas, (28) Argostolios, (29) Zakynthos, (30) Cythera; and the Cyclades are governed ecclesiastically from the sees of (31) Hermopolis, (32) Naxos, (33) Thera. In addition to these, there are as many as forty-nine bishoprics within New Greece (the provinces lately annexed from Turkey), which are subordinate not to Athens but to the Patriarch of Constantinople. Their ecclesiastical status was not changed with their political position: possibly because it was hoped that Constantinople would be within Greek territory so soon, that it was not worth while making any change. They are as follows:—Salonika, Kretes, Preveza, Mitylene, Sidero-Kastro (Demir-hissar), Samos, Zanthe, Edessa, Florina, Kozana, Paramythia, Kitron, Ierissos (Mt. Athos), Thasos, Lankada, Geromerion, Plomarion, Jannina, Berœa, Seres, Didymoteikhos, Methymna, Dryinopolis, Lemnos, Grevenæ, Cassandra, Nevrokopion, Konitza, Kampania, Souphlion, Zikhni, Genitsa, Ikaria, Pelagonia, Rodos, Drama, Alexandropolis, Chios, Maroneia (Dedeagatch), Kastoria, Sisanion, Elasson, Elevtheropolis, Ardamerion, Polyana, Kavalla, Nigritis, Metsovos, Psara.[21] Finally, there is a Metropolitan with seven suffragans in Crete.[22] The bishops are appointed by the Chief of the State, who selects one of the three names sent up by the Holy Synod. They are paid by the State. A bishop, as elsewhere in the Orthodox Church, must be over thirty years of age: unmarried, or a widower: and so, as a rule, from a monastery. The probability, therefore, is that he will not be a man of much culture: and this is unfortunate, for an educated clergy is, at present, the great need of the church in Greece. But, for all that, great respect is paid to the episcopal office.

The lower clergy are under the jurisdiction of the bishop: and amenable to his ecclesiastical court which takes cognizance of any offence against the Canon Law. They consist of several grades: archimandrites, who are unmarried: and others who must have married before ordination—whether priests, deacons or readers. A priest must be of not less than thirty years of age, and is ordinarily in charge of a parish. A deacon, who must be of not less than twenty-five years of age, has for his distinctive function the singing of the Gospel in the Liturgy: while the reader is charged with the reading of the Epistle. The clergy are paid by fees for baptisms, marriages and funerals: and by Easter dues. These sources of income, all told, afford them but a pittance: and they live in poverty. The son of the country priest is not infrequently the village shop-keeper or the local publican: and "priest's son devil's grandson" is a proverb significant of the expedients to which the families of the poverty-stricken and uneducated clergy are driven, in order to make a living. But the person and office of the priest is respected. He may be ignorant, but he is moral. He is poor, but contented: for he lives as a peasant among his flock who are peasants too. The services of his church are well attended: and its fabric is maintained at the expense of the community.

For the education of the clergy, there are, at present, but two Colleges, at Athens and at Arta. The Rizareion[23] at Athens is so called after its founders, George Rizares and his brother. They came from Epirus; made money in Russia: and left large bequests for the education of the clergy. The Rizareion was opened in 1844, and now has about a hundred students, from fifteen to twenty years of age. They receive a liberal education, in Arts and Theology: and the College is under the management of its own Council, though subject to the supervision of the Ministry of Education. But so good is the training, that many of its students are attracted to more lucrative careers than the priesthood : and only fifteen to twenty per cent proceed to Holy Orders.

Next to the bishop and the parish priest, the monasteries[24] have done most for religion in Greece. In 1833, they numbered as many as 593. " Their inhabitants were mostly picturesque, but idle, peasants " : and, next year, the Government " suppressed and nationalised all religious houses inhabited by less than six monks,"[25] numbering 412 in all. In 1905, there were 171 Religious Houses for men, 9 for women, and 34 " unorganised " monasteries : and their population consisted of 1,574 monks, with 631 novices and 910 servants, and 117 nuns, with 71 novices and 32 servants. Some houses are " cœnobitic " and the brethren live in community : others are " idiorhythmic," for the brethren do not have their meals in common. In either case, however, the monk, like the village priest, is usually a peasant and devoid of learning : but, like all Greeks, keenly interested in politics : and the whole monastic institute is under the control of the Minister of Education and Ecclesiastical Affairs.

Among the most famous monasteries are those of the Megaspelaion in the Peloponnese and those of Mt. Meteora in Thessaly : above all, those of the Monastic Republic on Mount Athos. The Megaspelaion is situate three to four miles N.E. of Kalavryta in the province of Achaia and Elis. It was founded by the Empress Euphrosyne, †1215, the wife of the Emperor Alexius III. (Angelus), 1195—1203 : and is well endowed with large estates in Elis. It has three hundred monks, and is famous for its picture of our Lady painted by St. Luke. The monastery of Galataké in Negropont (Eubœa) is also well off : and so are those of Pendeli and Petrake in Attica. But the monasteries of Mt. Meteora in Thessaly have lost their estates. They are situated to the N.E. of Kalabaka in the valley of the Salambria (Peneus). Looking down from the rocky summits on which they stand, and accessible only by basket and rope, they recall the turbulent days of their foundation : when security for the unarmed was only to be had at the price of such isolation. Most famous of all are the monasteries of Mount Athos: situate on the easternmost promontory of Chalkidike, and now part of Greece. The Republic includes twenty monasteries: seventeen of which are Greek, one Russian, one Bulgarian and one Serbian. Turkish from 1453—1912, the Holy Mountain was occupied by the Greek forces in November, 1912. Its monasteries are either cœnobitic, and ruled by an abbot who is elected by the brethren; or idiorhythmic, and administered by a band of overseers ($\dot{\epsilon}\pi i \tau \pi \rho o o \iota$) who are elected for a term of years. The peninsula, as a whole, is governed by a Council of four: and an Assembly of twenty members, one from each community.

Among the educated the influence of the Church in Greece has probably declined: but it remains strong among the peasants. They are devoted to the externals of religious observance: for worship is well maintained, and fasts are both frequent and rigorous. There are four chief fasts in the year: an Advent of forty days before Christmas; a Lent of forty-eight days before Easter; the Fast of the Holy Apostles, from the Monday after the octave of Pentecost to the Feast of St. Peter and St. Paul; and a fortnight's fast before the Falling Asleep of our Lady (August 15th). Besides, there are weekly fasts on Wednesday and Friday: and there are fasts too on the Vigil of the Epiphany (January 5th), the Beheading of St. John Baptist (August 29th), and Holy Cross Day (September 14th).

Rigorous in self-discipline, the Church in Greece is tolerant in its attitude towards other communions, except Roman Catholics and Bulgars. Hostility of Greek to Bulgar is traditional: and the Roman Catholics are disliked as proselytisers. Not, perhaps, without reason. For the Greek peasant is also devoted to his religion. He loves his own saints: St. Nicholas, the patron of Sailors, St. Elias, our Lady, St. George: besides, the local saints, St. Spiridon of Corfu, and our Lady of Kythera. He has a veneration too for " the Blessed ": a class of the second rank but venerable, like Luke the hermit of the tenth century whose memory is enshrined in the splendid monastery of Hosios Leukas near Stiris in Bœotia. And he reverences relics : and eikons, the restoration of their title to " salutation and honorific adoration,"[26] 843, being commemorated annually on the first Sunday in Lent, or " Orthodoxy Sunday." But in these devout observances the Greek only shares the religious habits of all Orthodox Christians.

§ 8. New developments[27] are taking place in the Church of Greece : where a reform, analogous to the movement for self-government in the Anglican Church, has come to pass. Hitherto, by a law dating from 1830, the government of the Church has been vested in the Sacred Synod. " This body was not, strictly speaking, a synod at all. It was a small committee of bishops, five to eight in number, of which the Metropolitan of Athens was president, and in which he was expected to act. The Bishops who composed the body, being nominated by the Government and removable from it . . . . at pleasure, were seldom inclined to do anything more than the mere routine work of the Church : while Parliament and the Government . . . though benevolent enough . . . had neither time nor capacity to take up Church questions. . . . The Church is " now " to be allowed self-government. . . . The governing body . . . is to be . . . the Synod . . . of all the bishops of the kingdom. This Synod, which is to meet at least once a year, is to pass any canons it desires. . . . How far its acts, *e.g.* in matters that concern . . . questions of property and the redistribution of ancient endowments . . . can be reviewed by the secular authority, is not quite clear. . . . The Synod will consist, at first, only of Bishops. The addition of clerical and lay Houses is a point for consideration. . . . The ' Sojourning Synod ' . . . is abolished. . . . This change has been brought about by ' Legislative Decree,' not by Act of Parliament. By Greek law, the Ministry has the power, when Parliament is not in session, of issuing orders of this sort . . . and this decree, like others, bears the name of the ' Chief ' of the Revolution, General Plastiras." But the probability is that it will be confirmed : for it " commands general approval. . . . ' We could not,' said one high in ecclesiastical office, 'have got this out of Parliament in ten years' work. There is something to be said for a *tyrannus* after all.' "

CHAPTER XV.

THE CHURCH OF RUSSIA OR THE PATRIARCHATE OF MOSCOW.

CHAPTER XV.

THE CHURCH OF RUSSIA OR THE PATRIARCHATE OF MOSCOW.

IN chapter viii. we have already dealt with Russian Christianity from the conversion of Russia under Vladimir I., 980—†1015, to the organisation of the Russian Church under his nephew, Yaroslav I., 1019—†54, and his successors. But only in summary: and the time has now come to pursue the story.

§ 1. And, first, of the Russian lands. Before the Tartar invasions of the thirteenth century, they included Great, Little, White, Red and Black Russia.

Of these territories, Great Russia—a name that first appeared in the thirteenth century—was the most important. Its nucleus was "The land-between-the-Rivers" of the Volga and the Oka, with Moscow, on the Moskva, a tributary of the Oka, for its centre. But it extended far and wide over the basin of the Volga; and included the cities of Tver on the upper Volga; Nizhni Novgorod (Lower Newtown, to distinguish it from old Novgorod) at the junction of that river with its tributary the Oka; Kazan, and Saratov, lower down the stream. It included also to the N.W. Pskov, together with old Novgorod (Newtown) on the Volkhov which runs from Lake Ilmen to Lake Ladoga, and afterwards Petrograd itself. Finnish elements were incorporated in its population.

To the S.W. of Great Russia lay Little Russia—a name that appears in the fourteenth century. It extended over the course of the Dniester, on whose upper waters lay Lvov (Lemberg), and over the lower course of the Dnieper; and had for its chief towns, Kiev on the Dnieper, Odessa on the Black Sea, Kharkov to the north, and Rostov on the Sea of Azov. On the west, Little Russia marched with the frontier of Poland; and so, by the Poles, was called the Ukraine or Border-land. Considerable Polish elements were incorporated with its population. It suffered, and declined in importance, from the time of the Tartar invasions.

To the N. of Little Russia, and to the S. and W. of Great Russia, lay White Russia. The northern part of it embraced the upper course of the Western Dvina (which flows into the Baltic at Riga and is to be distinguished from the Northern Dvina which finds an outlet into the White Sea at Archangel), and included the cities of Vilna and Minsk to the west. The southern districts lay between the upper Dnieper, with the towns of Smolensk and Moghilev on its banks, and its tributary the Beresina. Lithuania lay beyond the N.W. boundary; and there were Lithuanian elements mingled with the population of White Russia.

Red Russia covered Eastern Galicia, or Ruthenia, and lay between Volhynia and the Carpathians.

Black Russia was the district between the Beresina, the Pripet and the Niemen.

These regions together made up the Russian lands, and formed the original territories which, in course of time, expanded into the vast country known before the Great War as the Russian Empire of the Tsar Nicholas II., 1894—†1917. It stretched from the frontiers of the German and Austro-Hungarian Empires and Rumania, right across Russia in Europe and Siberia to the Pacific Ocean; and covered more than eight and a half million square miles with a population of about one hundred and eighty-three millions. But, since the Revolution of 1917, it has been reduced by the separation of " Succession States " to the north and west. These are Finland, to the north; Esthonia, Latvia and Lithuania, on the Baltic; and Poland. The remainder of the Russian Empire now consists of the Union of Soviet Republics, with a fringe of autonomous Republics and Provinces; the Union covering seven and a quarter million square miles, with a population of about one hundred and three millions.

§ 2. The ecclesiastical history of Russia[1] is, by common consent, divisible into six well-marked periods: (1) 989 —1237, the period of the diffusion of Christianity; (2) 1237—1461, the period of the Tartar domination, and of the development of northern Russia; (3) 1461—1589, the period of the two metropolitanates of Moscow and Kiev; (4) 1589—1700, the period of the Patriarchate of Moscow; (5) 1700—1917, the period of government by the Holy Synod; and, since the Revolution (6), of 1917, the period of the revived Patriarchate of Moscow.

§ 3. During the period of the diffusion of Christianity, 989—1237, the Grand Princes of the House of Rurik were the most important rulers of the country; and Kiev their capital. Vladimir I., 972—†1015, under whom took place the conversion of his people to Orthodox Christianity, was succeeded by his son Yaroslav I., 1016—†54.

His reign was an epoch of conquest and consolidation. Red Russia (Galicia) was recovered from Poland. The founding of Yuriev (=Georgetown, so called because the monastic name of Yaroslav was Yuri or George), now Dorpat in Latvia, extended Russian colonisation towards the Baltic; while the founding of Yaroslavl, on the upper Volga planted it among the Finns of the north. To the south, the repulse of the Pechenegs cleared the steppes of an harassing foe. Greater, however, than the achievements of Yaroslav in conquest or colonisation was his title to fame as " the Lawgiver." To him belongs the credit for the codification of Russian Law. He was responsible, on the one hand, for the beginnings of the *Pravda*—a civil and criminal code, applying to ecclesiastics, and dealing with such offences as murder, assault and damage to property; and, on the other, for the *Ordinances*. These were a digest of ecclesiastical law, and applied to all Russians who were Christians. They deal with sin rather than with crime; and legislate upon such matters as marriage and the status of women, necromancy and witchcraft. In both these codes, there is evidence of the influence of humanity and of definitely Christian principle. It is assumed that the family, rather than as hitherto the tribe, is the unit of society : and the rights of women are placed on a level equal with those of men. By a home and foreign policy of such distinction,

Yaroslav won recognition from the rest of Christendom; and the House of Rurik entered into intimate relations with Christian Princes of the West. Thus the sister of Yaroslav married Casimir I., King of Poland, 1040—†58; of his daughters, Elizabeth married Harald III. (Hardraada), King of Norway, 1047—†66. Anne became queen of Henry I. of France, 1031—†60; and Anastasia, queen of Andrew I. of Hungary, 1046—61. Princes of Sweden, Norway and England took refuge at his court; and both Olaf II. and Harald III. of Norway had reason to thank him for aid in trouble.

During the reign of Yaroslav, his capital, Kiev, reached the height of its prosperity. He built there the Cathedral of St. Sophia, and founded two religious houses, St. George for men, and St. Irene for women. About this time was founded the Pecherski Lavra at Kiev. It owes its origin to a Russian named Anthony, who went to Mount Athos in order to enter the monastic life. He was sent back home by his abbot after he had learned it; and began the solitary life in a cave (pech) near Kiev. From the cave of its founder sprang the oldest and first in rank of Russian monasteries. Besides the Pecherski monastery, there were seventeen others in Kiev during the twelfth century: and monasteries played a great part both in the spread of the Gospel and in keeping it alive. Kiev also became the seat of the metropolitanate; for, on the death of the metropolitan Theopemptus, 1037—†51, Yaroslav transferred the see from Pereyaslavl to Kiev and set up there Hilarion, a Russian, whose appointment was confirmed by the Œcumenical Patriarch Michael Cerularius, 1043—58. As Michael was, in great part, responsible for the final breach between East and West, his action riveted the dependence of the Russian Church upon Constantinople; and, until the end of the period now before us, the Church of Russia was governed by metropolitans of Kiev. There were twenty-four in all from Leo, 991—†1004, to Joseph, 1237, who disappeared in the siege of his city by the Tartars: and of these, all, with two exceptions, were Greek. The exceptions were Hilarion, 1051—? and Clement, 1147—†54: both of them men of eminence. For " Hilarion was one of the earliest native theological writers; while Clement was renowned for his conspicuous piety and his learning."[2]

Yaroslav was succeeded, after an interval of anarchy, by his grandson, Vladimir II., 1113—†25; surnamed Monomachus after his maternal grandfather, the Roman Emperor Constantine X. (Monomachus), 1042—†54. Vladimir inaugurated a fresh period of wise and firm administration. He beat off the Polovtsy, or Kumans of the steppes. He extended Russian colonisation among the Finns of the N.E. forests; and his literary bequests exhibit the Christian temper of his rule. " It is neither fasting nor solitude " he writes in his *Instruction* to his sons, " nor the monastic life that will procure you the life eternal . . . it is well-doing. Do not forget the poor, but nourish them. . . . Be a father to orphans, judge the cause of widows yourself. . . . Put to death no one, be he innocent or guilty; for nothing is more sacred than the soul of a Christian."[3]

Vladimir II. was the last of the powerful Princes of Kiev; and during the next hundred and seventy years (1054—1224) " which ensued between his death and the Tartar conquest, no less than 64 principalities had a more or less ephemeral existence, 293 princes put forward succession-claims, and their disputes led to 83 civil wars."[4] Kiev began to decline. In 1169 it was taken by rebel Russians from the north; and in 1203 it was taken again, and sacked, by the Polovtsy. Thus Little Russia became a desert. Two streams of migration set forth from the unhappy country. Some of its inhabitants trekked W. and N.W. to Red and White Russia—territories which passed to Poland and Lithuania, and were never recovered for Russia till the seventeenth century. Others drew off N. and N.E. towards the upper Volga and even as far as old Novgorod. From the settlements of this latter migration arose Moscow : and—in sharp contrast with the old and free Russia of rival republics and independent principalities—there arose too the Empire of the Tsars.

§ 4. This brings us to the second period, 1237—1461 :

the time of the Tartar domination and the development of northern Russia.

The Tartars were a Mongol race, whom Genghis Khan, 1206—†27, succeeded in uniting into one nation after forty years of obscure struggle. Advancing westward, they came into contact with the Polovtsy: who, though the hereditary enemies of the Russians, implored their help. " They have taken our country: to-morrow they will take yours." The Russians chivalrously answered to the appeal. But at the battle of the Kalka, 1224, a rivulet running into the Sea of Azov, the united armies were completely defeated. The Tartars did not at once pursue their advantage; but returned to complete the conquest of China. Meanwhile, the Russian princes went back to their habitual feuds; and, all unprepared, were helpless to resist the onset of the Tartars renewed thirteen years later. Between 1237—43, the Tartars subjugated all the Russian lands: and captured Kiev, 1240. They then founded on the Lower Volga a city called Sarai (=the castle), which became the capital of the Golden Horde (Orda=camp). Its Khan was the immediate overlord of the Russians; but, until 1260, he was himself the Viceroy of the Grand Khan in Mongolia.[5] Pagans when they entered Russia, the Tartars, c. 1272, embraced the religion of Islām. They were tolerant towards the religion of their subject people; but they showed themselves hard lords in secular affairs. They allowed the Russians to remain in possession of their lands. But their princes were compelled to visit the Golden Horde, and sometimes even the Grand Khan in China, for authorisation to rule and for the settlement of disputes; and while their subjects were required to pay the Tartar poll-tax, the principalities were bound to furnish the Mongol armies with troops on demand.[6]

The Russian Church at this epoch, was governed by metropolitans of all Russia, beginning with Cyril III., 1242—†81, until Jonah, 1448—†61; the first at Kiev: his two immediate successors, Maximus, 1285—†1305, and Peter, 1305—†26, at Vladimir, and the remainder from 1328 at Moscow. Vladimir is a city about a hundred miles E.N.E. of Moscow; and is situated on the Kliaswa, a tributary of the Oka which, in its turn, is an affluent of the Volga. It is to be distinguished from Vladimir-Volynski, far to the S.W. and now in Poland. After the fall of Kiev, Vladimir became for a time the capital of the House of Rurik. Thither the metropolitan followed the Court: and Maximus of Vladimir was the first of Russian metropolitans to take advantage of the friendly disposition manifested towards the clergy by the Tartar Khans. Already, in 1261, they had allowed their conquered subjects to set up a bishop at Sarai (Saratov) the capital of the horde. They now went further; and, at the request of Maximus, conceded to priests and monks exemption from the poll-tax: while, in 1313, his successor, Peter, secured a decree confirming the privileges of the Church and forbidding all and sundry to deprive it of its possessions. The yoke of the Tartars was galling enough to princes: but they were astute enough to see, in concessions to the clergy and the Church, a means of rendering it less onerous to the people.

The stay of Court and Metropolitan at Vladimir was brief—not more than a generation. For early in the fourteenth century the seat of government was transferred to Moscow. Various causes contributed to its rise. Thus Moscow owed much to geographical position. It lay between the Oka and the Volga, and also at the intersection of routes from Kiev to Novgorod, so that it was favourably situated for trade. The security of its position was also an advantage. Colonists from the ruined and enslaved south found safety in Moscow as in the centre of the land between the rivers. It was also out of reach of dangers far afield: such as those which beset Novgorod when its prince, Alexander Nevski, 1252—†63, beat off the Swedes, 1240, and the Teutonic Knights, 1242. Between 1238 and 1368, from the first Tartar assault to the first attack by the Lithuanians, only once did Moscow suffer at enemy hands, 1293. But neither growing population, trade nor security would alone account for the supremacy of Moscow. This was mainly due to the character and policy of its Princes. They were not particularly virtuous or courageous: and to rival princes mere robbers and enemies. But they rose to power because of their calculated subservience to the Tartar Khans; and, being men of cool judgment, in dealing with foreign overlords, models of temperance and precision at home, and good men of business, the Grand Princes of Moscow soon made their city the capital of Russia *de facto*, though Vladimir for a time remained so *de jure*.

First among such princes of the rising city of Moscow was the grandson of Alexander Nevski, the Grand Prince Ivan I. Kalita (=John the Purser), 1328—†41. John was nicknamed the Purser, because of his skill in finance. After obtaining the consent of the Tartars to his revival of the Grand Princedom at Moscow, he persuaded them, in order to make sure of their tribute, to place in his hands the financial supervision of the Russian principalities. His farming of the taxes was a step on the road to the subsequent authority of the Tsars over all the Russias; and, at the same time, Ivan strengthened his position at home by dropping the old system of inheritance by which Russian princes divided their lands as appanages among their sons, in favour of succession by right of primogeniture. Thus Ivan " established the idea of the State as one and indivisible." His ecclesiastical policy followed similar lines. Taking advantage of the preference of Peter, metropolitan of Vladimir, 1305—†28, for Moscow as a place of residence, he transferred the metropolitanate from the legal to the actual capital of Russia: and there Theognostes, 1328—†52, set up his throne as the first of twenty metropolitans of Moscow. Ivan then proceeded to give to his city the prestige of an ecclesiastical capital. He built churches for its adornment, notably the Church of the Assumption in the Kremlin. He and his successors procured the beatification of its earlier metropolitans: Peter, who forsook Vladimir for Moscow, and Alexis, successor to Theognostes, from 1354—†78. Monasteries also were founded in his, and his successors', days: which rendered the dominions of the Grand Prince of Moscow as celebrated for piety as the land of Kiev. They numbered as many as a hundred and eighty in all; but among the most famous are the monastery of Varlaam, on Lake Ladoga, founded in 1329 by Sergei and Germanus, and the monastery of the Trinity (Troitsa) founded in 1342 by St. Sergius, 1314—†92. The Troitsa became the chief monastic centre near Moscow; and, though forty miles from the city, did much to establish the growing pre-eminence of Moscow as the new capital of Russia. It also became "the mother of a rapidly increasing family of daughters, which spread widely northwards, and colonised the large unoccupied areas in that quarter with monks."[7] One of these was the monastery of Bielo-Ozero (the White Lake), north of Vologda, founded c. 1350, by St. Cyril, the friend and companion of St. Sergius. And a still more northerly offshoot was the Solovetski monastery in the White Sea. " It was founded in 1429 by Herman and Sabbati, hermits from Bielo-Ozero, on a small island in the White Sea: and served as the base of [missionary] operations among the Laplanders and other tribes along the coasts."[8] " By tradition, Russia was a missionary nation, and its church a missionary church. . . The monasteries were the chief evangelistic agencies. From the earliest days of Russia's conversion, these outposts were being pushed forward, civilising and Christianising, across the great open spaces, over the interminable steppes, and even up to the cold sea in the inhospitable north. Where any less concentrated or less continuous agency would have been useless, they succeeded; setting up a warm centre of light in a wide and cold area of darkness, and gradually extending their influence until the district was won."[9]

These movements, however, monastic and missionary, though beginning under Ivan Kalita, belong to the reigns of his successors: and we have forestalled events. Ivan Kalita was succeeded by his son Simeon the Proud, 1343 —†53; who continued his father's policy, secular and ecclesiastical. " He combined subservience to the Horde with domination over Russian princes, and assumed the title of Grand Prince of all the Russias. Aided by St. Alexis, metropolitan of Moscow, 1354—†78, he had bells cast for Moscow and Novgorod; adorned the three churches of the Kremlin with paintings; and did much to enhance the splendour proper to Moscow as an ecclesiastical metropolis." But his reign synchronised with the Black Death—that landmark in English history as well—and of this he died.

There followed six years of anarchy under his brother Ivan II., the Good, 1353—†9. But these came to an end with the accession of his son Dmitri Donskoi, 1362—†89. He won his surname at the battle of Kulikovo (=field of the woodcocks), on the Don, 1380. It was the first victory of Russians over Tartars, and the first dawn of ultimate deliverance from their yoke. Tartar raiding was henceforth to be held in check not by diplomacy as under Ivan Kalita, but by the sword: and the financial association of Russian principalities effected by Kalita was developed under his grandson into political union. Further, the spiritual leadership which Kalita had given to Moscow now bore fruit in the new national vigour displayed by Dmitri's successes against the Tartars. On his death, Moscow took rank as chief of the Russian principalities of the N.E.: and part of her greatness was due to the establishment in her ruling house of the principle of lineal inheritance in preference to collateral succession.

But, at this time, a rival to the future development of Moscow came suddenly to the front by the Union of Poland and Lithuania, 1386. Hedwig, Queen of Poland, 1384—†99, and still only a girl of 15, was forced by her nobles, from fear of Hungary, to accept the offer of marriage made to her by Iagailo (Jagellon), Duke of Lithuania, 1377—†1434. It was a master-stroke of policy on the part of the Poles: for, as the price of the crown of Poland the Duke accepted for his heathen realm conversion to Christianity, in its Roman form: on the same day, 4th March, 1388, he was christened and crowned King of Poland under the name of Ladislas V.,[10] and the union issued in the creation of the mighty Polish state of the Renaissance, the Reformation and the seventeenth century. The struggle, however, between Catholic Poland

and Orthodox Russia lay still in the future : and, whatever danger might afterwards arise in the West to Russia and Orthodoxy, under Dmitri Donskoi there began a great expansion to the N.E. by the missionary zeal of St. Stephen, bishop of Perm, 1383—†96. Perm is a town about 1130 miles N.E. of Moscow, and is situate on the Kama, an affluent of the Volga. The Ural mountains run through the province of Perm from north to south : and three-fourths of it are still forest. Stephen " was a Russian, born at Ustiug in the district of his subsequent work; and had the advantage of knowing from boyhood the language and life of his future converts. A great zeal for learning drew him into the monastery of St. Gregory at Rostov, 1365, and there his call to return as missionary to his old haunts became increasingly clear to him. Thirteen years were spent in preparation. He learnt Greek so as to be better equipped for dealing with the language and the work of translation. Also during his monastic career he reduced the barbarian language to system and writing, and made a large number of translations. After being ordained priest, and getting the necessary sanctions at Moscow, he went forth to the Zyrian people (c. 1378) and settled at Ust-Vym. Thence he went through all the Perm country; preaching, confounding the heathen magicians, and destroying the idols. He taught letters to the young men of the people, and trained them to be teachers and clergy—thus laying the foundations of the native church. In 1383 he was himself raised to the episcopate, and his influence and sphere of activity became larger. Not content with dispensing religion and a large-hearted charity to his flock within the limits of his diocese, he became their champion against attack and oppression both in Novgorod and in Moscow. On one such errand in 1396 death overtook him in Moscow after eighteen years of apostolic labour. He was buried in the famous Court Church of the Kremlin—St. Saviour's in the Wood—and was canonised by the Synod of 1549."[11]

Under Basil II., 1389—†1425, the expansion of Russia continued. Novgorod and Vladimir were brought under his suzerainty as dependent principalities. In 1392 he visited the Golden Horde to acquire Nizhni-Novgorod and Suzdal. And he reaped no little advantage from the irruption of Timour,[12] 1336—†1405. This Mongol conqueror, by the destruction of Sarai (Saratov) the capital of the Golden Horde, seriously weakened their power: and just as he relieved Constantinople at the battle of Angora, 1402, from the menaces of the Turk, so he relieved the pressure on Russia from the Tartars in the east. But on the west, a new menace arose from the successes of Poles and Lithuanians over the Teutonic Knights. At the great battle of Tannenberg, 15th July, 1410, Poland inflicted a decisive defeat upon the Order, absorbed its territories and so gained access to the sea. She was now a dangerous neighbour to the advance of Russia: while Polish Catholicism confronted Russian Orthodoxy.

Under Basil III., 1425—†62, a civil war of twenty years rendered any such advance impossible: but of more interest to the ecclesiastical history of Russia are the events that, in his reign, agitated Orthodoxy through its contact with the West. Pope Eugenius IV., 1431—†47, by the Councils of Ferrara, 1438, and Florence, 1439, hoped to re-establish the supremacy of the Papacy after its humiliation from the reforming Councils by bringing about the union between Latins and Greeks. It was a union, at that time, urgently desired by the Greeks, if only to obtain military aid from the West against the Turks. The Emperor, John VIII. (Palaeologus), 1425—†48, set sail for Italy, November, 1437; and among the prelates whom he found at Ferrara was Isidore, metropolitan of Moscow, 1436—41. Isidore was a Greek, born at Salonika. He had already had a share in the Council of Basel, and was interested in the coming Council. He was still Hegumen of the Convent of St. Demetrius in Constantinople when, a vacancy occurring in the see of Moscow, the Œcumenical Patriarch, Joseph II., 1416—†39, appointed him metropolitan and desired him to attend, in that capacity, at Ferrara. Isidore set out for Moscow, and arrived in April, 1437. He found Basil III. and his people well disposed. They wanted help from the West; and, like the Emperor and Patriarch of CP., were naïve enough to suppose that they would get it on their own terms, by prevailing upon the Latins to renounce their errors. Thus encouraged, Isidore proceeded on his journey by sea from Riga to Lübeck, and thence to Ferrara: where he arrived in time to take part in the Council both there and after its transference to Florence, 10th January, 1439. He does not appear to have been prominent, at first: but in the course of the discussions, he became convinced, with Bessarion, 1395—†1472 (a Greek of Trebizond) who was then archbishop of Nicæa, 1438, and afterwards became Cardinal and Latin Patriarch of Constantinople, 1463) of the necessity of re-union on the Latin terms. Accordingly, Isidore signed the Act of Union,[13] 5th July. He was created Cardinal; and dispatched by the Pope as his *Legatus a latere* to propagate the union throughout Lithuania, Livonia, Russia and Poland. Travelling leisurely through the intermediate countries, Isidore at last entered Moscow, March, 1441, as Cardinal Legate, preceded by a Latin Cross. He celebrated the liturgy at the Church of the Assumption in the Kremlin. He recited the name of Pope Eugenius before that of the Patriarch of Constantinople. And, at the end of the liturgy, his protodeacon read from the ambo the Florentine Act of Union. But he had miscalculated. Horror and consternation at the thought of union between Orthodox and Catholic, seized the congregation. Within four days after his arrival, Isidore was arrested. He was condemned and deposed by a Council, and imprisoned in the Chudov monastery. But in September, 1441, he escaped and made his way back to Rome: where he died, 1463, as Latin Patriarch of Constantinople. Ten years previously, Constantinople had been taken by the Turks. The way was thus left clear for Moscow to become the centre of Orthodoxy, for its efforts to break loose from Constantinople because that see was now compromised by the Florentine Act of Union with Rome; and for its ruler to step into the place of the East-Roman Emperor as the Christian Tsar.

§ 5. We now come to the third period, 1461—1589; of the two metropolitanates of Moscow and Kiev. The double series was actually inaugurated by the further activities of Isidore after his escape to Rome. He persuaded the Pope to send Gregory, one of his pupils, to be Uniate metropolitan of Kiev. This, of course, was distasteful to Moscow: and provoked the opposition of the Grand Prince, and the new metropolitan Jonah, 1448—†61. But to no purpose: for the Grand Duke of Lithuania was equally determined to keep his hold on Kiev. He set up Gregory in the see, 1458—†73; and demanded his recognition as metropolitan of Moscow also in place of Jonah on the ground that Jonah had been appointed by the Russian bishops without the consent of the Œcumenical Patriarch. The difficulty was resolved by Gregory himself who, in 1470, renounced his Uniate status and was accepted as Orthodox metropolitan of Kiev. The successors of Jonah, in their turn, acquiesced: by describing themselves henceforward as " metropolitans of Moscow and all Russia." So the double series of metropolitans at Moscow and Kiev was maintained till 1589. Its maintenance was due to the Russian people being politically divided between the two realms of Muscovy and Poland-Lithuania. While the Great Russians belonged to Muscovy, Poland-Lithuania had by now absorbed Little Russians and White Russians, Black and Red Russians: and Kiev, the old capital of Little Russia, lay within its borders. Further, Poland-Lithuania, as a Catholic State, was not inclined to tolerate too close a union between the Orthodox adherents of its archbishop at Kiev and the Orthodox State and Church of Moscow. In order that the metropolitans of Kiev should be kept in hand, they were not encouraged to reside there; and the fifteen, who followed each other in succession from Gregory, 1458—†73, to Onesiphorus, 1579—†89, lived more or less in exile from their see.

Events, however, were in progress which issued in the recovery of Kiev, and its re-union with Moscow and Russia. They are those which led to the creation of the Tsardom of Muscovy, 1462—1584. It was the work of the next three sovereigns:[14] Ivan the Great, Basil IV. and Ivan the Terrible.

Ivan III. (the Great[15]), 1462—†1505, began by suppressing the moribund republic of Novgorod, 1471; and absorbing the small principalities within reach of Moscow —1463, Yaroslavl; 1474, Rostov; 1485, Tver. Further to the N.E., Perm in 1472, and Vyatka in 1489, made their submission. Meanwhile, in 1480, the Tartar overlordship came to an end. " No part of *Rus* henceforth, beyond the limits of Lithuania-Poland, acknowledged a foreign master."[16] In the north and east, Ivan carried his conquests further afield; and, after repeated attempts, 1465—99, at last succeeded in annexing Yugra (N.W. Siberia) to his dominions. On the west, he drove the Lithuanians back behind the Sozh, 1503, a tributary of the Dnieper on its left bank; and recovered the territories which they had filched from Russia. Ivan was thus rightly styled " Re-uniter of Russian lands." He was also reorganiser of Russian rule. For he substituted a centralised government for disorder: very much as was done by his English contemporaries, the Yorkists and Tudors of the New Monarchy, 1471—1588. By getting rid of the Tartars, he made himself independent of any foreign power; and, in this sense, laid claim to the title " autocrat." Not that he had, as yet, attained an absolute authority within his realm. But that, in relation to other princes, he was now their equal, and a sovereign-ruler himself. As such, he obtained recognition: and so, for the first time, brought Russia into the comity of nations, whether of Western Europe or Islām. But by marriage with a Byzantine princess, 1472, Ivan III. obtained still more. Thomas Palaeologus, brother of Constantine XIII., the last East-Roman Emperor, had taken refuge in Rome. He died there; but left a daughter Zoe[17] (Sophia). The pope wished to find her a husband; and Paul II., 1464—†71, at the advice of Cardinal Bessarion, advised him to offer her in marriage to the Grand Prince of Russia. " Ivan and his boyards accepted the proposal with enthusiasm; it was God, no doubt, who had given him so illustrious a wife; ' a branch of the imperial tree which had formerly overshadowed all orthodox Christianity.' . . This daughter of emperors was destined to have an enormous influence on Ivan. It was she, no doubt, who taught him to 'penetrate the secret of autocracy.'.... 'How long am I to be the slave of the Tartars?' she would often ask."[18] She taught him also to look upon himself as the heir of the Cæsars, and upon Moscow as the only metropolis of Orthodoxy. Again, she brought in her train a crowd of Greek emigrants, who started a Renaissance in Russia. There were Italians also in her retinue; who re-built in Byzantine style the three churches in the Kremlin, of the Assumption, the Annunciation and St. Michael. As a symbol of his new dignity, and perhaps by right of his wife, Ivan took for the arms of Russia the double-headed eagle of Byzantium.

Basil IV., 1505—†33, succeeded; and carried on the policy of his father. He incorporated into his dominions the city-republic of Pskov, 1510, to the N.W.; the principalities of Ryazan, on the Oka, 1517, to the S.E. of Chernigov and Novgorod-Severşk, 1523, to the S.W.; and, 1514, he recovered from Lithuania the ancient city of Smolensk on the Dnieper.[19] At home, he swept away the last of the appanaged princes: and was the first of his house to assume the title: " Tsar and Autocrat of all the Russias." Not only the *boyars*, but the Church as well, felt the weight of his hand; and, of the three metropolitans of Moscow who held office during his reign, the first, Barlaam, 1511—21, resigned; the second, Porphyry, was thrown into prison; and only the third, Daniel, 1522—†39, continued at his post. Perhaps this was because he resembled in some degree his contemporary Cranmer, and was an adept in servility to tyrants; in particular, over their matrimonial projects. Basil IV. had long been married to Solomonia Saburova; but had no heir. He was anxious about the succession. The metropolitan consented not only to pronounce his divorce, but to permit his " re-marriage " to Helena Glinskaia. On 25th August, 1530, she bore him a son, who grew up to be Ivan the Terrible;[20] and three years later Basil IV. died.

The long reign of Ivan IV., 1533—†84, marks an epoch in the history of Russia. It is divisible into three periods, the first two of equal length; a minority of fourteen years, 1533—47; then another fourteen, in mid-career, 1547—61, of expansion abroad and reform at home both in State and Church; and finally the reign of terror, 1561—84, as a consequence of which his country fell back exhausted and the Tsar himself became indeed Ivan the Terrible.[21]

(i.) Ivan was a child of three years old at his accession; and for five years, 1533—8, so long as his mother lived, all went well. She took her uncle, Michael Glinski, for her adviser; and, while her family thus obtained power, they did not misuse it. But, on the death of the Empress Regent in 1538, their supremacy was resented; and for nine years, 1538—47, there ensued a period of contest for power between rival houses in which the *boyars* reduced their country to anarchy. Ivan, meanwhile, was growing up to manhood: an orphan, moody and suspicious; and a precocious youth, whose undisciplined inclinations it was the interest of the *boyars* to encourage. But an end came to anarchy when, at the age of seventeen, Ivan IV. suddenly declared himself of age and claimed the government in his own right.

(ii.) In his eighteenth year he had himself crowned at Moscow, 16th January, 1547. It was the first coronation of a Russian ruler as Tsar; and, shortly afterwards, he married, 3rd February, Anastasia Romanovna. From her brother, Nikita, sprang the Tsars of the House of Romanov, who held the throne till the Revolution of 1917. Anastasia made Ivan a faithful wife; but neither his coronation nor his marriage had any influence for the better upon his conduct. Suddenly, however, an improvement took place. A great fire in Moscow alarmed and sobered the Tsar. For there appeared a priest from Novgorod, named Silvester: who, after the manner of an Hebrew prophet, declared that the fire was a judgment of God upon the vices of Ivan and his people. And he bade the Tsar mend his ways, lest worse should befall him. Ivan had the sense to take the advice; and he began to act like an enlightened prince devoted to the welfare of his people. But he was aware of his inexperience: and, looking about for councillors, he kept Silvester at his side for ecclesiastical business, and entrusted secular affairs to a young noble named Adashev. By their advice, he inaugurated reforms both in State and Church. In 1550 he summoned a *Sobor,* or Assembly, " to deliberate on remedies for the terrible condition to which the oppression of the recent *boyar* régime had reduced the realm." The Assembly was of an administrative character; and " preliminary to the promulgation of Ivan's Code, which revived the law-book look of his grandfather,"[22] and aimed at some measure of local self-government. But the privilege had to be bought; and the local administration fell back into the hands of officials sent down from Moscow.

The attempt at ecclesiastical reform had not much better success. In 1551, Ivan IV. summoned the Council of the Hundred Chapters (Stoglav); so called because its decisions were arranged under a hundred heads. It met in the Kremlin, 1551; and there were present the metropolitan Macarius, 1542—†63, with nine bishops, besides archimandrites and nobles. Some of its enactments dealt with rites and ceremonies, and these may be reserved till we come to the reforms of the Patriarch Nikon, 1653—†67. It also dealt with other matters: church government and ecclesiastical courts, abuses in clerical life, monastic reform, and reforms concerning the life of the laity. In respect of ecclesiastical government, the legislation of the Council was directed to secure " a more effective supervision of the clergy and their dependents; to prevent the exaction of excessive fees and oppression by officials; to restrict their interference with the ecclesiastical courts proper, and regulate their own proper judicial action. In dealing with the abuses of clerical life the Council took steps not only to rebuke and correct scandals, but also to provide a better supply of efficient candidates for the priesthood by establishing better schools and enjoining upon the bishop more strictness in choosing candidates. Again, in dealing with monastic abuses the Council, besides attempting to ex-

ܐܝܫܝ ܡܪܝ ܫܡܥܘܢ
ܩܐܬܘܠܝܩܐ ܦܛܪܝܪܟܐ ܕܡܕܢܚܐ

THE ASSYRIAN PATRIARCH, ISSAI MAR SHIMUN.

See p. 424.]

tirpate scandals, introduced some reforms, *e.g.* it forbade the continuance of double monasteries which housed both monks and nuns; it curtailed the private privileges of the officers of monasteries; it recalled the religious to live in their monasteries, and not at large."[23] But, in this connection, the main business was how to prevent the Church from becoming the sole proprietor of Russian land. Many would have desired the secularisation of all monastic property, and the extension of State control over all Church lands. But Macarius and the clergy opposed these designs; and hindered any radical reform. "It was ordained," however, "that all allodial lands, which the *boyars* had made over to the Church without the sovereign's consent, should be restored; that all gifts made to it during Ivan's minority should be cancelled; and that, in future, the monasteries should not acquire certain kinds of estate without Imperial consent. Thus a limit was set to the growth of ecclesiastical property."[24] As to reform of the life of the laity, the aim of the Council was, as might be supposed, to put down immorality and superstition of various kinds.

As an appendix to this part of the Council's efforts, the *Domostroi* or Domestic Code, is of special interest. It stands in line with the *Instructions* bequeathed to his son by Vladimir (Monomachus), 1113—†25. "It was a new form of an old collection of domestic maxims given by a father to his son; the new edition was due to Silvester." Of this treatise, cc. 1—15, " set out the ideals of religion in the home, as a whole, the family prayers, the observance of fasts and festival, etc., together with duty to God and to the authorities ": cc. 16—30 " deal with mutual obligations within the family, the duties of husband and wife, parents and children "; cc. 31—65 are " concerned ... with details of domestic economy, the avoidance of vices and dangerous recreations and sports," and directions to a husband how to beat his wife. He is not to thrash her with a stick : but to take off her gown and beat her politely with a whip, while holding her by the hand! " The final chapter is in the form of an appeal from the writer to his son, that he should follow the example of his father." As a mirror of contemporary ideals and manners, the *Domostroi* is of curious but permanent interest. " But it suffered from the rigorism natural to a monastic reformer : so domestic life rebelled against it, and rendered it largely abortive."[25]

Its author was now out of favour. By 1553 the Tsar had come to lose confidence in his advisers Silvester and Adashev, suspecting them of too great sympathy with the *boyars*, from whom he had suffered so much in his youth. He now began to turn towards the further expansion of his empire : and this had, for one of its consequences, an extension of the Church. Three relics of the dominion of the Tartars still survived in the Khanates of Kazan, Astrakhan and the Crimea. In 1552, Ivan IV. accomplished the reconstitution of his military forces; and organised the *Streltsi,* or permanent garrison of Moscow, whom he equipped with fire-arms. He then conquered Kazan, 1553, on the upper Volga, to the east of Moscow —a city which Ivan the Great had captured, 1487, but had not annexed. It was incorporated into Russia; and formed into a new diocese, 1555. The memorial of his victory is still to be seen in the strange but beautiful church of St. Basil the Beatified which the Tsar caused to be erected as a thank-offering in the Red Square at Moscow. He next proceeded to the conquest of Astrakhan, 1554. He was now in possession of the whole course of the Volga; and it only remained for him to seize the Crimea, and so to reach the Black Sea. But the project was premature. The Tartars of the Crimea forestalled it by invading Russia, and burning Moscow, 1571. Ivan, meanwhile, had turned his arms to the N.W. With a view to an outlet on the Baltic, he wrested Livonia from the Teutonic Order, in 1557—60 : but could not hold it. The time for the expansion of Russia from sea to sea had not yet arrived. Ivan, however, recovered Polotsk from Lithuania, 1563; and another new diocese was formed there also.

(iii.) By this time a great change had come over Ivan IV.; which led to the third period of his reign,

1561—84. Within a few years, the restraining influences that surrounded him were removed in rapid succession: for the loss of the Tsarina Anastasia, 1560, was followed shortly by the death of the metropolitan Macarius, 1563. He felt completely alone : and the fears and hatreds of his boyhood seized upon him again. In order to protect himself against the *boyars,* he divided the administration of his empire into two parts. In 1564 he set up for part of the empire the *Oprichnina* or " Separate Establishment," over which he presided at the new Court in Alexandrov, a village near Moscow; and he left the *boyars* to carry on the government of the remainder in their *Zemstchina* or Council, at the old Court of Moscow. The *Oprichniki,* or servants of the new administration, became the agents of a reign of terror; and, with the Tsar for their abbot, lived a life of debauchery alternating with monastic exercises. Two metropolitans, Germanus, 1563—5, and Philip, 1565—†8, endeavoured to bring him to repentance. The former was quickly thrust aside : but Philip, who had been abbot of the austere Solovetski monastery in the solitudes of the White Sea, made a firmer stand. On the third Sunday in Lent of 1568, in the Uspenski Cathedral at Moscow, he refused to recognise the Tsar in the habit of the *Oprichniki;* and, after a second encounter, Ivan determined to get rid of him. He was put to death in a monastery at Tver. In 1570 the *Oprichniki* were let loose upon Tver. They completely devastated the city, and thence they proceeded to massacre the inhabitants of Novgorod.

Outbreaks of cruelty and murder, with intervals of remorse, continued for the rest of the reign; but Ivan retained his vigour, and undertook enterprises of lasting effect. He could not indeed maintain his hold upon Livonia : for after twenty years' war with Poland he was obliged to surrender it to that country, 1582. The Swedes to the north and the Poles to the west were, as yet, too strong to be reduced by Russian arms. But the Tsar was more successful to the S. and N. He beat back the Tartars of the Crimea after their advance upon Moscow: and, by the aid of the Cossack leader, Ermak, he annexed

Western Siberia, 1582. But the distant West also had its attractions for him: and trade was established between Russia and England by the adventurous mariners of Edward VI. and Elizabeth. Richard Chancellor made two voyages to Archangel, 1552; and thence to Moscow, 1553; while Sir Jerome Horsey went to Moscow, 1573, as clerk in the Russian Company. In 1580 he was sent home by Ivan to purchase munitions of war in England. He returned: and in 1585 was sent off again with dispatches to Elizabeth. In 1587 he came back to Moscow, and established a trade-monopoly with Russia for the English Company. The English traders were thus welcome to Ivan IV.; and, in the accounts of Russia they have left, occurs a description of the religion of the Russian people, worth quoting. It is by the English protestant Chancellor, and should be compared with the earlier and longer account by the Roman Catholic Sigismund Freiherr von Herberstein, 1486—†1566, who went twice to Moscow, in 1517, as ambassador of the Emperor Maximilian I., 1493—†1519, and in 1526 of the Archduke Ferdinand. Herberstein was charged by the Archduke to let him know " ubi conveniant vel discrepent in articulis fidei ac caerimoniis"; and hence the sketch of the Orthodox religion by silent contrast with the Catholic in his *Rerum Moscovitarum Commentarii*,[26] 1549. Chancellor's sketch is from the point of view of an English layman, half-pious, and half-puzzled, whose notions were those of the Reformation in England at its lowest ebb. It is as follows:—

" They doe observe the law of the Greekes with such excesse of superstition, as the like hath not bene heard of. They have no graven images in their churches, but all painted, to the intent they will not breake the commandement; but to their painted images they use such idolatrie, that the like was never heard of in England. They will neither worship nor honour any image that is made forth of their owne countrey. They have none other learning but their mother tongue, nor will suffer no other in their countrey among them. All their service in Churches is in their mother tongue. They have the old and new Testamente, which are daily read among them: and yet their superstition is no lesse. For when the Priests doe reade they have such tricks in their reading, that no man can understand them, nor no man giveth eare to them. For all the while the Priest readeth, the people sit down and one talke with another. But when the Priest is at service no man sitteth, but gagle and duck like so many Geese. And as for their prayers they have but little skill, but use to say *As bodi pomcle:* as much as to say, *Lord, have mercy upon me.* For the tenth man within the land cannot say the *Pater noster.* And as for the Creede, no man may be so bolde as to meddle therewith but in the Church: for they say it should not bee spoken of, but in the Churches. Speake to them of the Commandements, and they will say they were given to Moses in the law, which Christ hath now abrogated by his precious death and passion: therefore (say they) we observe little or none thereof. And I do beleeve them. For if they were examined of their Lawe and Commaundements together, they should agree but in fewe poynts. They have the Sacrament of the Lord's Supper in both kindes, and more ceremonies than we have. They present them in a dish in both kindes together, and carry them round about the Church upon the Priestes head, and so doe minister at all such times as any shall require. They be great offerers of Candles, and sometimes of money, which we call in England Soule pense, with more ceremonies than I am able to declare. They have foure Lents in the yeare, whereof our Lent is the greatest. Looke as we doe begin on the Wednesday, so they doe on the Munday before: And the weeke before that they call The Butter weeke: And in that weeke they eate nothing but Butter and milke. Howbeit, I beleeve there bee in no other countrey the like people for drunkennesse. . . . In these Lentes they eate neither Butter, Egges, Milke nor Cheese; but they are very straitely kept with Fish, Cabbages, and Rootes. And out of their Lents, they observe truely the Wednesdayes and Fridayes throughout the yeere: and on the Saturday they doe eate flesh. Furthermore, they have a great number of Religious men: which are blacke Monks, and they eate no flesh throughout the yeere, but fish, milke and Butter. By their order they should eate no fresh-fish; and in their Lents they eate nothing but Coleworts, Cabbages, salt Cowcumbers, with other rootes, as Radish and such like. Their drinke is like our peny ale, and is called Quass. They have service daily in their Churches: and use to goe to service two houres before day, and that is ended by day-light. At nine of the clock they goe to Masse: that ended to dinner; and after that to service again: and then to supper. You shall understand that at every dinner and supper they have declared the exposition of the Gospel that day: but how they wrest and twine the Scripture and that together by report it is wonderfull. As for whoredome and drunkennesse, there be none such living: and for extortion, they be the most abhominable under the sunne. Now judge of their holinesse. They have twise as much land as the Duke himselfe hath, but yet he is reasonable eeven with them, as thus: when they take bribes of any of the poore, and simple, he hath it by an order. When the Abbot of any of their houses dieth, then the Duke hath all his goods moveable and immoveable: so that the successor buieth all at the Duke's hands: and by this meane they be the best Fermers the Duke hath. Thus with their Religion I make an ende, trusting hereafter to know it better."[27]

Chancellor's view of it was critical but not unkind. It is a picture of lurid morals, mixed with genuine piety: and of a people not without traits of their sovereign Ivan the Terrible. One of his last outbreaks was to murder his son and heir, Ivan, in a fit of fury, 10th November, 1581. His second son, Theodore, was a weakling: and the third, Dmitri, by his last wife, Maria Nagaia, was but an infant. Thus Ivan himself brought his dynasty, the House of Rurik, to an end: and he died, 18th March, 1584, while playing chess, after an outburst of wrath at the wizards whom he had consulted, because they had told him that that day would be his last. Ivan sent a squire to tell them "the Emperor will burry or burne them all quick for their fals illucious and lies. The day is come: he is as hartt holl as ever he was. 'Sir, be not so wrathfull' [was their reply]. 'You know the daie is come and ends with the setting of the sun.' "[28]

§ 6. The fourth period of the history of the Church in Russia covers 1589—1700, and is the period of the Patriarchate of Moscow.

(i.) Politically, the period opened with thirty years of turmoil, 1584—1613, which intervened between the end of the House of Rurik and the accession of the House of Romanov. The end of the dynasty, 1584—1605, led to chaos known as the Time of Troubles, 1605—13; and the long struggle passed through three stages—dynastic, social and national—before order was restored in Church and State under the dyarchy of the first Romanovs— Michael the Tsar, 1613—†45, and his father, Philaret the Patriarch, 1619—†33.

(a.) Ivan the Terrible was succeeded by his son Theodore I., 1584—†98; but Theodore was a weakling. His brother-in-law, Boris Godunov, became the real ruler; though, at first, with the assistance and restraint of the Tsar's uncle, Nikita Romanov and others. Nikita died within a year; and Boris then took over the entire responsibility as Lord Protector of Russia. His policy as Regent, and afterwards as Tsar, was to favour the middle classes. They wanted land, and men to till it; and this led in 1597 to the formal introduction of serfdom. Meanwhile, the Empress-Mother, Anastasia Romanov, and the Tsarevitch Dmitri, had been relegated to Uglich, a town lying to the north of Moscow on the way to Yaroslavl. In 1591 the boy was found dead, with his throat cut; and the crime was attributed to Boris. He had a dangerous game to play, in order to hold his own against the suspicion that fell upon him. But he played it successfully. He banished Nikita's son, Theodore Romanov, first cousin of the weakling Tsar and connected through his wife Martha, the nun, with the old House of Rurik; and, having thus got rid of his chief rival, he ingratiated himself with the Sober or National Assembly and, supported by Job, Patriarch of Moscow, 1589—1605, was elected Tsar, 1598—1605. Thus the dynastic phase of the struggle ended in the extinction of the House of Rurik and the exclusion, for the time being, of the House of Romanov.

(b.) In its second, or social phase, the struggle for power developed into civil war; but was complicated by the intervention of foreign powers. A pretender, impersonating the murdered Tsarevitch, appeared in Poland, 1603. He turned out to be Gregory Otropiev, an unfrocked monk, who had formerly been in the service of the Romanovs: but he was a clever impostor. To conciliate friends, he professed himself a Roman Catholic, 1604; and played his part so well as to enlist the support of Sigismund III., King of Poland, 1587—†1632. Sigismund was the son of John III., King of Sweden, 1577—†92, and succeeded his father as King of Sweden, 1592—1604. But he had been brought up by the Jesuits, now all-powerful in Poland through having won back that country to the Counter-Reformation: whereas Sweden remained steadfastly Lutheran. Sigismund, accordingly, was repudiated by the Swedes; and, returning to Poland, was only too glad to be able to fish in troubled waters by espousing the cause of the False Dmitri I. As King of Poland-Lithuania, Sigismund hoped to win back parts of Lithuania recently annexed by Russia; and as ex-King of Sweden he looked to obtain Russian help to enable him to recover the throne he had lost. The False Dmitri I. could thus rely on Sigismund III.: and through him on the backing of the Roman Church: for Pope Clement VIII., 1592—†1605, would see in his enterprise a chance for bringing the Orthodox of Russia into union with the Holy See. Thus aided by powerful interests the pretender crossed the frontier, 1604, and soon attracted a following: particularly of peasants and cossacks. Boris died at this juncture: and should have been succeeded by his son, a handsome and promising lad of sixteen, who was proclaimed Tsar as Theodore II. He was supported by the Patriarch Job, 1589—1605, who issued his fulminations against the usurper. In spite of these, however, the army declared for the False Dmitri; and, while the populace seized and imprisoned the whole family of Godunovs, Dmitri entered Moscow and was acclaimed as Tsar, 1605

—†6. He at once proceeded to disgrace and remove the Patriarch Job in favour of Ignatius, whom he brought from Riazan to be Patriarch, 1605—6 : a Greek by birth, who had been educated in Rome and was, therefore, suspected of leanings towards re-union : and he got rid similarly of other partisans of Boris. But within a year he had succeeded in alienating all classes : the nobles, because of his favouritism; the clergy, because of his alliance with the Roman See; and the people, because of the patronage he bestowed on foreigners. In May, 1606, the False Dmitri I. was assassinated, by a band of conspirators under the leadership of Prince Vassili Shuiski, a lineal descendant of the old House of Rurik. They set up their chief as the Tsar Basil V., 1606—†10 : and so procured the triumph of that princely class against which the *Oprichnina,* or official nobility, of Ivan IV. had been directed. At the same time they displaced Ignatius, the Patriarch of the False Dmitri, in favour of Hermogenes, who thus became the third Patriarch of Moscow, 1606—11 : and signalised his promotion by having the real Dmitri canonised and transporting his relics to Moscow. But it was a short-lived triumph for the old *boyar* aristocracy. A second pretender appeared, False Dmitri II. : again with the support of the populace and of King Sigismund III. The King of Poland invaded Russia, headed off his enemies the Swedes who had intervened in favour of Basil V., and advanced upon Moscow. There the *boyars,* rather than accept the False Dmitri II., consented to acknowledge Sigismund's son, Ladislas,[29] as Tsar, on condition that he would become a member of the Orthodox Church : a condition which had been demanded by an embassy to Sigismund, headed by Philaret, now bishop of Rostov, but hitherto known as Theodore Romanov, nephew of Anastasia, the wife of Ivan the Terrible and cousin of his son, Theodore I. At this point, Sigismund showed his hand. He refused permission for his son Ladislas to go over to Orthodoxy; and declared that he would be Tsar himself. Then he sent off Philaret to safe custody in Poland : returned to Warsaw with the Tsar Basil V. in his train, where Basil died: and Russia, for the time being, had to acknowledge the Polish King as Tsar. So ended the second stage in the long struggle: and civil war between social classes issued in the enforced acceptance by prostrate Russia of a foreign rule.

(c.) The struggle, however, could not stop there. It changed its character and became a national movement against the foreigner. As such, it was headed by Hermogenes, the third Patriarch of Moscow, 1606—11: and Russian nationality was saved by the Russian church. The Poles were securely in possession of Moscow, and in March, 1611, beat off an attack by the First National Levy, of a hundred thousand men. But at the end of that year, a stronger movement began for the recovery of law and order and the restoration of Russia to the Russians. It found its rallying point in the Monastery of the Holy Trinity, founded 1382, in the forests some forty miles to the north of Moscow by the hermit Saint Sergius, and well-fortified. The monastery had already withstood a siege of sixteen months by Polish forces under the orders of the False Dmitri II., and it was then under the rule of the archimandrite Dionysius who, after the Poles had done to death the Patriarch Hermogenes, succeeded him as leader of the Russian Church. Dionysius sent forth missives in all directions, bidding the people unite for the overthrow of foreign domination and promising them help. A patriotic response came from the citizens of Nizhni Novgorod on the Volga: and under the leadership of their mayor, Cosmo Minin, a butcher by trade, there took shape the Second National Levy, 1612, well equipped both with money and arms. Advancing upon Moscow, they expelled the Poles from the capital in October: and sent out summonses to all parts of Russia for the meeting of a National Assembly to elect a Tsar. It met at Moscow, early in 1613: and the choice fell upon Michael Romanov, a lad of sixteen, and son of the exiled Theodore, now Philaret and in exile. Michael's " tender age . . . was sufficient to disarm suspicion. But . . . he had one supreme qualification which especially in the popular mind ensured his success. He was the first cousin once removed of the late Tsar Theodore I.," and his grandfather Nikita was the brother of Anatasia, the wife of Ivan the Terrible. This was enough to procure for the monarchy a firm foundation in the principle of legitimacy: and so to end the long struggle of warring factions. On 21st February, 1613, Michael was unanimously elected Tsar. His election marks the triumph of the *Oprichnina,* or official nobility, over the two forces that had brought Russia to the verge of ruin : revolutionary, represented by peasants and cossacks : and reactionary, represented by the *boyars.*

(d.) The reign of Michael Romanov, 1613—†45, marks the recovery of hereditary autocracy: and inaugurates a new epoch for Russia, which as yet was unprepared for any other form of stable government. Significant of the new epoch, and of the fear of renewed anarchy from which the election of Michael had delivered the country, was the title of *Autocrat* which he was the first of Russian rulers to assume. But owing to his inexperience and weakness of character, Russia might again have become the prey of anarchy, such as that which had afflicted her during the minority of Ivan IV., had it not been for the return from exile of Michael's abler father, Theodore Romanov. He had been taken as a hostage to Poland, 1610—8. He now became, as Philaret, the fourth Patriarch of Moscow, 1619—†33 : and co-regent with his son, for a period of Russian history known by consequence as the dyarchy. It was a period of consolidation, in self-defence. In 1617, Michael made terms with Sweden : and by the Treaty of Stolbovo, a village to the south of Lake Ladoga, the Swedes restored old Novgorod to Russia and recognised Michael as Tsar, in return for the cession of Ingria and Carelia districts to the south and east respectively of the Gulf of Finland. In 1618 he made a truce with Poland, on the basis of an exchange of prisoners, whence the return of his father Philaret : and the truce was confirmed by the Peace of Polyanovka, 5th June, 1634. By this agreement, Ladislas VII., as he now was, King of Poland, 1632—†48, in return for a money payment, the abandonment of Muscovite claims on Livonia and the cession of the towns of Smolensk, Seversk and Tchernigov, renounced all claim to the throne of Moscow and recognised the Grand Duke of Muscovy as Tsar. It was a heavy price to pay: for " in consequence of these treaties, Muscovy was completely cut off from the Baltic, besides losing her natural western frontiers, along the courses of the rivers Dnieper and Desna, which became, for a time, exclusively Polish streams."[30] Before they could be recovered, the Tsar Michael died in 1645. He was succeeded by his son Alexis: whose reign was eventful for the recovery by Russia of her Western provinces as well as for both gain and loss to the Church of Russia.

(e.) " The reign of Alexis, 1645—†76, witnessed not only the recovery of the recent acquisitions of Poland, but also the annexation of some of the borderlands which in race, language, sentiment and religion were Russian, but in consequence of the Lithuanian conquest had become part of the composite Polish-Lithuanian State."[31] Such districts were White Russia to the north, and Little Russia (or the Ukraine) to the south. In both these territories the Orthodox religion enjoyed legal safeguards: but " the increase of Polish influence in the Russian lands led to Roman propagandism actively carried on by the Jesuits, and to a long persecution of the Orthodox by those who aimed at union."[31] In the north this might have been successful: but in the south it was resisted by the Cossacks, a military population devoted to the Orthodox Faith. They rose against Poland. Their revolt, coupled with attacks directed from the north on Poland by the Swedes, reduced that country to the verge of disaster. These events " enabled Muscovy to recover from her ancient rival the territory ceded thirty-three years before: and the Peace of Andruszowo, 1667, exactly reversed the Peace of Polyanovka."[32] It restored to the Tsar Smolensk, Seversk and Tchernigov—the chief towns in White Russia—ceded in 1634: and it also gave him Little Russia up to the Dnieper together with the sacred city of Kiev.

(ii.) We now pass to the ecclesiastical counterpart of these gains to Russia.

(a.) One of them is the re-union of Kiev to the Patriarchate of Moscow. During the period of the two Metropolitanates, 1461—1589, the Metropolitanate of Moscow was confined to Great Russia, and its temper was strictly Russian and Orthodox. The Metropolitanate of Kiev, on the other hand, assimilated to some degree the culture of the West, and displayed some literary activity. Fifteen metropolitans succeeded one another at Kiev from Gregory, 1458—†73, to Onesiphorus, 1579—†89 : but they had hard work to maintain the position of their clergy against the pressure of the Jesuit propaganda. In order to save it, the metropolitan Michael and some of the clergy agreed to the union of the churches, accepting the authority of the Roman See, in return for the use of the vernacular and other privileges of Rite : for such were the terms of the Union of Brest-Litovsk, 1596. An Orthodox remnant maintained a stout resistance to the Union : but, for want of bishops and priests of their own, a steady stream passed over to the new Uniate body, until twenty years after the lapse of the metropolitanate by the desertion of Michael, an Orthodox hierarchy was reconstituted. Urgent representations, on behalf of the remnant, were made to the Œcumenical Patriarch : and he sent Theophanes, Patriarch of Jerusalem, to Little Russia in 1620. Theophanes consecrated Job Boretski to be Metropolitan of Kiev : and six bishops to fill the vacant and suppressed sees of Polotsk, Vladimir-Volynsk, Lutsk, Przemysl, Chelm and Pinsk.[33] The Orthodox cause then began to revive. It was vigorously opposed by such ardent Catholics as Josaphat Kuntsivich, bishop of Polotsk, 1618—†23. He tried to suppress all meetings for Orthodox worship, and was murdered at Vitebsk, 12th November, 1623, to be ultimately canonised, 29th June, 1867, by Pius IX. It was as vigorously defended by Orthodox champions : and by none more ably than by Peter Mogila, who became Metropolitan of Kiev, 1632 —†47. His *Orthodox Confession of Faith*[34] is one of the most authoritative documents of Orthodoxy. Thus the preservation of Orthodoxy in the Metropolitanate of Kiev was secured and its ancient prestige revived. In 1686 the Treaty of Moscow between Russia and Poland made the Tsar master of Kiev and Little Russia. The Patriarch of Moscow, Joachim, 1674—90, thereupon nominated Gedeon to be metropolitan of Kiev; and next year, 1687, Dionysius IV., Patriarch of Constantinople, 1671—†93, and Dositheus, Patriarch of Jerusalem, 1669—†1707, recognised the dependence of Kiev on Moscow. Not long afterwards the Patriarchate of Moscow came to an end: but it had done its work for the time in thus unifying the organisation of the Church in Russia.

(b.) We now turn from gain to loss: by schism, by rivalry between Patriarch and Tsar, and by the consequent abolition of the Patriarchate.

The Patriarchate of Moscow owes its inception to Boris Godunov. Anxious to obtain friends and supporters, in order to succeed the child Demetrius, he " secured the loyalty of the Church by a bold and clever stroke."[35] Jeremias II., Patriarch of Constantinople, 1572—†95, had come to Moscow, 1589, in order to solicit alms for the oppressed Christian subjects of the Sultan. Boris responded to his appeal: and induced him, in return, to consecrate a nominee of his own who was now Metropolitan to be Patriarch of Moscow: the Russian hierarchy henceforth to be competent to elect their own Patriarch. Thus Boris enhanced his own prestige as well as that of the Church in Russia: for the Patriarchate of Moscow was to take rank next to Jerusalem, the fifth of the ancient patriarchates. Indeed, it was to rank higher: and to be, in fact, for Orthodoxy, what Rome was for Catholicism. The Patriarchate of Old Rome was held to have lapsed because of the pope's defection from Orthodoxy: and the Patriarchate of New Rome to have lost respect, because of its being subject to the Turk and compromised by union with the Latins at Florence in 1439. Apart, then, from its having eclipsed Kiev, by the consecration of its metropolitan to be Patriarch, the Patriarchate of Moscow became the centre of the Russian Orthodox world. Eleven Patriarchs occupied the throne in succession: (1) Job, 1589—1605, the nominee of Boris; (2) Ignatius, 1605—6, the protégé of False Dmitri I.; (3) Hermogenes, 1606—11, the champion of the national uprising against the Polish supremacy; (4) Philaret, 1619—33, father of the first Tsar of the House of Romanov; (5) Josaphat, 1634—40; (6) Joseph, 1642—52; (7) Nikon, 1652—66, the reformer; (8) Josaphat, 1667—72; (9) Pitirim, 1672—3; (10) Joachim Savelov, 1674—90; and (11) Adrian, 1690—1700. Among the most important of these were Philaret and Joachim, because of their championship of Orthodoxy against Roman Catholicism, and Nikon, because of his reforming energy and his vindication of the rights of the Church against the State. Of these two, however, presently: for, at this point, it is convenient to note that the Patriarch exercised authority over metropolitans and bishops, whose sees were multiplied and suppressed in turn. Thus, in 1589, the creation of the Patriarchate was accompanied by the setting up of four metropolitanates for Novgorod, Kazan, Rostov and Krutiki:[36] of five[37] archbishoprics for Suzdal, Ryazan, Tver, Vologda and Smolensk: with eight bishoprics.[38] In 1602 was founded the see of Astrakhan, and in 1620 Siberia was given an episcopal see at Tobolsk. " In 1682 the Tsar Theodore III. proposed the establishment of twelve metropolitanates and seventy-two dioceses: but a council of bishops reduced the latter number to thirty-four, later to twenty-two, and thereafter to fourteen. There was a lack of funds for the support of the new dioceses, and at the end of the seventeenth century the Patriarchate of Moscow had thirteen metropolitanates, seven archbishoprics and two dioceses,"[39]

Philaret died in 1633. He had kept up a court which in splendour rivalled that of the Tsar: and as Patriarch and Co-regent had made his influence felt in Church and State. Thus, in secular affairs, while his son Michael had been elected Tsar on condition of ruling in accordance with the advice of the *boyars* and the assent of the Estates General and had kept his pledge, 1613—9, Philaret, on his return from exile, banished the leaders of the *boyars* and reduced the powers of the Estates to those of a merely consultative body. He had carried the same spirit into the affairs of the Church: and, 1620, without consulting the other Patriarchs, had ordered that all converts to Orthodoxy from other Confessions should be re-baptised. Men resented the increase of the power of the Church: it was certain to be contested. On the death of the Tsar Michael, 1645, no immediate opportunity occurred. For he was succeeded by his son, Alexis, 1645—†76, who was of mild disposition, and devoted to the interests of religion. But a reaction began: and Alexis was induced to adopt a policy of diminishing the prerogatives of clergy and religious. He prevented the increase of their wealth by a New Code which forbade the further acquisition of ecclesiastical property; and he reduced their independence by a Monastic Ordinance which limited their judicial privileges. The Tsar's attention, however, was diverted by wars with Poland, 1654—6. But a truce was made, 1656, by the treaty of Vilna: and next year, Alexis returned to Moscow—to take up the struggle with a personality more commanding even than Philaret—the seventh Patriarch of Moscow, by name Nikon, 1652—66.

Nikon,[40] whose proper name was Nikita Minin, was not, like Philaret, of princely, but of peasant, origin. Born of poor parents at Valmanovo, a village near Nizhni Novgorod, Nikon had been a secular priest before he returned to the monastic life in which he had served his novitiate as a boy. He retired as a hermit to the isle of Anzer in the White Sea; and thence to the Kozhuzersky monastery in the diocese of Novgorod. Of this House he became abbot in 1643. The business of his convent took him to Moscow: where, by his stature and his eloquence, he arrested the attention of the Tsar. Pious and impressionable, Alexis fell entirely under the influence of Nikon. He made him abbot of the wealthy Novospassky monastery at Moscow; and he became the Tsar's chief adviser. In 1649 he was promoted to be archbishop of Novgorod: where his pastoral zeal displayed itself in eloquent preaching—the clergy of that day did not preach, but read select homilies—and in the reform of the ceremonies and the music of the church. He also distinguished himself as one of the leading opponents of the New Code and of the civil organisation known as the Monastic Department. Notwithstanding this outspokenness on the part of Nikon, the Tsar determined, on the death of the Patriarch Joseph, to have him for his successor. Nikon was reluctant: for he foresaw clearly enough what was coming. But the Tsar would take no denial. He met him in the Cathedral of the Assumption; and, at the tomb of the Metropolitan Philip, 1565—8, the victim of Ivan the Terrible, extracted an unwilling consent: for Nikon only yielded after imposing on his electors an oath of obedience to himself in everything concerning the dogmas, canons and observances of the Church. Thus he became Patriarch, 1652.

For a few years, 1652—8, Tsar and Patriarch enjoyed each other's confidence: and were almost inseparable. "The Patriarch's authority is so great," says the traveller Adam Olearius, 1654, "that he in manner divides the Sovereignty with the Great Duke. He is the Supreme Judge of all Ecclesiastical Causes, and absolutely disposes of whatever concerns Religion, with such power that, in things relating to the Political Government, he reforms what he conceives prejudicial to Christian simplicity and good manners, without giving the Great Duke any accompt of it; who without any contestation commands the orders made by the Patriarch to be executed."[41] So long as these relations lasted, the anti-ecclesiastical measures of the *boyars* became a dead letter: and Nikon's influence was supreme. He was regent of the Empire during the absence of Alexis at the wars. He set himself to promote the advancement of education, in reliance upon Greek learning: and, in particular, to a much-needed reform of the service-books. But the manner of his proceedings, apart from their merits, made him many enemies. Nikon was a strong man, with the defects of his virtues: not merely tactlessness and want of sympathy, but harshness as well. Monks, clergy and laity alike resented the revision of the service-books. The *boyars* took offence at his opposition to their schemes of church-reform. There was general distaste for the severity of his rule. Moreover, the wars did not altogether go well. The Russians, indeed, could congratulate themselves on the recovery from Poland of White Russia, and of Little Russia with its ancient capital of Kiev, under the Treaty of Vilna, 1656. Poland was thus made to disgorge: but the task of beating Sweden and reaching the Baltic ended in failure, and Nikon earned fresh unpopularity by the collapse of his anti-Swedish policy. He was left without friends; and on the Tsar's return from the wars in 1657, everything turned upon whether Alexis would be man enough to stand by him. Events soon proved that he was not: for the former intimacy gave place to a coolness on the Tsar's part, and the hour of Nikon's opponents had come. As if fearing a renewal of his ascendancy, the Tsar refused to see him: and Nikon retired from the Court. On 19th July, 1658, he publicly divested himself of the patriarchal insignia, though he did not give up the office of Patriarch. It was a retirement, not a resignation: and Nikon, after first withdrawing to the Voskresensky monastery, removed far away to the Krestnoy monastery on the White Sea.

The Patriarch's enemies thereupon set themselves to procure his deposition; and synods were assembled where frivolous but malicious charges were made against him. In February, 1660, a Synod was held at Moscow to terminate the widowhood of the patriarchal see. It was resolved (a) that Nikon should be deposed from the patriarchal throne; (b) that he should be deprived of his episcopal orders; and (c) that steps should be taken for the appointment of his successor. It was urged in his defence that there was no precedent for depriving of his orders a bishop who had retired from his see; and that, if it was a question of electing a new patriarch, the Russian bishops had no right to judge their Patriarch without the concurrence of his fellow Patriarchs. They were called in: but, while they were on their way, the Tsar attempted to make him appear before a secular court composed of *boyars*. Nikon naturally declined; and he was attacked by raids on his property and persecution of his friends. In 1664 a dramatic turn was given to the course of events by the sudden appearance of the Patriarch in the Cathedral of the Assumption at Moscow. In accordance with custom he sent to summon the Tsar to the service; but he was told to return to the Voskresensky monastery, and there await the decision of the Patriarchs. Two of them at last arrived, the Patriarchs of Alexandria and Antioch: and a Synod was held, 16th November, 1666. Formal charges of no real weight were made against him: but the real matter at issue was studiously avoided, viz., the relations between Church and State. It goes without saying that the verdict went against him: for, on 12th December, the Council pronounced him guilty of reviling the Tsar and the Church, of deposing Paul, bishop of Kolomna, contrary to the canons and of beating his dependants. They sentenced him to be deprived of all his sacerdotal functions: and to be known henceforward simply as the monk Nikon. Banished to the Theropontov monastery at Bielo-Ozero (The White Lake), for fourteen years he remained in exile: while two men of minor calibre succeeded him on the patriarchal throne—Josaphat, 1667—72, and Pitirim, 1672—3. In 1676 the Tsar Alexis, who had at first befriended and afterwards deserted him, died; and was succeeded by a son feebler than himself—Theodore III., 1676—†82. The enemies of Nikon at once made it an occasion for harsher treatment of the exiled patriarch: and he was removed to stricter confinement. But the Tsar relented: and gave him leave to return to the Voskresensky monastery. Nikon started on the long journey from Bielo-Ozero southwards. But he never reached the goal: for he died at Yaroslavl, 17th August, 1681, on board the boat that was carrying him down the Volga. "To his suppression it was due that the Church in Russia was kept under by the State; and Peter the Great averted the rise of another Nikon by abolishing the Patriarchate, 1700." But it had served one purpose, before its extinction: for it had lasted long enough to receive Kiev back into the bosom of Orthodoxy, and so to secure the unification of the Russian Church.

We now pass from dissensions between the Crown and the Church, to dissensions within the Church: which also troubled the reign of Alexis. They, too, were connected with Nikon: and, in particular, with the reform of the service-books which others before him had attempted but he carried through. The Russian Church suffered then, as now, from formalism. It was Byzantine, but without Byzantine learning, for its language was not Greek but Old Slavonic. So its clergy were cut off from the springs of learning: and their ignorance, coupled with the backwardness and even bigotry of the people, induced a temper of fanatical opposition to reform. But there had been some lights in the darkness. Under Ivan III., 1462—†1505, there was Nil, a monk of Bielo-Ozero. He went to Mount Athos and learned Greek. Then he returned, and built a cell on the Sera, whence he is known as Nil Serski. He repudiated the use of external forms. In 1503 he proposed to disendow all Russian monasteries, on the ground that monks had nothing to do with worldly property. He submitted the Slavonic Scriptures and Lives of the Saints to a searching criticism, and pointed out the errors due to mistranslation. His pupil, Vassian Kosoi, applied similar criticism to the Slavonic version of the Byzantine Nomocanon or Canon Law; and was banished, 1531: for he had also become the centre of a movement for the reform of monasticism, and the prohibition of monastic estates. Vassian was aided, in his critical task, by a scholar more famous than himself, Maxim, the Greek, 1476—†1556. By birth an Epirote, he had been brought to Russia by Basil IV., 1505—†33: after visiting Italy in his youth, where he had made the acquaintance of Aldus the printer at Venice, and of Savonarola at Florence. Maxim carried back with him the spirit of Savonarola to Moscow: where he thought it his mission to put down both sin and error— in particular, the false renderings from the Greek which occurred in the Old Slavonic Service-Books. But this was held an insult to the saints who had used them.

Maxim replied with courage: by attacks on clergy and monks: and was thrown into prison, 1531.

The correction of the service-books which Maxim had suggested, became an object of solicitude to the Tsar Michael. He noticed the errors: and committed to Dionysius, a monk of the Convent of the Holy Trinity, the task of removing them. But his emendations in the text of the *Trebnik,* which, like the *Manuale* or *Rituale* of the West, contains the text of the offices in common use by the parish priest, created resentment: and little further was done till the days of the Patriarch Nikon. His attention was called not only to mistakes of translation, but to innovations which had crept into the Church of Russia, by Paisius, Patriarch of Jerusalem, 1645—61, who visited Moscow in 1649. Thus, it was the custom in Russia to make the sign of the Cross with two fingers; in Greece and the East with three, symbolic of the Trinity. Nikon at first hesitated. He appreciated the difficulties: and foresaw the storm. But he was convinced of the need for reform, and petitioned the Tsar to summon a synod for the correction of the liturgical books. And further visits of Greek Patriarchs forwarded the design. For soon after Paisius of Jerusalem there came Athanasius III., Patriarch of Constantinople, 1634—52, and Macarius III., Patriarch of Antioch, 1647—72, accompanied by his deacon and diarist, Paul. Meanwhile, a series of Councils was busy with the authorisation and publication of new service-books. A synod of 1654 ordained that the service-books were to be brought into conformity with the ancient Slavonic MSS. and " with the Greek books, the rubric and the holy Fathers." A synod of Lent, 1655, revised the Liturgy, and ordered that other ecclesiastical books should be so corrected. But the controversy now turned to matters of more popular concern than texts and books. There had come in of late through Kiev the influence of Latin ecclesiastical art, and ikons of this new type were in popular favour. Nikon, always on the side of Greek as against Latin culture, confiscated and destroyed them. This crusade against them, together with the destruction of the old books, as the new ones began to issue from the press, led to open resistance by the populace. Led by the party of the protopopes, who raised a cry of heresy against Nikon and the reforming Councils, they provoked the wrath of the Patriarch. His hand fell heavily on the offenders: and they were banished without trial. A third synod, of May, 1656, then intervened; and exasperated the conservatives by substituting for the old Russian tradition of crossing with two fingers an order that the sign of the cross was to be made with three fingers after the manner of the Greeks. But the Greeks, since the Council of Florence, were suspect as to their Orthodoxy: and, moreover, they were of no account as slaves of the Turk! The ferment became general: and the monasteries put themselves at the head of it. In particular, the Solovetski monastery, 1657, infected by the rebels who had been sent thither for punishment, refused absolutely to accept the new service-books. It became the centre of violent opposition: withstood a siege of several years: and, when at last it was taken, 1676, several of its monks were put to death for organising resistance to the Tsar. The resistance was coincident with the withdrawal of Nikon in 1658 from active participation in the government of the Church: and went on increasing till it had to be dealt with by the very Councils that effected his deposition. In 1666 a Synod pronounced " against the schismatics and troublers of the Church which have lately sprung up," and deposed the arch-priest Avvakum, one of the leaders of the opposition, before it proceeded, 12th December, to the deposition of the Patriarch Nikon himself. It then drew up and circulated for the use of the clergy a lengthy Ordinance concerning the books and the usages. Then the same Council, continuing into 1667, after appointing Nikon's successor " confirmed the liturgical decisions of the previous year (reinforced by the presence of the two Patriarchs of Alexandria and Antioch) and went on to a very full handling not only of the liturgical disputes, but also of all sorts of urgent church questions. Those who resisted the revision were formally anathematised, both clerical and lay alike." Thus Nikon was condemned: but his reforms were upheld.

They were upheld, however, at the price of schism (Raskol) and the schismatics (Raskolniki) or Old Believers, as they are called, represent to this day the conservatism of Nikon's time organised in opposition to the official Church. Their position resembles that of their contemporaries in England, who organised themselves as dissenters from the Church as restored in 1662: but with this difference. In England, it was the Church that was conservative and ritualistic: but these distinctions belonged in Russia to the Schismatics who were as often called the Old Ritualists as the Old Believers. To understand the breach between them and the Russian Church, account must be taken of the stagnation of secular culture in Russia, and of the ignorance and childish devotion to external trivialities which characterised either side. It was a stagnation for which every allowance has to be made, for it was due to the isolation of Russia from the rest of Europe during the thirteenth—fifteenth centuries. This isolation was consequent upon the removal of the capital from Kiev to Moscow, upon the Tartar Conquest which led to that transference, and upon the disappearance of the Byzantine Empire, after 1204, from the Russian orbit. Russian culture perished for lack of the old contact with the East Roman Empire. Then again the policy of Poland-Lithuania, in the days of its union and dominance, had been to keep Russia at arm's length, and at a distance from the culture of the west. The picture of Russian Society given in the *Travels* of Adam Olearius, 1646, gives a vivid impression of the result—its ignorance, boorishness, superstition, drunkenness and detestation of new ideas. The Raskolniki were the product of these surroundings. They flourished mainly in the districts furthest from the West, in Northern Russia and the region of the Volga. They represented antagonism to progress and western culture. They abhorred the "abominable German customs": classed Nikon's new ways with foreign dress and tobacco: and revolted from all his proceedings as from a conspiracy to replace Russian Orthodoxy by Latin heresy.

§ 7. The fifth period is that of government by the Holy Synod, 1700—1917, from the times of Peter the Great, 1689—†1725, to the Revolution.

Alexis III. died in 1676. He had been twice married. By his first wife, Maria Miloslavskaya, he had two sons: Theodore, born in 1662, and Ivan, born in 1666. She also bore him several daughters, one of whom was Sophia, †1689. By his second wife, Natalia Naryshkina, he had one son, Peter, born in 1672, and two daughters. There was no law of succession, as yet, in Russia; and in September, 1674, Alexis proclaimed his eldest son as his successor, under the title of Theodore III., 1676—†82. Theodore was only fourteen at his accession, and in feeble health. He died after a reign of six years; and the question of the succession had to be settled again. There were now two candidates for the throne, the half-brothers Ivan and Peter. Each was supported by his mother's relatives. As Ivan was even more of a weakling than Theodore, the Patriarch Joachim, 1674—90, with the *boyars,* declared for Peter, and the Naryshkins won the day. But they reckoned without Ivan's six sisters; and, in particular, without Sophia. She seized the reins of power and held them for seven years, 1682—9, during which, Ivan and Peter sat side by side as Tsars with Sophia as regent. Ivan became increasingly negligible: till, in August, 1689, Peter, who had reached the age of seventeen and was technically of age, determined to assert himself. He relegated Sophia to a convent. At last, by the death of Ivan V. in 1696, he occupied the throne alone.

Peter was a self-willed ruler: coarse and dissolute in his manner of life: and bent on introducing into Russia the civilisation of the West. He was thus no friend to religion; nor to the clergy of the Orthodox Church, whom he looked upon as reactionaries and obscurantists; and, since he had to live with them, he would run no risk of having to repeat the experiment of Alexis, his father, by letting himself be confronted by another Nikon. No patriarch should menace him with an authority rivalling his own. Accordingly, on the death of Adrian, 1690—†1700, Peter created the new office of " Exarch, *locum tenens* and administrator of the Patriarchal Throne," and appointed to it Stephen Yavorski. He had been trained in the Academy of Kiev, and stood for the learning of the West. For a time they worked together: for Peter looked upon Stephen as an enlightened person with a Western outlook. But they fell out in respect of Protestantism. Peter had much sympathy with Lutheranism, for he favoured the Germans: whereas Stephen, combining traditional Orthodoxy with a Jesuit training, looked upon everything Protestant with abhorrence. He was also drawn into political opposition to the Tsar: and eventually superseded, in Peter's favour, by Theophan Prokopovich, who was inclined to make terms with Protestantism. In 1718 Theophan became bishop of Pskov, and was the author of the *Spiritual Regulation*.[42] Promulgated by edict of 14th February, 1721, the *Regulation* placed the Patriarchate permanently in commission. " We therefore," says Peter in his edict, " having taken upon Us the care of the regulation of the clergy and the spiritual order, and not seeing any better way for it than a *Regulation* by a Synod, yet because this is too weighty a charge for any single person, to whom the Supreme Power is not hereditary, We appoint a Spiritual College, i.e., a Spiritual Synodical Administration, which is authorised to rectify, according to the Regulation here following, all spiritual affairs throughout the Russian Church."[43] Part I. of the Regulation " is an exposition of the advantage of government by a college rather than by an individual." Part II. " deals with the affairs of which the Spiritual College has cognizance "—reform and education—and " rules are given for preachers, and the ecclesiastical duties of the laity are defined."[44] In Part III. " the members of the Synod are taken in hand, and their duty, office and powers are " prescribed. Thus constituted, the Synod held its first meeting on 17th February, 1721. The Tsar is supreme judge; and is represented by a layman as Procurator of the Holy

Synod. He sat at a table apart, and had no voice in the doctrinal decisions of the Synod: for, as the eye of the Tsar, he was there merely to watch its proceedings and to obtain the sanction of the Tsar to its acts. So its Spiritual authority remained: and, when the Tsar applied to the Eastern Patriarchs for their approval, the Synod was " recognised, 23rd September, 1723, by the Patriarchs of Constantinople and Antioch as their ' brother,' and as a corporation competent to act in the same way as the four apostolic thrones." But, inevitably, the authority of the Procurator increased, while the independence of the Synod declined. And this process went on, though some Procurators were Protestants or rationalists, and others reactionaries such as Constantine Pobiedonostsev, 1881— †1905, whose aim was to coerce all religions professed in Russia to come within the fold of the Church. As to the constitution of the Holy Synod, it is not, strictly speaking, a Synod at all: but a " Spiritual College " consisting, at first, of a president and eleven members. It is, in fact, simply an " ecclesiastical committee," neither elected synodically, nor exercising synodical government. For there are no provinces in Russia: and the bishops " have no opportunity to co-operate or consult together." They are mere units, taking their orders from a " highly centralised ecclesiastical government,"[45] which, in effect, is one of the departments of state.

Nevertheless, this government *régime* did not stifle the progress of the Church in Russia.[46] In 1721 there were 18 " eparchies " or administrative departments. In 1764, these had grown, with the expansion of Russia, to 29; in 1801, to 36; and, at the opening of the twentieth century, to 65. They are ruled by the Metropolitans of Petrograd, Moscow and Kiev: and by archbishops and bishops of whom there were, in 1912, as many as 133. Of these, 66 are diocesan bishops and others bishop-vicars of eparchies or bishops-suffragan to the number of 45.

The clergy are divided into " white " or secular: and " black " or monastic.

The secular clergy, in 1912, numbered 45,000 priests (including 2,400 archpriests) and 15,000 deacons. Be-

sides, there were 44,000 singers : 60,000 churches and
chapels, with about 90 million Orthodox. The rest of the
population included some 2 million Old Believers,
13 million Mohammedans, 11 million Roman Catholics,
3 million Lutherans and 5 million Jews. Such was the
relative strength of the various religious bodies in Russia,
before the Revolution. What it is now, we have no
means of ascertaining.

The parochial clergy were supported mainly from local
sources—gifts, fees, glebe and the like : but some had
grants from the State. They were, however, hampered
by poverty; by want of education and lack of sound
vocation; by governmental oppression; by contempt and
social isolation; by family cares and, too often, by drink.
Nevertheless, the rural clergy held fast to their religion,
and maintained it among their flocks.

The "black," or monastic, clergy in the eighteenth
century were much reduced in number : especially by the
enactments of Peter the Great and his niece the Empress
Anna, 1730—†40. But they maintained their prestige.
Bishops and Professors were chosen from their ranks :
and the monasteries were both numerous and well-
endowed. In 1912 there were 298 monasteries recognised and subsidised by the Government, besides 154 for
which no such provision was made. They contained
9,317 monks and 8,266 novices. There were also 400
convents of women, with 12,652 nuns and 40,275 novices.
Many of these were Sisters of Charity, who served 184
hospitals and 148 asylums. But the lives of the regular
clergy, except in a few houses of strict observance, were
lax.

The clergy were educated at 185 schools, with 1,302
teachers, preparatory to the seminaries. Of seminaries,
there were 57 with 866 teachers and 20,500 students.
For higher education, there were the Ecclesiastical
Academies of Petrograd, Moscow, Kiev and Kazan, with
120 teachers and 862 students. These Academies had
good libraries, and professors of scientific distinction.
But the seminaries rarely exhibited any serious standard
of moral and intellectual attainment. Many of the

students lacked a true vocation; and numbers of them took part with the revolutionaries of 1906—8. As to the educative influence of the clergy, it has been slight; though they had large numbers of schools, primary and secondary. But allowance must be made for their difficulties. The Government would look with disfavour upon the display of too much zeal on the part of the clergy for the enlightenment of the people.

The depressing picture, however, is relieved by a succession of men of sanctity and learning in high places, and by a zeal for missions.

The Metropolitans Platon, 1775—†1812, and Philaret, 1821—†67, adorned the see of Moscow between them for nearly a century. Platon was a great preacher; and his *Orthodox Doctrine*,[47] 1765, together with the *Shorter* and *Longer Catechisms* of 1766 and 1776, have acquired, as recast by Philaret,[48] the position of authoritative text books and standard of Russian Orthodoxy. He was also the first writer to attempt a scientific *History of the Russian Church*, 1805. His pupil, Philaret,[49] carried on his work. After devoting himself to the circulation of the Scriptures in the vernacular, he put out a *Catechism*, 1823, at the request of the Holy Synod. To these pioneers succeeded Makari (Bulgakov), Metropolitan of Moscow, 1879—†82. " His fame rests upon two great books, the twelve volumes of his *History of the Russian Church* down to 1667, and the five volumes of his *Orthodox Dogmatic Theology*,"[50] 1853. Nor must we overlook the merits of two lay writers: A. S. Khomiakov, 1804—†60, and V. S. Soloviev, 1853—†1900. " They represent two opposite tendencies and, in a sense, carry on the traditional rivalry between the Little Russian " (Kiev) " and the Great Russian " (Moscow) " schools of theological thought." Khomiakov is Slavophil and Orthodox, passionately opposed to " the legalism of the Latins and the individualism of Western Protestantism." Soloviev is " well disposed towards Rome," and anxious for " a reconciliation between East and West."[51]

Finally, there is the missionary spirit of the Russian Church.[52] Ambrose Protasov, bishop of Kazan, 1816—

26, prepared the way, by teaching the native languages with a view to the propagation of the Gospel among the native tribes constantly included within the expanding empire of Russia. His policy was carried further by Nicholas Ilminski,[53] an expert in vernacular Tartar and kindred tongues. As a result of his zeal, and the efforts of the Kazan Translation Committee, the Scriptures and the Liturgy were disseminated in an ever-increasing number of native languages. The Altai Mission,[54] under the archimandrite Macarius, 1830—44, began the task of mastering the languages of Tartars, Kalmuks and others in Western Siberia. It was a slow process: but in 1865, when the Liturgy was first celebrated in the vernacular, progress became more rapid. The further East found its apostle in Innocent Veniaminov:[55] who became bishop of the new see of Kamchatka, 1840, until he was recalled to be Metropolitan of Moscow, 1868—†79, where he founded the Orthodox Missionary Society, 1870. Another great missionary was Nicholas Kosatkin. He founded the Orthodox Church in Japan, where he became bishop in Tokio, 1880—†1912. His mission weathered the storm of the Russo-Japanese War, 1904—5, and at his death its adherents numbered as many as 35,000.

Thus, oppressed though it was by the drab rule of the Holy Synod and held in leash by the all-powerful State, the Russian Church never suffered the lamp of sound learning to be extinguished or lost the light of true religion. At the revolution of 1917 it broke out into a new independence.

§ 8. The sixth and last period of the history of the Church in Russia is that of our own day. It began with the abdication of the Tsar Nicholas II., 1894—†1917, on 15th March, 1917. The government fell into the hands of Lenin and the Bolshevists. They are the enemies not merely of capitalism, but of religion. For a moment the Church forestalled them. On 28th August, 1917, a Council met in Moscow and resolved to restore the Patriarchate. On 1st November it elected Tikhon, Archbishop of Vilna, and afterwards metropolitan of Moscow, to be Patriarch. He was enthroned on 4th December; and held the perilous dignity till his death in April, 1925—too weak to prevent the persecution that ensued, but strong enough, as the rallying-point of Russian religion, to defeat its aims. By a decree of 23rd January, 1918, the Government disestablished the Church in Russia; confiscated all its property; and forbade the teaching of religion in the schools. They then proceeded to attack and murder the clergy; and no fewer than 28 bishops and 1,215 priests met a martyr's death, inflicted, in many cases, with horrible brutality. Unable, however, to break down the Church by a frontal attack, they have since resorted to the expedient of setting up a rival organisation called "The Living Church." It is officered by renegade clergy, and meant to break up the Orthodox Church by fostering dissensions within. But religion is still alive in the hearts of the Russian people; and there remains the hope that the Orthodox Church, reinvigorated by its sufferings and rooted in the affections of its people, may yet be the means for the salvation of Russia.

CHAPTER XVI.

THE "NESTORIANS,"
OTHERWISE
THE CHURCH OF THE EAST.

CATHOLICI AND PATRIARCHS OF THE EAST.

(From J. S. Assemani, *Bibliotheca Orientalium* III. i. 611 sqq.: Romae, 1725.)

1. Thomas, Apostle of the East
* * * *
11. Simeon Bar-Sabaë, †341.
12. Sciaadostus, †342 [Sahdost]
13. Barbaseminus, †346 [Barba'Semin]. See vacant, 346—83.
14. Tomarsa, 383—92
15. Cajuma, 395—9 [Qayoma]
16. Isaac, 399—410
17. Achaeus, 410—5 [Ahaï]
18. Iahbalaha I., 415—20
19. Maanes, 420 [Ma'na]
20. Marabochtus, 421 [Farbokt]
21. Dadjesus, 421—56 [Dadiso']
22. Babuaeus, 457—484 [Babowaï]
23. Acacius, 485—96
24. Babaeus, 497—502/3 [Babaï]
25. Silas, 505—23 [Sila]
26, 27. Narses et Elisaeus, 524—39
28. Paulus, 539
29. Mar Aba I., 540—52
30. Joseph, 552—67
31. Ezechiel, 570—81
32. Jesujabus, 582—95 [Iso'yabh I.]
33. Sabarjesus I., 596—604 [Sabriso' I.]
34. Gregorius, 605—8. See vacant, 608—28.
35. Jesujabus II., 628—43 [Iso'yabh II.]*
36. Maremes, 647—50
37. Jesujabus III., 650—60 [Iso'yabh III.]
38. Georgius, 660—80
39. Joannes, 680—2
40, 41. Ananjesus, 685—99: Joannes, 692. See vacant, 700—14.
42. Saliba-Zacha, 714—28. See vacant, 728—31.
43. Phetion, 731—41
44. Mar Aba II., 742—52
45. Surinus, 754
46. Jacobus, 754—73
47. Ananjesus II., 774—8
48. Timothy I., 778—820
49. Josue, 820—4
50. Georgius, 825—9. See vacant, 829—32.
51. Sabarjesus II., 832—6 [Sabriso' II.]
52. Abraham, 836—49. See vacant, 849—52.
53. Theodosius, 852—8
54. Sergius, 860—72
55. Enos, 877—84
56. Joannes, 884—92
57. Joannes, 892—8
58. Joannes, 900—5
59. Abraham, 905—37

*Up to this point, corrections have been made from J. Labourt, *Le Christianisme dans l'empire perse*, 353—4.

HIS BEATITUDE MAR IGNATIUS, ELIAS, PATRIARCH OF ANTIOCH AND OF THE
SYRIANS
(*i.e.*, of the Syrian-Orthodox or Jacobite Church).

See p. 438.]

60. Emmanuel, 938—60
61. Israel, 962
62. Ebedjesus I., 963—86 ['Abdiso I.]
63. Mares, 987—1001
64. Joannes, 1001—1011
65. Joannes, 1013—20
66. Jesujabus IV., 1021—5 [Iso'yabh IV.]
67. Elias I., 1028—49
68. Joannes, 1050—7
69. Sabarjesus III., 1063—72 [Sabriso' III.]
70. Ebedjesus II., 1074—90 ['Abdiso' II.]
71. Machicha, 1091—1108
72. Elias II., 1111—32
73. Barsuma, 1134—6
74. Ebedjesus III., 1138—47 ['Abdiso III.]
75. Jesujabus V., 1148—74 [Iso'yabh V.]
76. Elias IV., 1175—89
77. Iahbalaha II., 1190—1222
78. Sabarjesus IV., 1222—5 [Sabriso' IV.]
79. Sabarjesus V., 1226—57 [Sabriso' V.]
80. Machicha, 1257—65
81. Denha, 1265—81
82. Iahbalaha III., 1281—1317 [ex genere Turcorum in regione Cataje natus]
83. Timotheus II., 1318—? [for the rest to 1725, see M. Le Quien, *Oriens Christianus,* ii. 1152 sqq.]. [Hucusque ex Barhebraeo, 1226—†86, Mari, et Amro; J.S.A. III. i. 620.]

CHAPTER XVI.

The "Nestorians," otherwise the Church of the East.

§ 1. By the opening of the seventh century, the Church in Persia[1] had a place in Christendom and a genius of its own.

It had a hierarchy as strongly organised as that of its neighbour across the Roman frontier. Provinces corresponded to the great territorial divisions of the Persian Empire, and dioceses to the administrative and judicial districts. Without counting the patriarchal diocese, there were five metropolitan sees in 410: Beit Lapat, Nisibis, Perat, Arbela and Karka of Beit Slokh:[2] to which were added, between 550—600, Rêw-Ardashir for Persia proper and Merw for Khorasan.[3] By 630 these five provinces probably included not less than a hundred dioceses.[4] First among these was the see of Seleucia-Ctesiphon.[5] Its bishop adopted the title of Catholicus in order to mark his independence of all foreign jurisdiction; and in 424 declared his Church independent of the Western Fathers.[6] By the title Patriarch, he proclaimed himself the equal of the Bishops of Rome, Alexandria and Antioch.[7] Moreover, he was the supreme authority within his own communion. Next to him in rank stood the bishop of Kaskar;[8] who administered the patriarchate *sede vacante* and summoned the electoral college to proceed to the choice of a successor.[9] The metropolitan was the regional delegate of the Catholicus. The bishops, of whom there was but one in each town,[10] were masters each in his own diocese. To the precision with which the relations of patriarch, metropolitan and bishop were thus regulated, the Church of the East owes both its persistence and its prestige.[11] Synodical government also contributed to its vigour:[12] and so, too, did the ownership and administration of all ecclesiastical property by the bishop.[13] Such property was considerable: for the bishop's cathedral was usually surrounded by schools, library and hospital.[14] The episcopate also had absolute control of the monastic order.[15] It was of the cœnobitic or Pachomian type; and had been reinvigorated by the reforms of Abraham of Kaskar,[16] 491—†586, which, by the era of the Moslem conquest, had taken root in some sixty monasteries.[17] To their numbers and vitality, the Church of the East owed much of its power to resist for so long the assaults of Islām, as well as to maintain its dogmatic tradition against the Monophysites.[18]

As for doctrine, the Church of the East retained the Nicene Creed, but did not acknowledge the Councils of Ephesus and Chalcedon. It professed adherence to a formulary[19] of the Synod of Acacius, 486, which, while capable of interpretation in harmony with the Chalcedonian Definition, differed from it, though only by omission. The formulary omits the mention of Mary as Mother of God.[20] In the School of Nisibis,[21] the Church of the East had its own theological traditions: and looked back with reverence to Theodore of Mopsuestia, †428, as its "doctor" in chief.[22] In worship, it held to the common standards of Christendom: for the oldest of its three liturgies goes back to a date prior to the irruption of Nestorianism into Persia, though the other two are ascribed to Theodore and Nestorius.

Thus it was, on the whole, an allegiance to names rather than things that distinguished the Church in Persia from its Orthodox rival across the Romano-Persian frontier.[23] But it was a Church sufficiently *sui generis,* in organisation, belief and worship, to stand well with the Persian State: for "the one pre-occupation of the Persian Government towards the Christians was to have none but 'heretics' within its borders. Of what sort, did not matter. Their Armenian subjects were Monophysites; and their Aramaean subjects were Nestorians. But neither the one nor the other agreed with the subjects of the neighbouring Empire: and, further, they did not agree with each other. This was a double advantage"[24] to the Persian Government; and not without its attraction to the Church in Persia. And so things stood on the eve of the overthrow of the Persian Empire.

§ 2. The Persians, alarmed by the destruction of the Roman armies under Heraclius at the battle of the Yarmūk, 636, determined to take the offensive. They crossed the Euphrates in force; but at Kadesia[25] (Kādisīya) they suffered a defeat, 637; and the Arabs pushed on to Seleucia-Ctesiphon or, as they called it, Mada'in. Presently the whole of Irak was in their hands, including Mosul, 641. In 642 they invaded the plateau of Iran. Here the decisive battle took place at Nihāwand, near the ancient Ecbatana; and afterwards the Arabs pressed forward to the capture of the Median cities of Hamadān, Ray, and Ispahān. The resistance they met with proved stronger in Persia where the Aryan element in the population prevailed than among the Semitic inhabitants of Irak. But, on the assassination of the last King of Persia, Iazdgerd III., 632—†52, whom the Arabs had driven before them, 648, to the Turkish frontier, the Empire of the Sassanidae, 226—652, was finally extinguished: and Islām dominated Central Asia as far as Khorasan.

§ 3. It was a change of masters for the Church of the East; but not a serious blow. For, from the seventh to the fourteenth century, it carried its missionary conquests right across Asia as far as Pekin; and for their progress we have the evidence[26] of chronologers and historians, of the sites of bishoprics, and of travellers from the West.

To begin with the literary evidence. In 549, Mar Aba I., Patriarch of Seleucia-Ctesiphon, 540—†52, sent a bishop to the Hephthalite (White) Huns (Turks) on either side of the river Oxus; and, a century later, Elijah, Metropolitan of Merw, converted, in 644, communities of Turks in Khorasan. Contemporary with Elijah was the Patriarch Iso'yabh III., 650—60: who mentions "more than twenty bishops and two archbishops in the East" (i.e., beyond the Oxus) as owning his allegiance.[27] His successor, Timothy I., 778—†820, then residing, as did later Patriarchs, at Bagdad, consecrated a Metropolitan "for the King of the Turks,"[28] a bishop "for the Turks,"[29] and another for Thibet. He tells a correspondent that "many monks crossed the sea and went to the Indians and the Chinese with only staff and scrip." And he informs him of the death of the Metropolitan of China. According to Thomas of Marga,[30] who, about 840, wrote a series of monastic biographies similar to those contained in *The Lausiac History* of Palladius, the Patriarch Timothy also dispatched eighty monks, some of whom he consecrated bishops, to the heathen of Dailam and Gilan on the south of the Caspian Sea and gave them for a Metropolitan Subhaliso'. In 1009, 'Abdiso', Metropolitan of Merw, wrote to inform the Patriarch John that twenty thousand Turks and Mongols had come over to the Christian faith; and consulted him about the kind of food they were to eat in Lent.[31] They were a people called Kharaites (Kheraits),[32] who lay to the N.E., on the river Orkhon, to the south of Lake Baikal.

Early in the thirteenth century, Genghis Khan[33] became Emperor of the Mongols, 1206—†27, with his capital at Karakorum.[34] In 1216 he took possession of Pekin. Then, turning westward, in 1219 he captured Tashkent, Nur, Bukhārā, Samarkand and Balkh; and in 1224 defeated the Russians on the Kalka,[35] a river which runs into the sea of Azov. But he returned to his own country in the following year. His incursions, however, laid open the East to the commercial and missionary enterprise of Europe. A friend of St. Francis of Assisi, 1182—†1226, Friar John Pian de Carpine[36] penetrated to Karakorum, 1246, as the envoy of Pope Innocent IV., 1241—†54; to be followed by Friar William of Rubruck,[37] ?1216—?†60, the emissary of Louis IX. (St. Louis), King of France, 1226—†70 to the Grand Khan, 1253; and finally, by the celebrated Venetian traveller, Marco Polo,[38] 1256—†1323, who spent eighteen years in China, 1275—93. From their reports it appears that two powerful divisions of the Turco-Tartar race,[39] the Uighurs, to the east of Lake Balkash, and the Kheraits, further east still, and already mentioned, were Christian: as also were the Naimans who included nine powerful clans, in the Altai mountains, and the Merkites to the south-west of Lake Baikal.

Evidence from the sites of bishoprics supports this story of missionary expansion. Of sees bordering on the river Oxus, there lay to the west some twenty-one in all: including Ray (about thirty miles to the south-east of Teheran), with Herat, Merw, Naishapur and Tus in Khorasan; while to the east, in Turkestan, Mongolia, Manchuria, North China and S.E. Siberia, the list of 'Amr, written c. 1340, assigns Metropolitans to (12) China, (13) India, (18) Samarkand, (19) Turkestan, (23) Khān Bālik and Fālik,[40] (24) Tangut, (25) Kashgar and Nuākith: adding that each had from twelve to six suffragans. This would make a total of some forty to eighty bishoprics; while the principal cities described as the seats of Metropolitans are Samarkand in Sogdiana, Kashgar in Turkestan, Katai (Cathay) in North China, Tangut in the present province of Kan-su, and Khān Bālik, now Pekin. At the opening of the fourteenth century, the Patriarch Iahbalaha III.,[41] 1281—†1317, who was himself of Chinese origin, ruled over a hierarchy of twenty-five Metropolitans which would mean some two hundred to two hundred and fifty bishops; and we may gain a vivid impression of the vitality of the Church of the East and of the interest it excited in Europe from the account written by Rabban Saumā, whom he recommended to Argoun[42] Khan, Prince of the Mongols, as envoy to the West in order to concert an alliance for the taking of Jerusalem. Saumā started in March, 1287. He was received by the Emperor Andronicus II., 1282—1328, at Constantinople,[43] and then went on to Rome. The Pope, Honorius IV., 1285—†7, was just dead: so Saumā continued his journey to Paris where he was received by Philip IV. of France,[44] 1285—†1314, and to Gascony, where he had an audience of Edward I.[45] of England, 1272—†1307. On his return, he passed through Rome, where he was not only entertained by Pope Nicholas IV., 1288—†92, but allowed to make his communion at the papal Mass on Palm Sunday and given permission to celebrate his own. " The language is different," exclaimed the unsuspecting Romans, " but the rite is the same."[46] And so the envoy got back safely, with presents of relics and money, but no alliance, to his own land.[47]

Before he arrived, the western Mongols[48] had given in their adherence to Islām; and within the next hundred years the far-flung Christianity of the East was all but destroyed. Asia, at the opening of the fourteenth century was divided between several Mongol States, under the Grand Khan at Pekin. He himself ruled directly over Mongolia, China, Thibet and northern Indo-China. Persia and Armenia acknowledged the sway of the successors of Hulagu, grandson of Ghenghis Khan. Russia, with the lands of the Caspian and the Ural, were in possession of the Kiptchak[49] or Golden Horde: while Transoxiana and Chinese Turkestan belonged to the descendants of Jagatai, a son of Ghenghis Khan. One of their emirs, Tamerlane, or Timour[50] the Lame, 1336—†1405, possessed himself in 1369 of Transoxiana; and then entered upon a career of conquest during which he devastated the whole of Asia. In 1391—5 he wiped out the Khanate of the Golden Horde, and so, involuntarily, delivered Russia.[51] Then, turning east, he invaded India,[52] 1398—9. Next, he swept westward again; and, by the defeat of the Sultan Bāyāzid I., 1389—†1403, at Angora, 1402, he prolonged for fifty years the life of the Roman Empire at Constantinople.[53] Thence he returned to Samarkand: and, 1405, died on his way to the conquest of China.[54] His campaigns had one disastrous effect: they overwhelmed the Church of the East under the avalanche of Islām. Such remnants as were left took refuge in the mountains of Kurdistan. In the fifteenth century the Patriarchate became hereditary, from uncle to nephew; and in 1551 there broke out a schism,[55] which issued in two successions. The one is now represented by Mar Elias, the Uniate Patriarch of Babylon, living at Mosul; and the other by Mar Shimūn, the Patriarch of the East whose seat, since the eighteenth century, has been at Qudshanis, a village in the highlands of the river Zab. From 1885—1914 his clergy and people, who lived on either side of the frontier between Turkey and Persia, in the region between Lake Van, Lake Urmi and Mosul, were fostered and educated by the mission sent out by the Archbishop of Canterbury.[56] They fought on the side of the allies during the Great War; but, in the nationalist reaction which took place in Turkey after it, they were almost exterminated by the Turks. They are now reduced to about forty thousand refugees, who have found a new home under British protection in the plains of Irak. Meanwhile, their Patriarch, a young man of about one and twenty, named Issai Mar Shimūn XXI.,[57] was, till lately, in England as a ward of the Archbishop of Canterbury, pursuing his studies at St. Augustine's in that city. He has now returned home.

CHAPTER XVII.

THE MONOPHYSITES.

(I.) Armenians. (II.) Jacobites. (III.) Christians of Malabar. (IV.) Copts. (V.) Abyssinians.

PATRIARCHS OF ALEXANDRIA: FROM A.D. 451.

GREEKS (Orthodox).

Proterius	452—7
Timothy II. (Salofaciolus)	460—82
John I. (Talaia)	482
Paul	537—42
Zoilus	542—51
Apollinaris	551—70
John II.	570—80
Eulogius	580—607
Theodore Scribo	607—9
John III. (the Almoner)	609—19
George	620—30
Cyrus	630—43
Peter II.	643—52

[Vacant, 75 years.]

Cosmas I.	727—67
Politian	767—801
Eustathius	801—5
Christophorus	805—36
Sophronius I.	836—59
Michael I.	859—71
Michael II.	871—903
Christodulus	906—32
Eutychius	933—40
Sophronius II.	?
Isaac	?
Job	?
Elias I.	c. 969
Arsenius	?
George, or Theophilus	c. 1019
Alexander II., or Leontius	c. 1059
John IV.	c. 1084
Sabas	?
Theodosius	?
Cyril II.	?
Eulogius II.	?

COPTS (Monophysite).

Timothy II. (The Cat)	457—77
Peter III. (Mongus)	477—90
Athanasius II.	490—7
John I.	497—506
John II.	506—17
Dioscorus II.	517—9
Timothy III.	519—36
Theodosius I.	536—67
Peter IV.	567—70
Damian	570—603
Anastasius	603—14
Andronicus	614—22
Benjamin	623—62
Agatho	662—80
John III.	680—9
Isaac	690—3
Simon I.	694—701
Alexander II.	703—26
Cosmas I.	726—7
Theodore	727—38
Michael I.	743—66
Menas I.	766—75
John IV.	775—99
Mark II.	799—819
Jacob	819—36
Simon II.	836—7
Joseph	837—50
Michael II.	850—1
Cosmas II.	851—9
Sanutius I.	859—70
Michael III.	881—906
Gabriel I.	913—23
Cosmas III.	923—34
Macarius I.	934—52
Theophanes	954—8
Menas II.	958—76
Ephraim	977—81
Philotheus, or Theophilus	981—1005
Zacharias	1005—1032
Sanutius II.	1032—47
Christodulus	1047—77
Cyril II.	1078—92
Michael IV.	1092—1102
Macarius II.	1102—29
Gabriel II.	1131—46
Michael V.	1146—7

GREEKS (Orthodox).		COPTS (Monophysite).	
Sophronius III.	c. 1166	John V.	1147—64
Elias II. or Alfterus	c. 1180	Mark III.	1164—89
Mark II.	c. 1195	John VI.	1189—1216
Nicholas I.	c. 1210	Cyril III.	1235—43
Gregory I.	?	Athanasius III.	1251—61
Nicholas II.	c. 1260	John VII. (1st time)	1262—9
		Gabriel III.	1269—71
Athanasius III.	1276—1308	John VII. (2nd time)	1271—93
		Theodosius II.	1293—9
		John VIII.	1300—20
Gregory II.	c. 1320	John IX.	1320—6
		Benjamin II.	1327—39
Gregory III.	?	Peter V.	1340—8
Niphon	c. 1367	Mark IV.	1348—63
Mark III.	?	John X.	1363—9
Nicholas III.	?	Gabriel IV.	1369—78
Gregory IV.	?	Matthew I.	1378—1401
		Gabriel V.	1401—18
Philotheus I.	1437—50	John XI.	1418—41
		Matthew II.	c. 1450
Athanasius IV.	?	Gabriel VI.	?
		Michael VI.	?
Philotheus II.	c. 1523	John XII.	?
Gregory V.	?	John XIII.	?
Joachim I.	c. 1564	Gabriel VII.	1526—69
Silvester	c. 1574	John XIV.	1570—85
Meletius Pigas	1592—1602	Gabriel VIII.	1585—1602
Cyril Lucar	1602—21	Mark V.	1602—18
Gerasimus I.	1621—36	John XV.	?
Metrophanes	1636—9	Matthew III.	c. 1637
Nicephorus	1639—43		
Joannicius	1643—65	Mark VI.	1645—60
Joachim II.	1665—70	Matthew IV.	1660—76
Paisius	1675—85		
Parthenius	1685—9		
Gerasimus II.	1689—1710	John XVI.	1676—1718
Samuel	1710—24	Peter VI.	1718—26
Cosmas II.	1724—37	John XVII.	1727—45
Cosmas III.	1737—46		
Matthew	1746—66	Mark VII.	1745—70
Cyprian	1766—82	John XVIII.	1770—97
Gerasimus III.	1783—8		
Parthenius II.	1788—1805	Mark VIII.	1797—1809
Theophilus	1805—25	Peter VII.	1809—54
Hierotheus I.	1825—45		
[Artemius]	1845—7		
Hierotheus II.	1847—58	Cyril IV.	1854—61
Callinicus	1858—61		
James	1861—6	Demetrius II.	1862—75
Nicanor	1866—70		
Sophronius IV.	1870—99	Cyril V.	1875—1927
Photius	1900—25		
Meletius	1925—		

CHAPTER XVII.

The Monophysites.

(I.) Armenians. (II.) Jacobites. (III.) Christians of Malabar. (IV.) Copts. (V.) Abyssinians.

In the fifth century the Church of the East broke away into independence of Byzantine Christendom. Its people became known as Nestorians. The separation of the Monophysites declared itself about the same time; for, from the fifth century, Monophysitism was adopted as the official creed of the ancient and national Church of Armenia, while in Syria, the Jacobites, in the sixth century, set up an organised Church of their own. In Egypt, the Copts had been in sympathy with Monophysite from the days of Cyril and Dioscorus. In the seventh century, the majority took advantage of the Arab conquest, 642, to detach themselves finally from Constantinople, leaving to the Orthodox Patriarch of Alexandria a mere handful of adherents known as Melkites, or Imperialists.

§ 1. Armenia[1] was the first country to become possessed of a national Church.

(i.) Its conversion[2] was due to King Tiridates III., 261—†317. Quite early in his reign there were Christians in Armenia; for Dionysius, bishop of Alexandria, 247—†65, wrote to them on the subject of penance.[3] A generation later the Emperor Maximin, 311—†3, attempted to force some Armenian Christians to sacrifice to idols. They were " allies of the Romans."[4] The advantages of such an alliance weighed seriously with Tiridates; for no sooner had Constantine and Licinius given peace to the Empire by the Edict of Milan,[5] 313, than the king made a treaty with the Romans, 314. He had already calculated that to bring over his people to the Christian religion would assure him of the support of

Constantine against the pressure of Persia on his eastern frontier; and he resolved upon the conversion of his country. He found his agent in St. Gregory the Illuminator, †324, himself an Armenian prince who had fled during the Persian occupation to Cæsarea in Cappadocia, where he was converted to Christianity and received a Greek and a Christian education. Here, at the instance of Tiridates, he obtained from archbishop Leontius consecration to the episcopate, 302, and became the apostle of Armenia. The country was now "attached to the Empire by the double ties of policy and religion."[6] Its conversion proceeded apace. The neighbouring churches supplied the teachers. From the west, i.e., from Lesser Armenia and Cappadocia, came Greek-speaking clergy and catechists; while Armenia owed as much—perhaps even before the mission of Gregory—to missionaries of the Syriac tongue. They came from Edessa and Nisibis; and penetrated the country from the south. According to Faustus Byzantinus, an Armenian writer of the fourth century, the profession of true Christianity was confined to those who could read Greek or Syriac;[7] but illiterate as it was, the nation as a whole was rapidly incorporated into the organisation of the Church, which simply took over the arrangements existing for the native cults. Temples with their endowments, which were considerable, became churches; their priests became Christian clergy; and, at the head of the hierarchy, Gregory was installed as Catholicus. An hereditary priesthood with animal sacrifices, continuing side by side with the Unbloody Sacrifice of the Eucharist, remained as witnesses of the ease and the superficial character of the conversion. But it was more than sufficient for the moment. It gave to the Armenians under Tiridates a cohesion which enabled them to resist the onset of Persia and the religious propaganda of Mazdaïsm; and it ultimately secured to them, against similar pressure from Arabs, Mongols and Turks in succession, a tradition of unity by which their nation and their religion have been preserved together.

On the death of Constantine, 337, the advantages to be

counted upon from an alliance with Rome became uncertain; and Arsaces, King of Armenia, 337—†67, made it his policy to hold the balance even between Rome and Persia. The defeat of Julian by the Persians, 363, led the Romans to withdraw their protectorate over Armenia; and a reversion to paganism took place under Pap, 367—†74, the son and successor of Arsaces. It was directed against the reforms of the Catholicus, Nerses I., 362—†73. Great-grandson of St. Gregory the Illuminator, he had been brought up at Cæsarea; and was consecrated there by the exarch Eusebius, 362—†70, whose chaplain, St. Basil, assisted at the consecration. Nerses, on returning home, could not but contrast with the austere religion of Cæsarea the paganism veiled under profession of Christianity which satisfied the ideals of his fellow countryman. At the Synod of Ashtishat,[8] 365, he set on foot a series of reforms which aimed at securing stricter marriage-laws, the abolition of heathen customs at funerals, the provision of hospices for sick and poor. Nerses also set up schools for education in Greek and Syriac; multiplied convents both of men and of women; and was, in fact, the restorer, if not the originator, of the monastic life in Armenia.[9] It was an enlightened programme; but it invited the hostility of the Court, and led to the pagan reaction. With this was connected the breach with Cæsarea: for Basil, now archbishop, 370—†9, refused to consecrate Faustus, a bishop of the Court party, for an Armenian see. The candidate went off and procured consecration from Anthimus of Tyana,[10] the rival of St. Basil, whose claims were ignored: and, from this time forward, the consecration of the Catholicus of Armenia was lost to Cæsarea. Pap, however, failed to maintain his throne: and was assassinated. The country then became once more the prey of rivalries between Rome and Persia: until neither side could stand it any longer. In 387, Theodosius I., 379—†95, and Sapor III., 383—†8, agreed upon a partition. The Romans retained one fifth of the country which was added to the civil Diocese of Pontus; while the remaining four-fifths were handed over to Persia: and Greater, or Persarmenia,

The Monophysites

continued a vassal state of Persia, under an Arsacid prince, until 428.

(ii.) A period of anarchy and foreign domination,[11] 428—885, ensued: during which the country was administered by *marzbans,* or governors, sometimes of Persian, sometimes of Armenian, birth.

In Greater Armenia the Persian government inaugurated a persecution which aimed at the breaking down of Armenian nationality. It met with a manful resistance; and Sahak (Isaac) who, after an interval of fifteen years, succeeded his father, Nerses I., as Catholicus, 388—†439, became the rallying-point of every patriotic interest, Christian or nationalist. Discipline and education flourished under his rule. In collaboration with a disciple of Nerses, Mesrob by name, 354—†441, who, in 404, invented the Armenian alphabet, the Catholicus provided his people with a national literature, and with the means of worship in their mother-tongue. For translations of the Scriptures from the Septuagint and from Syriac, appeared, 404—33, in the vernacular: "an event," says Gibbon, "which relaxed the connexion of the Church and nation with Constantinople."[12] These translations were succeeded, from 433 onwards to the death of Sahak, by liturgical books in Armenian; though the Armenian Liturgy,[13] while possessing peculiarities of its own, e.g., the Old Testament lesson and the unmixed chalice, is really a variant of the Byzantine rite. Both these movements—the Scriptures in the vernacular and the substitution in worship, for rites followed within the Empire whether Byzantine in Greek or Antiochene in Syriac, of a liturgy in the mother-tongue—encouraged the drift of the Church of Armenia towards independence of, and even hostility to, the Church of the Romans. At the time of the Council of Chalcedon, the drift became a torrent. Two years before the Council, the Armenians were suddenly confronted by the edict[14] of Iazdgerd II., King of Persia, 438—†57, the purpose of which was to enforce Mazdaïsm upon all his subjects and to crush out Christianity in Armenia. The Emperor Marcian, 450—†7, preoccupied with his Council, could give them no help; and naturally they felt little interest in its proceedings. After prolonged struggles they recovered their independence: and, at the Synod of Valarshapat, 491, the Catholicus Babken I., 490—†515, repudiated the decisions of Chalcedon, in company with Armenian, Georgian, and Albanian bishops. The condemnation was an echo of the *Henoticon*, 482; and a bid, no doubt, for the support of the Empire which, under that instrument, had become, in effect, though not in terms, officially Monophysite. It was fear of Persia, rather than calculated heresy, which led to this result; though it was also due to defect of the Armenian language. The question at Chalcedon turned upon the difference between Person and Nature: whereas for these two terms an Armenian had but one. When the Empire veered round again under the House of Justin, 518—610, to the Chalcedonian standard, the Church of Armenia would feel that it had a creed different from that of the Romans; and could confidently assure its Persian overlords that Armenians, though Christian subjects of Persia, were neither disloyal nor in secret sympathy with fellow-Christians over the border. Accordingly, they reaffirmed the rejection of the Council of Chalcedon at the two Synods of Dvin, 527 and 551: and, in spite of the assistance against Persia which was rendered to them by the Empire in 571—8, and again in 591, the repudiation of Chalcedon was renewed in 596 and again in 616. The victories of Heraclius over the Persians, 632, restored Armenia to the Romans; and a forced but temporary reunion took place at the Synod of Erzerum, 633, presided over by the Catholicus Esdras, 630—†41, in the presence of Heraclius, though without mention of Chalcedon on either side. But his victories were completely wiped out by the Arab conquest, 654; when Armenia passed under the yoke of the Caliphs. Again, in self-defence, followed fresh repudiations of Chalcedon under the Catholicus Elias, 703—17, and at the Council of Manazkert (now Melasgerd), 728, under the Catholicus John of Odsun, 717—†28, with twenty bishops.[15]

(iii.) A period of autonomy, 885—1046, succeeded the

The Monophysites

epoch of foreign domination. The Caliphs had administered the country through *osdikans* or governors, sometimes of Arab and sometimes of Armenian extraction. One of these governors, who belonged to the Jewish family of the Bagratids succeeded in founding a native dynasty and ascended the throne as Ashod I., 885—†90. The dynasty lasted till Gagig II., 1040—†79. Other branches of the Bagratid family set up principalities at Kars, 962—1080; and in Georgia, where Bagratid princes maintained independence till the Russian conquest, 1801. But the Arab invasions drove many members of noble families to Constantinople; where several became generals of Byzantine armies; and some even Emperors—Leo V., 813—†20, known as the Armenian, the "Macedonian," Basil I., 867—†86, of Armenian extraction, and the great soldier John Tzimisces, 969—†76. Armenia, in fact, supplied the best soldiers of the Imperial armies; and this led to the drawing together of Armenia and the Byzantine Empire. Both were now threatened by the Seljuk Turks; and twice the Emperor Basil II., 976—†1025, invaded Armenia, in 991 and again in 1021, in order to make the Armenian fortresses, garrisoned by imperial troops, the first line of defence against these new foes. His policy failed under his feebler successors. It was avenged on both the Empire and Armenia by the great disaster at Manazkert, 1071, to the north of Lake Van. Armenia then became part of the Seljuk dominions. In 1157 it was split up into petty states ruled by Arabs, Kurds and Turks; until these were swept away, 1235, by the invasion of the Mongols. The country thereupon became the prey of nomads and marauders: till its ruin was completed, c. 1400, by the ravages of Timur. Many of its inhabitants fled to the mountains, where, to save their lives, they embraced Islām; and others to Cilicia, where the Bagratid Ruben had founded a principality in 1080, which afterwards developed into the kingdom of Lesser Armenia.

(iv.) A fourth period is represented by this kingdom of Armeno-Cilicia, 1080—1340, under Rubenian and

Hethumian princes. It was a period of successful struggle with the Byzantine Empire, and of losing contest with Seljuks and Mamluks, in reliance upon the Latin kingdoms of Syria.

(v.) During a fifth period, 1340—73, the kingdom of Armeno-Cilicia fell under the rule of the crusading family of the Lusignans. By supporting the crusaders and by trade with Italian republics, it had prolonged its stormy existence for three hundred years; when it was finally destroyed by the Mamluks of Egypt, 1375.

(vi.) From 1375—1473, Armenia "suffered the horrors of a Tartar invasion under Tamerlane, and finally passed under the yoke of the Turks."[16]

(vii.) Its last epoch runs from that date to the present day. Like other Christian communities subject to the Sultan, the Armenians were organised as a *millet* or nation. They were placed at first under the Armenian bishop of Brusa, who presently became Armenian Patriarch of Constantinople, 1461. Meanwhile, the Catholicus had several times changed his patriarchal seat.[17] He was at Ashtishat, to the S.W., or at Valarshapat, to the N.E., 301—478; at Dvin, to the north-east of Mt. Ararat, 478—931; at Agthamar, an island in Lake Van, 931—67; at Arkina, 968—92; in the city of Ani, on a tributary of the Araxes, to the N.W. of Dvin, 992—1054; at Tavplour, 1054—65; at Dzamntave, 1065—87; at Siavler, 1105—66; in Armeno-Cilicia, first at Hromkla, 1166—1293, and then at Sis, 1293—1441. But since 1441 he had established himself in the monastery of Etchmiadzin[18] (="The Only-begotten has descended") at the old royal capital of Valarshapat, and near Erivan, the capital of the Soviet Republic of Armenia. Besides the Catholicus, there is another Patriarch at Sis[19] who assumed the title during a temporary schism, 1440, and, as the price of accommodation, was allowed to keep it. A third owner of the title is the Armenian Patriarch of Constantinople,[20] who received it, 1461. A fourth is the Armenian Patriarch of Jerusalem[21] who adopted it in the eighteenth century; and a fifth is the titular Patriarch of Agthamar.[22] Russian intervention, 1828, secured the subordination of the Patriarch of Constantinople to the Catholicus: who is thus the ecclesiastical chief of the hierarchy and of all Armenians.

After the Russo-Turkish War of 1877—8, Russia encouraged the formation of patriotic committees in Armenia to work for an independent state under Russian protection which was to include Russian, Persian and Turkish Armenia. But on the assassination of the Tsar Alexander II., 1855—†81, the scheme of a separate state collapsed; and all hope of self-government for Armenia under Russian protection came to an end. Under Alexander III., 1881—†94, autocracy, alarmed at the ingratitude displayed by the murder of Alexander the Liberator, reverted to reaction. The movement for independence among Armenians became, through disappointment, a revolutionary enterprise; and in 1893, revolutionary placards were posted at Yuzgat and Marsivan, to the N.E. of Asia Minor. Next year the Turkish government retaliated by massacres.[23] An attempt of the British government to intervene and to press reforms upon the Porte came to nothing; for France and Russia refused their support. The failure offered a welcome opportunity to the Sultan Abdul Hamid II., 1876—1908; and in 1896 further massacres ensued which were carefully organised and carried out according to plan. Only Gregorian and Protestant Armenians were attacked; for the Uniate Armenians enjoyed the protection of France, and the Orthodox Armenians were sheltered by Russia. Between 1894—6 as many as 100,000 Armenians perished. Again at Mush, 1904, and at Van, 1908, similar horrors were enacted; the lower orders, who hated the Armenians as successful traders, being excited by cupidity against the victims. On the deposition of Abdul Hamid, 1908, the new régime professed an equal respect for all religions: but that did not prevent another outbreak at Adana, 1909, which cost the lives of 20,000 Armenians. Between 1915—20, the same policy of extermination was pursued by Talaat Bey and the Young Turks; and it has continued under the Kemalist régime since 1920. In the process of getting rid of Christian minorities, the Armenians of

Turkey have been reduced from 1,800,000 in 1895, to 281,000 in 1922; of whom 100,000 live at Constantinople. Scattered throughout the world are some 3,000,000 in all; the majority of whom still find their national and religious unity centred in the Catholicus at Etchmiadzin.

§ 2. The Jacobites[24] of Syria owe their origin to the sympathy of the Empress Theodora with Monophysitism, and their name to her *protégé*, James Baradaeus,[25] 490— †577. James was born at Tella, a town of Osrhoëne, about fifty-five miles due east of Edessa. and became a monk in the Syrian monastery of Phasil, i.e., the Quarry[26] near that city. He was an educated man; for he spoke Greek, Syriac and Arabic with equal facility. He was also an ascetic, with unrivalled powers of physical endurance. Devoted to the memory of Severus, Patriarch of Antioch, 512—8 (†539), the chief theologian of the Monophysites, and of his own fellow-townsman, John, bishop of Tella,[27] 512—9 (†538), whom Severus had entrusted with the task of ordaining Monophysite clergy, James was just the man to carry on this mission. His appointment to it was urged upon Theodora by Aretas, 530—†72, Emir of the Ghassanid Arabs and a zealous Monophysite, who visited Constantinople, 542—3. Accordingly, James was consecrated in secret by the Monophysite, Theodosius, once Patriarch of Alexandria, 536, but then in exile, 537—†67, at Lake Dercos, near the capital. He was given a roving commission to consecrate and organise a Monophysite hierarchy; and, as not less than three bishops are normally required for the consecration of a bishop, colleagues were supplied for him—Theodore for work among the Arabs, and two monks, Conon of Cilicia and Eugenius of Isauria. James was then smuggled out of Constantinople by the Emir Aretas; and set forth upon his life's work. Travelling everywhere on foot, and clothed in the ragged mulecloth which gave him his name of Bar-adai (the ragged), he exercised his episcopate for five-and-thirty years, 542—†77. In the course of it, he consecrated two Patriarchs of Antioch,[28] Sergius of Tella, 543—6, and Paul the Black, 542—†78, with eighty-nine bishops; and ordained, as some said, no fewer than one hundred thousand priests. From nonconforming members of the Church the Monophysites of Syria thus became a communion of separatists: until every official or Orthodox prelate found himself confronted by a rival bishop, with his clergy. Efforts were made, as by the Emperor, Justin II., 565—†78, through John of Callinicus, Count of the East, to reconcile the dissidents; but by the time when James died in the desert between Gaza and Egypt, the breach had become irreparable. When the Arab conquest of Syria, 638, finally severed the East from the Roman Empire, the Jacobites were free to go their own way.

Their subsequent history has been one of varied fortune. Unlike the Nestorians, they have never been a large body. But they have had their periods of expansion. Thus, at the end of the sixth century, they obtained a footing in Persia.[29] From Tagrit on the Tigris, and the famous monastery of Mar Mattai,[30] to the N.E. of Mosul, in the heart of the Nestorian country, they sent out their missionaries on all sides; and Sirin, the queen of Chosroes II., 590—†628, was a Jacobite Christian. In the seventh century, Maruta,[31] a monk who had been a zealous missionary and became metropolitan of Tagrit, 629—49, ruled over twelve suffragans in Persia and erected three new sees.[32] In the twelfth century the Patriarch had as many as twenty metropolitans and one hundred bishops in Syria, Asia Minor and Cyprus; while there were eighteen sees under the Mafrian (metropolitan) of the East. The Jacobites also had their epochs of distinction. Thus they produced a "brilliant school of liturgical science"; and "Dionysius bar Salībī[33] (†1171), Bishop of Amida (Diabekr) is famous as the author of a treatise[34] (the Liturgy of St. James) such as no other church could show in the Middle Ages. The result of this is that we know more about the history of the Jacobite rite than of any other."[35] The writing of historical works also engaged their attention; and contemporary with Dionysius was Michael I., Patriarch of Antioch, 1166—†99, whose *Chronicle*[36] is the chief source for Nestorian and Jacobite history. In the thirteenth century, his nephew, John Abu'l-Faraj, otherwise Gregory Barhebraeus,[37] 1226—†86 (for he was of Jewish descent), rose to great eminence both in medicine and literature. His best-known work is his *Universal History*, of which Parts II. and III.,[38] though based in great part on Michael, are invaluable sources for the history both of Jacobites and Nestorians. But, with Barhebraeus, the great days of the Jacobites passed away. In the fourteenth and fifteenth centuries, their strength was reduced, partly by persecution from the Moslems and partly by dissensions among themselves. At the present time they number not more than from 150,000 to 200,000 :[39] most of them between the upper Tigris, to N. and E., and the cities of Diabekr, Mardin and Nisibis, to W. and S.[40] Their ecclesiastical chief is entitled "Patriarch of Antioch" :[41] and, since the thirteenth century, Monophysite Patriarchs of Antioch have regularly taken the name of Ignatius,[42] after Ignatius, the martyr bishop of that see. The Patriarch lives at Mardin: but his church stands about five miles to the east of that city, at Deir-el-Za'aferan[43] (the Saffron Monastery), which has been the headquarters of the Syrian Patriarchs since Michael I.

Under the Patriarch are eight metropolitans—the title being purely honorary—for Jerusalem, Mosul, Mar Mattai (the abbot), Mardin Urfa (Edessa), Kharput and two without fixed sees: besides three bishops.[44] Most of the community speak Arabic: which has largely invaded their liturgy. But the liturgy itself is a Syriac form of the ancient Antiochene rite; and is commonly known as the Syriac St. James.[45] It has the usual features of that family: the cue for the celebrant taken from the Sanctus being "Holy";[46] and the Great Intercession coming between the Invocation and the Communion.[47] But the Jacobites have added features of their own. The words "who wast crucified for us" are inserted into the *Trisagion*;[48] and as many as sixty-four different forms of anaphora are in print.[49] But very few of them are in actual use.

§ 3. Closely connected, since the seventeenth century,

The Monophysites

with the Jacobites of Syria are the Syrians of Malabar,[50] sometimes called the Christians of St. Thomas. But they have only a legendary title to the Apostle's name; or, indeed, to any apostolic foundation.

(i.) In the first period of their history, they appear as one of the churches which owe their origin to the missionary zeal of the Church of the East. Cosmas Indicopleustes,[51] a merchant of Alexandria and possibly himself a Nestorian, made voyages to Arabia and East Africa, c. 520, for purposes of trade. He never got as far as India himself; but owes his information about it to what he learned from his fellow-travellers. Afterwards, he became a monk in Mt. Sinai; and then wrote, c. 547, his *Christian Topography,* containing accounts of his voyages made five-and-twenty years before. Here he tells us of the island named Taprobana (Ceylon), and how it had "a church of Christians, with clergy and faithful." He does not know whether there are churches further on: but there are " at Male " (sc. the Malabar coast) " where pepper is grown. In Calliane (Quilon) also, there is a bishop: customarily ordained in Persia. So, too, in the isle of Dioscoris (Socotra), where the people talk Greek, there are clergy to be found who were ordained in, and sent thither from, Persia. I had a talk with some of these Greek-speaking islanders, when we were on our way to Ethiopia."[52] So it is clear enough that the Christians of Malabar were one of the many missions founded by the Church of the East. Their bishops would be dependent upon the Catholicus of Seleucia-Ctesiphon; and to that extent they would rank as Nestorian. At the opening of the ninth century, the Catholicus Timothy I., 778—820, refers to the flourishing church of India which owned his authority:[53] while towards its close our own King Alfred, 871—†91, came into contact with the Christians of St. Thomas. The Danes were besieging London when he made a vow that, if they were compelled to raise the siege, he would send offerings to Rome, and also to India in honour of St. Thomas and St. Bartholomew. He sent them in 883 by a bishop who went first to Rome and then on to Malabar, where he offered the gifts, and returned with presents of jewels and pepper.[54] In the fourteenth century Marco Polo, 1256—†1323, describes the pepper-coast of Malabar;[55] and, though he says nothing of Christians there, he knows that there are Christians in India.[56] Archaeological evidence that they were of Persian origin is the fifth century cross at Mailapur, near Madras, with an inscription in Pahlavi,[57] and, in design, very similar to that of the Nestorian monument of 781 at Si-ngan-fu in N. China;[58] while that they had their own organisation is clear from the charter of privileges granted by a Hindu prince of the eighth century to "the metropolitan of India."[59]

(ii.) The second period of their history belongs to the epoch of Portuguese rule in southern India. On 20th May, 1498, Vasco da Gama, 1460—†1524, arrived off Calicut, and established himself for six months on the Malabar coast. On a second expedition in 1500 he arrived with 13 ships and 1,200 soldiers; and had instructions "to begin with preaching and, if that failed, to proceed to the sword." He made a stay at Calicut; and set up factories there and at Cochin. On his third voyage, 1502, he allied himself with the rajahs of Cochin and Cannamore against Calicut: and so secured a firmer hold in southern India. Next year, followed three expeditions from Portugal, one of them led by Alphonso d'Albuquerque, 1453—†1515, who became Viceroy in 1509. He seized Goa, 1510; which became, 1530, the capital of Portuguese India, the see of a bishop, 1534, and of an archbishop, 1557. Then followed, 1560, the setting up of the Inquisition; and upon the arrival of Aleixo de Menezes as archbishop of Goa, 1595—†1611, an intensive campaign for the union of the Syrians with the Roman See. They then consisted of a flock of about 200,000 in number, with 1,500 churches, under their metropolitan, Mar Joseph, whose see was at Angamale, inland from Cranganur. In 1599 at the Diocesan Synod of Diamper, now Udayamperūr,[60] some twelve miles south-east of Cochin, the Church of Malabar was required to renounce Nestorianism and all connexion with the Catholicus of the East, as well as to submit to the authority of the Roman Church: but the submission was accompanied with provision for much-needed reforms.[61] The majority acquiesced: and the whole Church remained Uniate till the Portuguese domination was put down by the Dutch. They captured Quilon, 1661: took Cranganur, 1662; and, 1663, made themselves masters of Cochin and the whole Malabar coast.

(iii.) With the supremacy of the Dutch, we enter upon the third period of the history of the Syrians of Malabar. A minority were non-Uniates: and the change of masters left them free to act for themselves. No sooner did they observe signs of the weakening hold of Portugal than, in 1653, they met at Alengat and renounced the communion of the Roman Catholic bishop of Cranganur. They then elected one Thomas, of the archidiaconal family of Palakomatta, to be their bishop; and tried to obtain his consecration from the Nestorians in Mesopotamia. But the Government was on the watch, and foiled their plans. They then turned to the Coptic Patriarch in Egypt. He sent them a Monophysite Syrian bishop, named Aitahalla. But he was caught, and put to death. Thomas might now have despaired of consecration, had it not been for the overthrow of the Portuguese dominion in India by Holland. The Dutch took Quilon, in 1661: in 1662 they captured Cranganur; in 1663 they made themselves masters of Cochin and the whole coast of Malabar. These victories at once reversed the ecclesiastical situation: and Thomas at last could be consecrated. But instead of applying to the Nestorians, he allowed himself to be consecrated by Gregory, a Jacobite bishop of Jerusalem, who came to India and ordained him metropolitan, 1665. Thus from Nestorians the Syrians became Monophysites: and are now in communion with the Jacobite Patriarch of Antioch. Such a *volte face* is without parallel in the history of the Church. But probably it meant much less than appears. It is very doubtful how far "Nestorianism" and "Monophysitism" represent more than a traditional adherence on the part of the communities so labelled. In any case, we can hardly be surprised at people being ready to accept the one or the other—whichever offered immediate relief from the attentions of the Inquisition.

The subsequent history of the Malabar Christians is a melancholy record of dissension.[62] The Uniates, of course, went on, and are now a body of some 400,000. But the non-Uniate Syrians of Malabar have been perpetually at strife among themselves. Their two chief divisions taken together number about the same as the Uniates; but their Church life is at a low ebb. Their rite[63] is that of the Syrian Jacobites, with variable Anaphoras—six in all:[64] and Syriac their liturgical language. But their pronunciation of it is peculiar: as one would expect from a people who talk Malayalam.

§ 4. The Copts are the next to engage our attention. Up to the middle of the seventh century their history is simply that of the Patriarchate of Alexandria, and has already been dealt with.[65] So we continue as from the Arab conquest of Egypt, 639—642:[66] when the country became part of the dominions of the Omayyad Caliphs, 661—749. They belonged to the Sunni[67] division of Mohammedans, and ruled from Damascus.

(i.) From 641—868 the province of Egypt was subject to their authority. But it sat lightly on the Governor, and left him in practice independent, so long as he paid the necessary tribute. At the time of the conquest Benjamin was the Coptic Patriarch, 623—62. He received a safe-conduct from 'Amr, 641—4: " There is protection and security for the place where Benjamin, the Patriarch of the Coptic Christians is, and peace from God; therefore let him come forth secure and tranquil, and administer the affairs of his Church, and the government of his nation."[68] Armed with these powers, Benjamin collected his scattered flock. He taught and reformed them; and built and restored churches and monasteries.[69] He also sent to Ethiopia the metropolitan Cyril, together with Teklahaimanot, the founder of monasticism in that country.[70] In so doing, he continued to exercise the jurisdiction which, from the first, the see of Alexandria had enjoyed in Abyssinia.

The Monophysites

Benjamin was succeeded by Agatho, 662—80. He converted the Gaïnites—an extreme sect of Monophysites—to its more normal form:[71] and rebuilt the church of St. Mark in Alexandria which had been burnt at the taking of the city.[72]

With John III., 680—9, the Copts had their first taste of the harsher treatment to which, as a nation of rayahs, they were at any time exposed. The Governor, 'Abd-el-'Azīz, 685—705, finding himself in want of money, demanded of the Patriarch 100,000 denarii. He burnt his feet in a brazier till he produced a tenth of this sum, which was all he could raise.[73]

Alexander II., 703—26, was branded[74] and mulcted of 6,000.

Upon his death, the Melkite Patriarchate, extinct since Peter II., 643—†52, was restored in the person of Cosmas, 727—†67. He solemnly abjured monotheletism, 743, with which Cyrus the Caucasian, Patriarch and Prefect of Egypt[75] under Heraclius, had been tainted. But the abjuration brought him no accession of strength. The numbers of his flock continued small; nor could he find the requisite three consecrators in Egypt for the prelates of his Court. He had to get them ordained at Tyre.[76] Nevertheless, his line continued: and from this time onwards, to the present day, the two successions, Melkite and Coptic, have existed side by side, until they are now represented respectively by Meletius, 1925—, formerly archbishop of Athens and Patriarch of Constantinople, and by Cyril V., 1875—†1927. But the history of both successions exhibits the same pitiful tale of persecution at the caprice of the ruler; and the marvel is, not that instances of apostasy were many, but that generation after generation stood firm when by turning Mohammedan any Christian could escape.

(ii.) The Fātimid Caliphs succeeded to power, 969, and maintained themselves in Egypt till 1171. They were of the Shīa division of Moslems;[77] and more tolerant than their predecessors.

The Patriarch Ephraim, 977—81, was a favourite at Court. He put down simony and concubinage: the two evils rampant among his clergy; and rebuilt the ruined church of St. Mercurius outside Fustāt.[78]

During the patriarchate of Zacharias, 1005—32, toleration gave way to horrible persecution under the Caliph El-Hākim, 996—1021. He destroyed 3,000 churches, and caused great numbers to apostatise; though the patriarch himself escaped with his life.[79]

His successor, Shenut II., 1032—47, displayed the deterioration of character easily explained, if not excused, by the constant oppression under which the Copts had to live. It had become customary for candidates for the Patriarchate to offer bribes to the clergy who elected, as well as to the Caliph who confirmed the election. In order to recoup himself, the Patriarch would sell bishoprics to the highest bidder. Shenut went so far as to summon a Synod and force it to declare this system lawful, together with its consequence—the sale of holy orders.[80]

A natural result was that many of his flock seceded to the Melkites, till Christodulus, 1047—77, took in hand some measure of reform. His Code of thirty-one canons,[81] indeed, does not deal with the crying offence of simony; but it provides for a renewal of discipline among both clergy and laity. He was the first Coptic Patriarch to establish himself at Cairo; where his successors reside to the present day.

Under Michael IV., 1092—1102, Egypt felt the first impact of the Crusades. They brought the Copts into conflict with the Latins; and they led to the overthrow of the enfeebled Fātimid dynasty.

(iii.) It was succeeded by Saladin and his successors: known from his name, Yūsuf 'ibn Ayyūb [Joseph, son of Job], as the Ayyūbids,[82] 1171—1250. Saladin belonged to the Sunni division of Moslems; and his rule was harsh. He forbade Christians to hold government posts, or any public office. He renewed the laws against the display on the outside of churches of any symbol of the Christian religion, such as bells and crosses. He prohibited Christians from celebrating processions in public.

The Patriarch, Gabriel II., 1131—46, put out a Code

of thirty canons,[83] which are still part of the Coptic Canon Law.

Under Cyril III., 1235—43, simony again made its appearance as a flagrant abuse.[84] Persecution, too, broke out again: with apostasies. One of them was that of the bishop of Sandafah.[85] It is no small credit to the loyalty of the Coptic episcopate that this is the first and only known instance of a bishop apostatising.

(iv.) The overthrow of the Ayyūbids led to the rule of the Mamlūks, 1250—1517. They were a bodyguard of Seljuk Turks, who seized upon power: and called Mamlūks, or slaves, for such had been their condition. Anarchy, licence and tyranny—as might be expected from slaves turned sovereigns—distinguished or disgraced their rule. During their tenure, the Patriarch Gabriel V., 1401—18, wrote an explanation of the Coptic rite;[86] and John XI., 1418—41, showed some disposition for reunion, perhaps in hope of protection, by sending Andrew, abbot of St. Anthony, to the Council of Florence, 1439. The Council proclaimed a union with the monophysites of Syria and Egypt; and the abbot was one of the signatories to the decree.[87]

(v.) The Mamlūks were overthrown by the Ottoman Turks, 1517—1914. They held Egypt under a Vali, or Governor, dispatched from Constantinople; till, in the eighteenth century, the Governor was chosen, for about a hundred years, from the Mamlūks or bodyguard. In 1811, Mohammed Ali exterminated the Mamlūks: and, by a firman of the Sultan, became hereditary Governor, 1841. He was succeeded by Ismail, 1863—79, who received the title of Khedive by a firman of 1867. But Ismail's extravagance involved him in financial embarrassment, and he was forced to abdicate in favour of his son, Tewfik, 1879—92. In 1882 the battle of Tel-el-Kebir led to the British occupation of the country. The Copts obtained their freedom: and shared in the prosperity which dawned upon Egypt with the new administration. Since the Turkish conquest they had lived on, in accordance with the custom of the Ottoman Empire, as a millet or nation of rayahs. Their bishops paid the usual fee, and obtained a *berat* from the government. The laity paid a poll-tax. They declined in numbers: and are still a minority of the population: 834,474 out of 12,404,942, though the total number of Christians in Egypt amounts to 1,026,107. But since 1882 they have enjoyed peace, protection and religious freedom. The majority are peasants: but, of the better educated, numbers are clerks and professional men, while their leaders are well-to-do merchants. All speak Arabic: Coptic having disappeared; except in their service-books, where the two languages are given in parallel columns. The Patriarch is now elected by twelve bishops who form his Court. In 1897, there were eighteen dioceses. The bishops are celibate, being taken from the monastic order. Many of the clergy are uneducated: and cannot read Arabic, much less Coptic. There are numerous monasteries:[88] St. Mercurius in Old Cairo; four in the Nitrian desert; two, St. Antony and his friend St. Paul near the Red Sea. A reforming party has made its appearance with the growth of education. They demand education for the clergy, and the right of control, especially in finance, for the laity. But the late Patriarch Cyril V. withheld his sympathy. In respect of the doctrine of the Person of our Lord the Copts are still officially Monophysite;[89] but, otherwise, they hold the creed of the other historic churches of Christendom, as do the Orthodox: differing from the Roman Catholic Church only in respect of the papacy and the *Filioque*.

It remains briefly to describe their Liturgy. It is a descendant of the parent-rite of Egypt, i.e., of the now disused Liturgy of St. Mark.[90] This rite is in Greek; and the Coptic Liturgies began as translations of it. They take three forms, each being an *anaphora* attached to a common *pro-anaphora*. The first and most important is *The Liturgy of the Coptic Jacobites,* including the *Anaphora of St. Mark or St. Cyril*.[91] It is, in fact, a Coptic form of the Greek of St. Mark. A good deal of it is still in Greek. But it is now in use only in Advent and Lent. The second has the *anaphora* of St. Gregory Nazianzen.[92] It is used at Christmas, Epiphany and Easter; and has the peculiarity of being addressed throughout to our Lord. The third has the *anaphora* of St. Basil,[93] and is a shortened and adapted form of the Byzantine Liturgy of St. Basil. It is in this form that the Coptic Liturgy is ordinarily celebrated. The Coptic St. Mark manifests the usual Alexandrine features: the Great Intercession between Preface and *Sanctus*,[94] with " full " for the cue to be taken up from the *Sanctus* by the celebrant,[95] while the *Sanctus* has no *Benedictus* to follow—again an Egyptian peculiarity.[96] But the ordinary Coptic Liturgy exhibits further peculiarities of its own. The Invocation is addressed to our Lord:[97] and the Great Intercession reverts from its Egyptian place between Preface and Sanctus to a position between the Consecration and the Communion,[98] where one would expect it in a rite based upon a Byzantine, i.e., ultimately, an Antiochene, original.

§ 5. Last to be considered of the Monophysite churches, and closely associated from the first with the Patriarchate of Alexandria, is the Church of Abyssinia.[99]

Geographically, Abyssinia is an oval-shaped country to the W. of the Red Sea: from E. to W. some 230 miles broad in the N., and towards the S. extending to 900 miles. Its western portion is a mountainous mass: and, where the mountains are seen from the Red Sea, they look like the walls of a vast fortress rising to heights from 8,000 to 11,000 feet. It is bounded by the Anglo-Egyptian Sudan to the W., Kenya to the S., and, to S.E. and N., by Italian, British and French possessions on the Indian Ocean and the Red Sea. Within these bounds are three zones of climate: first, the low valleys, with great heat and heavy rainfall in the summer, but otherwise arid like the Sudan; then a middle zone of 6,000 to 8,000 feet, which forms the larger and most populous part of the country, with rich pastures and an equable temperature, not much higher than that of the Mediterranean lands; and a third, or cold, zone, 8,000 feet and over, with variable temperature and chilly nights.

Ethnologically, the Agas, or Freemen, form the basal stock of the nation. But they have intermarried with Berbers and Sudanese to the West and with Semitic peoples such as Arabs and Himyarites, from across the Red Sea, on the East. In the fourth century these latter conquered the East coast of Africa opposite: and settled in the province called after them, Amhara. Galla tribes overran these regions in the fifteenth and sixteenth centuries. The mixture of races led the Arabs to name the country *Habesh,* "a heap of sweepings"; whence our name—Abyssinia.

Politically, Abyssinia consisted, at first, of four provinces: called, from N. to S., Tigré, Amhara, Gojam and Shoa—originally four small kingdoms under the *Negus-sé-neghest,* i.e. the king of the kings of Ethiopia. Its population is now about seven million. Its civil capital was, at first, Axum in Tigré, now in ruins and once the ecclesiastical capital too; then, since the middle ages, Gondar, in Amhara; and, since 1892, Addis Ababa in Shoa. The official and spoken language is Amharic: but Ge'ez is the liturgical and literary language—both, in origin, Semitic: but, unlike other Semitic tongues, written and read from left to right.[100]

The conversion of Abyssinia is described by Rufinus, a presbyter of Aquileia, †410. A philosopher of Tyre, by name Meropius, sailed forth to see the world. He took with him two boys, Frumentius and Aedesius. Their ship touched at a port, probably Adulis, now Harkiko, not far from Massawa on the Red Sea; but it was boarded by the natives, and Meropius, with most of the ship's company, was put to death. But the boys were spared: and taken to the king. He made Frumentius his chancellor and Aedesius his cup-bearer. On his death, the queen was anxious to retain them in her service during the minority of her son. They consented to remain; and Frumentius took advantage of his position to obtain freedom of worship for Roman merchants trading in the country, and encouraged them to build churches. At length, the young prince came of age; and Frumentius and Aedesius claimed their liberty. They returned home: Aedesius to Tyre, where he proceeded to Holy Orders: while Frumentius hastened to tell all that had happened to St. Athanasius, and urged him to provide a bishop for

His Beatitude the Lord Photius, Patriarch and Pope of Alexandria, and
Œcumenical Judge.
Born 1858. Consecrated Archbishop of Nazareth 1899. Died 6th Sept., 1925.—R.I

See p. 473.]

Abyssinia. Athanasius dealt with him as Pharaoh, when he promoted his adviser Joseph: for he consecrated him bishop and sent him back to preside over the church which he had helped to form in Abyssinia. Rufinus tells us that he had the story from the lips of Aedesius himself.[101]

The story is happily confirmed from an independent and trustworthy source; for St. Athanasius, in his *Apology to Constantius*, written in 357, has preserved a letter which the Emperor had lately sent to two princes of Axum, urging them to "send the bishop Frumentius at once to Egypt" for an enquiry into the circumstances of his appointment (evidently treated as recent) by George, the Arian intruder into the see of Alexandria.[102] There is evidence of another attempt to propagate Arianism in Abyssinia by Theophilus the Indian.[103] He was a native of Ceylon and an indefatigable Arian missionary who enjoyed the favour of Constantine, 337—†61, both on that account and for the wonderful cure he had wrought upon the Empress Eusebia,[104] †360. But his attempt to seduce Abyssinia had as little success as that of his patron. We know nothing of the work of Frumentius on his return as bishop. But Christianity was probably confined at first to the cities of the coast, such as Adulis, and of the north, such as Axum, while it would find its chief supporters among the Roman merchants who frequented their markets.

In the second half of the fifth century, we have the evidence of inscriptions for the conversion of King Tzânâ [? Ezânâ]. In the sixth, King Andog, at war with the Himyarites, near Aden, vowed to become a Christian if he should be victorious: and sent to the Emperor Justinian for a bishop. The Emperor sent a prelate named John, from Alexandria, who baptised the King and his nobles.[105]

So far, Abyssinian Christianity was Orthodox. But early in the sixth century began its connexion with Monophysitism. About 500, according to authors of the fifteenth century, arrived the Nine Saints from Rûm, i.e. from the Roman Empire. They were monks, with Syrian names. They established their monasteries in the northern parts of the country: where, in consequence of their labours, Christianity took root and flourished. They translated the Scriptures, and especially the New Testament, into Ge'ez. The text of their translation is held to suggest a Syrian rather than an Egyptian original: and points to Syria as the country from which they came. It is probable that with them came Monophysite influences as well.

Whatever the labours, joint or single, of John and the Nine Saints, they had much success. For early in the sixth century, the Court and the country round had become Christian. Cosmas Indicopleustes, writing c. 547, records the fact:[106] and the christianisation of Abyssinia may have been powerfully assisted by the protectorate which, at that time, the Roman Empire extended over the country in order to prevent it falling under the control of the Persians. Presently, we hear of a cathedral at Axum; and, also, in the sixth century, of Yared who set up a school of ecclesiastical chant there.

From the sixth to the twelfth century, we have little information about Abyssinia because of its isolation. But we know that the Metropolitan, or Abuna [=our father] continued in dependence upon Alexandria. In the seventh century, the Coptic Patriarch Benjamin I., 623—62, sent one of his monks, Cyril, to be Abuna:[107] and the Copts managed to keep the appointment in their own hands by not allowing the number of Abyssinian bishops to exceed seven: a number insufficient, according to the canons, for the consecration of a primate. So John,[108] in 826, was consecrated Abuna by James, Coptic Patriarch of Alexandria, 819—36. He was driven into exile by the king: who, however, asked pardon of the Patriarch Joseph, 837—50, and, in return, obtained James. About a century later, Cosmas III., Patriarch of Alexandria, 923—34, consecrated Peter as Abuna. He was ousted by a vagabond monk named Menas, who produced forged letters from the Patriarch and so took his place. But the fraud was discovered. Menas paid the penalty with his life. And a disciple of Peter was enthroned in his stead.[109]

About the year 1000, after the short reign of a

The Monophysites

pagan (or Jewish) queen, accompanied by persecution, Michael, otherwise Habib (Agapius), became Abuna, 1135. During his primacy, the king endeavoured to get the hierarchy enlarged, so as to obtain a number of native bishops sufficient to consecrate the Abuna at home, and so get rid of dependence upon Alexandria. He failed in his enterprise: but the dynasty continued Christian till 1150. The second half of that century is memorable for the zeal of Tekla Hāymānot, who laboured for the conversion of southern Abyssinia where paganism was still in possession.

Toward the end of the thirteenth century, Christianity was strong under the Salomonian dynasty:[110] and about 1300 the Abuna was Abba Salâmâ. He put out a revision of the text of the Gospels translated into Ge'ez. Victorious campaigns relieved the pressure of Islām. The monks increased in numbers: among whom was Ewostâtêwos, †1332, an ardent missionary who destroyed twelve sacred trees dedicated to local divinities; and Marqorêwos (Mercurius), who evangelised the pagans of Sarawe, to the N. of Axum. Between 1300—50 Abuna James sent twelve monks to evangelise Shoa; and, about the same time, they made attempts to reform the court and the nobles; where simony, corrupt morals and irregular marriages prevailed. The king, 'Amda Seyon, 1314—†43, retaliated by persecution directed against the monks of Dabra Libanos:[111] whose abbot, Anorêwos (Honorius) had pronounced him excommunicate.

About 1490 the Portuguese[112] made their first contact with Abyssinia: when Dom Pedro de Covilham arrived with a letter in search of Prester John! His arrival coincided with movements of aggression against Abyssinia on the part of Mohammedan neighbours; and, 1507, the Negus sent Matthew, an Armenian, to Portugal, with a request for aid. At length, in 1520, a Portuguese fleet, with Matthew on board, entered the Red Sea; and sent an embassy to visit the Negus David II., 1508—40. They stayed in the country for six years. After their departure, Mohammedan invaders poured in from the S.E., and forced David, 1528, to take refuge in the mountains. In answer to a further appeal for help, a Portuguese fleet under Admiral Stephen da Gama arrived from India at Massawa, February, 1541; and in July, Christopher, his brother, advanced to the aid of the Abyssinians, with a force of 450 musketeers. He met with a reverse in August, 1542, and was killed; but in the end the invaders were defeated, 21st February, 1543. Some twenty years later, the Jesuits entered the country, 1562. One of them, Pedro Paez, was a man of tact and judgment. He won his way at Court: and, at length, in the presence of his successor, Affonso Mendez, who was sent out by Pope Gregory XV., 1621—3, as Patriarch of Ethiopia, the Negus Susneos (Sisinius), 1607—†32, made his submission to the Roman See, 11th December, 1626.[113] But national feeling was offended by this loss of independence: and the people rallied to the opposition led by Abuna and the monks. Mendez, moreover, proved less diplomatic than his predecessor; and, on the accession of Fasilidas (Basilides), 1632—67, the Jesuits were expelled. The Church of Abyssinia which had thus for a time became a Uniate Church, reverted to its traditional association with the Copts and Monophysitism.

The Abyssinians, like other Monophysites, accept the first three Œcumenical Councils, but repudiate the fourth. They also reject the *Filioque,* in common with the Eastern Churches as a whole. They admit the Seven Sacraments, like the Copts. Among the seven is Holy Orders, which are bestowed by Abuna: who comes from Egypt, and is often ignorant of Ge'ez. He is chosen from the monks of St. Antony, and consecrated by the Coptic Patriarch of Alexandria. He consecrates the bishops: but is forbidden to raise the episcopate to a number exceeding seven. " This, as the event proved, was a most unwise regulation. It was apparently adopted at first by the jealousy of Alexandria, lest Axum should constitute itself a patriarchate. As twelve bishops were canonically required for the consecration of a patriarch, the limitation to seven entirely obviated this danger. But it has caused two great evils. It has prevented the spread of the Gospel in Africa. And [it] has been the occasion of the

[Monophysite] heresy in the Abyssinian Church."[114] Besides conferring Holy Orders, Abuna crowns the Negus, issues dispensations, and hears causes on appeal. And he maintains great state, being supported by lands and large revenues.

Second to Abuna in dignity, and more of a national potentate than his foreign superior is the *Echage*, or archbishop. He is the abbot of the monastery of Dabra Libanos in Shoa.

Monks are numerous: some, hermits following the rule of St. Antony: others, following the rule of St. Pachomius, live in community.[115] There are two orders—of Teklahaimanot and Ewostâtêwos. There are also Abyssinian monks in Egypt and at Jerusalem.

Conservative because of their age-long isolation, the Abyssinians have retained customs once prevalent in early days—the communion of infants from the chalice, the observance of Sabbath as well as Sunday, and the celebration of the Agapé. Feasts are numerous: but so, too, are Fasts, and very strict. They keep Wednesdays and Fridays, except in Eastertide: as well as seasonal fasts. Similar causes will account for the survival of Judaising practices among them: for infants of both sexes are circumcised before they are baptised, and there are persons under Nazarite vows.

Their rite is the Liturgy of the Twelve Apostles,[116] in Ethiopic. It is "fundamentally identical with the Coptic Liturgy of St. Cyril."[117] In addition to this they have varying anaphoras, of which fifteen are known.[118] They are attributed to various authors: and some of them show Syrian influence.[119]

For sixteen centuries the Church of Abyssinia has been held together by powerful forces—geographical isolation, national pride, tenacity of its past, and a warlike spirit. But it has maintained its traditions at the price of a low level of enlightenment and a backward Christianity. It is doubtful to what extent it will be able to resist the disintegration which now threatens it from penetration by the materialised civilisation of the yet distant West or from Moslem propaganda nearer home.

CHAPTER XVIII.

THE UNIATES.

CHAPTER XVIII.

THE UNIATES.

WE have now finished the history of the Churches of Eastern Christendom, orthodox and heretical. But there remains a body of Eastern Christians known as Uniates: of whom, if this book is to be complete, we must give a brief account. Brief it must be: but fuller detail may be found in the writings of the late Dr. Adrian Fortescue, a ripe scholar with a lively style. His sympathies in respect of the Orthodox[1] are limited, though he has some compassion for the Lesser Eastern Churches.[2] But he is whole-hearted in his championship of the Uniates;[3] and defends them against detractors, Latin or Anglican.

§ 1. A Uniate is a Christian of any Eastern rite in union with the Pope. He is a Roman Catholic who belongs not to the Latin but to an Eastern rite.

Thus the first note of a Uniate Church is its union with Rome; and its second is its retention of its ancient rite: and Uniates differ from other Eastern Christians in that they are in communion with the Roman See, and from Latins in that they follow other rites.

Thirdly, a Uniate Church, besides being encouraged to retain its own rite with such modifications as touch faith and order, i.e. the Catholic Creed and the Roman Primacy, is also organised under a hierarchy of its own. There is, however, one exception to this rule, in the case of the Italo-Greeks of Southern Italy, Sicily and Corsica. They do not fulfil all the conditions which constitute a Uniate Church: for they have no diocesan bishops of their own; but are organised under the local bishop who provides them, through an auxiliary bishop of their rite, with clergy capable of officiating in accordance with it. They are, in fact, members of the Roman Patriarchate in Italy, Sicily or Corsica who, in consequence of older arrangements made in the days when the Emperor

Leo III., 717—†41, tried, for political reasons, to claim them for the Patriarchate of Constantinople,[4] were encouraged to resist by being allowed to continue their use of the Byzantine Liturgy in communion with the Roman See.

A fourth point to observe in connexion with Uniate Churches is the relation of rite to Patriarchate. Had Leo succeeded, Italo-Greeks would, of course, have continued to worship according to their customary rite. In the West, there was no such rule as that rite follows Patriarchate: but a wider liberty. Membership in the Roman Patriarchate did not necessarily carry with it use of the Latin rite; and thus the Italo-Greeks, on coming under the Latin hierarchy, were left no less free to enjoy their own rite, as they do to this day, than were the churches of North Italy, Gaul and Spain to use their ancient Milanese, Gallican and Mozarabic rites, though these regions were taken as forming part of the Roman Patriarchate. The Western policy was, in fact, less rigid than the Eastern: it did not require uniformity of rite. Thus Pope Nicholas I., 858—†67, affirms that he has no sort of objection to people following different customs so long as there is nothing in them opposed to the holy canons.[5] Michael Cerularius, on the other hand, Patriarch of Constantinople, 1043—58, began his quarrel with Pope Leo IX., 1049—†54, by shutting up the Latin churches at Constantinople.[6] And liberty has been in the main, the policy of the Roman See in dealing with individuals and churches seeking recognition by it. Uncompromising in respect of faith and order, the Popes have been generous in regard to variety of usage in worship. They do not require the universal use either of the Latin language or of the Roman liturgy: a wise policy well illustrated by the well known advice of Pope Gregory the Great, 590—†604, to Augustine:[7] and set forth, with great clearness, in the legislation for Uniates of great popes such as Benedict XIV., 1740—†58, and Leo XIII., 1878—†1903. Thus, in *Allatae sunt*,[8] of 26th July, 1755, Benedict begins by reviewing the way in which his predecessors have dealt with the churches of the East, and says that union for them has always been arranged so that "errors opposed to the Catholic Faith were rooted out; but it has never been attempted to do any injury to the venerable Eastern rite";[9] and he concludes with the words: "We desire earnestly that they should become Catholics, not that they should become Latins."[10] The bull of Benedict was addressed to Roman Catholic missionaries in the East, to warn them against encroaching upon its ancient rites. In *Orientalium dignitas*,[11] of 30th November, 1894, Leo XIII. took up the warning, and reinforced it under penalties: "Any Latin missionary who shall have persuaded an Eastern Christian to adopt the Latin rite shall incur, *ipso facto,* suspension *a divinis,* and all other penalties threatened in the Constitution *Demandatam*"[12] of Benedict XIV.

And this brings us to the origin of the Uniate Churches. For the most part they owe their formation to Latin missionaries of the sixteenth and seventeenth centuries; and, except in one or two cases, such as that of the Malabar Uniates whose succession is that of the ancient Malabar Church brought over at the Synod of Diamper, 1599, there is no continuity between Uniates of the present day and the ancient churches of the East. They have been given Patriarchs and bishops of their own; who live side by side with other hierarchies of the place, orthodox or heretical. With the exception of the Maronites, they represent sections detached from these ancient Churches, sometimes by proselytism, sometimes in consequence of native schisms, and united to the see of Rome.[13] The reasons for such proceedings are such as can readily be understood, and often such as are entitled to discriminating, though respectful, sympathy. To Christians groaning under oppression, the desire for political protection from Roman Catholic powers with spheres of influence in the East has been a great inducement. Again, the resources of the Roman Church, in men and money; its higher standard of education and culture; the wealth of its spiritual zeal and devotional life—in short, its great prestige—have exercised a just and powerful attraction: and have given to Uniates of the East, who do not number more than 6,500,000, an influence out of all proportion to their numerical strength.

§ 2. We now pass to describe briefly the Uniate Churches of the East. They are eight in number: seven of them Churches corresponding to one or other of the Orthodox or Eastern Churches, and one—the Maronite Church—which has no such counterpart.

(i.) First among them are the Byzantine Uniates. They all use the Byzantine rite: but are organised into seven groups.

(1.) First, those in Syria and Egypt who are now called "Melkites," by a change in the application of that title. Originally, a " Melkite " meant a Christian who accepted the Emperor's religion, i.e. the Council of Chalcedon, as opposed to a Monophysite. But it is now commonly used for Uniates of the Byzantine rite in Syria and Egypt. They number[14] about 120,000, under a Patriarch of Antioch, who administers, and bears the title of Patriarch of, Alexandria and Jerusalem as well. He resides sometimes at Damascus and sometimes at Cairo. He rules over eleven dioceses: all in Syria, for he has no suffragan in Egypt or Palestine. He represents the original line of Patriarchs of Antioch. He and his people use Arabic as their liturgical language, with fragments of Greek. They are, in point of wealth and education, one of the most prosperous and advanced communities of the Near East.

(2.) There are a few hundred Byzantine Uniates in Turkey and Greece. They use Greek for their liturgical language; and depend on Latin delegates at Constantinople and Athens.

(3.) There is one Georgian congregation at Constantinople, the last remnant of the old Georgian Church, absorbed by Russia in 1811, but restored since the revolution of 1917.[15] They use their own language in the Liturgy, and obey the Latin delegate.

(4.) The Ruthenians " are the largest single body of Uniates. They are about 3,500,000 in number, three million in Galicia and the rest in what used to be Hungary. Most are now in Poland. Their intellectual centre is Lemberg. . . . In their Liturgies they use the Slavonic language."[16]

(5.) So do the Bulgarian Uniates, to the number of about 15,000, under two Vicars Apostolic.

(6.) Of Rumanian Uniates there are about 750,000, chiefly in Transylvania. They have four bishops; and use their own language in the Liturgy.

(7.) Finally, there are the Italo-Greeks, to the number of about 50,000. They are the remnant of the old church of Greater Greece, but with an admixture of Albanian immigrants, who, for fear of the Turks, crossed to Italy in the fifteenth and sixteenth centuries. They belong chiefly to Calabria and Sicily, though there is a small colony of about 600 Greeks at Cargese in Corsica. They have no diocesan bishops of their own, but are subject to Latin Ordinaries. These, however, have three ordaining bishops, as auxiliaries, in Rome, Calabria and Sicily;[17] and thus their traditional rite is maintained. But still more effectively is it maintained by the Greek College at Rome, founded by Pope Gregory XIII., 1572—†85; and at the monastery of Grotta Ferrata, near Frascati, just outside Rome, where the Byzantine Liturgy " is now to be seen and heard celebrated perfectly and sung exquisitely."[18] Their liturgical language is Greek.

(ii.) Second are the Chaldeans, who are Uniates converted from Nestorianism. They date from the sixteenth century, and are governed by the Patriarch of Babylon who lives at Mosul: and stands in the succession to the ancient Catholicus of the East. He is assisted by two archbishops and ten bishops: who rule over a community estimated at 50,000. Their liturgical books are in Syriac, slightly revised from the old Nestorian books.

(iii.) Third come the Uniate Copts, who number about 20,000.[19] From 1781 they were under a Vicar Apostolic. But, in 1895, they received from Leo XIII. a Patriarch of Alexandria, who lives at Cairo: and is assisted by two bishops, of Hermopolis and Thebes. They use the Coptic rite.

(iv.) A few Abyssinians are Uniates: but a Vicar Apostolic at present suffices for their supervision. He lives at Keren. Their rite is not the Ethiopic, which is not yet in order for satisfactory use. They temporarily employ the Latin Mass, translated into their own language.

(v.) The Catholic Syrian Church dates from 1781; and owes its origin to a schism among the Jacobites, one section of whom asked for recognition from Rome. In 1830, they were constituted a *millet* by the Turkish Government. The Uniate Patriarch of Antioch[20] lives at Beirut, though most of his flock dwell in Mesopotamia. They consist of about 25,000 families: and are governed by three archbishops and six bishops. They also have five monasteries.

(vi.) The Uniate Church of Malabar was formed by the Synod of Diamper, 1599. It has about 200,000 members:[21] under the archbishop of Ernakulam, with three bishops of Changanacherry, Kottayam and Tricur. Their rite is the Syriac Liturgy.

(vii.) Most influential of the Uniates are the Catholic Armenians. They number about 300,000: and are scattered about the Levant. Since 1830, they have had for their chief the Uniate Patriarch of Constantinople, who also holds the patriarchate of Cilicia. He presides over a hierarchy of three titular archbishops and fourteen bishops, of whom one has his see at Alexandria and the other as far afield as Ispahan. To this community belong the Mechitarists, a congregation founded, 1711, by an Armenian named Mechitar of Sebaste (Siwas). They follow the rule of St. Benedict: and their centre is at the monastery on the island of San Lazzaro, near Venice. They have missions all over the Levant; and are famous for their literary activity and their learning.

(viii.) Last to be mentioned are the Maronites.[22] They were formed round the monasteries of the Lebanon named after John Maro,[23] who died in the fifth century. They separated from the ancient see of Antioch, because they became Monotheletes. But in the twelfth century they were united to the Roman see. Since the fifteenth century they have been orthodox; and, ever since 1516, alone among Eastern Churches, they have maintained their fidelity to that obedience. They number about 250,000. Their head is "the Maronite Patriarch of Antioch and all the East." Alone among Uniates, they are not a community detached from one of the schismatic churches of the East. Their Patriarch is a successor to the monothelete rivals of the old line, who, therefore, in no way represents the original patriarchate. He is the civil head of his nation or *millet:* and lives in winter at Bkerke near Beirut. He rules over a hierarchy of nine bishops: some of whose sees, here printed in italics, are titular archbishoprics—*Aleppo; Beirut; Cyprus; Damascus; Sidon; Tripoli; Tyre;* Baalbek; Ghibail and Botri. There are also several titular bishops: and convents both of men and women. Their mother tongue is Arabic: their liturgical language is Syriac. "They use a Syrian rite of the type of the Liturgy of St. James, but with many modifications in the Roman direction. Thus they use unleavened bread, and receive communion under one kind, and the ancient epiklesis is reduced to a prayer for the spiritual benefit of the communicants. Many modern Roman devotions are common among the Maronites— Benediction, Stations, the Rosary, etc."[24]

CHAPTER XIX.

CONCLUSION.

(1.) FAITH. (3.) WORSHIP.
(2.) GOVERNMENT. (4.) RE-UNION.

CHAPTER XIX.

Conclusion.

WE have now finished the history of the Churches of Eastern Christendom: Orthodox, Heretical and Uniate. Omitting the last, they fall into two groups: twelve in communion with each other, and, except Bulgaria, with the Œcumenical Patriarchate:[1] and six others, Nestorian or Monophysite, separate from it.[2] Except in so far as Nestorians and Monophysites retain their distinctive tenets about the relation of "Person" and "Nature" in Jesus Christ, the Eastern Churches, as a whole, retain all those marks of the Faith, Order and Worship of the Church as it was at the opening of the fifth century which justify their claim to rank with historic Christendom. They are held by the Roman Church to be all alike in schism; but that Church acknowledges their Orders and Sacraments to be valid: while their Creed, except for Western[3] and Roman[4] additions to it, is the same. Their liturgies, moreover, are rites belonging to ancient families of liturgies of which the Roman rite is one. The Eastern Churches, however, do not constitute one body: for Orthodox and Heretical, Nestorian and Monophysite, maintain an existence separate from each other.

The Orthodox Churches, on the contrary, though severally organised, constitute one body: because they possess a common Faith, Government and Worship.[5]

§ 1. The common Faith is based on Holy Scripture; the dogmatic decisions of the Seven Œcumenical Councils;[6] and the Fathers, especially the *De Fide Orthodoxa*[7] of St. John Damascene († before 754). Secondary authorities, widely accepted, are the Expositions of Faith such as *The Orthodox Confession*[8] (1638) of Peter Mogila, Metropolitan of Kiev, 1632—†47, and *The Confession*[9] (1672) of Dositheus, Patriarch of Jerusalem, 1669—†1707. These, with others, are sometimes spoken of as the Symbolical Books of Orthodoxy. But the term is borrowed from Protestant theologians and is not strictly appropriate. In the Orthodox Church there is but one *Symbolum*, the " Nicene " Creed, of supreme authority; and these Expositions do not occupy that position of authoritative standards of reference which is occupied by the *Augsburg Confession* among Lutherans or the *Westminster Confession* among Scottish Calvinists.[10] A further bond in the Faith is supplied by various Catechisms of local origin but widespread influence, such as the *Longer Catechism*[11] of Philaret, Metropolitan of Moscow, 1820—†67, which was adopted by the Holy Synod in 1839, and " sent to all the Eastern Patriarchs and other Churches of the same Rite and Communion."[12] There are also dogmatic works of theologians, belonging to particular churches, but men of recognised authority in all, such as those of Macarius[13] (Bulgakov), Metropolitan of Moscow, 1879—†82, or of Chrestos Androutsos, now Professor in the University of Athens.[14] The Orthodox also maintain their connexion with historic Christendom by their adhesion to the Seven Sacraments—Baptism, Unction with chrism, Communion, Penitence, Orders, Matrimony and Unction with oil; and by a deep devotion to the Saints whose feasts they keep, whose icons they venerate, whose relics they treasure and to whose shrines they go on pilgrimage.

§ 2. In respect of Government, they have similar bonds in common. Its lines are laid down in the Canons, the Fathers and the Imperial Laws. Of these, the chief collection is the *Nomocanon*, a collection combining the canons of the Church and the laws of the State, originating in the sixth century, but re-issued in 883, and commonly, but doubtfully, ascribed to Photius,[15] Patriarch of Constantinople, 857—67. Besides the usual Orders of clergy, and a considerable part taken in ecclesiastical government by the laity, Orthodoxy maintains its continuity with the ancient Church by its retention of Monasticism.[16] There are no Monastic Orders as in the West, and no Congregations. But monks all observe the Rule of St. Basil,[17] archbishop of Cæsarea in Cappadocia, 370—

†9; and it has been characteristic of Eastern Monasticism, since the Council of Chalcedon,[18] that monasteries and convents are subject to the bishop; except in the case of *stauropegia* or monasteries in foreign lands immediately dependent on the Œcumenical Patriarch, and monasteries of Imperial foundation. Monks are either cenobitic, i.e. live the common life, with meals in common and a common purse; or idiorhythmic, where each member of the community dwells apart, though under the spiritual jurisdiction of the abbot. The centre of each church is the bishop, but the basis of ecclesiastical administration is the synod. And, while the several churches maintain their own corporate or national organisation and are, so far, independent or autocephalous, they are all (except Bulgaria, since 1870) in communion with the Œcumenical Patriarch, and all in communion with each other. The powers of the Œcumenical Patriarch are limited; and, though once he enjoyed a wider and more definite authority, this has been reduced bit by bit as each national church acquired autocephaly. But he still retains the right of consecrating the Holy Chrism and sending it to the several churches, except in Russia where it is consecrated by the Patriarch of Moscow. Orthodoxy thus, in point of government, is a loosely organised body: but still a fraternity of churches under the common leadership of the five Eastern Patriarchs—Constantinople, Alexandria, Antioch, Jerusalem and Moscow.

§ 3. A third bond of connexion between the Orthodox churches is their common worship. There is, indeed, no one liturgical language, as is Latin, with all the churches of the Roman obedience, except the Uniate. But each race retains its own tongue—not necessarily, indeed rarely, the vernacular. Churches are built on the same plan: there is a sanctuary, separated off from the people's part of the building by the Iconostasis—usually a solid, and generally a richly decorated, screen; adorned with icons, or pictures, of the saints. Feasts are classified in dignity according as they commemorate our Lord, or the Mother of God, or the Saints. Easter, Christmas, and the Assumption are preceded by long fasts: the other fast-days being Wednesday and Friday, the 14th September, the 29th August, and the eve of the Epiphany: and fasting is rigorous. The Lord's Day begins with its vigil on Saturday evening: a custom co-eval with Christianity which, to the great detriment of the observance of Sunday in England, the West has lost: and, while all business ceases on the Vigil, shops and places of amusement open again as soon as the Sunday Mass is over.[19] The Mass, of course, is the principal service of Sunday: and there is no such service as Low Mass.

The Liturgy is the centre of worship with Orthodox, as with all Catholics, Roman or Anglican. But, whereas communion is common, and increasing, at Mass in the West, it is rare in Orthodox countries. This is due to the long and strict fast required in preparation for it. Four times a year among the Slavs, and once a year among the Rumanians is now the common custom.[20] The Liturgy is the Byzantine rite in one or other of its forms: (1) the Liturgy of St. Basil,[21] of which at least the anaphora is almost certainly the work of St. Basil, archbishop of Cæsarea in Cappadocia, 370—†9, " is used only ten times in the year, at the vigils of Christmas, Epiphany and Easter, on the first five Sundays in Lent, and Maundy Thursday, and on the feast of St. Basil (January 1st) ": (2) the Liturgy of the Presanctified,[22] which was written probably in the sixth century, is used throughout Lent and Passiontide, except on Saturdays, Sundays, the Annunciation and Maundy Thursday: it is identical in structure with the others except that . . . . after the Great Entrance—in which here the consecrated Gifts reserved from the Liturgy of the preceding Sunday are brought from the Prothesis to the altar—everything is omitted until the Prayer before the Lord's Prayer: but ordinarily (3) the Liturgy of St. Chrysostom.[23] " The original text of the Liturgy is Greek: and this is used by the Greek Orthodox everywhere: in the kingdom, in Turkey, in Syria and Palestine, and in Egypt. A Slavonic version of the Greek is used in Russia, in Bulgaria, in Serbia, Bosnia and Montenegro, and by the Orthodox of Herzegovina and Dalmatia. The Slavonic was also used in Rumania until the seventeenth century, when a Rumanian version was adopted."[24] Preaching has almost disappeared: though there is a tendency towards its revival in Russia. Opportunities, indeed, of instruction are few: and Meletius II., now Patriarch of Alexandria, at a meeting with Anglican theologians in Oxford, where the Eastern and Western views of Confirmation were, amongst other things, under discussion, deplored the fact that in Greece—he was then Metropolitan of Athens—there was no such opportunity of giving instruction with them as with us, in preparation for Confirmation: for, in the East, the faithful are still, as in primitive times, baptised, confirmed and communicated as infants. On the other hand, " the religious life of the people never requires, as so often in this country, to be kept alive by the energy of the clergy. The drunken village pope has become a typical character in fiction—and, unfortunately, he is not unknown in real life—but if, in England, the parson is immoral or incompetent, the church is deserted; in Russia, the pope is compelled by the people to perform the ministrations which he alone can do. Their religion comes from themselves, and they are taught it " not by preaching but " as part of the traditions which they inherit."[25] Common to all the churches are the books for other offices[26]—the *Typikon*, or book of rules for the conduct of the services, the *Euchologion*, or book of prayers for occasional rites, and the *Horologion*, containing the Canonical Hours. Music is vocal and idiorhythmic; and instrumental music, like graven images as distinct from pictures, is forbidden.

If we are to sum up the characteristics of Orthodoxy in a short sentence, perhaps it would give a fair impression to say that in doctrine its system is traditional, with little room for development; that in government, it holds together by a loose administrative system and so contrasts with the more centralised organisation of the Roman Catholic Church; and that, in worship, it gives little scope to preaching, and so ignores what is all in all to the protestant sects. In one word, the Orthodox Church, in its general aspect, is more than anything else a society for worship.

§ 4. And as to prospects of re-union. The main obstacle to it lies in the conservatism of the Eastern Churches. Rooted as they are in centuries of separation from each other, there is not much chance of approximation between Orthodox and Heretical: until, on either side, the clergy are better educated, and the laity are delivered from the narrow outlook consequent upon the oppression and poverty under which for so long they have lived. In respect of re-union with the Roman Church, traditions of contempt for Latins on the part of the East and of ill-usage meted out to Greeks on the part of the West, have produced an atmosphere in the East, which is now the feebler portion of Catholic Christendom, of rooted antagonism. Greeks, when culture belonged to Constantinople, looked upon Latins as barbarians: and Latins retaliated by the infliction of barbarous ill-treatment on the Orthodox at the capture of Constantinople, 1204, which has never been forgotten or forgiven: very much as in England an anti-Roman tradition has been perpetuated by our memories of the reign of Mary, the Armada, the Gunpowder Plot and the fatuousness of James II. Orthodoxy, moreover, came to be identified with Hellenic nationalism: and this is no less a bar to unity within some Oriental churches, e.g. in Jerusalem between the Fraternity of the Holy Sepulchre, which is Greek, and the Arabophone laity, than to union between Orthodoxy and the Roman Catholic Church. In support of these animosities, theological differences, e.g. as to the *Filioque*, have been maintained in a controversial spirit: whereas, if the Latins were wrong in putting it into the Creed,[27] the Greeks are equally wrong in supposing that it necessarily implies two sources of Godhead, and in overlooking both the use which their own theologians[28] make of language equivalent to it as well as the testimony borne both by the phrase itself and by its origin to the co-equality of the Son with the Father denied by Arianism.[29] The differences, if the past could be forgotten, might easily be adjusted: for, behind the difference of expression, there is, in reality, no difference of faith. A similar accommodation might also be made, without difficulty, in respect

At Westminster Abbey, June 29, 1925.

of the different senses attached to the term Transubstantiation[30] which both Orthodox and Catholic use in order to secure their common belief in the real presence of the Body and Blood of our Lord after consecration: while as to what effects the consecration—whether the Words of Institution, or the Invocation of the Holy Spirit—this is merely the result of emphasising one rather than another of the topics included in the recital of thanksgiving for Redemption over the elements, which is what really effects the consecration—the Institution on Maundy Thursday, or the illapse of the Spirit at Pentecost.

On the other hand, there are forces now making for better understanding. The miseries of Eastern Christendom under the Turk and, since the Great War, in Russia as well as among Armenians and East Syrians, have led the East to turn for sympathy towards the West. Certainly, this sympathy is hardly promoted by the ardent propaganda long maintained in order to detach Uniates from the various Eastern Churches; and, at present, intensified in Poland and western Russia with a view to making converts from Orthodoxy. But this propaganda has been accompanied by generous charity on the part of the Holy See: so that East now looks to West as to a friend in time of distress. Similarly, in respect of relations between Orthodox and Anglicans, there has been in recent years a rapid movement towards mutual recognition and an ultimate re-union. The East now understands that Anglicans do not proselytise, and that we belong not to the lineage of continental protestantism but to the historic churches of Christendom. By an application of their doctrine of economy they have begun to recognise our Orders as "possessing the same validity as those of the Roman, Old Catholic, and Armenian Churches possess."[31] And the demonstration of fundamental unity at the sixteen hundredth anniversary of the Council of Nicæa, when two of the five Eastern Patriarchs—Photius of Alexandria and Damianus of Jerusalem—attended a Solemn Eucharist in Westminster Abbey, on St. Peter's Day, 1925,[32] may be hailed as the first-fruits of an intercourse that cannot but ultimately ripen into mutual intercommunion.

NOTES.

CHAPTER I.

1. See it in my *Documents illustrative of the History of the Church*, ii. No. 214.   **2.** Mansi, *Concilia* vii. 173 B.   **3.** For paragraphs 1 and 2 of this chapter, see my *History of the Church to A.D. 461*, III. c. xx.., where complete references to the authorities will be found.   **4.** J. B. Bury, *Later Roman Empire* (ed. 1923) i. 236—9.   **5.** The Dynasty of Leo, see *ib.* p. xviii.

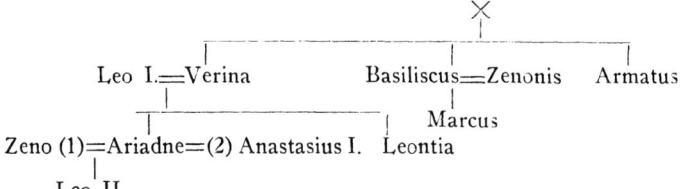

```
                              ×
      ┌───────────────────────┼──────────────────┐
      │                       │                  │
   Leo I.=Verina      Basiliscus=Zenonis      Armatus
      │                       │
      │                    Marcus
   ┌──┴─────────────────────┐
 Zeno (1)=Ariadne=(2) Anastasius I.   Leontia
      │
    Leo II.
```

6. Bury, *op. cit.* i. 317.   **7.** *Ib.* 322.   **8.** The Monophysites were the opponents of the Council of Chalcedon and its doctrine of two Natures in the one Person of Jesus Christ. They held that He was "of two Natures" before the Incarnation but denied that after it He is "in two Natures." Zealous for the unity of His being, clung to an unguarded phrase of St. Cyril of Alexandria—"One Nature incarnate of the Word": and hence were called Monophysites. Chalcedonians are Dyophysites.   **9.** Gibbon, c. xlvii. n. 74 (v. 128, ed. Bury, 1896).   **10.** *Documents* ii. No. 235.   **11.** Mansi vii. 487 sqq.   **12.** *Ib.* 509 sqq.   **13.** *Ib.* 505 sqq.   **14.** *Ib.* 520 sq.   **15.** *Ib.* 514 sq.   **16.** Leo, *Ep.* cxiii. § 3.   **17.** Leo, *Ep.* cxvii. § 3.   **18.** Leo, *Ep.* cxxiv.   **19.** Leo, *Ep.* xxviii.: tr. in my *Documents* ii. No. 209.   **20.** Leo, *Ep.* cxxiii.   **21.** Leo, *Ep.* cxliv. § 1.   **22.** Leo, *Epp.* cxlv.—cxlvii.   **23.** Leo, *Epp.* cxlviii.—cl.   **24.** Leo, *Ep.* clvii. § 2.   **25.** Leo, *Ep.* clxv.   **26.** *D.C.B.* iii. 665.   **27.** So W. A. Wigram, *Separation of the Monophysites*, 27, reviewing such suggestions as "white-cap" (Bury), "wobble-cap" (Fortescue), etc.   **28.** Leo, *Epp.* clxxi.—clxxiii.   **29.** Simplicius, *Ep.* xi. (*P.L.* lviii. 49 c).   **30.** *Documents* ii. No. 234.   **31.** Cyril Al., *Epp.* lvii., lviii.   **32.** *Chron. Z.M.* vii. 7.   **33.** Justinian, *Codex* I. iii. 29.   **34.** See it in Evagrius, *H.E.* iii. 7.   **35.** Simplicius, *Ep.* viii.   **36.** *Ib. Ep.* xix.   **37.** Simplicius, *Ep.* xvii.   **38.** J. B. Bury, *L.R.E.* i. 429 sqq.   **39.** The memory of Severus is still solemnly honoured in all the Jacobite Communions, by whom he is regarded as second only to Cyril and Dioscorus, *D.C.B.* iv. 637 q.v. *cf.* Duchesne, *L'église au VIme siècle* 19 sqq.   **40.** See it in Brightman *Liturgies*, 535 n. 1, at the beginning of the Mass of the Catechumens (Byz. viii. cent.).   **41.** Duchesne, *op. cit.* 30: Hefele—Leclercq, *Conciles* § 225 (ii. 1015): and Bury, *op. cit.* i. 440 n. 6. **42.** Duchesne, *op. cit.* 37: Bury, *op. cit.* i. 447 sqq. **43.** For this correspondence see Bury 450 n. 3, with references and dates to the originals in the *Collectio Avellana* of imperial and papal letters 367—553, which was made in Rome in the latter half of the sixth century. They are now edited in *Corp. Script. Eccl. Lat.* vol. xxxv. (Vienna, 1895—8). **44.** Justin was from Scupi, the capital of the province of Dardania in Latin Illyricum—which was papal and strongly Chalcedonian. Hence the reaction. Duchesne, *op. cit.* 44. **45.** Beginning with a letter from Justin to Pope Hormisdas (Hormisdas, Ep. xli.) in which he announces his accession, A. Thiel, *Epp. Rom. Pont. Gen.* i. 830 = *Coll. Avell. Ep.* 141. The correspondence = *Coll. Avell.* 105—243, but the order is given only in Thiel: see Duchesne, *op. cit.* 48 n. 1. **46.** For these demands, see letter of 11th Aug. 515: Hormisdas *Ep.* vii. (Thiel 755) and an extract in C. Mirbt, *Quellen zur Geschichte des Papsttums*[4] No. 195. **47.** Hormisdas. *Ep.* lxxviii. (*P.L.* lxiii. 512 c) = *Ep.* cxl. § 6 (Thiel, 970) = *Ep.* ccxxxviii. § 16 of *Coll. Avell.* (*C.S.E.L.* xxxv. 738): see Jaffé, *Regesta,* No. 860.

CHAPTER II.

1. On the "Constitution of the Monarchy," see J. B. Bury, *The Later Roman Empire*[2] (1923), c. 1. **2.** J. B. Bury, *L.R.E.*[2] i. 17. **3.** "Each Emperor nominated one of the two consuls for the year," *ib.* **4.** "The northernmost point of the Emperor's actual possessions was near the modern Galatz, or further east, where the Danube discharges itself into the Black Sea. That river was its northern boundary, and .. Belgrade ... its northernmost point towards the west; and what is now Ragusa was its highest port on the Adriatic. The Grecian peninsula, with the adjacent islands and Crete, formed the whole of its possessions in Europe. The strength of the Empire lay in the fertile provinces of Asia... a frontier which stretched from the south-eastern corner of the Black Sea ... on by the Euphrates ... reached its most southern point in the extremity of the Sinaitic peninsula.... Of the African possessions of the Empire no more remained than Egypt." W. H. Hutton, *The Church in the Sixth Century,* 13 sq. **5.** *Dict. Gr. and Rom. Biogr.* ii. 677—8. **6.** Born at Bederiana (Bader) near Scupi (Usküb) in Serbia in A.D. 452: *L.R.E.*[2] ii. 18. **7.** *L.R.E.*[2] i. 446. **8.** *Ib.* i. 436. **9.** *L.R.E.*[2] ii. 21. **10.** *Coll. Avell. Ep.* 141 (*C.S.E.L.* xxxv.): *L.R.E.*[2] ii. 18. **11.** *L.R.E.*[2] ii. 16. **12.** *Ib.* 19. **13.** Justin's sister was the wife of Sabbatius, who lived at the neighbouring village of Tauresium (now Taor): and they had two children, Peter Sabbatius and Vigilantia. Justin brought his nephew to CP., where he took the adoptive name of Justinian, *ib.* 19. **14.** The re-union with Rome, which involved the abandonment of the *Henoticon* of Zeno, the restoration of the prestige of the Council of Chalcedon and the persecution of the Monophysites, was the great inaugural act of the new dynasty, *ib.* ii. 20, and for details *ib.* 372 sqq. and *Coll. Avell. Epp.* 142—81. (a) Synod of CP. 518 decided that Monophysite bishops should be expelled; (b) John II., Patriarch of CP. 518—20, in April, 519, wrote to Pope Hormisdas, 514—†23 anathematising Acacius, *Coll. Avell. Ep.* 159; (c) Pope Hormisdas reminds the Emperor, 9th July, 519, that he still had to "correct" the churches of Alexandria and Antioch (*Coll. Avell. Ep.* 168): hence the persecution of Monophysites. **15.** *L.R.E.*² ii. 25 n. 4. Βασίλευς ἀκοίμητος or ὁ πάντων βασιλέων ἀγρυπνότατος. **16.** Αὐτοκράτωρ ὀνόματί τε καὶ πράγματι ἀπεδέδεικτο *ib.* 27 n. 1. **17.** *L.R.E.*² ii. 27 sqq. **18.** Doubtful: see *L.R.E.*² ii. 29. **19.** She procured Novel 14, A.D. 535, forbidding the "white-slave" trade; and maintained the Convent of Μετάνοια in a palace on the Asiatic side of the Bosporus, for rescue work, *L.R.E.*² ii. 32. **20.** *L.R.E.*² ii. 39 sqq. **21.** Novel 8, of A.D. 535 : *L.R.E.*² ii. 30 and note 3. **22.** For the Persian Wars, *L.R.E.*² ii. 75 sqq.: and map, p. 94. **23.** Now Lazistan : it was then Lazica, or Cholcis, the westernmost of three Kingdoms which lay South of the Caucasus between the Black Sea and the Caspian : the centre being Iberia (Georgia) and the easternmost, Albania : *ib.* 80. The importance of Lazica to the Romans was that it was a barrier against (1) the barbarians N. of the Caucasus, and (2) the Persians trying to advance through Iberia to the sea. *ib.* 80. **24.** The treaty made no change in the frontiers between R. and P. Armenia. Armenian Christians were tolerated by Chosroes I. : but the Armenian Church was drifting apart from CP. and Rome. In 491 they approved the *Henoticon* of Zeno. In 527 the Catholicus Narses secured the condemnation of the Two Natures, see Le Quien, *Or. Chr.* i. 1381—4 and Tournebize, *Hist. de l'Arménie*, i. 90—1. In 551 the Synod of Dvin confirmed the independence of the Armenian Church and began a reform of the calendar : according to which the Armenian era begins 11/7/552. The schism had political consequences. Greek influence declined in Persarmenia, to the profit of Chosroes and the loss of Justinian, *L.R.E.*² ii. 88 sq. **25.** The most important provision of the treaty was that Persia agreed to resign Lazica to the Romans : and for the others, see *L.R.E.*² ii. 121 sqq. **26.** For the reconquest of Africa, see *L.R.E.*² ii. 124 sqq. **27.** *Ib.* 286 sqq. **28.** For genealogy, *ib.* 125, n. 5. **29.** For her regency, *ib.* 159 sqq. **30.** He left about £14,590,000 in the treasury at his death, *L.R.E.*² i. 446. **31.** Really, his first cousin once removed, *L.R.E.*² ii. 125. **32.** For the reconquest of Italy, see *L.R.E.*² ii. 151 sqq. **33.** He entered the city by the Porta Asinaria, close to the Basilica of the Lateran, *ib.* 180. **34.** " Munera nomini tuo, Domine, cum gratiarum actione deferimus qui nos ab infestis hostibus liberatos paschale sacramentum secura tribuisti mente suscipere. Per." *Sacr. Leon:* p. 73 ll, 19—21 (ed. C. L. Feltoe), and see L. Duchesne, *Christian Worship*,⁶ 137. **35.** And is probably contemporary with St. Benedict : who was born, 480, at Nursia, in an Apennine valley, about 20 miles east of Spoleto : took up his abode at Sublaqueum (Subiaco) as a hermit, where he founded 12 monasteries : thence to Monte Cassino, in Campania, 528—†43. *Ib.* ii. 224. **36.** *Ib.* 236 sqq. **37.** *Ib.* 249 sqq. **38.** Or Tadinum, the modern village Gualdo Tadino, *L.R.E.*² ii. 264 : now called the battle of Busta Gallorum—see map, *ib.* 261. **39.** Mons Lactarius, *ib.* 270 sqq. The *History* of Procopius ends with this battle and the story is taken up by Agathias 536—†82, for the years 552—8 : see K. Krumbacher, *Gesch. der Byz. Litt.* § 100.

40. *L.R.E.*² ii. 274.   41. For its reorganisation, see the Pragmatic Sanction of Justinian, addressed to Narses and Antiochus, Prefect of Italy, 554: ap. *L.R.E.*² ii. 282.   42. *L.R.E.*² ii. 284.   43. *L.R.E.*² ii. 395 sqq.   44. *L.R.E.*² i. 231 sqq.: and text *Theodosiani Libri* XVI. edd. Mommsen and Meyer (Berlin, 1895, 2 vols.).   45. Now contained in *Corpus Juris Civilis*, edd. Krüger, Mommsen and Schöll (3 vols. Berlin, 1872—80).   46. *Haec quae*, prefixed to the Code, *Corp. Jur. Civ.* ii. 1.   47. This code was rendered authoritative by *Summa reipublicae* of 7th April, 529, q.v. in *Corp. Jur. Civ.* ii. 2—3. 48. This final code was rendered authoritative by *Cordi nobis* of 16th November, 1534: *ib.* 4.   49. *Cod. Just.* I. xvii. 1 (*Corp. Jur. Civ.* ii. pp. xiii.—xiv. and ii. 69—74).   50. *Corp. Jur. Civ.* vol. i. 51. By *Omnem reipublicae* and *Dedit nobis* (*Corp. Jur. Civ.* i. pp. xv. —xxix.).   52. *Corp. Jur. Civ.* vol. i. pp. 1 sqq.: ed. P. Krüger. 53. By *Imperatoriam majestatem* of 21st November, 533, addressed to "cupidae legum juventuti," *ib.* p. 1.   54. *Corp. Jur. Civ.* vol. iii. edd. R. Schöll and G. Kroll.

CHAPTER III.

1. "The fifth œcumenical Council differed from the four which preceded it in that, while they pronounced on issues which divided Christendom and which called for an authoritative decision of the Church, the Fifth dealt with a question which had been artificially created.... Justinian summoned it to confirm a theological decision of his own." *L.R.E.*² 391—2.   2. Brightman, *Liturgies* i. 369, 1. 20. 3. L. Duchesne, *Christian Worship*,⁵ 197.   4. Ἅγιος ὁ Θεός, ἅγιος ἰσχυρός, ἅγιος ἀθάνατος, ἐλέησον ἡμᾶς, Mansi vi. 936 C.   5. J. Pargoire, *L'église byzantine*, 26; Bury, *L.R.E.*² ii. 376; Bardenhewer, *Patrology*, 548. They had also desired the condemnation of Faustus, bishop of Reji (now Riez, in Provence) 452—?†90, as an advocate of Semi-Pelagianism, *ib.* 548, 600 sq. and my *Hist. Ch.* ii. 158: see their *Liber ad Fulgentium* § 28 (Fulg. *op.* 285: *P.L.* lxv. 451); Hefele—Leclercq § 208 (ii. 874); J. Tixeront, *History of Dogmas* iii. 124 sqq.   6. Krumbacher, pp. 55 sq.; Bardenhewer 548; his works are in *P.G.* lxxxvi. 73—158.   7. Krumbacher § 7; Bardenhewer § 102; his works in *P.G.* lxxxvi. 1185—2016; and note *L.R.E.*² ii. 373 n. 3. As to whether Leontius the Scythian monk is to be identified with L. of B. and the relative of Vitalian, see *ib.* 375 n. 1.   8. Εἷς τῆς ἁγίας τριάδος ἔπαθε σαρκί: Unus de Trinitate passus [crucifixus] est in carne. The formula was a reassertion of Cyril's Twelfth Anathematism— Εἴ τις οὐχ ὁμολογεῖ τὸν τοῦ Θεοῦ Λόγον παθόντα σαρκὶ καὶ ἐσταυρωμένου σαρκ ὶ... ἀνάθεμα ἔστω. 9. *L.R.E.*² ii. 372: the correspondence is in *Coll. Avell. Epp.* 142—81 (*C.S.E.L.* xxxv.).   10. Described in *Coll. Avell. Ep.* 167 (*C.S.E.L.* xxxv. 618 sqq.).   11. See John Maxentius, *Ep. ad legatos sedis apostolicae* (*P.G.* lxxxvi. 75—8).   12. *Liber ad Fulgentium*=Fulg. *Ep.* xvi. (*Op.* 277—85: *P.L.* lxv. 442— 51).   13. Fulgentius *Ep.* xvii. (*Op.* 286—327: *P.L.* lxxxv. 451— 98).   14. Hormisdas, *Ep.* lxx. (*P.L.* lxiii. 492 sq.): Jaffé No. 850.

15. Hormisdas, *Ep.* lxxix. § 2 (*P.L.* lxiii. 513 D)—nisi forte mavult quisquam dubitare quam credere, certare quam nosse, sequi dubia quam servare decreta [sc. of the Co. of Chalcedon and Pope Leo I.] and *Ep. Rom. Pont.* 961 (ed. A. Theiner), and Jaffé No. 857. **16.** Kidd, *Ch. Hist.* iii. 188. **17.** *Salvatorem et Dominum: Cod.* I. i. 6 § 7 (*Corp. Jur. Civ.* ii. 8). **18.** *Inter claras: Cod.* I. i. 8 (*Corp. Jur. Civ.* ii. 10—12) : Jaffé No. 884 : *P.L.* lxvi. 17 sqq. and 20 sqq.— " Quod, quia apostolicae doctrinae convenit, nostra auctoritate confirmamus." **19.** Bardenhewer, 618. The Roman deacon Anatolius consulted the deacon F.F., who replied that he saw no objection to the decree: *P.L.* lxvii. 889 sqq. **20.** Proclus *Ep.* ii. § 10 (*P.G.* lxv. 865 c.). **21.** Quoted in W. H. Hutton, *The Church of the Sixth Century,* 147. **22.** F. E. Brightman, *Lit.* i. 365 sq. **23.** *English Hymnal,* No. 325. **24.** *Documents* i. No. 126. **25.** So Augustinianism is the excess of speculation on the part of St. Augustine over those parts of his system which re-affirm the traditional teaching of the Church about sin and grace. **26.** Kidd, *Ch. Hist.* i. 426 sq. **27.** *Ib.* ii. 429 sqq. **28.** *L.R.E.*[2] ii. 380 sqq. : Tixeront,' *Hist. Dogm.* iii. 129 sqq. **29.** To hold an enquiry, at the instance of Theodora, into the circumstances attending the death of a deacon who had headed an opposition to the Orthodox Patriarch Paul of Alexandria, 538—42. Pelagius presided at a synod of Gaza for this purpose at Easter, 542 : Mansi viii. 1164 : Hefele § 254. **30.** Hefele § 255 (ii. 1182 sqq. ed. Leclercq) : Mansi ix. 488—533; *P.G.* lxxxvi. i. 945—89; Pargoire, 34. **31.** Hefele, § § 256—7 (ii. 1187 sqq.; ed. Leclercq). **32.** *Ib.* § 274 (iii. 121 : ed. Leclercq). **33.** Pargoire, 39. **34.** Hefele § § 258—66 (iii. 1 sqq. : ed. Leclercq) ; Tixeront, iii. 130 sqq.; Pargoire, 36 sqq.; *L.R.E.*[2] ii. 383 sqq. **35.** Theodore was a secret Monophysite as well as an Origenist : and he was warmly seconded by Theodora, *L.R.E.*[2] ii. 384. **36.** Our authority for this statement is Liberatus, *Breviarium,* c. xxiv (*P.L.* lxviii. 1049). He was a deacon of Carthage who, 560—6, wrote a concise history of Nestorianism and Monophysitism from 428—553. It is somewhat prejudiced in favour of the former, i.e., of the *Three Chapters:* Bardenhewer, § 116, No. 6. Text in *P.L.* lxviii. 969—1050. **37.** W. H. Hutton, *The Church of the Sixth Century,* 164. **38.** Kidd, *Ch. Hist.* iii. 201. **39.** *Ib.* 250. **40.** *Ib.* 261 sq. : and *Documents* ii. p. 267. **41.** Kidd, *Ch. Hist.* iii. 235. **42.** *Ib.* 271. **43.** *Ib.* 192. **44.** *Ib.* 329. **45.** Now lost : *L.R.E.*[2] ii. 384 n. 1 : but its contents are recoverable [see Tixeront iii. 130 n. 21 and Hefele—Leclercq § 258 (iii. 16)] from Facundus, bishop of Hermiane in Byzacena, *Pro defensione trium capitularum* [A.D. 546—8] *P.L.* lxvii. 527—852. **46.** Mansi ix. 375 D, 376 A : Hefele—Leclercq § 274 (iii. 106). **47.** *L.R.E.*[2] ii. 378. **48.** Only fragments remain, q.v. in Hefele § 259 ; iii. 26 (ed. Leclercq); Tixeront iii. 132. **49.** Hefele—Leclercq iii. 27. **50.** *Ib.* 28 sq.—Theodora died shortly afterwards, on 28th June, 548. **51.** He not only withstood the edict of Justinian of 544, against the *Three Chapters* but wrote c. 546—8 *Pro defensione trium capitularum,* and presented it to the Emperor. It is not Nestorianism which he seeks to defend but the credit of Chalcedon which he believed to be impugned by the Emperor's edict. Bardenhewer, § 116 No. 1. **52.** Hefele § 260 (iii. 31 sqq. : ed. Leclercq). **53.** *Ib.* § 261 (iii. 37 sqq. : ed. Leclercq) : for the oath, see Mansi ix. 363 D.

54. Mansi ix. 537—82; *P.G.* lxxxvi. i. 993—1035; Hefele § 263 (iii. 43 sqq. ed. H. Leclercq); Tixeront, *Hist. Dogm.* iii. 133 sqq.
55. Cyril *Ep.* 2 ad Nest. (*Op.* ix. 31: *P.G.* lxxvi. 60 sq.); Kidd, *Ch. Hist.* iii. 236, 265, 274, 283: for Justinian's acceptance of it, see *P.G.* lxxxvi. (1) 1001 A, and for his explanation, *ibid.* **56.** Justinian, *Conf. rectae fidei* (*P.G.* lxxxvi. i. 1003 B.C.). **57.** *Ib.* 1005 B.
58. Leontius, *Adv. Nest. et Eut.* i. (*P.G.* lxxxvi. ii. 1277 D): Bardenhewer § 102. **59.** His human nature never had an hypostasis of its own nor was it without an hypostasis but it ἐν τῇ ὑποστάσει τοῦ Λόγου τὴν ἀρχὴν τῆς ὑπάρξεως ἔλαβεν—Mansi ix. 556 D: *P.G.* lxxxvi. i. 1011 B. **60.** Hefele—Leclercq § 264 (iii. 56 sqq.).
61. Mansi ix. 50—5: *P.L.* lxix. 53—9: Hefele § 265 (iii. 61 sqq.: ed Leclercq). **62.** Mansi ix. 63—5: *P.L.* lxix. 63 sq.: Hefele § 266 (iii. 64 sqq.: ed. Leclercq). **63.** Hefele § 267 (iii. 68 sqq.) **64.** *Ib.* § 269 (iii. 84 sq.). **65.** *Ib.* § 270 (iii. 85 sqq.). **66.** *Ib.* § 271 (iii. 90 sqq.). **67.** Mansi ix. 61—106: *P.L.* lxix. 67—114: Hefele § 272 (iii. 93 sqq.). **68.** Hefele § 273 (iii. 101 sqq.). **69.** *Ib.* § 274 (iii. 105 sqq.). **70.** Mansi ix. 414—9: *P.L.* lxix. 122—8: Hefele § 276 (iii. 137). **71.** Mansi ix. 457—88; *P.L.* lxix. 143—78: Hefele § 276 (iii. 138 sq.). **72.** Hefele § 277 (iii. 141 sq.): Tixeront iii. 143 sq.
73. Hefele § § 278—83 (iii. 146 sqq.). Not until the Synod of Aquileia, A.D. 700, under Pope Sergius I. 687—†701. **74.** *Cf.* P. Batiffol, *L'empereur Justinien et le siège apostolique* in *Recherches de la Science religieuse*, t. xvi. 193—264 (1926). **75.** *L.R.E.*² ii. 393. **76.** Evagrius *H.E.* iv. cc. 39, 40 (*Op.* 421 sqq.: *P.G.* lxxxvi. (2) 2781 sqq.). **77.** J. Wordsworth: *The One Religion*, 68. **78.** Pargoire, 28 sq. **79.** Hefele—Leclercq § 245 (ii. 1120 sqq.). **80.** The edict of 15th March, 533 *Salvatorem et dominum:* Cod. I. vi. In § 7 he condemns μὴ ὁμολογοῦντας τὸν δεσπότην ἡμῶν Ι.Χ. τὸν υἱὸν τοῦ Θεοῦ καὶ Θεὸν ἡμῶν, τὸν σαρκωθέντα καὶ ἐνανθρωπήσαντα καὶ σταυρωθέντα ἕνα εἶναι τῆς ἁγίας καὶ ὁμοουσίου Τριάδος (*Corp. Jur. Civ.* ii. 8). **81.** Hefele—Leclercq § 250 (ii. 1142 sqq.). **82.** *Novel* xlii. (*Corp. Jur. Civ.* iii. 263 sqq.) or Mansi viii. 1149—56. **83.** Pargoire, 31 sqq. **84.** Eutychius †939, Patriarch of Alexandria, *Annales* 311 (*P.G.* cxi. 1105 B). **85.** Pargoire, 32 sq. **86.** Tella (or Tela), otherwise Constantina, was a city in the Province of Osrhoëne, whose metropolitical see was Edessa: M. Le Quien, *Or. Chr.* ii. 967. John was bishop there 503—†48. He took part, as a follower of Severus of Antioch, in the colloquy at CP. 533, *ib.* 969 sq. **87.** *L.R.E.*² ii. 391. **88.** Mansi viii. 1163—76: Hefele—Leclercq § 250 (ii. 1154).
89. Liberatus, *Breviarium* c. xix. (*P.L.* lxviii. 1033 sq.)—by "corruption" they meant not only a tendency to decomposition but passibility, i.e., capability of suffering pain and such things as hunger, thirst, and of experiencing the impulse of honest passions (πάθη ἀδιάβλητα) such as fear, joy, etc. Tixeront, *Hist. Dogm.* iii. 109. This puts the question into a more sympathetic guise for us, and makes it more intelligible. **90.** Liberatus, *Breviarium*, c. xix. (*P.L.* lxviii. 1034): Tixeront, *Hist. Dogm.* iii. 121 sq.
91. Lk. ii. 52. **92.** Timothy [a presbyter of CP., early in vii. cent.] *De receptione haereticorum* [*P.G.* lxxxvi. (1) 44]. **93.** R. L. Ottley, *Doctrine of the Incarnation*, ii. 122.

CHAPTER IV.

1. *Novella* xlii. § 1. (*Corpus Jur. Civ.* iii. 264: Berolini, 1895.)
2. For this division of heretics into two classes, less and more serious: see *Cod.* I. v. 21 § 2. **3.** *Cod.* I. v. 11; 12 § 3; 16.
4. *Cod.* I. v. 18 § 3. **5.** *Cod.* I. v. 14. **6.** *Cod.* I. iv. 20. **7.** *Cod.* I. v. 17; xviii. § 10; xix. § 4; xxi. § 1. **8.** *Cod.* I. v. 12 § 6. **9.** *Ibid.* and v. 21. **10.** *Cod.* I. x. 2. **11.** *Cod.* I. xi. 10. **12.** *Ibid.* § 1.
13. *Ibid.* § 2. **14.** *Cum recta* (7th March, 533): *Cod.* I. iv. § 3.
15. *Venerabilem ecclesiam* (1st August, 535). **16.** *Dudum quidem* (1st April, 535). It is addressed to Epiphanius, Patriarch of CP. 520—†35, after the rebuilding of St. Sophia (532 to 537), which had been burnt in the Nika riot (531), i.e., St. Sophia and its three churches annexed. **17.** *Nov.* iii. c. 1. For "ushers" (ostiarii) not reckoned among the clergy, see L. Duchesne, *Chr. Worship*[5] 344.
18. *Jam quidem* (of 18th May, 535). **19.** *Multis et variis* (14th April, 535). **20.** *D.C.B.* iii. 558. **21.** *Nov.* cxxxi. § 1. **22.** *Primum esse*, of 4th April, 544. **23.** *Verbo nobis*, of 18th August, 537.
24. *Unam nobis*, of 7th May, 541. **25.** *Rem non insuetam*, of 6th August, 536. **26.** *Maxima quidem,* of 16th March, 535: tr. J. C. Ayer, *A source-book for Ancient Church History*, 554.
27. *Si leges* (26th April, 565): *Nov.* cxxxvii. c. 6, tr. J. C. Ayer, *op. cit.* 555. "The custom of saying the Anaphora inaudibly was apparently gaining ground in the sixth century, and Justinian attempted to check it." F. E. Brightman, *Liturgies*, i. 533 l. 17.
28. *De gubernatione,* of 1st May, 546, tr. J. C. Ayer, 557. **29.** *Cod.* I. i. 7 § 2. **30.** *Inter claras* of 6th June, 533: *Cod.* I. i. 8 § 8.
31. "Summi pontificatus apicem": *Nov.* ix. Praef., of 14th April, 535. **32.** "Fontem sacerdotii" *ibid.* **33.** Venerandae sedi summi Ap. Petri: *ibid.* § 3. **34.** E. Denny, *Papalism*, § 809. **35.** *Nov.* cxxxi. c. 2; cf. *Nov.* cix. Praef. (7th May, 541) and *Nov.* cxxiii. c. 3 (1st May, 546). **36.** *Cod.* I. ii. 24 Praef. **37.** C. J. Hefele, *Councils* iv. 174 sq. **38.** *Cod.* I. ii. 6. **39.** To Epiphanius, 520—†35, in *Cod.* I. i. 7; I. iv. 34; *Nov.* iii., v., vi.; to Anthimus, 535—6, in *Nov.* xvi.; and to Menas, 536—†52, in *Nov.* lv., lvii. **40.** C. J. Hefele, *Councils*, iv. 415. **41.** Gregory *Epp.* Lib. V. Ind. xiii. *Ep.* xx. (*Op.* iii. 748: *P.L.* lxxvii. 746 A.): tr. F. H. Dudden, *Gregory the Great*, ii. 213. **42.** *Nov.* xi. of 14th April, 535. **43.** *Nov.* xi—antistes non solum metropolitanus sed archiepiscopus. **44.** Thdt. *H.E.* V. xxviii. § 2. **45.** In the tenth century there were 57 metropolitans, 49 archbishops and 514 bishoprics. C. Diehl, *Byzance*, 180. **46.** *Cod.* I. iii. 42. **47.** *Nov.* vi. (16th March, 535); *Nov.* cxxiii. (1st May, 546); *Nov.* cxxxi. c. 13 (18th March, 545); and *Nov.* cxxxvii. (26th March, 565). **48.** *Nov.* cxxiii. § 1 and *Nov.* cxxxvii. § 1. **49.** *Nov.* cxxiii. c. 19 (1st May, 546). **50.** *Nov.* lxxxiii. c. 1 (18th May, 539) and cxxiii. c. 21 (1st May, 546).
51. *Nov.* cxxiii. c. 13 (1st May, 546). **52.** *Nov.* vi. cc. 5, 6 (16th March, 535). **53.** *Nov.* cxxiii. cc. 29, 30 (1st May, 546). **54.** *Nov.* vi. c. 8 and *Nov.* cxxiii. c. 17. **55.** *Nov.* iii. c. 1 (1st April, 535).
56. *Singularis vita* of 4th March, 539.—*Nov.* cxxxiii. c. 1. **57.** "Hanc minimam inchoationis regulam."—*S. Benedicti Regula Monachorum*, c. lxxiii. **58.** *Nov.* v. cc. 1, 9 (20th March, 535) and *Nov.* cxxxiii. c. 4 (4th March, 539). **59.** *Nov.* lix. c. 4 (3rd November, 537).
60. *Nov.* cxxiii. c. 36 (1st May, 546). **61.** *Nov.* cxxxiii. c. 3 (4th

March, 539). **62.** *Nov.* lxxix. (11th March, 539). **63.** *Nov.* v. c. 2 (20th March, 535): *Nov.* cxxiii. c. 35 (1st May, 546). **64.** *Nov.* lxvii. c. 1 (1st May, 538). **65.** *Nov.* lvii. c. 2 (3rd November, 537); *Nov.* cxxiii. 18 (1st May, 546). **66.** *Nov.* iii. Praef. (1st April, 535). **67.** *Nov.* lviii. (3rd November, 537) and *Nov.* cxxxi. c. 8 (4th April, 544). **68.** *Nov.* cxli. (15th March, 539). **69.** *Nov.* cxvii. c. 10 (18th December, 542). **70.** *Ibid.* c. 9. Wife may divorce husband for (1) Treason, (2) Attempt on her life, (3) On her chastity, (4) If he has charged her with adultery but is unable to prove it, (5) If he takes another woman to live in the house. **71.** F. E. Brightman, *Liturgies* i. 113—43, 144—188, 194—244. **72.** *Ibid.*, 126—31, 165—75, 228—31. **73.** *Ibid.*, 132 line 11; 176 line 5; 232 line 3. **74.** *Ibid.*, 31—68, 69—109. **75.** *Ibid.*, 54—8, 89—96. **76.** *Ibid.*, 51, 86. **77.** *Ibid.*, 309—411. **78.** *Ibid.*, 353—99. **79.** *Ibid.*, 345—52. **80.** *Ibid.*, 527—34. **81.** Brightman, *Lit.* i. 377. **82.** *Nov.* cxxxvii. c. 6 (26th March, 565). **83.** *Cod.* I. iii. 41 § 24. **84.** O. Bardenhewer, *Patrology*, 562. **85.** Paul Maas, *Frühbyzantinische Kirchenpoesie*, 23 sqq. (Lietzmann's *Kleine Texte* No. 52/53). **86.** *Nov.* cxxiii. c. 32. **87.** *Nov.* cxxxiii. c. 3 § 1. **88.** *Nov.* cxxiii. c. 32. **89.** *Cod.* I. iv. 22 § 1. **90.** *Nov.* viii. ad fin. **91.** Places of pilgrimage were Jerusalem and Sinai: and the shrines of 10,000 Angels at Germia in Galatia visited by Justinian in October, 563, of St. John at Ephesus and of St. Thecla at Seleucia. **92.** *Cod.* I. iii. 18: Bingham, *Ant.* III. ix. **93.** Otherwise "lecticarii" (because of the bier on which they carried the corpse "seu decani" because they were a College at CP.). *Nov.* xliii. praef. (1st June, 536) or "Collegiati" *Cod.* XI. xviii. praef. and Bingham, *Ant.* III. viii. **94.** *Nov.* cxlii. **95.** *Nov.* xiv. **96.** *Nov.* cxli. **97.** *Cod.* III. xliii. **98.** *Nov.* lxxvii. **99.** *Nov.* VI. i. 5 § 9; VI. iv.; LVI.; CXXIII. ii. § 1; iii.; xvi.

CHAPTER V.

1. *Cf.* M. Manitius, *Gesch. der Lat. Litt. des Mittelalters*, i. 168—70.
2. *In laudem Justini* ii. 265 (*Mon. Germ. Hist.: Auct. ant.* III. ii. 133).
  Nulla fuit iam cura senis: iam frigidus omnis
  Alterius vitae solo fervebat amore.
  In caelum mens omnis erat.
3. Evagrius *H.E.* v. 4 (*P.G.* lxxxvi. 2794—2802). **4.** John of Ephesus, *E.H.* i. 5 (tr. R. Payne Smith: Oxford, 1860). **5.** *Ib.* iii. 11. **6.** For Maurice, see *Dict. Gk. and Rom. Biography*, ii. 975—8. "Righteous art Thou, and true are Thy judgments," were his last words, just before the murder of himself and his five sons, 27th November, 602. **7.** Evagrius, *H.E.* v. 19 (*P.G.* lxxxvi. 2832). **8.** John Eph. v. 22. **9.** "It is worthy of note that at this period the Emperors, feeling that their authority rested on an insecure footing, formed close alliances with the Patriarchs, who possessed immense influence with the people. Justin was prepared to adopt the ecclesiastical policy of John of Sirimis, Tiberius was ready to support Eutychius, and now we find Maurice standing fast by John Nesteutes in his contest with the see of Rome." J. B. Bury, *Later Roman Empire* (ed. 1889), ii. 85. **10.** John Eph., *H.E.* i. 42. **11.** Evagrius, *H.E.* v. 4 (*Op.* 430; *P.L.* lxxxvi. 2800 B) —περὶ πρόσωπα ἢ συλλαβὰς i.e. about One or two "Persons" in Christ (Catholicism v. Nestori-

anism), or whether He was Ἐκ δύο φύσεων (Eutychians and Monophysites only) or Ἐν δύο φύσεσιν (Catholics). But συλλαβὰς may also include a reference to the question whether His body was φθάρτος or ἄφθαρτος. **12.** Bardenhewer, *Patrology*, 171. **13.** John Eph., *H.E.* i. 1. **14.** John Eph., *H.E.* iii. 36. **15.** *Ib.* ii. 44. **16.** *Ib.* ii. 50. **17.** Bury's Gibbon, vol. V. app. i. (p. 496). **18.** *Ibid.* **19.** John Eph., *H.E.* i. 5. **20.** John Eph., *H.E.* i. 10. **21.** *Ib.* i. 14. **22.** *Ib.* i. 17. **23.** *Ib.* i. 16. **24.** *Ib.* i. 17. **25.** *Ib.* i. 15. **26.** This was one step in attaining pre-eminence for New Rome: the other was, by the title Œc. Patr., to place it on a level with Old Rome. CP. succeeded in eclipsing Alexandria, Antioch and Jerusalem (all depressed by schism and Mohammedan conquest) but never in rivalling Old Rome: for the Popes were free and the Patriarchs dependent upon the Emperor: *cf.* John Eph., *H.E.* i. 11. **27.** John Eph., *H. E.* i. 11. **28.** "Diacrinomeni." **29.** *Ib.* i. 37. **30.** John Eph., *H.E.* ii. 35: iii. 17. **31.** "Corpus nostrum," said Eutychius, "in illa resurrectionis gloria erit impalpabile, ventis aereque subtilius." Greg. Magn., *Moralium* xiv. § 72 (*Op.* i. 465: *P.L.* lxxv. 1077C): *cf.* John Eph., *H.E.* iii. 17. **32.** Lk. xxiv. 39. **33.** 1 Cor. xv. 50. The whole discussion in § § 72—3 turns on 1 Cor. xv.; and is very interesting in view of modern differences of opinion about the resurrection-body. **34.** Greg. Magn. *Moralium*, xiv. § 74 (*Op.* i. 466, 1079B). **35.** John Eph., *H.E.* iii. 20. **36.** *Ib.* ii. 37. **37.** *Ib.* iii. 21. **38.** Gregory wrote against it to John, to Maurice and to the Empress Constantina, *Epp.* V. xviii., xx., xxi.: also to the Patriarchs of Alexandria and Antioch, *Ep.* xliii. (*Op.* iii. 741 sqq.; *P.G.* lxxvii. 738 sqq.). To Gregory it meant "sole bishop"; but to the "easterns, accustomed to high-flown compliments .. it had no such tremendous significance": on the controversy, see F. H. Dudden, *Gregory the Great*, ii. 209—19. **39.** For the Armenian Church, see: H. Gelzer, *Die Anfänge der armenischen Kirche* in *Berichte der sächsischen Gesellschaft der Wissenschaften zu Leipzig*: Phil. Hist. Classe, 1895, i. and ii. pp. 109—74; Fr. Tournebize, *Histoire politique et religieuse de l'Arménie* in *Revue de l'Orient chrétien*, 1902—4 (vol. vii. [1902] pp. 26, 277, 508; vol. viii. [1903] pp. 206, 577, and vol. ix. [1904] pp. 107, 212, 393, 537); S. Weber, *Die Katholische Kirche in Armenien* (Herder, 1903). **40.** *Documents*, ii. No. 210. **41.** Evagrius, *H.E.* iii. 14, and *Documents* ii. No. 235. **42.** Tournebize gives the names and dates of the Catholici from v.—vii. cent., as follows:—Moses I., 457—65; Kioud, 465—75; Christopher I., 475—80; John I., 480—7; Babken I., 487—92 [? 490—515]; Samuel, 492—502; Mousché, 502—10; Sahag, (Isaac) II., 510—5; Christopher II., 515—21; Ghevout (Leontius), 521—4; Nerses II., 524—?; John II., ?; Moses II., 549—79; Abraham I., 594—600; John III., 600—17; Gomidan, 617—25; Christopher III., 625—?; *R.O.C.* vii. 537. **43.** Evagrius, *H.E.* v. 7 (*Op.* 433 sq.: *P.G.* lxxxvi. 2805 sqq.): *cf.* cc. 8—15 and John of Eph. *H.E.*, ii. 18—24. **44.** F. E. Brightman, *Liturgies* i. 571. **45.** *Ibid.* 341 l. 21 (ix. cent.); 394 l. 12. **46.** *Encycl. Brit.*[11] ii. 589: *cf. Rituale Armenorum* (edd. F. C. Conybeare and A. J. Maclean) pp. 65 sqq. for the rites, and canons about animal sacrifices. **47.** *Orat ii. De resurrectione Domini* (*Op.* iii.: *P.G.* xlvi. 627—52). **48.** The Jacobite Patriarch of Antioch now resides near Mardin, in the "Saffron Monastery," or at Mardin, according to O. H. Parry, *Six months in* *a Syrian Monastery*, c. v. (Horace Cox, 1895). He rules about 200,000, once in Turkey: and they are to be found chiefly in Mesopotamia, in the N.E. corner between Diabekr, Mardin, Jezireh to the S.W. and the Tigris to the N.E., i.e., in the hilly region of Jebel Tur (Parry, c. xiii. and map p. 169); but also near Damascus, and at Mosul. **49.** John Eph., *H.E.* i. 41. **50.** *Enc. R.E.* xii. 173: For their liturgy, see Brightman i. 69 sqq.; Features of their worship are (1) leavened bread; (2) reservation for the sick, but only for communion on the same day; (3) little children are baptised, confirmed and communicated; (4) antidoron; (5) Vesture of alb, amice, undivided stole, yellow shoes, and a chasuble split down the front and buckled with silver at the neck; (6) insertion of "who wast crucified for us" into "The Trisagion"; but this is addressed to the Son and not to the Trinity; (7) strict fasts—Advent, Lent, W. and F. in each week, and others. **51.** J. Labourt, *Le christianisme dans l'empire perse*, cc. v.—vii.; W. A. Wigram, *The Assyrian Church*, cc. ix., x.; L. Duchesne, *L'église au VIme siècle*, c. ix. **52.** "Assumed rather than expressed in formal documents": Wigram, 90. For this "Synod of Mar Isaac" 399—†410, see J. B. Chabot, *Synodicon Orientale*, 253 sqq. (*Notices et Extraits des MSS. de la Bibliothèque Nationale*, vol. xxxvii. [Paris, 1902]); Wigram, 89 sqq. **53.** *S.O.* 285 sqq.—"Synod of Dad-ishu," Catholicus 421—†56; *Documents illustrative of the History of the Church*, ii. No. 155. **54.** *Ibid.* No. 235. **55.** *Ibid.* No. 236. **56.** R. H. Connolly, *The Liturgical Homilies of Narsai* (Texts and Studies VIII. i. Cambr. 1909). **57.** Borrowed by Ishu-Yahb III., Catholicus 647—†58, who had travelled in the West, from the churches of the Roman Empire. Connolly, xlix. **58.** Brightman, *Lit. E. and W.*, i. 247—305. **59.** *Ibid.* 287. **60.** *Ibid.* 285. **61.** Renaudot, *Lit. Orient. Collectio* ii. 610—5. **62.** *Ibid.* 620—35. **63.** *E.R.E.* xii. 177. **64.** Connolly, 5 sq. It is spoken of as "thundered forth" by the people. **65.** The practice of reciting it in the Liturgy may have been introduced by Narsai himself: *ibid.* lxii. n. 1. **66.** *Ibid.* pp. 10—12: and app. I. 90 (by E. Bishop). **67.** *Ibid.* pp. 13—18: and app. V. According to Justinian, *Novel* cxxxvii. c. vi. ["Jubemus omnes et episcopos et presbyteros non tacite, sed ea voce quae a fideli populo exaudiatur sacram oblationem precesque in sancti baptismate adhibitas faciant"] "the recital of the canon aloud was the traditional and still universal practice" in his Empire. At Rome, and at CP., the canon had come to be said inaudibly by the end of the eighth century (App. v. 124 sq.) **68.** Connolly, 4. **69.** *Ib.* 12. **70.** *Ib.* 4, 12. **71.** *Ib.* 22 sq.—On this ceremonial splendour, see app. I. 88 sqq. **72.** *Ib.* 117. **73.** App. iv. 117 sqq. **74.** Synode de Mar Acacius [Catholicus 485—†96] A.D. 486. Canon I.: *S.O.* 301 sq. Wigram, 164; *Documents* ii. No. 236. "Acacius's Confession of Faith is derived from the theology of Antioch; between it and the Formula of Union in 433 or that of the Council of Chalcedon there are only shades of expression. However, the term 'Mother of God' was avoided." L. Duchesne, *The Early History of the Church*, iii. 393. **75.** Synode de Mar Babai, A.D. 497; *S.O.* 312. **76.** Wigram, 208. **77.** Duchesne, *L'église au VIme siècle*, 315 sqq. **78.** *S.O.* 556. **79.** Council of Mar Abha, can. 40: *S.O.* 561. **80.** Or "perambulatory synod," Oct., 540: W. 192: *S.O.* 320 sqq. **81.** *S.O.* 550 sqq.: W. 189. **82.** *S.O.* 332 sqq.; W. 195. **83.** *S.O.*

553 sqq.: W. 197 sq. **84.** W. 198. **85.** Synod of Joseph, 554; *S.O.* 354; W. 210. **86.** His Council (*S.O.* 368 sqq.) of 576 gives a valuable picture of church life at the time, in its 39 canons. **87.** Synode de Mar Jesuyabh I. A.D. 585, canon II. *S.O.* 398 sq.: W. 219. **88.** W. 220. **89.** Duchesne, *op. cit.* 329. **90.** *Enc. Br.*¹¹ vii. 113—6. **91.** Dio. Al. *ap.* Eus. *H.E.* VI. xli. § 19. **92.** *H.D.B.* i. 668 sqq. **93.** J. Leipoldt, *Schenute von Atripe, und die Enstehung des national Agyptischen Christentums*, in *T.* and *U.* N.F., Bd. x. Heft 1 (Leipzig, 1903). **94.** J. G. Milne, *A History of Egypt under Roman rule*, v. 104, 158 (Methuen, 1898). Schnoudi was born 333; accompanied Cyril to the Council of Ephesus, 431 and died 451, at the age of 118: Leipoldt, *ut sup.*, pp. 44—6. Schenute bedeutet für die Weltgeschichte nichts, für die Kopten alles. (1) S. hat seinem Volke eine Nationalkirche geschenkt. (2) S. hat seinem Volke eine Nationallitteratur gegeben. (3) S. hat durch sein persönliches Vorbild und seine straffe Organisierung der Klosterarbeit gezeigt, wie unter den damaligen Verhältnissen die wirtschaftliche Not zu lindern war.—Leipoldt, *ut. sup.*, p. 191. **95.** In 321, Alexander had 100—Socr. *H.E.* I. vi. § 13: in 369, Ath. mentions 90. *Ad Afros* § 10. **96.** J. M. Neale, *Patriarchate of Alexandria*, ii. 1—60. **97.** B. J. Kidd, *Hist. Ch. to A.D. 461*, iii. 402 sqq. **98.** W. B. in *D.C.B.* iv. 1031—3. **99.** *D.C.B.* iv. 1033—4. **100.** *Documents* ii. No. 234. **101.** *D.C.B.* iii. 347—8. **102.** *Documents*, ii. No. 235. **103.** *D.C.B.* iv. 336—8. **104.** Duchesne, *op. cit.* 338 sqq. **105.** " Dans sa résidence forcée près du lac de Dercos (near CP.) le patriarche T. présidait à tout le mouvement monophysite." Duchesne *op. cit.* 338. **106.** *D.C.B.* iv. 250. **107.** *D.C.B.* iv. 1221. **108.** *D.C.B.* iii. 348. **109.** *D.C.B.* ii. 283. Duchesne, *op. cit.* 377: under whom " Coptes et Melkites vivaient ensemble tant bien que mal": *ib.* 376. **110.** *D.C.B.* iv. 925. **111.** *D.C.B.* iii. 348 **112.** " Communis filius" of A.D. 598: Greg. Magn., *Epp.* lib. viii. *Ind.* ii. *ep.* 30 (*Op.* iii. 919; *P.L.* lxxvii. 932 B.C.): Jaffé No. 1518. **113.** Cyrus had been metropolitan of Phasis in Lazica: whence his name " the Caucasian " Kaukios or Al Muqawkaz—Duchesne, *op. cit.* 400, 414, 424. **114.** *Enc. R.E.* iv. 118. **115.** F. E. Brightman, *Liturgies* i. 185: from the Anaphora of St. Cyril—"the most ancient" of the Coptic rites. " By joining to the Anaphora of St. Cyril the Ordinary of the Coptic Mass, we obtain a Coptic liturgy which is the exact counterpart of the Greek Liturgy of St. Mark ": and is printed in Brightman, pp. 144—88 as the Liturgy of the Coptic Jacobites: see L. Duchesne, *Chr. Worship*⁵ 81.

CHAPTER VI.

1. This victory was the occasion of " the most celebrated of all the hymns of the Greek Church, the so-called Greek *Te Deum:* ὕμνος ἀκάθιστος. It is a hymn of thanksgiving to B.V.M. for her deliverance of CP. and the Empire from the Avars. Its author was the Patriarch Sergius; and it is so called because all stand while it is sung: whereas at other hymns (καθίσματα) they sit."—Bardenhewer, 564. **2.** *D.C.B.* iv. 617—8. **3.** *D.C.B.* i. 775. Phasis (=Poti) at the mouth of the River Phasis (now Rion) and at the western terminus of the Trans-caucasian Railway from the Black Sea to Baku on the Caspian. It was geographically in Cholcis (or Lazica). **4.** Le Quien, *Oriens Christianus*, ii. 1361—3. **5.** Mansi x. 991—8 : A. Hahn, *Symbole*, § 234. **6.** *D.C.B.* iv. 320—3 ; J. Tixeront, *Hist. Dogm.*, iii. 153 sqq. ; Hefele, *Councils*, v. 1 sqq. **7.** Οὐ κατὰ θεὸν τὰ θεῖα δράσας, οὐ τὰ ἀνθρώπεια κατὰ ἄνθρωπον, ἀλλ' ἀνδρωθέντος θεοῦ, καινήν τινα τὴν θεανδρικὴν ἐνέργειαν ἡμῖν πεπολιτευομένος Ps.-Dion. *Ep.* iv. (*Op.* i. 590 ; *P.G.* iii. 1072 C). **8.** Persians till 629 ; Saracens after 634. **9.** See the letter of Sergius to Honorius in Mansi xi. 529 sqq. **10.** *Ib.* 529 C. **11.** Μίαν ἡγεμονικὴν ἐνέργειαν *ib.* 561 C. **12.** "A cette idée (one operation), les Monophysites arrivaient en partant de l'unité de nature, leur dogme fondamental ; Serge, qui retenait le décret de Chalcedoine, ne pouvait suivre ce chemin ; il partait de l'unité de personne, et, *rattachant la faculté d'agir non pas à la nature, mais à la personne*, il concluait tout comme les dissidents à l'unité ' d'energie.' "—Duchesne, *op. cit.* 392. **13.** *Ib.* 529 E. **14.** Letter of Cyrus to Sergius, *ib.* 561 E. **15.** *Ib.* 563—8 ; and A. Hahn, *Symbole*, § 232 : tr. J. C. Ayer, *Source-Book*, 661 sq. ; and Hefele v. 19 sq. **16.** Καὶ τὸν αὐτὸν ἕνα Χριστὸν καὶ υἱὸν ἐνεργοῦντα τὰ θεοπρεπῆ καὶ ἀνθρώπινα μιᾷ θεανδρικῇ ἐνεργείᾳ κατὰ τὸν ἐν ἁγίοις Διονύσιον. It will be noticed that Ps.-D. had not said μιᾷ but καινῇ. **17.** *Vita Maximi* c. x. (*P.G.* xc. 77 D) : Hefele v. 21. **18.** O. Bardenhewer, *Patrology*, 564—5. **19.** *Ib.* 576—9. **20.** Mansi xi. 532 D. **21.** *Ib.* 533 A. **22.** *Ib.* 536 D. **23.** Mansi xi. 461—509 and Sophronius, *Op. ap. P.G.* lxxxvii. 3, col. 3147—3200 and A. Hahn, *Symbole*, § 233 ; Hefele v. 41 sqq. The letter was adopted 28th March, 681, at the 13th session of the sixth Œcumenical Council : Mansi xi. 556 C, D. **24.** Mansi xi. 537 A. **25.** Mansi xi. 537—44, in the Greek : the Latin original is lost : see also *P.L.* lxxx. 470—4 and Hefele v. 27—32. **26.** "Unam voluntatem fatemur D. N. I. C." Hefele v. 29. He ought to have said : (a.) "We must not ascribe two *contrarias voluntates* to Christ, for He did not assume the *natura humana vitiata;* (b.) but, nevertheless, there are in Christ *two wills*, the divine and the incorrupt human." He erred by omission : and the Monotheletes made the most of it. Hefele v. 36. His error was not in stating what was false—but in want of explicitness in stating (b.) i.e., what is true. It was *ex cathedra*, Hefele v. 61. **27.** Jn. vi. 38. **28.** Mk. xiv. 36. **29.** Mansi xi. 541 A. **30.** Extant only in fragments : for which see Mansi xi. 579—82 and *P.L.* lxxx. 474—6, Hefele v. 49 sqq. **31.** Mansi xi. 582 A. **32.** Mansi xi. 582 C. **33.** Mansi x. 992—7 : A. Hahn, *Symbole*, § 234 ; Hefele v. 62 sqq. **34.** Mansi xi. 994 E. **35.** ἀλλ' ὁπότε καὶ οἵαν καὶ ὅσην αὐτὸς ὁ Θεὸς Λόγος ἠβούλετο *ib.* 996 C. **36.** By Co. of CP. under Sergius, September—December, 638 (Mansi x. 1000) ; and under Pyrrhus (Patriarch of CP. 638—41 and †655) in 639 (*ib.* 1001—4). **37.** Gibbon c. l. (v. 311 sqq. ed. J. B. Bury, 1896). **38.** *Ib.* c. li. (v. 397 sqq.). **39.** *C.M.H.*, vol. iii. c. x. **40.** Al-Madina "the city" : which is an abbreviation of Madinat-an-Nabi "the City of the Prophet," *ib.* iii. 312 n. 1. **41.** J. C. Ayers, *Source-Book*, 654. **42.** *Ib.* 657 sq. **43.** "*Islam* is the infinitive, and *Muslim* or ' Moslem ' the participle, of a verb which signifies 'to deliver' or 'to commit entirely' something or person to someone else ; authoritatively interpreted in this connection as 'to deliver the face to God,' *i.e.* to turn to God only in prayer and worship, to the exclusion of all other objects of devotion. Hence the words are equivalent to 'monotheism' and 'monotheist.'" D. S. Margoliouth, *Mohammedanism*, p. 1. **44.** J. C. Ayers, 655. **45.** "There is no God but Allah" and "Mohammed is the messenger of Allah": Margoliouth, p. 1. **46.** Deut. iv. 4 and the Nicene Creed. **47.** *C.M.H.* ii. c. xi. **48.** Gibbon c. li. (v. 409 sq.). **49.** *Ib.* 415 sqq. The chronology is very uncertain: see app. 21. **50.** *C.M.H.* ii. 342 sqq. **51.** Gibbon, c. li. (v. 444 sqq.). **52.** *Ib.* 459 sqq.: capture of Carthage, 698; final conquest of Africa, 709. **53.** Duchesne, *op. cit.* c. xii. **54.** Mansi x. 709—60; Maximus, *Op.* ii. 159—95 (*P.G.* xci. 287—354); Hefele § 303 (E.T. vol. v.; Hefele—Leclercq, vol. iii. pt. i.). **55.** Mansi x. 712 D.: for "will" belonging to "person" and not to "nature" see above, p. 107 n. 12. **56.** Hefele § 304. (1) From Numidia, Byzacene and Mauretania to Pope Theodore (Mansi x. 919—22); (2) from Byzacene to Constans II. (Mansi x. 925—30); (3) from "Africa" to Paul II. of CP. (*ib.* 925 D.): (4) from Victor, Primate of Carthage 646—? to Pope Theodore (*ib.* 943—50). **57. Only Paul's reply is extant** (*ib.* 1019—26). **58.** *Ib.* 878 E. **59.** Text in Mansi x. 1029—32; C. Kirch, *Enchiridion* Nos. 972—3; tr. Ayers, 662—4: Hefele, § 306. **60.** Mansi x. 863—1186; Hefele § 307. **61.** "Duas eiusdem sicuti naturas, unitas inconfuse, ita et duas naturales voluntates, divinam et humanam." Mansi x. 1150 D. **62.** *Ib.* 1158 sq.; tr. Ayers, 664 sq. **63.** *Ib.* 1169—84. **64.** *Ib.* 789—98. **65.** Mansi xi. 195—202. **66.** Hefele § 313. This document was a collection of signatures, not a synodal letter: see L. Duchesne, *op. cit.* 464 n. 1. **67.** W. Bright, *Chapters in Early English Church History.* **68.** Mansi xi. 294 B. **69.** Bede, *H.E.* iii. 17: Mansi xi. 175—7. **70.** Mansi xi. 234—86. **71.** *Ib.* 235 C. **72.** Mansi x. 235 D. **73.** *Ib.* 238 A. **74.** *Ib.* 239 B, C. **75.** "Nevertheless, not as I will but as thou wilt", Mt. xxvi. 39; Lk. xxii. 42; "I seek not mine own will, but the will of him that sent me," Jn. v. 30; "Not to do mine own will, but the will of him that sent me," Jn. vi. 38; and passages which describe our Lord's obedience, Lk. ii. 51; Phil. ii. 8. **76.** *Ib.* 278 C. **77.** *Ib.* 286—315. **78.** *Ib.* 202—3. **79.** *Ib.* 189—718: Hefele § § 315—23. **80.** οἷά τε συμφωνούσας (utpote consonantes) Mansi xi. 636 D. **81.** *Ib.* 640 A.; Hahn § 150; Ayers, 670. **82.** Mansi xi. 556 C.; Hefele § 324; Ayers, 671: date 13th session, 28/3/680. **83.** E. Denny, *Papalism*, § § 798, 962—till the eleventh century. **84.** *Supra* p. 108 n. 26. "Duas voluntates haud absolute denegavit, sed tantummodo contrarias, cuiusmodi in *nobis* ex corrupto naturae statu reperiuntur" is the defence of Petavius, *De Inc.* I. xxi. 11. **85.** *Cf.* E. Denny, *Papalism*, § § 782 sqq.: and Dom J. Chapman, O.S.B., *The condemnation of Pope Honorius* (reprinted from the *Dublin Review*) and published by the [Roman] Catholic Truth Society, 1907, at 3d. **86.** R. L. Ottley, *Doctrine of the Incarnation*, ii. 127. **87.** So St. Thomas Aq.—"Ad perfectionem humanae naturae pertinet voluntas, quae est naturalis eius potentia. ... Unde necesse est dicere quod Filius Dei humanam voluntatem assumpserit cum humana natura." *Summa* III. q. xviii. art. 1. But he adds that the "voluntas naturalis," or instinctive wish to avoid suffering, obeyed the "voluntas rationalis" and the Divine will, so that there was no "contrarietas voluntatum," *ib.* art. 6: W. Bright,

Sermons of St. Leo,[2] 174 : who also refers to Hooker *E.P.* V. xlviii. §9, and H. P. Liddon, *B.L.* 265 sq.   **88.** R. C. Trench, *Hulsean Lectures*, 1845—6,[6] 182 n. 1 (Macmillan, 1880).   **89.** Mansi xi. 921—1006; Hefelé § 327 (v. 221 sqq. E. Tr.; III. i. 560 sqq. ed. Leclercq). **90.** c. 39.   **91.** J. Pargoire, *L'église byzantine*, § 23.   **92.** *Ib.* § 24. **93.** Mansi x. 920 B, C.   **94.** *Ib.* 896 B, C.   **95.** *Ib.* 893 C, D. **96.** Maximus, *Op.* ii. 76 (*P.G.* xci. 144 C.).   **97.** Mansi xi. 241 C. **98.** *Ib.* 655 D.   **99.** Pargoire, ii. § 26.   **100.** Agnellus, *Lib. Pont. Eccl. Rav.* § 112 (*Script. Rerum Langobard.* saec. VI.—IX. [ap. *Mon. Germ. Hist.*] pp. 350—3).   **101.** *Ib.* p. 350 n. 8.   **102.** Pargoire, ii. § 27 : the canons hostile to Rome are given and discussed in J. S. Assemani, *Bibliotheca Juris Orientalis*, § cclxxxi. sqq. (i. 413 sqq.— Romae 1762). They are chiefly cc. 2, 13, 36, 55. Hence this synod was not received at Rome. Hefelé § 328.   **103.** *Ib.* § 29.   **104.** Mansi x. 581— 2: Honorius *Ep.* viii. (*P.L.* lxxx. 478).   **105.** Mansi xi. 16, 18 sq. **106.** c. 36.   **107.** c. 38.   **108.** Pargoire ii. § 30.   **109.** c. 37.   **110.** c. 8. **111.** c. 35.   **112.** cc. 19, 20.   **113.** cc. 12, 48.   **114.** c. 3. **115.** Pargoire, ii. § 31.   **116.** c. 13.   **117.** c. 13.   **118.** cc. 14, 15. **119.** c. 3.   **120.** c. 9.   **121.** c. 24.   **122.** cc. 24, 51.   **123.** c. 50. **124.** c. 86.   **125.** c. 24.   **126.** c. 5.   **127.** c. 21.   **128.** c. 27. **129.** c. 33.   **130.** c. 22.   **131.** c. 23.   **132.** c. 10.   **133.** c. 34= Chalc. 18.   **134.** c. 17.   **135.** c. 18.   **136.** c. 16.   **137.** c. 7. **138.** Pargoire, ii. § 33.   **139.** c. 43.   **140.** c. 40.   **141.** c. 44. **142.** c. 46.   **143.** c. 47.   **144.** c. 42.   **145.** c. 45.   **146.** c. 49. **147.** καλόγηροι, caloyers.   **148.**=Westerns in c. 30. Our own abp. Theodore of Tarsus, 668—†90, is a good example of this. **149.** Letter of the Emp. Constantine IV. to Pope Donus, 676—†8 in Mansi x. 200 B.   **150.** Pargoire § § 34, 35.   **151.** c. 71, i.e., outlandish, ?Oriental, or ?Slavonic.   **152.** c. 51.   **153.** c. 62. **154.** c. 65.   **155.** c. 61.   **156.** c. 60.   **157.** c. 77.   **158.** c. 94. **159.** c. 100.   **160.** c. 96.   **161.** J. B. Bury, *Later Roman Empire*, ii. 325.   **162.** *Ib.* ii. 396.   **163.** *Ib.* ii. 393 n. 2.   **164.** Pargoire p. 221.   **165.** Pargoire ii. § 19.   **166.** *Ib.* ii. § 36.   **167.** c. 80. **168.** c. 90.   **169.** Nic. c. 20.   **170.** c. 73.   **171.** c. 82.   **172.** c. 70. **173.** c. 75.   **174.** Pargoire ii. § 37.   **175.** c. 78.   **176.** c. 84. **177.** Except with the consent of the bishop when it may be administered in private oratories, cc. 31, 59.   **178.** c. 95=CP. 7 (381). Manichaeans, Valentinians, Marcionites.   **179.** c. 95.   **180.** c. 102. **181.** c. 53.   **182.** c. 55.   **183.** c. 98.   **184.** c. 72.   **185.** c. 87. **186.** c. 91.   **187.** c. 92.   **188.** c. 93.   **189.** c. 83.   **190.** c. 23. **191.** c. 58.   **192.** c. 29.   **193.** c. 101.   **194.** F. E. Brightman, *Liturgies*, i. 102 sq., 396.   **195.** Text in *ib.* 534—9, App. P. : Pargoire ii. § 39.   **196.** e.g. that the Liturgy is not to be celebrated in private oratories, c. 31.   **197.** c. 81.   **198.** c. 75.   **199.** Not alluded to by Maximus, etc.; but they were there before the seventh century, see Brightman, 528.   **200.** c. 99.   **201.** c. 28.   **202.** c. 57.   **203.** c. 32. **204.** c. 55.   **205.** c. 101.   **206.** c. 101.   **207.** Brightman, 536 sq., 539.   **208.** c. 52.   **209.** c. 74.   **210.** c. 74.   **211.** c. 76.   **212.** c. 16. **213.** Pargoire, ii § 40.   **214.** c. 99.   **215.** c. 97.   **216.** c. 76.   **217.** c. 88. **218.** c. 69.   **219.** Brightman, *Lit.* i. 537.   **220.** Pargoire ii. § 41. **221.** c. 82.   **222.** c. 55.   **223.** cc. 80, 90.   **224.** c. 89.   **225.** c. 66. **226.** cc. 55, 56. No fasting, as in Rome, on Saturdays in Lent; and no eating of eggs and cheese, these are animal food, after the manner of Armenians.   **227.** Pargoire ii. § 42.   **228.** *Ib.* § 43.

229. *Ib.* § 45.   **230.** *P.G.* lxxxvii. iii. 2851—3112.   **231.** Supra p. 108 n. 23.   **232.** C. Diehl, *Hist. de l'Empire byzantine,* 56 sqq.   **233.** J. B. Bury, *Later Roman Empire,* ii. 275—8.   **234.** *Ib.* 331 sqq.   **235.** *Ib.* 278 sqq.   **236.** *Ib.* 339 sqq.   **237.** *Ib.* 343.   **238.** J. B. Bury, *Later Roman Empire,* ii. 304.   **239.** C. Diehl, 62 sqq.   **240.** Hefele § 328 : Bury, 366.   **241.** e.g., Bury, 325, 329, 361, 363, 367, 389.   **242.** *Ib.* 387—9.   " Leo III. made an attack upon superstition the basis of his policy of reform.... The increase of ecclesiastical influence in the Empire is one of the most striking features of the seventh century; and as the dignitaries of the Church readily acquiesced in the growth of superstition, to which they were themselves inclined, the prospect of reform seemed almost hopeless, as it would be necessary to carry it out in spite of the institution with which the spiritual life of the age was interwoven. The Isaurian Emperors in the eighth century undertook the task, but the obloquy which has ever attached to their names among the orthodox shows how much the undertaking cost them."

CHAPTER VII.

1. Gibbon c. xlix. (v. 278).   **2.** *Ib.* 244.   **3.** *Enc. Brit.*[11] xv. 774. " The Khazars were generally on friendly terms with the Roman Empire and on hostile terms with the Saracen caliphate." Bury, *L.R.E.* ii. 409.   **4.** The junction of the lines from CP. and Smyrna towards Koniah and Bagdad; about 200 miles E. of Smyrna. **5.** C. Diehl, *Hist. de l'Empire byz.*, 66 : ἔδει μᾶλλον αὐτοῖς τὰς ἀνδρείας τούτων ἐξειπεῖν, τὰς κατὰ τῶν πολεμίων νίκας, τὰς βαρβαρικὰς ὑποπτώσεις, τὴν τοῦ ὑπηκόου περιποίησιν, τὰς βουλὰς, τὰ τρόπαια, τὰς κοσμικὰς συστάσεις, τὰς πολιτικὰς καταστάσεις, τὰς τῶν πόλεων ἐπανορθώσεις κ.τ.λ. Mansi xiii. 356 B.   **6.** J. B. Bury, *Later Roman Empire,* ii. 408 sqq.   **7.** Bury reckons 7 in Asia : (1) Opsikion, (2) Anatolic, (3) Thracesian, (4) Armeniac, (5) Cibyraiot, (6) Bucellarian, (7) Coloneia ; and four in Europe : (1) Thrace, (2) Macedonia, (3) Hellas, (4) Sicily and S. Italy : *L.R.E.* ii. 350 sq. **8.** Bury, *L.R.E.* ii. 421 and n. 3.   **9.** Gibbon (ed. J. B. Bury) vol. v. app. 12; *L.R.E.* ii. 418 sqq.   **10.** Νόμος Ῥοδίων ναυτικὸς *(Jus Navale Rhodiorum) ap.* J. M. Pardessus, *Us et coutumes de la mer* vol. i. c. 6 (Paris, 1847) and W. Ashburner, *The Rhodian Sea-Law* (Clar. Press, 1909, 18/- n.).   **11.** i.e., " A compendious selection *(ecloga)* of the laws, made by the wise Emperors Leo and Constantine, from the Institutes, Digesta, Codex and Novels of the great Justinian ; and an improvement thereof in the direction of humanity (εἰς τὸ φιλανθρωπότερον)" is the full title. Text in A. G. Montferratus, *Ecloga Leonis et Constantini,* (Athens, 1899) : account in Bury's Gibbon v. app. xi. and his *L.R.E.* ii. 412 sqq. **12.** *Novel* xv. § 1*(Novellae* i. 80 : ed. Teubner, 1881). The Empire had lost Syria in the East, Africa in the South, and the northern provinces of the Balkan peninsula; so that it was becoming entirely Greek.   **13.** Bury's Gibbon v. 526. *Cf.* the preface to the *Ecloga* in Monferratus 1—5, tr. in Bury, *L.R.E.* ii. 412 sqq.   **14.** Tit B. § § 14, 15 (Monferratus, 14): (1) Wife's adultery, (2) husband's impotence,

(3) plots against life of one spouse by the other, (4) leprosy.
15. Mt. v. 29. **16.** Exod. xxi. 24. **17.** Gen. iv. 24. **18.** Tit. xvii.
§ 2 (Monferratus, 41). **19.** *Ib.* § 11 (M. 43). **20.** *Ib.* § 39 (M. 48).
21. *Ib.* § 19 (M. 44). **22.** *Ib.* § 20 (M. 44). **23.** See " The relation of Christianity to art" in B. F. Westcott, *The Epistles of St. John*, pp. 331—74. **24.** Jerome, *Adv. Vigilantium* § 4 : B. J. Kidd, *Hist. Ch.* iii. 38. **25.** Bury's Gibbon ii. 547 app. 10. **26.** A. Harnack, *History of Dogma*, ii. 144 : see C. Gore, *The Body of Christ*, 89.
27. " Placuit picturas in ecclesia non esse debere, ne quod colitur et adoratur in parietibus depingatur." *Conc. Illib.* c. 36 (Mansi ii. 11 D).
28. Eus., *Ep.* ii. (ad Constantinam Augustam): *Op.* ii. (*P.G.* xx. 1548 B). **29.** Epiph. *Ep. ad Joann. Hier.* § 9 (*Op.* iii. 263 : *P.G.* xliii. 390 C)=Jerome, *Ep.* li. § 9. On the doubt, see J. Tixeront, *Hist. Dogm.* iii. 431 n. 47. **30.** " Adoramus omnes crucem et, per ipsam, illum cuius est crux : non tamen crucem coadorare dicimus cum Christo, nec per hoc una est crucis et Christi natura " : Rusticus, *Contra acephalos disputatio* (*P.L.* lxvii. 1218 C). **31.** *H.E.* iv. c. 26 (*Op.* 404 : *P.G.* lxxxvi. ii. 2745). **32.** *Peregrinatio Silviae:* text in L. Duchesne, *Chr. Worship*,[5] 510. **33.** Acts xix. 35. **34.** Evagrius *H.E.* iv. 27 (*Op.* 406; *P.G.* LXXXVI. ii. 2748 sq.). **35.** *Mors Pilati* [c. 350] *ap.* C. de Tischendorf, *Evangelia Apocrypha*[2] 457. **36.** J. Tixeront, *Les origines de l'église d'Edesse*, 122 (Paris, 1888).
37. Simeon, *Ep. ad Justinum II.* (*P.G.* LXXXVI. ii. 3217 A). **38.** *Acta* ii. § 18 (*Op.* i.: *P.G.* xc. 156 A, B). **39.** Leontius of Neapolis, *Sermo.* III. (*P.G.* xc. 1608—9). **40.** Michael II., 820—†9, to Louis I., 814—†40 : Mansi xiv. 420 B.C. **41.** T. Hodgkin, *Italy and her invaders*, vi. 432 n. 9 : Bury, *E.R.E.* 117. **42.** Nacolia (in Phrygia Salutaris) is now Sidi Ghazi—W. M. Ramsay, *Hist. Geogr. A.M.*, 144. **43.** Claudiopolis (Bithynium)=now Boli. **44.** Germanus, *Ep.* ii. (*P.G.* xcviii. 157 C). **45.** J. B. Bury, *L.R.E.* ii. 437. **46.** T. Hodgkin, *Italy and her invaders*,[2] vi. 446. **47.** Text in Mansi xii. 959—74; *P.L.* lxxxix. 511—24; Jaffé Nos. 2180—2 : for their spuriousness, L. Duchesne, *Liber Pontificalis* i. 413 sq. : and T. Hodgkin, *Italy and her invaders*, vi. 501 sqq. Note E. **48.** Germanus *Ep.* iv. (*P.G.* xcviii. 163—88). **49.** *Ib.* 168 C. **50.** *Ib.* 168 D.
51. *Ib.* 172 C. **52.** *Ib.* 172 D. **53.** *Ib.* 174 D. **54.** *Ib.* 185 B.
55. *Ib.* 188 A. **56.** Text of the *Orations* in *Op.* i. 307—90 (*P.G.* xciv. 1231—1420) : tr. M. H. Allies, *St. John Damascene on Miracles:* see also the summary of their argument in his *De fide orthodoxa* iv. § 16 (*Op.* i. 279—82 : *P.G.* xciv. 1167—76) tr. *N.* and *P.N.F.* and J. C. Ayers, *Source Book* 691; for summaries of the argument, see *D.C.B.* iii. 651 sqq. and J. Tixeront, *Hist. Dogm.* iii. 444 sqq.
57. *Orat.* i. § 4 (1236 C) οὐ τὴν ἀόρατον εἰκονίζω θεότητα, ἀλλ' εἰκονίζω Θεοῦ τὴν ὁραθεῖσαν σάρκα. **58.** Μὴ κάκιζε τὴν ὕλην· οὐ γὰρ ἄτιμος § 16 (1245 C). **59.** Ἡ γὰρ τῆς εἰκόνος τιμὴ πρὸς τὸ πρωτότυπον διαβαίνει (1252 D) quoting Basil *De Sp. sancto* § 45 (*Op.* iv. 38; *P.G.* xxxii. 149 C). **60** ἡ τῆς λατρείας προσκύνησις and ἡ ἐκ τιμῆς προσαγομένη τοῖς κατά τι ἀξίωμα ὑπερέχουσιν § 8 (1240 B). **61.** *Orat.* ii. § 5 (*Op.* i. 331 sq. : *P.G.* xciv. 1288 A, B). **62.** *Orat.* i. § 16 (1248 B). **63.** *Ib.* i. § 16 (1246 C). **64.** *Ib.* ii. § 19 (130 6B). **65.** Οὐδὲ μία χελιδὼν ἔαρ ποιεῖ : *Ib.* i. § 25 (1257 B) : Greg. Naz. *Orat.*, xxxviii. *(sic.)* but I cannot find it there: and it comes from Aristotle, *Ethics* I. vii. § 16. **66.** *Ib.* i. § 27 (1260 sqq.). **67.** *Ib.* i. § 17 (1248 C).
68. *Ib.* i. § 27 (1264 B). **69.** *Ib.* ii. § 14 (1300 B). **70.** *Ib.* i.

§ 27 (1281 B).   **71.** *Ib.* ii. § 12 (1296 C).   **72.** Hodgkin, vi. 461.
73. Mansi xii. 299—300 : Hefele § 333.   **74.** Hodgkin, vi. 463—5.
75. *Supra* § 2.   **76.** Hefele § 336 : Mansi xiii. 205—363.   Its *acta*
are embodied there in those of the sixth session of Nicæa II.; where
its decrees were read by Gregory, Bp. of Neocæsarea *(italics)* followed
by a refutation read by John the Deacon (rom).   **77.** And metropolitan of Pamphylia II.   **78.** Exod. xx. 4; Deut. v. 8; Mansi xiii.
283 C.   **79.** Rom. i. 23—5 : Mansi xiii. 285 B.   **80.** Mansi xiii. 255 A.
81. *Ib.* 251 A, 259 B.   **82.** *Ib.* 261—3.   **83.** *Ib.* 356 D.   **84.** Hefele
§ 339.   **85.** *E.R.E.* vii. 79 : J. B. Bury, *L.R.E.* ii. 477 ; Hefele § 344.
86. Bury, *L.R.E.* ii. 494 sqq.   **87.** Bury, *L.R.E.* ii. 458.   **88.** Mansi
xiii. 985 B.   **89.** *Ib.* 986 A : Hefele § 345.   **90.** Hadrian *Ep.* lvi.
(*Deus, qui dixit*: 26th Oct., 785) in *P.L.* xcvi. 1215—34 : Mansi xii.
1055—72 : Jaffé No. 2448 : Hefele § 345 (vi. 349 sqq.).   **91.** Hefele § 346.
92. Mansi xii. 951 sqq. : Hefele § § 347—57.   **93.** Session IV.
H. § 351.   **94.** This is significant of his policy : eccl. independence
in questions of dogma, but supremacy of the State in all matters of
law and administration—a " tiers parti " between the absolutism of
Justinian, Leo III. and Const. V. and the independence advocated by
Theodore of the Studium †828 : Bury, *Eastern Roman Empire*, 31 sq.
95. Mansi xiii. 203—64 : Hefele § 353.   **96.** Mansi xiii. 373—400 :
H. § 354.   **97.** Ἀσπασμὸν καὶ τιμητικὴν προσκύνησιν, οὐ μὴν τὴν
κατὰ πίστιν ἡμῶν λατρείαν ἣ πρέπει μόνῃ τῇ θείᾳ φύσει Mansi xiii.
377 D.   **98.** *Ib.* 400 C.   **99.** *Ib.* 420 sq. : Hefele vi. 379.
100. J. B. Bury, *L.R.E.* ii. 483.   **101.** *Ib.* 493.   **102.** *Ib.*
506—8.   **103.** J. B. Bury, *The Eastern Roman Empire*, 802—67,
c. 1, § 1.   **104.** Bury, *E.R.E.* 9, 38.   **105.** N., like his father, was
an Imperial Secretary : whence, perhaps, his moderation. As to his
learning, he wrote (1) a *Breviarium*, covering A.D. 602—769 (*P.G.*
c. 863—94) and (2) a *Chronographia Brevis* to A.D. 829 (*ib.* 995—
1060) : see K. Krumbacher, *Geschichte der Byz. Litt.* 71 sq., 349 sq.
106. For whom, see Alice Gardner, *Theodore of Studium* (Arnold,
1905) : works in *P.G.* xcix.   His life : b. 759; influence of his
mother's brother Plato, abbot of Saccundium, led him, 781, to enter
monastic profession; 787, ordained priest; 799, abbot of Studium;
795—7, first banishment; 809—11, second; 815—21, third; 826, death :
see Krumbacher, 147 sqq., 712 sqq.   His line was Papalism to avoid
Cæsaropapism : Bury, 66.   **107.** To Leo III., 795—†816, "in more than
Byzantine terms of adulation " (Gardner, 126) in *Ep.* II. xxxiii.
(*P.G.* xcix. 1017—22; and to Paschal I., 817—†24, in [817—8], *Epp.*
II. xii., xiii. (*P.G.* xcix. 1151—6).   Leo " declined to commit himself." Bury, *E.R.E.* 37.   **108.** Bury, *E.R.E.* 39 sqq.   **109.** *Ib.* 352—
3 : he survived till †845.   **110.** *Ib.* 62.   **111.** *Ib.* 67.   **112.** *Ib.* 68.
113. *Ib.* 69, who gives the decree : and references to further
authorities.   **114.** Best evidence in Theodore St. *Ep.* II. xii. and xiv.
to Pope Paschal I. and the Patriarch of Alexandria (*P.G.* xcix.
1151—60); Bury, 71 sqq.   **115.** Michael the Amorian married, as his
second wife, Euphrosyne, the daughter of Constantine VI.
116. Bury 113.   **117.** "Conjurer with a dish."   **118.** This is a revised
account of the " persecution," acc. to B. 135—43.   **119.** Bury, 145
and n. 4. Logothete of the Course=Postmaster General.   **120.** *Ib.*
147 sq. : Mansi xiv. 787—8.   **121.** H. H. Milman, *Lat. Chr.*[4] ii. 342.
122. *Enc. Brit.*[11] xx. 959—62 s. v. " Paulicians " by F. C. Conybeare :
and Bury, *E.R.E.* 276—8. See also Hastings, *E.R.E.* ix. 695—8.

123. *Codex Scorialensis* in the Library of the Escorial *E.R.E.* ix. 695.   **124.** F. C. Conybeare, *The Key of Truth*, cvi.   **125.** *Ib.* cxvi.   **126.** J. E. Bury, *E.R.E.* 278 n. 2.   **127.** "The Paulicians are best understood as a section in that continuous stream of anti-Catholic and anti-hierarchical thought and life which runs parallel with the stream of orthodox doctrine and organisation practically throughout the history of the Church." *E.R.E.* ix. 697.   **128.** J. B. Bury, *E.R.E.* 379 n. 3.   **129.** *Ib.* 395 sq.: see Map IV. A in K. Heussi and H. Mulert, *Atlas zur Kirchengeschichte*.   **130.** *Enc. Brit.*[11] xviii. 817. **131.** J. B. Bury, *E.R.E.* 392—401.   **132.** "His functions were partly those of a Minister of Foreign Affairs": J. B. Bury, *Sclavonic Settlements*, p. 42 (S.P.C.K.: 1920).   **133.** Pope John VIII., 872— †82, wrote twice to Methodius forbidding him to say Mass in Slavonic, and requiring it to be said either in Greek or in Latin. Jaffé No. 2978 (May, 873) and No. 3268 (14th June, 879). He then sent for Methodius, who came to Rome and offered explanation. These Pope John accepted: and changed mild remonstrance into willing approval. See Jaffé No. 3319, of June, 880.   **134.** Bury, *E.R.E.* 401.   **135.** John VIII. *Ep.* ccxciii. (*P.L.* cxxvi. 906 C) Jaffé No. 3319.   **136.** The date is fixed by (1) Pope Nicholas I. who speaks of the conversion of Boris as a project in *Ep.* lxi. § 12 (*P.L.* cxix. 875 C.: Jaffé No. 2758) of May, 864; (2) Hincmar, *Annales ad ann*, 864, says it is expected in Germany, *Mon. Germ. Hist. Scriptorum*, i. 465, ed. G. H. Pertz; and (3) Photius, *Ep.* xiii. § 4 (*P.G.* cii. 724) who writing at the end of 866 says it is not quite two years since the Bulgarians became Christians.   **137.** *Enc. Brit.*[11] iv. 772.   **138.** *See below*, cap. xiii. § 7.   **139.** Under whom "the policy of the Franks . . . aimed at the extension of their power over the Slavonic states on their S. E. frontier," and particularly "destroying the independence of the Slavonic Kingdom of Great Moravia." J. B. Bury, *E.R.E.* 382 sq.   **140.** *Ib.* 386.   **141.** J. B. Bury, *E.R.E.* 387 sqq.   **142.** Nicholas I. *Responsa ad Bulgaros*, 14, 106.   **143.** Photius, *Epp.* I. viii. (*Op.* ii.: *P.G.* cii. 627—96). **144.** *Responsa*, 106.   **145.** *Responsa*, 37, 76.   **146.** Text in Nicholas *Ep.* xcvii. (*P.L.* cxix. 978—1016) and Mansi xv. 401—34: Jaffé No. 2812.   **147.** Matt. xvi. 19; xviii. 18.   **148.** J. B. Bury, *E.R.E.* 392.   **149.** Photius *Epp.* I. xiii. § § 3, 4 (*Op.* ii.: *P.G.* cii. 724). **150.** I. Silbernagl, *Verfassung* . . . . . *Kirchen des Orients*, § 38. **151.** J. C. Robertson, *Hist. Chr. Ch.* iii. 443. Bulgaria was (1) converted by Latin bishops, 866—70, chief of whom was Formosus, afterwards pope, 891—†6; (2) next taught by Greek bishops, 870—86; and (3) finally by Slavonic bishops, 886 onwards, Gorazd, Nahum, Clement, Sabbas, Angelar, etc., the followers of St. Methodius who, on his death, were expelled from Moravia: *Dict. Th. Cath.* ii. 1181: of these, Gorazd and Clement were the first two archbishops of Bulgaria. Under Boris and his son Symeon, they carried the work and the traditions of C. and M. throughout Bulgaria: and acclimatised the Slavonic Liturgy there, which afterwards spread throughout all Slav peoples.   **152.** J. B. Bury, *E.R.E.* 419. **153.** *Ibid.* c. vi. "Photius and Ignatius."   **154.** J. B. Bury, *E.R.E.* 14 n. 2.   **155.** "To Bardas belongs the credit of having systematically undertaken the task of establishing a school of learning. He revived . . . the University of CP., which had been instituted by Theodosius II., and allowed to decay and disappear under the Heraclian and Isaurian dynasties." Leo the mathematician, afterwards abp. of Thessalonica, 840—3; Photius, Patriarch of CP., 858—69; and Constantine (Cyril), Apostle of the Slavs, †869, were its three eminent teachers : it was known as "The School of Magnaura," being housed in the palace of that name. " Since the age of Theophilus and Bardas ... there was no interruption ... in the literary activity of the Greeks, till the final fall of CP." *Ib.* 435, 439. **156.** Hauck-Herzog, *Realencyclopädie*[3] XV. 374—393 : *Enc. Brit.*[11] xxi. 483 sq. : and K. Krumbacher, *Gesch. der Byz. Litt.* 73—9, 515—24. **157.** His aunt by marriage was a sister of the Empress, *ib.* 156 n. 1. **158.** Photius, *Op.* iii.—iv. 1—545 B (*P.G.* ciii. 41—1588 : civ. 9—356) : tr. J. H. Freese. **159.** This was quite a safe assumption. "The possession of literary education by laymen generally and women was a deep-reaching distinction between Byzantine civilisation and the barbarous West, where the field of letters was monopolised by ecclesiastics. It constituted one of the most indisputable claims of Byzantium to superiority, and it had an important social result ... layman and cleric met on common ground; and ecclesiastics never obtained the influence, or played the part, in administration and politics which their virtually exclusive possession of letters procured for them in Western Europe": J. B. Bury, *E.R.E.* 434 sq. **160.** Photius, *Op.* i. (*P.G.* cii. 45—1172). **161.** Antioch, at this time, was vacant: so the Ἐνθρονιστικὴ Ἐπιστολὴ was addressed to the Steward and Chaplain of the See, q.v. in Photius, *Op.* ii.(*P.G.* cii. 1017—24). **162.** Nicholas *Ep.* iv. (*P.L.* cxix. 776 D) : Bury, *E.R.E.* 193 n. 2. **163.** Photius *Ep.* I. i. (*Op.* ii. *P.G.* cii. 585—94). **164.** Bury *E.R.E.* 193. **165.** They are the first to be called " *Legati a latere.*" Hefele—Leclercq iv. i. 273. **166.** Nicholas I. *Ep.*4 (*P.L.* cxix. 773—9) : Mansi xv. 162—7; Jaffé No. 2682; H. § 464. **167.** Bury *E.R.E.* 195 n. 1. **168.** Nich. *Ep.* 4 (*P.L.* cxix. 779 A). **169.** Nicholas I. *Ep.* 5 (*P.L.* cxix. 780) : *Omnis utilitas:* Mansi xv. 168. **170.** Bury *E.R.E.* 195 n. 1. **171.** Ἀφαιρεῖται ἀφ' ἡμῶν τὸ ἥμιτυ τῆς ἀρχῆς : Photius *Ep.* iii. (To Bardas)—*Op.* ii. (*P.G.* cii. 620 D). **172.** "Longa exsilia et diuturnas pediculorum comestiones," Nich. *Ep.* 12 (*P.L.* cxix. 790 A). **173.** Mansi xv. 595—8 : Hefele—Leclercq § 464, IV. i. 275. **174.** Photius *Epp.* I. ii. (*Op.* ii. *P.G.* cii. 593—618). **175.** Hefele § 464. **176.** *Quod igitur, Ep.* ii. (*P.L.* cxix. 783—5) ; Mansi xv. 168—70; Jaffé 2690. **177.** *Postquam beato Petro: Ep.* 12 (*P.L.* cxix. 785—90) : Mansi xv. 174—8 : Jaffé 2691. **178.** *Serenissimi imperii: Ep.* 13 (*P.L.* cxix. 790—4) : Mansi xv. 170—4 : Jaffé 2692. **179.** Et ideo consequens est ut quod ab hujus sedis rectoribus plena auctoritate sancitur, nullius consuetudinis praepediente occasione proprias tantum sequendo voluntates, removeatur; sed firmius et inconcusse teneat—*Ep.* 12 (*P.L.* cxix. 786 C) : to Photius. **180.** Mansi xvi. 293—302. **181.** *Acta* in Nicholas *Ep.* xlvi. (*P.L.* cxix. 850—5); Mansi xv. 178—82 : Jaffé i. p. 350; Hefele—Leclercq § 470, IV. i. 326 sqq. **182.** The Emperor's letter is lost: but recoverable from *Proposueramus quidem*=Nicholas I. *Ep.* 86 (*P.L.* cxix. 926—62). The Pope describes it as "tota blasphemiis, tota injuriis plena " (927 A) : Mansi xv. 186—216; Hefele § 476. **183.** *P.L.* cxix. 932 C. **184.** *Ib.* **185.** Hefele § 479 (ed. Leclercq IV. i. 442 sqq.). **186.** Photius *Ep.* xiii. § § 4—27 (*Op.* ii. *P.G.* cii. 723—32). The real cause lay deeper, in the total denial of the papal supremacy by the Greeks; and their unequivocal assertion that, with the Empire, that supremacy had passed to CP.: H. H. Milman, *Lat. Chr.*[4] iii. 166: *cf.* Nicholas I. to Hincmar of Rheims: Cum etiam glorientur [sc. the Greeks] et perhibeant quando de Romana Urbe Imperatores olim Constantinopolim sunt translati, hinc et primatum R. sedis ad Constantinopolitanam ecclesiam transmigrasse et cum dignitatibus regiis etiam ecclesiae Romanae privilegia: *Ep.* cii. [A.D. 867] (*P.L.* cxix. 1157 B). **187.** Photius *Ep.* xiii. § 37 (*Op.* ii.: *P.G.* cii. 738 C). **188.** Hefele § 469 (Leclercq IV. i. 332). **189.** The marriage took place at Christmas, 862: Hefele § 466 (Leclercq IV. i. 295). **190.** Mansi xv. 649—58 [Nicholas *Ep. Scelus quod*] 30th Oct., 867: Jaffé No. 2748; and Nicholas *Ep.* clv. (*P.L.* cxix. 1167 B)=*Ep.* lviii. in Mansi xv. 336 D: of 31st Oct., 867, Jaffé No. 2886: Hefele § 470 (Leclercq IV. i. 333). **191.** Hefele § 470 (Leclercq IV. i. 336—7). **192.** Mansi xv. 803—4; Hefele § 479 (Leclercq IV. i. 448). **193.** Mansi xvi. 1 sqq. Hefele § § 487—95 (Leclercq IV. i. 480 sqq.) **194.** At the seventh session, 29th Oct., they anathematised Photius: Mansi xvi. 133 B, C., and Hefele § 491. **195.** Hefele § 496. **196.** Paul, bishop of Ancona, and Eugenius, bishop of Ostia: commissioned 16th April, 878, by *Benedictus Deus* of John VIII. to Basil I.: *Ep.* cxiii. (*P.L.* cxxvi. 766 C): Mansi xvii. 70 B: Jaffé No. 3135. **197.** Pope John wanted the aid of the Emperor Basil against the Saracens: *Ep.* cxiv.—*Scimus, venerabilis*—of 26th February, 878—*P.L.* cxxvi. 767: Mansi xvii. 70: Jaffé No. 3118: Hefele § 496 (Leclercq IV. i. 562). **198.** In the fifth session, 26th Jan., 880; Mansi xvii. 508 B.: H. § 498 (H. Leclercq IV. i. 601). **199.** In letters of 13th August, 880, to (1) the Emperor—*Post innumeras*, and (2) Photius—*Hoc nostri: Epp.* ccxcvi., ccxcvii. (*P.L.* cxxvi. 909—11); Mansi xvii. 184—7; Hefele § 498 (Leclercq IV. i. 605—6). **200.** Mansi xvi. 449 A, B: Hefele § 499 (Leclercq IV. i. 607). **201.** Hefele § 499 (Leclercq IV. i. 609 n. 2). **202.** For this date, *ib.* p. 612.

CHAPTER VIII.

1. Du Cange, *Fam. Byz.* xx. (*Corp. Byz.* xxiv. 124). **2.** Du Cange, *Fam. Byz.* No. xxii. **3.** *Ib.* No. xxi.: Bury's Gibbon v. 210 n. 48 **4.** *Ib.* No. xxii. **5.** *Ib.* No. xxiii. **6.** The favourite of the Empress Helena. **7.** Du Cange, *Fam. Byz.* xx. (*Corp. Byz.* xxiv. 124): Bury's Gibbon v. 215 n. 56. **8.** *Enc. Br.*[11] iv. 119 sqq.: see also Gibbon c. liv. n. 32 (vi. 122 ed. Bury) and app. 6 "The Paulician heresy," for very diverse views. **9.** Now Eski Stambul, 22 kilometres south of Shumla—Gibbon c. lv. n. 90 (v. 160, ed. Bury). **10.** J. Gay, *L'Italie méridionale et l'empire byzantine, 867—1071* (Paris, 1904). **11.** Gay, 52. **12.** Gay, 109. **13.** Gay, 110. **14.** *Ib.* 114. **15.** *Ib.* 132. **16.** *Ib.* 162 sq. **17.** The ancient Cannae: *ib.* 411. **18.** *Ib.* 254 sqq., 376 sqq. Basilians *v.* Benedictines. **19.** *Ib.* 184 sqq. **20.** *Ib.* 304 sq. **21.** *Ib.* 319. **22.** *Ib.* 337—40. **23.** *Ib.* 422. **24.** *Ib.* 428—9. **25.** G. Finlay, *Hist. Byz. Emp.* 357 (Dent: Everyman's Library). **26.** Gay, 375. **27.** *Ib.* 374. **28.** The Croats entered Croatia, 634—8. ... In 806, N. and N.E. districts were added to the Empire of the Franks, and thus won for the Western Church. ... In 877 the Croats were temporarily subdued by the Byzantine Emperor, Basil I.; and became Orthodox Christians. *Enc. Br.*[11]. vii. 474.   **29.** " From the eighth to the twelfth century, the bulk of the Serbs were under either Bulgarian or Greek suzerainty, while the Serbo-Croat provinces of Dalmatia acknowledged either Venetian or Hungarian supremacy... The Bulgarian danger and the ... successful operations of Basil I. determined the Serbian Zhupans to acknowledge" him and "the entire Serbian people embraced Christianity 871—5": *Enc. Brit.*[11] xxiv. 691.   **30.** H. Gelzer, *ap.* Krumbacher, *Byz. Litt.* 997.   **31.** See C. R. Beazley, N. Forbes and G. A. Birkett, *Russia from the Varangians to the Bolsheviks* (Clar. Press, 1918); W. H. Frere, *Links in the chain of Russian Church History* (Faith Press, 1918); W. F. Reddaway, *Introduction to the study of Russian History* (S.P.C.K., 1920: "Helps for students of History," No. 25); A. Ramband, *Hist. de la Russie*[6] (Paris, 1914); E. Tr. by Mrs. L. B. Lang (Sampson Low, 1879); R. F. Bigg-Wither, *A Short History of the Church of Russia* (S.P.C.K., 1920); A. N. Mouravieff, *A Hist. of the Church of Russia,* tr. R. W. Blackmore (Oxford, 1842); H. Y. Reyburn, *The Story of the Russian Church* (Melrose, 1924); G. F. Maclear, *Hist. Chr. Missions during the Middle Ages* (Macmillan, 1863); J. B. Mozley, in *The Christian Remembrancer,* X. 245 sqq., and A. M. H. J. Stokvis, *Manuel* ii. 336.

THE GRAND DUKES OF KIEV.

(1) Rurik 862—†79   (2) Oleg 879—†912

(3) Igor I. 912—†45=Olga, regent 945—64 (†969)

(4) Sviatoslav I. 945—†73

(5) Yaropolk 973—†80   (6) Vladimir I. 980—†1015

(7) Sviatopolk I. 1015—†9.   (8) Yaroslav I. 1019—†54

32. Beazley, 3 sq.   **33.** It covers the years 850—1110; and was written by an unknown monk of the Pecherskaia Lavra at Kiev, c. 1100: Frere, 5, n. 2.   **34.** " Nestor," *Chr.* xv.   **35.** *Chr. de Nestor* xvi.—" In the fourteenth year of Michael " III., i.e., 865. **36.** Photius, *De Rossorum incursione homiliae duae,* ap. *Fragm. Hist. Graec.* v. 162—73.   **37.** *Chr. de Nestor* xviii.   **38.** Photius *Ep.* I. xiii. § 35 (*Op.* ii.: *P.G.* cii. 736 sq.).   **39.** Const. Porph., *De cerimoniis aulae Byzantinae* ii. 15 (*Op.* i. 343 sqq.; *P.G.* cxii. 1107 sqq.). **40.** *Chr. de Nestor* xxxi.   **41.** *Ib.* xxxviii.   **42.** *Ib.*   **43.** *Ib.* **44.** *Chr. de Nestor* xl.   **45.** *Ib.* xli.   **46.** *Ib.* xl.   **47.** *Ib.* xli. **48.** *Chr. de Nestor* xlii.   **49.** *Ib.* xliii.   **50.** W. H. Frere, *Links in the chain of Russian Church History,* 19 n. 2: q.v. for the rest of this paragraph.   **51.** J. Pargoire, *L'église byzantine,* 78. John had formerly been a barrister (scholasticus) at Antioch: K. Krumbacher, *Gesch. der byz. Litt.*[2] 607.   **52.** *Ib.* 202.   **53.** *Ib.* 318.   **54.** Photius, *Op.* iv.: *P.G.* civ. 975—1218; K. K. assigns it to Th. Bestes, 1090. **55.** *P.G.* cxxxiv., cxxxv. for his *Annals:* cxxxvii., cxxxviii. for his comments.   **56.** *P.G.* cxxxvii., cxxxviii.: Theodore Balsamon, Patriarch of Antioch, †1204 K.K. 607.   **57.** *P.G.* cxliv. 959—cxlv. 212. Its title is: *Syntagma alphabeticum rerum omnium quae in* ....

canonibus comprehenduntur, K.K. 608. **58.** The Lateran Synod of April, 863: see Hefele § 470 (ed. Leclercq, iv. 326 sqq.); and *supra* c. vii. § 10 (p. 174 n. 181). **59.** *Ib.* § 476. **60.** In spite of seven more letters of 13th Nov., 866, all sent by Pope Nicholas to important persons at CP., Hefele § 477. **61.** Paul, bishop of Populonia in Tuscany, and Formosus, bishop of Porto, sent, Nov., 866, with the *Responsa ad consulta Bulgarorum:* Hefele § 478. **62.** Photius *Ep.* xiii. (*Op.* ii.; *P.G.* cii. 721—42). **63.** Hefele § 479 (*Conciles,* ed. Leclercq iv. 448). **64.** Hefele § 481. **65.** *Ib.* §§ 487—93. **66.** At the seventh session—Hefele § 491. **67.** Hefele § 498. **68.** For the works of Leo VI. (Philosophus), see *P.G.* cvii: and for the eccl. hist. of his reign, see *Vita Euthymii*, written soon after his death, 917 (ed. C. de Boor, 1888). Bury's Gibbon v. 504 and Krumbacher, *Gesch. der byz. Litt.* 312 sq. **69.** See note of H. Leclercq in Hefele § 499: *Conciles* iv. 609 n. 2. **70.** *Fam. Byz.* 119 in *Corp. Byz.* xxiv. **71.** Mansi xvi. 425—38. It contains a complete survey of the life of Photius, from the Ignatian side. **72.** *Ib.* 433 C. **73.** *Ib.* 436 D. **74.** Mansi xvi. 436 E. **75.** For the letters of Nicholas I., see *P.G.* cxi. 1—392: and Krumbacher, 458 sq. **76.** Daughter of Stylianus Zautzes, like Basil—a "Macedonian" of Armenian descent—to whom Basil, on his deathbed, committed the charge of the State. He received the title Basileopator, on the marriage of Zoe to Leo, 894, and died 896. Bury's Gibbon, v. 206 n. 41. **77.** Second *Novel* of Basil I.: see J. A. B. Mortreuil, *Hist. du droit byz.* 565—1453 (2 vols. Paris, 1843) ii. 280. **78.** For his fourth wife: although he had himself forbidden third marriages. *Const.* xc. (*P.G.* cvii. 603). **79.** L. Duchesne, *The Churches separated from Rome*, 154. **80.** q.v. in *P.G.* cvii. 367 sq., or in J. Leunclavius, *Jus Graeco-Romanum*, Francofurti, 1596, ii. 88—102, and note esp. § lvii. [J. Loewenklau, 1533—†93.] **81.** H. Gelzer, *Abriss* ap. K. Krumbacher, *Gesch. der byz. Litt.* 976. **82.** H. H. Milman, *Latin Christianity*, iii. 279 sqq. **83.** J. B. Bury in *Enc. Brit.*[11] xxiii. 521. **84.** *Ib.* 575. **85.** *Ib.* 521. **86.** Nicholas *Ep.* liii. (to Pope John X., 914—†29): *P.G.* cxi. 249 A. **87.** Mansi xviii. 331—42; or J. Leunclavius, *Jus Graeco-Romanum* i. 104—8; Mortreuil ii. 348—9. **88.** *Ibid. Epp.* liii.—lvi.: and lxxvii. **89.** q.v. in *P.G.* cix. 225—370; cxii., cxiii.: and, for introduction, K. Krumbacher, *Gesch. der byz. Litt.* 252 sqq. **90.** For the reigns of Romanus II., Nicephorus II. and John Tzimisces, i.e., for 959—76, the chief authority is the history of Leo Diaconus (Leo Asiaticus). He was born 950; accompanied Basil II. in the wars against Bulgaria, 986, and wrote after 992. His history is the work of a contemporary, dependent upon personal knowledge of eye-witnesses and on his own observation—not on previous writers: Bury's Gibbon v. 504; Krumbacher, 266 sqq. The text is in *P.G.* cxvii. 635—926. For the reign of R. II. see cc. i.—iv. of G. L. Schlumberger, *Un empereur byzantine au Xme siècle* (Paris, 1890). **91.** Leo Diaconus, *Hist.* iii. 8 (*P.G.* cxvii. 732 A). **92.** *Ib.* iii. 9 (*P.G.* cxvii. 733 A). **93.** *Fam. Byz.* xxi. (*Corp. Byz.* xxiv. 126): and for the detailed history of his reign, G. L. Schlumberger, *Un empereur byzantine au Xme siècle: Nicéphore Phocas*, 1890. **94.** *Novel* 2, ap. J. A. B. Mortreuil, *Hist. du droit byz.* ii. 353: and, for comments, G. L. Schlumberger, *Un emp. byz.* 389 sq. **95.** G. Finlay, *Hist. Gr.* ii. 328 sq. **96.** G. L. Schlumberger, *Un emp. byz.* 312 sqq. **97.** Krumbacher, 315; Bury's Gibbon v. 212 n. 52:

and for his aid in money, Schlumberger, 387. **98**. M. Le Quien, *Oriens Christianus* ii. 1377—9. Similar proceedings under Romanus III. (Argyrus) 1028—†34 led to a day of reckoning. The Syrians went over in large numbers to Islam; and so prepared the way for the great loss of eastern provinces consequent upon the Turkish victory at Manazkert, 1071. Gelzer in Krumbacher, 999. **99**. Leo Diaconus v. 5—8 (*P.G.* cxvii. 780—9). **100**. Finlay, iii. 334. **101**. Gibbon, c. xlviii. n. 53 (ed. Bury v. 214). **102**. Finlay, iii. 338 sq.: Gibbon, c. liv. (vi. 121 : ed. Bury). **103**. Gibbon, c. lv. (vi. 160 : ed. Bury). **104**. *Ib.* c. xlviii. n. 56 (ed. Bury v. 215). **105**. On the details see *ib.* c. xlviii. n. 58 (v. 216) from G. Schlumberger, *L'épopée byzantine*, cc. vi., vii., xi., which covers the reigns of John Tzimisces and the first thirteen years of Basil II **106**. Text in J. Leunclavius, *Jus Graeco-Rom.* i. 113—7 : Mortreuil ii. 353. **107**. J. Leunclavius, *Jus. Gr.-Rom.* i. 117—8; J. A. B. Mortreuil, *Hist. du droit byz.* ii. 357. **108**. Gibbon c. lv. n. 100 (vi. 164) for date. **109**. For details, see *ib.* c. lv. n. 23 (vi. 136) : Finlay iii. 368 sqq. **110**. Finlay iii. 384 sqq. **111**. *Ib.* 386. **112**. *Ib.* 368. **113**. Gibbon, c. xlviii. (v. 217). **114**. J. Leunclavius, *Jus. Graeco-Rom.* ii. 155—8 : Mortreuil ii. 330 sqq. **115**. Mortreuil ii. 333. **116**. The *latifundia* were the ruin of the Empire in the eleventh century. They were cultivated by bondsmen and slaves. Under Melik-Shah, 1072—92, his cousin Suleiman gave them their freedom on payment of a poll-tax: and so bound the provinces conquered after Manazkert, 1071, to the Turkish interest : Krumbacher, 1012. **117**. *Novel* I. : J. Leunclavius, *Jus. Gr.-Rom.* ii. 138—41 : Mortreuil ii. 336—8. **118**. *Novel* I. : J. Leunclavius, *Jus. Gr.-Rom.* ii. 167—8 : Mortreuil ii. 350. **119**. *Novel* III. : J. Leunclavius, *Jus. Gr.-Rom.* ii. 170—1 : Mortreuil ii. 354. **120**. *Fam. Byz.* xxi. (*Corp. Byz.* xxiv. 126 sq.). **121**. *Fam. Byz.* xxiii. (*Corp. Byz.* xxiv. 129). **122**. G. L. Schlumberger, *L'épopée byzantine* i. 397. **123**. *Ib.* i. 423. **124**. *Ib.* i. 693. **125**. *Novel* II. : J. Leunclavius, *Jus. Gr.-Rom.* ii. 172—9 : Mortreuil ii. 358. **126**. *Fam. Byz.* xxviii. (*Corp. Byz.* xxiv. 142 sqq.). **127**. *Novel* II. : J. Leunclavius, *Jus. Gr.-Rom.* i. 113—7 : Mortreuil ii. 353. **128**. *Novel* I. : J. Leunclavius, *Jus. Gr.-Rom.* i. 117—8 : Mortreuil ii. 357. **129**. J. Leunclavius, *Jus. Gr.-Rom.* i. 104—8. **130**. Formosus, *Ep.* ii. (*P.L.* cxxix. 840 A). **131**. H. Gelzer, *Abriss* c. vi. (K. Krumbacher, *Gesch. der byz. Litt.* 998—1014) : J. B. Bury : "Roman Emperors from Basil II. to Komnenos" in *E.H.R.* iv. (1889) 41—64, 251—85. **132**. For their portrait and character, see G. L. Schlumberger, *L'ép. byz.* iii. 391 sq., and for their times, J. B. Bury, "Roman Emperors from Basil II. to Isaac Komnenos" in *Engl. Hist. Review* iv. 41—64, 251—85, Nos. 13, 14 : Jan. and April, 1889. **133**. *Fam. Byz.* xix. (*Corp. Byz.* xxiv. 122). **134**. *Ib.* xxiv. (*Corp. Byz.* xxiv. 131). **135**. G. L. Schlumberger, *L'épopée byzantine* iii. 529—42. **136**. *Fam. Byz.* xxiii. (*Corp. Byz.* xxiv. 129) : she was the niece of his second wife : for the event, G. L. Schlumberger, *L'ép. byz.* iii. 419. **137**. Michael (Stratioticus) VI. 1056—7 : Isaac I. [M.] (Comnenus) 1057—9; Constantine XI. [B.] (Ducas) 1059—67; Romanus IV. [M.] (Diogenes) 1067—71; Michael VII. [B.] (Ducas) [Parapinaces] 1071—8; Nicephorus III. (Botaniates) 1078—81. For genealogy, see H. B. George, *Genealogical Tables*[4] No. xlviii. [M.=military party : B.=bureaucratic party : Michael Cerularius (M.) set up I.C. : Psellus (B.)=P.M. of M. VII.]. **138**. "Konstan-

KK

tin XI. eröffnet die Dukasära, die unglückliche Epoche der herschen den Bureaukraten, Rhetoren u. Gelehrten," etc., see Krumbacher 1006 sq. **139.** They were "driven into Europe from the lower Ural at the end of the ninth century and wandered about the northern frontiers of the Byzantine Empire for about 300 years," *Enc. Brit.*[11] xxvii. 470. **140.** G. L. Schlumberger, *L'épopée byz.* iii. 201 : K. 1004. **141.** *Ib.* iii. 287 sqq. : H. Gelzer *ap.* K. Krumbacher, 1001. **142.** Its consequence was the separation of the autocephalous church of Ochrida, Krumbacher, 1002. **143.** *Ib.* iii. 311 sqq.; 446 sqq. **144.** Gibbon, c. lvi. (vi. 184 sqq.) : see map, p. 174. **145.** He was fourth son of Tancred de Hauteville : Stokvis iii. 698 : [Guiscard (Wiscard)=Wise] and H. B. George, *Genealogical Tables*[4] xiii. and xlix.* **146.** Catapan, i.e., κατεπάνω τῶν ἀξιωμάτων : he who is placed over the dignities, or the officer who governed Calabria and Apulia under the Byz. Emperors. **147.** G. L. Schlumberger, *L'ép. byz.* iii. 435 : by his victory at Monopoli (Krumbacher 1003). **148.** It was in consequence of the animosities between E. and W. enkindled in these wars that the breach between Leo IX. and Michael Cerularius occurred : Krumbacher 1003 sq. **149.** Gibbon c. lvii. (vi. 231 sqq. ed. Bury). **150.** Since the Romans took Ani, 1045. The Orthodox clergy greedily seized the bishoprics and abbeys; summoned the Catholicus Peter, †1056 to CP.; and interfered with the choice of his successor. Krumbacher, 1004. **151.** *Ib.* c. lvii. (vi. 236) n. 30. **152.** Krumbacher, 1010. **153.** Finlay iii. 48 sq. **154.** Krumbacher, 1003 : *E.H.R.* iv. 271. **155.** Krumbacher, 1005 : *E.H.R.* iv. 272 sq. **156.** Harald III. (Hardraada), "Man of hard counsel" King of Norway, 1047—†66. He was the uterine brother of Olaf II. (St. Olaf, †1030); and, after their defeat, fled to Russia, then dominated by his countrymen the Varangians. He took service in the Varangian Guard under Romanus III. (Argyrus) and his wife, the Empress Zoe, 1028—†50 : amassed great wealth as mercenary and pirate; and was imprisoned by Zoe to make him disgorge it. But he escaped to Russia, and thence to Sweden : where he plotted to dethrone Magnus I., son of St. Olaf, and King of Norway, 1030—†47. He succeeded : and built Opslo (Christiania) 1048 as a naval base against the Danes. Defeated by them, 1062, he accepted the invitation of Tostig, brother of Harold, King of England, to invade the country. He was defeated and slain at Stamford Bridge, on the Derwent, between York and Malton, 25th Sept., 1066. **157.** Krumbacher § 184 (pp. 433 sqq.) : *E.H.R.* iv. 42 sqq. His *History* covers 976—1077 and from 1034 has "the value of contemporary history." **158** Krumbacher, § 78 (pp. 170 sqq.) : *E.H.R.* iv. 268 : he was Joannes Nomophylax, the scholiast on the *Basilika*. **159.** Its original founder was Theodosius II., 408—†50; but it lasted only for 300 years, being closed by the Iconoclast Leo III., 717—†41, because the professors refused to support his religious doctrines, *E.H.R.* iv. 266 sq. **160.** *E.H.R.* iv. 265 sqq. **161.** *E.H.R.* iv. 59 sqq. Of the five brothers, John possessed the most political talent, Michael IV. the most religion and virtue (he was ascetic, and, like Theodora and Justinian, spent large sums on the reclamation of prostitutes), while the other three (all eunuchs) were Nicetas, Constantine and George. The whole family were very unpopular; and Michael IV. was involved in their unpopularity. Michael V. (nephew of M. IV. and adopted son of Zoe, known as Calaphates) was the first to turn against them, 1041—2; then the plotters who tried to substitute Cerularius. **162.** *E.H.R.* iv. 282. **163.** The claim of the patriarch of CP. to the title of "ecumenical" was first raised in the reign of Maurice, 582—†602, and was then resisted by Gregory I., 590—†604. The claim was of practical value in so far as it was connected with the subordination of the sees of Alexandria and Antioch to CP.; and thus Leo IX. writes that it is intolerable "quod nova ambitione Al. et Ant. patriarchas antiquis suae dignitatis privilegiis privare contendens contra fas et jus suo dominio subjugare conaretur"(*Ep.* cii. : *P.L.* cxliii. 774 B.). An attempt was made in 1024 to bribe the pope [the covetous John XIX.] into conceding the coveted title to the Byzantine bishop : *E.H.R.* iv. 283 n. 95 : and see M. Le Quien, *Or. Chr.* i. 89. **164.** A general account of the schism is given by Michael Psellus, in his *Logos Epitaphios* on Michael Cerularius q.v. in K. N. Sathas *Bibliotheca Graeca Medii Aevi,* iv. 303—87. **165.** *Ib.* 283. **166.** L. Bréhier, *Le schisme oriental du XIe siècle;* G. Schlumberger, *L'épopée byzantine* iii. 681 sqq.; Hefele, *Conciles* § 548 (ed. H. Leclercq IV. ii. 1076 sqq.). Texts in Cornelius Will, *Acta et scripta* (Lipsiae, 1861). **167.** Now San Paolo di Civitate, in the province of Foggia or Capitanate, in Apulia. **168.** It was his duty to do so, as the head of the Church to which they belonged. So H. Gelzer holds that Michael Cerularius acted under provocation (ap. Krumbacher 1003) : L. Bréhier, on the contrary, looks upon him as the attacking party. G. Schlumberger iii. 706 n. 5. But there was no love lost on either side : and it is not of serious moment who began it. Each was ready enough to take it up, and carry it on. **169.** Will, No. I.; *P.L.* cxliii. 793—8. **170.** Wibert, *Vita Leonis* IX. ii. § 9 (*P.L.* cxliii. 498 A). **171.** Will, No. II. : Mansi xix. 635—56; *P.L.* cxliii. 744—69; Jaffé, No. 4302. **172.** Text in C. Mirbt, *Quellen*[4] No. 228 : translation in E. F. Henderson, *Select Hist. Documents of the Middle Ages,* 319 sqq. : on it, see E. Denny, *Papalism,* § 1179. **173.** Will, No. III.; Mansi xix. 667—7; *P.L.* cxliii. 777—81; Jaffé No. 4333. **174.** Will, No. IV.; Mansi xix. 663—6; *P.L.* cxliii. 773—7. **175.** See supra 209 n. 163. **176.** Will, No. V. : *P.L.* cxliii. 931—74. **177.** Will, No. VI. : *P.L.* cxliii. 973—84. **178.** Will, No. VII. : *P.L.* cxliii. 983—1000. **179.** *Ib.* § 35 (Will, p. 150). **180.** Will, No. VIII. : *P.L.* cxliii. 1001—4; C. Mirbt, *Quellen zur Geschichte der Papsttums*[4] No. 268. **181.** Will, No. IX. **182.** Exodus v. 21. **183.** *Commemoratio* ap. C. Will 152 A, line 12. **184.** *Ib.* 152 B, line 7. **185.** Will, No. XI. **186.** M. Le Quien, *Or. Chr.* ii. 754. **187.** Will, Nos. XII.—XVII. **188.** L. Bréhier, *Le schisme oriental,* xxiv. sq. **189.** *P.L.* xiii. 374. **190.** J. B. Bury, in *E.H.R.* iv. 284, quoting Psellus, *Epitaph,* 354 (K. N. Sathas, *Bibl. Gr. Med. Aevi.,* vol. iv.). **191.** *Fam. Byz.* xxviii. (*Corp. Byz.* xxiv. 143). He was the son of Manuel Comnenus, a favourite officer of Basil II.; was educated in the monastery of the Studium; and then began his career in the Emperor's body-guard. Under the eye of the indefatigable Basil he learned the steady application to business and the active warlike habits of that prince; but with these virtues he acquired also something of the grave, melancholy and inflexible character of his patron. Finlay iii. 8. **192.** "He had been a general of some reputation, and an efficient member of the official establishment" but "he was a man of advanced age and limited capacity. The prime minister and the eunuchs of Theodora had suggested his nomination, because it promised to place on the throne one who could not avoid being an instrument in their hands," *ib.* ii. 449. **193.** *E.H.R.* iv. 284 sq. **194.** Finlay iii. 1—52. The authorities are: (1) John Scylitzes † c. 1090, and wrote a history of A.D. 811—1079. He was thus contemporary with the events from Isaac I. (Comnenus) to Alexius I. (Comnenus)—see Krumbacher § 151: Anna Comnena, 1083—†?, wrote, c. 1148, the history of the times of her father, Alexius Comnenus, 1069—1118: see Krumbacher § 121. **195.** "An avaricious pedant," Finlay iii. 13. **196.** He married the widow of Constantine XI., Eudocia Macrembolitissa, who was left with three little sons and wanted a guardian for them. *Ib.* iii. 23 sq. **197.** "The peck-filcher" because of his avarice. He sold wheat at short weight. He was "a learned grammarian, but a worthless sovereign." *Ib.* iii. 37 sq. See also *Fam. Byz.* xxvi. (*Corp. Byz.* xxiv. 137). **198.** Thus, by the fall of Bari, 15th April, 1071, four years after the Norman Conquest of England, another Norman conqueror put an end to the authority of the Roman Empire of the East in Italy. *Ib.* iii. 37. **199.** *Ib.* iii. 45 sq. **200.** *Ib.* iii. 47 sq. **201.** *Fam. Byz.* xxviii. (*Corp. Byz.* xxiv. 147). **202.** Finlay iii. 53—218: H. B. George, *Genealogical Tables*[4] No. xlviii.

CHAPTER IX.

1. Authorities for the Comneni: Nicephorus Bryennius, 1062—†1137, *Hist. of Alexius Comnenus,* covering 1070—9 (Krumbacher § 120; Bury's Gibbon, v. 506), and his wife, Anna Comnena, 1083—?†1150, who completed the work of her husband by (1148) writing the history of her father, 1069—1118, in the *Alexiad* (Krumbacher § 121: Bury's Gibbon v. 506); John Cinnamus, 1143—?†90, private secretary of Manuel I., 1143—†80, whose history covers 1118—76 (Krumbacher § 122; Bury's Gibbon v. 507); Nicetas Acominatus, c. 1150—?†1215, who filled most important posts under the Angeli, last of all Great Logothete, 1204, and wrote a history of 1180—1206; which, unlike those of Anna and Cinnamus, is fair to the Crusaders (Krumbacher § 123; Bury's Gibbon v. 507), and Gibbon c. xlviii. (v. 226 sqq.); H. Gelzer, in Krumbacher pp. 1014 sqq.: C. W. C. Oman, 256 sqq.; C. Diehl, 139 sqq.; E. A. Foord, *Byz. Emp.* 331 sqq.; Finlay, iii. 53 sqq. **2.** R. L. Poole, *Hist. Atlas of Modern Europe,* Map lxxiii. [Empire 1025—1472]. **3.** Gelzer, *Abriss, ap.* Krumbacher 1015 sqq. **4.** At Lebunion, 29th April, 1091. The European provinces were now clear of invaders, but they must have suffered greatly. **5.** Gelzer, *Abriss, ap.* Krumbacher, 1020 sqq. **6.** Gibbon c. xlviii. (v. 228). **7.** After his defeat, at Myriokephalon, Manuel asked for water. They brought it, with a crimson tinge. "Christian blood!" said the Emperor, as he dropped the glass in horror. "What of that, your Majesty?" was the reply. "You have drunk your subjects' blood all your reign!" **8.** Gibbon c. xlviii. n. 72 (v. 239 ed. Bury). **9.** *Ib.* v. 242. **10.** Gibbon cc. lviii., lix.; L. Bréhier, *L'église et l'Orient au Moyen Age: Les Croisades* (Paris, 1907); E. Barker, *The Crusades* (Clar. Press, 1923); Hefele—Leclercq, *Conciles* § 601 (v. 406 sqq.). **11.** The phrase is that of Guibert, *Gesta Dei per Francos* i. § 1. ap. *Recueil des Hist. des Croisades* [Historiens Occidentaux] iv. 124 E: [Guibert b. 1053: abbot of Nugent, 1104: see Gibbon vi. 524] Fulcher of Chartres, *Historia Hierosolymitana* (ed. H. Hagenmeyer, 1913: also in *P.L.* clv. 821—940: written 1127) says that Urban II. promised "remissio peccatorum" to all who lost their lives in the Crusade: see I. iii. 5; I. iv. 3. [a diary, of the highest importance: see Bury's Gibbon vi. 524]. **12.** Eus *V.C.* iii. 25—40. **13.** *Ib.* 42—3. **14.** *Ib.* 41. **15.** *Itineraria Hierosolymitana:* saec. iv.—viii. (ed. P. Geyer, Vindobonae, 1898) 1—33 (*C.S.E.L.* xxxix.): "*Itinerarium Burdigalense.*" **16.** J. Pargoire, *L'église byzantine,* 114. **17.** Cyril *Ep. ad Constantium* [of 7th May, 351] § 3 (*Op.* ii. 436: ed. G. C. Reischl). **18.** *S. Silviae peregrinatio ad loca sancta* (*C.S.E.L.* xxxix. 35—101). **19.** Jerome *Ep.* xlvii. [A.D. 393] § 2 (*Op.* i. 211: *P.L.* xxii. 493). **20.** *De situ terrae sanctae* (*C.S.E.L.* xxxix. 135—55). **21.** *Antonini Placentini Itinerarium* (*C.S.E.L.* xxxix. 156—218). **22.** *C.S.E.L.* xxxix. 219—97. **23.** Willibald: b. 700: sent, 705, to monastery of Bishop's Waltham in Hampshire; c. 720 went with his brother Wunebald and his father *ad limina apostolorum,* and thence to the East: see his *Odoeporicon* (or Itinerary) in *Acta SS.,* 7th July, ii. 501—12, tr. Thomas Wright, *Early Travels in Palestine,* 13—22 (Bohn's Library, 1848). He afterwards was consecrated bishop of Eichstädt, 741—†86, by his fellow-countryman, St. Boniface. **24.** Einhard, *Annales,* A.D. 800 (*Mon. Germ. Hist.,* Script. i. 187, ed. G. H. Pertz). **25.** Einhard, *Vita Caroli* § 16 (*Mon. Germ. Hist.,* Script ii. 451, ed. G. H. Pertz). **26.** Bernard, *Itinerarium* § 10 (*P.L.* cxxi. 571 sq.): tr. in T. Wright, *Early Travels in Palestine,* 26. **27.** M. Le Quien, *Oriens Christianus* iii. 496 B. **28.** *Vita Lietberti* c. 41 ap. *Mon. Germ. Hist.,* Script. vii. 536 n. 22. **29.** *P.L.* cxlix. 961 C: Jaffé No. 4342. **30.** *Annales Altahenses Majores* A.D. 1065 (*Mon. Germ. Hist.,* Script. xx. 815 line 23). **31.** Milman, *Latin Chr.*° iii. 398 sq.; G. F. Maclear, *Chr. Missions in the Middle Ages,* 286 n. 3 (Macmillan, 1863). **32.** Jaffé No. 4789. **33.** *Ib.* No. 4823. **34.** *Ib.* No. 4826. **35.** *Ib.* No. 4876. **36.** *Ib.* No. 4904. **37.** At the Council of Rome, 24th—28th Feb., 1075; H. H. Milman, *Latin Chr.*°: iv. 56 sqq. The strife issued in the Concordat of Worms, 23rd Sept., 1122, q.v. in Mirbt, *Quellen*⁴ No. 305. **38.** Jaffé, No. 4926. **39.** See H. Hagenmeyer, *Chronologie de la première croisade* ap. *Revue de l'Orient Latin* vi. 214—93 and vii. 273—478. **40.** Anna Comnena, *Alexias* vii. (*Op.* 201—2; *P.G.* cxxxi. 564—8). **41.** Bernold, *Chron.* ad ann 1095 ap. Mansi, *Concilia* xx. 802 E: Hefele—Leclercq § 601 (v. 419). **42.** Mansi xx. 815—920; Hefele—Leclercq § 601 (V. i. 398 sqq.): C. Mirbt, *Quellen*⁴ No. 300. **43.** Jaffé No. 5608. **44.** Gibbon c. lviii. (vi. 278 sq.). **45.** *Ib.* c. lviii. (vi. 280): so called since he was born at St. Gilles [Giles] a town of Lower Languedoc between Nîmes and the Rhone. **46.** *Ib.* c. lviii. (vi. 281 sq.). **47.** Three vessels left Genoa, 15th July, and reached Antioch 17th Nov., 1097: Hagenmeyer, *Chron.* Nos. 174, 210: (*Revue* vi. 499, 518). **48.** The Genoese fleet arrived at Joppa 17th June, 1099 (*Chron.* 392: vii. 468). **49.** Godfrey of Bouillon did homage, 20th Jan., 1097 (Hagenmeyer, *Chron.* 113; *Revue* vi. 268), and Raymond, though he refused homage, promised that he would attempt nothing against either the honour or the life of the Emperor, 26th April. *Chron.* 141 (*ib.* 281).

50. For the routes of these and later Crusaders see map in Bury's Gibbon vi. 294. **51.** Gibbon compares him to a jackal and the Crusaders to the lion: and says he was amply recompensed by the benefits he derived from the exploits of the Franks—clix. (vi. 322). **52.** Their route lay through Synnada, Philomelium, Iconium, Heraclea, Tarsus, Antioch, Emesa, [Homs], Tripolis, Beyrout, Sidon, Tyre, Cæsarea, Ramlah, to Jerusalem. **53.** Hagenmeyer, *Chron.* 265 (*Revue* vii. 285). **54.** He left the main army of the Crusaders for this purpose, about 17th Oct., 1097 (see Hagenmeyer, *Chron.* 199: *Revue* vi. 512); reached Edessa 20th Feb., 1098 (*Chron.* 239 *ib.* 539) and took the citadel, 8th March (*Chron.* 247, *ib.* 547). **55.** Robert II., Duke of Normandy, 1087—†1134, eldest son of William the Conqueror, and brother of William Rufus and Henry I. **56.** They started 1st March, 1099: Hagenmeyer, *Chron.* 356 (vii. 443): on 19th May (Ascension Day), they were at Beyrout (*Chron.* 353: vii. 456); at Cæsarea, 29th May (Whit-Sunday), (*Chron.* 379: vii. 459); 7th June, at Jerusalem: which they began to invest (*Chron.* 385: vii. 463). **57.** His election to this office took place about 22nd July, 1099 (*Chron.* 409: vii. 481). **58.** M. Le Quien. *Oriens Christianus* iii. 499. **59.** He was elected 1st Aug., 1099 (*Chron.* 413: vii. 484); but was speedily followed by Dagobert, abp. of Pisa, 26th—31st Dec. (*Chron.* 439; vii. 500): see also M. Le Quien, *Or. Chr.* iii. 1243. **60.** Authorities: see Gibbon c. lix. (vi. 324) n. 10. One of the most important is Odo de Deuil, *De Ludovici VII. profectione in Orientem* (*P.L.* clxxxv. 1201—46), a monk of St. Denis, who was attached to Louis by Suger, abbot of St. Denis (b. 1082) and succeeded him as abbot 1152. Deuil is a suburb to the N. of Paris. **61.** Eugenius *Ep.* xlviii. (*P.L.* clxxx. 1065 A): Jaffé No. 8796. **62.** E. Barker, *The Crusades*, 52. **63.** On the behaviour of Manuel I. and his subjects towards their " formidable guests," see Gibbon c. lix. (vi. 327 sq.). **64.** Gibbon c. lix. (vi. 329) n. 10: and map p. 294. **65.** Gibbon c. lix. [vi. 330], where he arrived 2nd Feb., 1148: map p. 294. **66.** Gibbon c. lix. (vi. 336—9). **67.** Al-Adid Abu-Muhammad Abd-Allah 1160—†71: he died 13th Sept., 1171. **68.** Ayyub=Job. **69.** Saladin was not recognised by the Caliph of Bagdad (Sunnite) till 1175, Gibbon c. lix. n. 58 (vi. 341). **70.** Gibbon c. lix. (vi. 339 sqq.). **71.** A. M. H. J. Stokvis, iii. 731: he married Theodora, the sister of Isaac II., and afterwards became King of Jerusalem, 1192: H. B. George, *Tables* xlviii. and l. **72.** Gibbon c. lix. (vi. 348). **73.** Letters of Gregory VIII. [1187] in Jaffé Nos. 16018, 16019, of 29th Oct., 1187. **74.** *Annales Marbacenses* A.D. 1188 (*Mon. Germ.*, Script. xvii. 164). **75.** " Ordinance of the Saladin Tithe" A.D. 1188 in W. Stubbs, *Select Charters*[8] 159. **76.** For the third Crusade, the authority is Nicetas [see above, p. 221 n. 1] who differs from Anna Comnena, in that he is surprisingly fair to the Crusaders: see Bury's Gibbon v. 507 and vi. 325 (c. lix. n. 11). **77.** Thence to Sozopolis, Philomelium, Iconium, Laranda, Seleucia: between which two last places ran the Calycadnus (Saleph, now Geuk Su) river, where the Emperor lost his life: map in Gibbon vi. 294: c. lix n. 30 (vi. 331). **78.** Guy (b. 1140, d. 1194) was King of Jerusalem, 1186—92, and first King of Cyprus. Lusignan is in the Department of Vienne, about 15 miles S.E. of Poitiers. **79.** The chief authorities are Nicetas Acominatus (see above: 221 n. 1) and Sir Geoffrey de Villehardouin, 1155—†1213,

Notes 503

Marshal of Theobald, Count of Champagne. His *Conquest of Constantinople* was thought by Gibbon to be a naïve and candid narrative; but it is really an "official" version of, rather apology for, what happened: see Bury's Gibbon vi. 528. The edition is *La Conquête de Constantinople* par Geoffroi de Villehardouin: par M. Natalis de Wailly (Paris, 1872). **80.** L. von Ranke. **81.** Innocent III. *Epp.* I. xi. (*P.L.* ccxciv. 9 sq.) : A. Potthast, *Regesta Pont. Rom.* i. No. 18. **82.** *Epp.* I. cccliii. (*P.L.* ccxiv. 325—7): Potthast, No. 349. **83.** *Epp.* I. cccliv. (*P.L.* ccxiv. 327—9): Potthast, No. 350. **84.** *Gesta Innocentii III.* § lxxxiii. (*P.L.* ccxiv. p. cxxxi.). **85.** Hatched by Philip and Boniface: see Gibbon c. lx. nn. 53, 63 (vi. 385, 388). **86.** Innocent III. *Epp.* V. ccxxii. (*P.L.* ccxiv. 1124 D): Potthast No. 1763. Otto was the son of Henry the Lion, Duke of Saxony, 1142—80 [†1195] whose great-grandmother was Gertrude, heiress of Brunswick: see H. B. George, *Tables* xvi. A. **87.** Gibbon c. lx. n. 51 : ed. Bury vi. 385. **88.** Simon IV., Count of Montfort, Earl of Leicester and Count of Toulouse. His fourth son was the Simon de Montfort, Earl of Leicester, killed at Evesham, 1265. **89.** *Epp.* VI. ci. (*P.L.* ccxiv. 107 A, B): Potthast No. 1948. **90.** Innocent III. *Epp. VIII.* cxxvi. Quomodo enim Graecorum Ecclesia, quantumcunque afflictionibus et persecutionibus affligatur, ad unitatem ecclesiasticam et devotionem sedis apostolicae revertetur, quae in Latinis nonnisi perditionis exempla et opera tenebrarum aspexit, ut jam merito illos abhorreat plus quam canes. Illi etenim, qui non quae sua sunt sed quae Jesu Christi quaerere credebantur, gladios quos exercere debuerant in paganos, Christianorum sanguine cruentantes, nec religioni nec aetati nec sexui pepercerunt, incestus adulteria et fornicationes in oculis hominum exercentes, et tam matronas quam virgines etiam deo dicatas exponentes spurcitias garcionum (*P.L.* ccxv. 701 B) Potthast No. 2564. **91.** *Epp.* VII. cliv. (*P.L.* ccxv. 456 A).

CHAPTER X.

1. For this partition, see Gibbon, c. lxi. nn. 1, 8 (vi. 413, 6). **2.** By purchase from the Marquis of Montferrat, 12th Aug., 1204 : *ib.* c. lxi n. 11 (vi. 417). **3.** *Ib.* c. lxi. (vi. 417). **4.** Otto, 1205—25; Guy I., 1225—63, etc. : see Stokvis ii. 465. **5.** Guillaume I., 1205—9; Geoffrey I., 1209—18; G. II., 1218—45; Guillaume II., 1245—78 : Stokvis, ii. 472. **6.** Michael I. was the natural son of Constantine Angelus, uncle of the Emperors Isaac II., 1185—95, and Alexius III., 1195—1203. He and his successors assumed the name of Comnenus Angelus Ducas. He was murdered 1214, and was succeeded by his brother Theodore (Emp. of Thessalonica, 1222—43), 1214—30 [†1254] : *Ib.* c. lxi. n. 27 (vi. 421); he by his brother Manuel, 1230—7 [†1241] ; then by Michael II. (son of Michael I.), 1237—†71 : see A. M. H. J. Stokvis, ii. 457—8. **7.** Stokvis, ii. 456. **8.** Gibbon c. lxii. (vi. 455 sqq.). The authorities are :—(1) George Acropolites, b. at CP. 1217, to Nicæa 1235, Grand Logothete 1244 and tutor to Theodore II. (Lascaris), reputed Gk. Emp. at Co. of Lyons, 1245, for re-union of E. and W., d. 1282. His history covers 1203—61, and so is a continuation of Nicetas. It is the work of a contemporary, in a good position to know (Krumbacher § 125 : Bury's Gibbon vi. 518). (2) George Pachymeres 1242—†1310: continuator of George Acropolites, beginning at 1255 and carrying on to 1308 : too theological : but that reflects the main interest of his time (Krumbacher § 126 : Bury's Gibbon vi. 518). (3) Nicephorus Blemmydes, 1198—†1272, was, beside George Acropolites, the most important literary figure at the court of the Emperor of Nicæa : took part in controversies with Latins under John III. (Vatatzes) : tutor to young prince Theodore : a pedant : (Krumbacher § 186 : Bury's Gibbon vi. 519). **9.** Gibbon c. lxi. n. 41; Lituni or Lamia is just N. of the Pass of Thermopylæ : for this event, see L. Bréhier, *L'église et l'Orient du Moyen Age*, 173. **10.** To the South of Cyzicus. It is now Maniyas, on the lake of that name: see Finlay iii. 286. **11.** Gibbon c. lxi. (vi. 124 sq.). **12.** Gibbon c. lxi. **13.** From Demetrius, son of Boniface, Marquis of Montferrat : Gibbon, c. lxi. (vi. 431) and 438 n. 69. **14.** In Macedonia, to the E. of Thessalonica. **15.** "Able and humane": Gibbon c. lxi. n. 53 (vi. 433). **16.** Near the Strymon (Struma) to the N.E. of Thessalonica. **17.** Gibbon c. lxi. (vi. 431). **18.** Gibbon c. lxi. n. 69 (vi. 438). The Thessalonian Empire thus lasted 1222—†43. Epirus split off from the Empire of Th. 1236—7, under Michael II. (a bastard son of Michael I.) whose Despotate survived the Empire. **19.** He seems to have suffered from a cerebral disease, and was subject to fits of epilepsy. Gibbon c. lxii. n. 11 (vi. 459). **20.** A natural son of the Western Emperor Frederick II. 1214—†50. **21.** Near Kastoria in Macedonia : Gibbon c. lxi. n. 71 (vi. 439). **22.** Near Smyrna : Gibbon c. lxii. n. 25 (vi. 464). **23.** Hefele § 602 (v. i. 459, ed. Leclercq). **24.** Eadmer, *Vita Anselmi* ii. 47 : Anselm, *Op.* (*P.L.* clviii. 102 sq.). **25.** Anselm, *Op.* i. 49—61 (*P.L.* clviii. 285—326). **26.** Anselm, *Op.* i. 135—7 (*P.L.* clviii. 541—8). **27.** Innocent *Epp.* VIII. lv. (*P.L.* ccxv. 623 A) : Potthast No. 2498. **28.** *Ib.* (*P.L.* ccxv. 623 C). **29.** W. Norden, *Das Papsttum und Byzanz*, 348 sqq. **30.** Hefele § 662 (*Conciles* v. 1565 sqq.). **31.** Mansi xxiii. 47—56. **32.** *Fraternitatis tuae* (Mansi xxiii. 559 : Potthast No. 8981) : Fleury, *Hist. Eccl.* XXIV. xx. (xvii. 45 sqq.). **33.** Mansi xxiii. 48 sq. **34.** σὲ τὸν ἁγιώτατον πάπαν τὸν τοῦ ὑψηλοτάτου θρόνου τὴν προεδρίαν λαχόντα : *ib.* 49 A.—**35.** *Ib.* 53 A. **36.** *Ib.* 53 D. **37.** *Ib.* 53 D. **38.** Baronius—Raynaldi, *Annales* ad ann. 1232 § L. (vol. ii. 72) : Fleury xvii. 46 sq. **39.** Mansi xxiii. 58 A. **40.** *Ib.* 58 B. **41.** *Ib.* 59 A. **42.** *Ib.* 59 B. **43.** Mansi xxiii. 59—62; Potthast No. 9198 : Hefele, *Conciles* v. 1567. **44.** For these proceedings see their "Relatio" in L. Wadding (an Irish Franciscan, 1588—†1657] or Vadingus, *Annales Minorum* ii. 224 sqq. : Mansi xxiii. 277—320; Hefele § 662 (v. 1567—72); Fleury lib. XXIV. cc. xx., xxix.—xxxii. (xvii. 43 sqq.). **45.** On 20th Jan., 1234 : see Mansi xxiii. 283. **46.** Ath. *Exp. Fidei* § 4 (*Op.* i. 81 : *P.G.* xxv. 208 A). D. Stone, *Outlines of Christian Dogma*, Note 3, p. 276. **47.** Cyril Al., *Ep.* xvii. [3 ad Nest. § 10] (*Op.* ix. 74 : *P.G.* lxxvi. 117 C). D. Stone, *Outlines of Christian Dogma*, Note 3, p. 276. **48.** D. Stone, *Outlines*, 29. **49.** *Filioque* first appears at a Synod of Toledo, 447 [de utroque processit: Leo *Ep.* xv. § 1 : *Op.* i. 697; *P.L.* liv. 681 A], and was part of a creed introduced in 589 by the third Co. of Toledo to be sung at the Mass [Canon 3], without any suspicion that it was not in the original. This was done in protest against Arianism. From Spain, the *Filioque* travelled to France and

Germany. Charlemagne adopted it in his private chapel, and defended it in writing. The Synod of Aix, 809, sent a petition to Pope Leo III., 795—†816, to sanction its insertion into the Creed, who refused: but the habit of reciting the Creed with this addition continued to make way, and at last, in 1014, "exactly 200 years after the death of Charlemagne, the Emperor Henry II., 1002—†24, prevailed upon Benedict VIII., 1012—†24, to adopt the German use of chanting the Symbol at the Holy Mysteries."—H. B. Swete, *Hist. Doctr. of the Procession of H.S.*, 225.

CHAPTER XI.

1. More exactly, "The Greek Empire consisted of several detached provinces, when Cantacuzenos seated himself on the throne; and the inhabitants of these different parts could only communicate freely by sea.... (1) CP. and Thrace, (2) Thessalonica, with Chalcidice and its three peninsulas, Cassandra, Longos and "Αγιον "Ορος, (3) A part of Vallachian Thessaly and Albanian Epirus, which formed a small imperial province interposed between the Serbian Empire and the Catalan Duchy of Athens and Neopatros, (4) the Greek province in the Peloponnesus=Despotate of Misithra, about one-third of the peninsula: (5) a few fragments: islands in the Ægæan not seized by Venetians, Genoese or Knights of St. John, and the cities of Philadelphia and Phocæa which, though surrounded by Turks, still held to CP." Finlay iv. 447—8, quoted in Bury's Gibbon vi. 502 n. 34. **2.** Gibbon, c. lxii. **3.** Hefele—Leclercq § § 676—7 (VI. i. 153—218). **4.** His followers, the Arsenites, kept up their horror of the Palaeologi; and continued "forty-eight years in an obstinate schism," 1266—1312. Gibbon, c. lxii. **5.** Manfred was a natural son of the Emperor Frederick II., 1214—†50, and a Hohenstaufen. **6.** Gibbon, c. lxii. (vi. 474 sqq.: ed. Bury). **7.** Mansi xxiv. 39—42; Potthast, *Regesta* 20527. **8.** Mansi xxiv. 42—50; Potthast, *Regesta* Nos. 20630—1. **9.** Mansi xxiv. 51—6. **10.** Potthast, *Regesta* 20760. **11.** Works in *P.G.* cxli.: those of his opponent Gregory II., 1283—9, *ibid.* cxlii. **12.** See list in C. Mirbt, *Quellen*[4] No. 760. **13.** Mansi xxiv. 62; Potthast ii. 1677. **14.** Mansi xxiv. 64; Potthast ii. 1680. **15.** Mansi xxiv. 65, 67—74. **16.** Mansi xxiv. 73—4. **17.** Potthast No. 21465. **18.** *Ib.* No. 21478. **19.** Fleury, *H.E.* xviii. 252—8. **20.** Mansi xxiv. 105: Potthast, *Regesta* No. 21815. **21.** Gibbon c. lxii. (vi. 476, ed. Bury). **22.** *Ib.* p. 477. **23.** Gibbon c. lxiii. (vi. 487 sqq.) who says: "The long reign of Andronicus the Elder is chiefly memorable by the disputes of the Greek church, the invasion of the Catalans, and the rise of the Ottoman Power." See also *D.G.R.B.* i. 174: K. Krumbacher, *Gesch. der Byz. Litt.* 1054—6. **24.** Raynaldus iv. 417. **25.** Gibbon c. lxii. (vi. 479 sqq.). **26.** Gibbon c. lxiv. (vii. 24 sqq. ed. Bury). **27.** Du Cange, *Familiae Augustae Byzantinae: Corp. Byz.* xxiv. 194. **28.** For Barlaam, see K. Krumbacher, *Gesch. der Byz. Litt.* 100. In CP., 1339—41, he was "Orthodox," and wrote against the "Catholics": on his return to Calabria, he became a "Catholic" again, and became bp. of Gerace. A. Fortescue, *The Uniate Eastern Churches,* 108 (Burns, Oates and Washbourne, 1923).

(For his works, see *P.G.* cli. 1255—1364) and Hefele—Leclercq, *Conciles* § 707 (vi. 842). **29.** A town of now 10,670 people in the province of Reggio Calabria. **30.** See his *Oratio pro unione Avenione habita coram Benedicto PP. XII.: P.G.* cli. 1332—42; or Raynaldus, ad ann. 1339 Nos. xx.—xxiv. (vi. 168—70); summarised in Fleury, *Hist. Eccl.* lib. xcv. c. 1 (vol. xx. pp. 1—8), and Gibbon vii. 84, and Hefele—Leclercq, *Conciles*, vi. 842. **31.** *P.G.* cli. 1332 A. **32.** Gibbon c. lxvi. (vii. 85 sq.). **33.** *Ib.* c. lxvi. n. 4 (vii. 85). **34.** A. Fortescue, in *The Catholic Encyclopædia* s.v. "Hesychasm": and Fleury, *H.E.* Book xcv. c. ix. **35.** K. Krumbacher, *Gesch. der Byz. Litt.* 43. **36.** Krumbacher, 152 sqq. **37.** *Ib.* 103 sq.: *P.G.* cl., cli. **38.** Krumbacher, 100: *P.G.* cli. **39** *P.G.* cli. 1314—30. **40.** *P.G.* cli. 1255—80 (in Latin): he had previously written against it in Greek (1255—8) Περὶ τῆς τοῦ Πάπα ἀρχῆς **41.** *P.G.* cli. 1301—14. **42.** Krumbacher, 100 sq. **43.** Krumbacher, 101. **44.** M. Le Quien, *Oriens Christianus* i. 297—300. **45.** Mansi xxv. 1147 sq.: Fleury *H.E.* Lib. xcv. c. ix. (xx. 24): Hefele—Leclercq, *Conciles* § 707 (vi. 844 sqq.) **46.** κύριε I.X., Ύἱὲ τοῦ Θεοῦ, Ύἱὲ τοῦ Θεοῦ, ἐλέησον ἡμᾶς. **47.** To the Hesychasts, support was given by the Emp. John V. (Cantacuzene), 1347—54, and the Patriarchs of his usurpation, Isidore I., 1347—9, Callistus I., 1350—4, and Philotheus, 1354—5: and others, Krumbacher, 101. **48.** Gibbon c. lxiii. (vi. 495). **49.** For the family of Cantacuzene, see *Fam. Byz.* No. xliii. (*Corp. Byz.* xxiv. 208 sqq.) and *D.G.R.B.* i. 595. John Cantacuzene married Irene, grand-daughter of John Asan II., King of Bulgaria, 1218—41. **50.** Text in *P.G.* cliii. and cliv. 1—370: see Gibbon c. lxiii. (vi. 489) and Krumbacher 298—300. **51.** Jo. Cant., *Hist.* iii. c. 30 (*Op.* 447: *P.G.* cliii. 877 A): Gibbon c. lxiii. (vi. 496). **52.** Text in *P.G.* cxlviii. 119—1450, cxlix. 1—502: Bury's appendix i. in his Gibbon vi. 518; Krumbacher, 295 sq. **53.** Serbia was the strongest power in the peninsula under Stephen; and its boundaries extended from the Danube to the gulf of Arta. In 1346 he was crowned at Skopia as "Tsar of the Serbs and Greeks": and raised his abp. to the rank of Patriarch. Moreover, he did for Serbia what Yaroslav did for Russia, and gave it a code of laws: see Gibbon c. lxiii. n. 31 (vi. 500). The civil war between John V. (Palaeologus) and John Cantacuzene gave him his opportunity. **54.** Hefele—Leclercq, *Conciles* § 709 (vi. 908). **55.** Fleury *H.E.* xcv. c. xl. (xx. 77): Hefele—Leclercq § 709 (vi. 908). **56.** *Ib.* xcv. c. xli. (xx. 79). **57.** Le Quien, *Or. Chr.* i. 301. **58.** *Ib.* 302 sq. **59.** Fleury *H.E.* xcvi. c. i. (xx. 112 sqq.). **60.** *Ib.* xcvi. c. 2 (xx. 118). **61.** *Ib.* xcvi. c. 28 (xx. 157 sq.). **62.** John Cantacuzene, *Hist.* iv. c. 9 (*Op.* ii. 732 sqq.: *P.G.* cliv. 61 sqq.): Gibbon c. lxvi. (vii. 86 sq.): *C. Med. Hist.* iv. 616 sq. **63.** Gibbon c. lxiv. (vii. 38). **64.** Raynaldus, ad ann. 1355 No. xxxiv. (vi. 631—2): date, 15th Dec., 1355. **65.** *Ib.* ad ann. 1356 No. xxxiii.—xxxiv. (vii. 17 sq.). **66.** *Ib.* No. xxxv. (vii. 19). **67.** *C.M.H.* iv. 617: Helefe—Leclercq, §710 (vi. 930 sq.): Fleury xcvi. c. 29 (xx. 158 sqq.). Gibbon c. lxiv. (vii. 87 sq.). **68.** Gibbon c. lxiv. n. 79 (vii. 30). **69.** *Ib.* n. 81 (vii. 31). **70.** Fleury xcvii. c. 5 (xx. 221) for his return to Rome from Avignon, 16th Oct., 1367. **71.** Ipsa quoque S.R.E. summum et plenum primatum et principatum super universam catholicam ecclesiam obtinet, quem se ab ipso Domino in beato Petro Apostolorum principe seu vertice, cujus Romanus

Pontifex est successor, cum plena potestate recepisse, veraciter et humiliter recognoscit. Et sicut prae ceteris tenetur fidei veritatem defendere, sic et si quae de fide subortae fuerint quaestiones, suo debent judicio definiri : ad quam potest gravatus quilibet in negotiis, ad forum ecclesiasticum pertinentibus, appellare. Raynaldus, ad. ann. 1369 n. II. (vii. 172) : Fleury *H.E.* xcvii. c. 13 (xx. 235). W. Norden, *Das Papsttum und Byzanz* 709; L. Bréhier, *L'église et l'Orient*, 317. **72.** Gibbon c. lxiv. n. 81 (vii. 31). **73.** Gibbon c. lxiv. (vii. 33) n. 85. **74.** L. Bréhier, *L'église et l'Orient*, 319 : Fleury *H.E.* xcix. c. 16 (xx. 453). It rendered Bayazid master of the Balkan peninsula. **75.** Gibbon c. lxv. (vii. 42 sqq.). **76.** Fleury civ. c. 106 (xxi. 484). **77.** L. Bréhier, *L'église et l'Orient*, 325. **78.** Georgius Phrantzes [1401—†77] *Chronicon* ii. 13 (*Op.* 178 sq. : *P.G.* clvi. 784 B). He was Secretary to Emp. Manuel II., and wrote the history of 1258— 1476 : anti-Turk of course; and anti-Latin, because the Latins looked upon the fall of CP. as a punishment of the Greeks for their schism ! See Krumbacher §134 (pp. 307—8) : and for the other two authorities for this period, *ib.* § § 132, 3. (1) Laonicus Chalco[co]ndyles, an Athenian of good family, † after 1463, wrote his *History* of 1298—1463 (*P.G.* clix.). (2) Ducas, Secretary of the Genoese Podesta at Phocæa, before the fall of CP. He was a supporter of the union of E. with W., as the best safeguard against the Turk, and wrote his *History* of 1341—1402 (*P.G.* clvii. 739—1166). **79.** He was thrice married to (1) Anne, of Russia, † 1417; (2) Sophia, d. of John II., Marquis of Montferrat, divorced 1426; and (3) Maria Comnena, † 1439. **80.** Theodore, Despot of Selymbria, † 1458; Andronicus, Despot of Thessalonica, † 1429; Demetrius, Despot of the Peloponnese, †1471; Thomas, Despot of Achaia, †1465; Michael : *Fam. Byz.* xl. (*Corp. Byz.* xxiv. 198 sq.). **81.** Mansi xxix. 165—9; Hefele—Leclercq, *Conciles* § 807 (vii. 954). **82.** Hefele—Leclercq, § § 807, 808, 810 (vii. 951 sqq.); M. Creighton, *Hist. Papacy* ii. 322 sqq. (ed. 1897) : and his note on the authorities for Ferrara and Florence, *ib.* 382 sqq. (1) On the Latin side, the Acts of the Council in Mansi xxxi.; (2) on the side of the Unionist Greeks, the " Acta Græca" probably by Bessarion; and (3) Sylvester Syropulus' *Memoirs*. He was in attendance on the Patriarch Joseph. **83.** Creighton ii. 329. **84.** Hefele—Leclercq §810 (vii. 965). **85.** Krumbacher § 44. He was a friend of the union and an opponent of Mark. **86.** Krumbacher § 41. He was an opponent of the union. **87.** Krumbacher § 42 : a friend of the union. **88.** Hefele—Leclercq, § 810 (vii. 968). **89.** Hefele—Leclercq, § 810 (vii. 973). **90.** Third session, 14th Oct.: *ib.* 974. **91.** Eleventh session, 11th Nov.: *ib.* 984. **92.** *Ib.* 986. **93.** *Ib.* § 811 (vii. 987 sqq.). **94.** *Ib.* 988. **95.** Or of Ragusa, Provincial of the Dominicans of Lombardy. **96.** *Ib.* 993. **97.** Krumbacher § 12 : Mansi xxxi. 877 B : Hefele— Leclercq § 811 (vii. 994) : and Maximus, *Op.* ii. 70 (*P.G.* xci. 136 A). **98.** Creighton ii. 344. **99.** Mansi xxxi. 1000 A. **100.** Hefele— Leclercq, § 812 (vii. 1009) : Mansi xxxi. 1000 B.C. **101.** On 4th June, the Greeks adopted this formula : Συμφωνοῦμεν ὑμῖν καὶ ἣν προσθήκην λέγετε ἐν τῷ ἱερῷ συμβόλῳ, ἐστὶν ἀπὸ τῶν ἁγίων, καὶ συγχωροῦμεν αὐτὴν, καὶ ἑνούμεθα ὑμῖν, καὶ λέγομεν ὅτι ἐκπορεύεται τὸ πνεῦμα τὸ ἅγιον ἐκ πάτρος καὶ υἱοῦ, ὡς ἀπὸ μιᾶς ἀρχῆς καὶ αἰτίας Mansi xxxi. 1001 C. **102.** Mansi xxxi. 1008 sq.: Hefele— Leclercq § 813 (vii. 1014 sq.). **103.** Mansi xxxi. 1004 D : Hefele—

Leclercq § 812 (vii. 1012).   **104.** Mansi xxxi. 1017 C; Hefele—
Leclercq § 814   (vii. 1025).   **105.** Mansi xxxi. 1017 E.
106. Οἰκονομήσατε ἡμᾶς ἀπελθεῖν : *ib.* 1017 E.   **107.** Mansi xxxi.
1020 C: H.—L. § 814 (vii. 1026).   **108.** H.—L. § 814 (vii. 1026).
109. *Ib.* § 815 (vii. 1030—1).   **110.** *Laetentur Coeli* in Mansi xxxi. 1025
—34 : H.—L. § 816 (vii. 1032 sqq.) : Mirbt⁴ No. 400. § 2. In nomine igitur
sanctae Trinitatis, Patris et Filii et Spiritus Sancti, hoc sacro appro-
bante Florentino concilio definimus, ut haec fidei veritas ab omnibus
christianis credatur et suscipiatur, sicque omnes profiteantur.
§ 3. Quod Spiritus Sanctus ex Patre et Filio aeternaliter est, et
essentiam suam suumque esse subsistens habet ex Patre simul et
Filio et ex utroque aeternaliter tanquam ab uno principio et unica
spiratione procedit. Declarantes quod id quod sancti doctores et
patres dicunt ex Patre per Filium procedere Spiritum Sanctum, ad
hanc intelligentiam tendit, ut per hoc significetur Filium quoque esse
secundum Graecos quidem causam, secundum Latinos vero princi-
pium, subsistentiae Spiritus Sancti sicut et Patrem. Et quoniam
omnia quae Patris sunt Pater ipse unigenito Filio suo gignendo dedit
praeter esse Patrem, hoc ipsum quod Spiritus Sanctus procedit ex
Filio, ipse Filius a Patre aeternaliter genitus est. Definimus insuper
explicationem verborum illorum " Filioque " veritatis declarandae
gratia, imminente tunc necessitate, licite ac rationabiliter symbolo,
fuisse appositam. § 4. Item, in azymo sive fermentato pane triticeo
corpus Christi veraciter confici . . . § 5. Item, si vere poenitentes in
Dei caritate decesserint, antequam dignis poenitentiae fructibus de
commissis satisfecerint et omissis, eorum animas poenis purgatorii post
mortem purgari : et ut a poenis huiusmodi releventur, prodesse eis
fidelium vivorum suffragia, missarum scilicet sacrificia, orationis et
eleemosynas et alia pietatis officia, quae a fidelibus pro aliis fidelibus
fieri consueverunt secundum ecclesiae instituta. . . . . . § 8. Item
definimus, sanctam apostolicam sedem et Romanum Pontificem in universum orbem tenere primatum et ipsum Pontificem Romanum successorem esse beati Petri principis apostolorum, et verum Christi vicarium, totiusque ecclesiae caput
et omnium christianorum patrem et doctorem existere, et ipsi in
beato Petro pascendi, regendi ac gubernandi universalem ecclesiam
a D.N.I.C. plenam potestatem traditam esse, quemadmodum etiam
in gestis oecumenicorum conciliorum et in sacris canonibus con-
tinctur. § 9. Renovantes insuper ordinem traditum in canonibus
ceterorum venerabilium patriarcharum, ut patriarcha Constantinopolitanus secundus sit post sanctissimum Romanum Pontificem,
tertius vero Alexandrinus, quartus autem Antiochenus et quintus
Hierosolymitanus, salvis videlicet omnibus privilegiis et iuribus
eorum.   **111.** Mansi xxxi. 1047—60 : H.—L. § 823 (vii. 1079 sq.) :
Mirbt⁴ No. 401. **112.** H.—L. § 823 (vii. 1087). **113.** Gibbon c. lxvii. (vii.
134 sqq.). **114.** *Ibid.* vii. 140 sqq. **115.** So called from his mother Irene,
who was the daughter of Constantine Dragases, a prince of Serbia.
Gibbon c. lxvii. n. 52 (vii. 154).   **116.** Gibbon c. lxviii. (vii. 163).
117. The fanatic Greeks regarded this as pollution. St. Sophia was
deserted both by clergy and people : " and the first minister of the
Empire . . . was heard to declare that he had rather ,behold in CP.
the turban of Mahomet than the pope's tiara or a cardinal's hat."
Gibbon c. lxviii. (vii. 177).   **118.** *Ib.* c. lxviii. n. 85 (vii. 183).

CHAPTER XII.

1. See "Eastern Churches" by A. Fortescue in *The Catholic Encyclopædia*, v. 230—40, and "Orientalische Kirche" by F. Kattenbusch in Hauck-Herzog *Realencyclopädie*,[2] xiv. 436—67 : "Eastern Church" in Hastings' *Encyclopædia of Religion and Ethics*, v. 134—6; "Greek Orthodox Church," *ib.* vi. 425—35; and L. Pullan, *Religion since the Reformation*, Lecture VII. (Clar. Press, 1923). **2.** J. A. Douglas, *The Relations of the Anglican Churches with the Eastern-Orthodox*, 170 sqq. **3.** Formed of 200,000 Serbs who in 1690 migrated from the Patriarchate of Ipek, *E.R.E.* vi. 430. **4.** " Became autocephalous in 1766 when the Patriarchate of Ipek, of which it formed a part, was abolished." *E.R.E.* vi. 430. **5.** "Severed from the archbishopric of Carlowitz in 1864, to satisfy the nationalist tendencies of the Rumanians." *E.R.E.* vi. 431. **6.** *E.R.E.* vi. 431. **7.** Greg. Naz., *Orat.* xliii. § 58 (*Op.* ii. 813 : *P.G.* xxxvi. 572 A). **8.** Canon. 17 (Mansi vii. 365 B). **9.** Canon 38 (*ib.* xi. 960—1). **10.** W. Bright, *Notes on the Canons*, 176. **11.** Innocent, *Ep.* xxiv. § 2— "Nam quod sciscitaris, utrum divisis imperiali iudicio provinciis, ut duae metropoles fiant, sic duo metropolitani episcopi debeant nominari, non esse vere visum est ad mobilitatem necessitatum mundanarum Dei ecclesiam commutari " (*P.L.* xx. 548 sq.), A.D. 415 : Jaffé No. 310. **12.** W. Bright, *op. cit.* 177. **13.** Vicomte de la Jonquière, *Histoire de l'Empire Ottoman* (Hachette, Paris, 2 vols. 1914) : D. G. Hogarth, *The Balkans*, 319 sqq. **14.** In the angle between the Danube and its tributary the Drave, to the S.W. of Hungary. **15.** See B. J. Kidd, *Documents of the Continental Reformation*, pp. 181, 185, 245, 302. **16.** *Ibid.* 341. **17.** " The practical result of the great victory at Lepanto was that it enabled the Venetians to purchase peace early in 1573, by paying the Sultan 300,000 ducats." G. Finlay, *History of Greece*, v. 85 (Oxford, 1877). **18.** Otherwise Zeideva, near Komorn : which is in Hungary, between Pressburg and Buda-Pesth, on the Danube. **19.** He does not appear to have been called the Sultan till the sixteenth century. **20.** Krumbacher, § 45. **21.** Manuel Malaxos, *Historia Politica CP.* pp. 14—16, and *Hist. Patriarchica*, pp. 107—9 (*Corp. Script. Hist. Byz.* xxiv. 26—9, 78—82 : Bonn, 1849). M. M. of Nauplia wrote c. 1550—78 : and his *Hist. Patr.* covers the years 1454—78 : Krumbacher § 167. **22.** *E.R.E.* vi. 428. **23.** He " enjoyed more power than he enjoyed under a Christian sovereign, and he began to wear on his brow a jewelled crown similar to that of the departed emperors." L. Pullan, *op. cit.* 197. **24.** viz. : 1. Athens, 2. Thebes, 3. Naupactus, 4. Corfu, 5. Patras, 6. Lacedaemon, 7. Argos (Nauplia), 8. Paros and Naxos, 9. Andros, 10. Chalcis (Euboea), 11. Pharsala, 12. Larissa, 13. Monemvasia. C. D. Cobham, *Patriarchs of CP.* 67 n. 1 : see also, for later modifications, Isidor Silbernagl, *Verfassung ünd gegenwärtiger Bestand samtlicher Kirchen des Orients*[2] (Regensburg, 1904) § 34. **25.** Cobham, 67 n. 1; Silbernagl § 19. **26.** viz. : Ephesus (3), Heraclea (3), Salonika (5), Crete (8), Smyrna (1). **27.** These were Gennadius II., 1454—6; Isidore II., 1456—63; [Sophronius I., 1463—4] ; Joasaph I. (Kokkas), 1464—6; Mark II. (Xylocaraves), 1466—7, and for their freedom from simony, see *Hist. Patr.* 124 (*Corp. Scr. Hist. Byz.* xxiv. 102). **28.** " Mohammed II. accepted the purchase-money, and allowed the Greeks to introduce that black stain of simony into their hierarchy which soon spread over their whole ecclesiastical establishment. From this time simony became a part of the constitution of the Orthodox Church." G. Finlay, *Hist. Gr.* v. 140. **29.** Manuel Malaxos, *Hist. Patr.* 125 (*C.S.H.B.* xxiv. 103 sq.). **30.** He became Patriarch 1472—5 and again 1482—6. **31.** M. M., *Hist. Patr.* 126 (*C.S.H.B.* xxiv. 106). **32.** He became Dionysius I., 1467—72. **33.** Raphael I., 1475—6: for whom see M. M., *Hist. Patr.* c. viii. (*C.S.H.B.* xxiv. 113). **34.** πεσκέσιον: H.P. c. vii. (*C.S.H.B.* xxiv. 112). **35.** χαράτζιον (Kharaj): H.P. c. vii. (*C.S.H.B.* xxiv. 112). **36.** M. M., *Hist. Patr.* xix. (*C.S.H.B.* xxiv. 154). **37.** "No more selfish and degraded class of men has ever held power than .. the Phanariot Greeks of CP.," and "the Greek hierarchy only shared the character of the class from which it was selected": G. Finlay, *Hist. Gr.* v. 150. **38.** "The patriarch and the bishops purchased their dignities, and repaid themselves by selling ecclesiastical rank and privileges; the priests purchased holy orders, and sold licences to marry. The laity paid for marriages, divorces, baptisms, pardons, and dispensations of many kinds to their bishops. The extent to which patriarchs and bishops interfered in family disputes and questions of property is proved by contemporary documents." G. Finlay, *Hist. Gr.* v. 156: and "the whole system was intended to be a means of extorting money": Pullan, 214. **39.** M. M., *Hist. Patr.* c. iii. (*C.S.H.B.* xxiv. 98). **40.** *Ib.* c. ix. (*C.S.H.B.* xxiv. 113). His nose was slit. **41.** G. Finlay, *Hist. Gr.* vi. 186. **42.** "To the conduct [of the secular clergy] we must attribute the confidence which the agricultural population retained in the promises of the Gospel, and their firm persistence in a persecuted faith. The grace of God operated by their means to preserve Christianity under the domination of the Othomans": *ib.* v. 152. **43.** A. Baudrillart, *Dict. d'Hist. et Géogr. Eccl.* ii. 289 sqq. for the history of the patriarchate (and for a list of the Patriarchs, Orthodox and Coptic, see *ib.* pp. 365—7) and *Dict. Théol. Catholique* i. 786 —824. **44.** Hauck-Herzog, *Realencyclopädie*[3] (1904) xiv. 446: A. Vacant and E. Mangenot, *Dict. Théol. Catholique* i. *E.R.E.* vi. 429. **45.** And in the nineteenth at CP. **46.** I. Silbernagl § 12, i.e. since 1846. Before that date he was appointed by the religious authorities of CP. He is now elected by the Orthodox of Egypt. The Greek Orthodox have their Cathedral and three churches in Alexandria; and say the liturgy in Greek. The Syrian Orthodox have one church, and a liturgy in Arabic: *Dict. Hist. Géogr.* ii. 363. **47.** *Ib.* § 19 B. **48.** See s.v. "Antioche" in A. Baudrillart, *Dict. d'Histoire et de Géographie Ecclésiastiques* iii. 563—703; *E.R.E.* vi. 431. **49.** But the Orthodox Patriarchate, in 570, contained twelve metropolitan sees, with suffragans: (1) Tyre, 13; (2) Tarsus, 7; (3) Edessa, 11; (4) Apamea, 7; (5) Hierapolis-Mabug, 9; (6) Bosra, 19; (7) Anazarbus, 8; (8) Seleucia in Isauria, 24; (9) Damascus, 11; (10) Amida-Diabekr, 8; (11) Sergiopolis, 5; (12) Dara, 3; and see map in *Dict. H. G.* ii. 607. **50.** *Échos d'Orient chrétien* iii. 223 sq., quoted in A. Fortescue, *O.E.C.* 287 n. 1. **51.** The double-succession, Orthodox and Melkite, begins in 1724: *D.H.G.* iii. 700. "Melkites"=(1) those who accepted the Emperor's religion as opposed to the Monophysites: (2) after schisms of ninth and eleventh centuries it was used for "Catholics" and Orthodox, in E.: (3) it is now commonly used for the "Catholics" only and means "Uniates of the Byzantine rite in Syria and Egypt": A. Fortescue, *Uniate Eastern Churches*, 185 sq. **52.** Silbernagl § 13. **53.** Or 316,000, with 14 sees: *E.R.E.* vi. 431.

54. *Ib.* § 19 C. They are (1) Aleppo, (2) Amida (Diabekr), (3) Arcadia (Akkar), (4) Beirut, (5) Homs, (6) Epiphania (Hama), (7) Laodicea (Latakiyeh), (8) Seleucia, (9) Tarsus (Adana), (10) Theodosiopolis (Erzerum=Arx Romanorum), (11) Tripoli, (12) Tyre and Sidon. Silbernagl § 19 B : Fortescue 287. *D.H.G.* iii. 684 for map which gives a different enumeration :—(1) Tarsus-Adana, (2) Aleppo, (3) Laodicea, (4) Hama, (5) Akkar, (6) Homs, (7) Tripoli, (8) Beirut, (9) Zahle-Baalbek, (10) Tyre-Sidon, (11) Damascus, (12) Amida (Diabekr), (13) Theodosiopolis (Erzerum). **55.** Pullan 217. **56.** *E.R.E.* vi. 431. **57.** Acts xii. 17, xv. 13, xxi. 18; Gal. ii. 9. **58.** *S. Silviae Peregrinatio* in *C.S.E.L.* xxxix. *Itinera Hierosol:* 35—101; or *The Pilgrimage of Etheria*, edd. M. L. McClure and C. L. Feltoe (S.P.C.K., 1920): B. J. Kidd, *Documents* ii. No. 88. **59.** τὴν ἀκολουθίαν τῆς τιμῆς, τῇ μητροπόλει σωζομένου τοῦ οἰκείου ἀξιώματος. Nicene Canon, 7. **60.** Theodoret *H.E.* II. xxvi. § 6. **61.** B. J. Kidd, *Hist. Ch.* iii. 331. **62.** Mansi, iv. 1312 D, E. **63.** *Ib.* vii. 180 B, C, D. **64.** Kidd, *Hist. Ch.* iii. 331 sq. **65.** *E.R.E.* vi. 432, reckons fifteen. **66.** Silbernagl § 19 D. **67.** *Report of the Commission appointed by the Government of Palestine to enquire into the affairs of the Orthodox Patriarchate of Jerusalem,* p. 9 (Clar. Press, 1921). **68.** *Ib.* 9. **69.** *Ib.* 8. **70.** *Report,* 9. **71.** In the Valley of the Kidron, between Jerusalem and the Dead Sea. Its founder was St. Sabas, 439—531. **72.** *Ib.* 10 sq. **73.** *Report,* 14 n. 1. **74.** L. Pullan, *Religion since the Reformation,* 217 sq. **75.** *Ib.* 218. **76.** *Report,* 222. **77.** *Ib.* 228. **78.** *Ib.* 229. **79.** *Ib.* 231. **80.** *Ib.* 235. **81.** *Dict. Théol. Catholique* i. 2424—72; *Cath. Enc.* iv. 589—91; J. Hackett, *A History of the Orthodox Church of Cyprus* (1901). **82.** Acts iv. 36. Theodore Lector, *H.E.* ii. 2 (*Op.* 571 : *P.G.* lxxvi. 184), c. 500—50. George Cedrenus, *Hist. Compendium* (*Op.* 618—619 : *P.G.* cxxi. 673 B), c. 1200. Joel, *Chronographia* (*Op.* 43 : *P.G.* cxxxix. 264 C), c. 1204—61. Nicephorus Callistus, *H.E.* xvi. 37 (*Op.* 716: *P.G.* cxlvii. 200 C), early fourteenth century. **83.** Acts xiii. 1—12. **84.** Socr *H.E.* i. 12 (*Op.* 39—40: *P.G.* lxvii. 104—5). **85.** Nos. 190, 191, in the list in C. H. Turner, *Eccl. Or. Mon. Jur. Ant.* I. i. 80—1. **86.** B. J. Kidd, *Hist. Ch. to A.D.* 461, iii. 248 sq. **87.** *Et onus et honor* of c. 415 : Innocent *Ep.* xxiv. (*P.L.* xx. 547—51): Jaffé, No. 310. **88.** Cyprios sane asseris olim Arianae impietatis potentia fatigatos non tenuisse Nicaenos canones (5 et 6) in ordinandis sibi episcopis, et usque adhuc praesumptum, ut suo arbitratu ordinent, neminem consulentes. Quocirca persuademus eis, ut curent juxta canonum fidem catholicam sapere, atque unum cum caeteris sentire provinciis, ut appareat sancti Spiritus gratia ipsos quoque ut omnes Ecclesias gubernari, *ib.* § 3 (*P.L.* xx. 549 A). **89.** Fleury, Bk. xxiii. c. 26. **90.** Mansi iv. 1467. **91.** *Ib.* 1467 sq. **92.** See his sermon preached before the Council at Ephesus : Actio I., c. xi. : (Mansi iv. 1245—8). **93.** Mansi iv. 1465 sqq. **94.** κατὰ τοὺς κανόνας τῶν ὁσίων πατέρων καὶ τὴν ἀρχαίαν συνήθειαν : Canon 8, Mansi iv. 1469 B : W. Bright, *Canons*^{2} xxix. sq., 135—9. **95.** Theodore Lector, *H.E.* [c. 500—50] ii. 2 (*Op.* 571 : *P.G.* lxxvi. 184); George Cedrenus, *Hist. Compend.* [c. 1200] (*Op.* 618—9 : *P.G.* cxxi. 673 B); Joel, *Chronographia* [c. 1204—61] (*Op.* 43 : *P.G.* cxxxix. 264 C), and Nicephorus Callistus, *H.E.* [early fourteenth century] xvi. 37 (*Op.* 716 : *P.G.* cxlvii. 200 C). **96.** So the Council in Trullo [A.D. 692] c. 39 which reads ὥστε τὴν Νέαν Ἰουστινιανούπολιν

512   The Churches of Eastern Christendom

τὸ δίκαιον ἔχειν τῆς Κωνσταντινουπόλεως, as quoted in J. Hackett, *Orthodox Church of Cyprus*, 38 n. 1 : read τὸ δίκαιον ἔχειν τῆς Κωνσταντίνεων πόλεως. Nimirum "utque N. I. jus habeat Constantiensium civitatis sive Constantiae," *i.e.* Salamis, *ib.* 43 n. 1. **97.** George Cedrenus, *Hist. Compend.* (*Op.* 363 : *P.G.* cxxi. 97 B). **98.** Hackett, 331 sqq. **99.** *Ib.* 345 sqq. **100.** *Ib.* 348 sqq. **101.** Hackett, 339 sqq. **102.** *Ib.* 59 sqq. **103.** A Latin hierarchy was set up 1196, with a metropolitan at Nikosia, and suffragans at Limassol, Paphos and Famagusta. They were endowed out of the spoils of the Orthodox. Hackett, 75. **104.** *Ib.* 172 sq. **105.** *Ib.* 190 sqq. **106.** *Ib.* 184. **107.** *Ib.* 186. **108.** *Ib.* 194 sq. **109.** Hackett, 229. **110.** *Ib.* 231. **111.** *E.R.E.* vi. 429. **112.** Cf. "The Church of Cyprus" by T. Papaporphyrion in *The Christian East*, vol. ii. No. 1 (April, 1921) pp. 22 sqq. **113.** Silbernagl § 14 : A. Fortescue, *O.E.C.* 310 sqq. : *E.R.E.* vi. 429.

CHAPTER XIII.

1. D. G. Hogarth, *The Balkans*, 23 sqq. : *Cambridge Mediæval History* IV. cc. viii. and xvi. ; Gibbon, c. lv. ed. Bury, vol. vi. ; *Dictionnaire de Théologie Catholique*, edd. A. Vacant and E. Mangenot, ii. 1174—1236, s.v. "Bulgarie" : R. Ll. James, *Dict. Eastern Orthodox Church*, 26 sq. **2.** Nicephorus, *Breviarium*, p. 38 (*P.G.* c. 929 sqq.) : on this work see Krumbacher § 146. **3.** So Bury in Gibbon, vol. vi. app. 11. **4.** Le Quien, *Oriens Christianus* ii. 24 sq. **5.** *E.R.E.* vi. 430. **6.** In *Ep.* viii. (*Op.* ii. : *P.G.* cii. 627—96) "De officio principis." Probably Boris knew that the Western Emperor was crowned by *his* patriarch, the Bishop of Rome, and the Eastern Emperor by *his*, the Bishop of CP. How, then, could Boris himself be an Emperor's equal, without his own Patriarch? Hence his request, and its refusal both by Photius and Pope Nicholas, as afterwards by Pope Hadrian II., 867—†72. **7.** Photius *Ep.* xiii. §§ 3, 4 (*Op.* ii. : *P.G.* cii. 724, B, C). This letter helps to fix the dates. He says that there were scarcely two years between the conversion of the country by the Greeks and the arrival of the Latin missionaries. **8.** Mansi xvi. 10—13. **9.** So complains Pope Hadrian II., *Ep.* xxxvi. (A.D. 871, Nov. 10th) *P.L.* cxxii. 1310 C : Jaffé No. 2943. **10.** See the *Vita Clementis*, c. xx. in *P.G.* cxxvi. 1228 B. It is the work of a contemporary, in the tenth century : see Krumbacher, § 88, p. 199. **11.** Ochrida, is the ancient Lychnidus which had a bishop in 519. The name Achrida (now Ochrida) is "posterior to that date." The autonomous archbishopric, or patriarchate, was fixed here from 981—1767 : see s.v. "Achrida" in A. Baudrillart, *Dict. d'Hist. et de Géogr. Eccl.* i. 321. **12.** See list of the archbishops 1018—1767 in *ib.* 323 sq. : or *Dict. Th. Cath.* ii. 1203 : some of them were men of distinction : but the preoccupations of all were the same, viz. : (1) the elimination of everything Bulgar in favour of everything Greek; (2) the maintenance of their ancient privilege against the Patriarch of CP. ; *Dict. Th. Cath.* ii. 1185 sq. **13.** *D.H.G.E.* i. 328. Under Boris, 852—88, there were 7; under Peter, 927—69, 28; under Samuel, 976—1014, 16; *Dict. Th. Cath.* ii. 1185. **14.** *C.M.H.* iv. 243. **15.** See his letters in A. Theiner, *Monumenta vetera Slavorum Meridianorum* I. No. xxvi.

Notes

p. 16, xxxvi. p. 21. **16.** Innocent replied 24th Feb., 1204 to Kalojan and to Abp. Basil: Theiner I. Nos., xl., xli. The consecration of the Abp. took place 7th Nov., and the Coronation of the King 8th Nov., 1204: Theiner I. No. lxi. p. 40. **17.** Prêslav and Velbuzd: Theiner I. No. xlv. p. 29. **18.** Vidin, Nish, Branichevo, Usküb. **19.** L. Pullan, *Religion since the Reformation*, 216 sq. **20.** See good map of these sees in *Dict. Th. Cath.* ii. 1038. **21.** For a good map of modern Jugoslavia, see *Southern Slav Monuments: I. The Serbian Orthodox Church*, by M. J. Pupin, with an introduction by Sir T. G. Jackson, Bart. (Murray, 1918). **22.** *Enc. Brit.*[11] xxxii. 112 (ed. 1922). **23.** *The Balkans* (ed. D. G. Hogarth), 79 sqq.: *C.M.H.* IV. cc. xvii., xviii. **24.** *Op.* ii. 86—105 (*P.G.* cxii. 247—312): reprinted in J. B. Bury, *The early history of the Slavonic Settlements in Dalmatia, Croatia and Serbia* (S.P.C.K., 1920: Texts for Students, No. 18). **25.** J. B. Bury, *ib.* p. vi. **26.** Bury's Gibbon, v. app. 11. **27.** *Ibid.* vi. app. 12. **28.** L. Pullan, *Religion since the Reformation*, 215 sq., for this process of Hellenisation in Serbia. **29.** The Patriarch fled to Carlowitz, then in the Habsburg dominions, where his successors were recognised by the Austrian Empire, but only with the rank of metropolitan. In 1849, the patriarchate was restored, but with diminished jurisdiction. The Patriarchs therefore remained outside, and were even inimical to, the national movement; and had no control over the Orthodox Church of Serbia itself until 1879: when the Church of Serbia was recognised by the Phanar as autocephalous: see § 13. **30.** L. Pullan, *Religion since the Reformation*, 219 sqq. **31.** A. Mousset, *Le Royaume Serbe-Croate-Slovene* (Paris, 1926). **32.** *The Christian East*, Dec., 1922, p. 188. **33.** *Ib.* May, 1923, p. 112.

CHAPTER XIV.

1. N. Jorga, *A history of Roumania:* tr. J. McCabe (T. Fisher Unwin, 1925). **2.** H. Schiller, *Geschichte der römischer Kaiserzeit* i. 554, quoted in Gibbon (ed. Bury) i. 449. **3.** Gibbon, c. x. (ed. Bury, i. 249). **4.** *Ib.* c. x. n. 106 (i. 260). **5.** *Ib.* c. xi. (i. 294). **6.** *Ib.* c. xxxv. (iii. 476). **7.** The great profits gained by the illegal exercise of power made the name of Phanariot a byword for the basest servility, corruption and rapacity ... and the Phanariots [*Hospodars* or *Voivodes* first appointed for Moldavia, 1712, and for Wallachia, 1716—see list in Finlay v. 295 sqq.], intent only on accumulating money and enjoying their power, rendered the native inhabitants of the Principalities the most wretched portion of the sultan's subjects (*ib.* 243): and L. Pullan, *Religion since the Reformation*, 216. **8.** For this information I am indebted to Col. S. S. Butler, C.M.G., D.S.O., Military Attaché of the British Legation, Bucharest. **9.** *The Christian East*, June, 1920, pp. 94—7. **10.** See map in W. Miller, *A history of the Greek people, 1821—1921* (Methuen, 1922), 142: and *Enc. Brit.*[11] xii. 468 sqq. **11.** W. Miller, *Hist. Gr. People*, 128. **12.** Area of England=50,851; Wales, 7,467; E. and W., 58,318. **13.** A. J. Toynbee in *The Balkans*, 181 sqq. **14.** G. Finlay, *History of Greece*[1] V. cc. i.—iii. **15.** *Ib.* c. iv. **16.** W. Miller, *The Turkish Restoration in Greece*, 1718—97 (Helps for

514 *The Churches of Eastern Christendom*

Students of History, No. 38: S.P.C.K., 1921). **17.** G. Finlay, V. c. v. **18.** *Ib.* vols. VI., VII.: W. Miller, *Hist. Gr. People, 1821—1921*, and *Greek Life in Town and Country* (G. Newnes, 1905, 316 n.). **19.** W. Miller, *Greek Life in Town and Country*, c. iv. (Newnes, 1905). **20.** *E.R.E.* vi. 429. **21.** I am indebted for this information on the episcopate of Greece to the Rev. Dr. W. A. Wigram, Chaplain of the British Legation, Athens. **22.** *The Statesman's Year-Book*, 1924: 983 sq. **23.** *The Christian East*, May, 1923. **24.** *Ib.* April, 1921. **25.** W. Miller, *Hist. Gr. People*, 26. **26.** ἀσπασμος καὶ τιμητικὴ προσκύνησις : see the Definition of the Second Council of Nicæa, 787 (Seventh Œcumenical) in Mansi xiii. 730 B. **27.** *The Christian East*, Feb., 1924.

CHAPTER XV.

1. *The Catholic Encyclopædia*, xiii. 261—4. **2.** W. H. Frere, *Links in the Chain of Russian Church History*, 14. **3.** A. Rambaud, *History of Russia*, i. 106. **4.** *Enc. Brit.*[11] xxiii. 892. **5.** For the Tartar conquest, see A. Rambaud, *Hist. Russia*, i. 153 sqq.: Beazley, Forbes and Birkett, *Russia*, 51 sqq. **6.** Rambaud, i. 171 sqq.; Beazley, etc., 58 sq. **7.** W. H. Frere, *Links in the Chain of Russian Church History*, 36. **8.** *Ib.* 156 n. 2. **9.** *Ib.* 156. **10.** Jagellon became Ladislas V., King of Poland, 1385—†1434: see H. B. George, *Tables*[4] No. xli. **11.** W. H. Frere, *Links in the Chain of Russian Church History*, 26 n. 2. **12.** Otherwise, Tamerlane=Timour Leng =Timour the lame. **13.** q.v. in C. Mirbt, *Quellen*[4] No. 400. **14.** Cf. J. B. Bury, "Russia, 1462—1652," in *Cambr. Med. Hist.* V. c. xvi. **15.** He "deserves his title" because "he brought to a virtual completion . . . the two chief enterprises which had engaged the energies of his predecessors—the emancipation of Russia from the slackening yoke of the Tartars, and the gathering of Russian territory under the wing of Moscow," *ib.* 478. **16.** R. Beazley, Forbes and Birkett, *Russia*, 77. **17.** *Fam. Byz.* xl.: (*Corp. Script. Byz.* xxiv. 202). **18.** A. Rambaud, *Hist. Russia*, i. 245: but these "consequences" of the marriage are repudiated by Bury in. *C.M.H.* V. 482 sqq. **19.** He also maintained relations with foreign courts: and Sigismund, Freiherr von Herberstein, 1486—†1566, who, as ambassador of the Emperor Maximilian, 1493—†1519, twice visited Moscow, has left us an intimate description of Russia in his *Rerum Moscovitarum Commentarii*, published in 1549 (see tr. in *Notes upon Russia*, ed. R. H. Major, Hakluyt Society's publications, series i. No. 10). **20.** "In the West he will always be known as Ivan the Terrible; but the epithet is misleading; for the Russian word which it translates means 'to be feared' in the sense in which we are bidden to fear God, as a stern master, not as an ogre." *C.M.H.* v. 488. **21.** See K. Waliozewski, *Ivan the Terrible* (tr. Lady Mary Loyd, Heineman, 1904). **22.** *C.M.H.* v. 492. **23.** W. H. Frere, *Links in the Chain of Russian Church History*, 74 n. 1. **24.** *C.M.H.* v. 489. **25.** W. H. Frere, *Links in the Chain of Russian Church History*, 75, n 1. **26.** Translated into English in *Notes upon Russia*, ed. R. H. Major (Hakluyt Society, 2 vols., 1851—2). For another sketch, from the point of view of a Lutheran, see Adam Olearius, *Voyages and*

Notes

Travels of the Ambassadors from the Duke of Holstein to the Great Duke of Muscovy, 1633—9 (E. Tr. by John Davies, London, 1662), pp. 124—145. **27**. Hakluyt's *Voyages*, i. 264 sqq. (ed. J. Masefield—Everyman's Library). **28**. Sir Jerome Horsey, his Travels: in Hakluyt Society, No. 20—*Russia at the close of the Sixteenth Century*, 201 (ed. E. A. Bond, 1856). **29**. Afterwards Ladislas VII., King of Poland, 1632—†48. **30**. R. L. Poole, *Atlas* No. xlix. **31**. *C.M.H.* v. 504. **32**. R. L. Poole, *Hist. Atlas of Modern Europe*, No. xlix. **33**. Polotsk is in Western Russia: and the other five now in Poland. **34**. "Orthodoxa Confessio Fidei Catholicae et Apostolicae Ecclesiae Orientalis": in E. J. Kimmel, *Libri Symbolici Ecclesiae Orientalis* (Jenae, 1843) 45—324: or *Monumenta Fidei Ecclesiae Orientalis* (Jenae, 1850) 45—324. **35**. N. Forbes, in *Russia*, 137. **36**. ="Kroutits," i.e., the Steeps (though often called, as before, bishops of Sarai and Podonsk): sc. the steep banks of the Moskva: where their residence stood, for on the fall of Sarai they transferred their seat to Moscow, and acted as Vicars to the Metropolitan. Mouravieff, 93 sq. and 383. **37**. Or ? six: + Nizhni Novgorod, Mouravieff, 130. **38**. Kolomna, Bransk, Pskov, Riev of Vladimir, Ustiog, Bielo-Ozero, Dmitroff: Mouraviev, 130. **39**. *Catholic Encyclopædia*, xiii. 262. **40**. A. N. Mouravieff, *Hist. Ch. in Russia*, tr. R. W. Blackmore, pp. 193 sqq.: W. H. Frere, *Links in the Chain of Russian Church History*, 111 sqq.: *Enc. Brit.*[11] xix. 691 sqq. **41**. Adam Olearius, *Voyages and Travels*: tr. J. Davies (London, 1662), 138 sq. Adam Oelschläger [Olearius] 1599—†1671, was secretary to the embassy sent by Duke Frederick III. of Schleswig-Holstein-Gottorp to Muscovy, Tartary and Persia. **42**. Printed in T. Consett, *The Present State and Regulations of the Church of Russia* (London, 1729). **43**. Consett, 3, 4. **44**. W. H. Frere, *Links in the Chain of Russian Church History*, 129 sq. **45**. *Ib.* 132. **46**. The figures following are taken from the *Catholic Encyclopædia* xiii. 261—4. They do not quite tally with another set of figures given in Frere, *Links in the Chain of Russian Church History*, 189 n. 1; but the two sets approximate. **47**. Tr. in R. Pinkerton, *The Present State of the Church in Russia* (Edinburgh, 1814) 37 sqq. **48**. Tr. in R. W. Blackmore, *The Doctrine of the Russian Church* (London, 1845). **49**. Philaret (Basil Drosdof) was born at Kolomna, near Moscow, 1782; became Rector of the Academy of St. Petersburg, 1812, Bishop of Reval, 1817, Archbishop of Tver, 1819, and of Yaroslavl, 1820, then Metropolitan of Moscow, 1821—†67. It was he who drafted the edict by which, 19th March, 1861, Alexander II., 1855—†81, emancipated some 23 million serfs. **50**. W. H. Frere, *Links in the Chain of Russian Church History*, 175; and Macaire, *Théologie Dogmatique Orthodoxe* (2 vols., Paris, 1859—60). **51**. W. H. Frere, *Links in the Chain of Russian Church History*, 175 sq. **52**. E. Smirnov, *Russian Orthodox Missions* (Rivington, 1903). **53**. *Ib.* 30 sqq. **54**. *Ib.* 17 sq. **55**. *Ib.* 21 sqq.

CHAPTER XVI.

1. See J. Labourt, *Le Christianisme dans l'empire perse:* and above, ch. v. § 8. **2**. Synod of Isaac, 410: canon xxi. *Synodicon Orientale*, 272, ed. J. B. Chabot. **3**. Synod of Joseph, 554, *ibid.* 367.

4. Labourt, 327. **5.** Canon xxi. of Synod of Isaac: *Syn. Or.* 272. **6.** Synod of Dadiso‛, 424: *Syn. Or.* 295 sq.; Kidd, *Documents* ii. No. 155. **7.** *Ibid.* **8.** Described by the Synod of Isaac, in respect of the Catholicus: "il est son bras droit et son auxiliaire": *Syn. Or.* 272. **9.** Synod of Joseph, 554: canon xxi.: *Syn. Or.* 365. **10.** Synod of Isaac, 410: *Syn. Or.* 258. **11.** Labourt, 333. **12.** *Ib.* 333 sq. **13.** *Ib.* 337. **14.** Labourt, 338. **15.** *Ib.* 324. **16.** *Ib.* 315 sqq. **17.** *Ib.* 320—mostly in the north, especially in Adiabene. For the history of Persian Monasticism, see *Le livre de la Chasteté* [ed. J. B. Chabot (Rome, 1896)] by Iso‛denah, bp. of Bassora (end of eighth century); and *The Book of Governors* by Thomas of Marga (ninth century) [ed. E. M. Budge, London, 1893], and Labourt, c. xi. **18.** *Ib.* 324. **19.** *S.O.* 302; Kidd, *Documents*, ii. No. 236. **20.** "Acacius's . . . Confession of Faith is derived from the theology of Antioch; between it and the Formula of Union in 433 or that of the Council of Chalcedon there are only shades of expression. However, the term 'Mother of God' was avoided." L. Duchesne, *Early Hist. Ch.* iii. 393. **21.** Labourt, c. x.: Duchesne, *L'église au VIme siècle*, 310. **22.** "Nous définissons donc... qu'il n'est permis à aucun homme, à quelque ordre ecclésiastique qu'il appartienne, de diffamer ce docteur de l'église [sc. Theodore], en secret ou en public, ni de rejeter ses saints écrits, ni d'accepter cet autre commentaire" [sc. by Henana of Adiabene, a doctor of the School of Nisibis c. 570]. Synod of Iso‛yabh I., A.D. 580: canon II. (*S.O.* 400): renewed at the Synods of 596 and 605 by the Patriarchs Sabriso I. and Gregory (*S.O.* 459, 475): see Duchesne, *op. cit.* 327. **23.** "Avec elle [sc. the Church of the Roman Empire] on n'avait aucune relation officielle; mais c'était toute la dissidence, car aucun anathème n'avait était lancé ni d'un côté, ni de l'autre." *Ib.* 326. **24.** Duchesne, *op. cit.* 326 sq. **25.** Situated on the edge of the cultivated land, near the present Meshed Ali, on a canal W. of the Euphrates, and about 90 miles south of Bagdad. **26.** Collected in A. Mingana, *The early spread of Christianity in Central Asia and the Far East* (Manchester University Press, 1925). **27.** Mingana, app. I. **28.** H. Labourt, *De Timotheo I. Nestorianorum Patriarcha (728—823) et Christianorum orientalium condicione sub Caliphis Abbasidis* (Parisus, 1904), p. 43. The Abbasid Caliphs ruled at Bagdad from 750—1258: but became insignificant after 860. **29.** *Ibid.* **30.** Thomas of Marga was secretary to the Patriarch Abraham, 837—50, and by him was made bishop of Marga, and afterwards metropolitan of Beth Garmai: see W. Wright, *Syriac Literature*, 219. **31.** See Barhebraeus, *Chronicon Ecclesiasticum*, (edd. J. B. Abbeloos et T. J. Lamy, Lovanii, 1872—7) iii. 280—2. Gregory Barhebraeus, or Abu'l-Faraj, 1226—†86, was a maphrian of the Jacobite church, and "one of the most learned and versatile men that Syria ever produced" (W. Wright, *A Short History of Syriac Literature*, 265). He wrote his *Chronicle* in Syriac c. 1240 (Part I. Secular: II. Antioch: III. East Syrians). **32.** "The kingdom of the mysterious Prester John, who has been identified wiith Wang Khan, is placed in their land." *C.M.H.* iv. 650: and Gibbon c. lxiv. n. 3 (ed. J. B. Bury, 1896, vol. vii. p. 2). **33.** Temujin, was his proper name: "Ghenghis" or "Chingiz" means "Great": see for his conquests, Gibbon c. lxiv. (ed. Bury, vol. 7). **34.** In the territory of the Naimans, *C.M.H.* iv. 631. For the Mongols, see *C.M.H.* iv. c. 20: and map No. 46. "The Mongol Empire about 1250." **35.** See above, ch. xv. § 4.   **36.** See *Libellus historicus Joannis de Plano Carpini* in *Texts and Versions of John de Plano Carpini*, pp. 43—74 [ed. for the Hakluyt Society by C. R. Beazley, 1903]; and translation in W. W. Rockhill (Hakluyt Society, 1900) 1 sqq. with map. **37.** Latin text in Beazley *op. cit.* 144—83: and tr. in *ib.* 184—234, and in Rockhill *op. cit.* 40 sqq.   **38.** *Travels*,² edd. H. Yule and H. Cordier (London, 1921): or *Everyman's Library*, vol. 306. **39.** There were five sections of Turks under Oghuz Khan: (1) Kiptchaks or Kumans; (2) Kankali, N. of lake Aral, between the Ural river and Lake Balkash; (3) Naimans, S. of the Ob and Yenisei rivers, in whose district was the famous town of Karakorum. They were subjects of "Prester John"; (4) Uighurs—one of the centres of Nestorian Christianity; (5) Merkites, *C.M.H.* iv. 631.   **40.** So they are numbered in the "Notitia episcopatuum Orientis ex Amro" in *Bibl. Or.* ii. 458.   **41.** J. S. Assemani, *Bibliotheca Orientalis* III. i. 620: see also J. B. Chabot, *Histoire de Mar Jabalaha* III. (Paris, 1895), reprinted from *Revue de l'Orient Latin* i. 566—610, ii. 73—142, 235—304 (Paris, 1893—4): with Chronological Table ii. 301 sq. **42.** Argoun, 1284—†91, was grandson of Hulagu, 1251, himself grandson of Ghengis Khan. See table in *R.O.L.* i. 572.   **43.** *Hist de Mar. J.* c. vi.   **44.** *Ib.* (*R.O.L.* ii. 106).   **45.** *Ib.* (*R.O.L.* ii. 110). At Bordeaux, where Edward I. communicated at Rabban Sauma's [Nestorian] Mass.   **46.** *Ib.* (*R.O.L.* ii. 114—5).   **47.** *Ib.* (*R.O.L.* ii. 120—1).   **48.** Two grandsons of Ghenghis Khan were (1) Hulagu (b. 1216), 1256—†65, who ruled over Persia, Mesopotamia and Asia Minor: captured Bagdad 1258 and put an end to the Abbasid Caliphate there: and became a Mohammedan; and (2) Kublai Khan, 1259—†94, who transferred his capital from Karakorum to Pekin, and became a Buddhist.   **49.** Otherwise known as Kumans from Kumistan in Persia (*C.M.H.* iv. 631) and as the Polovtsy to the Russians: "in the ninth century their expansion brought them to the Volga, and . . . . they made themselves a thorn in the side of Russia, until their incorporation . . . in the Golden Horde during the thirteenth century," *ib.* 631.   **50.** Gibbon, c. lxv.: *C.M.H.* iv. 650 sqq.   **51.** Bury's Gibbon, vii. 48 (c. lxv. n. 3).   **52.** *Ib.* vii. 50 sq. **53.** *Ib.* vii. 52 sqq.   **54.** *Ib.* vii. 68.   **55.** J. S. Assemani, *Bibl. Orient.* iii. 621; A. Fortescue, *The Lesser Eastern Churches*, 101 sqq. **56.** A. J. Maclean and W. H. Browne, *The Catholicos of the East and his people* (S.P.C.K., 1892).   **57.** *The Christian East*, April, 1926: photograph, and pp. 44 sqq.

CHAPTER XVII.

1. *Dictionnaire de Théologie catholique*, edd. A. Vacant et E. Mangenot (Paris, 1899—   ), i. 1888—1968; *Dictionnaire d'Histoire et de Géographie ecclésiastiques*, ed. A. Baudrillart (Paris, 1925), iv. 290—391; *Enc. Brit.*¹¹ ii. 564 sqq.   **2.** B. J. Kidd, *Hist. Ch. to A.D. 461*, iii. 419 sqq.   **3.** Eus. *H.E.* VI. xlvi. § 2. **4.** *Ib.* IX. viii. § 2.   **5.** Kidd, *Documents* i. No. 182. **6.** Gibbon, c. xviii. (ed. Bury, ii. 226).   **7.** Faust, Byz., *Hist. Arm.*, iii. § 13.   **8.** *D.H.G.E.*, iv. 297: Kidd, *Documents*, ii. No. 118. Ashtishat was in Taron, to the south-west of Armenia.

It had been the religious centre of Armenian paganism. In the fourth century it was the ecclesiastical capital of the country, and the place for synods; Valarshapat being the civil capital. In the fifth century, it was succeeded by Dwin, to the N.E. **9.** For a list of Armenian monasteries, see *D.H.G.E.* iv. 377 sqq. **10.** Basil, *Epp.* cxx.—cxxii. (*Op.* iv. 211—3 : *P.G.* xxxii. 537—44). **11.** For these periods in Armenian History, see *C.M.H.* iv. 154. **12.** Gibbon, c. xxxii. n. 83 (iii. 392, ed. Bury). **13.** Brightman, *Liturgies*, 412—57. **14.** Kidd, *Documents*, ii. No. 210. **15.** Whence Germanus, Patriarch of CP., 715—†30, in his reply to John of Odsun, sets himself to show that the phrase of St. Cyril—Μία φύσις τοῦ Λόγου σεσαρκωμένη —really meant "one Person of the Word [and that] Incarnate" and is not incompatible, in the thought of St. Cyril, with the distinction of the two Natures : see Germanus, *Ep. ad Armenos,* § 10 (*P.G.* xcviii. 140). **16.** *C.M.H.* iv. 155. It was during this period that the Armenians were received at the Council of Florence, 1439; when Eugenius IV. addressed to them the *Decretum pro Armenis* of 22nd Nov., 1439, or instruction on the sacraments, parts of which, especially § 15, on Holy Orders, are now rather embarrassing : see it in C. Mirbt, *Quellen zur Geschichte des Papsttums,*[4] No. 401. **17.** For a list of the Catholici, see M. Le Quien, *Oriens Christianus,* i. 1371—1416; *D.T.C.* i. 1922—4; *D.H.G.E.* iv. 371 sqq. **18.** He had 28 dioceses before 1915; including Armenians in Europe (6,000) and America (50,000). **19.** For a list of the Patriarchs of Sis, see *D.H.G.E.* iv. 373 sq. He had 15 dioceses. **20.** For those of CP., *ib.* iv. 376 sq. He had 51 dioceses (CP. 150,000). **21.** For those of Jerusalem, *ib.* iv. 375 sq. He had 4 dioceses (Jerusalem 3,000). **22.** With two dioceses—for these statistics, see *D.H.G.E.* iv. 367 sq. **23.** See, in detail, *D.H.G.E.,* iv. 346 sqq. : *Enc. Brit.*[11] ii. 567 sq. **24.** The chief modern books are O. H. Parry, *Six months in a Syrian Monastery,* 279 sqq. (Cox, 1895); A. Fortescue, *The Lesser Eastern Churches,* 323 sqq. (C.T.S., 1913) and s.v. "Eastern Churches" in *Cath. Enc.* v. 233 sq.; W. A. Wigram, *The Separation of the Monophysites* (Faith Press, 1923); and L. Duchesne, *L'église au VIme siècle,* c. x. (Paris, 1926); the sources being the *Chronicle of Michael the Syrian* (twelfth century), the *Chronicle of Gregory Barhebraeus* (thirteenth century), and the material in J. S. Assemani, *B.O.* ii. (Rome, 1721). **25.** *D.C.B.* iii. 328—32. **26.** Parry, 291. **27.** *B.O.* ii. 53. **28.** Cf. the "Catalogus Patriarcharum Syro-Jacobitarum" in J. S. Assemani *Bibl. Or.* ii. 479. They begin with Severus 512—8, and go down to Ignatius XXVII. (77 in all) down to the author's time (1721). **29.** For the Jacobites in Persia, see J. Labourt, *Le Chr. dans l'empire perse,* 217—221, 239—41. **30.** G. P. Badger, *The Nestorians and their Rituals,* i. 96 sqq. : Parry, *op. cit.* c. xix. **31.** J. S. Assemani, *Bibl. Or.* ii. 418—20 : and for a list of the Mafrians or "Primates Orientis," see *ib.* 482—4. On the office of Mafrian, see Parry, *op. cit.* 317 sq. **32.** Labourt gives the list, but thinks it too long for the seventh century, *op. cit.* 241. **33.** Bishop of Mar'ash, 1145; transferred to Amida, where he died, 1171; see *Bibl. Or.* ii. 156—211 : W. Wright, *Syriac Literature,* 246. **34.** For his *Expositio Missae,* see *Bibl. Or.* ii. 176—208. **35.** Fortescue, *L.E.C.* 331. **36.** *Chronique de Michel le Syrien,* Patriarche Jacobite d'Antioch (1166—1199), ed. J. B. Chabot (3 vols., Paris, 1899—1924). **37.** O. H. Parry, *op. cit.* 300. **38.** *Gregorii Barhebraei Chronicon Ecclesiasticum,* edd. J. B. Abbeloos et T. J.

Lamy (3 vols., Lovanii, 1872—7). **39**. Parry, *op. cit.* 346. **40**. *Ibid.* c. xiii. : " Jebel Tur—the mountain home of the Syrians," and map. **41**. "And of all the Jacobite Churches of Syria and the East." *Ibid.* 314. " The East" here refers to the Syrian Christians in India—some 300,000 in number—for whom see *ib.* 347 sqq. **42**. Beginning with Ignatius III., 1264—†82 : Assemani, *Bibl. Or.* ii. 480. **43**. Described in O. H. Parry, *op. cit.* c. ix. **44**. Fortescue, *L.E.C.* 340. **45**. Text in F. E. Brightman, *Liturgies,* i. 68—110. **46**. " Even as in truth thou art holy," etc.; *ib.* 86. **47**. *Ib.* 89—96. **48**. *Ib.* 77. **49**. *Ib.* lviii. sq. **50**. James Hough, *Hist. Chr. in India* (2 vols., London, 1839); G. B. Howard, *The Christians of St. Thomas and their Liturgies* (Parker, 1864); A. Fortescue, *L.E.C.,* 353 sqq.; W. J. Richards, *The Indian Christians of St. Thomas* (1908). **51**. On whom, see O. Bardenhewer, *Patrology,* 555 sq.; K. Krumbacher, *Gesch. der Byz. Litt.,* § 171. **52**. Cosmas Indicopleustes, *Topographia Christiana,* iii. (*Op.* 178 sq. : *P.G.* lxxxviii. 169 A, B). **53**. H. Labourt, *De Timotheo I.,* pp. 41 sq. **54**. *Anglo-Saxon Chronicle,* A.D. 883, ii. 66 (ed. B. Thorpe, 1861) : and William of Malmesbury, *Gesta regum Anglorum* ii. § 122 (ed. W. Stubbs, i. 130). **55**. *Travels* Bk. III., ch. xxv. : ii. 389 (edd. H. Yule and H. Cordier). **56**. *Ib.* Bk. III. c. xviii. **57**. A. Fortescue, *L.E.C.* 361 sq. **58**. *Ib.* 107. **59**. *Ib.* 352 sq. **60**. See *Survey of India:* Malabar district and Cochin and Travancore State : No. 58, C 1 and 5 (Map Record and Issue Office, 13 Wood St., Calcutta). **61**. For the Synod of Diamper, see Latin text in Mansi, *Concilia,* xxxv. 1161—1368 (Parisiis, 1902); and tr. in Hough, *op. cit.* ii. 511—683. **62**. " The Christians form at least a quarter of the population of two small states—Travancore and Cochin, and their number is nearly a million. Unhappily, they are divided into four separate bodies. First, there is the main body which claims to represent unchanged the ancient Church, . . . perhaps a quarter of a million. Then there are " the Uniates ". . . probably the most numerous body of the four. Thirdly, there is a secession from" the main body "who have come under Protestant influences, and are known as the Mar Thomas Syrians. And lastly there is a small body which seceded from Rome in 1880 and obtained a bishop from those Assyrian Christians to whom the Archbishop of Canterbury sent his mission. It is with the first of these four communities with which we of the Oxford Mission [to Calcutta] have had most to do. In 1913 they invited us to send delegates to their students' conference and to hold a Retreat for their priests; and every year since then the invitation has been repeated and, whenever possible, accepted." Fr. E. F. Browne, in *The Christian East,* Feb., 1924, p. 47. **63**. F. E. Brightman, *Liturgies,* 69 sqq.; G. B. Howard, *op. cit.* 191 sqq. **64**. Howard, *op. cit.* 222 sqq. **65**. Ch. i. and v. § 9. For the Coptic and Melkite Patriarchs, from this date onwards, see Le Quien, *Or. Chr.* ii. 412 sqq. : *D.H.G.E.* ii. 365 sqq., and the list prefixed to this chapter. **66**. For the Copts, see Eutychius [Orthodox Patriarch of Alexandria, 933—†40], *Contextio Gemmarum* [a history of the world to 938] *P.G.* cxi. 889—1156; Severus [Monophysite Bishop of Al-Ushmunain], *History of the Patriarchs of Alexandria* [Arabic : tr. B. T. A. Evetts] in *Patrologia Orientalis* I. 99—214, 381—518, V. 1—215, X. 357—552 [from St. Mark to Joseph, †849] : E. Renaudot [1646—†1720] *Hist. Patr. Al. Iac.* (Parissis, 1713), based on Severus; J. M. Neale, *History of the Patriarchate of Alexandria;* A. P. Stanley, *Lectures on the Eastern*

520   The Churches of Eastern Christendom

Church, c. i.; J. M. Fuller, s.v. "Coptic Church" in D.C.B. i. 664—86; A. Fortescue, L.E.C. 214 sqq.; and D.H.G.E. ii. 326 sqq. See also, for the general setting, S. Lane-Poole, *A history of Egypt in the middle ages*, 640—1517 (Methuen, 1901).   67. "Sunnites, literally, those of the path, *sunna*, i.e. followers of the Prophet's directions. . . . They accept the orthodox tradition as well as the Koran: and predominate in Arabia, the Turkish Empire, the north of Africa, Turkestan, Afghanistan and the Mohammedan parts of India, and the east of Africa." *Enc. Brit.*[11] xxvi. 103.   68. *P.O.* i. 495 sq. 69. *Ib.* 500.   70. Renaudot, *Hist. Patr. Al.* 170 sq.   71. *Ib.* 172 sq. 72. *P.O.* i. 494.   73. *P.O.* v. 13 sqq.   74. *Ib.*   75. *P.O.* i. 491 n. 1. 76. Eutychius, *Annales* 387 sq. (*P.G.* cxi. 1123).   77. The Shi'ites are so called from *shi'a*, a party. They hold the hereditary principle, and maintain that the lawful head of Islam should be a descendant of the Prophet, through his daughter, Fatima, and his son-in-law, 'Ali ibn 'Abi-Talib. Theirs is now the official religion of Persia. For a table of the Fatimids, see S. Lane-Poole, *op. cit.* 116.   78. S. Lane-Poole, *Hist. Egypt*, 119. Fustat, "the camp" of 'Amr, near Cairo. It remained the capital until the building of Cairo, 969, *ib.* 17. 79. E. Renaudot, *op. cit.* 413.   80. *Ib.* 413.   81. *Ib.* 421 sqq.   82. For a table of the Ayyubids, see S. Lane-Poole, *op. cit.* 212.   83. Renaudot, *op. cit.* 513.   84. *Ib.* 578 sq.   85. *Ib.* 592. He had been excommunicated by the Patriarch for a moral offence; and, to escape the penalty, turned Moslem.   86. Le Quien, *Or. Chr.* ii. 499 E. 87. *Decretum pro Jacobitis* (*Cantate Domino*, 4th Feb., 1441, of Eugenius IV.) in Denzinger-Bannwart[14-18], *Enchiridion*, 703—5. See Mansi xxxi. B, coll. 1734—43.   88. See A. J. Butler, *The Ancient Coptic Churches of Egypt* (Clar. Press, 1884), and *The Churches and Monasteries of Egypt*, attributed to Abû Sâlih, the Armenian: edd. B. T. A. Evetts and A. J. Butler (Clar. Press, 1895).   89. The present authorised Coptic Catechism of 1912 teaches that our Lord "became one only Person, one only distinct substance, one only nature, with one will and one operation"—quoted in Fortescue, *L.E.F.* 260. 90. Text in Brightman, *Liturgies* 113—143; see L. Duchesne, *Chr. Worship* (ed. 1903), 80. "Once used by the Egyptian Melkites, it was replaced by the Byzantine rite in the thirteenth century." A. Fortescue, *The Mass* (1912), 97.   91. Text in Brightman, *Lit.* 144—88; Duchesne, 80 sq., who says: It "is evidently the most ancient. . . . It alone of the three presents certain features characteristic of the Alexandrine Liturgy. . . . It reproduces often the text of the Liturgy of St. Mark word for word. By joining to the *anaphora* of St. Cyril the Ordinary of the Coptic Mass, we obtain a Coptic Liturgy which is the exact counterpart of the Greek Liturgy of St. Mark."   92. Text in E. Renaudot, *Lit. Or. Collectio* (ed. 1847) i. 25—37.   93. Text in *ib.* i. 1—25.   94. Brightman, 165—75. 95. *Ib.* 176, line 5.   96. *Ib.* 176, line 3.   97. Rogamus te Christe Deus noster, nos peccatores indigni servi tui, et adoramus te per beneplacitum bonitatis tuae, ut adveniat Spiritus sanctus tuus super nos, et super haec dona praeposita, et sanctificet ea, efficiatque ea Sancta Sanctorum tuorum. Renaudot i. 15.   98. *Ib.* 16—18. 99. *Dict. Th. Cath.* v. 922—69; *D.H.G.E.* i. 210—27: *D.C.B.* ii. 232—41; *Cath. Enc.* i. 75—9; Fortescue, *L.E.C.* 293 sqq.; *Enc. Brit.*[11] i. 82—96; and M. Geddes, *The Church History of Ethiopia* (London, 1696). Geddes was a Chancellor of Sarum who wrote "this History to be of some use to all Protestant countreys, which may therein, as in a glass, see what treatment they are to expect from Popery, whenever the Supream Power is in its hands." But, allowing for this, his facts are useful. **100.** *Enc. Brit.*[11] i. 88 sq. **101.** Rufinus, *H.E.* i. 9 (*Op.* 230—2: *P.L.* xxi. 478—80). **102.** Ath., *Apol. ad Const.* § 31 (*Op.* i. 250: *P.G.* xxv. 636 sq.). **103.** Philostorgius, *H.E.* iii. who mentions his missions to the Homerites (Himyarites) § 4 and to Axum § 6 (*P.G.* lxv. 484—5). **104.** Corporis morumque pulchritudine pluribus antistante et in culmine tam celso humana, cuius favore justissimo exemptum periculis declaratumque Caesarem retulimus Julianum. Amm. Marc. *Res Gestae* XXI. vi. 4. **105.** John Malalas, *Chronographia* [written c. 573] xviii. (*Op.* 433: *P.G.* xcvii. 640 sq.): see K. Krumbacher, *Gesch. der Byz. Litt.* § 140. **106.** Cosmas Indicopleustes, *Top. Chr.* iii. (*Op.* 179: *P.G.* lxxxviii. 169 C). **107.** E. Renaudot, *Hist. Patr. Al.*, 170. **108.** For the list of the Abunas, so far as they are known, from John onwards, see *D.H.G.E.*, i. 224. The late Abuna was Mattheos, who died on 4th Dec., 1926, after being Abuna for 47 years, 1879—1926. **109.** Renaudot, *op. cit.* 339. **110.** It began with Salomon I., 1285—94: for the list of the kings who followed, see A. M. H. Stokvis, *Manuel d'Histoire*, i. 443. **111.** To the N. of Addis Ababa, in Shoa. **112.** *Enc. Brit.*[11] i. 90. **113.** Geddes, 339. **114.** J. M. Neale, *Hist. Patr. Ab.* i. 156 sq.: and cf. E. Renaudot, *Lit. Or. Collectio* i. 418 sq. **115.** For Egyptian monasticism, as represented by Antony and Pachomius in the fourth century, see my *History of the Church to A.D. 461*, ii. 102 sq. **116.** Text in Brightman, *Liturgies*, 194—244: and see S. A. B. Mercer, *The Ethiopic Liturgy* (Milwaukee, 1915). **117.** L. Duchesne, *Christian Worship*,[2] 81. **118.** Brightman, lxxiii. sq. **119.** A. Fortescue, *The Mass*, 97.

CHAPTER XVIII.

1. A. Fortescue, *The Orthodox Eastern Church* (C.T.S., 1912). **2.** *Ib. The Lesser Eastern Churches* (C.T.S., 1913). **3.** *Cath. Enc.* v. 235 sqq. and *The Uniate Eastern Churches* (Burns, Oates and Washbourne, 1923): unfortunately not finished. It deals only with the Italo-Greeks, and the Melkites: and Stephen Gaselee, *The Uniates and their rites* (Alcuin Club, 1925, 2/-). **4.** See above Ch. vii. § 4. He wanted to round off his empire, and make the Patriarchate of Constantinople con-terminous with the Roman Empire of the East. In the eleventh century the Normans wrested Southern Italy from the East Roman Empire: see above, Ch. viii. § 6. **5.** Nicholas I. *Ep.* xii. [to Photius, 862] (*P.L.* cxix. 789 C). **6.** Leo IX. *Ep.* c. § 29 (*P.L.* cxliii. 764 A). Leo says that he did not retaliate by interfering with churches and monasteries of the Greek rite at Rome. **7.** Gregory, *Epp.* XI. lxiv. (*Op.* iii. 1152: *P.L.* lxxvii. 1187 A). **8.** Benedict XIV., *Bullarium* iv. 123—36. **9.** § 6 (*ib.* 124). **10.** § 48 (*ib.* 136). **11.** Leo XIII., *Acta* V. 303—11 (Brugis, 1898). **12.** *Ib.* § 1 (v. 306 sq.). **13.** "Roman Catholic controversialists like to allow it to be thought—they are generally too wise to state it openly—that any given body of Uniates is an original, faithful remnant which has remained true to Rome and refused to go into schism; whereas most (though not all Uniates) . . . have been detached by Roman missionaries from their own mother Church, and the way has been made easy for them to enter into communion with Rome by leaving them as much as possible of their own rites and customs." Gaselee, 13. **14.** I give the numbers mainly from Gaselee, as his is the latest reckoning; but, as he says, "it is exceedingly difficult to make even an approximately accurate estimate": p. 7. **15.** For the history of the Church in Georgia, see my *History of the Church to A.D. 461*, iii. 414 sqq. **16.** Gaselee, *op. cit.* 7. **17.** They are attached to the three seminaries of these Italo-Greeks or Italo-Albanians, viz. (1) The Greek College at Rome; (2) the Calabrian College at San Benedetto Ullano; and (3) the Greek-Albanian College at Palermo: the whole procedure being regulated by *Etsi Pastoralis*, of Benedict XIV. (26th May, 1742): see his *Bullarium* i. 75 sqq. But the College in Calabria is now secularised. Gaselee, 10. **18.** A. Fortescue, *The Uniate Eastern Churches*, 150, and Gaselee, pp. 11—12. **19.** This is Fortescue's figure: Gaselee says Uniate Copts and Abyssinians together "may amount to 5,000 in all": p. 8. **20.** Thus there are in all no less than six Patriarchs of Antioch: (1) The Orthodox Patriarch: and five others, viz. the (2) Jacobite Patriarch and four papal (3) of the Latin rite (titular: lives in Rome), (4) Melkite, (5) Syrian Uniate, (6) Maronite. **21.** This is Fortescue's figure: Gaselee says that 100,000 is "a serious over-estimate," p. 8. **22.** *Cath. Enc.* ix. 683—8; s.v. "Maronites" by J. Labourt. **23.** Theodoret, *Hist.Rel.* c. xvi. (*Op.* iii. 1222—4: *P.G.* lxxxii. 1417—20). The monastery which commemorates his name is Beit-Marun, between Apamea and Emesa, on the right bank of the Orontes. It dates from the sixth century. **24.** Addis and Arnold, *Catholic Dictionary*,[9] 549 sq.

CHAPTER XIX.

1. The churches of (1) Constantinople, (2) Alexandria, (3) Antioch, (4) Jerusalem, (5) Cyprus, (6) Russia, (7) Georgia, (8) Greece, (9) Bulgaria, (10) Rumania, (11) Jugo-slavia, (12) Sinai. Of these, five are Greek (CP., Al., Cyprus, Greece, Sinai); three are Slavic (Russia, Bulgaria, Jugo-slavia); one Rumanic (Rumania); and two Arabic (Antioch and Jerusalem). **2.** They are (1) East Syrians, (2) Armenians, (3) Jacobites, (4) Malabar, (5) Copts, (6) Abyssinians. **3.** The *Filioque* in "who proceedeth from the Father *and the Son.*" **4.** Those of the Creed of Pope Pius IV., 1564: see it in C. Mirbt, *Quellen*[4] No. 480, or in *Can. et decret. Conc. Trid.*, 226 sq. (Lipsiae, 1876), or at the beginning of the new *Codex iuris canonici* (Romae, 1918). **5.** J. Hastings, *E.R.E.* s.v. "Eastern Church," v. 134—6 (1912), and "Greek Orthodox Church," vi. 425—35 (1913): A. C. Headlam, *The Teaching of the Russian Church* (Rivington, 1897); L. Pullan, *Religion since the Reformation*, c. vii. (Clar. Press. 1923); and F. Gavin, *Greek Orthodox Thought* (Milwaukee, 1923). **6.** These are (1) Nicæa I., 325; (2) CP. I., 381; (3) Ephesus, 431; (4) Chalcedon, 451; (5) CP. II., 553; (6) CP. III., 680; (7) Nicæa II., 787. The Roman Catholic Church reckons thirteen more: see list in Mirbt, *Quellen*[4] No. 760. For tr. see *The Seven Œc. Co.* (Nicene and Post-Nicene Fathers, vol. xiv.). **7.** Text in *Op.* i. 123—304 (*P.G.* xciv. 789—1228) : tr. in *N. and P.-N.F.*, vol. ix. **8.** Text in E. J. Kimmel, *Monumenta Fidei Ecclesiae Orientalis* (Jenae, 1850), 56—324. **9.** Text in *ib.* 425—87. **10.** R. W. Blackmore, *The Doctrine of the Russian Church* (Aberdeen, 1845), p. viii. **11.** Tr. in *ib.* 29—142 : and, with it, cf. his less known *Harmony of Anglican Doctrine with the Doctrine of the . . . Church of the East* (Aberdeen, 1846). **12.** *Ib.* vi. **13.** *Introduction à la théologie orthodoxe* (Paris, 1857), and *Théologie dogmatique orthodoxe* (Paris, 1860). **14.** Δογματικὴ τῆς ὀρθοδόξου ἀνατολ ικ ῆ ς'Ἐκκλησιάς (Athens, 1907), Συμβολικὴ, etc. **15.** Called the *Syntagma* of Photius, but of which he was " probably neither the new editor nor the author," *Cambr. Med. Hist.* iv. 718 : and see K. Krumbacher, *Gesch. der Byz. Litt.* § 258. **16.** H. F. Tozer, *The Church and the Eastern Empire,* c. viii. **17.** E. F. Morison, *St. Basil and his Rule* (Clar. Press, 1912), and W. K. L. Clarke, *St. Basil the Great,* 69—74 (Cambr. Press, 1913) : and my *History* ii. 238. **18.** Canon 4 : W. Bright, *Canons of the First Four Councils*[2] 140 sqq. : and my *History,* iii. 329. **19.** W. B. Trevelyan, *Sunday,* 185 sq. **20.** L. Pullan, *Religion since the Reformation,* 195. **21.** Brightman, *Liturgies,* 400—11. **22.** *Ib.* 345—52. **23.** *Ib.* 353—99 : and tr. F. E. Brightman, *The Divine Liturgy of St. John Chrysostom* (Faith Press, 1922) : see, too, A. Riley, *A guide to the Divine Liturgy in the East* (Mowbray, 1922). Note that " St. Basil and St. Chrysostom are not distinct 'liturgies' but rather two 'masses' of the same liturgy." Brightman, *op. cit.* p. v. **24.** Brightman, *The Divine Lit.,* vi. **25.** A. C. Headlam, *The Teaching of the Russian Church,* 28. **26.** *Ib.* 35 sqq. **27.** It was admitted by Benedict VIII., 1012—†24, in 1014, under pressure from Spanish and German custom of long standing. *D.C.B.* iii. 133. **28.** St. Athanasius and St. Cyril of Alexandria : see D. Stone, *Outlines of Dogma,* n. 3, pp. 276 sqq. " It may be doubted whether there has ever been an essential difference between the East and the West on this subject. . . . It is difficult to think that Easterns have ever meant that the Son was passive in the procession, while Westerns have certainly not meant that there were two *principia* " in the Godhead. **29.** *D.C.B.* iii. 129. **30.** Cyril Lucar, in denying Transubstantiation, rejected the Real Presence (*Conf.* c. xvii. : Kimmel, *Mon. Fid. Eccl. Or.,* i. 35—7). The *Orthodox Confession* of Peter Mogila reasserted the traditional doctrine of the East in those matters in which Cyril Lucar had denied or modified it (*Conf.* i. 56 and 107 : Kimmel i. 125 sq., 180—4)—and " accepted the word 'Transubstantiation' which Cyril Lucar had repudiated, probably using it, as he had used it, simply to denote the change of the elements by consecration into Christ's body and blood." This, however, is to attach to it a less technical meaning than belongs to it in Latin theology ; but the purpose is the same—to safeguard the Real Presence. See further, D. Stone, *Doctrine of the Holy Eucharist,* i. 175 sqq. : L. Pullan, *Religion since the Reformation,* 201 sq. : A. C. Headlam, *Teaching of the Russian Church,* 8 sqq. **31.** By the Church of Constantinople, 28th July, 1922, and by the Churches of Jerusalem and Cyprus, 12th March and 20th March, 1923—see the letters in *The Christian East* of October, 1922 and August, 1923. **32.** *Ib.* (Sept., 1925).

INDEX.

Abyssinia, Church of : 100, 297, 442, 447 sqq.
Acacian Schism (484—519), The : 17 sqq., 25, 28
Acacius, Catholicus of "The East" (485—†96) : 92 sq.
Acacius, Patr. CP. (471—†89) : 4, 11, 14 sqq., 18
Acephali, The : 50
Accœmetæ, The : 13 sq., 37
Achaia, Principality of : 247, 251, 267
"Adoration" : meaning of, 142, 144
Agapetus, Pope (535—†6) : 63
Agatho, Pope (678—†82) : 119 sq., 124
Agnoetae, The : 51
Ajnadain, Battle of : 113
Aktistetae, The : 51
Albania : 341 and see "Epirus, Despotate of"
Alexander III., Pope (1159—†81) : 223
Alexandria, Patriarchs of : 2, 23, 79, 98, 102, 137, 180, 220, 246, 261, 296, 426 sq., 443
  Church of : 305 sqq.
Alexis (Romanov : Tsar, 1645—†76) : 396 sqq., 400 sqq.
Alexius I. (Comnenus : Emp. 1081—†1118) : 215, 222, 228
Alexius III. (Angelus : Emp. 1195—†1203) : 224, 236 sqq., 361
Alexius IV. (Angelus : Emp. †1204) : 239 sqq.
Alexius V. (Murtzuphlus : Emp. 1204) : 241
Alfred, King of England (871—†91) : 439
Almsgiving : 165
Anarchy : The First (695—717), 103, 134 ; The Second (802—20), 134, 152 sqq., 320 ; The Third (1025—81), 182 sq., 204 sq., 221, 227
Anastasius, Emp. (491—†518) : 17 sqq., 25, 28, 37
Anastasius of Sinai (640—700) : 132
Anatolius, Patr. CP. (449—58) : 8 sq.
Ancyra (Angora), Battle of (1402) : 265, 284, 378, 423
Andronicus I. (Comnenus : Emp. 1183—†5) : 223
Andronicus II. (Palaeologus : Emp. 1282—1328) : 265, 271 sq., 422
Andronicus III. (Palaeologus : Emp. 1328—†41) : 265, 271, 273 sq., 277
Androutsos, Professor, of Athens : 468
Angeli, Dynasty of the : 218
Angels, *Cultus* of : 74, 131
Animal sacrifices : 90, 429
Anselm, abp. of Canterbury (1093—†1109) : 252 sq.
Anthimus, Patr. CP. (535—†6) : 56
Antioch, Patriarchs of : 2, 23, 79, 102, 137, 180, 220, 246, 261, 296, 306 ; Jacobite Patriarchs of, 438, 441 ; Church of, 306 sq. ; Christology of, 12, 42
Antonina, wife of Belisarius : 55
Aphthartodocetism : 35, 48 sqq., 51, 85, 91

Apocrisiarius: 16, 40, 44, 66, 88
"Archbishop," Meaning of title of : 63 sq.
Arians : 56, 449
Armenia : 83, 134, 156 sq., 184 sq., 188, 207, 221; Church of, 88 sqq., 130, 197, 203, 297, 428 sqq.; seat of the Catholicus of, 434; massacres of Armenians, 435 sq.; Uniates, 462
Art : Byzantine, 68, 129, 131, 150; influence of paganism on, 147, Russian, 382
Assyrians : see "East-Syrians" and "Persia"
Astrakhan, Conquest of (1554) : 386
Athanasius of Trebizond : 201
Athens : University of, 58; Duchy of, 247
Athos, Monasteries of Mt. : 201, 361 sq., 404
Autocephalous churches : 63, 123
Avars, The : 80, 82, 105, 158, 346
Ayyubids, Dynasty of (1169—1341) : 234, 444
Azymes : 210, 252 sq., 288

Babylon, Uniate Patriarch of : 423
Bagdad : Caliphs of : 139, 155, 203, 225
Baldwin, Count of Edessa (1098—1100) : 229 sq.
Baldwin I., Latin Emp. of CP. (1204—†5) : 242 sq., 248, 325
Balkan : League (1912), 330, 340
 War (First : 1912—3), 330, 340, 352, 357
 (Second : 1913), 331, 341, 352, 357
Baptism : Rites of, 93, 165; necessity of, 129
Baptisteries : 69
Baradæus (Baradai), see "James"
Bardas, Cæsar (862—†6) : 156, 169, 173, 175
Bardas Phocas : 183 sq., 199, 203
Bardas Sclerus : 183, 203
Barlaam, bp. of Gerace (1341—†8) : 274 sqq.
Barsumas (Barsoma), metr. of Nisibis (420—†92) : 91 sq.
Basil, Rule of St. : 468
Basil I., Emp. (867—†86) : 181 sq., 183, 194 sq., 334, 433
Basil II. (Bulgaroctonus : Emp. 976—†1025) : 181 sq., 186 sq., 202 sqq., 324, 334, 433
Basil II., Grand Prince of Moscow (1389—†1425) : 377 sq.
Basil III., Grand Prince of Moscow (1425—†62) : 378 sq.
Basil IV., Grand Prince of Moscow (1505—†33) : 382 sq.
Basil V., Tsar (1606—†10) : 393
Basil Lecapenus (944—88) : 181, 183, 202
Basil "the Bird" : 183, 199
Basilika of Leo VI. (Emp. 886—†912) : 199
Bayazid I., Sultan (1389—†1403) : 282 sqq., 423
Belgrade (Singidunum) : 81, 339
 Patriarchate of : 342
Belisarius (†565) : 27 sqq., 55
Benedict XII. (Pope 1334—†42) : 274 sq.
Benedict XIV. (Pope : 1740—†58) : 458
Benjamin, Coptic Patr. Al. (623—62) : 442, 450
Berlin, Treaty of (1878) : 330, 339, 357
Bernard, St. (†1153) : 232
Bessarion, Cardinal (†1472) : 286 sqq., 379
Bishop, Duties of a : 64, 125

Blues and Greens: 27
Bogomils: see "Paulicians"
Bohemond, Prince of Antioch (†1111): 229 sq.
Boris I., King of the Bulgars (852—88): 158, 161, 165, 168, 195, 320
Boris II., King of the Bulgars (969—†76): 186
Boris Godunov, Tsar (1598—†1605): 391 sqq., 398
Bosnia and Herzegovina: 298, 332, 334, 337, 339 sq.
Bregalnitza, Battle of the (1913): 331
Bringas, Joseph: 183, 200
Bucharest, Treaty of (1913): 341
Bulgaria: 319 sqq.
    Church of: 324, 327 sqq.
    Exarchate of (1870): 329
    Uniates of: 461
Byzantinism: 61, 171, 209
Bulgars, The: 17, 118, 132, 140, 153, 155, 157, 184 sq., 202 sq., 206, 249 sqq., 264, 282, 301, 319, 327, 341
    Conversion of: 139, 160 sqq., 321 sqq., 346
    Kings of: 179, 220, 245, 249, 341

Cæsaropapism: 48, 55, 61, 117
Caliphs: Ommayad, 139, 442 sq.
    Abbasid, 139, 155, 225
    Fatimite, 226, 231, 443 sq.
Canonisation: 75, 201
Canon Law: 194, 445
Carlowitz, Church of: 298, 332
Catalans, The: 272
Catapan: of S. Italy, 206
    of Cyprus, 226
Catholici: of Armenia, 89; of "the East," 92; 416 sqq.
Ceremonial splendour: 93
Ceylon: 439, 449
Chalcedon, Reaction after: 3 sqq.
Chancellor, Richard (†1556): 388 sq.
Charlemagne (Emp. 800—†14): 152, 155, 158, 225
Charles, Count of Anjou (†1285): 268
Charles, King of Rumania (1881—†1915): 349
Chataldja Lines: 17, 320, 331
Cherson: 187, 190 sq.
China: Nestorian missions in, 421 sq.; Nestorian monument in, 440
Church and State, Relations of: 153, 171, 197 sqq., 201 sqq., 204, 209, 214, 254, 298 sq.
    In Russia, 399 sq., 410, 413 sq.
Church, arrangements of a: 71, 131, 470
Civitate, Battle of (1053): 209
Clement IV. (Pope, 1265—†8): 268
Clement V. (Pope, 1305—†14): 272
Clement VIII. (Pope, 1592—†1605): 392
Clerics: Privileges of, 65; marriage of, 65, 94, 125; maintenance of, 65; trading by, 65; numbers of, 65; duties and morals of, 126; corporate interests of, 204 sq.
Code: of Justinian I., 31, 58 sq.; of Leo III. (1) agrarian, 140, 330; (2) nautical, 141, 330; (3) the *Ecloga,* 141
Codex Theodosianus: 31

Cœnobites: 67, 362, 419, 469
Communion: fast before, 129, 165, 470; rarity of, 470
Comneni, Dynasty of the: 204, 215, 218 sqq., 244
Confession: private, 69
Confirmation: 69, 129
Conrad, Marquis of Montferrat (1183—†92): 235 sqq.
Constans II., Emp. (642—†68): 103, 114 sqq.
Constantine IV. (Pogonatus: Emp. 668—†85): 103, 115, 118 sqq., 156
Constantine V., Emp. (741—†75): 138 sqq., 149 sqq., 156
Constantine VI., Emp. (780—†97): 150
Constantine VII. (Porphyrogenitus: Emp. 945—†59): 182, 189, 197, 199 sq., 333
Constantine IX., Emp. (1025—†8): 205
Constantine X. (Monomachus: Emp. 1042—†54): 206, 209 sqq., 226
Constantine XI. (Ducas: Emp. 1059—†67): 214
Constantine XIII. (Dragases: Emp. 1448—†53): 266, 290 sqq., 381
Constantine, King of Greece (1913—†23): 357 sq.
Constantine, bp. of Nacolia (c. 720): 144 sqq.
Constantine the Philosopher: see "Cyril, St."
Constantinople: Patriarchs of, 2, 23, 79, 102, 137, 180, 204 sq., 220, 245, 261, 294 sqq.; see of, 62 sq., 167, 176, 196, 209; number of sees dependent on, 64, 123 sq.; number of clergy in, 65; capture of (1204), 241 sq.; Latin Emps. of, 245; Latin Patriarchs of, 245; Fall of (1453), 290; position of Patriarch after Mohammedan Conquest, 302 sq.
Coptic Church: 96 sqq., 297, 442 sqq.
Corpus Juris Civilis: 32
Cosmas Indicopleustes (c. 547): 439, 450
Councils: Chalcedon (451), 3, 44, 46, 95, 298; CP. (553), 38, 41, 46 sqq., 55; relation of Emperor to, 55; civil sanction to, 3, 60; Valarshapat (491), 88, 432; Dvin (525, 551, 591), 88 sq., 432; Seleucia-Ctesiphon (410), 91; Markabta of the Arabs (424), 91; Acacius (486), 93, 419; Babai (497), 93; Ishu-yabh (c. 590), 94; CP. (680), 109, 115, 120 sqq.; Rome (679), 120; Hatfield (680), 120; *In Trullo* (692), 123, 194, 298; Nicæa (787), 140, 151, 194; Rome (731), 149; Hieria (753), 151, 153; CP. (869), 168; CP. (861), 173, 197; Lateran (863), 174 sq., 194; CP. (867), 174 sq., 195; CP. (869), 175, 195; Vladimir (1274), 194; CP. (879—80), 197; CP. (920), 199; CP. (1054), 213; Piacenza (1095), 228; Clermont (1095), 229; Bari (1098), 252 sq.; Lyons (1274), 258, 269 sq., Florence (1439) 258, 266, 271, 285 sqq. 378 sqq., 445; Ferrara (1438), 266, 285 sq., 378 sqq.; Constance (1415), 284; Seres (1351), 337; of a Hundred Chapters (1551), 384; Moscow (1660), 402; (1666), 403, 406; (1917), 413; Ashtishat (365), 430; Erzerum (633), 432; Manzikert (728), 432; Diamper (1599), 440, 459, 462
Counter-Reformation, The: 392, 396 sq.
Crete: 183 sq., 200, 247, 354, 359
Crimea, The: 386 sq.
Crimean War, The (1854—6): 327, 356
Croats: 106, 128, 132, 186 sq., 332
Cross, The: 74, 113, 128, 143, 166, 224 sq.
Crusades, The: 224 sqq., 444
Cyprus: 140, 184, 226, 235; Church of, 63, 123, 297, 310 sqq.
Cyril, St. (827—†69): 139, 157 sqq., 330, 333

Index

Cyril V., Coptic Patr. Al. (1875—†1927) : 443, 446
Cyrus, the Caucasian (Mukaukis), bp. of Phasis and Patr. Al. (630—†43) : 98, 106 sq., 114, 443
Czernagora, Church of : 298
Czernowitz, Church of : 298

Dadyeshu, Catholicus of Seleucia-Ctesiphon (†456) : 43
Damascus, Caliphs of : 114, 139, 442
Dandolo, The Doge Enrico (1192—†1205) : 238
Dazimon, Battle of (838) : 155
Decretum pro Armenis (1439) : 289
Definitio Fidei of Chalcedon : 3, 419
Deaconesses : 65
Departed, Prayers for the Faithful : 73
Digamists : 125
Digest, The : 32
Dionysius bar Salibi (†1171) : 437
Dioscorus, Patr. Al. (444—51) : 5, 8, 96
Diptychs, The : 130, 199, 256, 269
"Distinguishers" (Diacrinomeni) : 87
Divine Office, The : 72 sq.
Divorce : 69, 141, 164, 169, 199
Dmitri (Demetrius : †1590) : 390 sq.
Dmitri I., The False : 392 sqq.
Dmitri II., The False : 393
Dmitri Donskoi, Grand Prince of Moscow (1362—†89) : 376 sq.
Dobrudja, The : 36, 331, 345 sq., 348
Docetism : 12, 51
Dodecanese, The : 351
Domestic Code, The (1551) : 385
Donation of Constantine, The : 210
Dositheus, Patriarch of Jerusalem : his *Confession* (1672) : 467
Dushan, Stephen, King of the Serbs (1331—†55) : 264 sq., 277, 326, 336 sq., 341, 345
Dutch in India, The : 441 sq.

East and West, Differences between : cultural, 133, 207, 472; ecclesiastical, 133, 168 sqq., 205, 207 sqq., 236, 253, 285
"East, Church of the " : see " Nestorians " and " Persia "
East-Syrians, Church of the : see " Persia " and " Nestorians "
Ecclesiastical and civil divisions : 298
Ecloga of Leo III. (717—†41) : 141, 198
Economy, Doctrine of : 473
Ecthesis (638), The : 103, 106, 109, 115 sq.
Edessa : School of, 92 sq.; capture of, 114, 232; Jacobite see of, 438
Egypt : Mohammedan conquest of, 99, 114 sq., 442
Empire, The Roman : constitution of, 24, 152, 182; extent of, 24 sq., 187, 203, 263; organisation of, 119, 132; ethnography of, 132; becomes Greek, 132; religion its dominant interest, 133; losses of, 134, 154 sq., 206 sq., 221; diplomacy of, 187 sq.; decay of (c. 1025), 203 sqq., 264 sq.
Encyclical of Basiliscus, The : 11, 14, 97
Entrance : The Little, 35, 72, 130; The Great, 72, 130
Epirus, Despotate of : 247 sqq., 263, 266
Episcopal sees, Number of : 64

MM

Etchmiadzin: 88, 434
Ethiopia: see "Abyssinia"
Eudocia, Empress (421—†60): 5 sq.
Eudoxia, Empress (437—†c. 470): 7
Eugenius IV., Pope (1431—†47): 285 sqq., 378 sq.
Euphemius, Patr. CP. (490—6); 17
Euphrosyne, Empress (†1215): 361
Euthymius, St. (377—†473): 5
Eutychius, Patr. CP. (577—†82): 87 sq.
Evagrius: *Hist. Eccl.*, of: 86, 143
Ewostâtêwos (Eustathius: †1332): 451 sq.

Facundus, bp. of Hermiane (sixth cent.): 44
Fans, The liturgical: 130
Fasts and Feasts: 74 sq., 132, 164, 469
Ferdinand, King of Bulgaria (1887—   ): 330 sqq., 340
Ferdinand, King of Rumania (1914—†27): 349
Feudalism: 203, 207, 224, 248
Filioque, The: 196, 252 sqq., 271, 276, 286 sqq., 446, 452, 472
Formosus, Pope (891—†6): 205
Franciscan missionaries: 421
Frederick I. (Barbarossa: Emp. 1152—†90): 223, 235 sqq., 325
Frederick II., Emp. (1214—†50): 251, 267
Frumentius, first bp. of Ethiopia (c. 350): 448 sq.
Fulgentius Ferrandus (sixth cent.): 38, 44
Fulgentius of Ruspe (†533): 37
Fulk, parish priest of Neuilly (†1201): 237

Garigliano, Battle of the (915): 187
Genghis Khan (1206—†27): 372, 421
Gennadius II., Patr. CP. (1453—6): 302 sqq.
George I., King of Greece (1863—†1913): 356 sq.
George II., King of Greece (1923—4): 358
George Phrantzes (†1477): 284 sq.
Georgia: 89, 221, 298, 432, 460
Germanus I., Patr. CP. (715—30): 146 sqq.
Germanus II., Patr. CP. (1222—40): 254 sqq.
Godfrey of Bouillon (†1100): 229 sqq.
Golden Horde, The: 372, 378, 423
Gorazd, abp. of Bulgaria (ninth cent.): 322
Gospel-narratives of the Resurrection: 91
Grand Company, The: see "Catalans"
Grand Khan of the Mongols, The: 372
Great War, The (1914—8): 331, 342, 473
Greece: 301, 330 sq., 341, 351 sqq.
    Church of: 298, 303, 358 sqq., 471
    Sees of: 358 sq.
"Greek Fire": 115
Greens and Blues: 27
Gregory I., Pope (590—†604): 63, 66, 82, 84, 87 sq., 163, 458
Gregory III., Pope (731—†41): 148 sq.
Gregory VII., Pope (1073—†85): 209, 213, 227 sq.
Gregory IX., Pope (1227—†41): 253 sqq.
Gregory V., Patr. CP. (1818—†21): 305
Gregory Asbestas, abp. Syracuse (855—†63): 170

Gregory Akindynos (fourteenth cent.) : 276, 278
Gregory Barhebraeus (†1286) : 438
Gregory Palamas, abp. Thessalonica (1349—†60) : 276, 278
Grotta Ferrata : 461
Guiscard, Robert (†1085) : 206
Guy of Lusignan, King of Jerusalem and Cyprus (†1194) : 235

Hadrian I., Pope (772—†95) : 151
Hadrian II., Pope (867—†72) : 159, 195
Harold Hardraada, King of Norway, (1047—†66) : 208
Harun Arraschid, Caliph (786—†809) : 150 sqq., 225
Hellenism : 133 sq., 141, 174, 176, 181, 186, 202, 334, 472
Henoticians, The : 50
Henoticon, The : 5, 16 sqq., 25, 50, 89, 92, 98, 104, 432
Henry IV., Emp. (1056—†1106) : 228 sq.
Henry VI., Emp. (1190—†7) : 236 sq.
Heraclius, Emp. (610—†41) : 74, 84, 99, 103 sqq., 225, 333, 420
　Dynasty of, 102 sqq.
Herberstein, Freiherr von (†1566) : 388
Heresies, religious and rationalistic : 48
Heresy, treatment of : 58 sq.
Hermannstadt, Church of : 298
Hermogenes, Patriarch of Moscow (1606—11) : 394
Hesychasm : 275 sq., 278
Hierarchy, Grades of : 64 sq., 125 sq.
Home Synod, The : 9, 40, 64, 125
Honorius, Pope (625—†38) : 108 sqq., 122, 124
Honorius IV., Pope (1285—†7) : 422
Hormisdas, Pope (514—†23) : 19, 25, 37, 63
Horsey, Sir Jerome (†1627) : 388
Humbert, Cardinal (†1063) : 210 sqq.
Hungary : 235, 290, 299, 337, 347
　Conversion of : 227, 334
Hymns : 73

Iahbalaha III., Patriarch of the East (1281—†1317) : 422
Ibas, bp. of Edessa (†457) : 42 sqq., 47
Iberia : see " Georgia "
Iconoclasm : 138 sqq.
Icons : see " Images "
" Idiorhythmic " monasticism : 362, 469
Ignatius, Patr. CP. (847—58) : 168 sqq., 194 sq., 322
Illyricum, Ecclesiastical position of : 63, 125, 149, 151, 172 sq., 198, 321 sq.
Images : 128, 142 sqq., 363, 468, 471
Impersonality of our Lord's human nature : 45 sq.
" In two Natures " : 6, 8, 50
Incense and Lights : 73
Infallibility, Papal : 122
Infants, Baptism, Confirmation and Communion of : 69, 471
Innocent I., Pope (402—†17) : 298, 311
Innocent III., Pope (1198—†1216) : 236 sqq., 253, 325, 335
Innocent IV., Pope (1241—†54) : 421
Innocent VI., Pope (1352—†62) : 280

532   Index

Inquisition, The: 440, 442
Institutes, The: of Gaïus, 31; of Justinian, 31
Invocation of the Holy Spirit: 288, 473
Ipek: see "Pec"
Irene, Empress (797—†802): 138 sq., 150
Isaac I. (Comnenus: Emp. 1057—†9): 214
Isaac II. (Angelus: Emp. 1185—†95): 224, 235 sq., 324
Isaurian Dynasty (717—867), The: 136
Isidore, Cardinal (†1463): 286 sqq., 290, 378 sq.
Islam: advance of, 103; meaning of, 112; see "Mohammedanism"
Italy, Byzantines in: 29 sq., 186 sqq.
Itinerary: of the Bordeaux Pilgrim (339), 224; of Bernard (870), 225
Ivan I. (Kalita, 1328—†41): Grand Prince of Moscow: 374 sqq.
Ivan III. (the Great, 1462—†1505): 381
Ivan IV. (the Terrible, 1533—†84): 382 sqq.

Jacobites: 91, 289, 297, 436 sqq., 441, 462
Jagellon, Duke of Lithuania (1377—†1434): 376 sqq.
James Baradaeus (Baradai): 90, 436
Jerusalem, Patriarchs of: 2, 23, 79, 102, 137, 180, 220, 246, 261, 296
    Armenian Patriarch of: 434
    Capture of: (637), 113, 225; (1099), 231
    Kings of: 230 sq.
    Church of: 307 sqq.
Jesuits, The: 396 sq., 409, 452
Jews and Samaritans: 57, 60
Joachim II., Patr. CP. (1860—3): 328
Joannitsa (Kalojan, Tsar of the Bulgars: 1197—†1207): 249 sqq., 325, 335
Joasaph I., Patr. CP. (1464—6): 305
John I. (Tzimisces: Emp. 969—†76): 181, 184, 200 sqq., 323, 334, 433
John II., Emp. (1118—†43): 222
John III. (Ducas Vatatzes: Emp. 1222—†54): 249 sqq.
John V. (Palaeologus: Emp. 1341—†91): 265, 271, 277 sq., 280 sq.
John VI. (Cantacuzene: Emp. 1347—54): 265, 277 sqq.
John VIII. (Palaeologus: Emp. 1425—†48): 285 sq., 378 sq.
John Asan II., Tsar of the Bulgars (1218—†41): 250 sq., 324 sqq., 334
John XXI., Pope (1276—†7): 270
John XI. (Beccus: Patr. CP. 1275—82): 270, 272
John, bp. of Ephesus (†c. 585): 57 sq., 81, 85 sq., 90
John, bp. of Tella (†538): 50, 436
John Kurkuas (920—†42): 183 sq.
John Moschus (†619): 132
John of Damascus, St. (c. 750): 147 sqq., 467
John Scholasticus, Patr. CP. (566—†97): 85, 193 sq.
John Talaia, Patr. Al. (482): 16
John the Faster, Patr. CP. (582—†95): 63, 84
John the Orphanotrophus (c. 1050): 208
John Xiphilinus, Patr. CP. (1064—†75): 208
Jugoslavia, Church of: 333 sqq., and see "Serbia"
Julian, bp. of Halicarnassus (†536): 90 sq.
Justin I., Emp. (518—†27): 18 sqq.; House of, 22
Justin II., Emp. (565—†78): 80 sq., 85, 89, 437
Justinian I., Emp. (527—†65): 24 sqq.; his recovery of Africa, 28 sqq.; of Italy, 29 sq.; his legal reforms, 30 sqq.; as

theologian 35 sqq.; hymn of, 39; *Adv. Origenem*, 40 sq.; *Confessio rectae fidei*, 45; his Cæsaropapism, 47; his aphthartodocetism, 48 sqq.; Church and State under, 55 sqq.; architects of, 68; successors of, 80 sqq.
Justinian II., Emp. (685—95): 104, 122 sq., 156, 311
Justiniana, Prima: 63
Juvenal, Patr. Jer. (451—†8): 5 sq., 307

Kaaba, The: 147
Kairowan: 114
Kalka, Battle of the (1224): 372, 421
Kazan: Conquest of (1553), 386; Ambrose, bp. of (1816—26), 412 sq.
Khazars, The: 139, 157, 188, 190
Khomiakov, A. S. (†1860): 412
Kiev: 188, 191 sqq., 370, 372, 396 sqq., 405
  metropolitans of, 370, 397
  and Moscow, joint metropolitanates of (1461—1589), 379 sqq.
  School of, 412
Kiptchak, The: see "Golden Horde"
Kiss of Peace, The: 130
Klokotinitza, Battle of: 250
Kontakia: 73
Koran, The: 110 sq.
Kosovo, Battle of (1389): 282, 337, 341, (1448) 290
Krum, King of the Bulgars (802—†15): 155, 161, 185, 319
Ktistolatrae, The: 51
Kulikovo, Battle of (1380): 376
Kumanovo, Battle of (1912): 330, 341
Kuntsivich, St. Josaphat (†1623): 397

Lausanne, Treaty of (1923): 303, 352
Law, Influence of Christianity on: 142, 167
Lazica: 27, 83, 107, 124, 139
Legitimacy, Conception of: 181 sq., 205
Leo I., Emp. (457—†74): 3, 8
Leo I., Pope (440—†61): 6, 8, 87, 120
Leo IX., Pope (1048—†54): 209 sqq.
Leo XIII., Pope (1878—†1903): 458
Leo III., Emp. (the Isaurian: 717—†41): 134, 138 sqq., 146 sqq., 195 333, 458
Leo IV. (the Khazar: Emp. 775—†80): 138, 150
Leo V. (the Armenian: Emp. 813—†20): 138, 153, 155, 157, 161, 320, 433
Leo the mathematician: 158
Leo VI. (The Philosopher: Emp. 886—†912): 182, 184, 187, 196 sqq.
Leo, Archbishop of Ochrida: 210 sqq.
Leo Tornicius, Revolt of (1047): 208
Leonine Sacramentary, The: 29
Leontius of Byzantium (†543): 37, 45, 106
Lepanto, Battle of (1571): 300
Lights and Incense: 73
Litanies: 73
Lithuania: 376 sqq., 380, 382, 386, 396
Liturgies: see *Rites*
Lombards, The: 83

Macarius, Metropolitan of Moscow (1879—†82): 412, 468
Macedonian Dynasty, The: 178 sqq., 226
Malabar, Christians of: 439 sqq., 459
Mamluks, The (1250—1517): 445 sq.
Maniaces, George: 206 sq.
Manichæans: 56 sq., 185
Manuel I. (Comnenus: Emp. 1143—†80): 223, 334
Manuel II. (Palaeologus: Emp. 1391—†1425): 283 sqq.
Manzikert (Manazkert), Battle of (1071): 207, 214, 221, 227, 433
Mar Abha, Catholicus of "The East" (540—†52): 94 sq.
Marcian, Emp. (450—†7): 3 sqq., 89, 431
Maria Maggiore, Church of S.: 172
Mark, abp. of Ephesus (†1443): 286 sqq.
Maronites: 462 sq.
Marqorêwos (Mercurius: fourteenth cent.): 451
Martha the nun (seventeenth cent.): 391
Martin I., Pope (649—†55): 117
Martin V., Pope (1417—†31): 284
Martyrius, Patr. Ant. (459—70): 13, 36
Martyropolis (Maïferkat): 83
Maruta, metropolitan of Tagrit (629—49): 437
Matrimony, Holy: 69, 141, 163 sq.
Maurice, Emp. (582—†602): 63, 82 sq., 84, 89 sq.
Maxim the Greek (1476—†1556): 404 sq.
Maximus the Confessor (580—†662): 107 sqq., 115, 124, 130, 132, 144, 287
Mazdaïsm: 89, 429, 431
Mecca: 110 sqq.
Mechitarists: 462
Medina: 110 sqq.
Megaspelaion, Monastery of: 355, 361
Meletius II., Orthodox Patr. Al. (1925—   ): 433, 471
Melkites (=Royalists): 10, 49, 96, 428, 443; (=Uniates of the Byzantine rite), 460
Menas, Patr. CP. (†552): 40 sq., 46
Mesembria (Misivri): Defeat of the Bulgars at (817), 155, 320
Mesrob (†441): 431
Meteora, Monasteries of Mt.: 361
Methodius I., Patr. CP. (843—†7): 154 sq., 169 sqq.
Methodius, St. (825—†85): 139, 158 sqq., 322, 330, 333
Michael I. (Rhangabe: Emp. 811—3): 153, 155, 169
Michael II. (The Stammerer: Emp. 820—†9): 138, 153
Michael III. (the Drunkard: Emp. 842—†67): 138, 154, 157, 162, 168 sqq., 175, 188, 194, 320
Michael VIII. (Palaeologus: Emp. 1259—†82): 252, 264 sq., 266 sqq.
Michael I., King of Rumania (1927—   ): 349
Michael (Romanov: Tsar, 1613—†45): 395 sq.
Michael Cerularius, Patr. CP. (1043—†58): 205 sqq., 370, 458
Michael Psellus (1018—†96): 208, 213, 215
Missions: 128, 157 sqq., 187, 375, 376 sq., 412, 420 sqq., 437, 439, 449, 451 sq.
Mitrovitsa (Sirmium): 81
Mixed Chalice: 130
Mohacz, Battle of (1526): 299, 337
Mohammed II., Sultan (1451—†81): 290 sqq., 299 sqq.

Index

Mohammedanism : 109 sqq., 190, 372, 423
    sects of : 226, 234
Moldavia : 347 sqq.
Monasticism : 5, 13 sq., 39 sq., 66 sqq., 126 sq., 132, 145, 153, 171, 193, 200 sq., 204, 361 sqq., 374 sq., 385 sqq., 411, 419, 442, 446, 451 sq., 462, 468 sq.
Monemvasia (Malvoisie) : 81, 278 sq., 286
Monenergism : 107 sqq., 133
Mongols, The : 372 sqq., 378, 423, 433
Monophysites : 4 sqq., 10, 18, 27, 35, 48 sqq., 66, 70, 84 sqq., 88 sqq, 104, 107, 113, 201, 297, 425 sqq., 432, 441, 446, 449 sq., 452
Monophysitism : Periods of, 104
Monotheletism : 106 sqq., 115 sq., 133, 462 sq.
Montanists : 57
Montenegro : 330 sq., 338 sq., 340
    Church of : 298, 332
Morals : 75, 127
Moravia, conversion of : 158, 333
Morosini, Latin Patr. of CP. (1205—†11) : 242
Moscow : rise of, 373, 376, 379, 382
    metropolitans of : 374
    and Kiev, joint metropolitanates of : 379 sqq., 396
    Patriarchate of (1589—1700) : 392 sqq., 396, 398 sq.
Mukaukis : see " Cyrus "
Music : 471
Myriokephalon, Battle of (1176) : 223
Mystagogia of Maximus the Confessor, The : 129

Narsai (†502) : 91 sq.
National Churches : 104, 159, 211, 301 ; see " Philetism "
Nationalism : 176, 472
Navarino, Battle of (1827) : 356
Nemanja, Dynasty of (twelfth—fourteenth cent.) : 334 sq.
Nerses I., Catholicus of Armenia (362—†73) : 430 sq.
Nestor, Chronicle of: 188
Nestorians, The : 92 sqq., 415 sqq., missions of, 420 sqq.
Nicæa, Emperors of : 245 sqq.
Nicephorus I. (Emp. 802—†11) : 152 sqq., 155, 157, 171, 320
Nicephorus II. (Phocas : Emp. 963—†9) : 182, 184 sq., 200 sqq., 204, 323
Nicephorus I., Patr. CP. (806—†15) : 153, 171, 319
Nicephorus Gregoras (†c. 1359) : 276 sq.
Nicholas I., Pope (858—†67) : 139, 162 sqq., 171 sqq., 195, 321, 458
Nicholas IV., Pope (1288—†92) : 422
Nicholas II., Tsar of Russia (1894—†1917) : 368, 413 sq.
Nihawand, Battle of (642) : 420
Nikon, Patriarch of Moscow (1652—66) : 399 sqq.
Nil Serski (c. 1500) : 404
Nisibis : 83, 92, 184, 419, 438
Nomocanon, The : 85, 193, 404, 468
Normans, The : 206 sq., 210, 215, 221, 227 sq., 236
Novels: of Justinian, 32, 59 sq.; of Basil II., 203; of Romanus I., 203
Novgorod : Old, 188, 367, 373, 377, 387, 399
    New (Nizhni), 367, 378, 394, 400
Novi-Bazar, *Sandjak* of : 339 sq.

536 Index

Nubia, Conversion of : 100

Ochrida : 186, 200, 210, 303, 323, 327, 330 sq., 337 sq., 342, 348
Œcumenical Patriarch : 63, 84, 211
"Of two Natures" : 8
Old Believers, The : 407
Olearius, Adam (c. 1650) : 401, 407
Olga, Grand Duchess of Kiev (†969) : 189, 200
Omar, The Caliph (634—†43) : 113 sq.
"One nature of the Word [and that] incarnate " : 45
"One of the Trinity was crucified in the flesh " : 37; "became Incarnate," 38
"One theandric operation " : 106
Oprichniki, The : 387
Oprichnina, The : 387, 393, 395
Ordination : 61, 69, 125 sq., 473
Origenism : 39 sqq., 311
Orthodoxy : Characteristics of, 133, 159, 181, 202, 298, 408, 412, 471;
    Sunday of, 154; extent of, 254; Symbolical Books of, 397, 468;
    common Faith of, 467 sq.; Government of, 469 sq.; worship
    of, 470 sq.; prospects of re-union with, 472 sq.
Ostrogoths, The : 28 sq.
Ottoman : Sultans : 260
    Turks : 265 sqq., 299 sqq., 445 sqq.

Paganism : 56 sq., 166, 190
Palaeologi, Dynasty of the : 244, 260 sqq.
Palestine, Monks of : 5, 9, 39 sq., 66
Pallium, The : 166
Pandects, The : see *Digest*
Pankalia (979), Battle of : 204
Pantheon, The : 118
Patriarchates : 62 sq., 469; and rites, 458
Patzinaks : see " Petchenegs "
Paul II., Pope (1464—†71) : 381
Paulicians, The : 143, 156 sq., 162, 185, 202, 222, 323, 334
Peć (Ipek), See of : 303, 337 sq.
Pelagius I., Pope (555—†60) : 40, 66
Penance : 69, 129, 165
Peregrinatio S. Silviae [Etheriae] : 225, 307
Periods of ecclesiastical history, 451—695 : 104
Persecution : 56 sqq., 85 sq., 91, 117, 153, 156 sq., 414, 431, 435 sq.,
    438, 443 sq., 451
Persia : Rome and, 27, 83, 89, 104 sq., 227, 419, 430
    Church of : 43, 92 sqq., 297, 418 sqq.
" Person " and " Nature " : 45 sq., 116, 467
Petchenegs : 188, 206, 222, 228, 323, 369
Peter Mogila, metropolitan of Kiev (1632—†47) : 397; *Orthodox Confession* of, 398, 467
Peter Mongus, Patr. Al. (477—90) : 15 sqq.
Peter the Fuller, Patr. Ant. (468—†78) : 14 sqq., 36, 312
Peter the Great, Tsar (1689—†1725) : 408 sqq.
Phanar, The : 305

Index

Phanariots, The: 305, 307, 327, 338, 348, 355
Philaret, Metropolitan of Moscow (1821—†67): 412, 468
Philaret, Patriarch of Moscow (1619—†33): 391 sqq., 399
Philetism: 301, 305, 330
Philiké Hetaerea, The: 355
Phocas, House of: 199
Photius, Patr. CP. (857—67 and 878—86): 139, 157 sqq., 162 sqq., 168 sqq., 189, 194 sqq., 205, 321, 468
Phthartolatrae, The: 51, 90
Pilgrims: 5, 131, 224 sqq., 468
Pius V., Pope (1566—†72): 300
Platon, Metropolitan of Moscow (1775—†1812): 412
Pobiedonostsev, Constantine (1881—†1905): 410
Poimanenus, Battle of (1204): 249 sq.
Poland: 376 sqq., 386, 390, 395 sqq., 402, 460
 and Lithuania, 380, 396
Polo, Marco (1256—†1323): 421, 440
Polovtsy, The: 372
Polyeuctus, Patr. CP. (956—70): 200 sqq.
Popes, List of: 2, 23, 79, 102, 137, 180, 219, 246, 260
Pornocracy (tenth cent.), The: 198
Porphyrogeniti, The: 182, 205
Portuguese: in India, 440 sq.; in Abyssinia, 451 sqq.
Possessor, an African bp.: 37
Pratum Spirituale, The: 132
Preaching, Rarity of: 471
Processions: see "Litanies"
Proclus, abp. CP. (434—†6), *Tome* of: 38
Procopius, The *Secret History* of: 26
Proterius, Patr. Al. (452—†7): 7 sqq., 96 sq.
Pseudo-Dionysius (c. 500): 106
Pulcheria, Emp. (450—†3): 3
Purgatory: 286

Raskolniki, The: 407
Ravenna: 30, 68 sq., 82, 124, 146, 148
Raymond, Count of Toulouse (†1105): 229 sqq.
Reformation, The: 300
Relics, *Cultus* of: 74 sq., 144, 468
Responsa ad Bulgaros (866): 163 sqq., 321
Responsales: see *Apocrisiarii*
Resurrection-body: 87 sq.
Reunion of E. and W., Attempts at: 223, 227, 237, 252 sqq., 267, 274 sq., 279, 281, 285 sqq., 397, 412, 440 sq., 445, 452; prospects of, 472
Revolt of Nika (532): 26
Richard I., King of England (1189—†99): 235 sqq.
Rite and Patriarchate, Relation between: 458
Rites: Byzantine: 35, 39, 70 sq., 90, 129 sq., 460 sq., 470 sq.
 Alexandrine: 70, 445 sqq., 452
 West-Syrian: 70, 437 sq., 442
 Armenian: 90, 431
 East-Syrian: 93
Roger de Flor: 265, 272

Roman See: Primacy of, 62, 124, 153, 166, 171, 174, 210, 254 sq.; importance of, 119, 176, 194; patrimony of, 149, 172, 195; ignored by Emp. Leo VI., 198; tolerance of, 210, 458
Romanov, House of (1547—1917): 383 sqq.
Romanus I. (Lecapenus: Emp. 919—44): 199, 322
Romanus III. (Argyrus: Emp. 1028—†34): 205 sq.
Romanus IV. (Diogenes: Emp. 1067—†71): 207, 214
Romanus the Melodist (c. 550): 73
Rostislav, Prince of Moravia: 158, 161, 320
Rumania: 301, 345 sqq.
 Church of: 298, 348 sqq., 470
 Sees of: 349
Rurik, House of: 188, 369, 373, 390 sqq.
Russia: Conversion of, 188 sqq., 203; organisation of Church in, 192; monasteries of, 193, 374 sq.; Canon Law of, 193 sq.; Church of, 297, 368 sqq.; and Turkey, 300 sq., 327, 330, 354 sq.; the Russian lands, 367 sq.; missionary spirit of, 375, 412 sq.; moral and social conditions in, 388 sq.; sees of, 399; ignorance of the clergy in, 404; Service-books of, 405 sq.; isolation of, 407; Holy Synod of, 408 sqq.; expansion of Church in, 410
Russians: 188, 202, 323
Russo-Turkish War (1877—8): 330, 357, 435
Rusticus, deacon of (c. 553): 143
Ruthenians, The: 460 sq.

Sabbath not the Lord's Day: 164
Sacraments: administration of the, 69, 129; the Seven, 468
St. Sophia: 68 sq., 242, 290 sq.
St. Thomas, Christians of: see "Malabar"
Saints: intercession of, 149; devotion to, 468
Saladin (†1193): 234 sq., 444
Samuel, Tsar of the Bulgars (976—†1014): 186, 203, 206, 323, 334
Saracens: 110 sqq., 125, 139, 149, 155, 183, 186 sq., 203, 225, 227, 313
Sardica: see "Sofia"
Sassanidae, Dynasty of the (226—652): 420
Sauma, Rabban (thirteenth cent.): 422
Sava, St. (†1236): 336
Script: Glagolitic, 159; Cyrillic, 159
Scriptures, Translation of the: 159
Scupi: see Skoplje.
Scythian monks, The: 36 sqq.
Seleucia-Ctesiphon, See of: 418
Seljuk Turks, The: 206, 221, 227 sq., 249, 433, 446
Serbia: Church of, 298, 322 sqq., 332 sqq.; episcopal sees of, 342
Serbs: 106, 128, 132, 187, 206, 221, 223, 264 sq., 280, 282, 301, 324, 326, 330 sq., 332 sqq.
 Kings of the: 220, 245, 260
 Dynasties of: 339
Sergius, Patr. CP. (610—†38): 105 sq., 130
Service-books: *Typikon, Euchologion, Horologion:* 471
Severus, Patr. Ant. (512—8): 18, 38, 49 sq., 90 sq., 106, 436
Sèvres, Treaty of (1920): 352, 357
Shiites: 226, 234, 443
Shimun XXI., Mar (Patriarch of the East): 424
Siberia: Annexation of Western (1582): 388; missions in, 413

Sicily: 203, 207, 267
Sigismund III., King of Poland (1587—†1632): 392 sq.
Simeon Stylites, St.: 7, 9
Simeon, Tsar of the Bulgars (893—†927): 185, 322 sq., 334
Simony: 304 sqq., 444
Simplicius, Pope (468—†83): 10, 15 sq.
Sinai, Church of Mt.: 63, 297, 308, 316
Singidunum (Belgrade): 81
Sirmium (Mitrovitsa): 81
Skoplje: 26, 324 sq., 331, 335, 337, 341 sq.
Slavs, The: 82, 132, 140, 157, 202, 331, 346
Slivnitza, Battle of (1885): 340 sq.
Slovenes: 332
Socotra: 439
Sofia: 155, 161, 184, 323
Solitaries: 5, 9, 66
Soloviev, V. S. (†1900): 412
Sophia, Empress (sixth cent.): 81
Sophia (Palaeologus), wife of Ivan III. (1472): 381
Sophronius, Patr. Jerusalem (634—†8): 106 sqq., 113, 124, 131 sq.
Statuary as distinct from pictures illegitimate: 147
Stephen, bp. of Perm (1383—†96), St.: 377
Suleiman the Magnificent, Sultan (1520—†66): 299
Sunday, Observance of: 164, 470
Sunnites: 226, 234, 442
Sviatoslav I., Grand Duke of Kiev (945—†73): 185, 189, 323
Swatopluk, Prince of Moravia (870—†94): 160
Sweden: 392, 395
Syllaeum, Battle of: 115
Syria: 90 sq.; Mohammedan conquest of, 113, 437; culture of, 145; Melkites (Uniates) of, 460

Tannenberg, Battle of (1410): 378
Tarasius, Patr. of CP. (784—†806): 151, 169, 171
Tartars, The: 191 sq., 372 sq., 376, 413
Teklahaimanot: 442, 451 sq.
Tetragamy, The: 197 sq., 199, 204
Teutonic Knights, Order of the: 378, 386
Themes: 119, 132, 140
Theoctistus, Logothete of the Course (†856): 154, 158, 169
Theodora, Empress (†548): 26 sqq., 44, 49, 55, 73 sq., 436
Theodora, Empress (842—†67): 138, 154, 157, 169 sq.
Theodora, Empress (1054—†6): 182, 205, 214, 226
Theodore I. (Lascaris: Emp. 1206—†22): 249 sq.
Theodore II. (Lascaris: Emp. 1254—†8): 251 sq.
Theodore I., Tsar of Russia (1584—†98): 390 sqq.
Theodore, abbot of the Studium (†826): 153 sqq.
Theodore Ascidas, abp. of Cæsarea in Cappadocia (†558): 40 sqq., 47
Theodore, bp. of Mopsuestia (†428): 42 sqq., 46, 419
Theodore of Santabaren, Abbot: 196
Theodore of Tarsus, Abp. Cant. (668—†90): 118, 120
Theodore, Pope (642—†9): 116
Theodoret, bp. of Cyrus (†458): 42 sqq., 47
Theodosius, bp. of Ephesus (c. 720): 144
Theopaschitism: 35 sqq.

Theophano, Empress of Romanus II. (959—†63): 182, 200, 202
Theophano, Empress of Otto II. (973—†83): 187
Theophilus, Emp. (829—†42): 138, 153, 156 sq., 171
Thessalonica: Kingdom of, 247
　　Empire of, 247 sq.
Thomas, bp. of Claudiopolis (c. 720): 144, 147
Three Chapters, The: 42 sqq., 55, 104, 143
Tiberius II., Emp. (578—†82): 80 sq., 85
Tikhon, Patriarch of Moscow (1917—†25): 414
"Time of Troubles," The (1605—13): 391 sqq.
Timothy Salofaciolus, Patr. Al. (†482): 10 sq., 15, 97
Timothy the Cat, Patr. Al. (457—77): 8 sqq., 15, 97
Timour (Tamerlane: 1336—†1405): 265, 378, 423, 433
Tirnovo, See of: 303, 325, 330 sq.
Tomus Unionis (920), The: 199, 204
Trade-routes: 238, 264, 388, 421, 439 sq.
Trajan, Emp. (98—†117): 346
Transubstantiation: 473
Trebnik, The: 405
Trebizond, Emps. of: 245 sq.
Trisagion, The: 18, 35 sq., 71, 130, 438
Turkish Empire: 299
Type (648), The: 103, 116 sq., 133

Unction: 69
Uniates, The: 457 sqq.
Universities: Athens, 58; CP., 156, 208
Unworthiness of the minister: 165
Urban II., Pope (1088—†99): 228
Urban IV., Pope (1261—†4): 267 sq.
Urban V., Pope (1362—†70): 281
Usküb: *see* Skoplje

Valentinian III., Emp. (425—†55): 6, 28
Vandals, The: 28 sq., 56, 60
Vassian Kosoi (sixteenth cent.): 404
Velbuzd, Battle of (1330): 326, 336, 347
Velimirovic, Dr. Nikolai, bp. of Ochrida: 342
Venice: 155, 186 sq., 206, 222, 238 sqq., 247, 249, 263, 265, 273, 281, 286, 314, 335, 352 sqq., 462
Venizelos, M.: 330, 340 sq., 357
Veronica, Veil of St.: 144
Vigilius, Pope (538—†55): 44 sqq., 55, 66, 143
Viminacium (Kostolats): 81
Visigoths, The: 28 sq.
Vitalian, Pope (657—†72): 118
Vladimir I., Grand Prince of Kiev (980—†1015): 189 sqq., 203, 369
Vladimir II. (1113—†25): 371 sq.

Wallachia: 347 sqq.
War, Christianity and: 166
"West-Syrians": see "Jacobites"
"Who wast crucified for us": 18, 36, 438
Wilfrid, bp. of York (679): 120
Worship of the Church: 68 sqq., 128 sq.